W9-AAO-953

AP® WORLD HISTORY: MODERN
PREMIUM PREP

2023 Edition

The Staff of The Princeton Review

PrincetonReview.com

Penguin
Random
House

The Princeton Review
110 East 42nd St, 7th Floor
New York, NY 10017

Published in the United States by Penguin Random House LLC, New York.

Terms of Service: The Princeton Review Online Companion Tools ("Student Tools") for retail books are available for only the two most recent editions of that book. Student Tools may be activated only once per eligible book purchased, for a total of 24 months of access. Activation of Student Tools more than once per book is in direct violation of these Terms of Service and may result in discontinuation of access to Student Tools Services.

ISBN: 978-0-593-45094-9
eBook ISBN: 978-0-593-45121-2
ISSN: 2691-1485

AP is a trademark registered and owned by the College Board, which is not affiliated with, and does not endorse, this product.

The Princeton Review is not affiliated with Princeton University.

The material in this book is up-to-date at the time of publication. However, changes may have been instituted by the testing body in the test after this book was published.

If there are any important late-breaking developments, changes, or corrections to the materials in this book, we will post that information online in the Student Tools. Register your book and check your Student Tools to see if there are any updates posted there.

Permission has been granted to reprint portions of the following:

Excerpts from *THE WRETCHED OF THE EARTH* by Frantz Fanon, English translation © 1963 by Présence Africaine. Used by permission of Grove/Atlantic, Inc. Any third party use of this material, outside of this publication, is prohibited.

Excerpt "Mi Opinion" from A Nation of Women: *An Early Feminist Speaks Out* by Luisa Capetillo, translation © 2004. Reprinted by permission of Arte Público Press, University of Houston.

Editor: Orion McBean
Production Artist: Deborah Weber
Production Editors: Lee Elder and Emily Epstein White
Content Contributor: Jason Morgan

Printed in the United States of America.

10   9   8   7   6   5   4   3   2

2023 Edition

The Princeton Review Publishing Team
Rob Franek, Editor-in-Chief
David Soto, Senior Director, Data Operations
Stephen Koch, Senior Manager, Data Operations
Deborah Weber, Director of Production
Jason Ullmeyer, Production Design Manager
Jennifer Chapman, Senior Production Artist
Selena Coppock, Director of Editorial
Aaron Riccio, Senior Editor
Meave Shelton, Senior Editor
Chris Chimera, Editor
Orion McBean, Editor
Patricia Murphy, Editor
Laura Rose, Editor
Alexa Schmitt Bugler, Editorial Assistant

Penguin Random House Publishing Team
Tom Russell, VP, Publisher
Alison Stoltzfus, Senior Director, Publishing
Brett Wright, Senior Editor
Emily Hoffman, Assistant Managing Editor
Ellen Reed, Production Manager
Suzanne Lee, Designer
Eugenia Lo, Publishing Assistant

For customer service, please contact **editorialsupport@review.com**, and be sure to include:

- full title of the book

- ISBN

- page number

Acknowledgments

The Princeton Review would like to extend special thanks to Jason Morgan for his valuable contributions to the 2023 edition of this book. We are also, as always, very appreciative of the time and attention given to each page by Deborah Weber, Lee Elder, and Emily Epstein White.

Contents

Get More (Free) Content
at **PrincetonReview.com/prep**

As easy as 1•2•3

1 Go to PrincetonReview.com/prep or scan the **QR code** and enter the following ISBN for your book: **9780593450949**

2 Answer a few simple questions to set up an exclusive Princeton Review account. *(If you already have one, you can just log in.)*

3 Enjoy access to your **FREE** content!

Once you've registered, you can...

- Access and print Practice Tests A and B with the corresponding Answers and Explanations
- Access comprehensive study guides, extra bubble sheets for the practice tests in the book, and lists of need-to-know World History terms
- Get valuable advice about the college application process, including tips for writing a great essay and where to apply for financial aid

- If you're still choosing between colleges, use our searchable rankings of *The Best 388 Colleges* to find out more information about your dream school.

- Check to see if there have been any corrections or updates to this edition

- Get our take on any recent or pending updates to the AP World History: Modern Exam

Need to report a potential **content** issue?

Contact **EditorialSupport@review.com** and include:

- full title of the book
- ISBN
- page number

Need to report a **technical** issue?

Contact **TPRStudentTech@review.com** and provide:

- your full name
- email address used to register the book
- full book title and ISBN
- Operating system (Mac/PC) and browser (Chrome, Firefox, Safari, etc.)

Look For These Icons Throughout The Book

 ONLINE ARTICLES

 ONLINE PRACTICE TESTS

 PROVEN TECHNIQUES

 APPLIED STRATEGIES

 STUDY BREAK

 OTHER REFERENCES

 ONLINE VIDEO

Part I
Using This
Book to Improve
Your AP Score

- Preview: Your Knowledge, Your Expectations
- Your Guide to Using This Book
- How to Begin

PREVIEW: YOUR KNOWLEDGE, YOUR EXPECTATIONS

Your route to a high score on the AP World History: Modern Exam depends a lot how you plan to use this book. Start thinking about your plan by responding to the following questions.

1. Rate your level of confidence about your knowledge of the content tested by the AP World History: Modern Exam:

   A. Very confident—I know it all
   B. I'm pretty confident, but there are topics for which I could use help
   C. Not confident—I need quite a bit of support
   D. I'm not sure

2. If you have a goal score in mind, circle your goal score for the AP World History: Modern Exam:

   5   4   3   2   1   I'm not sure yet

3. What do you expect to learn from this book? Circle all that apply to you.

   A. A general overview of the test and what to expect
   B. Strategies for how to approach the test
   C. The content tested by this exam
   D. I'm not sure yet

YOUR GUIDE TO USING THIS BOOK

This book is organized to provide as much—or as little—support as you need, so you can use this book in whatever way will be most helpful to improving your score on the AP World History: Modern Exam.

- The remainder of **Part I** will provide guidance on how to use this book and help you determine your strengths and weaknesses

- **Part II** of this book contains Practice Test 1, the Diagnostic Answer Key, answers and explanations for each question, and a scoring guide. We recommend that you take this test before going any further in order to realistically determine
  o your starting point right now
  o which question types you're ready for and which you might need to practice
  o which content topics you are familiar with and which you should carefully review

  Once you have nailed down your strengths and weaknesses with regard to this exam, you can focus your test preparation, build a study plan, and be efficient with your time. Our Diagnostic Answer Key will assist you with this process.

- **Part III** of this book will
  - provide information about the structure, scoring, and content of the AP World History: Modern Exam
  - help you to make a study plan
  - point you toward additional resources

- **Part IV** of this book will explore various strategies such as
  - how to attack multiple-choice questions
  - how to write effective essays
  - how to manage your time to maximize the number of points available to you

- **Part V** of this book covers the content you need for the AP World History: Modern Exam.

- **Part VI** of this book contains three additional practice tests, along with their answers and explanations. If you skipped Practice Test 1, we recommend that you do all four (with at least a day or two between them) so that you can measure your progress. Additionally, taking these tests will help to identify any external issues: if you get a certain type of question wrong more than once, you probably need to review it. If you get it wrong only once, you may have run out of time or been distracted by something. In either case, reviewing your practice test results will allow you to focus on the factors that caused the discrepancy in scores and to be as prepared as possible on the day of the test.

You may choose to use some parts of this book over others, or you may work through the entire book. The ways in which you use this book will depend on your needs and how much time you have. Now let's look at how to make this determination.

Extend Your Practice!
Head over to your Student Tools, our online hub for additional resources, to download your two online practice tests. Follow the instructions on the Get More (Free) Content page at the beginning of this book to access this content and more!

HOW TO BEGIN

1. **Take Practice Test 1**

    Before you can decide how to use this book, you need to take a practice test. Doing so will give you insight into your strengths and weaknesses, and the test will also help you make an effective study plan. If you're feeling test-phobic, remind yourself that a practice test is a tool for diagnosing yourself—it's not how well you do that matters but how you use information gleaned from your performance to guide your preparation.

    So, before you read further, take Practice Test 1 starting at page 9 of this book. Be sure to do so in one sitting, following the instructions that appear before the test.

2. **Check Your Answers**

    Using the Diagnostic Answer Key on page 39, follow our three-step process to identify your strengths and weaknesses with regard to the tested topics. This will help you determine which content review chapters to prioritize when studying this book. Don't worry about the explanations for now, and don't worry about missed questions. We'll get to that soon.

3. **Reflect on the Test**

    After you take your first test, respond to the following questions:

    *   How much time did you spend on the multiple-choice questions?

    *   How much time did you spend on the short answers and essays?

    *   How many multiple-choice questions did you miss?

    *   Do you feel you had the knowledge to address the subject matter of the short answers and essays?

    *   Do you feel you wrote well-organized, thoughtful short-answer responses and essays?

4. **Read Part III of This Book and Complete the Self-Evaluation**

    Part III will provide information about how the test is structured and scored. It will also set out areas of content that are tested.

    As you read Part III, reevaluate your answers to the questions above. At the end of Part III, you will revisit and refine the questions you answer above. You will then be able to make a study plan, based on your needs and time available, that will allow you to use this book most effectively.

Bonus Tips and Tricks...
Check us out on YouTube for test taking tips and tricks to help you ace your next exam at www.youtube.com/ThePrincetonReview

5. Engage with Parts IV and V as Needed

Notice the word *engage*. You'll get more out of this book if you use it intentionally than if you read it passively, hoping for an improved score through osmosis.

The strategy chapters in Part IV will help you think about your approach to the question types on this exam. This part will open with a reminder to think about how you approach questions now and then close with a reflection section asking you to think about how or whether you will change your approach in the future.

The content chapters in Part V are designed to provide a review of the content tested on the AP World History: Modern Exam, including the level of detail you need to know and how the content is tested. You will have the opportunity to assess your mastery of the content of each chapter through test-appropriate drill questions.

6. Take Another Test and Assess Your Performance

Once you feel you have developed the strategies you need and gained the knowledge you lacked, you should take Practice Test 2, which starts on page 333. You should do so in one sitting, following the instructions at the beginning of the test.

When you are done, check your answers to the multiple-choice sections. Ask a teacher to read your essays and provide feedback.

Once you have taken the test, reflect on the areas on which you still need to work, and revisit the chapters in this book that address those deficiencies. Then, try your hand at Practice Tests 3 and 4 in this book and, if needed, Practice Tests A and B online, to track your progress and see where you still need improvement. Through this type of reflection and engagement, you will continue to improve.

7. Keep Working

In addition to this book and its online Student Tools, there are other resources available to you, including a wealth of information on AP Students, the official site of the AP Exams. You can continue to explore areas that can stand improvement and engage in those areas right up to the day of the test. For updates and information on the AP World History: Modern Exam, as well as free practice, check out its home page: <u>apstudents. collegeboard.org/courses/ap-world-history-modern/assessment</u>.

Need Some Guidance?
If you're looking for a way to get the most out of your studying, check out our free study guide for this exam, which you can access via your Student Tools. See the Get More (Free) Content page for step-by-step instructions for downloading your bonus materials.

AP Students
The AP Students home page is <u>apstudents. collegeboard.org/home</u>

Part II
Practice Test 1

- Practice Test 1
- Practice Test 1: Diagnostic Answer Key and Explanations
- How to Score Practice Test 1

Practice Test 1

Completely darken bubbles with a No. 2 pencil. If you make a mistake, be sure to erase mark completely. Erase all stray marks.

1.

YOUR NAME:
(Print) _____
Last   First   M.I.

SIGNATURE: _____   DATE: ___ / ___ / ___

HOME ADDRESS:
(Print) _____
Number and Street

_____
City   State   Zip Code

PHONE NO.: _____

IMPORTANT: Please fill in these boxes exactly as shown on the back cover of your test book.

2. TEST FORM

3. TEST CODE   **4. REGISTRATION NUMBER**

⓪	Ⓐ	Ⓙ	⓪	⓪	⓪	⓪	⓪	⓪	⓪	⓪
①	Ⓑ	Ⓚ	①	①	①	①	①	①	①	①
②	Ⓒ	Ⓛ	②	②	②	②	②	②	②	②
③	Ⓓ	Ⓜ	③	③	③	③	③	③	③	③
④	Ⓔ	Ⓝ	④	④	④	④	④	④	④	④
⑤	Ⓕ	Ⓞ	⑤	⑤	⑤	⑤	⑤	⑤	⑤	⑤
⑥	Ⓖ	Ⓟ	⑥	⑥	⑥	⑥	⑥	⑥	⑥	⑥
⑦	Ⓗ	Ⓠ	⑦	⑦	⑦	⑦	⑦	⑦	⑦	⑦
⑧	Ⓘ	Ⓡ	⑧	⑧	⑧	⑧	⑧	⑧	⑧	⑧
⑨			⑨	⑨	⑨	⑨	⑨	⑨	⑨	⑨

5. YOUR NAME

First 4 letters of last name				FIRST INIT	MID INIT
Ⓐ	Ⓐ	Ⓐ	Ⓐ	Ⓐ	Ⓐ
Ⓑ	Ⓑ	Ⓑ	Ⓑ	Ⓑ	Ⓑ
Ⓒ	Ⓒ	Ⓒ	Ⓒ	Ⓒ	Ⓒ
Ⓓ	Ⓓ	Ⓓ	Ⓓ	Ⓓ	Ⓓ
Ⓔ	Ⓔ	Ⓔ	Ⓔ	Ⓔ	Ⓔ
Ⓕ	Ⓕ	Ⓕ	Ⓕ	Ⓕ	Ⓕ
Ⓖ	Ⓖ	Ⓖ	Ⓖ	Ⓖ	Ⓖ
Ⓗ	Ⓗ	Ⓗ	Ⓗ	Ⓗ	Ⓗ
Ⓘ	Ⓘ	Ⓘ	Ⓘ	Ⓘ	Ⓘ
Ⓙ	Ⓙ	Ⓙ	Ⓙ	Ⓙ	Ⓙ
Ⓚ	Ⓚ	Ⓚ	Ⓚ	Ⓚ	Ⓚ
Ⓛ	Ⓛ	Ⓛ	Ⓛ	Ⓛ	Ⓛ
Ⓜ	Ⓜ	Ⓜ	Ⓜ	Ⓜ	Ⓜ
Ⓝ	Ⓝ	Ⓝ	Ⓝ	Ⓝ	Ⓝ
Ⓞ	Ⓞ	Ⓞ	Ⓞ	Ⓞ	Ⓞ
Ⓟ	Ⓟ	Ⓟ	Ⓟ	Ⓟ	Ⓟ
Ⓠ	Ⓠ	Ⓠ	Ⓠ	Ⓠ	Ⓠ
Ⓡ	Ⓡ	Ⓡ	Ⓡ	Ⓡ	Ⓡ
Ⓢ	Ⓢ	Ⓢ	Ⓢ	Ⓢ	Ⓢ
Ⓣ	Ⓣ	Ⓣ	Ⓣ	Ⓣ	Ⓣ
Ⓤ	Ⓤ	Ⓤ	Ⓤ	Ⓤ	Ⓤ
Ⓥ	Ⓥ	Ⓥ	Ⓥ	Ⓥ	Ⓥ
Ⓦ	Ⓦ	Ⓦ	Ⓦ	Ⓦ	Ⓦ
Ⓧ	Ⓧ	Ⓧ	Ⓧ	Ⓧ	Ⓧ
Ⓨ	Ⓨ	Ⓨ	Ⓨ	Ⓨ	Ⓨ
Ⓩ	Ⓩ	Ⓩ	Ⓩ	Ⓩ	Ⓩ

6. DATE OF BIRTH

Month	Day		Year	
◯ JAN				
◯ FEB	⓪	⓪	⓪	⓪
◯ MAR	①	①	①	①
◯ APR	②	②	②	②
◯ MAY	③	③	③	③
◯ JUN		④	④	④
◯ JUL		⑤	⑤	⑤
◯ AUG		⑥	⑥	⑥
◯ SEP		⑦	⑦	⑦
◯ OCT		⑧	⑧	⑧
◯ NOV		⑨	⑨	⑨
◯ DEC				

7. GENDER
◯ MALE
◯ FEMALE

The Princeton Review®

1. Ⓐ Ⓑ Ⓒ Ⓓ
2. Ⓐ Ⓑ Ⓒ Ⓓ
3. Ⓐ Ⓑ Ⓒ Ⓓ
4. Ⓐ Ⓑ Ⓒ Ⓓ
5. Ⓐ Ⓑ Ⓒ Ⓓ
6. Ⓐ Ⓑ Ⓒ Ⓓ
7. Ⓐ Ⓑ Ⓒ Ⓓ
8. Ⓐ Ⓑ Ⓒ Ⓓ
9. Ⓐ Ⓑ Ⓒ Ⓓ
10. Ⓐ Ⓑ Ⓒ Ⓓ
11. Ⓐ Ⓑ Ⓒ Ⓓ
12. Ⓐ Ⓑ Ⓒ Ⓓ
13. Ⓐ Ⓑ Ⓒ Ⓓ
14. Ⓐ Ⓑ Ⓒ Ⓓ
15. Ⓐ Ⓑ Ⓒ Ⓓ
16. Ⓐ Ⓑ Ⓒ Ⓓ
17. Ⓐ Ⓑ Ⓒ Ⓓ
18. Ⓐ Ⓑ Ⓒ Ⓓ

19. Ⓐ Ⓑ Ⓒ Ⓓ
20. Ⓐ Ⓑ Ⓒ Ⓓ
21. Ⓐ Ⓑ Ⓒ Ⓓ
22. Ⓐ Ⓑ Ⓒ Ⓓ
23. Ⓐ Ⓑ Ⓒ Ⓓ
24. Ⓐ Ⓑ Ⓒ Ⓓ
25. Ⓐ Ⓑ Ⓒ Ⓓ
26. Ⓐ Ⓑ Ⓒ Ⓓ
27. Ⓐ Ⓑ Ⓒ Ⓓ
28. Ⓐ Ⓑ Ⓒ Ⓓ
29. Ⓐ Ⓑ Ⓒ Ⓓ
30. Ⓐ Ⓑ Ⓒ Ⓓ
31. Ⓐ Ⓑ Ⓒ Ⓓ
32. Ⓐ Ⓑ Ⓒ Ⓓ
33. Ⓐ Ⓑ Ⓒ Ⓓ
34. Ⓐ Ⓑ Ⓒ Ⓓ
35. Ⓐ Ⓑ Ⓒ Ⓓ
36. Ⓐ Ⓑ Ⓒ Ⓓ

37. Ⓐ Ⓑ Ⓒ Ⓓ
38. Ⓐ Ⓑ Ⓒ Ⓓ
39. Ⓐ Ⓑ Ⓒ Ⓓ
40. Ⓐ Ⓑ Ⓒ Ⓓ
41. Ⓐ Ⓑ Ⓒ Ⓓ
42. Ⓐ Ⓑ Ⓒ Ⓓ
43. Ⓐ Ⓑ Ⓒ Ⓓ
44. Ⓐ Ⓑ Ⓒ Ⓓ
45. Ⓐ Ⓑ Ⓒ Ⓓ
46. Ⓐ Ⓑ Ⓒ Ⓓ
47. Ⓐ Ⓑ Ⓒ Ⓓ
48. Ⓐ Ⓑ Ⓒ Ⓓ
49. Ⓐ Ⓑ Ⓒ Ⓓ
50. Ⓐ Ⓑ Ⓒ Ⓓ
51. Ⓐ Ⓑ Ⓒ Ⓓ
52. Ⓐ Ⓑ Ⓒ Ⓓ
53. Ⓐ Ⓑ Ⓒ Ⓓ
54. Ⓐ Ⓑ Ⓒ Ⓓ

55. Ⓐ Ⓑ Ⓒ Ⓓ

AP® World History: Modern Exam

SECTION I, PART A: Multiple Choice

DO NOT OPEN THIS BOOKLET UNTIL YOU ARE TOLD TO DO SO.

At a Glance

Time
55 minutes
Number of Questions
55
Percent of Total Score
40%
Writing Instrument
Pencil required

Instructions

Section I, Part A of this exam contains 55 multiple-choice questions. Fill in only the ovals for numbers 1 through 55 on your answer sheet.

Indicate all of your answers to the multiple-choice questions on the answer sheet. No credit will be given for anything written in this exam booklet, but you may use the booklet for notes or scratch work. After you have decided which of the suggested answers is best, completely fill in the corresponding oval on the answer sheet. Give only one answer to each question. If you change an answer, be sure that the previous mark is erased completely. Here is a sample question and answer.

Sample Question   Sample Answer

Chicago is a   Ⓐ ● Ⓒ Ⓓ
(A) state
(B) city
(C) country
(D) continent

Use your time effectively, working as quickly as you can without losing accuracy. Do not spend too much time on any one question. Go on to other questions and come back to the ones you have not answered if you have time. It is not expected that everyone will know the answers to all the multiple-choice questions.

Your total score on the multiple-choice section is based only on the number of questions answered correctly. Points are not deducted for incorrect answers or unanswered questions.

SECTION I, PART B: Short Answer

At a Glance

Time
40 minutes
Number of Questions
3
Percent of Total Score
20%
Writing Instrument
Pen with black or dark blue ink

Instructions

Section I, Part B of this exam consists of 4 short-answer questions, of which you will answer 3. Answer all parts of Questions 1 and 2, and then choose to answer EITHER Question 3 or Question 4. Write your responses on a separate sheet of paper.

After the exam, you must apply the label that corresponds to the last short-essay question you answered—Question 3 or 4. For example, if you answered Question 3, apply the label ③ . Failure to do so may delay your score.

WORLD HISTORY: MODERN

Section I, Part A

Time—55 minutes

55 Questions

Directions: Each of the questions or incomplete statements below is followed by either four suggested answers or completions. Select the one that is best in each case and then fill in the appropriate letter in the corresponding space on the answer sheet.

Questions 1–4 refer to the passage below.

6. After our death [Charles VI], and from that time forward, the crown and kingdom of France, with all their rights and appurtenances, shall be vested permanently in our son [son-in-law], King Henry [of England], and his heirs.

7.....The power and authority to govern and to control the public affairs of the said kingdom shall, during our lifetime, be vested in our son, King Henry, with the advice of the nobles and wise men who are obedient to us, and who have consideration for the advancement and honor of the said kingdom....

24.....[It is agreed] that the two kingdoms shall be governed from the time that our said son, or any of his heirs shall assume the crown, not divided between different kings at the same time, but under one person who shall be king and sovereign lord of both kingdoms; observing all pledges and all other things to each kingdom its rights, liberties or customs, usages and laws, not submitting in any manner one kingdom to the other.

29. In consideration of the frightful and astounding crimes and misdeeds committed against the kingdom of France by Charles, the said Dauphin, it is agreed that we, our son Henry, and also our very dear son Philip, duke of Burgundy, will never treat for peace or amity with the said Charles.

Treaty of Troyes, 1420

1. The Treaty of Troyes can best be understood in the context of which of the following?

   (A) The Thirty Years War
   (B) The War of Spanish Succession
   (C) The English Civil War
   (D) The Hundred Years' War

2. The intended outcome of the treaty can best be summarized in which of the following ways?

   (A) England withdrew from France.
   (B) The French monarchy would rule over England.
   (C) England gained control over the French monarchy.
   (D) England would retain limited control over French territory.

3. Which of the following was a consequence of the treaty?

   (A) The French surrendered to the English army.
   (B) The French monarchy ended until the fifteenth century.
   (C) The French were inspired to strengthen their military resistance against England's rule.
   (D) The French ceded internal government control to the Huguenots.

4. Which of the following was a long-term consequence of this conflict between France and England?

   (A) French monarchical power became more centralized.
   (B) Both France and England moved toward stronger parliamentary systems.
   (C) Catholic influence in France subsided.
   (D) The English monarchy was severely weakened.

GO ON TO THE NEXT PAGE.

Questions 5–8 refer to the passage below.

The people are Idolaters; and since they were conquered by the Great Kaan they use paper-money. Both men and women are fair and comely, and for the most part clothe themselves in silk, so vast is the supply of that material, both from the whole district of Kinsay, and from the imports by traders from other provinces. And you must know they eat every kind of flesh, even that of dogs and other unclean beasts, which nothing would induce a Christian to eat.

Since the Great Kaan occupied the city he has ordained that each of the 12,000 bridges should be provided with a guard of ten men, in case of any disturbance, or of any being so rash as to plot treason or insurrection against him. Each guard is provided with a hollow instrument of wood and with a metal basin, and with a time-keeper to enable them to know the hour of the day or night. And so when one hour of the night is past the sentry strikes one on the wooden instrument and on the basin, so that the whole quarter of the city is made aware that one hour of the night is gone. At the second hour he gives two strokes, and so on, keeping always wide awake and on the look out. In the morning again, from the sunrise, they begin to count anew, and strike one hour as they did in the night, and so on hour after hour.

The Glories Of Kinsay [Hangchow], Marco Polo, c. 1300

5. According to Marco Polo, Kinsay was governed with an emphasis on which of the following?

(A) A strong economy

(B) Reinforced security

(C) Cultural homogeneity

(D) Isolationism

6. Marco Polo visited Kinsay during which of the following dynasties?

(A) Song

(B) Yuan

(C) Ming

(D) Qing

7. The reference to silk clothing is evidence of which of the following insights about Kinsay's occupiers?

(A) The occupiers were advanced in manufacturing.

(B) The occupiers reformed the economic structure of China.

(C) The occupiers trained in Chinese traditional fabric making.

(D) The occupiers tolerated local customs.

8. Which of the following represents an ongoing historical trend that benefited Marco Polo at the time this account was written?

(A) The trade connection established by the Mongol empire enabled the free passage and trading opportunities that allowed Marco Polo to complete his journey.

(B) The spread of the Black Plague limited meaningful interaction between would-be trade partners from separate regions of Euro-Asia.

(C) The resurgence of the Silk Road allowed for easier overland trade during the rule of the Yuan Dynasty.

(D) The success of the transatlantic trade boosted interest in exploring the Far East, leading to many wealthy Europeans financing opportunities for explorers to travel to Asia.

GO ON TO THE NEXT PAGE.

Questions 9–12 refer to the image below.

Siege of Esztergom 1543 Produced by Sebastian Vrancx (1573–1647)

*The painting depicts a campaign by Suleiman I against the city of Esztergom
(located in modern-day Hungary) against the Holy Roman Empire.*

9. The event portrayed in the image above occurred in the context of which of the following Islamic empires?

  (A) Mughal

  (B) Safavid

  (C) Ottoman

  (D) Abbasid

10. Sulieman was able to successfully invade Esztergom due to which of the following factors?

  (A) Esztergom had poorly defended ocean borders.

  (B) Sulieman's army was welcomed into the region by the large Muslim population, which considered his arrival a liberation.

  (C) The Turks had already taken Austria, which allowed for simple access into Hungary.

  (D) The political instability during the Protestant Reformation greatly weakened the Holy Roman Empire.

11. Which of the following was a consequence of the event portrayed in the image?

  (A) The Ottoman Empire reached its greatest heights by expanding into Central Europe.

  (B) Much of the religious landscape of Eastern Europe was split between the Orthodox Christian Church and Islam.

  (C) Suleiman I abdicated his throne, unable to control his empire following a military defeat.

  (D) The Turks attempted to further penetrate Europe before acknowledging the futility of doing so.

12. Which of the following was an important continuity underlying the conflict depicted in this painting?

  (A) Military conflicts in pursuit of expanded empires

  (B) Violent campaigns aimed at converting conquered people to a different religion

  (C) Warfare as a means of controlling overseas trade

  (D) Battles over disputed territories amidst the fall of empires

GO ON TO THE NEXT PAGE.

Questions 13–16 refer to the passage below.

…it is not unreasonable to conclude that the Japanese and Korean peoples formed for a long time one and the same nation. The recent annexation of Korea by Japan is therefore not the incorporation of two different countries inhabited by different races, but, it may rather be said to be the reunion of two sections of the one and same nation after a long period of separation. Indeed it is nothing more nor less than the old state of things restored. … In developing the industry of an infantile nation, it is advisable to begin the work by undertaking the improvement of the agricultural industry, and this has been diligently carried on since Japan assumed the protectorate of the Korean Empire.

Komatsu Midori, "The Old People and the New Government," in *Transactions of the Korea Branch of the Royal Asiatic Society,* 1912

13. The situation described in the passage resulted from which of the following events?

    (A) The Treaty of Shimonoseki
    (B) The Meiji Restoration
    (C) The Treaty of Kanagawa
    (D) The White Lotus Rebellions

14. The passage can best be used as evidence for which of the following trends?

    (A) Western nations' success in establishing spheres of influence in Asia
    (B) Japan's use of propaganda to win over the allegiance of the Korean people
    (C) Japan and Korea's common distrust of the nationalist Chinese government
    (D) Japan's neutrality in the affairs of mainland China

15. This passage is best understood in the context of which of the following?

    (A) Japan's rise to imperial power
    (B) The opening of Japan's contact with the West
    (C) Korea's long struggle to unify with Japan
    (D) China's nationalist reforms

16. Which of the following would best support the author's assertion that Japan and Korea are a "reunion of two sections"?

    (A) A linguistic textbook that details the differences between the Japanese and Korean languages
    (B) Survey information that demarcates the historical boundaries of Japan and Korea
    (C) War records outlining casualties experienced by each nation
    (D) A census document from a previous century that shows names common to both countries

GO ON TO THE NEXT PAGE.

Questions 17–20 refer to the map below.

Path Map of a Late Fifteenth Century Voyage.

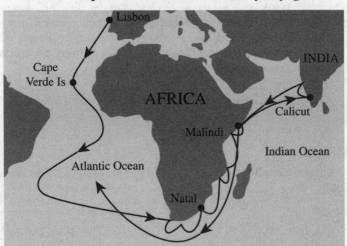

17. The voyage as shown in the map most clearly demonstrates which of the following developments of the time period?

    (A) The strength of European business ventures in India during the sixteenth century
    (B) A lack of interest in the New World on the part of Portuguese explorers
    (C) The inaccessibility of Muslim lands at the dawn of the sixteenth century
    (D) Portuguese dominance in sea exploration during the late fifteenth and early sixteenth centuries

18. Which of the following conclusions about the early sixteenth century is most directly supported by the map?

    (A) Portugal was primarily interested in exploration of the African and Asian coasts.
    (B) Vasco da Gama was the first European to embark on intercontinental travel by sea.
    (C) European nations began to look outward for economic opportunities.
    (D) Europeans began mass migrations to distant lands in the early sixteenth century.

19. Which of the following is an accurate statement concerning Asian nations' interactions with European powers throughout the sixteenth century?

    (A) Japan actively engaged with Portuguese traders and missionaries throughout the century.
    (B) India long resisted European attempts to establish ports along its coast.
    (C) Ming rulers successfully maintained an isolationist policy despite European attempts to create more trade with China.
    (D) Asian countries exclusively had interactions with Spanish and Portuguese traders throughout the sixteenth century before other European nations finally became interested in exploring the East.

20. Which of the following best explains the impact of the trade relationship between the Portuguese and Africans in the sixteenth century?

    (A) Unlike other European nations, the Portuguese mostly ignored the trading opportunities available in Africa, and instead chose to focus on economic expansion in Asia.
    (B) The Portuguese engaged in trade for gold and salt, but unlike other European powers, refused to participate in the slave trade.
    (C) The Portuguese set up ports along the western and southern African coasts which led to beneficial economic opportunities for many African people.
    (D) The Portuguese exploited human labor by bringing enslaved Africans to Europe.

GO ON TO THE NEXT PAGE.

Questions 21–25 refer to the passage below.

Since the Sung dynasty had lost the throne and Heaven had cut off their sacrifice, the Yuan [Mongol] dynasty had risen from the desert to enter and rule over Zhongguo [China] for more than a hundred years, when Heaven, wearied of their misgovernment and debauchery, thought also fit to turn their fate to ruin, and the affairs of Zhongguo were in a state of disorder for eighteen years. But when the nation began to arouse itself, We…conceived the patriotic idea to save the people, and it pleased the Creator to grant that Our civil and military officers effected their passage across eastward to the left side of the River. We have then been engaged in war for fourteen years; …We have established peace in the Empire, and restored the old boundaries of Zhongguo. We were selected by Our people to occupy the Imperial throne of Zhongguo under the dynastic title of 'the Great Ming,' … We now send a native of your country…to hand you this Manifesto. Although We are not equal in wisdom to our ancient rulers whose virtue was recognized all over the universe, We cannot but let the world know Our intention to maintain peace within the four seas. It is on this ground alone that We have issued this Manifesto.

Manifesto of Accession as First Ming Emperor, 1372 C.E. (Sent to Byzantine Emperor)

21. This manifesto was created in the wake of which of the following events?

(A) The Ming seizing control of China following the defeat of the Mongol government

(B) A peaceful transfer of power from the Yuan rulers to the Ming emperor

(C) The defeat of the Sung Dynasty by an alliance of Mongol and Ming warriors

(D) The rise of Mongol power in China after years of violent struggle

22. In which of the following ways did the Ming Dynasty differ from the previous ruling dynasty?

(A) The Ming was interested in expanding its borders, while the Yuan was largely isolationist.

(B) The Ming ruled over a period of economic and cultural stagnation, while the Yuan oversaw a Chinese Golden Age of artistic and technological innovation.

(C) The Ming placed emphasis on local and internal economic trade, while the Yuan employed seafarers to seek out trade partners abroad.

(D) The Ming returned China to its Confucian roots, while the Yuan respected, but did not fully embrace the tenets of Confucianism.

23. Which of the following best characterizes the author's tone in the passage?

(A) Vengeful over the costs of fourteen years of warfare

(B) Confident in his assurance of a long-term peace

(C) Joyful over the rise of a new dynasty

(D) Concerned about the instability of the Ming empire

24. Which of the following reasons best describes the Ming Emperor's interest in writing to the Byzantine Emperor?

(A) To alert the Byzantines that China no longer wishes to engage in expansionary wars

(B) To share news of the rise of the Mongols who now rule China

(C) To offer an invitation into a more active economic relationship

(D) To warn to the Byzantine emperor not to challenge China's borders

25. The Ming Emperor's assertion that he "pleased the Creator" is a reference to which traditional Chinese ruling concept?

(A) Filial piety

(B) Legalism

(C) Mandate of Heaven

(D) Neo-Confucianism

GO ON TO THE NEXT PAGE.

Questions 26–30 refer to the passage below.

The new Imperialism has nowhere extended the political and civil liberties of the mother country to any part of the vast territories which, since 1870, have fallen under the government of Western civilised Powers. Politically, the new Imperialism is an expansion of autocracy.

Taking the growth of Imperialism as illustrated in the recent expansion of Great Britain and of the chief continental Powers, we find the distinction between Imperialism and colonization…closely borne out by facts and figures, and warranting the following general judgments: —

First—Almost the whole of recent imperial expansion is occupied with the political absorption of tropical or sub-tropical lands in which white men will not settle with their families.

Second—Nearly all the lands are thickly peopled by "lower races."

Thus this recent imperial expansion stands entirely distinct from the colonisation of sparsely peopled lands in temperate zones, where white colonists carry with them the modes of government, the industrial and other arts of the civilisation of the mother country. The "occupation" of these new territories is comprised in the presence of a small minority of white men, officials, traders, and industrial organisers, exercising political and economic sway over great hordes of population regarded as inferior and as incapable of exercising any considerable rights of self-government, in politics or industry.

Imperialism, A Study by English economist John A. Hobson (1902)

26. British interest in imperial claims in South African were accelerated by which of the following?

    (A) Worries about rebellions in Great Britain's sub-Saharan colonies

    (B) A need to establish geographically useful bases in the run-up to World War I

    (C) The discovery of gold by the Boers

    (D) Fears stemming from the German Empire quickly colonizing lands near South Africa

27. How is the "small minority of white men" mentioned in the passage best understood contextually?

    (A) Representatives of the colonizing nations who hold disproportionate amounts of power in host countries

    (B) Rebels who oppose the imperial presence of their home countries in colonized lands

    (C) Settlers from a colonizing nation who face oppression upon settling in a host country

    (D) Missionaries who attempt to introduce Christianity to a region that had not yet been exposed to it

28. The author of this text expresses a belief in which of the following as a distinction between colonization and imperialism?

    (A) Colonization typically occurs in tropical or sub-tropical lands, while the new imperialism occurs primarily in temperate zones.

    (B) Colonization traditionally involves the transfer of tools and methods to help the colonized country, while imperialism involves a denial of rights to the people of the host country.

    (C) Colonization occurs in lands in which white people would not settle with their families, while imperialism can exist anywhere so long as the settlers can exercise political and economic sway.

    (D) Colonization promotes democracy in host countries, while imperialism is, at its core, an expansion of autocracy.

GO ON TO THE NEXT PAGE.

29. Which of the following was a key distinction between European imperialism in sub-tropical lands and the European spheres of influence that were established in China?

    (A) In China, Europeans maintained an equal balance of trade, while in sub-tropical countries, European traders relied on exploitation and unfair practices.

    (B) In China, merchants from Europe typically could not make much profit; however, they could often greatly enrich themselves by establishing businesses in sub-tropical nations.

    (C) In China, the European style of mercantilism was rejected, but merchants in sub-tropical lands often welcomed European traders.

    (D) In China, Europeans focused only on exploiting the region for money, while in sub-tropical regions, Europeans attempted to influence and change the host country's culture.

30. The passage is best understood in the context of which of the following historical events?

    (A) The Berlin Conference
    (B) World War I
    (C) The Boer War
    (D) The Treaty of Cordoba

GO ON TO THE NEXT PAGE.

Questions 31–34 refer to the passage below.

I believe strongly and sincerely that with the deep-rooted wisdom and dignity, the innate respect for human lives, the intense humanity that is our heritage, the African race, united under one federal government, will emerge not as just another world bloc to flaunt its wealth and strength, but as a Great Power whose greatness is indestructible because it is built not on fear, envy and suspicion, nor won at the expense of others, but founded on hope, trust, friendship and directed to the good of all mankind. The emergence of such a mighty stabilising force in this strife-worn world should be regarded not as the shadowy dream of a visionary, but as a practical proposition, which the peoples of Africa can, and should, translate into reality. There is a tide in the affairs of every people when the moment strikes for political action. Such was the moment in the history of the United States of America when the Founding Fathers saw beyond the petty wranglings of the separate states and created a Union. This is our chance. We must act now. Tomorrow may be too late and the opportunity will have passed, and with it the hope of free Africa's survival.

I Speak of Freedom: A Statement of African Ideology by Kwame Nkrumah, 1961

31. Kwame Nkrumah most directly advocates a belief in which of the following ideologies?

(A) Marxism
(B) Pan-Africanism
(C) Neoliberalism
(D) Nationalism

32. Which of the following explains why the author references the United States?

(A) To offer a criticism of a dominant imperial power
(B) To demonstrate the achievability of his vision with a historical example
(C) To dismiss the vision of the United States' Founding Fathers as futile
(D) To argue that it is too late to follow the model laid out in American history

33. A historian researching the process of African decolonization would most likely find this passage useful as a source of information about which of the following?

(A) Perspectives of African politicians on the importance of the sovereignty of individual nations
(B) How leaders of decolonization movements in Africa viewed the roles of other African nations in the decolonization process
(C) The influence of the United States on decolonized nations in Africa
(D) The difficulty of maintaining a decolonized Africa amidst the wealth and strength of the world's great powers

34. Kwame Nkrumah saw his vision most closely achieved by which of the following occurrences?

(A) African countries' acceptance into the United Nations
(B) The spread of influence by non-governmental organizations throughout Africa
(C) The implementation of the African Union
(D) The creation of the Organization of African Unity

GO ON TO THE NEXT PAGE.

Questions 35–38 refer to the passage below.

Blessed be the sacred Land
Happy be the bounteous realm
Symbol of high resolve
Land of Pakistan
Blessed be thou citadel of faith

The order of this sacred land
Is the might of the brotherhood of the People
May the nation, the country, and the state
Shine in glory everlasting
Blessed be the goal of our ambition

This Flag of the Crescent and Star
Leads the way to progress and perfection
Interpreter of our past, glory of our present
Inspiration of our future

National Anthem of Pakistan, approved by the Government in August 1954

35. The "brotherhood of the People" mentioned in the national anthem is a reference to which of the following?

   (A) Colonized peoples
   (B) All persons living on the Indian subcontinent
   (C) Pakistanis and their former colonizers
   (D) Muslims

36. The creation of Pakistan was most acutely attributed to which of the following?

   (A) Mohandas Gandhi
   (B) The United Nations
   (C) British colonialists
   (D) The Muslim League

37. Which of the following was a result of the establishment of Pakistan and India as two separate countries?

   (A) Migrations in the millions stemming from religious violence
   (B) The establishment of a common government to oversee tensions between the two nations
   (C) The establishment of separate state religions in Pakistan and India
   (D) An agreement between Mohandas Gandhi and Muhammad Ali Jinnah to allow free passage between the two nations via the Kashmir region

38. The arrangement made between the Pakistanis and Indians in 1947 was most similar to which of the following historical arrangements?

   (A) The military arrangement between Germany and Japan during World War II
   (B) The political arrangement between the Soviet Union and Poland at the start of the Cold War
   (C) The geographical arrangement between Jews and Muslims in Palestine
   (D) The colonial arrangement between France and Indochina in the first part of the twentieth century

GO ON TO THE NEXT PAGE.

Questions 39–41 refer to the passage below.

My lord, you may have seen before this, by the maps of Asia, how great every way is the extent of the empire of the Great Mogul, which is commonly called India or Indostan…

In this…country there are sundry nations which the Mogul is not full master of, most of them still retaining their particular sovereigns and lords that neither obey him nor pay him tribute but from constraint; many that do little, some that do nothing at all, and some also that receive tribute from him. . .

Such are the Pathans, a Mohammedan people issued from the side of the river Ganges toward Bengal, who before the invasion of the Moguls in India had taken their time to make themselves potent in many place, and chiefly at Delhi, and to render many rajahs thereabout their tributaries. These Pathans are fierce and warlike, and even the meanest of them, though they be but waiting men and porters, are still of a very high spirit…

An Account of India and the Great Moghul, by François Bernier, 1655 CE

39. According to Bernier, the relationship between the Pathans (commonly referred to as Pashtuns) and the Mughal empire can best be described in which of the following ways?

(A) The Pathans, a minority group under the Mughal Empire, are forced to pay tribute to live under the Mughal rule.

(B) The Mughal Empire and the Pathans are the two primary sovereign entities in India, and thus they retain a peaceful relationship largely by leaving one another alone.

(C) The Mughal Empire is deferential to the Pathans, with whom the empire wishes to avoid conflict.

(D) The Mughal Empire and the Pathans, separated by their religions, retain a mutual respect for one another.

40. This passage could be used as evidence for which of the following conclusions?

(A) The Mughal Empire thrived by exercising total control over the people living within its borders.

(B) The Pathans were key to assisting the Mughal emperors in their hold on power in the Indian subcontinent.

(C) Hindu subjects of the Mughal Empire tended to not pay tribute to the emperor.

(D) The Mughal Empire maintained its stability during this period largely due to its hand-off governing style with regards to minority groups.

41. Which of the following led to an easing of tensions between Muslims and Hindus in the Indian subcontinent from the mid-sixteenth to the mid-seventeenth centuries?

(A) The death of Emperor Akbar

(B) The Mughal government's suspension of the use of the *jizya*

(C) Economic success following the establishment of the British East India Company

(D) The reforms of Emperor Aurangzeb

GO ON TO THE NEXT PAGE.

Questions 42–44 refer to the passage below.

> Where is the German's fatherland?
> Then name, oh, name the mighty land!
> Wherever is heard the German tongue,
> And German hymns to God are sung!
> This is the land, thy Hermann's land;
> This, German, is thy fatherland.
> This is the German's fatherland,
> Where faith is in the plighted hand,
> Where truth lives in each eye of blue,
> And every heart is staunch and true.
> This is the land, the honest land,
> The honest German's fatherland.
> This is the land, the one true land,
> O God, to aid be thou at hand!
> And fire each heart, and nerve each arm,
> To shield our German homes from harm,
> To shield the land, the one true land,
> One Deutschland and one fatherland!

"The German Fatherland" by Ernst Moritz Arndt,
a popular German folk song in the late nineteenth century.

42. The final verse of this song is most clearly a reference to which of the following events?

    (A) The end of the Concert of Europe
    (B) The consolidation of the German Catholic territories under Prussian rule
    (C) The German Empire's imperialist expansion into other parts of the world
    (D) The establishment of the Frankfurt Parliament

43. Ideas similar to those expressed in the passage have directly contributed to the development of which of the following aspects of late nineteenth-century nationalism?

    (A) Religious zealotry
    (B) Belief in racial superiority
    (C) Isolationism
    (D) Widespread democratization

44. A historian would likely categorize this song as part of which of the following?

    (A) The Volkisch Movement
    (B) The Self-Strengthening Movement
    (C) Kulturkampf
    (D) The People's Will

GO ON TO THE NEXT PAGE.

Questions 45–47 refer to the two passages below.

Source 1

I want to say to you who think women cannot succeed, we have brought the government of England to this position, that it has to face this alternative; either women are to be killed or women are to have the vote. I ask American men in this meeting, what would you say if in your State you were faced with that alternative, that you must either kill them or give them their citizenship, —women, many of whom you respect, women whom you know have lived useful lives, women whom you know, even if you do not know them personally, are animated with the highest motives, women who are in pursuit of liberty and the power to do useful public service? Well, there is only one answer to that alternative; there is only one way out of it, unless you are prepared to put back civilization two or three generations; you must give those women the vote. Now that is the outcome of our civil war.

"Militant Suffragist," Emmeline Pankhurst, 1913

Source 2

A woman whose husband owns a sugar mill or hacienda and calls herself a Spiritist or Christian should not seek to load herself down with jewelry, nor make useless purchases. She should visit the families of her peons, who produce the wealth she and her husband possess and who continue increasing it, and observe how they live, if they lack items that are useful or necessary, like chairs, beds, and other utensils. And she should notice if their roof doesn't leak, and if the inhabitants can live in the house in sanitary conditions, that it is sufficiently clean so that she would want to live there herself. And if you find opposition from your husband, if he is cruel and egotistical and becomes an obstacle to your great and just aspirations, do not blame him and do not fear him; because in him, you will see the symbol of ignorance, trying to hold on to its power. Oh woman! You will set a great and dignified example by breaking traditional customs, which are unjust and tyrannical, the symbols of ignorance, in order to establish the realm of Freedom, Equality, and Fraternity, symbols of truth and justice!

"Mi Opinion" Luisa Capetillo, 1911

45. Source 1 suggests that which of the following was true about the women's right to vote in the early part of the twentieth century?

   (A) The British granted women the right to vote before the Americans did.
   (B) Only England and the United States had taken a serious look at the women's right to vote by the early twentieth century.
   (C) Women's right to vote was becoming widespread in Western democracies in the early twentieth century.
   (D) Debates over the right to vote for women would lead to civil war within the United States.

46. In Source 2, Capetillo's view of the struggle for women's rights is most directly influenced by which of the following ideologies?

   (A) Nationalism
   (B) Marxism
   (C) Anti-colonialism
   (D) Capitalism

47. Which of the following is a key distinction between the two sources?

   (A) Capetillo downplays the immediacy of the struggle for women's rights, while Pankhurst demonstrates that equal rights is a grave issue that must not wait any longer.
   (B) Capetillo discusses economic and social obstacles women face, while Pankhurst advocates more specifically for suffrage.
   (C) Capetillo does not mention the role of men in the debate, while Pankhurst directs her comments toward men.
   (D) Capetillo claims that women must break away from traditional customs, while Pankhurst holds a more conservative approach that relies on gradualism and tradition.

GO ON TO THE NEXT PAGE.

Questions 48–51 refer to the image below.

"Telling the Italians!", Produced by Clifford Berryman, American Cartoonist, 1938.

48. This cartoon is best understood in the context of which of the following events?

    (A) Treaty of Brest-Litovsk
    (B) Tripartite Pact
    (C) Anti-Comintern Pact
    (D) The Munich Conference

49. The cartoonist implies which of the following claims about Mussolini?

    (A) He was responsible for Germany's military successes.
    (B) He was primarily responsible for the start of World War II.
    (C) He employs propaganda to mislead his people.
    (D) He held more popularity in Europe than did Hitler.

50. Mussolini and Hitler shared which of the following common factors in their rise to power?

    (A) They both benefited politically from weak economies in their countries.
    (B) They were both democratically elected to the heads of their governments.
    (C) Each leader initially gained popularity by appealing to their country's socialist parties.
    (D) Both were trained in prestigious military schools, laying the groundwork for expert usage of militaries to gain and hold onto power.

51. In contrast to Hitler, Mussolini focused on which of the following strategies?

    (A) Creating non-aggression pacts with powerful nations
    (B) Manipulation of the national news media for political benefit
    (C) Emphasis of the superiority of one race over others
    (D) Expansion into Northern Africa

GO ON TO THE NEXT PAGE.

Questions 52–55 refer to the passages below.

<u>Source 1</u>

It goes without saying that in that event the U.S. government cannot fail to call to stern account those immediately responsible for the deliberate violation of the Soviet Union's national frontiers by American planes. . . It is natural that under these conditions we are unable to work at the conference, unable to work at it because we see from what positions it is desired to talk to us— under threat of aggressive intelligence flights. Everyone knows that spying flights are undertaken for intelligence purposes with a view to starting war. Accordingly, we reject the conditions in which the United States is placing us. We cannot take part in any negotiations, not even in the settlement of questions which are already ripe, because we see that the U.S. has no desire to reach agreement. . . .We wish to be rightly understood by the peoples of all countries of the globe, by public opinion. The Soviet Union is not abandoning its efforts for agreement, and we are sure that reasonable agreements are possible, but evidently at some other, not this particular time. . . .The Soviet government is profoundly convinced that if not this U.S. government, then another, and if not another, then a third, will understand that there is no other solution than peaceful co-existence of the two systems, the capitalist and the socialist. It is either peaceful co-existence, or war, which would spell disaster for those now engaging in an aggressive policy.

Nikita Khrushchev: Summit Conference Statement, May 16, 1960

<u>Source 2</u>

…at this morning's private session, despite the violence and inaccuracy of Mr. Khrushchev's statements, I replied to him in the following terms: In my statement of May 11th and in the statement of Secretary Herter of May 9th the position of the United States was made clear with respect to the distasteful necessity of espionage activities in a world where nations distrust each other's intentions. We pointed out that these activities had no aggressive intent but rather were to assure the safety of the United States and the free world against surprise attack by a power which boasts of its ability to devastate the United States and other countries by missiles armed with atomic warheads.

Dwight Eisenhower: Summit Conference Statement, May 16, 1960

52. This passage is most clearly an example of which of the following?

   (A) A debate over allowable missile placements
   (B) Talks in the lead-up to a military conflict
   (C) A summit focused on a hypothetical situation involving international spying
   (D) Negotiations aimed at easing tensions during the Cold War

53. According to the passage, Khrushchev and Eisenhower are meeting in the wake of which of the following incidents?

   (A) The Soviet Union used spies on American soil.
   (B) The Soviet Union aggressively expanded its influence into sovereign European nations.
   (C) The Soviet Union had threatened nuclear war against the United States
   (D) The Soviet Union captured an American espionage plane.

54. According to the passages, Khrushchev and Eisenhower disagree in which of the following ways?

   (A) Khrushchev argues for the end of the Cold War, while Eisenhower posits that it will continue indefinitely.
   (B) Khrushchev maintains that the Soviet Union has a right to defend itself with espionage measures, while Eisenhower counters that no such right exists.
   (C) Khrushchev claims that American spying measures are aggressive acts, while Eisenhower insists they are preventative.
   (D) Khrushchev makes a distinction between spying and national defense, while Eisenhower debunks any such distinction.

55. According to the passage, Khrushchev maintains which of the following viewpoints about capitalism?

   (A) Capitalism is an evil that must be done away with.
   (B) Capitalism can and should coexist with socialism.
   (C) Capitalism will one day turn the Cold War into a dangerous, direct conflict.
   (D) Capitalism is key to maintaining a peaceful balance in the world.

GO ON TO THE NEXT PAGE.

WORLD HISTORY: MODERN

SECTION I, Part B

Time—40 minutes

Directions: Answer Question 1 **and** Question 2. Answer **either** Question 3 **or** Question 4.

Use complete sentences; an outline or bulleted list alone is not acceptable. On test day, you will be able to plan your answers in the exam booklet, but only your responses in the corresponding boxes on the free-response answer sheet will be scored.

Use the two passages below to answer all parts of the question that follows.

<u>Source 1</u>

His first anxiety after his arrival was about the rebellion—in what it consisted, what the insurgents meant, who dared to instigate such a crime. And as nobody could answer accurately upon all points, and some pleaded their own ignorance, others the obstinacy of the Streltsi, he began to have suspicions of everybody's loyalty…. No day, holy or profane, were the inquisitors idle; every day was deemed fit and lawful for torturing. There were as many scourges as there were accused, and every inquisitor was a butcher.

> Diary of Johann Georg von Korb, ambassador from Emperor Leopold I to Czar Peter the Great in 1699

<u>Source 2</u>

The tsar labored at the reform of fashions, or, more properly speaking, of dress. Until that time the Russians had always worn long beards, which they cherished and preserved with much care, allowing them to hang down on their bosoms, without even cutting the moustache. With these long beards they wore the hair very short, except the ecclesiastics, who, to distinguish themselves, wore it very long. The tsar, in order to reform that custom, ordered that gentlemen, merchants, and other subjects, except priests and peasants, should each pay a tax of one hundred rubles a year if they wished to keep their beards; the commoners had to pay one kopek each. Officials were stationed at the gates of the towns to collect that tax, which the Russians regarded as an enormous sin on the part of the tsar and as a thing which tended to the abolition of their religion.

> *Life of Peter the Great*, by French historian Jean Rousset de Missy, c. 1730

1. a) Identify and explain ONE piece of historical evidence that would support Source 1's evaluation of Peter the Great's approach to governing.

b) Identify and explain ONE piece of historical evidence that would support Source 2's evaluation of Peter the Great's approach to governing.

c) From the two evaluations above, select the one that, in your opinion, is more accurate to the true governing style of Peter the Great. Briefly explain your choice using additional evidence beyond that used to answer (a) or (b).

GO ON TO THE NEXT PAGE.

Answer all parts of the question that follows.

2. a) Identify and explain TWO ways in which Enlightenment philosophies influenced reaction to the Industrial Revolution.

   b) Identify and explain TWO ways that nation-states increased their power through the Industrial Revolution.

   c) Identify and explain TWO ways that the Industrial Revolution impacted the social and economic lives of the working class.

GO ON TO THE NEXT PAGE.

Question 3 or 4

Directions: Answer **either** Question 3 **or** Question 4.

Answer all parts of the question that follows.

Painting of Mansa Musa holding a gold coin from the 1375 Catalan Atlas.

3. a) Identify and explain ONE symbol presented in the image above.

   b) Identify and explain ONE way in which the Mansa Musa was able to expand the Malian Empire.

   c) Identify and explain ONE reason for the success of the Malian Empire.

GO ON TO THE NEXT PAGE.

Answer all parts of the question that follows.

G20 Map, September 26, 1999

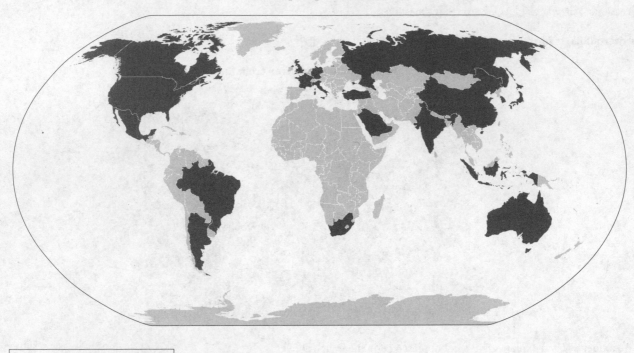

■ = countries part of the G20
■ = countries not part of the G20

4. a) Identify and explain TWO factors that account for the development of the division shown on the map.

   b) Identify and explain ONE goal of the G20.

   c) Identify and explain ONE factor blocking the G20's objectives.

END OF SECTION I

The Exam

AP® World History: Modern Exam

DO NOT OPEN THIS BOOKLET UNTIL YOU ARE TOLD TO DO SO.

Instructions

The questions for Section II are printed in the Questions and Documents booklet. You may use that booklet to organize your answers and for scratch work, but you must write your answers in this Section II: Free Response booklet. No credit will be given for any work written in the Questions and Documents booklet.

The proctor will announce the beginning and end of the reading period. You are advised to spend the 15-minute period reading the question and planning your answer to Question 1, the document-based question. If you have time, you may also read Questions 2, 3, and 4.

Section II of this exam requires answers in essay form. Write clearly and legibly. Circle the number of the question you are answering at the top of each page in this booklet. Begin each answer on a new page. Do not skip lines. Cross out any errors you make; crossed-out work will not be scored.

Manage your time carefully. The proctor will announce the suggested time for each part, but you may proceed freely from one part to the next. Go on to the long essay question if you finish Question 1 early. You may review your responses if you finish before the end of the exam is announced.

After the exam, you must apply the label that corresponds to the long-essay question you answered—Question 2, 3, or 4. For example, if you answered Question 2, apply the label 2 . Failure to do so may delay your score.

At a Glance

Total Time
1 hour, 40 minutes
Number of Questions
2
Writing Instrument
Pen with black or dark blue ink

Question 1 (DBQ): Mandatory

Suggested Reading and Writing Time
60 minutes
Percent of Total Score
25%

Question 2, 3, or 4 (Long Essay): Choose ONE Question

Answer either Question 2, 3, or 4
Suggested Time
40 minutes
Percent of Total Score
15%

WORLD HISTORY: MODERN

SECTION II

Total Time—1 hour, 40 minutes

Question 1 (Document-Based Question)

Suggested reading and writing time: 1 hour

It is suggested that you spend 15 minutes reading the documents and 45 minutes writing your response. Note: You may begin writing your response before the reading period is over.

Directions: Question 1 is based on the accompanying documents. The documents have been edited for the purpose of this exercise.

In your response you should do the following.

• Respond to the prompt with a historically defensible thesis or claim that establishes a line of reasoning.

• Describe a broader historical context relevant to the prompt.

• Support an argument in response to the prompt using at least six documents.

• Use at least one additional piece of specific historical evidence (beyond that found in the documents) relevant to an argument about the prompt.

• For at least three documents, explain how or why the document's point of view, purpose, historical situation, and/or audience is relevant to an argument.

• Use evidence to corroborate, qualify, or modify an argument that addresses the prompt.

Begin your response to this question at the top of a new page in the separate Free Response booklet and fill in the appropriate circle at the top of each page to indicate the question number.

GO ON TO THE NEXT PAGE.

1. Using the documents and your knowledge of world history, evaluate the extent to which decolonization transformed diplomacy in the twentieth century.

Document 1

Source: The "Loi-Cadre" of June 23, 1956

Without prejudice to the expected reform of Title VIII of the Constitution, in order to give the overseas peoples a more direct share in the management of their own interests, measures of administrative decentralization and devolution shall be introduced within the territories, groups of territories and central services under the jurisdiction of the Ministry of France Overseas. To this end, decrees taken . . . on the basis of the report given by the Minister of France Overseas and, on occasion, by the Ministers concerned, may:

1) Modify the role and powers of administration and management of the general governments with a view to transforming them into coordinating bodies…

2) Institute government councils in all the territories…

3) Grant broadened deliberative powers…

4) Determine the conditions of the institution…

Document 2

Source: Declaration on Granting Independence to Colonial Countries and Peoples, 1960

General Assembly Resolution 1514 (XV), December 14, 1960 The General Assembly:

Mindful of the determination proclaimed by the peoples of the world in the Charter of the United Nations to reaffirm faith in fundamental human rights, in the dignity and worth of the human person,…Solemnly proclaims the necessity of bringing to a speedy and unconditional end colonialism in all its forms and manifestations; And to this end Declares that: 1. The subjection of peoples to alien subjugation, domination and exploitation constitutes a denial of fundamental human rights, is contrary to the Charter of the United Nations and is an impediment to the promotion of world peace and co-operation. 2. All peoples have the right to self-determination; by virtue of that right they freely determine their political status and freely pursue their economic, social and cultural development. 3. Inadequacy of political, economic, social or educational preparedness should never serve as a pretext for delaying independence. 4. All armed action or repressive measures of all kinds directed against dependent peoples shall cease in order to enable them to exercise peacefully and freely their right to complete independence, and the integrity of their national territory shall be respected.

GO ON TO THE NEXT PAGE.

Document 3

Source: British Government Statement on its policy In Burma, May 1945

The considered policy of His Majesty's Government of promoting full self -government in Burma has frequently been declared. It Is and has consistently been our aim to assist her political development till she can sustain the responsibilities of complete self-government within the British Commonwealth and consequently attain a status equal to that of the Dominions and of this country. 2. Inevitably Burma's progress towards full self -government has been interrupted and set back by, the Japanese invasion and the long interval of enemy occupation and active warfare in her territories, during which she has suffered grave damage not only in the form of material destruction but in a shattering of the foundations of her economic and social life. It is, of course, upon these foundations that a political structure rests, and until the foundations are once' again firm the political institutions which were in operation before the Japanese invasion cannot be restored. . . .3. Until these foundations are restored sufficiently, to enable the first essential political process to be undertaken, that is for a General Election to be held, it is not possible to re-establish a Burmese Government as it existed till 1941. It is accordingly necessary, so long as the government of the country cannot be carried on in accordance with the provisions of the 1935 Act, that recourse should continue to be had to the provisions of Section 139, under which the administration is carried on by the Governor in direct responsibility to His Majesty's Government. . . . But though this initial period of controlled government is necessary, His Majesty's Government are anxious that all the functions of government should not in fact be concentrated in the Governor, but that he should be provided with definite means of obtaining Burmese assistance and advice in the discharge of them and have power to associate with himself representatives of Burmese opinion in executive and legislative capacities.

Document 4

Source: Map depicting Colonial Affiliations of Africa and India before 1945.

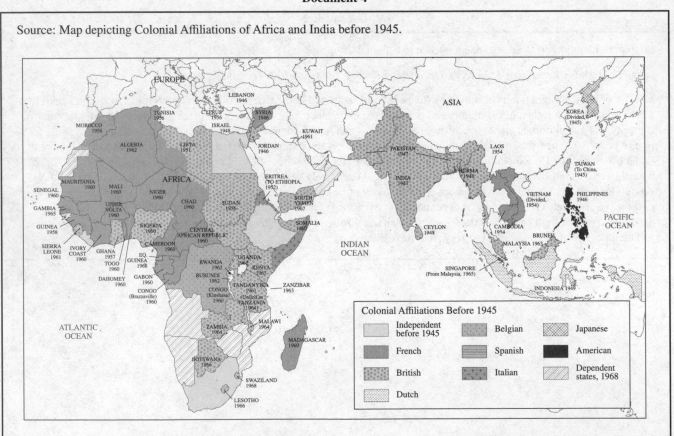

GO ON TO THE NEXT PAGE.

Document 5

Source: President Sukarno of Indonesia's speech at the opening of the Bandung Conference, April 18 1955

…today we are faced with a situation where the well-being of mankind is not always the primary consideration. Many who are in places of high power think, rather, of controlling the world. Yes, we are living in a world of fear. The life of man today is corroded and made bitter by fear. Fear of the future, fear of the hydrogen bomb, fear of ideologies. Perhaps this fear is a greater danger than the danger itself, because it is fear which drives men to act foolishly, to act thoughtlessly, to act danger-ously. . . .All of us, I am certain, are united by more important things than those which superficially divide us. We are united, for instance, by a common detestation of colonialism in whatever form it appears. We are united by a common detestation of racialism. And we are united by a common determination to preserve and stabilise peace in the world.

Document 6

Source: Jawaharlal Nehru's December 18, 1956 speech in Washington D.C.

I speak of India because it is my country and I have some right to speak for her. But many other countries in Asia tell the same story, for Asia today is resurgent, and these countries which long lay under foreign yoke have won back their independence and are fired by a new spirit and strive toward new ideals. To them, as to us, independence is as vital as the breath they take to sustain life, and colonialism, in any form, or anywhere, is abhorrent . . . Peace and freedom have become indivisible, and the world cannot continue for long partly free and partly subject. In this atomic age peace has also become a test of human survival. Recently we have witnessed two tragedies which have powerfully affected men and women all over the world. These are the tragedies in Egypt and Hungary. Our deeply felt sympathies must go out to those who have suffered or are suffering, and all of us must do our utmost to help them and to assist in solving these problems in a peaceful and constructive way. But even these tragedies have one hopeful aspect, for they have demonstrated that the most powerful countries cannot revert to old colonial methods or impose their domination over weak countries. World opinion has shown that it can organize itself to resist such outrages. Perhaps, as an outcome of these tragedies, freedom will be enlarged and will have a more assured basis. The preservation of peace forms the central aim of India's policy. It is in the pursuit of this policy that we have chosen the path of nonalinement [nonalignment] in any military or like pact of alliance. Nonalinement does not mean passivity of mind or action, lack of faith or conviction. It does not mean submission to what we consider evil. It is a positive and dynamic approach to such problems that confront us.

GO ON TO THE NEXT PAGE.

Document 7

Source: Speech at *The First Afro-Asian People's Solidarity Conference*, Anwar el Sadat, 1957

The idea of Afro-Asian Solidarity did not emanate out of naught, so as to be born and see daylight at Bandung all of a sudden. But before materializing as an historical event, it was an impression and an innate volition instinctively developing in the mind of the colonized and the exploited—the human being whom imperialism had reduced to a typefied specimen of a subjugated specie and bondsman recognisable in every colonized country. Indeed the idea of solidarity was deeply rooted in the hearts of those subjected peoples, continually aspiring through diverse national movements to smash the fetters of bondage and redeem their salvation. In the course of time these national movements were destined to meet, to consolidate and to react with one another, purposefully in some instances, but unconsciously and spontaneously in the majority of cases. It is evident therefore, that the Bandung Conference was not a haphazard event, but rather a natural psychological factor which led to the awakening of the peoples of Africa and Asia and roused them from their slumber to solve the problem of their very existence and survival, and to resume the struggle for the recovery of their liberty and freedom.

…Gone for ever is the era where the future of war and peace was decided upon in a few European capitals, because today we happen to be strong enough to make the decision ourselves in that respect. Our weight in the international balance has now become preponderant. Only think of the colossal number of our people, our natural resources, the vastness of the area covered by our respective countries, and our strategic positions.

END OF DOCUMENTS FOR QUESTION 1

GO ON TO THE NEXT PAGE.

Question 2, 3, or 4 (Long Essay)

Suggested writing time: 40 minutes

Directions: Answer Question 2 **or** Question 3 **or** Question 4.

In your response you should do the following.

- Respond to the prompt with a historically defensible thesis or claim that establishes a line of reasoning.

- Describe a broader historical context relevant to the prompt.

- Support an argument in response to the prompt using specific and relevant examples of evidence.

- Use historical reasoning (e.g., comparison, causation, continuity or change over time) to frame or structure an argument that addresses the prompt.

- Use evidence to corroborate, qualify, or modify an argument that addresses the prompt.

2. In the period 1200 C.E. to 1600 C.E., rapidly developing technologies led to increased regional and transregional trade. Develop an argument that evaluates the extent to which the new technology contributed to an increase in trade in this time period.

3. In the period 1500 C.E. to 1750 C.E., nations' influence expanded and global interaction increased. Certain Asian states were able to resist this influence and contact. Develop an argument that evaluates the reasons some Asian nations were able to remain relatively untouched by outside influences.

4. In the period after 1900, the movements championing women's equality varied, with many states adopting policies to offer more opportunities to women. Develop an argument that evaluates the extent to which one or more states reacted to a gender equality movement.

WHEN YOU FINISH WRITING,
CHECK YOUR WORK ON SECTION II IF TIME PERMITS.

STOP
END OF EXAM

Practice Test 1:
Diagnostic
Answer Key and
Explanations

PRACTICE TEST 1: DIAGNOSTIC ANSWER KEY

Let's take a look at how you did on Practice Test 1. Follow the three-step process in the diagnostic answer key below and go read the explanations for any questions you got wrong or you struggled with but got correct. Once you finish working through the answer key and the explanations, go to the next chapter to make your study plan.

 **Check your answers and mark any correct answers with a ✔ in the appropriate column.**

Section I, Part A: Multiple Choice Questions							
Q #	Ans.	✔	Chapter #, Unit Title	Q #	Ans.	✔	Chapter #, Unit Title
1	D		**6,** Unit 1: The Global Tapestry	29	D		**8,** Unit 6: Consequences of Industrialization
2	C		**6,** Unit 1: The Global Tapestry	30	A		**8,** Unit 6: Consequences of Industrialization
3	C		**6,** Unit 1: The Global Tapestry	31	B		**9,** Unit 8: Cold War and Decolonization
4	A		**6,** Unit 1: The Global Tapestry	32	B		**9,** Unit 8: Cold War and Decolonization
5	B		**6,** Unit 2: Networks of Exchange	33	B		**9,** Unit 8: Cold War and Decolonization
6	B		**6,** Unit 2: Networks of Exchange	34	D		**9,** Unit 8: Cold War and Decolonization
7	D		**6,** Unit 2: Networks of Exchange	35	D		**9,** Unit 8: Cold War and Decolonization
8	A		**6,** Unit 2: Networks of Exchange	36	D		**9,** Unit 8: Cold War and Decolonization
9	C		**7,** Unit 3: Land-Based Empires	37	A		**9,** Unit 8: Cold War and Decolonization
10	D		**7,** Unit 3: Land-Based Empires	38	C		**9,** Unit 8: Cold War and Decolonization
11	D		**7,** Unit 3: Land-Based Empires	39	C		**7,** Unit 3: Land-Based Empires
12	A		**7,** Unit 3: Land-Based Empires	40	D		**7,** Unit 3: Land-Based Empires
13	A		**8,** Unit 6: Consequences of Industrialization	41	B		**7,** Unit 3: Land-Based Empires
14	B		**8,** Unit 6: Consequences of Industrialization	42	B		**8,** Unit 5: Revolutions
15	A		**8,** Unit 6: Consequences of Industrialization	43	B		**8,** Unit 5: Revolutions
16	D		**8,** Unit 6: Consequences of Industrialization	44	A		**8,** Unit 5: Revolutions
17	D		**7,** Unit 4: Transoceanic Interconnections	45	A		**9,** Unit 7: Global Conflict
18	C		**7,** Unit 4: Transoceanic Interconnections	46	B		**9,** Unit 7: Global Conflict
19	A		**7,** Unit 4: Transoceanic Interconnections	47	B		**9,** Unit 7: Global Conflict
20	D		**7,** Unit 4: Transoceanic Interconnections	48	D		**9,** Unit 7: Global Conflict
21	A		**6,** Unit 1: The Global Tapestry	49	C		**9,** Unit 7: Global Conflict
22	D		**6,** Unit 1: The Global Tapestry	50	A		**9,** Unit 7: Global Conflict
23	C		**6,** Unit 1: The Global Tapestry	51	D		**9,** Unit 7: Global Conflict
24	A		**6,** Unit 1: The Global Tapestry	52	D		**9,** Unit 8: Cold War and Decolonization
25	C		**6,** Unit 1: The Global Tapestry	53	D		**9,** Unit 8: Cold War and Decolonization
26	C		**8,** Unit 6: Consequences of Industrialization	54	C		**9,** Unit 8: Cold War and Decolonization
27	A		**8,** Unit 6: Consequences of Industrialization	55	B		**9,** Unit 8: Cold War and Decolonization
28	B		**8,** Unit 6: Consequences of Industrialization				

Section I, Part B: Short-Answer Questions			
Q #	Ans.	✔	Chapter #, Unit Title
1	See Explanation		**7,** Unit 3: Land-Based Empires
2	See Explanation		**8,** Unit 5: Revolutions
3	See Explanation		**6,** Unit 2: Networks of Exchange
4	See Explanation		**9,** Unit 9: Globalization
Section II : DBQ and Long-Essay Questions			
1	See Explanation		**9,** Unit 8: Cold War and Decolonization
2	See Explanation		**6,** Unit 2: Networks of Exchange
3	See Explanation		**7,** Unit 4: Transoceanic Interconnections
4	See Explanation		**9,** Unit 7: Global Conflict

 **Tally your correct answers from Step 1 by chapter. For each chapter, write the number of correct answers in the appropriate box. Then, divide your correct answers by the number of total questions (which we've provided) to get your percent correct.**

CHAPTER 6: UNIT 1 TEST SELF-EVALUATION

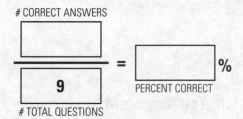

CORRECT ANSWERS

9
TOTAL QUESTIONS

= PERCENT CORRECT %

CHAPTER 7: UNIT 3 TEST SELF-EVALUATION

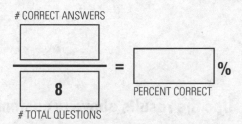

CORRECT ANSWERS

8
TOTAL QUESTIONS

= PERCENT CORRECT %

CHAPTER 6: UNIT 2 TEST SELF-EVALUATION

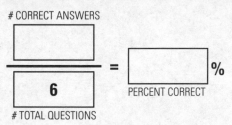

CORRECT ANSWERS

6
TOTAL QUESTIONS

= PERCENT CORRECT %

CHAPTER 7: UNIT 4 TEST SELF-EVALUATION

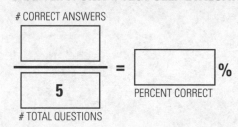

CORRECT ANSWERS

5
TOTAL QUESTIONS

= PERCENT CORRECT %

CHAPTER 8: UNIT 5 TEST SELF-EVALUATION

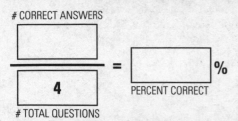

CORRECT ANSWERS

4

TOTAL QUESTIONS

=

%

PERCENT CORRECT

CHAPTER 8: UNIT 6 TEST SELF-EVALUATION

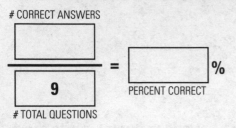

CORRECT ANSWERS

9

TOTAL QUESTIONS

=

%

PERCENT CORRECT

CHAPTER 9: UNIT 7 TEST SELF-EVALUATION

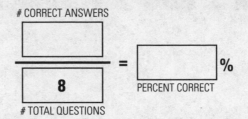

CORRECT ANSWERS

8

TOTAL QUESTIONS

=

%

PERCENT CORRECT

CHAPTER 9: UNIT 8 TEST SELF-EVALUATION

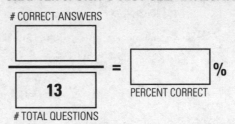

CORRECT ANSWERS

13

TOTAL QUESTIONS

=

%

PERCENT CORRECT

CHAPTER 9: UNIT 9 TEST SELF-EVALUATION

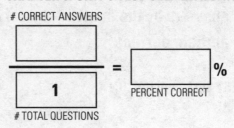

CORRECT ANSWERS

1

TOTAL QUESTIONS

=

%

PERCENT CORRECT

 **STEP 3** >> **Use the results above to customize your study plan. You may want to start with, or give more attention to, the chapters with the lowest percents correct.**

PRACTICE TEST 1 EXPLANATIONS

Section I, Part A: Multiple-Choice Questions

1. **D**   The passage was created in the early 15th century, which would chronologically align with the Hundred Years' War. Choice (D) is correct. Choices (A), (B), and (C) can each be eliminated as they occurred centuries after this text was written.

2. **C**   While it may not have been the long-term outcome of the war, the passage states that the "crown and kingdom of France" is to "be permanently" given to the King of England. This is consistent with (C), which is the correct response. The treaty is written by the English, from a position of leverage. Eliminate (A) and (B), as they imply English defeat prior to this treaty. Finally, eliminate (D) since limited control over French territory is an understatement when the treaty actually called for the English gaining the power of the French crown.

3. **C**   This treaty was not the end of the Hundred Years' War by any stretch. Recall the story of Joan of Arc and how the French eventually pushed the English armies out. Choice (C) is therefore correct. Also eliminate (A) and (D) as they would indicate a French defeat at the end of the Hundred Years' War. Choice (B) is also incorrect since the French monarchy did not disappear with this treaty, and was actually strengthened by the war.

4. **A**   Following this war, the French unified their territory and established their monarchy as a stronger central authority. Choice (A) is correct. The English monarchy continued while sharing power with parliament, though the power of the English monarchy in the 15th and 16th centuries could hardly be described as "severely" weakening. Eliminate (B) and (D). Finally, France remained a Catholic country, so (C) is incorrect.

5. **B**   The text notes that Kinsay's government increased guards on the city's bridges to secure against disturbance, treason, and insurrection. Choice (B) is therefore correct. There are passing mentions to paper money and vast imports from traders, but no real discussion of whether the government of Kinsay emphasized maintaining a strong economy. Eliminate (A). Knowing that the China that Marco Polo visited was run by the Mongols, you could eliminate (C) and (D). The Mongols tolerated diverse cultures and focused on connecting, trading, and fighting with foreigners, not remaining isolated.

6. **B**   Marco Polo's visit to China was during the Mongol rule, which created the Yuan Dynasty. Choice (B) is correct. Eliminate (A), as the Mongols overthrew the Song, and (C) and (D), both of which followed Mongol rule in China.

7. **D**   The Mongols were notable for their respect for and adoption of local customs. Silk clothing, which had long been produced in China, would have been seen by the Mongols as a beneficial trade item that the native Chinese could offer Yuan society. Choice (D) is correct. Also, eliminate (C), as the Mongol rulers would have left such crafts to the experts—the native Chinese. Further, the Mongols were not known for technological innovations independent from conquered cultures, so (A) and (B) are inconsistent with Mongol history.

8. **A** The Mongols had, for the first time ever, connected the continents of Asia and Europe under a single empire. This allowed for easier passage for traders moving to other parts of the empire. Choice (A) is correct. Choice (B) can be eliminated as any limitation on interactions between trade partners would not have benefited Marco Polo. Choice (C) is a true statement, but is not relevant to the journey of Marco Polo, a sea traveler. Eliminate it. Finally, Marco Polo predated transatlantic trade by about two centuries, so (D) should be eliminated.

9. **C** Suleiman I was emperor of the Ottoman Empire, based in modern-day Turkey. Choice (C) is correct. The Mughal (India) and Safavid (Persia) empires would have to go through the Ottoman to invade eastern and central Europe, so it is not likely that they would be featured in this image. Eliminate (A) and (B). The Abbasid Dynasty ended in the 13th century, so it would not be possible for either of the armies depicted to represent the Abbasids. Choice (D) is incorrect.

10. **D** The Protestant Reformation had left much of the lands of central Europe politically fractured. Choice (D) is therefore correct. Eliminate (C), as the Ottomans attempted (and failed) to take Austria *after* the battles in Hungary. Central Europe had long been Christian (even if the Protestant Reformation helped create separate sects), so (B) is incorrect. As we should know, Hungary is landlocked, so (A) can also be easily eliminated.

11. **D** Choice (D) is correct as Suleiman's army stopped trying to expand into Europe shortly after this battle. The Ottomans were defeated in Austria, so they never really penetrated Central Europe militarily or created much change in Eastern Europe culturally. Eliminate (A) and (B). Suleiman never gave up his power, and he died as emperor amidst his campaigns into European territory. Choice (C) is incorrect.

12. **A** The trend consistent with Islamic "Gunpowder" empires of this era was land expansion using advanced military technology. Choice (A) is correct as it is most consistent with this trend. Since the focus of these battles was land expansion, (B), (C), and (D) can be eliminated.

13. **A** In 1876, Korea declared its independence from a deeply weakened China. Japan, seeing an opportunity to establish its dominance in East Asia, declared war with Qing China. Following the war, the two parties signed the Treaty of Shimonoseki. The victorious Japan, with its sights set on imperial expansion, demanded that China hand over control of Taiwan. Japan then focused on establishing these territories that were recently liberated as key components of its eventual Pacific empire. Choice (A) is correct. The Meiji Restoration involved a rapid Westernization of Japan and occurred some 50 years prior to Japan's war with China. Eliminate (B). Choice (C) is incorrect since the Treaty of Kanagawa involved Japan opening its trade with the West, and did not concern Korea. The White Lotus Rebellion also did not involve Korea, and was instead an internal rebellion in China aimed at overthrowing the Qing Dynasty. Eliminate (D).

14. **B** With imperial hopes, Japan attempted to lure Koreans into support for the Japanese Empire. This text describes a cultural and racial homogeneity between Japan and Korea. Of course, it is clear that Japan's end game was imperial expansion on the Asia mainland. Choice (B) best captures

this cynical viewpoint. There is no mention of Western nations, so (A) can be eliminated. Also eliminate (C) as there is no mention of China within this text. Finally, considering this was written in the wake of the Sino-Japanese war, Japan was certainly not neutral in the affairs of mainland China. Eliminate (D).

15. **A** In the early 20th century, Japan had begun its rise to imperial power, which included colonizing Korea. This passage shows Japan laying the groundwork for such a campaign. Choice (A) is correct. Once it industrialized in the late 19th century, Japan did not see much of a need to continue contact with the West, so (B) can be eliminated. There was not a major movement within Korea to unify with Japan; rather, it was handed over as one nation's colony to another. Choice (C) is incorrect. The passage does not concern China. Choice (D) can be eliminated.

16. **D** The author claims that the Japanese and Koreans are actually part of a common nationality, now finally reunited. The author would best be supported by evidence that shows some commonalities between the two nations. Choice (D), evidence of common names, would best demonstrate some shared origin between Japan and Korea. Choices (A) and (B) would highlight differences, so they can be eliminated. Finally, (C) would not be relevant to uncovering commonalities between Korea and Japan. Eliminate it.

17. **D** The Portuguese were the first Europeans to finance expeditions to Africa and Asia, and Portugal's Vasco da Gama embarked on one of the earliest Portuguese explorations of these regions. Choice (D) is correct. The European companies based in India were not fully established until the late 16th and early 17th centuries. Eliminate (A). You may also eliminate (B) since the Portuguese explored the New World (Brazil, for instance) during this time period, as well as Africa and Asia. Finally eliminate (C) as India was under control of an Islamic sultanate (the Delhi Sultanate) and was still quite accessible to explorers.

18. **C** The late 15th and early 16th centuries were the dawn of the European Age of Exploration. This map shows one notable explorer, but serves to represent a larger trend of the European powers of the time. Choice (C) is correct. Portugal's exploration expanded beyond just Africa and Asia, and included the Americas. Eliminate (A). There were other explorers before Vasco da Gama, notably Bartholomew Dias. Choice (B) is incorrect. Choice (D) is also incorrect; although the early 16th century was a time of exploration, mass migrations to the new colonies did not occur.

19. **A** Portuguese Jesuits and traders created a thriving port district in Nagasaki that allowed for some westernization until the Tokugawa Shogunate changed all that in 1600. Choice (A) is correct. European powers successfully established ports in India without much resistance. Choice (B) is incorrect. The Ming did not have much power by the 16th century and European nations were able to establish trade in the formerly isolationist country (the Portuguese set up a colony in Macao, for instance). Choice (C) is incorrect. Asian nations had interactions with other European powers during the 16th century. Think of the establishment of the Dutch East India Company in 1600—it did not come out of nowhere! Eliminate (D).

20. **D** The Portuguese began the overseas slave trade by bringing enslaved people from Africa to Europe. Choice (D) is correct. By extension, (B) can be eliminated. Portugal maintained its presence in Africa, as well as Asia, so (A) is incorrect. Finally, eliminate (C), as the Portuguese involvement in the slave trade would indicate that Portuguese presence in Africa was not beneficial to Africans.

21. **A** The passage states that "Heaven, wearied of [the Mongol's] misgovernment and debauchery, thought also fit to turn their fate to ruin." The author describes the Mongol government's fall and China's descension into 18 years of war before the Ming established peace. Choice (A) is most consistent with this context. Since years of war took place between dynasties, (B) is incorrect. The author does mention the defeat of the Sung and the rise of the Mongols, but this occurred over a century before the manifesto was written. Eliminate (C) and (D).

22. **D** The Ming found importance in turning China away from outside influence (the Mongols, after all were outsiders to the native Chinese) and toward more traditional Chinese culture. A key part of that culture is Confucianism. Choice (D) is correct. Choice (A) is incorrect because the Ming became increasingly isolationist, unlike the expansionist Mongol dynasty. Choice (B) is incorrect because the Ming oversaw a Golden Age, not the Yuan (the Mongol absorbed, though largely did not create, new art and technologies). Finally, eliminate (C)—while the Ming were mostly viewed as isolationist, one of the most famous figures in Chinese history is Zheng He, a Ming seafarer.

23. **C** The author revels in the glory ("We were selected by Our people to occupy the Imperial throne of Zhongguo under the dynastic title of 'the Great Ming'") that following years of war, his new empire reigns. Choice (C) is correct. Choice (A) is incorrect as his tone is positive and not bitter. Choice (B) seems tempting due to the discussion of maintaining peace. However, this is a hope that the author gives with some humility ("Although We are not equal in wisdom to our ancient rulers whose virtue was recognized all over the universe, We cannot but let the world know Our intention to maintain peace within the four seas"). Eliminate it. Choice (D) is incorrect because the Ming empire is new and, at the time the passage was written, would have been viewed as dominant.

24. **A** The second half of the passage, which indicates that China has restored its old boundaries (in contrast to the rule of the more belligerent Mongols) and seeks peace, conveys a sense that the author is hoping to alter the Byzantine emperor's view of China. Choice (A) is correct. Accordingly, you can eliminate (D). Choice (B) is incorrect because the Mongols had recently been overthrown by the Ming. And (C) is incorrect as the passage makes no mention of trade.

25. **C** There has long been the idea in Chinese history that the ruling dynasty has power because of divine approval (similar to the European "divine right of kings"). This concept, which the author references, is known as the Mandate of Heaven. Choice (C) is correct. Choice (A) has to do with respect for elders, so it can be eliminated. Legalism, which has played into Chinese history over time, refers to a strict system of governing by using rewards and punishments. Eliminate (B). Choice (D), neo-Confucianism, was embraced by the Ming Dynasty, but is not related to the more divine concept that the author alludes to.

26. **C** The British engaged in battle with the Boers over South Africa following the discovery of gold and diamonds in a region known as the Transvaal. Choice (C) is correct. Eliminate (A) since the threat of rebellions against the British colonizers in Africa did not materialize until the 20th century. Choice (B) is incorrect because the British established their presence in South Africa long before anyone considered the possibility of a world war. Finally, eliminate (D), as the fears that motivated the German Empire to claim parts of the southern region of Africa were on the part of the Germans, who thought the British might expand their claims to land, not the other way around.

27. **A** The author describes the "small minority of white men" as occupiers who hold "sway over great hordes of population." This is most consistent with (A), which is the correct answer. Since this group holds power and represents the imperial presence, (B) and (C) are incorrect. Finally, (D) is incorrect since the group is mentioned alongside officials, traders, and industrial organizers, all economic stakeholders, rather than religious officials.

28. **B** The author states that "imperial expansion stands entirely distinct from the colonization," the latter of which he claims is characterized by a system in which "white colonists carry with them the modes of government, the industrial and other arts of the civilisation of the mother country." In other words, colonization represents an effort (be it misguided) to benefit the host country while imperialism is, as the author puts it, "an expansion of autocracy." Choice (B) is correct.

29. **D** Europeans in China were looking for an economic advantage in a region with major trade activity, while imperialists in sub-Saharan Africa, for instance, attempted to change the culture of those nations to best benefit the imperial power. Choice (D) is therefore correct. European traders found China to be a profitable place in which they could expand their mercantile reach, so (B) and (C) can be eliminated. Finally, spheres of influence in China greatly benefited non-Chinese nations over China, so (A) can be eliminated.

30. **A** In 1884, the powers of Europe carved out boundaries in Africa to sort out conflicts over their imperial reaches. The author is critiquing the process of imperialism at this time because an entire continent had been exploited in a race for colonies. Choice (A) is correct. World War I had not yet occurred, so (B) is incorrect. While this passage was written at the time of the Boer War, it does not directly reference that conflict as closely as it does the fallout from the Berlin Conference. Eliminate (C). The Treaty of Cordoba established Mexico's independence from Spain, and is therefore not terribly relevant to this passage. Eliminate (D).

31. **B** In this passage, Kwame Nkrumah calls for all of Africa to be "united under one federal government." This unity of African nations is known as Pan-Africanism. Choice (B) is correct. While Nkrumah was a Marxist, this ideology is not as apparent in this passage as is Pan-Africanism. Eliminate (A). Neoliberalism is a belief in free markets. This would definitely contrast with Nkrumah's Marxist leanings. Eliminate (C). Choice (D) is incorrect as Nkrumah advocates Pan-Nationalism, rather than allegiance to only Ghana.

32. **B** Nkrumah writes about a "moment in the history of the United States of America when the Founding Fathers saw beyond the petty wranglings of the separate states" to draw a parallel with the relationships among the nations of Africa. He posits that the nations could come together with similar success to the separate states which became the United States. Choice (B) is correct. Since he seems to admire the American model and uses it as something toward which Africa should strive, (C) and (D) can be eliminated. Nkrumah does not mention the United States' imperialism, so (A) can also be eliminated.

33. **B** In this text, Kwame Nkrumah looks outside of his home country of Ghana and toward the larger good of Africa as a whole. To do this, Nkrumah, a decolonization leader himself, must speak to what he sees is best for his country's neighbors around the continent. Choice (B) is correct as it best aligns with this purpose. While Nkrumah may believe in the sovereignty of individual African nations, in this text, he advocates unity among the nations of Africa, which would not be an opportunity for him to emphasize sovereignty. Choice (A) is incorrect. Choice (C) is incorrect as it is a misreading of a historical example offered by Nkrumah in this passage. Finally, the reference to "Great Powers" is about a possibility for Africa to be one, not a discussion of other powers around the world. Eliminate (D).

34. **D** Kwame Nkrumah's work best came into fruition with the establishment of the Organization of African Unity, of which he was the head. Choice (D) is correct. Be careful not to confuse it with the African Union, which the OAU ultimately transformed into during the early part of the 21st century (long after Nkrumah had died). Eliminate (C). Choice (A) is incorrect since many African nations were already a part of the United Nations (UN) at the time this passage was written (including Nkrumah's home country of Ghana). Choice (B) is also incorrect because Nkrumah was not discussing non-governmental organizations (NGOs) in this passage, but rather the actual unity of African nations into a single governing state.

35. **D** Pakistan was founded as a Muslim nation. Before the reference to "the brotherhood of the People," the anthem refers to Pakistan as "sacred land." In this context, the song is referring to Muslims by mentioning a "brotherhood of the People." Choice (D) is correct. Choice (A) can be eliminated because Pakistan, since its founding, was never colonized. Choice (B) is incorrect because the anthem does not reference others on the continent (Indians, for instance). Choice (C) is half correct, but the "former colonizers" part would not be included in the brotherhood. Eliminate it.

36. **D** In the years leading up to the liberation of the Indian subcontinent, the Muslim League advocated for a separate land for India's Muslims should decolonization become a reality. Choice (D) is correct. Mohandas Gandhi had dreamed of a unified India consisting of both Hindus and Muslims. Eliminate (A). The United Nations did not negotiate the partition of India, so (B) is incorrect. Finally, eliminate (C) as the British colonists were not in position to determine the division of Indian land.

37. **A** Upon the partition of India, millions of people moved or were forced to flee due to religiously motivated violence. Essentially, India and Pakistan exchanged millions of citizens, with practitioners of each religion moving to the nation where their religion was dominant. Choice (A) is therefore correct. The partition of the land made for strict geographical and governmental boundaries.

Eliminate (B). Unlike Pakistan, India did not establish a state religion. Choice (C) is incorrect. Finally, eliminate (D) as Ghandi and Jinnah made no such agreement and the Kashmir region remains the subject of contentious dispute among the two nations.

38. **C** The arrangement between Pakistanis and Indians can be described as one of geographical boundaries that separate groups with different religious identities and strong conflict from one another. This is most similar to the situation between Israel and Palestine. Choice (C) is the most accurate. India and Pakistan do not share a pact, so (A) and (B) are incorrect. Further, they do not have a colonial relationship to one another, so (D) is incorrect.

39. **C** In the second paragraph, the text states that some nations within the Mughal Empire do not pay tribute to the emperor, and even collect tribute from him. One such group, the Pathans, are described as warlike and capable of collecting tribute from rajahs. The Mughal are therefore best described as deferential (showing respect) toward the Pathans. Choice (C) is correct. The passage therefore contradicts (A), as the Pathans do not pay tribute to the emperor. Eliminate it. Choice (B) is incorrect because the passage notes that the groups do interact through payments to the Pathans. Finally, (D) is incorrect as both groups are the same religion—both are Muslims (the Pathans are described as Mohammedan).

40. **D** It is evident from the passage that the Mughal Empire did not exercise complete control over all who lived within its borders. Certain nations within the empire were not asked to pay tribute, and the Mughals even paid tribute to some of those smaller nations. This is most consistent with the conclusion in (D), which is the correct answer. This information also contradicts (A), so eliminate it. There is no evidence in this passage that the Pathans assisted the Mughals. Eliminate (B). Finally, the text does not discuss how Hindu subjects were treated. Eliminate (C).

41. **B** In the second half of the 16th century, Akbar, the Mughal emperor, attempted reforms to allow for the coexistence of both Muslims and Hindus. One particular measure he took was to eliminate the *jizya*, the head tax on Hindus. Choice (B) is therefore correct. Since Akbar was viewed as one who oversaw a more peaceful coexistence between the two religions, (A) is incorrect. The establishment of the British East India Company led to further outside control of India, which would not have any specific impact on the relationship between Muslims and Hindus during this time period. Eliminate (C). Choice (D) is incorrect because the reign of Aurangzeb was characterized by persecution of Hindus (and the reinstatement of the *jizya*.)

42. **B** The reference to one Deutschland (Germany) calls back to the time following the Franco-Prussian War in which the German Empire united the individual German states. Choice (B) is correct. The Concert of Europe refers to a balance of power maintained by the nations of the continent. The Concert of Europe ended in the middle of the 19th century following a series of revolutions and military conflicts. Eliminate (A). The final verse of the song references "one true land," which is the actual lands of Europe that fall under German power, not the far-off regions of German exploration. Choice (C) is incorrect. By the time this song was popularized, the Frankfurt Parliament was a distant memory—a failed attempt to unify German lands in 1848. Eliminate (D).

43. **B** One way the Germans unified is through a shared idea of racial superiority (the song even mentions a physical feature traditionally attributed to Germans: blue eyes). Choice (B) is correct. While the German Empire was predominantly Christian, it would not be considered "zealous" in terms of its religious beliefs. Eliminate (A). The Germans, despite Bismarck's wishes, engaged in some overseas empire building. Eliminate (C). Finally, the empire slowed down any democratic reforms when it consolidated power in Emperor William II. Choice (D) is therefore incorrect.

44. **A** The Volkisch Movement took German nationalism, in the form of arts, culture, and history, combined it with a sense of ethnic superiority, and accelerated a sense of German pride that built toward the rise of Nazi Germany in the 20th century. This song would definitely fall under the category of building German pride and nationalist fervor. Choice (A) is correct. Choice (B) is incorrect because the Self-Strengthening Movement was a Chinese attempt at military reform, not a source of German pride. Choice (C) is incorrect, as Kulturkampf was a conflict between Bismarck and the Catholic Church over the control of church appointees in Germany. Finally, eliminate (D), as the People's Will was a Russian anti-czarist movement.

45. **A** The opening line of this selection is a plea to American men that states "you who think women cannot succeed, we have brought the government of England to this position." The position Pankhurst refers to is women's suffrage. Therefore, British women already had the right to vote before it was guaranteed to American women. Choice (A) is correct. There is no evidence in the passage that all countries beyond the two discussed had neglected to take a look at women's suffrage. Eliminate (B). There is also no evidence in the text about how widespread the movement was becoming in other Western democracies. Eliminate (C). Choice (D) is incorrect since it misreads Pankhurst's reference in the final sentence to "our civil war," which was not a literal reference to one developing within the United States.

46. **B** Capetillo's focus on visiting women who had less, yet produced the wealth that the upper class possess, points us in the direction of Marxism. Choice (B) is correct. One could also infer from this that she was a strong critic of capitalism. Eliminate (D). Capetillo's focus on class struggle and breaking with tradition does not include a call for nationalism. Eliminate (A). While, of course, Capetillo opposed colonialism, it is not mentioned in this passage. Eliminate (C).

47. **B** In Source 2, Capetillo discusses the importance of fellowship with women of different social classes, as well as breaking with traditions. She is discussing women's roles in society more generally. However, Pankhurst avoids this generality and hones in on a specific political issue: the right to vote. Choice (B) is correct. Eliminate (A) as Capetillo clearly shows the urgency of the struggle for equal rights through an emotional appeal to women. Choice (C) can be eliminated since Capetillo mentions husbands. Finally, while the first half of (D) is true, the second half, that Pankhurst, who advocates expanding who has the right to vote in the United States, is anything but gradual and traditional. Eliminate (D).

48. **D** Germany invaded Austria in 1938 before setting its sights on the Sudetenland of Czechoslovakia. At the Munich Conference of 1938, which included Hitler, Mussolini, and Prime Minister Neville Chamberlain of England, Hitler was given the Sudetenland, without the consent of Czechoslovakia, in return for the promise to cease his expansionist activities. The cartoon shows Hitler placing Austria in his bag, which would set this cartoon right at the time of the Munich Conference. Choice (D) is correct. The Treaty of Brest-Litovsk was a World War I era treaty that set the stage for Russia's exit from the war. Eliminate (A). The Tripartite Pact signed by Germany, Italy, and Japan did not occur until two years after this cartoon was created. Eliminate (B). The Anti-Comintern Pact signed between Germany, Italy, and Japan focused on a mutual defense against Russia and had nothing to do with Austria. Eliminate (C).

49. **C** The cartoon lampoons Mussolini attempting to take credit for the expansionist work of Germany. The caption shows that he is trying to convince Italians that he is responsible. Choice (C) best aligns with this idea. Choices (A) and (B) are incorrect, as they misunderstand the satirical nature of the cartoon and take the image too literally. The cartoon does not comment on how Europeans felt about Mussolini vis-à-vis Hitler. Eliminate (D).

50. **A** Postwar economies in Italy and Germany, combined with the effects of the economic depression experienced around the world in the 1930s, were fertile grounds for two future dictators to exploit people's anxieties and advance their political positions in times of extreme uncertainty. Choice (A) is correct. While Hitler was democratically elected to chancellor of Germany in 1932, Mussolini was appointed prime minister of Italy by King Victor Emmanuel III, who faced threats from Mussolini's supporters. Eliminate (B). Mussolini's National Fascist Party aggressively sought out socialists due to the party's loyalty to factory owners. And by the time Hitler rose to power, the Weimar Republic was outright hostile to socialists. Eliminate (C). Neither Hitler nor Mussolini attended military school. In fact, Mussolini fled Italy in his youth to avoid compulsory military service. Choice (D) is incorrect.

51. **D** While Hitler's expansion was largely limited to European lands, Mussolini expanded into Northern Africa (Ethiopia and Somalia, for instance). Choice (D) is correct. Hitler signed a non-aggression pact with the Soviet Union. Eliminate (A). Both also engaged in the use of propaganda, so (B) is incorrect. Finally, Hitler's rise to power was largely propped up by his claims of Germany's racial superiority. Choice (C) is incorrect.

52. **D** During their arms race, both the United States and the Soviet Union engaged in talks to limit the possibility of mutually assured destruction. This summit was one such talk. Choice (D) is correct. There is no evidence in the text that the heads of state are discussing missile placement in this summit. Eliminate (A). The United States and the Soviet Union never engaged in an outright military conflict. Choice (B) is incorrect. The espionage discussed in this passage was based on a real, not hypothetical, event in which a U.S. plane was caught doing surveillance in Soviet airspace. Choice (C) is incorrect.

53. **D** Khrushchev describes the meeting occurring "under threat of aggressive intelligence flights," accusing the United States of participating in a secretive spy plane program. Choice (D) is correct. Since the Soviets are accusing the Americans of spying, (A) is incorrect. There is no discussion of Soviet influence in Europe within this passage, so (B) can be eliminated. Finally, eliminate (D) since this passage is a debate about spy planes, not nuclear war.

54. **C** While Khrushchev describes the spy planes as "aggressive," Eisenhower counters that the flights "had no aggressive intent but rather were to assure the safety of the United States." This evidence is consistent with (C), which is the correct answer. Eisenhower does not say anything about the Cold War going on indefinitely, so (A) is incorrect. Choices (B) and (D) are incorrect because they credit Khrushchev with Eisenhower's perspective.

55. **B** Khrushchev states that "there is no other solution than peaceful co-existence of the two systems, the capitalist and the socialist." He therefore envisions a world in which both countries' economic systems could exist. Choice (B) is correct. The statement should let us eliminate any answer choice that is hostile to capitalism, such as (A) and (C). Finally, recall that Khrushchev's system nonetheless stands in contrast to capitalism. Eliminate (D).

Section I, Part B: Short-Answer Questions

Question 1

a) The version of Peter the Great conveyed in Source 1 is that of a brutal, paranoid monarch. Evidence from Russian history that could support this view would be any of the following:

- He brutally tortured political dissidents who opposed his Westernization.

- He disallowed opposition parties.

- He ordered the death of his son.

- He exploited the serf class, turning them effectively into enslaved people.

b) The version of Peter the Great conveyed in Source 2 is that of a Westernizing reformer. Evidence from Russian history that could support this view would be any of the following:

- He built Russia's first navy.

- He moved Russia's capital to St. Petersburg to be more accessible to the West.

- Russia recruited Western European engineers, scientists, architects, and artists.

- Women of the nobility were forced to dress in Western fashions.

- Men were forced to shave their beards.

c) Feel free to use any of the evidence in the bullet points listed above, if you did not already use them for parts (a) and (b), to portray which aspect of Peter the Great's ruling style he should be most known for. Explain how your examples typify Peter the Great's governing.

Question 2

a) There are plenty of ways in which the Enlightenment-inspired liberal reforms helped inform reactions to rapid industrialization, but you need to write about only TWO of them. You can include any of the following:

- In Britain and the United States, where the impact of the Enlightenment was strong, reforms to the free-market system, such as child labor laws and unionism, took root, lessening the negative impact of capitalism on workers. (The British Parliament passed laws, such as the Factory Act of 1883.)

- In other countries such as Russia, Marxist ideas grew popular among a small group of urban intellectuals—eventually including Vladimir Lenin—who believed they could lead a workers' revolution and end the tyranny of the czars.

- Elsewhere, Marxism impacted social thought and intermixed with capitalist thought to create economic systems that were partly socialist (in which the government owned some of the means of production) and partly capitalist (in which individuals owned some of the means of production).

- Social mobility—the ability of a person to work his way up from one social class to the next—became more commonplace.

- The slave trade was abolished, which meant that no new enslaved people were transported from Africa, though the ownership of existing enslaved people continued. In 1833, the British outlawed slavery, and three decades later, it was outlawed in the United States.

b) You need to identify TWO primary ways that the Industrial Revolution helped increase the power of nation-states. There is much to choose from:

- Industrial nations amassed incredible wealth by colonizing regions with natural resources, and then taking those resources without compensating the native peoples. The resources were sent back to Europe, where they were made into finished products to be sent back and sold to the colonies. The more colonies a nation had, the richer it became.

- Countries with industrial technology had advanced military weapons and capacity, and were therefore easily able to conquer people who did not have this technology.

- The Industrial Revolution helped propel Great Britain to its undisputed ranking as the most powerful nation in the 19th century. The revolution also spread through much of mainland Europe, especially Belgium, France, and Germany, as well as to Japan and ultimately to the country that would eclipse Britain as the most industrialized—the United States.

- The more factories that developed in favorable locations, the larger cities grew. In 1800, along with London, the Chinese cities of Beijing (Peking) and Canton ranked in the top three, but just 100 years later, 9 of the 10 largest cities in the world were in Europe or the United States.

c) There are many possible responses to this question.

- People who'd been working in agriculture and handicrafts were slowly brought into working with mechanized manufacturing.

- To obtain these industrial jobs, rural working people were forced to move into the cities, particularly in the nineteenth century.

- Employment became precarious, as factories opened and closed with no notice given to workers.

- The children of the working class were often forced to labor in factories as well, in unsafe conditions.

- Though the rural environment had been clean, the newly industrialized cities were hotbeds of air and water pollution.

Question 3

a) The symbols you may want to identify include the gold coin (representing the gold deposits of Africa), a mosque (indicative of Mansa Musa's Islamic faith), or castles and crowns (demonstrating his power over a West African empire).

b) One way that Mansa Musa expanded Malian power is through the establishment of one of the wealthiest cities of the time—Timbuktu. As the capital of Mali, this city, founded on the gold and salt resources of the Sahara, attracted merchants from around the world. Controlling the gold trade in general allowed Mansa Musa to harness great economic and political power.

Further, Mansa Musa used Islam as a unifying force throughout the reaches of Western Africa. Also, don't neglect his journey to Mecca, which attracted attention for Mali across the Islamic world.

c) There are many possible responses to this question.

- The abundant natural resources of the western African region, particularly gold and salt.

- The heavy taxation that Mansa Musa placed on imports and exports paid for the empire's infrastructure, especially the water supply in Timbuktu, the chief city of the empire.

- The decentralized structure of the Malian Empire. The farflung provinces were given a large amount of power to rule themselves.

- A capable military, supported by the tax revenue, that projected power through its region and beyond.

Question 4

a) For this question, try to figure out what the G20 countries have in common that the non-G20 countries do not. Your job is to account for some of the reasons that this divide exists. This map of G20 countries shows a contrast between nations. For instance, centuries of imperialism, as well as a variety of decolonization practices, could explain why many countries in Africa, still considered economically developing, are not included in the G20. Some formerly colonized regions, such as China and India, are included. Perhaps explain why they break the pattern. You could explain why some post-colonial countries have been economically successful, while others have not.

b) The G20 is a forum for the world's major industrialized democracies. Be sure to explain that this summit of the world's most powerful leaders meets annually to discuss issues of mutual or global concern such as climate change, terrorism, and trade.

c) There are many possible responses to this question.

- Rising nationalism and insufficient cooperation has made it more difficult for the G20 to face global challenges.

- The power of private industry to influence national policy often slows down efforts to change societal structures, especially in the sector of climate change and energy policy.

- Recently, the economic downturn caused by the coronavirus pandemic has caused many countries, especially the ones in emerging markets, to rethink their commitment to global challenges.

Section II: Document-Based Question (DBQ)

A strong essay for this prompt would demonstrate how the complex nature of 20th-century diplomacy was further complicated by decolonization movements. The best essays will use all seven documents to show the diversity of reactions to navigating the inevitable movement toward decolonization in a post–World War II environment. A couple documents that might be useful for setting the stage for this essay, while also developing some context on the views and realities of decolonization, would be Document 2, in which the United Nations decries colonialism in 1960, and Document 4, which gives you a visual representation of the formerly colonized world. Two of the documents are from the perspectives of colonizing powers: Document 1 shows France caving to anti-colonial pressure and giving some degree of self-rule to its colonies, while Document 3 demonstrates hesitation by the British in giving full self-rule to Burma under the guise of protecting it from Japan. A strong essay would show the commonalities between these documents, and highlight the key contextual differences in their author's motivations. The remaining documents come from the perspectives of formerly colonized nations. Document 5 and Document 7 give us examples of how formerly colonized nations in Africa and Asia attempted to create strength through unity in a Western-dominated world. Use these to assist your analysis of how the decolonized world may have seen itself vis-à-vis the developed world. Finally, the major post–World War II diplomatic issue is the Cold War, and one document specifically references the role of a formerly colonized nation, India, in choosing sides during the Cold War. Document 6 reveals that India chose nonalignment for its own strategic purposes. To create a successful DBQ, organize all of these ideas in a way that takes the reader through both the context of decolonization and the motivations of all parties in creating a diplomatically strategic postwar world.

Long Essay

Question 2

A strong essay will use examples of emerging technologies during the years 1200 to 1600 to show how trade increased. The key, however, will be your analysis, which will evaluate the extent to which it affected trade. To do this, be sure to tie each example of a new technology to how it aligns with specific countries furthering their economic reach.

Some examples of technologies you might want to use could include:

- Astrolabe
- Sextant
- Guns and cannons
- Magnetic compass
- Cotton sails
- Lateen sails
- Sternpost rudder
- Three-masted caravels

Some examples of increased economic action during this period may include:

- Indian Ocean trade routes
- The Silk Road
- The Hanseatic League
- Great Zimbabwe
- Mongol trade routes
- Trans-Saharan trade and Timbuktu
- Connections made by Chinese explorers (Xuanzang and Zheng He)
- European exploration (Marco Polo, Vespucci, de Leon, Balboa, Magellan, Drake, Verrazzano, Cabot, Hudson, Columbus, and da Gama)
- Travels of Ibn Batutta
- Trade ports in India
- Trade ports in Nagasaki, Japan

Question 3

For this essay, you should develop a thesis statement featuring a couple specific reasons or an overarching general reason as to why certain Asian countries were untouched by outside influences during this period. Under the umbrella of that thesis statement, use some specific examples to illustrate the phenomenon.

One example could be how Ming China abruptly stopped its naval voyages and, as a society, increasingly turned inward. Historians see this trend as a reaction to the outside rule of the Mongols during the Yuan Dynasty. Ming China was interested in reclaiming what was traditionally Chinese, free from outside influence.

Japan is another key example. Under the Tokugawa Shogunate's National Seclusion Policy, Japanese were prohibited from traveling abroad, and most foreigners were prohibited from visiting Japan. Western trade was interrupted and Christian missionaries persecuted. Japan became increasingly secluded for nearly 200 years.

An important component of this essay is to analyze these examples fully by evaluating *why* these nations remained successfully untouched during their periods of seclusion. This could be accomplished in a couple ways. For one, you could compare these nations to other parts of the non-Western world that were not able to resist outside influences. Another analytical approach should involve the reasons China and Japan wanted to remain free from outside trade and cultural interactions.

Question 4

A successful essay will discuss how well nations afforded women rights and opportunities in the 20th century. Be sure to fully analyze your examples by tying them to specific historical movements and trends. The prompt allows you to make the scope of your discussion as narrow or as broad as you wish. Regardless, there are some key trends that should be noted in your essay. For instance, the integration and global connectedness of the world made access to education and political freedoms far more widespread, especially among the middle and upper classes.

One obvious topic to discuss is women's suffrage. There are many historical occurrences that accelerated this process around the world, so the way you present suffrage can come in many forms. World Wars saw many women begin to work outside the home in factories, for instance. This created a new public role for women that opened up doors for allowing women to participate more directly in society in terms of voting and educational opportunities (United States and Great Britain). By mid-century, this trend was seen in other parts of Europe as well as in Latin America, India, China, and Japan.

Communist countries provided opportunities to women that were not always available in capitalist societies. The equality demanded in a classless society resulted in considerable advances for women. Revolutions in Russia, China, and Cuba created educational opportunities for women in professions such as medicine. Women were also generally given equal legal rights including those of inheritance, divorce, and child rearing. Keep your analysis focused on how the ideals of communism were consistent with women's liberation. The strongest essays will also analyze how the realities for women in many of these countries were not always as progressive as the ideals.

You may also want to cover some Islamic societies, which have presented complicated cases for women's rights. Iran, for example, was quite progressive following the rise of Reza Shah until the Iranian Revolution in 1979. It was possible that within a single woman's lifetime, she went from an extremely traditional, oppressive society to one in which she could vote, dress less traditionally, divorce her husband, become educated, and pursue a career. Of course, after the Iranian Revolution, those reforms were reversed immediately.

Feel free to wrap up with connections to the dawn of the 21st century to fully evaluate the extent to which women's equality exists around the world.

HOW TO SCORE PRACTICE TEST 1

Section IA: Multiple Choice

	× 1.090 =	
Number Correct (out of 55)		Weighted Section I Score (Do not round)

Section IB: Short Answer

Question 1:

_____ × 3.3333 = _____

(out of 3)   (Do not round)

Question 2:

_____ × 3.3333 = _____

(out of 3)   (Do not round)

Question 3 or 4:

_____ × 3.3333 = _____

(out of 3)   (Do not round)

AP Score Conversion Chart World History	
Composite Score Range	AP Score
107–150	5
90–106	4
73–89	3
56–72	2
0–55	1

Section II: Document-Based Question

Question 1:

_____ × 5.3571 = _____

(out of 7)   (Do not round)

Section II: Long Essay

Question 2, 3, or 4:

_____ × 3.750 = _____

(out of 6)   (Do not round)

Composite Score

Weighted Section IA Score	+	Weighted Section IB Score	+	Weighted DBQ Score	+	Weighted Long Essay Score	=	Composite Score (Round to the nearest whole number)

Part III
About the AP World History: Modern Exam

THE STRUCTURE OF THE AP WORLD HISTORY: MODERN EXAM

The AP World History: Modern Exam is 3 hours and 15 minutes long and broken up into two sections, each of which consists of two parts. Your performance on these four parts, outlined in the table below, is compiled and weighted to find your overall exam score.

Structure of the AP World History: Modern Exam				
Section	**Description**	**Number of Questions**	**Time Allotted**	**Percentage of Total Exam Score**
Section I	Part A: Multiple Choice	55	55 minutes	40%
	Part B: Short Answer	3	40 minutes	20%
Reading Period			15 minutes	
Section II	Part A: DBQ	1	45 minutes	25%
	Part B: Long Essay	1	40 minutes	15%

Here's what to expect in each of these sections.

- **Multiple Choice**: Questions will be grouped into sets of two to five and based on primary or secondary sources, including excerpts from historical documents or writings, images, graphs, maps, and so on. Each set of questions will be based on a different piece of source material. You'll have 55 minutes to answer 55 multiple-choice questions. This section will test your ability to analyze and engage with the source materials while recalling what you already know about world history.

- **Short Answer**: You will answer three of the four questions in this section. Questions 1 and 2 are required, and then for the third and final question, you will choose between Questions 3 and 4. These questions will require you to respond to a primary or secondary source, a historian's argument, or a general proposition about world history. Your response should be about a paragraph in length. The time allotted for this section is 40 minutes.

- **Document-Based Question (DBQ)**: Here you'll be presented with a variety of historical documents that are intended to show the complexity of a particular historical issue. You will need to develop a thesis that responds to the question prompt, and support that thesis with evidence from both the documents and your knowledge of world history. To earn the best score, you should incorporate outside knowledge and be able to relate the issues discussed in the documents to a larger theme, issue, or time period. The 60-minute timeframe for this section includes a suggested 15-minute reading period so that you can familiarize yourself with the question and documents.

- **Long Essay**: You'll be given a choice of three essay options, and you must choose one to answer. The long essay is similar to the DBQ in that you must develop a thesis and use historical evidence to support an argument, but there will not be any documents on which you must base your response. Instead, you will need to draw upon your own knowledge of topics you learned in your AP World History class. You'll have 40 minutes to write this essay.

HOW THE AP WORLD HISTORY: MODERN EXAM IS SCORED

Each of the four parts of the exam is weighted differently to determine your overall score.

Test Section	Percentage of Overall Score
Multiple Choice	40%
Short Answer	20%
DBQ	25%
Long Essay	15%

Rubrics are provided for both the DBQ and long essay in later chapters.

Once the multiple-choice section of your test has been scanned and your essays have been scored by readers, College Board converts your results to the standard AP Exam 1 to 5. A score of 4 or 5 will most likely get you what you want from the college or university you'll attend—college credit for World History. A score of 3 is considered passing and might get you college credit; then again, it might not. Therefore, your goal is to get at least a 3, preferably a 4 or 5. If you receive below a 3, it is highly unlikely that you will get college credit for your high school AP course, but you still get a grade for that class. A good grade in an AP class always looks good on your transcript.

The tricky part about the 1 to 5 scoring system is that it is designed to compare you to everyone else who took the AP World History: Modern Exam during a given year. But if the test that year was particularly tough, the top 20 percent or so of scorers will still score 4s and 5s. In other words, if all the scaled scores are somewhat low, the top end will still earn high marks. Of course, the opposite is also true—if everyone does an excellent job, some people will still end up with 1s and 2s.

For your reference, here is the College Board's score distribution data from the 2019 and 2020 AP World History: Modern Exam administrations.

Score	2021 Percentage	Credit Recommendation	College Grade Equivalent
5	9.7%	Extremely Well Qualified	A
4	18.5%	Very Well qualified	A−, B+, B
3	24.0%	Qualified	B−, C+, C
2	28.9%	Possibly Qualified	−
1	19.0%	No Recommendation	−

Scores taken from May 2021 test administration. Data taken from the College Board website.

OVERVIEW OF CONTENT TOPICS

The AP World History: Modern Exam divides all history into four major periods from about 800 years ago to the present.

Chronological Period	Units
Period 1 c. 1200 c.e. to c. 1450	Unit 1: The Global Tapestry
	Unit 2: Networks of Exchange
Period 2 c. 1450 to c. 1750	Unit 3: Land-Based Empires
	Unit 4: Transoceanic Interconnections
Period 3 c. 1750 to c. 1900	Unit 5: Revolutions
	Unit 6: Consequences of Industrialization
Period 4 c. 1900 to the present	Unit 7: Global Conflict
	Unit 8: Cold War and Decolonization
	Unit 9: Globalization

The review of history included in this book divides world history into four chapters for each period, while each chapter is further divided into the nine units it covers. So we've got you all covered!

The Free-Response Questions (a.k.a. the Essays)

There are three types of essays on the AP World History: Modern Exam. The short-answer questions are the first type. You need to answer three of these, which require you to respond to a primary source, a historian's argument, sources such as data or maps, or general propositions about world history.

The second type of essay is the Document-Based Question (DBQ), a question based on seven primary-source documents. You must formulate a thesis or claim in response to a prompt, and then support your thesis using evidence from the documents, as well as outside examples. You should incorporate as many of the given documents as possible into your response.

The third type is the long essay, which is probably more like the type of question you might see on a classroom test. For this essay, you are given three options, and you must answer one. This essay requires you draw upon your knowledge of world history and what you learned in your AP World History: Modern course to respond to a historical issue.

What Do They Want From Me?

What is the AP World History: Modern Exam really testing? In a nutshell: can you make connections between different societies over different periods of time? In other words, for any given period of history, can you explain who was doing what? How did what they were doing affect the rest of the world? What changed about the society during this period of time? To show what you know about world history, keep this big-picture perspective in mind as you study and answer multiple-choice questions or construct essays. To help you do this, keep an eye out for certain recurring themes throughout the different time periods. Specifically, be on the lookout for the following:

- How did people interact with their environment? Why did they live where they did? How did they get there? What tools, technology, and resources were available to them? How was the landscape changed by humans?
- What new ideas, thoughts, and styles came into existence? How did these cultural developments influence people and technology (for example: new religious beliefs or Renaissance thought)?
- How did different societies get along—or not get along—within a time period? Who took over whom? How did leaders justify their power? Who revolted or was likely to revolt? Were they successful?
- How did economic systems develop, and what did they depend on in terms of agriculture, trade, labor, industrialization, and the demands of consumers?
- Who had power and who did not within a given culture and why? What was the status of women? What racial and ethnic constructions were present?

Got a Question?
For answers to all your test prep questions and additional test taking tips, subscribe to our YouTube channel at www.youtube.com/ThePrincetonReview

The College Board says that the AP World History: Modern Course and Exam addresses six main themes of world history:
1. Humans and the Environment
2. Cultural Developments and Interactions
3. Governance
4. Economic Systems
5. Social Interactions and Organization
6. Technology and Innovation

For each time period covered in Part V of this book, you will find boxes that identify the major themes in the box at the left, plus a Big Picture overview and a Pulling It All Together summary for each period. The introduction to Part V will fill you in on how to use these tools as you study.

Furthermore, the College Board states that the AP World History: Modern Exam is designed to test six specific skills, including

1. Developments and Processes—Identify and explain historical developments and processes.
2. Sourcing and Situation—Analyze sourcing and situation of primary and secondary sources.
3. Claims and Evidence in Sources—Analyze arguments in primary and secondary sources.
4. Contextualization—Analyze the context of historical events, developments, or processes.
5. Making Connections—Using historical reasoning processes (comparison, causation, continuity, and change), analyze patterns and connections between and among historical developments and processes.
6. Argumentation—Develop an argument.

HOW AP EXAMS ARE USED

Different colleges use AP Exams in different ways, so it is important that you go to a particular college's website to determine how it uses AP Exams. The three items below represent the main ways in which AP Exam scores can be used:

- **College Credit**. Some colleges will give you college credit if you score well on an AP Exam. These credits count toward your graduation requirements, meaning that you can take fewer courses while in college. Given the cost of college, this could be quite a benefit, indeed.

- **Satisfy Requirements**. Some colleges will allow you to "place out" of certain requirements if you do well on an AP Exam, even if they do not give you actual college credits. For example, you might not need to take an introductory-level course, or perhaps you might not need to take a class in a certain discipline at all.

- **Admissions Plus**. Even if your AP Exam will not result in college credit or even allow you to place out of certain courses, most colleges will respect your decision to push yourself by taking an AP Course or even an AP Exam outside of a course. A high score on an AP Exam shows mastery of more difficult content than is taught in many high school courses, and colleges may take that into account during the admissions process.

OTHER RESOURCES

There are many resources available to help you improve your score on the AP World History: Modern Exam, not the least of which are your teachers. If you are taking an AP class, you may be able to get extra attention from your teacher, such as obtaining feedback on your essays. If you are not in an AP course, reach out to a teacher who teaches World History, and ask whether the teacher will review your essays or otherwise help you with content.

Another wonderful resource is **AP Students**, the official site of the AP Exams. The scope of the information at this site is quite broad and includes:

- the updated course description, which provides details on what content is covered and sample questions
- the latest AP Environmental Science Free-Response and Scoring Guidelines
- access to AP Classroom if you are enrolled in a course (teacher assistance required)
- free-response prompts from previous years and exam tips

The AP Students home page address is apstudents.collegeboard.org.

The AP World History: Modern home page for students is apstudents.collegeboard.org/apcourse/ap-world-history.

Finally, The Princeton Review offers tutoring for the AP World History: Modern Exam. Our expert instructors can help you refine your strategic approach and add to your content knowledge. For more information, call 1-800-2REVIEW or visit www.PrincetonReview.com.

Check for Updates!
The College Board's AP Students home page for the AP World History: Modern Exam has a wealth of resources, including the latest information on how the 2023 Exam will be administered. We recommend you check for updates on their site!

DESIGNING YOUR STUDY PLAN

In Part I, you identified some areas of potential improvement. Let's now delve further into your performance on Practice Test 1, with the goal of developing a study plan appropriate to your needs and time commitment.

Read the answers and explanations associated with the multiple-choice questions (starting on page 43). After you have done so, respond to the following questions:

- Review the Overview of Content Topics on page 62 and, next to each one, indicate your rank of the topic as follows: "1" means "I need a lot of work on this," "2" means "I need to beef up my knowledge," and "3" means "I know this topic well."

- How many days/weeks/months away is your AP World History: Modern Exam?

- What time of day is your best, most focused study time?

- How much time per day/week/month will you devote to preparing for your AP World History: Modern Exam?

- When will you do this preparation? (Be as specific as possible: Mondays and Wednesdays from 3:00 to 4:00 P.M., for example.)

- Based on the answers above, will you focus on strategy (Part IV), content (Part V), or both?

- What are your overall goals in using this book?

Part IV
Test-Taking Strategies for the AP World History: Modern Exam

PREVIEW

Review your responses to the three questions on page 2 of Part I and then respond to the following questions:

- How many multiple-choice questions did you miss even though you knew the answer?

- On how many multiple-choice questions did you guess randomly?

- How many multiple-choice questions did you miss after eliminating some answers and guessing based on the remaining answers?

- Did you create an outline before you wrote each essay?

- Did you find any of the essays easier or harder than the others—and, if so, why?

Study Aids Online!
We've created step-by-step study plans so you can use this book to your best advantage. Head over to your Student Tools (see the "Get More (Free) Content" page for instructions) to get started!

HOW TO USE THE CHAPTERS IN THIS PART

For the following Strategy chapters, think about what you are doing now before you read the chapters. As you read and engage in the directed practice, be sure to appreciate the ways you can change your approach. At the end of Part IV, you will have the opportunity to reflect on how you will change your approach.

Chapter 1
How to Approach
the Multiple-Choice
Questions

THE BASICS

The multiple-choice part of the exam will consist of sets of two to five questions that are tied to primary sources, secondary sources, or historical issues. The directions will be pretty simple. They will likely be similar to the following:

> **Directions:** Each of the questions or incomplete statements below is followed by four suggested answers or completions. Select the one that is best in each case and then fill in the corresponding space on the answer sheet.

In short, you are being asked to evaluate a provided document or source and answer a series of questions. Once you select an answer, you will fill in the appropriate bubble on a separate answer sheet. You will *not* be given credit for answers you record in your test booklet (e.g., by circling them) but not on your answer sheet. Part A of Section I (the multiple-choice questions) consists of 55 questions, and Part B (the short-answer questions) contains four questions. You have 1 hour and 35 minutes to complete these two sections, so time management is key. The College Board breaks it down as follows: 55 minutes for the multiple-choice section, and 40 minutes for the short answers.

> The AP World History: Modern Exam tests your ability to read, analyze, and draw conclusions about primary sources as well as their connection to historical events and ideas. The questions in the multiple-choice section will all be based in some way on a primary source, whether a chart of information, an excerpt from a historical document or text, a photograph, or a map— the list goes on!

TYPES OF SOURCES

Unlike many AP Exams, the multiple-choice questions on the AP World History: Modern Exam appear in sets associated with a primary source, secondary source, or historical issue. Primary sources are original materials, which provide a firsthand account or perspective. Many of the primary sources that you are likely to see on the exam will include direct excerpts from historical literary works, documents from ancient history, legislation, inscriptions, letters, and speeches. Secondary sources are pieces of information that relate to or are discussed in reference to information presented elsewhere (not firsthand information). Examples of secondary sources include historical perspectives on events, historical criticisms, artwork or cartoons, photographs, or retrospective analyses. Additional sources used on the exam may include charts or graphs that depict key historical relationships.

Here is an example of a primary source you may see on the AP World History: Modern Exam:

Questions 13–15 refer to the passage below.

The Laws of Genghis Khan

1. It is ordered to believe that there is only one God, creator of heaven and earth, who alone gives life and death, riches and poverty as pleases Him—and who has over everything an absolute power.
2. Leaders of a religion, preachers, monks, persons who are dedicated to religious practice, the criers of mosques, physicians and those who bathe the bodies of the dead are to be freed from public charges.
3. It is forbidden under penalty of death that any one, whoever he may be, shall be proclaimed emperor unless he has been elected previously by the princes, khans, officers and other Mongol nobles in a general council.
4. It is forbidden chieftains of nations and clans subject to the Mongols to hold honorary titles.
5. Forbidden to ever make peace with a monarch, a prince or a people who have not submitted.

The series of legal prescriptions from The Laws of Genghis Khan, excerpted above, outlines a few aspects of the Mongol legal system. On the AP World History: Modern Exam, you will be given primary sources like these that address key events or issues in world history. The accompanying questions will evaluate these sources from the perspective of the thematic learning objectives described in Part III of this book. Throughout this chapter, we have provided additional examples that represent the diversity of sources you may see on the exam. We will now discuss how to tackle the questions stemming from these sources.

TYPES OF QUESTIONS

The questions in the multiple-choice section will center on one or more key themes addressed by the source document provided for each set of questions. The majority of the questions will be pretty straightforward once the context of the source is understood. For instance, an example question stemming from the text quoted above may appear as follows:

13. The excerpt provided is best understood in the context of which of the following?

    (A) The Prussian consolidation of power in the mid 19th century
    (B) The resistance of minority groups throughout Eastern Europe
    (C) The need for improved trade regulations throughout continental Europe
    (D) The creation of new states in response a renewed sense of nationalism throughout Europe

Often the test writers will throw in trickier, less straightforward questions, such as NOT/EXCEPT questions. For these types of questions, you are looking for the answer that is NOT true. Approach these as you would a simple "true or false" question. Take a look at the following EXCEPT multiple-choice question.

Questions 4–7 refer to the passage below.

"Whereas, Most Christian, High, Excellent, and Powerful Princes, King and Queen of Spain and of the Islands of the Sea, our Sovereigns, this present year 1492, after your Highnesses had terminated the war with the Moors reigning in Europe, the same having been brought to an end in the great city of Granada, where on the second day of January, this present year, I saw the royal banners of your Highnesses planted by force of arms upon the towers of the Alhambra, which is the fortress of that city, and saw the Moorish king come out at the gate of the city and kiss the hands of your Highnesses, and of the Prince my Sovereign; and in the present month, in consequence of the information which I had given your Highnesses respecting the countries of India and of a Prince, called Great Can, which in our language signifies King of Kings, how, at many times he, and his predecessors had sent to Rome soliciting instructors who might teach him our holy faith, and the holy Father had never granted his request, whereby great numbers of people were lost, believing in idolatry and doctrines of perdition. Your Highnesses, as Catholic Christians, and princes who love and promote the holy Christian faith, and are enemies of the doctrine of Mahomet, and of all idolatry and heresy, determined to send me, Christopher Columbus, to the above-mentioned countries of India, to see the said princes, people, and territories, and to learn their disposition and the proper method of converting them to our holy faith; and furthermore directed that I should not proceed by land to the East, as is customary, but by a Westerly route, in which direction we have hitherto no certain evidence that any one has gone."

Christopher Columbus, personal journal, 1492

4. The effects of European exploration of the Americas included all of the following EXCEPT

   (A) the exchange of information about crops and other food items
   (B) the widespread conversion of Europeans to Native American religious belief systems
   (C) the introduction of new weapons to Native American tribes
   (D) the decimation of the Native American population due to diseases brought by the Europeans

A few times during the multiple-choice section, you will be asked to interpret an illustration source, often a map or other type of graphic. These questions are usually pretty easy. The key is not to try to read too much between the lines. To save time, read the question first, and then go to the graphic. This way you will know what you are looking for!

Here is an example of a map source and associated question.

Questions 33–35 refer to the map below.

Voyage Map of Ibn Battuta's and Marco Polo's travels, 13th and 14th Centuries.

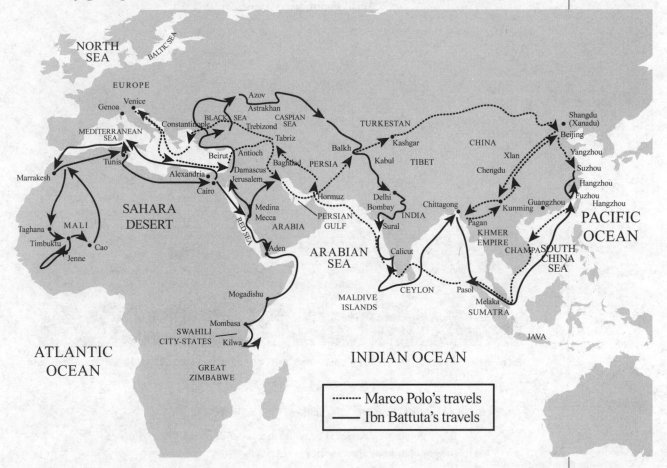

33. According to the map above, how does the voyage of Ibn Battuta compare to that of Marco Polo?

   (A) Marco Polo began his journey before Ibn Battuta.

   (B) Ibn Battuta spent considerable time on the Swahili Coast, while that area was largely avoided by Marco Polo.

   (C) Unlike Ibn Battuta, Marco Polo's voyage explored the port cities of China.

   (D) Ibn Battuta's voyage took him through Islamic lands, unlike the voyage of Marco Polo.

Finally, there will be a few questions on your test asking you to interpret a graph or chart. These are usually very straightforward, unless they are "EXCEPT" or "NOT" questions. Those tend to be time-consuming, and even strong students should probably do those at the end, if time permits. When you answer one of these chart or graph questions, realize that more than one answer might be valid, but only one will be supported by the information in the chart or graph.

The following is an example of a graph question.

Questions 40–44 refer to the table below.

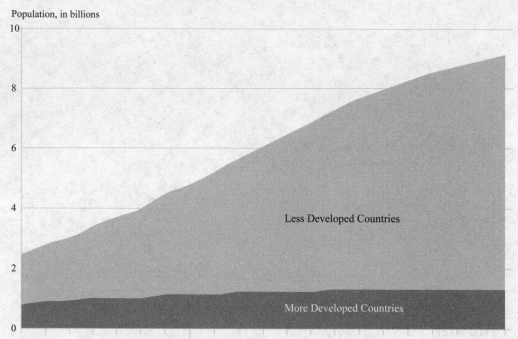

World Population Growth, 1950–2050

40. It can be inferred from the information in the table above that

    (A)   the population of Africa is growing at a faster rate than that of Europe

    (B)   the population of all countries is declining

    (C)   the population of China is growing more quickly than that of any other nation

    (D)   the population of more developed countries is greater than that of less developed countries

The Big Picture

One of the most important characteristics of the AP World History: Modern multiple-choice section is that the questions and answers are designed to illustrate basic principles of world history. These principles are evaluated through the five thematic learning objectives mentioned in Part III. Multiple-choice questions will NOT ask about exceptions to historical trends; the test ignores these because the test writers are trying to find out whether you have mastered the important generalizations that can be drawn from history. They do not want to know whether you have memorized your textbook (they already know that you haven't). Talk of historical exceptions is welcome in the essay section, though. Students who discuss exceptions in their essays often impress the readers. More on that later.

Overall, you should always keep the **big picture** in mind as you take this exam. As you approach questions, use the sources provided to help you focus on key points or themes that are being questioned. Even if you cannot remember the specific event or concept being tested, you should be able to answer the question by remembering the general social and political trends of the era and using the information that may be ascertained from the source. Let's look at a couple of illustrative examples.

Think Big
Remembering general concepts and major events of a given time and place in history can be the key to choosing the right answers in the multiple-choice section. Even if you're not familiar with a specific source, being familiar with the general trends of the time period and place can help you BIG time.

Questions 51–54 refer to the passages below.

"From the beginning of my coming to stay in Egypt I heard talk of the arrival of this sultan Musa on his Pilgrimage and found the Cairenes eager to recount what they had seem of the Africans' prodigal spending. I asked the emir Abu…and he told me of the opulence, manly virtues, and piety of his sultan. "When I went out to meet him {he said} that is, on behalf of the mighty sultan al-Malik al-Nasir, he did me extreme honour and treated me with the greatest courtesy. He addressed me, however, only through an interpreter despite his perfect ability to speak in the Arabic tongue. Then he forwarded to the royal treasury many loads of unworked native gold and other valuables."

—al-Umari's description of the visit to Cairo in 1324
by Mansa Musa, the King of Mali.

51. A primary effect of pilgrimages such as Mansa Musa's was

   (A) repression of religion

   (B) cultural diffusion

   (C) intolerance directed toward travelers from foreign lands

   (D) economic stagnation

The strategy used to answer this question is Process of Elimination, or POE for short. We'll go into this strategy in more detail in a few pages!

Here's How to Crack It

At first glance, this question may appear to require you to remember a lot of details about Mansa Musa's travels. It's not really all that tricky, though. To answer this question correctly, you need to remember only the big picture about the Islamic world during this period (and of course, you need to remember that the "Pilgrimage" the author refers to is the Islamic tradition of *hajj*—the trek taken by Muslims to the holy city of Mecca).

When you take a close look at the question stem, you can see that the point of the question is to figure out which answer choice correctly describes the historical relevance of people from around the Islamic world traveling to a common location. Choice (A) does not make sense; Muslims traveled through Muslim lands to fulfill an Islamic tradition. Mansa Musa would not encounter cities that would repress his faith along his travels. Eliminate it. Choice (C) is contradictory to how cities treated fellow Muslims—pilgrims were welcome to pass through without difficulty or taxation, so you can eliminate that option as well. Choice (D) contradicts the text. The passage describes Mansa Musa both encountering and throwing around plenty of wealth, so eliminate (D). Choice (B) is the only remaining option and is the correct answer. If there is one thing to know about Islamic travelers in this period, it is that they took traditions from their homelands to new locations while bringing back ideas, materials, and innovations from their travels to their homelands. This describes cultural diffusion.

Let's look at another example.

Questions 13–14 refer to the passage below.

"And here it becomes evident that the bourgeoisie is unfit any longer to be the ruling class in society and to impose its conditions of existence upon society as an over-riding law. It is unfit to rule because it is incompetent to assure an existence to its slave within his slavery, because it cannot help letting him sink into such a state that it has to feed him instead of being fed by him. Society can no longer live under this bourgeoisie; in other words, its existence is no longer compatible with society.

The essential condition for the existence, and for the sway of the bourgeois class, is the formation and augmentation of capital; the condition for capital is wage-labor. Wage-labor rests exclusively on competition between the laborers. The advance of industry, whose involuntary promoter is the bourgeoisie, replaces the isolation of the laborers, due to competition, by their revolutionary combination, due to association. The development of modern industry, therefore, cuts from under its feet the very foundation on which the bourgeoisie produces and appropriates products. What the bourgeoisie therefore produces, above all, are its own grave diggers. Its fall and the victory of the proletariat are equally inevitable."

13. The quotation above appears in which of the following?

(A) Martin Luther's "Letter to Pope Leo X"
(B) John Stuart Mill's *On Liberty*
(C) Jean-Jacques Rousseau's *The Social Contract*
(D) Karl Marx and Friedrich Engels' *The Communist Manifesto*

Here's How to Crack It

The first thing you may notice is that this question is pretty difficult; the quotation is one long sentence filled with archaic language and syntax. However, if you key in on the big picture, this question isn't all that hard, provided you've prepared for the exam. The central concept of the quotation, to oversimplify quite a bit, is that there is some sort of conflict between different classes in society and that the bourgeoisie (read: upper/middle classes who are the ones with capital, i.e., money) is bad.

Now let's take a look at the answer choices. Martin Luther's "Letter to Pope Leo X," (A), is a religious treatise that attempts to clarify Luther's intentions to the Roman Catholic Church. The terminology of the quotation, such as "capital," "the advance of industry," and "bourgeoisie," should tell you that this text does not focus on Christianity but is rather a discussion of economic matters. Eliminate (A). John Stuart Mill's *On Liberty*, (B), is a philosophical work published in 1859 that emphasizes the importance of individuality and the liberty of individual citizens in opposition to tyrannical government. Choice (B) could match the correct time period, but the quote itself doesn't mention liberty or individualism, so eliminate it. Rousseau's *The Social Contract*, (C), is a treatise published in 1752 that discusses the conditions in which a society can form a legitimate political authority. Without knowing specifics, this might appear to be a possible answer, but (D) is better: *The Communist Manifesto*, published in 1848, theorizes that human history is characterized by class struggle and that the problems of the capitalist mode of production will lead to socialism and eventually communism. Even if you didn't recognize the quote right away, the fact that the author consistently repeats the term "bourgeoisie" and ends with a prediction about the "victory of the proletariat" (i.e., working class) should key you into the fact that you are dealing with a text about communism.

Process of Elimination (POE)

If it seems that we are focusing more on eliminating incorrect answers than on finding the correct answers, you're right. This is because eliminating wrong answers is the most efficient way to take a multiple-choice exam. We call this strategy **Process of Elimination (POE)**. You should use this technique to whittle down the answer choices to one, because incorrect answers are much easier to identify than correct ones. When you look for the correct answer among the answer choices, you have a tendency to try to justify how each answer *might* be correct. You'll adopt a forgiving attitude in a situation in which tough assertiveness is rewarded. Eliminate incorrect answers. Terminate them with extreme prejudice. Remember that "half wrong is all wrong," and mark up the test as you do this. You are probably used to teachers telling you not to write on the test. This test, however, is yours to mark up, and that will make it easier for you to decide what to guess. If you have done your job well, only the correct answer will be left standing at the end.

Remember POE
Process of Elimination, or POE, is an effective strategy when it comes to guessing on questions you're not completely sure about. If you can't eliminate any answer choices right off the bat, it's best to skip the question and come back to it later.

Common Sense Can Help

Sometimes an answer choice on the multiple-choice section contradicts common sense. Eliminate those answers. Evaluate the question below, which stems from a source on trade between Europe, Africa, and the Americas during the Age of Exploration. Which of the answer choices to the question below lack common sense?

―――――――――○―――――――――

12. According to the passage, which of the following best explains the most important effect that transatlantic exploration had on societies in the New World?

    (A) The rapid decrease in the population of native peoples was due to the arrival of disease and the use of firepower.

    (B) The immediate commercial success of corn forced individuals in the Americas to defend themselves against repeated attacks by the Chinese, who wanted to take control of the corn trade.

    (C) The development of cotton cultivation led to increased numbers of conquistadors seeking fortune in the Americas.

    (D) Difficulties assimilating with the native population led to a full retreat by European explorers.

Here's How to Crack It

Even if you didn't completely understand the passage (which would precede this question on the actual exam), common sense should allow you to eliminate (B) immediately. Even if you don't know much about the American civilizations that preceded European encounters, hopefully you do know that the Chinese never attacked the Americas. Now let's consider the other answer choices. Was cotton the most important crop in the Americas? No one knows exactly (evidence of early cotton production has been found in Mexico and parts of South America) but gold (remember the legend of El Dorado?), not cotton, was the primary motivation for conquistadors to explore the New World. Eliminate (C). Choice (D) is completely backwards and violates common sense. The tragic outcome of the conquistadors was that they brutally attacked native populations, particularly those who refused to assimilate to European norms. Eliminate (D). The correct answer is (A).

―――――――――○―――――――――

Context Clues

Some questions contain context clues or vocabulary words that will either lead you to the correct answer or at least help you eliminate an incorrect answer. Look at the passage and question below.

Questions 38–41 refer to the passage below.

"To close off employment possibilities and respectable occupations to the most numerous and useful class is like killing genius and talents, and forcing them to run away from an ungrateful home. However, in our current constitution, only nobles enjoy all prerogatives like landed wealth, honors, dignities, graces, pensions, retirements, responsibility for government, and free schools. . . . These [privileges] constitute the favors the State lavishes exclusively on the nobility, at the expense of the Third Estate.

The nobility enjoys and owns everything, and would like to free itself from everything. However, if the nobility commands the army, the Third Estate makes it up. If nobility pours a drop of blood, the Third Estate spreads rivers of it. The nobility empties the royal treasury, the Third Estate fills it up. Finally, the Third Estate pays everything and does not enjoy anything."

> —*Cahier de doléances* ["list of grievances"]
> drawn up in the sénéchaussée of Aix-en-Provence, 1789.

38. The point of view expressed in the quotation above is most likely that of

   (A) a Spanish explorer preparing to embark upon a journey
   (B) a Dutch merchant considering trading options in southern Europe
   (C) a Frenchman reflecting on the inequity evident in his country
   (D) a Russian peasant petitioning the repressive tsarist government

Here's How to Crack It

If you feel like you entered this passage in the middle of a longer discussion and have no idea what a "sénéchaussée" is, don't worry. There are a few big context clues in the bibliographical information that might give you enough of a framework to answer this question correctly. The title of this text is *Cahier de doléances*. The year it was written is 1789, and the passage mentions buzzwords such as the Third Estate and nobility. Do any of the answer choices have nothing to do with this topic? First, eliminate (B). There is no mention of anyone or anything Dutch in the text. Choice (A) seems pretty unlikely, too. There is nothing in the text about exploration. Furthermore, the Age of Exploration was much earlier than 1789. Choice (D) might look plausible if you notice the complaints about the oppositional relationship between the State and those who do not rank in the nobility, but the title of the passage makes it clear that this passage is from a French, not Russian, author. Eliminate (D). The correct answer, (C), makes the most sense because the Third Estate felt the distribution of wealth and privileges was unequal in the Ancient Regime of Louis XVI so it would be logical for a list of grievances to reflect upon such inequity in the run-up to the French Revolution.

Here are the answers to the questions in this chapter.

13. C
4. B
33. D
40. A
51. B
13. D
12. A
38. C

Summary

○ The multiple-choice section consists of sets of two to five questions, which are tied to primary sources, secondary sources, or historical issues.

○ Familiarize yourself with the different types of questions that will appear on the multiple-choice section. Be aware that you will see many questions about political, social, cultural, economic, and religious history. Tailor your studies accordingly.

○ Look for "big picture" answers. Correct answers on the multiple-choice section confirm important trends in world history. This section will not ask you about weird exceptions that contradict those trends. It also will not ask you about military history featured on the History Channel. You will not be required to perform miraculous feats of memorization; however, you must be thoroughly familiar with all the basics of world history.

○ Use Process of Elimination (POE) when working on a question you're not sure about. Once you have eliminated some choices and convinced yourself that you cannot eliminate any other incorrect answers, you should guess and move on to the next question.

○ Use common sense, and look for context clues.

Chapter 2
Essay Basics and How to Approach the Short-Answer Questions

OVERVIEW

There are three types of essay questions on the AP World History: Modern Exam: the short-answer questions, the document-based question (DBQ), and the long essay question. In this chapter we will review some essay basics and discuss the short-answer section in more detail. In the chapters that follow, we will discuss the DBQ and the long essay question more in depth.

Reasons to Be Optimistic About the Free-Response Questions

AP graders know that you are given very little time to write the DBQ and the long essay question. They also know that you don't have enough time to cover the broad scope of the subject matter tested by the question. The fact is, many long books have been written about any one subject that you might be asked about on the DBQ and the long essay.

The College Board's AP World History Course Description (which can be downloaded from the College Board's AP Students website) advises students to write an essay that has a well-developed thesis, provides support for the thesis with specific examples, addresses all parts of the question, and is well organized. Therefore, expressing good ideas and presenting valid evidence in support of those ideas is hugely important. Making sure that you mention every single relevant piece of historical information is not so important.

Also, you should remember that graders are not given a lot of time to read your essays. When they gather to read the exams, each grader goes through more than 100 essays per day. No one could possibly give detailed attention to all points in your essay when he or she is reading at such a fast clip. What he or she can see in such a brief reading is whether you have something intelligent to say and whether you have the ability to say it well. As many teachers and professors will tell you, when you read several bad essays, you tend to give those that are not completely awful more credit than they possibly deserve.

ESSAY BASICS: WHAT ARE THE AP ESSAY GRADERS LOOKING FOR?

In conversations with those who grade AP World History: Modern Exams, it is clear that what they want above all else is for you to address the question. In some of your classes, you may have gotten into the habit of throwing everything but the kitchen sink into an essay without truly addressing the question at hand. Do not try to fudge your way through the essay. The graders are all experts in history, and you will not be able to fool them into thinking you know more than you actually do.

It is also very important to focus on the phrasing of the question. Some students are so anxious to get going that they start writing as soon as they know the general subject of the question, and many of these students lose points because their essays do not answer the question. Take, for example, an essay question that asks you to discuss the effects of technological advances on the ability of European explorers to travel more widely around the globe in the 15th century. If you are an overanxious test taker, you might start rattling off everything you know about the Age of Exploration. No matter how well this essay is written, you will lose points for one simple reason—not answering the question!

Furthermore, a good essay does more than rattle off facts. Just as the multiple-choice questions seek to draw out certain general principles or the "big picture" of world history, the essay questions seek to do the same. The readers want to see that you understand some of the fundamental issues in world history and that you can successfully discuss this material in a coherent manner.

If all this sounds intimidating, read on! There are a few simple things you can do to improve your grade on the AP essays.

Things That Make Any Essay Better

There are two essential components to writing a successful timed essay. First, plan what you are going to write before you start writing! Second, use a number of tried-and-true writing techniques that will make your essay appear well organized, well thought out, and well written. This section is about those techniques.

Before You Start Writing

Read the question carefully. Underline key words and circle dates. Then brainstorm for one or two minutes. Write down everything that comes to mind in your test booklet. (There is room in the margins and at the top and bottom of the pages.) Look at your notes and consider the results of your brainstorming session as you decide what point you will argue in your essay; that argument is going to be your thesis. Tailor your argument to your information, but by no means choose an argument that you know is wrong or with which you disagree. If you do either of these things, your essay probably won't be a successful or effective one. Finally, sort the results of your brainstorm. Some of what you wrote down will be "big picture" conclusions, some will be historical facts that can be used as evidence to support your conclusions, and some will be irrelevant points that you can discard.

Next, make an outline. You should plan to write one paragraph for each of the short-answer questions and five paragraphs each for the DBQ and long essay. Plan to go into special detail in each of the paragraphs on the DBQ. (Remember, you will have the documents and your outside knowledge to discuss on the DBQ. Plus, you will have more time.) For the essays in Section II of the exam, your first paragraph should contain your thesis statement, in which you directly answer the question in just a few sentences. Your second, third, and fourth paragraphs should each contain one argument (for a total of three) that supports that statement, along with historical evidence to support those arguments. The fifth paragraph should contain your conclusion and reiterate your answer to the question.

Before you start to write your outline, you will have to decide what type of argument you are going to make. Here are some of the classics.

Circle Key Words
When you read a question, circle or underline key words and phrases that you can refer back to easily when you begin to create your outline and then write the essay.

1. Make Three Good Points

This is the simplest strategy. Look at the results of your brainstorming session, and pick the three best points supporting your position. Make each of these points the subject of one paragraph. Make the weakest of the three points the subject of the second paragraph, and save the strongest point for the fourth paragraph. If your three points are interrelated and there is a natural sequence to arguing them, then by all means use that sequence; otherwise, try to save your strongest point for last. Begin each paragraph by stating one of your three points, and then spend the rest of the paragraph supporting it. Use specific, supporting examples whenever possible. Your first paragraph should state what you intend to argue. Your final paragraph should explain why you have proven what you set out to prove.

2. Make a Chronological Argument

Many questions lend themselves to a chronological treatment. Questions about the development of a political, social, or economic trend can hardly be answered any other way. When you make a chronological argument, look for important transitions and use them to start new paragraphs. A five-paragraph essay about the events leading up to the French Revolution, for example, might start with an introductory discussion of France and the role of royal absolutism. This is also where you should state your thesis. The second paragraph might then discuss the economic crisis that led to the calling of the Estates-General. The third paragraph could deal with concern among members of the third estate that their interests might not be represented at Versailles, despite the vital economic role they played in 18th-century France. The fourth paragraph could be concerned with the events leading up to and including the King's agreement to meet the three estates at a National Assembly. Your conclusion in this type of essay should restate the essay question and answer it. For example, if the question asks whether the French Revolution was inevitable, you should answer "yes" or "no" in this paragraph.

3. Identify Similarities and Differences

Some questions, particularly the long essay question, ask you to compare events, issues, and/or cultural practices. Very often, the way the question is phrased will suggest the best organization for your essay. Take, for example, a question that asks you to compare the impact of three events and issues on the decision to execute the English monarch Charles I in 1649. This question requires you to set the historical scene prior to the three events/issues you are about to discuss. Continue by devoting one paragraph to each of the three, and conclude by comparing and contrasting the relative importance of each. Again, be sure to answer the question in your final paragraph.

Other questions will provide options. If you are asked to compare Italian and Northern European humanism during the Renaissance, you might open with a thesis stating the essential similarity or difference between the two. Then, you could devote one paragraph each to a summary of certain trends and authors, while in the fourth paragraph you could point out the major similarities and differences between Italian and Northern European humanism. In the final paragraph, you could draw your conclusion (for example, "their similarities were more significant than their differences," or vice versa). Or, using another angle altogether, you might start with a thesis, then discuss in the body of your essay three pertinent philosophical, religious, or political issues, then discuss how Italian humanists dealt with such questions, then move on to the Northern European humanists, and wrap up with an overview of your argument for your conclusion.

4. Use the Straw Dog Argument

For this technique, choose a couple of arguments that someone taking the position opposite yours would take. State those opposing arguments, and then tear them down. Remember that proving your opposition wrong does not mean that you have proved that you yourself are correct; that is why you should choose only a few opposing arguments to refute. Summarize your opponent's arguments in paragraph two, dismiss them in paragraph three, and use paragraph four to make the argument for your side. Or, use one paragraph each to summarize and dismiss each of your opponent's arguments, and then make the case for your side in your concluding paragraph. Acknowledging both sides of an argument, even when you choose one over the other, is a good indicator that you understand that historical issues are complex and can be interpreted in more than one way, something teachers and graders like to see.

Conclusion

No matter which format you choose, remember to organize your essay so that the first paragraph addresses the question and states how you are going to answer it. (That is your thesis.) The second, third, and fourth paragraphs should each be organized around a single argument that supports your thesis, and each of these arguments must be supported by historical evidence. Your final paragraph ties the essay up into a nice, neat package. Your concluding paragraph should also answer the question. And remember, stay positive!

As you are writing, observe the following guidelines:

- **Keep sentences as simple as possible.** Long sentences get convoluted very quickly and will give your graders a headache, putting them in a bad mood.

- **Write clearly and neatly.** As long as we are discussing your graders' moods, here is an easy way to put them in good ones. Graders look at a lot of chicken scratch; it strains their eyes and makes them grumpy. Neatly written essays make them happy. When you cross out, do it neatly. If you are making any major edits—if you want to insert a paragraph in the middle of your essay, for example—make sure you indicate these changes clearly.

- **Define your terms.** Most questions require you to use terms that mean different things to different people. One person's "liberal" is another person's "conservative" and yet another person's "extremist." What one person considers "expansionism," another might call "colonialism" or "imperialism." The folks who grade the test want to know what you think these terms mean. When you use them, define them. Take particular care to define any such terms that appear in the question. Almost all official College Board materials emphasize this point, so do not forget it. Be sure to define any term that you suspect can be defined in more than one way.

- **Use transition words to show where you are going.** When continuing an idea, use words such as *furthermore, also,* and *in addition.* When changing the flow of thought, use words such as *however* and *yet.* Transition words make your essay easier to understand by clarifying your intentions. Better yet, they indicate to the graders that you know how to make a coherent, persuasive argument.

- **Use structural indicators to organize your paragraphs.** Another way to clarify your intentions is to organize your essay around structural indicators. For example, if you are making a number of related points, number them ("First… Second…And last…"). If you are writing a compare/contrast essay, use the indicators *on the one hand* and *on the other hand.*

- **Stick to your outline.** Unless you get an absolutely brilliant idea while you are writing, do not deviate from your outline. If you do, you will risk winding up with an incoherent essay.

- **Try to prove one "big picture" idea per paragraph.** Keep it simple. Each paragraph should make one point and then substantiate that point with historical evidence and examples.

> **Essay Essential**
> Don't underestimate the power of a neat essay. If your handwriting is questionable, try to print as clearly as possible.

- **Back up your ideas with examples.** Yes, we have said it already, but it bears repeating: do not just throw ideas out there and hope that you are right (unless you are absolutely desperate). You will score big points if you substantiate your claims with facts and specific examples.

- **Try to fill the essay form.** An overly short essay will hurt you more than one that is overly long.

- **Make sure your first and last paragraphs directly address the question.** Nothing will cost you points faster than if the graders decide you did not answer the question. It is always a safe move to start your final paragraph by answering the question. If you have written a good essay, that answer will serve as a legitimate conclusion.

- **Always place every essay into a historical context.** For example, if you are given an essay asking you to compare and contrast Newton's and Einstein's ideas on the universe, don't make it an essay on science. Instead, show how each of these men was a product of his respective time period, and show how their ideas influenced their contemporaries as well as future generations.

> Remember, the short-answer section contains four questions, but you need to answer only three. Questions 1 and 2 are required, and then you choose EITHER Question 3 or Question 4.

SHORT-ANSWER BASICS

The short-answer section of the exam (Part B of Section I) involves answering three short-answer questions in which you will respond to a primary source, historical argument, data or maps, or general propositions about world history. The questions may have multiple components, and you will be required to address all parts of a given question. Since these are short-answer prompts, you are not required to develop and support a thesis statement.

Time Crunch

Perhaps the biggest challenge of the short-answer section is the time allotted. You have a total of 40 minutes to answer three questions. You'll be given up to a page to write each essay, but it is not necessary to fill all of the provided space. Quality matters more than quantity, though a longer essay will likely look more impressive to the reader. So there is no time to dawdle on the short essays! You must keep brainstorming to a minimum (no more than two or three minutes in total), and keep your pencil moving!

Strategy for Answering the Short-Answer Questions

The short-answer questions will consist of multiple parts, which center on a key learning objective. Some questions may give you the opportunity to choose from among several topics. For the questions that do not give you the opportunity to pick from a list of choice topics, read the question and each of the parts carefully. Many of these questions will resemble the following example.

3. Use the image below to answer all parts of the question that follows.

The Shah Mosque in Isfahan, Iran, 1611–1629

The image above shows the Shah Mosque in Isfahan, Iran. The mosque was constructed between 1611 and 1629.

a) Briefly explain how mosques such as the one pictured above are evidence of Islamic influence across parts of Asia, Africa, and Europe in the fifteenth through eighteenth centuries.

b) Briefly explain the role of mosques such as the one pictured above in the religious and political dynamics of early modern (fifteenth through eighteenth centuries) Islamic civilizations.

Here's How to Crack It
1. Think.

You've probably seen photos of mosques like this before. The first step is to make sure to read the information provided under the photograph very carefully and glean whatever you can from that information. In the case of the photograph pictured above, note that we are dealing with a mosque in Iran, built in the early part of the 17th century. Next, let's turn to the questions. Part (a) wants you to explain this photograph in terms of Islamic influence, while part (b) wants you to contextualize the photograph as it relates to early modern Islamic religious and political dynamics. Once you are sure that you understand the questions, brainstorm a little bit and jot down a few notes for yourself about key themes or concepts that relate to the questions asked.

For part (a), your brainstorming might look something like this:

- Islamic culture: known for architecture, math, science, medicine, etc.
- Islamic architecture—contains scripture, art, minarets, and domes
- Mosques built for worship (also denoted an Islamic presence/dominance in the area)
- Islamic culture spread throughout parts of Asia, Africa, and Europe and had a lot of influence on the cultures of those regions
- Muslims conquered Persia, where this mosque is located (Safavid Empire)
- Places conquered by Muslims sometimes adopted Arabic as well as Islamic intellectual/technological advancements

For part (b), your brainstorming might look something like this:

- Mosques built for worship
- Islamic empires maintained close ties between religion and politics
- As Islamic empires spread, government leaders ordered the construction of mosques in newly conquered regions
- Ottoman and Mughal rulers acted in accordance to Islamic law
- Civil laws were influenced by the Qur'an

2. Write.
Here is a sample short-answer response using some of the ideas outlined above:

In early modern Islamic cultures, religion dominated most aspects of daily life. Muslim leaders were, for the most part, quite devout, and dedicated significant resources to spreading the Islamic faith and honoring Allah. Because religion was such an important aspect of the Islamic empires, Muslims built mosques in major cities and towns in order to show the centrality of their faith. The establishment of mosques in conquered territories informed Muslims and non-Muslims alike of the dominant religion in the region. During the early modern period, Islamic empires expanded their influence in parts of Africa, Asia, and Europe. In places where Muslims had conquered, Islamic settlers had enormous cultural impact upon local populations. Some places adopted the Arabic language, and many places were also influenced by Islamic architecture, universities, libraries, scientific discoveries, and technologies.

Summary

○ Read questions carefully. Be sure you are answering the question that is asked. You must answer all parts of the question in order to get full credit.

○ Do not start writing until you have brainstormed, chosen a thesis, and written an outline. The only exception to this is the short-answer section; the questions there do not require a thesis, and you will not have enough time to write an outline.

○ Follow your outline. On the longer essays, stick to one important idea per paragraph. Support your ideas with historical evidence.

○ Write clearly and neatly. Do not write in long, overly complex sentences. Toss in a couple of "big" words you know you will not misuse. When in doubt, stick to simple syntax and vocabulary.

○ Use transition words to indicate continuity of thought and changes in the direction of your argument.

○ Provide a strong historical context. You may be faced with questions focusing on science, economics, philosophy, literature and art, religion, and other disciplines. Always remember that this is a history exam, so everything you discuss needs to be situated within a broader context.

Chapter 3
How to Approach
the Document-
Based Question
(DBQ)

IT'S ALL IN THE DOCUMENTS

The first essay you'll see in Section II of the AP World History: Modern Exam is the Document-Based Question (DBQ). As the name implies, this question is based on approximately seven documents centered on a historical topic or issue between the years 1450 and 2001. Your job is to work through the documents to determine how they relate to each other, what changes can be seen over time, how the author's background may have influenced the contents of the document, and so on.

The DBQ measures your ability to develop a thesis, support your thesis with historical evidence and your outside knowledge of world history, and make historical connections. In other words, you're being asked to think like a historian by analyzing primary sources and building an argument (in response to a given prompt) around those sources. The question is intended to test a specific skill, such as the ability to recognize trends throughout history or cause-and-effect relationships between historical events.

Before the start of the essay portion of the exam, there will be a reading period for you to read the DBQ documents and question. It is suggested that you spend 15 minutes reading the documents and 45 minutes writing your response, but you may begin writing before the 15-minute reading period is over. To do well on this essay, you need to know exactly what to do with those 15 minutes. And to do that you need to know exactly what you are expected to write. Let's begin by looking at the scoring rubric for the DBQ.

How the DBQ Is Scored

The DBQ is graded on a 7-point scale. Here's how those points are earned.

Task	Points Possible	Description
Thesis/Claim	1 point	To earn this point, the thesis must make a claim that *responds* to the prompt rather than restating or rephrasing the prompt. The thesis must consist of one or more sentences located in one place, either in the introduction or the conclusion.
Contextualization	1 point	To earn this point, the response must relate the topic of the prompt to broader historical events, developments, or processes that occur before, during, or continue after the time frame of the question. This point is not awarded for merely a phrase or reference.

Task	Points Possible	Description
Evidence	3 points	*Evidence from the Documents* To earn 1 point, the response must accurately describe—rather than simply quote—the content from at least 3* of the documents to address the topic of the prompt. To earn 2 points, the response must accurately describe—rather than simply quote—the content from at least 6* documents. In addition, the response must use the content of the documents to support an argument in response to the prompt. *Evidence Beyond the Documents* To earn the third point, the response must describe the evidence and must use more than a phrase or reference. This additional piece of evidence must be different from the evidence used to earn the point for contextualization.
Analysis and Reasoning	2 points	To earn 1 point, the response must explain how or why—rather than simply identifying—the document's point of view, purpose, historical situation, or audience is relevant to an argument about the prompt for each of the three documents sourced. To earn the other point, a response must demonstrate a complex understanding of the historical development that is the focus of the prompt, using evidence. This can be accomplished in a variety of ways, such as: • Explaining nuance of an issue by analyzing multiple variables • Explaining both similarity and difference, or explaining both continuity and change, or explaining multiple causes, or explaining both cause and effect • Explaining relevant and insightful connections within and across periods • Confirming the validity of an argument by corroborating multiple perspectives across themes • Qualifying or modifying an argument by considering diverse or alternative views or evidence This understanding must be part of the argument, not merely a phrase or reference.

*Rubric based on a DBQ with seven documents

What the Rubric Actually Means

Here's what you need to do to get a good score on the DBQ:

- Formulate a relevant thesis or claim and support that thesis with the documents, as well as outside examples not covered in the documents. Did you answer the question that was asked? Make sure that your thesis directly addresses the prompt and accurately describes the contents of your essay. Be sure that the documents can be used to support your claim—students often make the mistake of coming up with an interesting thesis only to find that the documents don't really support it.

- Analyze the documents. Your analysis must acknowledge the source of the documents and the author's point of view, purpose, and/or audience, which means that you must demonstrate that you understand the context of each source. You should also be able to explain the following:
  o What was the context (historical, political, or cultural environment) in which the document was authored? What else was going on around the author at the time this was written?
  o How does this author's perspective affect what he or she wrote and why? What is the author's position in society (gender, age, educational level, political or religious belief system)? How do these attributes inform what the author writes?
  o How does the content and tone of the document relate to that of the other documents? What does one document say that another doesn't? What accounts for these differences?
  o When was the document written? Who was the intended audience, and what was the author trying to express?

- Identify and explain additional examples and evidence that are not represented in the documents, and use them to support or expand your argument in some way. When brainstorming outside evidence and how to use it in your essay, consider the following questions:
  o What types of evidence offer information that is not already present?
  o What points of view are missing that would make your argument stronger? Consider groups typically not represented (women, the working class, peasants).
  o Why is this additional evidence important?

- Connect the topic of the prompt and the documents to broader historical themes, developments, or issues. You want to demonstrate your understanding of how the topic or issue at hand relates to other issues in world history.

So to write a decent DBQ essay, you need to write an essay that opens with a thesis, support that thesis with all of the documents, analyze the documents, include outside evidence and examples to bolster your argument, and make connections between the topic of the prompt and other historical issues and developments.

THE DOCUMENTS

Of course, before you can write anything, you need to work your way through the documents. *Working* the documents (not just reading them) is almost as important as writing the essay itself. Let's spend a few minutes learning exactly how to process, or work, the documents so that you can put together a high-scoring essay.

Work Those Documents

When the reading period begins, open up your test booklet to Part A of Section II (the DBQ). Study the DBQ directions in this book so that you do not have to spend a lot of time reading through them on test day. Still, you should do a quick scan of the directions to make sure they are the ones you are familiar with. Remember, the highest-scoring essays typically make use of all of the documents, so plan to use all of them in your essay. Also remember that not every document will be a passage of text. You may see images, charts, photographs, maps, and other visual sources as well.

Step 1: Process the Prompt

You cannot begin to think about the documents until you know what you are being asked to do. Read the question carefully. Underline the important details (such as time period, culture, location) and circle what you are supposed to analyze and the actions you need to take (for example, compare and contrast, change over time, and so on). You can also jot down any information about the question topic and time period that immediately springs to mind.

Give Me 15 Minutes and I'll Give You the World

Is 15 minutes really enough time to read through the documents? That depends on how well you know the topic. Most students will need the full 15 minutes to work through the documents and prepare to write the essay. But if those 15 minutes are up and you haven't finished planning your essay, keep working the documents. The actual writing of your essay will take less time if you are well prepared when you begin. Use the 15 minutes you are given plus any additional time you need (up to 10 more minutes) to plan your essay. Once you've gotten a handle on the documents and organized your thoughts, it will probably take you only about 20 to 30 minutes to actually write the essay.

Look at the following example of a DBQ:

1. Using the documents and your knowledge of world history, compare and contrast the attitudes toward women globally during the Industrial Period (1750–1900).

Based on the question, what do you know the documents are about?
Attitudes toward women in various cultures during the Industrial Period.

What are you being asked to do?
Compare and contrast the attitudes and look for any variances between cultures.

What could additional evidence do?
Clarify how existing attitudes affected women's daily lives.

But Where?

For the essay portion of the test, you will receive a booklet that contains the essay questions, space to plan your essays, and a sealed answer booklet. Use the spaces in the question booklet to do your prep work—outlining, summarizing documents, brainstorming. Don't be shy about what you write in the booklet—the graders won't see your notes. It's important to remember that you will receive credit only for what you write in the answer booklet. Even if your teachers in school sometimes give you credit for outlining, AP readers will not.

Step 2: Build a Framework

Once you've gotten a handle on the question, use it to create a framework for processing the documents you are about to read. For example, if a question asks you to compare and contrast two major religions, you would create a compare-and-contrast chart of the viewpoints in question. You can fill in the chart as you work through the documents. If the question focuses on change over time, create a space in which you can easily note any changes you come across. In the example above, the question asks you to both compare and contrast attitudes of different cultures and to look for any change over time—specifically, 1750–1900.

Your framework for this question might look like this:

Similarities in attitudes toward women	Differences in attitudes toward women

These first two steps should take about two minutes. Then it's time to hit the documents.

Step 3: Work the Documents

Notice that we are not telling you to simply read the documents. *Read* is too passive a word for what you need to do. As you read each document, summarize and analyze it in light of your framework (what you need to use it for). Look at the following document that goes with our example.

Document 1

Source: Lafcadio Hearn, *Glimpse of Unfamiliar Japan* (1894)

The girl begins her career as a slave, a pretty child bought from miserably poor parents under a contract, according to which her services may be claimed by the purchasers for eighteen, twenty, or even twenty-five years. She is fed, clothed, and trained in a house occupied only by geisha; and she passes the rest of her childhood under severe discipline. She is taught etiquette, grace, polite speech; she has daily lessons in dancing; and she is obliged to learn by heart a multitude of songs with their airs. Also she must learn games, the service of banquets, and weddings, the art of dressing and looking beautiful. Whatever physical gifts she may have are carefully cultivated.

First, circle the source, making note of the kind of text this is and its date. This document is from a book by a man who, based on his names and objective descriptions, appears to be an outsider to Japanese culture. What is the document's attitude about women? The emphasis here is on training. A woman must be fastidiously trained to become a proper geisha. Geishas begin their lives sold into slavery and then go through harsh training to perfect their craft.

You Read a Document. Now What?
Be sure to circle the source of the document, and note the type of text it is.

Let's see how this compares to the second document.

Document 2

Source: *The Sadler Report: Report from the Committee on the Bill to Regulate the Labour of Children in the Mills and Factories of the United Kingdom* (London: House of Commons, 1832).

—Have you recently seen any cruelties in the mills?

—Yes; not long since I was in a mill and I saw a girl severely beaten; at a mill called Hicklane Mill, in Batley; I happened to be in at the other end of the room, talking; and I heard the blows, and I looked that way, and saw the spinner beating one of the girls severely with a large stick.

…

—Do you find that the children, the females especially, are very early demoralized in them?

—They are.

This document came from the Sadler Report, written in 1832 as part of an investigation into child labor. What was the attitude toward women based on the Sadler Report? While boys and girls are both victims of harsh labor conditions, it appears that girls are targeted for extreme abuse.

Try working the next three documents.

Document 3

Source: *Parliamentary Papers* (Great Britain), 1842

Betty Harris, age 37: I was married at 32, and went into a colliery (coal mine) when I was married. I used to weave when I was about 12 years old; can neither read nor write. I work for Andrew Knowles…and make sometimes 7 [shillings] a week, sometimes not so much. I am a drawer [transporter of the coal car] and work from 6 in the morning to 6 at night. Stop about an hour at noon to eat my dinner; have bread and butter for dinner; I get no drink. I have two children but they are too young to work…I know a woman who has gone home and washed herself, taken to her bed, been delivered of a child, and gone to work again in under the week.

Document 4

Source: Hindu Widows' Remarriage Act (1856)

No marriage contracted between Hindus shall be invalid, and the issue of no such marriage shall be illegitimate, by reason of the woman having been previously married or betrothed to another person who was dead at the time of such marriage, any custom and any interpretation of Hindu Law to the contrary notwithstanding.

Document 5

Source: Captain Carette, a French military captain, gives his account of the French invasion of an Algier region known as Kabylia (1850).

Almost all [Kabyle] women follow their brothers and husbands [into battle]. They are even seen in the midst of the battle, encouraging the combatants with their cries, caring for the wounded, helping to carry the dead off the battlefield, sharing in the dangers of the struggle—in the pain of defeat or the joy of victory. Bloody examples prove the part that these women play in holy war [against the French army]. In December 1834, a Kabyle woman served as a foot soldier in an attack against a [French military] cavalry charge; her body was discovered among the dead afterwards. In a military confrontation in 1835, fourteen women were killed or wounded. Finally in June 1836, I saw the widow of a Kabyle religious leader, who had been killed the day before in combat, arrive at the head of a column of Berber warriors. She remained at the site of her husband's death weeping and wailing despite the fact that bullets [from French rifles] rained about her for an hour.

Visual Documents
Although the documents used for this example are all text-based sources, on the exam the documents may be a mix of text and visual sources, such as a map, political cartoon, graph, or other image.

What did you notice about these documents? Any differences or changes? Document 3, written in England in 1842, shows clearly the attitudes of that time and culture—women are simply viewed as labor working for the profit of businesses. Document 4 is the only document that seems to show some empowerment of women. Notice how in Document 4 the widows are freed from their "ownership" by their deceased husbands. Document 5 shows a culture in which women were even more empowered: women in Algiers fought alongside men, seemingly as equals.

Step 4: Frame the Documents

Once you've worked the documents (or as you go along), fill in your framework from what you've read. For example, using the four documents we just read, try filling in the compare-and-contrast chart.

Your chart should look something like this:

Similarities in attitudes toward women	Differences in attitudes toward women
All Documents—women subservient to men (with the exception of Doc 5). *All Documents—women far fewer legal rights (with the exception of Doc 5).*	*Doc 1—men in control, emphasis on training girls* *Doc 4—women gain more equal footing* *Doc 2 and 3—British women mistreated through labor* *Doc 4 and 5—Northern Africa and India provide examples of ways that women could be seen as equals*

What are the differences that we see in our examples so far? While the British and Japanese examples show women as second-class citizens, the India example and the Algier example give evidence that women could, at least at times and in some particular respects, be seen as equal to men. Although the question doesn't specifically mention it, we should also be aware of the influence of culture when it came to the treatment of women. Some differences that appear in these documents may be a result of not only a change in thought process over time but also a differing attitude of a particular culture. If we were to read the rest of the documents that accompany this question, we would likely see even greater changes in the attitudes toward and treatment of women.

Step 5: Analyze and Add

In order to get as many points as possible, you must analyze as many documents as possible. According to the DBQ scoring rubric, an essay will earn the most points if at least six documents (for a seven-document DBQ) are sufficiently discussed in your essay. You must also pull in outside examples and evidence that support your line of argumentation in some way.

Point of View

Analyzing the documents' points of view is an extremely important part of earning a high score on the DBQ. For example, in our sample documents, Documents 1 and 5 were written by European men based on their observations of women in other cultures. Could the fact that they are men coupled with the fact that they may have lacked a deeper understanding of the cultures they are observing have influenced what they chose to write? Absolutely. Look at Document 1 again.

Document 1

Source: Lafcadio Hearn, *Glimpse of Unfamiliar Japan* (1894)

The girl begins her career as a slave, a pretty child ought from miserably poor parents under a contract, according to which her services may be claimed by the purchasers for eighteen, twenty, or even twenty-five years. She is fed, clothed, and trained in a house occupied only by geisha; and she passes the rest of her childhood under severe discipline. She is taught etiquette, grace, polite speech; she has daily lessons in dancing; and she is obliged to learn by heart a multitude of songs with their airs. Also she must learn games, the service of banquets, and weddings, the art of dressing and looking beautiful. Whatever physical gifts she may have are carefully cultivated.

As you can see, the author focuses on the geisha's lack of freedom. He even refers to her as a slave, a word not even used in any of the other documents. While his designation may have been accurate, particularly in his own point of view, any gaps in his understanding of Japanese culture may yield a misunderstanding of how the Japanese, even the geishas themselves, view the practice. The culture in which he lived clearly influenced his point of view. These are the types of issues you want to bring into your analysis of point of view.

As mentioned above, you should pay attention to who wrote the documents and when they were written, as both of these factors can help you determine the point of view.

Outside Evidence and Examples

So as not to forget this step, make a note of it now, and then plan to include it as part of your opening thesis.

In order to assess how the attitudes of a culture affected women's daily lives during a certain period, what types of additional evidence would be helpful? What about either other examples of texts written by women that reflected their thoughts or daily experiences, or examples that would illustrate the daily responsibilities of women in the given period? *Be sure to explain why you feel this evidence will add to your analysis;* just describing an example will not earn you the point.

Step 6: Organize the Documents

So far you've processed the question, built a framework, worked the documents to fill in that framework, analyzed the documents for purpose, audience, and point of view, and determined the type of additional evidence you need and why. Now it's time to organize your documents so that you know which ones you are using as support, which ones you are analyzing and exactly how you plan to use them in connection with one another. This last step will act as the outline for your essay.

Use the following chart to organize your essay.

Thesis	You will open your essay with a thesis. In your thesis, reference the strongest supporting documents. As part of your outline, decide which documents represent the core of your thesis and include them in your opening paragraph. Also, jot down a few brief notes about your thesis before moving on. (Be sure to make your notes on scratch paper—not in the essay booklet.)
Support	List the documents that you plan to use to support your thesis. Include all the documents you mention in your thesis (in the first paragraph). Also feel free to include any other document that will lend additional support.
Group 1	First, group the documents in the most obvious way. For example, if you are asked to compare and contrast a set of documents, break the documents into two groups so that each group contains documents with similar features but the two groups clearly contrast each other.
Group 2	Regroup the documents in a way that shows some sort of insight into how the documents relate to each other. For example, if you first created groups by putting together documents with obvious similarities, regroup them in a way that shows something different or less obvious about the documents. If the question asks about change over time, regroup the documents to show how things changed over some period.
Number of Documents	Use this as a checklist to be sure you include all of the documents in your essay. List the number of documents you've been given; then go through each category and check off the document number as you come to it. If you finish your check and realize that you omitted one (or more) documents, go back to that document to determine how and where you can use it.
Outside Examples/ Evidence	Once you've grouped your documents, consider what other kind or kinds of outside evidence would add something interesting to the analysis of the question posed. Be sure to include reasons why a particular piece of evidence would be useful.

Use our sample documents to fill your own organizational chart. It might resemble something like the following:

DBQ Essay Organizational Chart

Your Turn!
Consider creating a chart like this one on test day as a way to plan your essay and organize your thoughts before writing.

	Document Number(s)	Comments
Thesis	Doc 1—male control, training women Doc 2—exploitive labor Doc 3—exploitive labor	Attitudes toward women between the years 1750 and 1900 were largely exploitive and intended to sustain patriarchies. Japan—emphasis on "training" geishas and women were subordinate to men. British women were largely abused as laborers.
Support	Documents 1, 2, and 3 Document 4 softer yet holds women in same position Document 5 to show difference in women's stature	
Group 1	1 & 2 versus 4 & 5	Shows complete subservience of women as compared to models from other cultures that emphasized more equality
Group 2	5 (and others) versus 1, 2, 3, & 4 (and others)	Shows a culture in which women were on equal footing with men (at least in the military)
Number	1, 2, 3, 4, 5, __, __	Check off each as it is used in your outline so that you know that you have used them all.
Outside Examples/ Evidence		A text that portrays a woman who lived during this period showing her defining herself as a citizen or individual rather than just as a laborer. Examples of women questioning their position in society, wanting more.

Remember that the DBQ you see on test day may contain more documents, which will make your essay groupings more diverse. The way you group the documents should support your thesis and show changes or contrast as well.

FORMULATING YOUR DBQ THESIS

The number-one rule for writing an AP essay thesis statement is to make sure you answer the question. Here are some other basic rules for writing an effective essay thesis.

- **Give Them What They Want**—Answer the question by restating key phrases from the question.

- **Show Them Where You Got It**—AP World History: Modern Exam essays are all about the evidence. Use your framework to support your assertions right from the beginning. Remember that evidence in your thesis is merely introductory—save the details for the body of the essay.

- **Help Them Get There**—Make a clear transition from your thesis to the body of your essay by using a phrase like, "To better understand the differences between these two societies…" or "To better understand the changes that occurred…." You might also want to suggest, describe, and justify the inclusion of the outside evidence or examples as part of this last sentence. That way you won't forget to include them, and they make for a good transition.

How Long Is 15 Minutes?

Right now this process may seem as if it will take two hours as opposed to 15 minutes. You need to practice doing it a few times to get a feel for how much time to spend on what. You may find that you can fill in your framework as you analyze the documents, or identify the documents' point of view as you go. The more you practice, the more efficient you will become. Remember, however, that analyzing the documents is as important as writing the essay. If you need to use the first 5 to 10 minutes of your writing time to finish your analysis or outline, it will be time well spent.

For our example, your thesis and introduction could be something like the following:

> From a review of the five documents presented, it is clear that the role of women in various cultures from 1750 to 1900 was primarily one of servitude or worse in comparison to our contemporary ideas about the rights of women. However, there is also evidence that in certain cultures women were seen less as second-class citizens and more as equals who deserved equal rights under the law and equal opportunities to serve their nations. In Great Britain and Japan, women were seen more as property than as people, and that only men reserved the rights afforded to citizens. However, as one observes other models of gender roles around the world, one realized that the full picture of women during the Industrial Period is far more complex than the exploitive actions of British and Japanese men would suggest.

When you write your thesis paragraph, imagine that a reader will read your essay only if he or she is convinced to do so by your first paragraph (no pressure). Then, use your framework to write the body of your essay. Your framework can act as both your outline and your checklist—once you've written the bulk of your essay, quickly scan through to make sure you didn't leave anything out. Finally, close with a recap of your points and get on to the next essay.

Before moving on to the next chapter, practice writing your own thesis statement for the sample DBQ in this chapter. Try to come up with as many as possible, and then evaluate them using the scoring rubric on pages 94 and 95.

HOW LONG SHOULD THIS GO ON?

You have 60 minutes for the DBQ. It's suggested you use the first 15 minutes to read the question and documents, and then use the remaining 45 minutes to write the essay. Note that you are allowed to begin writing before the 15-minute reading period is up, but we encourage you to use the full time to plan your essay. And if you're still in the planning stages when the 15 minutes are up, we recommend you spend no more than 10 additional minutes working through the documents and planning your essay. In other words, you should begin writing by 10 minutes into the essay-writing part of the test. You can write a great DBQ essay in 20 to 30 minutes, but you don't want to cut into writing time for the long essay (which we'll cover in the next chapter).

AP essay graders tell us that spending too much time on the DBQ is an obvious problem for many students. Blowing off the Long Essay question will seriously endanger your score! Remember, the DBQ accounts for 25% of your score, and the long essay question accounts for 15% of your score, so be sure to leave yourself adequate time to get to both questions!

PUT IT ALL TOGETHER

Now it's time to try your hand at a practice DBQ. Remember to use all the steps and not to shortchange the prework on the documents. The more comfortable you are with the documents, the easier it will be for you to write this essay. Try keeping track of your time by noting your start time, and then noting how long it takes you to analyze the documents. When you are finished with the essay, note the time you finished. This will give you a rough idea of how much time you need to shave off in practice.

When you have finished, ask a classmate to score your essay using the scoring rubric at the beginning of this chapter.

Directions: Question 1 is based on the accompanying documents. The documents have been edited for the purpose of this exercise.

In your response you should do the following.

- **Thesis/Claim:** Respond to the prompt with a historically defensible claim that establishes a line of reasoning.

- **Contextualization:** Describe a historical context relevant to the prompt.

- **Evidence:** Support an argument in response to the prompt using at least **six** documents. Use at least one additional piece of specific historical evidence (beyond that found in the documents) relevant to an argument about the prompt.

- **Analysis and Reasoning:** For at least **three** documents, explain how or why the document's point of view, purpose, historical situation, and/or audience is relevant to an argument. Demonstrate an understanding of the historical development that is the focus of the prompt, using evidence to support or modify an argument that addresses the question.

1. Using the documents and your knowledge of world history, analyze the rise of nationalism in Egypt and India in the early 20th century. What additional evidence would help your analysis of causes for the nationalist feelings in these nations?

Document 1

Source: Sir Rabindranath Tagore, *Nationalism*, 1918.

Rabindranath Tagore, Bengali poet, playwright, and novelist, who was one of the earliest non-European recipients of the Nobel Prize for literature, wrote the following:

Has not this truth already come home to you now when this cruel war has driven its claws into the vitals of Europe? When her hoard of wealth is bursting into smoke and her humanity is shattered on her battlefields? You ask in amazement what she has done to deserve this? The answer is, that the West has been systematically petrifying her moral nature in order to lay a solid foundation for her gigantic abstractions of efficiency. She has been all along starving the life of the personal man into that of the professional.

Document 2

Source: Mahatma Gandhi, 1909.

We hold the civilization that you support to be the reverse of civilization. We consider our civilization to be far superior to yours. If you realize this truth, it will be to your advantage and, if you do not, according to your own proverb, you should only live in our country in the same manner as we do. You must not do anything that is contrary to our religions. It is your duty as rulers that for the sake of the Hindus you should eschew beef, and for the sake of Mahomedans you should avoid bacon and ham. We have hitherto said nothing because we have been cowed down, but you need not consider that you have not hurt our feelings by your conduct. We are not expressing our sentiments either through base selfishness or fear, but because it is our duty now to speak out boldly. We consider your schools and courts to be useless. We want our own ancient schools and courts to be restored. The common language of India is not English but Hindi. You should, therefore, learn it. We can hold communication with you only in our national language.

Document 3

Source: *Ganesh Janani* by Abanindranath Tagore, 1907.

Document 4

Source: Sarojini Naidu, *An Indian Nationalist Condemns the British Empire*, 1920.

I speak to you today as standing arraigned because of the blood-guiltiness of those who have committed murder in my country. I need not go into the details. But I am going to speak to you as a woman about the wrongs committed against my sisters. Englishmen, you who pride yourselves upon your chivalry, you who hold more precious than your imperial treasures the honor and chastity of your women, will you sit still and leave unavenged the dishonour, and the insult and agony inflicted upon the veiled women of the Punjab?

The minions of Lord Chelmsford, the Viceroy, and his martial authorities rent the veil from the faces of the women of the Punjab. Not only were men mown down as if they were grass that is born to wither; but they tore asunder the cherished Purdah, the innermost privacy of the chaste womanhood of India. My sisters were stripped naked, they were flogged, they were outraged. These policies left your British democracy betrayed, dishonored, for no dishonor clings to the martyrs who suffered, but to the tyrants who inflicted the tyranny and pain. Should they hold their Empire by dishonoring the women of another nation or lose it out of the chivalry for their honor and chastity? The Bible asked, "What shall it profit a man to gain the whole world and lose his own soul?" You deserve no Empire. You have lost your soul; you have the stain of blood-guiltiness upon you; no nation that rules by tyranny is free; it is the slave of its own despotism.

Document 5

Source: Taha Hussein, Muslim literary figure and Egyptian nationalist, *The Future of Culture in Egypt,* 1938.

Now that we have succeeded in restoring the honor and self-respect that come with independence, it is our plain duty to protect what we have won. We must rear a generation of Egyptian youth who will never know the humiliation and shame that was the lot of their fathers. Some Egyptians object to Europeanization on the grounds that it threatens our national personality and glorious heritage. I do not naturally advocate rejection of the past or loss of identity in the Europeans;... the only time that we might have been absorbed by Europe was when we were extremely weak, ignorant, and possessed of the notion that the hat was superior to the turban and the fez because it always covered a more distinguished head!... Although great powers imposed their will on us for many centuries, they were unable to destroy our personality. I am merely asking that the preservatives of defense, religion, language, art, and history be strengthened by the adoption of Western techniques and ideas.

Document 6

Source: Preamble to the Constitution of the Kingdom of Egypt, 1923.

We, the King of Egypt,

Having, since mounting the throne of our ancestors and vowing to keep safe the trust which God Almighty has entrusted to us, always done our utmost to pursue the good of our nation, and pursue the path which we know will lead to its welfare and advancement and to deriving the enjoyments of free and civilized nations;

And since such end cannot be properly attained unless in a constitutional system similar to the most advanced constitutional systems in the world, under which our nation can happily and satisfactorily live and pursue the path of an absolutely free life, and which ensures active participation in running state affairs and overseeing the drafting and enforcement of laws, and brings a sense of comfort and assurance about our nation's present and future, while maintaining the national qualities and distinctions which constitute the great historical heritage thereof;

And as the fulfillment of such end has constantly been our desire and one of the greatest endeavors we are determined to seek so as to help our People's rise to the highest of standards which the People is readily qualified and capable of meeting, which befit the ancient historical greatness of our People, and which enable our People to attain the appropriate status among peoples of civilized nations....

Document 7

Source: Female nationalist protesters in Cairo, Egypt, 1919.

Summary

o The DBQ is the first part of Section II of the exam. It is worth 25% of your total score.

o On the new AP World History: Modern Exam, you have a total of 60 minutes to write this essay: 15 minutes for reading and planning your essay, and 45 minutes for writing it. Remember to pace yourself and be mindful of the time.

o The 15-minute reading period is not mandatory, and you can begin writing your essay before the 15 minutes are up. However, we recommend you use the full time allotted. A well-planned essay is much easier to write.

o The DBQ directions will tell you exactly what your essay needs to do in order to get full credit. Be familiar with these directions before you sit down to take the test. This way, you won't need to waste any time reading the directions on exam day. Still, we recommend you give them a scan just to make sure that they align with the directions you've been practicing with.

o Make sure your essay has a clear thesis statement, which should be in the first paragraph. This thesis statement is the basis of your argument; the goal of the essay is to "prove" that argument using the documents and outside evidence.

o Use as many documents as possible. In a DBQ that contains seven documents, you should incorporate six into your response. And don't simply mention the document; you need to explain it and use it to support or qualify your argument in some way in order to get full credit.

o Don't forget about outside evidence! The AP essay graders want to see a firm grasp of the material and an ability to connect the documents to other historical events and topics you've learned about in class.

Chapter 4
How to Approach
the Long Essay

Quick Note
On Section II of the exam, many students are tempted to ease up by the time they get to the long essay, or they invest all of their time in the DBQ because there's a lot of planning involved. Do not make this mistake. Reach down for the last bit of energy and finish strong!

OVERVIEW OF THE LONG ESSAY

Part B of Section II contains the long essay question. You will be given three essay prompts, and you must choose ONE to answer. These prompts may take the form of a historical statement or stance, which you must then support, modify, or refute in a written essay. As with the DBQ, you are required to develop and defend a relevant thesis. Many of the outlining approaches for the DBQ described in the previous chapter are also applicable for this essay. However, unlike the DBQ, the long essay does not include documents; your essay will instead be based entirely on your knowledge of AP World History and the themes and concepts discussed in your class. You will have 40 minutes to write this essay, which constitutes 15% of your total score.

A simple, defendable thesis accompanied by an organized essay that effectively analyzes the given subject should result in a high score. Do not write an essay that is simply descriptive, in which you regurgitate everything you know about the topic of the essay prompt. Purely descriptive essays rarely get a top score, as they usually fail to analyze, assess, and evaluate the historical issue or topic. Here is an example of a set of long essay questions:

2. Using specific examples, analyze continuities and changes in the dynamics of trade between China and other nations from 1200 C.E. to 1500 C.E.

3. Using specific examples, compare and contrast the relationships the Islamic Gunpowder Empires had with various non-Islamic groups between 1500 C.E. and 1800 C.E.

4. Using specific examples, evaluate the relationships between the upper and lower classes in Europe from 1700 C.E. to the present.

Check for Exam Updates
While preparing for the AP World History: Modern Exam, check the College Board website regularly for test updates, including changes to the exam format and scoring.

As you can see, long essay questions are designed to prompt analysis and evaluation of subject matter that you have learned in class. The subjects should be familiar, and the questions are straightforward. The highest score you can earn on the long essay is 6 points. On the following page you'll find the scoring rubric, which you can also download from the College Board website.

How the Long Essay Is Scored

The long essay is graded on a 6-point scale. Here's how those points are earned.

Task	Points Possible	Description
Thesis/Claim	1 point	To earn this point, the thesis must make a claim that responds to the prompt (rather than restating or rephrasing the prompt) with a historically defensible thesis/claim that establishes a line of reasoning. The thesis must consist of one or more sentences located in one place, either in the introduction or the conclusion.
Contextualization	1 point	To earn this point, the response must relate the topic of the prompt to broader historical events, developments, or processes that occur before, during, or continue after the time frame of the question, offering more historical context relevant to the prompt. This point is not awarded for merely a phrase or reference.
Evidence	2 points	To earn **1 point,** the response must identify specific historical examples of evidence relevant to the topic of the prompt. To earn **2 points,** the response must use specific and relevant examples of historical evidence to support an argument in response to the prompt.
Analysis and Reasoning	2 points	To earn the **first point,** the response must identify specific historical examples of evidence relevant to the topic of the prompt. To earn the **second point,** the response must use specific historical evidence to support an argument in response to the prompt. This can be accomplished in a variety of ways, such as: • Explaining nuance of an issue by analyzing multiple variables • Explaining both similarity and difference, or explaining both continuity and change, or explaining multiple causes, or explaining both cause and effect • Explaining relevant and insightful connections within and across periods • Confirming the validity of an argument by corroborating multiple perspectives across themes • Qualifying or modifying an argument by considering diverse or alternative views or evidence This understanding must be part of the argument, not merely a phrase or reference.

As you may have noticed, the long essay question is asking you to do many of the same tasks as the DBQ, just without the documents. AP graders want to see you make a thesis or claim, support that claim using historical evidence, and connect the historical issue with other developments in world history.

Choose to answer the question that you can write the most about. The more you know about the subject, the more you can say about it, and the better your essay score will be.

How to Write the Essays

We outlined a plan for writing longer essays in the previous chapter on the DBQ. These same directions apply here, though you will not need to worry about analyzing or incorporating specific documents into your response. As a refresher, here are the steps for structuring your essay:

1. Read the question and analyze it. Circle or underline important words and phrases in the question.

2. Create a grid or table in which to plan your essays and take notes.

3. Assess all of your notes and, based on that information, formulate a thesis statement.

4. Write a quick outline. Remember, you have only 40 minutes for the long essay question, so your outline should be brief. Write just enough so that you have a general idea of how your argument will be organized.

5. Write the essay.

Summary

o The long essay question is the last section of the test. You will be given three questions, and you must choose ONE to answer.

o Analyze the question you choose. Circle and/or underline important words and phrases. Once you understand the question, create a grid or columns in which to organize your notes on the essay.

o Formulate a thesis; then write an outline for your essay.

o Follow your outline (which should be brief, as you have only 40 minutes for this essay). Stick to one important idea per paragraph. Support your ideas with historical evidence.

o Write clearly and neatly. Do not write in overly complex sentences. Toss in a couple of "big" words that you know you will not misuse. When in doubt, stick to simple syntax and vocabulary.

o Use transition words to indicate continuity of thought and changes in the direction of your argument.

Chapter 5
Using Time Effectively to Maximize Points

BECOMING A BETTER TEST TAKER

Very few students stop to think about how to improve their test-taking skills. Most assume that if they study hard, they will test well, and if they do not study, they will do poorly. Most students continue to believe this even after experience teaches them otherwise. Have you ever studied really hard for an exam and then blown it on test day? Have you ever aced an exam for which you thought you weren't well prepared? Most students have had one, if not both, of these experiences. The lesson should be clear: factors other than your level of preparation influence your final test score. This chapter will provide you with some insights that will help you perform better on the AP World History: Modern Exam and on other exams as well.

PACING AND TIMING

A big part of scoring well on an exam is working at a consistent pace. The worst mistake made by inexperienced or unsavvy test takers is that they come to a question that stumps them, and, rather than just skip it, they panic and stall. Time stands still when you're working on a question you cannot answer, and it is not unusual for students to waste five minutes on a single question (especially a question involving a graph or the word EXCEPT) because they are too stubborn to cut their losses. It is important to be aware of how much time you have spent on a given question and on the section you are working on. There are several ways to improve your pacing and timing for the test:

- **Know your average pace.** While you prepare for the multiple-choice section of the exam, try to gauge how long you take on 5, 10, or 20 questions. Knowing how long you spend on average per question will help you identify how many questions you can answer effectively and how best to pace yourself for the test.

- **Have a watch or clock nearby.** You are permitted to have a watch or clock nearby to help you keep track of time. It is important to remember, however, that constantly checking the clock is in itself a waste of time and can be distracting. Devise a plan. Try checking the clock after every 15 or 30 questions to see if you are keeping the correct pace or whether you need to speed up; this will ensure that you're cognizant of the time but will not permit you to fall into the trap of dwelling on it.

- **Know when to move on.** Since all questions are scored equally, investing appreciable amounts of time on a single question is inefficient and can potentially deprive you of the chance to answer easier questions later on. If you are able to eliminate answer choices, do so, but don't worry about picking a random answer and moving on if you cannot find the correct answer. Remember, tests are like marathons; you do best when you work through them at a steady pace. You can always come back to a question you don't know. When you do, very often you will find that your previous mental block is gone, and you will wonder why the question perplexed you the first time around (as you gleefully move on to the next question). Even if you still don't know the answer, you will not have wasted valuable time you could have spent on easier questions.

- **Be selective.** You don't have to do any of the questions in a given section in order. If you are stumped by an essay or multiple-choice question, skip it or choose a different one. You may not have to answer every question correctly to achieve your desired score. Select the questions or essays that you can answer and work on them first. This will make you more efficient and give you the greatest chance of getting the most questions correct.

- **Use Process of Elimination on multiple-choice questions.** Many times, one or more answer choices can be eliminated. Every answer choice that can be eliminated increases the odds that you will answer the question correctly. Review Chapter 1 and make sure you're completely familiar with all the strategies you can use to find these incorrect answer choices and increase your odds of getting the question correct.

Remember, when all the questions on a test are of equal value, no one question is that important. Your overall goal for pacing is to get the most questions correct. Finally, you should set a realistic goal for your final score.

TEST ANXIETY

Everybody experiences anxiety before and during an exam. To a certain extent, test anxiety can be helpful. Some people find that they perform more quickly and efficiently under stress. If you have ever pulled an all-nighter to write a paper and ended up doing good work, you know the feeling.

Keep Calm

Trying to relax and de-stress is important not only on test day, but also during your test prep! As you work your way through this book, be sure to take intermittent study breaks to help yourself unwind and then refocus.

However, too much stress is definitely a bad thing. Hyperventilating during the test, for example, almost always leads to a lower score. If you find that you stress out during exams, here are a few preemptive actions you can take.

- **Take a reality check.** Evaluate your situation before the test begins. If you have studied hard, remind yourself that you are well prepared. Remember that many others taking the test are not as well prepared, and (in your classes, at least) you are being graded against them, so you have an advantage. If you didn't study, accept the fact that you will probably not ace the test. Make sure you get to every question you know something about. Don't stress out or fixate on how much you don't know. Your job is to score as high as you can by maximizing the benefits of what you do know. In either scenario, it is best to think of a test as if it were a game. How can you get the most points in the time allotted to you? Always answer questions you can answer easily and quickly before you answer those that will take more time.

- **Try to relax.** Slow, deep breathing works for almost everyone. Close your eyes, take a few, slow, deep breaths, and concentrate on nothing but your inhalation and exhalation for a few seconds. This is a basic form of meditation, and it should help you to clear your mind of stress and, as a result, concentrate better on the test. If you have ever taken yoga classes, you probably know some other good relaxation techniques. Use them when you can (obviously, anything that requires leaving your seat and, say, assuming a handstand position won't be allowed by any but the most free-spirited proctors).

- **Eliminate as many surprises as you can.** Make sure you know where the test will be given, when it starts, what type of questions are going to be asked, and how long the test will take. You don't want to be worrying about any of these things on test day or, even worse, after the test has already begun.

The best way to avoid stress is to study both the test material and the test itself. Congratulations! By buying or reading this book, you are taking a major step toward a stress-free AP World History: Modern Exam.

REFLECT
Respond to the following questions:

- How long will you spend on multiple-choice questions?

- How will you change your approach to multiple-choice questions?

- What is your multiple-choice guessing strategy?

- How much time will you spend on the short-answer questions?

- How much time will you spend on the DBQ? The long essay question?

- What will you do before you begin writing an essay?

- How will you change your approach to the essays?

- Will you seek further help outside of this book (such as a teacher, tutor, or AP Students) on how to approach multiple-choice questions, the essays, or a pacing strategy?

Part V
Content Review for the AP World History: Modern Exam

HOW TO USE THIS BOOK TO TAKE ON THE WORLD

Now that you know the kinds of questions to expect on the AP World History: Modern Exam, you're ready to take on the world!—or at least the review of AP World History. Part V of this book is designed to maximize your AP World History review. Here's how it is organized:

While You Read

As you read these content chapters, remember to underline key ideas or jot down notes in the margins. Remembering the key events and issues that took place during pivotal moments in history will help you when it comes to the source-based questions on the exam, which test your ability to tie a specific piece of evidence to a larger historical idea or theme.

- **Four Periods, Four Chapters.** The AP World History: Modern Exam divides world history into four distinct time periods, as we discussed in Part III. For ease of use, we have split our world history content review into these exact periods.

- **Get the Big Picture.** Each chapter begins with a "Stay Focused on the Big Picture" section so that you will—you guessed it—stay focused on the big picture while you review. To do well on this test, you're going to need to demonstrate not only that you have specific knowledge of people and events, but also that you understand how historical issues and events are connected. You'll also need to be able to think (and write) about concepts with a wide-angle lens, as well as use primary and secondary sources to investigate and analyze historical concepts and issues.

- **Make Those Connections.** Each chapter reviews the salient points of that period; the Compare Them, Contrast Them, Note the Change, and Focus On boxes help you make connections between different societies (that's the whole point of this test, remember?).

- **Pull It All Together.** Each chapter ends with a "Pulling It All Together" section to once again help you focus on the major points of the period.

KNOW WHERE YOU ARE IN THE WORLD

The AP World History: Modern Exam frequently refers to cultural regions of the world. So it is important to know where you are! The following map shows you the most commonly defined regions. Be aware that they don't always match up with physical boundaries. For example, parts of North Africa may be included when we're talking about the Middle East, and sub-Saharan Africa and Southeast Asia may be considered part of the Islamic world.

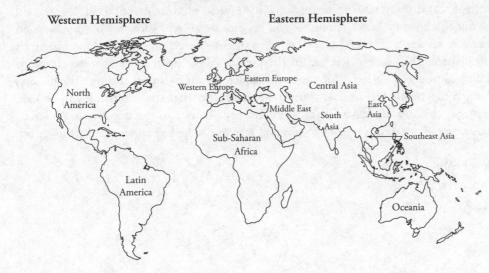

Geographic Regions of the World

Western Hemisphere   Eastern Hemisphere

North America
Western Europe
Eastern Europe
Central Asia
Middle East
South Asia
East Asia
Southeast Asia
Sub-Saharan Africa
Latin America
Oceania

HOW TO GET THE MOST OUT OF YOUR REVIEW

Here's what we suggest. Read through each chapter once. You'll probably remember most of the people, places, events, and concepts from your AP class. The chapters will help you review and pull together the major points. This review won't be as detailed as the book from your AP class, or else Part V would be as thick as your textbook, which would be kind of pointless. As you read through each chapter, consult your textbook if you've forgotten something entirely. After you finish going through a chapter once, spend some time in your AP textbook (or another world history source) going over the stuff you either didn't know or didn't remember. Then go back to the chapter to do mini-reviews of certain areas and to focus on the big-picture concepts and connections taking place in that period.

No, After You

It does not matter in which order you choose to review the material. If you love the Renaissance and hate the Middle Ages, review Chapter 7 first and Chapter 6 later. If you know that your knowledge of the Regional and Interregional Interactions era is lacking but you are pretty confident in what you know about recent history, dive into Chapter 6 first. This review is meant to be dynamic—we expect that you will return to it repeatedly as you prepare for your exam.

In addition, as we mentioned in the introduction to this book, you may wish to flip back and forth between your history review and your testing strategies practice. We would advise you to work through at least the multiple-choice section of Part IV before you get to the test, but it is really up to you. If you want to get a jump start on your history review and save the techniques for later, go ahead. On the other hand, you may wish to mix them up to see how our strategies help you gain points.

> **Noticing Themes > Memorizing Dates**
> The chapters that follow are filled with tons of dates, people, place names, events, and more. It can seem overwhelming, but remember that you do not need to memorize every fact about World History in order to do well on the exam. Instead, try to think conceptually about each era: what changed and what stayed the same? Pay attention to trends as well as cause-and-effect relationships between historical events.

No matter how you decide to organize your review, we do suggest that you continue to practice your test strategies and essay writing throughout the course of your preparation. As we said before, knowing this history is not enough—you need to be able to show what you know on test day. Once you review a chapter, practice writing an essay based on one of the comparisons or significant changes that took place within the period. Make up multiple-choice questions for a classmate and quiz each other. Once you've completed your first pass through the history, take a full-length diagnostic test so that you can get a feel for what the real thing will be like. The bottom line is this: do not leave all your test strategy practice to the last minute. Instead, use that practice to enhance your history review and zero in on the key concepts of each period.

Let the review begin…

Chapter 6
Period 1,
c. 1200 to c. 1450

Unit 1: The Global
       Tapestry
Unit 2: Networks
       of Exchange

I. CHAPTER OVERVIEW

Read through this chapter once; then go back and focus on the things that you're not entirely clear about. Here's the chapter outline.

I.   Chapter Overview

        You're reading it.

II.   Stay Focused on the Big Picture

        Organize the many events that occurred during the 250 years covered in this chapter into some big-picture concepts.

III.   Unit 1: The Global Tapestry

        Here's how we've organized the information.

        A. Review of History Within Civilizations
        B. Overview of the World's Major Religions in 1200
        C. Developments in the Middle East
        D. Developments in Europe
        E. The Emergence of Nation States
        F. Developments in Asia
        G. Developments in Africa
        H. Developments in the Americas

IV.   Unit 2: Networks of Exchange

        To do well on the AP World History: Modern Exam, you need to understand more than just the events that occurred within each region or civilization. You need to understand how they interacted with and affected each other. This gets very complicated, so we've given the topic its own section.

        Here's how we've organized it:

        A. Height of the Middle Ages: Trading and Crusading
        B. The Rise and Fall of the Mongols
        C. Mali and Songhai
        D. Chinese Technology
        E. Review of Interaction Among Cultures

V.   Technology and Innovations, 600 C.E.–1450

VI.   Changes and Continuities in the Role of Women

        The wealthier a society is, the less public presence and freedom women have.

VII.   Pulling It All Together

        A review of the review

II. STAY FOCUSED ON THE BIG PICTURE

As you review the details of the civilizations in this chapter for each unit, stay focused on the following four big-picture concepts:

For **Unit 1**, ask yourself:

1. Do cultural areas, as opposed to states or empires, better represent history? Cultural areas are those that share a common culture and don't necessarily respect geographical limitations. States, like city-states, nation-states (countries), and empires, have political boundaries, even if those boundaries aren't entirely agreed upon.

2. How does the environment impact human decision making? Pay attention to the way states respond to environmental changes. Do they move or send out raiding parties? Are they able to respond quickly and successfully to environmental changes?

For **Unit 2**, ask yourself:

3. How does change occur within societies? As you review all the information in this chapter, you'll notice a lot of talk about trading, migrations, and invasions. Pay attention to why people move around so much in the first place and the impact of these moves. Furthermore, don't forget that sometimes change occurs within a society because of internal developments, not because of external influences. Pay attention to that too.

4. How similar were the economic and trading practices that developed across cultures? Pay attention to monetary systems, trade routes, and trade practices. How did they link up?

III. UNIT 1: THE GLOBAL TAPESTRY

A. Review of History Within Civilizations

This period is defined by what rises out of the collapse of the classical civilizations and by the interactions—both positive and negative—that develop between new states. This period is one of tremendous growth in long-distance trade: the caravans of the various Silk Routes, the multiethnic Indian Ocean sailors, and the trips across the Sahara to West Africa all peak from 1200 to 1450 C.E. These 250 years were also defined by expansion of the trading empires of the Middle East and China. Remember interaction!

B. Overview of the World's Major Religions in 1200

Religions have been pretty significant movers in world history. With that in mind, it makes sense to get our bearings on the religious landscape of the world in 1200 since there are not many events we will cover in the upcoming chapters that are completely divorced from religion. As you review the major belief systems, keep a few things in mind:

1. Most of these belief systems have impacted world history from their inception through the present era. That said, the discussion here focuses on the impact of these systems during the ancient era. We'll talk more about the impact of these religions on later world events in subsequent chapters.

2. Most of the major religions have had schisms (divisions), resulting in a variety of subgroups and sects. The test writers will focus more on the overall religion than on particular sects (though there are a few exceptions that we'll get to in future chapters, such as the Protestant Reformation within Christianity and the rise of fundamentalism in Islam).

3. Focus not only on the theological or philosophical basis of each belief system, but also on the impact those belief systems had on social, political, cultural, and even military developments.

4. Pay attention to where each belief system started and where it spread. As merchants and warriors moved, so did their religious beliefs. By looking at where religions branched out or came into conflict with one another, you'll get a good understanding of which cultures frequently interacted with each other.

Religious Mysticism

Within religious traditions, there are adherents who focus on mystical, or transcendent, experiences that bring them closer to the divine (however that is defined by the religion). Buddhist monastics or Hindu Bhaktas (devotees of **Bhakti**), for instance, dedicate their lives to meditation such that it will help to break their attachment to the physical world. Mystics from the monastic tradition, such as Christian monks or Islamic **Sufis**, use their practices of prayer to strive for a direct experience with God.

Belief System	Cultures that Practiced It	Nuts and Bolts	Broader Impact
Buddhism	Eastern civilizations, most notably in India, China, Southeast Asia, and Japan practiced Buddhism.	• Buddhism was founded by a young Hindu prince named Siddhartha Gautama, who was born and lived in Nepal from 563 through 483 B.C.E. He rejected his wealth to search for the meaning of human suffering. After meditating under a sacred bodhi tree, he became the Buddha, or Enlightened One. • There is no supreme being in Buddhism. Rather, Buddhists follow the Four Noble Truths: all life is suffering; suffering is caused by desire; one can be freed of this desire; and one is freed of desire by following a prescribed path. • After the death of Buddha in 483 B.C.E., Buddhism split into two large movements, Theravada Buddhism and Mahayana Buddhism. • Theravada (Hinayana) Buddhism emphasizes meditation, simplicity, and an interpretation of nirvana as the renunciation of human consciousness and of the self. (Theravada means "the Way of the Elders.") • Mahayana Buddhism ("The Greater Vehicle") is a more complicated form of Buddhism, involving greater ritual than Buddha specified. Mahayana Buddhism appealed to people who believed that the original teachings of Buddha did not offer enough spiritual comfort; therefore, they began to hypothesize that other forms of salvation were possible. • Mahayana Buddhism's openness to the practices of other cultures allowed its spread to cover a much greater area than that of Theravada Buddhism.	• Because it rejected social hierarchies of castes, Buddhism appealed strongly to members of lower rank. And because Buddhism isn't attached to an underlying social structure, it can apply to almost anyone, anywhere. As a consequence, it spread rapidly to other cultures throughout Asia. • In India, Buddhism was eventually reabsorbed into Hinduism, which remained the dominant belief system there. • In China, Japan, and Southeast Asia, Buddhism continued to thrive. • Furthermore, as Buddhism spread via the trade routes, the cultures of Asia intertwined.

Belief System	Cultures that Practiced It	Nuts and Bolts	Broader Impact
Christianity	Originally a splinter group of Jews practiced the religion, but it quickly expanded into the non-Jewish community and throughout Europe, north-eastern Africa, and parts of the Middle East.	• Christianity came into existence with Jesus of Nazareth, a charismatic Jewish teacher who claimed to be the Messiah, a religious figure for whom Jews had long awaited. • Many people were attracted to his teachings of devotion to God and love for human beings. • The Roman and Jewish leaders were not among them, so in approximately 30 C.E., Jesus was crucified. • His followers believed that he rose from the dead and ascended into heaven, and Christianity was born. • Christianity is based on both the Old and New Testaments of the Bible. • Christians believe that Jesus Christ is the Son of God and that forgiveness of sins, and ultimately everlasting life, is achievable only through belief in the divinity, death, and resurrection of Christ. • The Christian view is that the world was made by a personal and sovereign God, but that the world has fallen from harmony with God's will. • Human beings are expected to seek to know God, to worship him, and to practice love and service to him and to other human beings.	• With its emphasis on compassion, grace through faith, and the promise of eternal life regardless of personal circumstances, Christianity appealed widely to the lower classes and women. • By the 3rd century C.E., Christianity had become the most influential religion in the Mediterranean basin. • Following a period of sporadic and localized persecution, it became legal within, and then the official religion of, the Roman Empire; it continued to branch northward and westward into regions beyond the boundaries of the Roman Empire. • In the ensuing centuries, this marriage of Christianity and empire would profoundly affect developments in a large segment of the world.

Belief System	Cultures that Practiced It	Nuts and Bolts	Broader Impact
Confucianism	Confucianism was developed specifically for the Chinese culture and was widely practiced throughout China from around 400 B.C.E. onward.	• Confucius was an educator and political advisor, and in this role he had a tremendous influence on China. • He attracted many followers, some of whom helped share his teachings and others who collected his thoughts and sayings in the Analects, which would come to have a profound influence on Chinese thinking both politically and culturally. • Though fundamentally moral and ethical in character, it is also thoroughly practical, dealing almost solely with the question of how to restore political and social order. Confucianism does not deal with large philosophical issues or with religious issues such as salvation or an afterlife. • Confucianism focuses on five fundamental relationships, which are considered the building blocks of society: ruler and subject, parent and child, husband and wife, older sibling and younger sibling, and friend and friend. • When each person in these relationships lives up to his or her obligations in those relationships, society is orderly and predictable.	• Because Confucianism was an ethical, social, and political belief system, rather than a theological system, it was compatible with other religions. In other words, a person could, for example, practice both Buddhism and Confucianism simultaneously. • This flexibility enabled Confucianism to flourish. Government leaders, too, embraced it, because it was intended to create an orderly society. • Its widespread acceptance eventually led to a distinctive Chinese culture in which communities became extremely tight-knit; members had duties and responsibilities to many others in the community from birth to death. • Confucianism did not, however, have a similar impact on the rest of the world, because it evolved only within the context of the Chinese culture.

Belief System	Cultures that Practiced It	Nuts and Bolts	Broader Impact
Hinduism	The various cultures of the Indian subcontinent practiced Hinduism.	• Hindus believe in one supreme force called Brahma, the creator, who is in all things. Hindu gods are manifestations of Brahma—notably Vishnu, the preserver, and Shiva, the destroyer. • The life goal of Hindus is to merge with Brahma. Because that task is considered impossible to accomplish in one lifetime, Hindus also believe that who you are in this life was determined by who you were in a past life, and that how you conduct yourself in your assigned role in this life will determine the role (caste) you are born into in a future life. • If you behave well and follow the *dharma* (the rules and obligations of the caste you're born into), you'll keep moving up the ladder toward unification with Brahma. If not, you'll drop down the ladder. This cycle of life, death, and rebirth continues until you achieve *moksha,* the highest state of being, one of perfect internal peace and release of the soul. • There is no one central sacred text in Hinduism, though the Vedas and the Upanishads, sources of prayers, verses, and descriptions of the origins of the universe, guide Hindus.	• Hinduism is a religion as well as a social system—the caste system. • Hinduism's close identification with the caste system and the Indian social structure and customs have prevented its acceptance in other parts of the world. • In recent years, modern Hindus are beginning to rebel against the strictures of the caste system. Nevertheless, Hinduism as a whole remains a powerful force. • Hinduism later spawned another religion—Buddhism.

Belief System	Cultures that Practiced It	Nuts and Bolts	Broader Impact
Islam	Followers of Islam, Muslims, were initially those living under the caliphates (Islamic kingdoms) in the Middle East, though the religion quickly spread to North Africa, central Asia, and parts of Europe.	• In the seventh century, a new monotheistic faith, called Islam, took hold in the Middle East. • **Muslims** believe that Allah (God) transmitted his words to the faithful through Muhammad, whose followers began to record those words in what came to be called the Qu'ran. • Muslims believe that salvation is won through submission to the will of God, and that this can be accomplished by following the Five Pillars of Islam: confession of faith; prayer five times per day; charity to the needy; fasting during the holy month of Ramadan; and pilgrimage to Mecca, a city in Saudi Arabia. • Early on, Islam split into two groups: Shia and Sunni. The split occurred over a disagreement about who should succeed Muhammad as the leader of the faith.	• Islam rapidly spread out of the city of Mecca into other parts of the Middle East and beyond under the Umayyad Dynasty. • The Umayyad Dynasty was replaced by the Abbasid Dynasty around 750, which continued the growth of Dar al Islam (the Islamic world).

Belief System	Cultures that Practiced It	Nuts and Bolts	Broader Impact
Judaism	The Hebrews, a tribe from the Middle East, were the original practitioners of Judaism.	• Judaism holds that God selected a group of people, the Hebrews, and made himself known to them. If they followed his laws, worshipped him, and were faithful, he would preserve them for all time. This group became the Jews, and Judaism became the first of the great monotheistic faiths. • Judaism is not centered on many of the concepts typically associated with a religion, although a belief in an afterlife, a set of traditions and doctrines, and philosophy are part of its makeup. At the center of Judaism is the awareness of a unique relationship with God. • Jewish people believe that they were created by a personal, sovereign God, as was the world, for them to live in and enjoy and in which they could exercise free will. The destiny of the world is paradise, reached by human beings with divine help. • Created in the image of God, human beings have an obligation to honor and serve God by following the texts of the Hebrew Bible, which include the Torah and other sacred texts that formed the basis of the Old Testament in Christianity. • The Hebrew Bible contained accounts of miracles, laws, historical chronicles, sacred poetry, and prophecies and formed a central part of Jewish religious practice and social custom. Thus, Judaism is both a set of religious guidelines and a cultural system.	• Judaism was the first of the major monotheistic faiths; as such, it spawned the other two major monotheistic religions, Christianity and Islam.

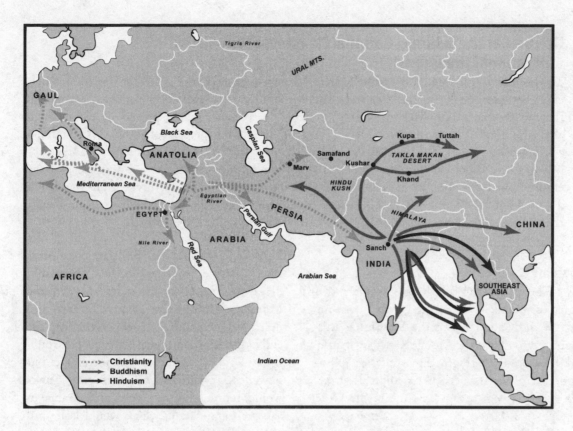

Map of World Religions, c. 600 c.e.

C. Developments in the Middle East

The Abbasid Dynasty: Golden Age to Remember

The **Abbasid Dynasty** reigned from 750 to 1258 c.e., that is, until the Islamic Empire was defeated by the Mongols (more on them later). Throughout this time, like all major empires, the Abbasids had many ups and downs, but they oversaw a golden age beginning in the early- to mid-9th century, during which the arts and sciences flourished. The Abbasids built a magnificent capital at **Baghdad** (modern-day Iraq), which became one of the great cultural centers of the world, highlighted by a grand library known as the House of Wisdom. Prior to its destruction by the Mongols, Baghdad was a center for innovations in mathematics, notably from **Nasir al-Din al-Tusi**, as well as medicine. Scholars in Baghdad preserved much of the classical knowledge from Ancient Greece and Rome, retransmitting it to Europe as Muslim contact with the European world increased.

Like most of the other ancient civilizations we've discussed so far, the Islamic Empire was built around trade. The merchants introduced the unique idea of credit to the empire's trade mechanisms to free them of the burden—and the danger—of carrying coins. Necessarily, they also developed a system of itemized receipts and bills, innovations that were later used in Europe and elsewhere.

Decline of the Islamic Caliphates: Internal Rivalries and Mongol Invasions

The Islamic Empire regularly endured internal struggles and civil war, often arising from differences between the Sunni and Shia sects, and from ethnic differences between diverse groups in the rapidly expanding Muslim world. Numerous rival factions and powers developed, and although none of these threatened Islam, they did destabilize the central authority at Baghdad and cut tax revenues. The final blows came when enslaved Turkish warriors revolted and established a new capital at Samarra in central Iraq, while other groups carved out pieces of the empire. There was a new Shia dynasty in northern Iran and constant threats from the Seljuk Turks, a nomadic Sunni group. Like the Romans before them, weakened by internal problems, the Abbasids also had external foes: the Persians, Europeans, and Byzantines.

Mamluks: Saving Islam?

While Islamic lands were being overrun by Mongol invaders, the fate of Islam was arguably at stake. One of the groups that rose from the ashes of the Abbasid Caliphate was the **Mamluks**. This group from Egypt managed to defeat the Mongols in a key battle near the town Nazareth before retreating to Egypt and establishing a sultanate that lasted until the 16th century—and with it the preservation of Islam during a very uncertain time in the Near East.

However, it would be the Islamic Empire's most distant enemy, the Mongols, who would defeat it. During the Crusades, in 1258, the **Mongols** overran the Islamic Empire and destroyed Baghdad, thereby signaling the end of the Abbasid Dynasty. Its people would flee to Egypt, where they remained intact but powerless. Eventually, the **Ottoman Turks** would reunite Egypt, Syria, and Arabia in a new Islamic state, which would last until 1918.

D. Developments in Europe

Developments in Europe and points east became quite complicated during the **Middle Ages**, which is the period after the fall of Rome and before the Renaissance. Developments in the Middle East, the Roman Empire, and eventually Christianity, was divided into two factions that split, reconnected, and then split again. Ultimately, the eastern Roman Empire, centered in Constantinople, became the highly centralized government known as the Byzantine Empire; in the west, on the other hand, the empire collapsed entirely, although the Christian religion retained a strong foothold. The important point to remember about all of this is that even though both segments of the empire followed Christianity, they practiced different forms of the religion; moreover, their populations competed for supremacy.

European Feudalism: Land Divided

Feudalism, the name of the European social, economic, and political system of the Middle Ages, had a strict hierarchy. At the top was a king, who had power over an entire territory called his kingdom. Beneath him were the **nobles**, who in exchange for military service and loyalty to the king were granted power over sections of the kingdom. The nobles, in turn, divided their lands into smaller sections under the control of lesser lords called **vassals**. The vassals could also split their lands into smaller pieces and give custody of them to subordinate vassals, who could divide their lands into even smaller pieces in the custody of even more subordinate vassals, and so on. Below the vassals were **peasants**, who worked the land. For this system to work, everyone had to fulfill obligations to others at different levels in the hierarchy: to serve in the military, produce food, or serve those who were at a higher level. If, say, you were a lesser-lord, you were obliged to your lord, and you were obliged to your vassals as well.

The estates that were granted to the vassals were called **fiefs**, and these later became known as **manors**. The lord and the peasants lived on the manor. The peasants worked the land on behalf of the lord, and in exchange the lord gave the peasants protection and a place to live. Many of the manors were remarkably self-sufficient. Everything that was needed to live was produced on them. Food was harvested, clothing and shoes were made, and so on. Advances made in the science of agriculture during this time helped the manors to succeed. One such advance, called the **three-field system**, centered on the rotation of three fields: one for the fall harvest, one for the spring harvest, and one not-seeded fallow harvest (the latter allowing the land to replenish its nutrients). In this way, manors were able to accumulate food surpluses and build on the success. Lords directed what was called the "Great Clearing," the clearing of huge areas of forest for the creation of more farmland.

The lord, as noted, owed his allegiance to the king but had direct contact with him only when the king called upon the lord to provide a service. Otherwise, the lord was in charge of his own manor—his own life. And though the various fiefs were, in theory, self-sustaining, and the lords all beholden to the same ruler, conflicts erupted between feudal lords on a regular basis (this is where the term feud comes from). The etiquette of these disputes and rules of engagement was highly refined and flowed from the **code of chivalry**, an honor system that strongly condemned betrayal and promoted mutual respect. Most of the lords (and knights, who were also considered part of the nobility) followed the code of chivalry.

The feudal system, like most of the civilizations, was male-dominated. Land equaled power, and only males could inherit land, so women were pretty much powerless. Specifically, when a lord died under the feudal system, his land and title passed down via **primogeniture**, to his eldest son. Even noblewomen had few rights, though they were socially elevated (and have come to be romanticized in literature). Women could inherit a fief, but they could not rule it. Furthermore, women's education was limited to domestic skills. As usual in most early societies, noblewomen were admired and valued primarily for their "feminine" traits—their beauty or compassion—but were regarded essentially as property to be protected or displayed.

Peasants (called **serfs**) in the feudal social system, whether male or female, had few rights. As manorial life evolved, an increasing number of peasants became tied to the land quite literally: they couldn't leave the manor without permission from their lord. Peasants were not quite enslaved, but not free either. Ironically, however, it was this "imprisonment" on the land that led to the serfs becoming highly skilled workers. In short, they learned how to do whatever it took to make the manor self-sufficient.

Contrast Them: Feudal Europe and the Islamic Empire

During the Abbasid Dynasty, Islamic merchants were trading with the world while European lords were governing their manors. Baghdad became a center of learning and art in the Islamic Empire, whereas small, secluded monasteries became centers of learning in the early Holy Roman Empire. In summary, it can be said that in the early Middle Ages, educated Europeans became very provincial, while educated Arabs became more worldly.

As many of the serfs became skilled in trades other than farming, and Europe slowly but surely started trading with the rest of the world, some of these skilled craftspeople began to earn extra income. Over time, this elevation in the status of craftspeople chipped away at the rigid social stratification of the manor system. When banking began in Europe, towns and cities started to gain momentum. The result was the emergence of a "middle class" made up of urban craftsmen and merchants. The success of this new middle class lured more people into towns in the hopes of making more money or learning new skills. By the 11th century, Western Europe was re-engaging with the world.

E. The Emergence of Nation-States

Keep in mind that during the Middle Ages, Western Europe wasn't organized into countries (nation-states); rather, it was broken up into feudal kingdoms. However, by the close of the Middle Ages, Western Europe began to organize along cultural and linguistic lines. People who spoke French aligned themselves with France. Those who spoke English united under the banner of England. We'll be talking a lot more about this in the next chapter, but for now just keep this general concept in mind.

The various parts of Europe took different paths to achieve statehood during the 13th century. In Germany, for example, the reigning family died out without a suitable successor to the emperorship, so the region entered a period known as an **interregnum** (a time between kings). Germany and Italy became decentralized in a group of strong, independent townships and kingdoms, similar to city-states. In this environment, merchants and tradespeople became more powerful. In northern Germany, for example, the Hanseatic League led the region's progress in international trade and commerce.

England, by contrast, unified much more quickly. Since the time of **William the Conqueror**, England had followed a tradition of a strong monarchy. However, during the rule of King John, powerful English nobles rebelled and forced him to sign the **Magna Carta** (1215 C.E.). This document reinstated the feudal rights of the nobles, but also extended the rule of law to other people in the country, namely the growing burgher class, laying the foundation for the Parliament. Initially, an assembly was established, made up of nobles who were responsible for representing the views of different parts of England on law-making and taxation issues. After a trial period, the Parliament was established. Later, it was divided into two branches: the House of Lords (nobles and clergy) and the House of Commons (knights and wealthy burghers). The House of Lords presided over legal issues and advised the king; the House of Commons was concerned with issues of trade and taxation. The result was that England established its identity pretty early on.

The formation of France was bound up with England. In 987, **King Hugh Capet** ruled only a small area around Paris; for the next 200 years or so, subsequent French kings expanded the territory. Beginning in the 12th century, England began to claim large parts of present-day France. The English occupation of the French-speaking territories led to revolts and, eventually, to French statehood. (The goal was to unite France under its own leadership.) This effort was spearheaded by an unlikely candidate.

As a teenager, farm girl **Joan of Arc** claimed to have heard voices that told her to liberate France from the hands of the English, who had by the early 15th century claimed the entire French territory. Remarkably, this uneducated youngster somehow managed to convince French authorities that she had been divinely inspired to lead men into battle, and they supplied her with military backing. With her army, she forced the British to retreat from Orleans, but was later captured by French opponents known as the Burgundians, tried by the English, and burned at the stake. Nevertheless, she had a significant impact on the **Hundred Years' War** (1337–1453) between England and France, which eventually resulted in England's withdrawal from France.

> **Bourbon Beginnings**
> After the Hundred Years' War, royal power in France became more centralized. Under a series of monarchs known as **Bourbons**, France was unified and became a major power on the European continent.

At around the same time, Spain was united by **Queen Isabella**, the ruler of Castile (present-day central Spain). Power in the Spanish-speaking region of Europe had been divided for two reasons: first, Castile was one of three independent Spanish kingdoms, and therefore no single ruler controlled the region, and second, the peasants were split along religious lines (mostly Christian and Muslim), because of the lasting influences of the Muslim conquest of the Iberian Peninsula during the Middle Ages. To overcome these obstacles, Isabella married **Ferdinand**, heir to the Spanish Kingdom of Aragon, in 1469, thus uniting most of Spain in a single monarchy. Rather than compete with the church for authority, Isabella and Ferdinand, both Christians, enlisted the Catholic Church as a strong ally. Spanish statehood thrived under the new monarchy, and the alignment with the Catholic Church effectively ended religious toleration in the region. The result was that non-Christians (predominantly Muslim and Jewish people) were forced to convert to Christianity or leave the country. This policy marked the beginning of the **Spanish Inquisition**. The consequences for non-Christian Spaniards were tragic; the consequences for the Spanish monarchy were huge. Newly unified and energized, Spain embarked on an imperial quest that led to tremendous wealth and glory, eventually resulting in the spread of the Spanish language, Spanish customs, and Christianity to much of the New World (as you will see in the next chapter).

Russia

At this time, Eastern Europe and Russia were very different from the West. The Eastern Orthodox Christians of this area spent much time and effort defending themselves from the colonization of various western invaders. It wasn't until 1242 C.E. that Russia succumbed to the **Tatars** (a group of Mongols from the east) under Genghis Khan. The Tatars ruled a large chunk of Russia for two centuries, leading to a cultural rift that further split Eastern and Western Europe.

By the 14th century, Mongol power started to decline and the Russian princes of Muscovy grew in power. By the late 1400s, Ivan III expanded Muscovy territory (the area surrounding Moscow) into much of modern-day Russia and declared himself **czar**, the Russian word for emperor or Caesar. As the center of the Eastern Orthodox Church, Moscow was declared the Third Rome, after the real Rome and Constantinople. By the mid-1500s, **Ivan the Terrible** had centralized power over the entire Russian sphere, ruling ruthlessly and using the secret police against his own nobles. The next chapter will go into more of the details about Russia. By this time, nationalism in Russia was well underway.

F. Developments in Asia

1. China and Nearby Regions

Two powerful Chinese dynasties during this period, the Song (960–1279 C.E.) and Ming (1368–1644 C.E.), developed Golden Ages. The **Ming Dynasty** came to power after a brief period of domination by Mongol invaders. You should understand from the outset that when we speak of China, we're actually talking about its influence throughout much of east and southeast Asia. We'll talk more specifically about Korea, Vietnam, and Cambodia in a minute. For now, you just need to understand that China had an enormous impact on cultural and political developments in those civilizations.

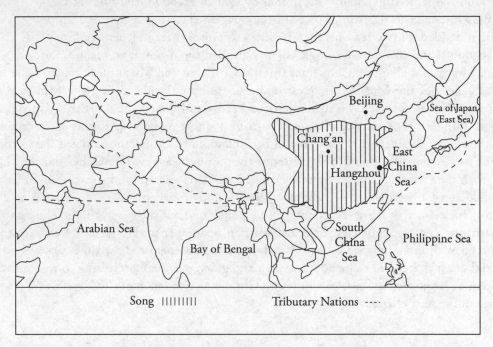

Extent of the Song (960–1279 C.E.) Dynasty

Chinese Women Under the Song Dynasty

During the Song Dynasty, adherence to a new Confucianism justified the subordination of women, and **foot binding** became a widespread practice. A woman's feet would be bound shortly after birth in an effort to keep them small—if kept bound for a long enough time, they wouldn't grow even as the rest of the body did. Large feet were considered masculine and ugly. This practice, which lasted for centuries among elite families, was not only painful, but also often deforming and sometimes crippling.

Religion in China: Diverse Beliefs

Following the fall of the Han Dynasty, there were a number of different religious influences in China, such as Nestorianism, Manichaeism, Zoroastrianism, and Islam. The religion that had the greatest impact by far was Buddhism, especially in two of its forms: Mahayana and Chan. Mahayana Buddhism appealed to many because of its emphasis on a peaceful and quiet existence and a life apart from worldly values. With its emphasis on meditation and appreciation of beauty, Chan (or Zen) Buddhism won converts in the educated classes, who generally followed the tenets of Confucianism.

Both the Confucians and the Daoists reacted strongly to the spread of Buddhism. Many Confucians saw Buddhism as a drain on both the treasury and the labor pool, especially because Buddhism dismissed the pursuit of material accumulation. The Daoists saw Buddhism as a rival religion that was winning over many of its adherents.

Neo-Confucianism in China

As China turned away from otherworldly ideas of the Buddhists during the early Song, new ideas about Confucian philosophy developed. Where older Confucianism had focused on practical politics and morality, the neo-Confucianists borrowed Buddhist ideas about the soul and the individual. This new tradition became the guiding doctrine of the Song Dynasty and the basis for civil service. At its core was a systematic approach to both the heavens and the role of individuals. Filial piety, the maintenance of proper roles, and loyalty to one's superiors were again emphasized.

2. Japan

Because Japan consists of four main islands off the coast of mainland Asia, it was relatively isolated for thousands of years. Ideas, religions, and material goods traveled between Japan and the rest of Asia, especially China, but the rate of exchange was relatively limited. Only in recent centuries has Japan allowed in Western influences.

Feudal Japan

The interesting thing about feudalism in Japan is that it developed at around the same time as feudalism in Western Europe, but it developed independently.

In 1192 C.E., Yoritomo Minamoto was given the title of chief general, or **shogun**, by the emperor. As with the Fujiwara family, the emperor was the figurehead but didn't hold the real power, which was in the hands of the shogun.

Contrast Them: China and Japan

Even though China influenced Japan enormously, it didn't penetrate Japanese identity. Birth was more important than outside influence or education. The aristocracy remained strong. Despite the widespread influence of Confucianism and Chan (now Zen) Buddhism, the Japanese continued to observe the rites of their indigenous religion, Shintoism.

Below the shogun in the pecking order were the **daimyo**, owners of large tracts of land (the counterparts of the lords of medieval Europe). The daimyo were powerful samurai, who were like knights. They were part warrior, part nobility. They, in turn, divided up their lands to lesser samurai (vassals), who in turn split their land up again. Peasants and artisans worked the fields and shops to support the samurai class. Just as in European feudalism, the hierarchy was bound together in a land-for-loyalty exchange.

Compare and Contrast Them: European and Japanese Feudalism

They were similar in terms of political structure, social structure, and honor code. They were different in terms of treatment of women and legal arrangement. In Europe, the feudal contract was just that, a contract. It was an arrangement of obligations enforced in law. In Japan, on the other hand, the feudal arrangement was based solely on group identity and loyalty. In both cases, the feudal arrangement was based on culture, and so the feudal system stayed around for a very long time.

The samurai followed a strict code of conduct known as the **Code of Bushido**, which was very similar to the code of chivalry in Europe. The code stressed loyalty, courage, and honor, so much so that if a samurai failed to meet his obligations under the code, he was expected to commit suicide.

Interestingly, unlike under European feudalism, women in Japan were not held in high esteem. Remember that in Europe, noblewomen were given few rights, but they were adored, at least to the extent that they were beautiful and possessed feminine traits. In contrast, Japanese women lost any freedom they had during the Fujiwara period and were forced to live harsher, more demeaning lives.

3. India

India was the birthplace of two major religions: Hinduism and Buddhism. In the 10th century, another major religion made its way to the Indus valley: Islam.

The Delhi Sultanate

After defeating the disorganized Hindus, the Islamic invaders set up shop in Delhi under their leader, the sultan. Hence, this kingdom is referred to as the **Delhi Sultanate**. For over 300 years beginning in about 1206 C.E., Islam spread throughout much of northern India. While many Hindus held on to their religious beliefs under this theoretically tolerant regime, individual sultans were highly offended by Hinduism's polytheistic ways and did their best to convert them. Like non-Muslims under the Umayyads in Arabia, non-Muslims under the sultans in India had to pay a tax. But more than that, the sultans were capable of religiously motivated destruction. Hindu temples were sometimes destroyed, and occasionally violence erupted in communities.

Despite the differences between the Islamic and Hindu cultures, an amazing amount of progress occurred in India under the sultans. Colleges were founded. Irrigation systems were vastly improved. Mosques were built, often with the help of Hindu architects and artists. Many Hindus in northern India converted to Islam. Sometimes the conversions were genuine; other times, they just made life easier. In any case, a considerable number of Hindus in northern India converted to Islam while the vast majority of Hindus in southern India held on to their traditions.

Rajput Kingdoms

Some Hindus in northern India continued to retain their identity despite the Islamic influence. Although the Rajputs' name comes from the term for "son of the king," those who were referred to as Rajputs actually descended from a variety of social and ethnic backgrounds. The **Rajput Kingdoms** consisted of several different Hindu principalities that were largely independent of one another. However, these kingdoms had to adhere to some degree of unity in order to put up resistance against the invading Muslim forces for several centuries from 1191 until the Rajput kingdoms were finally put down by the Muslim Mughal forces in 1527.

4. Southeast Asia

Religions of Asia spread over trade routes and laid the foundation for states established throughout South and Southeast Asia.

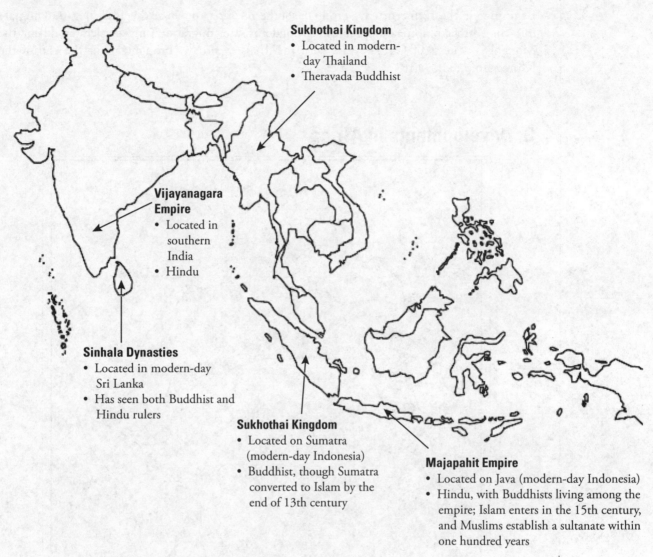

Sukhothai Kingdom
- Located in modern-day Thailand
- Theravada Buddhist

Vijayanagara Empire
- Located in southern India
- Hindu

Sinhala Dynasties
- Located in modern-day Sri Lanka
- Has seen both Buddhist and Hindu rulers

Sukhothai Kingdom
- Located on Sumatra (modern-day Indonesia)
- Buddhist, though Sumatra converted to Islam by the end of 13th century

Majapahit Empire
- Located on Java (modern-day Indonesia)
- Hindu, with Buddhists living among the empire; Islam enters in the 15th century, and Muslims establish a sultanate within one hundred years

State Building in South and Southeast Asia

It is no secret that Hinduism and Indian culture are intertwined. However, while Hinduism is unique for not spreading as the other religions we covered have done, there were a couple exceptions to this rule.

The **Khmer Empire,** established in the 9th century, was predominantly Hindu. That may not seem strange until you realize that the Khmer were located in Southeast Asia—in what is today Cambodia, Laos, and Thailand. Through the Indian Ocean trade network, Hindu beliefs were carried to Southeast Asia, becoming the centerpiece of the growing empire.

The Khmer were skilled at complex architecture. Their most impressive construction is a temple known as **Angor Wat,** which endeavored to represent the entire Hindu universe in a single stone structure.

The Khmer Empire enjoyed a prosperous economy, much of which was controlled by women. Further, the empire practiced tolerance of other religions. This was necessary due to the substantial Buddhist population that lived in Southeast Asia.

Beginning in the 12th century, a group in southern China known as the Thais began to migrate into the Khmer Empire and established kingdoms. This migration only accelerated during the Mongol conquests of China. Wars with the Thais eventually brought about the end of the Khmer Empire in 1431.

G. Developments in Africa

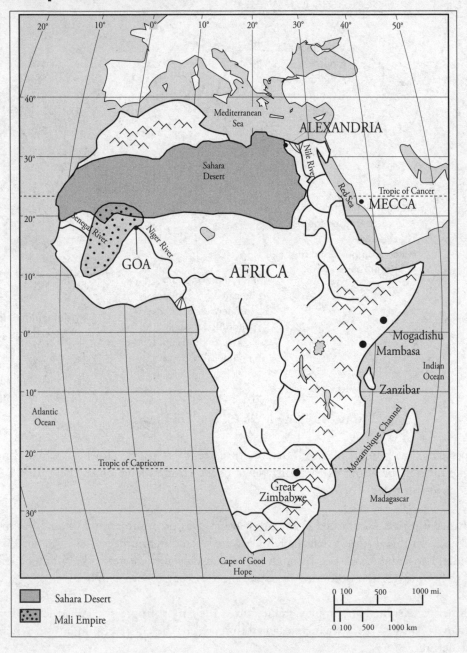

African Empires and Trade Cities

When the Islamic Empire spread across North Africa in the 7th and 8th centuries, African kingdoms began trading with the larger Mediterranean economy. Islamic traders penetrated the unforgiving Sahara desert and reached the fertile wealthy interior of Africa, called sub-Saharan (beneath the Sahara), while African traders pushed northward toward Carthage and Tripoli. Previously, the desert had acted as one gigantic "don't-want-to-deal-with-it" barrier, so people typically didn't. Increasingly, however, caravans of traders were willing to do what they had to do to get to the riches on the other side of the sand. At first, the west Africans were in search of salt, of which they had little but which existed in the Sahara. When they encountered the Islamic traders along the salt road, they started trading for a lot more than just salt. The consequence was an explosion of trade.

Hausa Kingdoms

Off the Niger River, in what is now Nigeria, a people known as the **Hausa** cultivated state systems in various kingdoms throughout the western part of central Africa. A solidly Islamic region by the 15th century, the Hausa kingdoms achieved economic stability and religious influence in much the same way that the kingdoms of Mali and Songhai did: through long trade. Due to its local resources, the Hausa established wealth through both the salt and leather trade, all while turning an otherwise agricultural economy into the mother that drove a thriving state. Due to its wealth and political centrality, the Hausa's most populous city, Kano, was a destination for traders who ventured through central and western Africa. A series of internal wars among the Hausa kingdoms ultimately led to its political and economic downturn by the 18th century.

H. Developments in the Americas

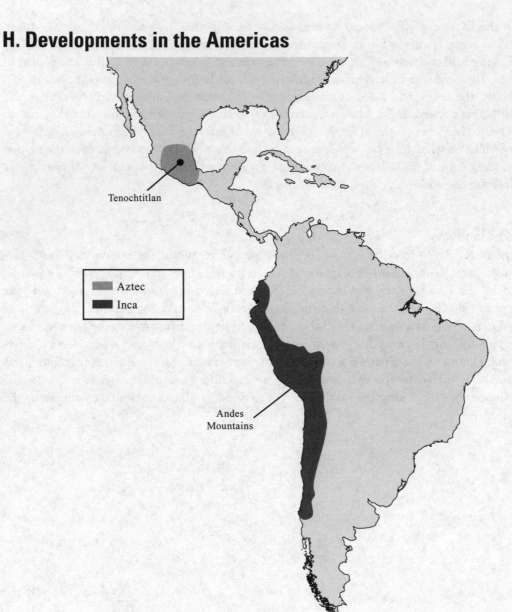

The American Civilizations

There were three great civilizations in what is now Central America and South America that developed before the arrival of the Europeans. One of the civilizations, the Maya, actually began around the time of the major classical civilizations. The other two civilizations, the Incas and Aztecs, were conquered by the Europeans after 1450. They will be discussed again in the next chapter. That said, we are including the latter two in this chapter so that you can review the cultural characteristics of these civilizations in one place. We'll talk about their conquests in the next chapter.

The Aztecs: Trade and Sacrifice

The Aztecs, also known as the Mexica, arrived in central Mexico in the mid-1200s and built their capital at **Tenochtitlan** (modern-day Mexico City). More than anything else, the Aztecs are known for their expansionist policy and professional army, which allowed them to dominate nearby states and demand heavy taxes and captives. Warriors were the elite in the Aztec social structure (the majority of the people were peasants and enslaved). Through conquest and alliances, the Aztecs built an empire of some 12 million people. Despite the huge size, they didn't use a bureaucratic form of government. The conquered areas were generally allowed to govern themselves, as long as they paid the tribute demanded of them. Roads were built to link the far-flung areas of the huge empire, and trade flourished.

Aztec women had a subordinate public role but could inherit property. Like women in almost all other traditional civilizations, Aztec women were primarily charged with running the household, but they were also involved in skilled crafts, especially weaving, and—to some extent—in commerce.

Notably, the Aztec religious system was tied to the military because one of the purposes of the military was to obtain victims for human sacrifice. Tens of thousands of men and women were killed annually; many would be sacrificed simultaneously for an important religious occasion, such as the dedication of a new temple.

The Inca: My Land Is Your Land

The Inca Empire, set in the Andes Mountains in Peru, was also expansionist in nature. At its zenith, it is thought to have controlled more than 2,000 miles of South American coastline. The Inca controlled this territory using a professional army, an established bureaucracy, a unified language, and a complex system of roads and tunnels.

Like the Maya (and the Aztecs), the Incas had no large animals, so the prime source of labor was human. A large proportion of the population was peasants, who worked the land or on construction projects. They were expected to give a proportion of their harvest to support the ruling classes and to provide famine relief. These surpluses eventually became large enough to support large cities. The capital at Cuzco may have had as many as 300,000 people in the late 1400s.

> ### Cahokia
> Located near the site of modern-day St. Louis, Cahokia was the largest North American city north of Mexico prior to the arrival of European settlers. In the 13th century, its population rivaled or surpassed that of any European city, and while it was abandoned a hundred years before the voyages of Columbus, no American city passed Cahokia's peak population mark until after the United States had achieved its independence. Cahokia was dominated by a huge earthwork known as Monks Mound, an artificial hill 100 feet high and covering 17 acres, consisting of soil transported to the site by hand in baskets.

Incan women were expected to help work the fields, weave cloth, and care for the household. They could pass property on to their daughters and even played a role in religion. The Inca were polytheistic, but the Sun god was the most important and was at the center of the state religion. Like the Aztecs, the Inca practiced human sacrifice, but in much smaller numbers, usually choosing instead to sacrifice material goods or animals. Incan religion also had a very strong moral quality, emphasizing rewards for good behavior and punishments for bad. Like the Egyptians, Incan rulers were mummified after death and became intermediaries between the gods and the people.

For the Inca, the concept of private property didn't exist. Rather, the ruler was viewed as having descended from the Sun and, therefore, owning everything on Earth. The military was very important because each new ruler needed to ensure his place in eternity by securing new land, and that meant conquest. There was a state bureaucracy, manned by the nobility, which controlled the empire by traveling on a complex system of roads.

The Inca were excellent builders, stone cutters, and miners. Their skills are evident from the ruins of the **Temple of the Sun** in Cuzco and the temples of **Machu Picchu**. They never developed a system of writing. However, they were able to record census data and keep an accounting of harvests on *quipu*, a set of knotted strings.

IV.   UNIT 2: NETWORKS OF EXCHANGE

A. Height of the Middle Ages: Trading and Crusading

Given the new importance of trade, towns with wealthy merchants arose near the once all-powerful manors. Towns were chartered on lands controlled by feudal lords (the charters gave the townspeople certain rights), and within the towns, the middle-class merchants, or **burghers**, became politically powerful. Like their manorial predecessors, the towns had a great deal of independence within the empire but were intrinsically more interdependent than the self-sufficient manors of the feudal system. Eventually, towns formed alliances, not unlike a city-state structure. One of the most significant alliances, the **Hanseatic League**, had an economic basis; established in 1358, it controlled trade throughout much of northern Europe. One effect of the interdependence of the towns was to initiate a drive toward nationhood; another was to increase social mobility and flexibility among the classes.

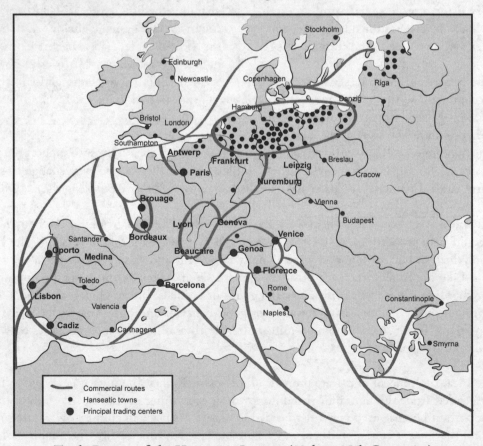

Trade Routes of the Hanseatic League (13th to 15th Centuries)

Among the greatest artistic achievements of the Middle Ages was its architecture, specifically its cathedrals. In the early Middle Ages, churches were built in the bulky Romanesque style; later architectural advancements led to what came to be called the Gothic style. Gothic cathedrals were designed to draw worshippers closer to God. To achieve this, architects of the day used "flying buttresses," which gave support for tall windows and vaulted ceilings. Over time, the cathedral became more than a place of worship; it became an art form and an arena for art.

The Birth of Scholasticism

Another important effect of people thinking more openly was the founding of universities, where men (not women) could study philosophy, law, and medicine, and learn from the advances made in Muslim cultures. In science, the ideas of Aristotle, Ptolemy, and other Greeks were brought to Europe through contacts with Islamic and Byzantine Empires (again, via trading and crusading). This progression, called **scholasticism**, also sometimes came into conflict with the church because it relied on reason rather than faith.

The church sponsored artists to adorn the inside of cathedrals with paintings and sculpture. Music, too, such as Gregorian chants, became an intrinsic part of ceremonies.

The **Crusades** were military campaigns undertaken by European Christians of the 11th through the 14th centuries to take over the Holy Land and convert Muslims and other non-Christians to Christianity). European contact with the Muslim world during the Crusades and over the trade routes helped spur new thought and broadened the perspective of these previously insular people. In time, people began to question organized religion (citing "reason"), which of course the church found threatening. This process of reasoning gave rise to **heresies**, religious practices or beliefs that do not conform to the traditional church doctrine. Sometimes what became defined as heresies were simply older beliefs that did not adapt to more mainstream changes in religious thought. In what may seem ironic today, many heretics wanted a return to the simpler ways of early Christianity; they rejected how worldly and wealthy the church had become.

Doubts about the supremacy of religious dogma continued to emerge until the beginning of the 13th century, when **Pope Innocent III** issued strict decrees on church doctrine. Under Innocent III, perceived heretics and Jews were frequently persecuted, and a fourth, ultimately unsuccessful crusade was attempted. During this crusade, which seemed motivated by greed, the Crusaders conquered—and sacked—the already Christian Constantinople, and declared a Latin Empire. (This empire was short-lived, lasting only some 50 years, and ended when the Byzantines overthrew the Latins in 1261.) A few years later, Pope Gregory IX set into motion the now-notorious **Inquisition**, a formalized interrogation and persecution process of perceived heretics. Punishment for so-called nonbelievers ranged from excommunication and exile to torture and execution. Because of the pervasiveness of the church and its ultimate power at this time, it is sometimes referred to as the **Universal Church** or the **Church Militant**.

Late in the 13th century, **Thomas Aquinas** (1225–1274 c.e.), a famous Christian theologian, made significant inroads in altering Christian thought. He wrote the *Summa Theologica*, which outlined his view that faith and reason are not in conflict, but that both are gifts from God and each can be used to enhance the other. His writings had a major impact on Christian thought, although the church remained a strict guardian of its own interpretations.

Focus On: The Bubonic Plague
Referred to as the Black Death, this epidemic originated in China, where it killed an estimated 35 million people. It spread rapidly through Europe in the mid-14th century. Its transmission was facilitated by new forms of commerce and trade, including Mongol control of the central Asian Silk Routes, that increased the interaction between Europe and Asia. First occurring in the 1330s, the epidemic spread westward with traders and merchants and arrived in Italian port cities as early as 1347. Crowded conditions in Europe's cities and the lack of adequate sanitation and medical knowledge all contributed to its rapid spread. Within only two years, more than a third of Europe's population was dead, and traditional social structures nearly collapsed. The dramatic changes brought by the epidemic sped up social and economic movements that were already impacting Europe. These included a shift toward a commercial economy, more individual freedoms, and development of new industries.

Urbanization

If trade is the way you make your living, chances are you are spending lots of time in cities. Traders and merchants needed a place to meet and conduct business and this period saw the growth of urban culture throughout the world, mostly as a result of trade contacts and networks. Along with trade, cities showcased the wealth and power of the rulers who both controlled and benefited from the trade. Urban centers usually developed along trade routes or in locations necessary for strategic defense.

In the early years, the most populous cities were in the Muslim world and China—cities that were part of the network of Silk Routes: Baghdad, Merv, and Chang'an. Prior to 1400, Constantinople was the only European city of any size and it was really considered part of the Eastern world. Along with their economic role, these cities became political and cultural centers for the new trade empires. After 1400, European cities begin to grow with Paris and the Italian city-states emerging as new trading powers.

B. The Rise and Fall of the Mongols

The Mongols, the epitome of a nomadic culture, existed as a society for a long time before they became a force on the broader world scene. The Mongols were superb horsemen and archers and probably could have been a world power early in the development of major civilizations. However, rivalries between tribes and clans kept them from unifying, so for centuries they fought with each other and remained fairly isolated from the rest of the world.

In the early 1200s, all that changed. Using his tremendous military and organizational skills, **Genghis Khan** (also spelled Chingiss Khan) unified the Mongol tribes and set them on a path of expansion that would lead to the largest empire the world had ever seen.

Genghis Khan unified several nomadic tribes of Mongolia and led the Mongol invasion of China in 1234, which was the beginning of the enormous Mongolian conquests. The **Mongol Empire** eventually spanned from the Pacific Ocean to Eastern Europe. Following the death of Genghis Khan, his followers splintered into different groups called hordes. The members of these hordes elected a new Great Khan after Ghenghis and his successor, but by the election of Kublai Khan these hordes, or Khanates, were largely independent of any sort of central leadership from the homeland in Mongolia proper. The **Golden Horde** conquered the region of modern-day

Russia. In China, **Kublai Khan** ruled. Mongols destroyed cities and were ruthless warriors, but once their domain was established, the empire was relatively peaceful. (This peace is sometimes called the *Pax Mongolica*.) The continuous empire allowed for the exchange of goods, ideas, and culture from one distant region to another. Mongols, who were illiterate, nomadic people prior to their conquests and education reforms brought about by Genghis Khan, eventually became assimilated into the cultures of the people they defeated.

Warning! You Are Now Entering a Golden-Age-Free Zone

One of the most striking things about the Mongols is that their empire was one of territory, infrastructure, and conquest, but not one of "culture." Because the Mongol Empire was so enormous and conquered so many different kinds of civilizations, it did not attempt to force a unified religion or way of life on its people. That being said, although the Mongols did not make many advances in the arts and sciences themselves, their superior infrastructure allowed for the exchange and spread of ideas. Genghis Khan also established the first pony express and postal system and gave tax breaks to teachers and clerics within his empire. In other ways, however, the Mongol Empire had a profoundly negative impact on conquered cultures, stifling cultural growth rather than contributing to it by having been so brutal in their initial raids.

Contrast Them: The Mongol Empire and All Other Major Civilizations

The Mongol Empire was larger than any of the empires that had existed up to that point in time. Yet rather than imposing its own cultural developments on the areas it conquered, it generally accepted or ignored those of the people it conquered. Unlike the sultans who took over India, the Mongols allowed their subjects to practice their own religions without interference. It should be pointed out that because the Mongol empire was so expansive, it tied much of the world together and served as a conduit across which ideas and culture spread from the Pacific to the Mediterranean and vice versa. It's just that it wasn't the Mongols' own culture.

Timur Wasn't Timid

In addition to invading Russia, Persia, Central Asia, and China, the Mongols also found time on their itinerary for a layover in India. They swept in under their leader, the untamed Timur Lang, who destroyed just about everything in sight and massacred thousands, and then just as quickly swept out. The sultanate was destroyed, but after **Timur Lang** (sometimes referred to as **Tamerlane**) returned to his capital in Samarkand, the Mongols pulled out as well. Just a few years later, the sultanate was restored. Islam continued to grow in India for the next few centuries under the Mongol Empire, even as many Hindus hung on to their beliefs. Look for more on this later.

How the Mongols Did It: No Rest Until Conquest

Imagine that you live in a village that lies in the path of an advancing Mongol horde. You've heard the stories. If you put up a fight, they'll pummel you. If you retreat to your house, they'll burn it. If you organize a resistance in your place of worship or civic building, they'll level it. You've also heard that if you just give in, they might spare your city, but they also might not. They're not really interested in changing your culture. So your only real choice, if you want to stay alive, is to give in. If you do, you may or may not be able to keep your life and your culture, but if you don't, you'll suffer a certainly grotesque death. What would you do?

In the 1200s and 1300s, a lot of people gave in, and those who did not met their death. The Mongols weren't called ruthless warriors for nothing. They knew how to fight, but they were more than fierce fighters. They were also highly organized and highly mobile. Unlike the much-feared Roman army, which in its heyday could cover about 25 miles per day, the Mongol horsemen could cover about 90. Their bows, designed to be launched from horseback, had a range of up to 300 yards, way more than anybody else's. Their armies were divided into units, which were further separated into light and heavy cavalries and scouting units. They were extremely motivated—Genghis Khan punished traitors swiftly and rewarded the courageous generously. They were stealthy—they had an extensive network of spies who scouted their enemies before battle. Finally, their goals were made unmistakably clear—the consequences of putting up a fight against the Mongols meant certain destruction of the entire village, so most learned not to resist. In short, they were really, really good at what they did: conquering.

The Mongol Impact

The Mongols were great diffusers of culture. In some cases, Mongols assimilated into the cultures they conquered. For example, in Persia, most Mongols became Muslim. Elsewhere, Mongolian culture remained separate from the conquered people. In China, for example, Kublai Khan, the grandson of Genghis, thwarted Mongolization by prohibiting intermarriage as well as forbidding Chinese to learn the Mongol language. When the Chinese finally kicked out the Mongols in 1368, they established the Ming Dynasty rooted in traditional Chinese identity and practices.

There were two major consequences of Mongol rule. The first is that Russia, which was conquered by the Golden Horde and treated as a vassal state, didn't unify or culturally develop as quickly as its European neighbors to the west. The second is that world trade, cultural diffusion, and global awareness grew. Think about it: the Mongol empire touched Europe and very nearly touched Japan. It stretched southward to Persia and India, making possible not only trade but also the transmission of the Black Death (Bubonic Plague) in the 14th century. This single empire touched nearly all the major civilizations of the day. So, as strange as it sounds, the often brutal Mongols, in their own way, brought the world together. By 1450, as the Mongol Empire was well in decline, the world would never again be disconnected.

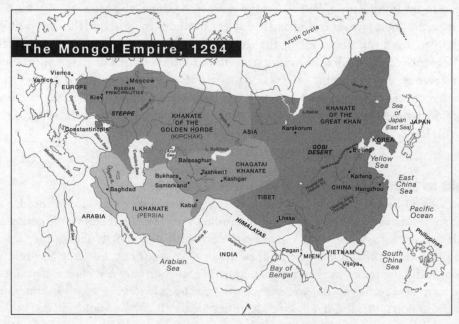

Map of the Mongol Khanates

C. Mali and Songhai

Why were the Islamic traders so interested in trading with west African kingdoms? Because in Mali (about 1200–1450 C.E.), there were tons, and we mean tons, of gold. A little sand in your eyes was probably worth some gold in your hand. So the Islamic traders kept coming. The constant trade brought more than just Islamic goods to Ghana and Mali; it brought Islam.

One of the greatest Malian rulers, **Mansa Musa**, built a capital at Timbuktu and expanded the kingdom well beyond the bounds of Ghana. In 1324, Musa made a pilgrimage to Mecca (remember the Five Pillars of Islam?) complete with an entourage of hundreds of gold-carrying servants and camels. The journey was so extravagant, so long, and so impressive to everyone who saw it that Musa became an overnight international sensation. Had the Musa moment occurred in the Internet age, you can bet it would have been all over social media.

The largest empire in west Africa was formed in the mid-15th century, when Songhai ruler Sonni Ali conquered the entire region and established the Songhai Empire. The Songhai Empire lasted until around 1600 C.E., and during its reign, Timbuktu became a major cultural center, complete with a university that drew scholars from around the Islamic world.

D. Chinese Technology

At the height of the Song Dynasty, China was relatively stable. One of the many reasons for the stability was the bureaucratic system that was based on merit through the use of the civil service examinations. Song rulers continued to modify the civil service examination, but kept it focused on Confucian principles, which created a large core of educated, talented, and loyal government workers. The Song also built an extensive transportation and communication network, including canals. They developed new business practices, including the introduction of paper money and letters of credit. All of this, of course, led to increased trade and cultural diffusion.

The Song Dynasty, under pressure from northern nomads, withdrew to the south and established a capital city at Hangzhou, the southern end of the Grand Canal. Here they concentrated on developing an industrial society, building on many of the ideas of the previous dynasty. An early form of **movable type** resulted in an increase in literacy and bureaucrats among the lower classes. Printed books also spread agricultural and technological knowledge, leading to an increase in productivity and population growth. By the 1100s, the Song were an urban population with some of the largest cities in the world. Their wealth was based in part on their powerful navy and their participation in international trade throughout southeast Asia.

During the Song Dynasty, new technologies were applied to the military. Gunpowder started to be used in primitive weapons. The magnetic compass, watertight bulkheads, and sternpost rudders made the Chinese junks, as their ships were called, the best of their time. The junks were also used as merchant ships, of course.

Between 800 and 1100, iron production increased tenfold to about 120,000 tons per year, rivaling the British production of iron centuries later (in the 1700s). Song technology also included the production of steel using water-wheel-driven bellows to produce the needed temperatures.

The introduction of Champa, a fast-ripening rice from Vietnam, linked with new agricultural techniques, increased food supplies. This led to a rapid population rise from 600 to 1200 C.E. China's population more than doubled, increasing from 45 million to 115 million. The urban centers expanded greatly.

E. Review of Interactions Among Cultures

The purpose of this section is to help you pull together the history from this time period and view it from a global perspective. The examples below are by no means an exhaustive list of the ways that civilizations or groups of people interacted from 1200 to 1450. To the contrary, they are examples that serve as a starting point in your studies. We strongly suggest that you add examples to the ones below as you work your way through this review and your materials from class.

Trade Networks and Cultural Diffusion

Trade has always been a big deal, historically speaking. Getting stuff and buying stuff is a huge incentive behind interactions. If you have everything you need and want, you can live in isolation. If you don't, and somebody else down the road has what you want, you've got two choices: take it or trade for it. If you're not into the whole conquest thing, then trading is probably your best option.

From 1200 to 1450, trade exploded onto the world scene—so much so that the world after 1450 is inseparable from global interaction. Let's quickly review the global trade routes.

- The Hanseatic League (more details in this section)
- The Silk Road (used heavily from about 1200 C.E. until about 1600 C.E.—more on that later)
- The land routes of the Mongols
- Trade between China and Japan
- Trade between India and Persia
- The Trans-Saharan trade routes between west Africa and the Islamic Empire

Remember, too, that trade was not only aided by better boats and better roads, but also by monetary systems, lines of credit, and accounting methods that helped business boom. Record keeping and money management are key. If you're able to keep records or borrow money, you are by definition establishing a business relationship that extends into the future. Once you start thinking about a regular business-trade relationship extending into the future, you can get people to invest in that future, and pretty soon the wheels of international business are going 'round and 'round.

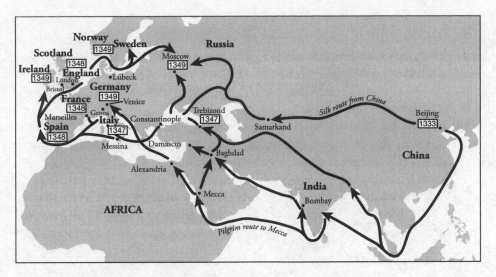

Spread of the Black Death (1333–1349 C.E.)

The trade routes are important, of course, not just because of their impact on business, but also because of their role in cultural diffusion. It is over the trade routes that religions and languages spread. It is over the trade routes that literature and art and ideas spread. And, unfortunately, it is over the trade routes that disease and plague sometimes spread. The **Bubonic Plague** (also called the Black Death) started in Asia in the 14th century and was carried by merchants along the trade routes all the way to Europe, where it destroyed entire communities and killed as many as one out of every three people in Western Europe. The Plague quickened the decline of feudal society because many manors weren't able to function.

In addition to the trade routes mentioned above, there's one that we haven't discussed in detail yet—the Indian Ocean Trade. It's important, so we'll go into it in some detail.

Indian Ocean Trade

Throughout the period covered in this chapter, the Persians and the Arabs dominated the **Indian Ocean Trade**. Their trade routes connected ports in western India to ports in the Persian Gulf, which in turn were connected to ports in eastern Africa.

Unlike boats that were used on the Mediterranean Sea, boats that sailed the Indian Ocean were, necessarily, more resilient to the large waves common in those waters. The

The benefits of the Indian Ocean trade network were not limited to coastal communities. **Great Zimbabwe** was a thriving city located in what is now Zimbabwe and Mozambique. From the 11th to 15th centuries, Great Zimbabwe served as a trading empire with river access to the southeastern coast of Africa. Great Zimbabwe's fortuitous location on the most direct route between Africa's gold mines and the Indian Ocean ports made it the de facto distributor of African gold to the rest of the world.

traders learned to understand the monsoon seasons and direction of the winds and scheduled their voyages accordingly. Despite these difficulties, the Indian Ocean trade routes were relatively safe, especially when compared to those on the Mediterranean, where constant warfare was a problem.

Since sailors often married the local women at the ends of their trade routes, cultures started to intermix rapidly. Many sailors took foreign wives home and created bilingual and bicultural families.

Vibrant Indian Ocean Communities

Some 1,000 years before Christopher Columbus crossed the Atlantic Ocean, a robust trade network developed across the Indian Ocean, leading to cultural diffusion between communities that were settled thousands of miles away from one another.

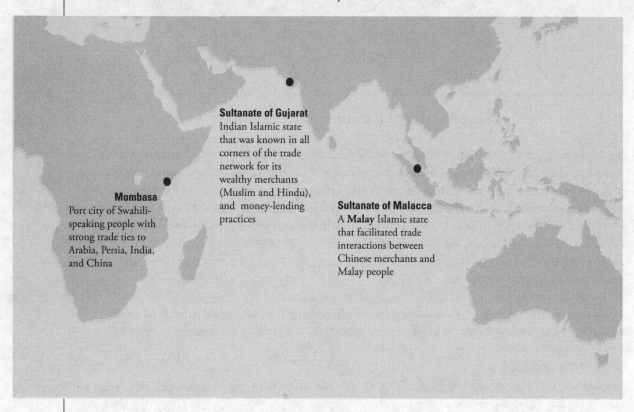

Mombasa
Port city of Swahili-speaking people with strong trade ties to Arabia, Persia, India, and China

Sultanate of Gujarat
Indian Islamic state that was known in all corners of the trade network for its wealthy merchants (Muslim and Hindu), and money-lending practices

Sultanate of Malacca
A **Malay** Islamic state that facilitated trade interactions between Chinese merchants and Malay people

Vibrant Indian Ocean Map

More on the Silk Road

You may already know that the Silk Road connected China to the Mediterranean cultures even way back in the early days of the Roman Empire. You also need to know that the Silk Road was used heavily again from about 1200 C.E. until about 1600 C.E., during the reign of the Mongols. The Silk Road was spotted with trade towns throughout Central Asia, such as **Kashgar** and **Samarkand**, as well as smaller inns, known as caravanserais, for travelers to rest and, as a result, exchange elements of culture with other travelers. Such transfers led to an effective numbering system arriving in Europe and a common script, known as Uyghur, that standardized much of the trade communication in Central Asia.

The important thing to know about the Silk Road is that it carried so much more than silk. It carried porcelain and paper. It carried military technologies. It carried religions, such as

Buddhism, Islam, and Christianity. It carried food. Because it extended so far and was used for so long, it's safe to say that East met West on the Silk Road. It's impossible to have a discussion about international trade and cultural diffusion without mentioning it by name.

More on the Hanseatic League

As you already know, the Hanseatic League was a collection of city-states in the Baltic and North Sea regions of Europe that banded together in 1241 c.e. to establish common trade practices, fight off pirates and foreign governments, and essentially establish a trade monopoly from the region to much of the rest of the world. It worked for a few hundred years. More than 100 cities joined the league. The result was enormous for two reasons. First, it resulted in a substantial middle class in northern Europe, a development that would drive changes in that region in later centuries (more on that in the next chapter). Second, it set a precedent for large, European trading operations that profoundly affected the Dutch and the English, which would also deeply affect the broader world in later centuries.

Was There a Global Trade Network?

If you think about it, after about 1200 c.e. or so, the world was very interconnected. Europe was trading with the Islamic world and Russia. The Islamic world was trading with Africa, India, and China. India was trading with China and eastern Africa. China was trading with Japan and southeast Europe. If you link up all the trade routes, goods could make their way from England to Persia to India to Japan. They could also travel to points north and south, from Muscovy to Mali.

The global network wasn't entirely controlled by one entity or laid out by one trading organization. It was more like a web of interconnected but highly independent parts. It required lots of managers at each site. It required people to be linked up through third and even fourth parties. No one person was managing it, yet almost all major civilizations (except those in the Americas) were a part of it. In short, it was like the Internet, only in geographic space instead of cyberspace.

Expansion of Religion and Empire: Culture Clash

One of the most significant influences on cultural interaction and diffusion has been the expansion of empires and the intentional diffusion of religion. Keep in mind that when we say intentional diffusion of religion, we mean methods like missionary work or religious warfare. This is opposed to the natural spread of religious ideas that occurs when people come into contact with each other, such as over trade routes.

When you think about it, the bulk of this chapter is about two things: the expansion of religion and empires leading to cultural contact, or the relative isolationism that resulted under the feudal systems in Europe and Japan. Another way to encapsulate this period: a time fueled by conquest and religious expansion. We've talked a lot about the efforts of expansionists that succeeded.

Other Reasons People Were on the Move

Interaction among and within civilizations occurred during this period in history for many reasons other than trade or conquest. As populations grew, people needed more room to spread out. This not only led to huge movements of people, such as the Germanic tribes into southern Europe, but also to more crowded conditions on the manor or in small towns. The result was the burgeoning of ever-larger cities; once the cities became larger, more opportunities were created there, which pulled more and more people in from the countryside.

Some cities grew not just because of a general population increase, but because they were intentionally established as centers of civilization. Think about the empires in this chapter. The eastern Roman Empire, which of course became the Byzantine Empire, was headquartered at Constantinople, which was specifically built as a center to draw people. In fact, capitals were moved all the time to create an aura of a rising empire. The Islamic Empire moved to Baghdad. The Mongols built a city at Samarkand, as did the Malians at Timbuktu, and the Aztecs at Tenochtitlan. The list goes on and on. Every time an empire built a new city to flaunt itself, it drew thousands of people. This is true especially to the degree that these civilizations built universities, which by their nature drew people from around the empire. That meant people who weren't living in the same city in the past were now living together. The result? More cultural diffusion.

Pilgrimages were a third reason that people during this time period were constantly on the move. Rome and Constantinople certainly attracted thousands to their grand cathedrals, but the Islamic duty to travel to Mecca was no doubt the most significant destination of religious pilgrimages. Imagine the thousands upon thousands who traveled from the vast reaches of the Islamic world. Imagine the amount of cultural diffusion that occurred as a result. Just think of Mansa Musa and you'll be convinced.

Notable Global Travelers

Xuanzang, a Chinese Buddhist monk, traveled throughout the T'ang Dynasty and into India to understand how Buddhism is practiced in different parts of Asia. **Marco Polo,** a merchant from Venice, made his way to China and back to Europe.

Islamic traveler **Ibn Battuta** experienced unbelievable adventures (seriously, his travels are more interesting than any Indiana Jones movie) on his way through the Islamic world into India and China before returning to Africa.

Margery Kempe, a Christian from England, documented her travels to religious sites throughout Europe and the Holy Land in a book chronicling her spiritual journey.

Each of these travelers wrote extensively of their journeys. When people in their homelands read about their travels, they developed an understanding of cultures in other parts of the world. Along their travels these three men and woman also brought elements of various cultures to their destination.

V. TECHNOLOGY AND INNOVATIONS, 600 C.E.–1450

It was interaction that led to innovation. This period is marked by expanding trade, expanding empires, and expanding interactions. All led to increased wealth, frequent cultural borrowing, and the development of new ideas. Many of these new innovations came from the eastern societies—China and India, filtered through the Islamic world. By 1450, most of these new ideas had made their way back to Europe, following the Crusaders, merchants, and missionaries.

Islamic World	China
paper mills (from China)	gunpowder cannons
universities	movable type
astrolabe and sextant	paper currency
algebra (from Greece)	porcelain
chess (from India)	terrace farming
modern soap formula	water-powered mills
guns and cannons (from China)	cotton sails
mechanical pendulum clock	water clock
distilled alcohol	magnetic compass
surgical instruments (syringe etc.)	state-run factories

Trade Networks and Agriculture

In addition to ideas that began to move around the world, trade networks moved agricultural products. Some of these would result in great environmental changes, influence trade networks, and motivate exploration and conquest.

VI. CHANGES AND CONTINUITIES IN THE ROLE OF WOMEN

The spread of Islam, the openness of Christianity and Buddhism, the development of new empires based on wealth and acquisition of property, and the revitalization of neo-Confucianism impacted the status of women around the world. Restrictions on women's freedoms depended on which caste or class they belonged to. At the uppermost levels, a woman could overcome the status of her gender and assume leadership roles if there was no male heir or if the male heir was very young. Generally, however, as societies became more urban and wealthy, women, especially those of the elite or upper classes, had their freedoms further restricted even as their status in society rose. This can be seen in the increased veiling of women in the Islamic world and among Christians in the Mediterranean world (especially Italy and Spain), the custom of foot binding in neo-Confucian China, and the young age of marriage in South Asia.

Trade and the arrival of new religions did not significantly change the role of women in African societies—as pastoral nomads, many of the African societies were relatively egalitarian. Even when sedentary lifestyles developed, women had a great deal of freedom and societies were sometimes matrilineal and matriarchal. Women commanded a bride-price rather than having to give a dowry, and were considered a valuable source of wealth. "Mother of the King" was a political office in many African societies, and women participated in specific religious rituals controlled solely by women. Although both Islam and Christianity found converts in Africa, women were less eager to convert than men and the practice of veiling was met with mixed reactions.

Changes in the status and role of women included access to more education as societies continued to prosper and interact. This is true of the Confucian cultures of China and Japan, where women were highly literate and expected to understand proper virtue and their role in the household. Overall, however, even when they were educated and wealthy, most women had far less power than their male counterparts and were subject to any number of cultural and legal restrictions.

Women's Status in Ancient Societies			
Europe	**Islam**	**India**	**China**
strict and patriarchal social divisions	equality in religion, but separate in mosque	strict patriarchal caste system	strict Confucian social order and guidelines for virtuous behavior
could inherit land and take oaths of vassalage, but property belonged to husband	received half inheritance of male children	child marriages	access to dowries and owned businesses
could bring a court case, but not participate in decision	testimony had less weight than that of males	practice of *sati* for widows	widow to remain with son; no property if remarried
division of labor; women in textiles		family textile labor	silk weaving as female occupation
Christian monogamy	concubines and seclusion in harems	marriage limited to caste members	concubines and seclusion in harems
education limited to upper-class males	literate society	education limited	literate society, but state education limited to men
did not recognize illegitimate children	all children are seen as legitimate		
veiling of upper class	veiling in public	*purdah*: veiling or seclusion	foot binding

VII.   PULLING IT ALL TOGETHER

There's no question that the spread and growth of religion had enormous consequences during this time period. There's also no question that the issue of centralization versus noncentralization seems to have an impact on a civilization. Look at what it meant for Europe, Japan, China, and India. Beyond the issues of interaction, centralization, and the growth of religion, there's something else you should be thinking about: how to organize the world in your head.

Today, we have clear boundaries between countries, but in addition to using those political boundaries, we talk of cultural regions all the time. We'll say things like "the West" or "the East." That's fine, but where's the dividing line? Is modern-day Russia part of the East or the West? What about Saudi Arabia? What about Japan?

Moreover, we often split even our own country into manageable pieces that don't have specific, exact geographic boundaries. In the United States, for example, when one refers to "the South," it's usually in reference to a culture rather than a specific geographical place. Is Florida part of "the South"? Northern Florida probably is, but the rest of Florida has a very different feel.

This kind of stuff is a big deal for the AP test writers. Sometimes it's easier to think about and write about history in terms of cultural areas rather than political boundaries. "The Islamic World," for example, is used to refer not only to countries that are predominately Muslim, but also communities and individuals within non-Muslim countries who participate in the culture of Islam. Or think about the "Jewish community." In the time period covered by this chapter, Jews were scattered throughout Europe, Africa, and Asia. There was no Jewish state, only a Jewish culture. Nevertheless, the Jewish culture maintained its identity.

You might want to think of the world in terms of major cultural divisions. Religions help. You can think of developments in the Christian sphere, the Islamic sphere, the Hindu sphere, and the Buddhist sphere. Don't forget, though, that some of these spheres overlap, and some of them coexist with other religions or belief systems like Confucianism and Buddhism. You can also think of developments in terms of expanding empires and feudal systems. Even more generally, think of the world in terms of cultures that interacted and those that did not.

However you choose to think about the world, whether in terms of cultural areas or structural similarities, the important thing is that you try to analyze the history. Doing so will force you to make comparisons between cultures, which is exactly the kind of critical thinking you need to do on the AP World History: Modern Exam. The more you think about how these cultures can be organized, the more familiar you'll be with world history.

CHAPTER 6 KEY TERMS

Bhakti	Bourbons	Pope Innocent III
Sufis	Hundred Years' War	Inquisition
Baghdad	Queen Isabella	Universal Church
Nasir al-Din al-Tusi	Ferdinand	Church Militant
Mamluks	Spanish Inquisition	Thomas Aquinas
Mongols	Tatars	Genghis Khan
Ottoman Turks	Czar	Mongol Empire
Middle Ages	Ivan the Terrible	Golden Horde
Feudalism	Ming Dynasty	Kublai Khan
nobles	foot binding	Timur Lang
vassals	shogun	Tamerlane
peasants	Code of Bushido	Mansa Musa
fiefs	Delhi Sultanate	movable type
manors	Rajput Kingdoms	Bubonic Plague
three-field system	Khmer Empire	Indian Ocean Trade
code of chivalry	Angor Wat	Great Zimbabwe
primogeniture	Hausa	Kashgar
serfs	Tenochtitlan	Samarkand
interregnum	Temple of the Sun	Xuanzang
William the Conqueror	Machu Picchu	Marco Polo
Magna Carta	burghers	Ibn Battuta
King Hugh Capet	Hanseatic League	Margery Kempe
Joan of Arc	Crusades	

Chapter 6 Drill

See the end of the chapter for the answers and explanations.

Questions 1–4 refer to the passage below.

The king rarely goes out; but, to chant the liturgy and worship, on every seventh day he proceeds by way of this tunnel to the hall of worship where, in performing divine service, he is attended by a suite of over fifty men. But few amongst the people know the king's face; if he goes out he sits on horseback, protected by an umbrella; the head of his horse is adorned with gold, jade, pearls and other jewels. Every year the king of the country of Ta-shih [citizens of the Caliphate] who is styled *Su-tan* [Sultan] sends tribute-bearers, and if in the country some trouble is apprehended, he gets the Ta-shih to use their military force in restoring order.

Passage regarding the city of Antioch from *A Description of Barbarian Nations, Records of Foreign People,* a 13th century Chinese text.

1. The text of this passage is best viewed as evidence of which of the following continuities of the thirteenth century?

   (A) Mongol destruction of Middle Eastern cultures
   (B) Christian dominance in Medieval Europe
   (C) An ongoing economic connection between East Asia and the Middle East
   (D) The strength of the caliphates' militaries over invading armies

2. The customs of the king, as described in the passage, are most strongly influenced by which of the following?

   (A) Christianity
   (B) Confucianism
   (C) Buddhism
   (D) Islam

3. Which of the following best explains the motivation behind sending out tribute-bearers?

   (A) To acknowledge control over certain foreign regions
   (B) To ensure ongoing wealth for the caliphate
   (C) To provoke military action
   (D) To maintain a balance of trade with other countries

4. This excerpt was written in the context of which of the following?

   (A) A decline in Silk Road trade activities
   (B) A Chinese Golden Age
   (C) Mongol control spanning from Europe to Asia
   (D) The spread of medieval Christendom

Questions 5–7 refer to the image below.

Woodcut of a traditional West African village along the Niger River, 14th century.

5. The people of this village most likely considered them-
    selves part of

    (A) the Song Dynasty
    (B) the Khmer Empire
    (C) the Mali Empire
    (D) the Hanseatic League

6. At the time, it is most likely that Arabic traders visited
    this village primarily to

    (A) purchase gold
    (B) capture enslaved people
    (C) enforce religious restrictions
    (D) avoid punitive taxes

7. To the outside world, this region's Islamic identity was
    emphasized most strongly by which of the following?

    (A) Its conquering of neighboring regions in the name
        of Allah
    (B) Its prohibition of consuming pork products
    (C) Its practice of praying five times per day
    (D) Mansa Kankan Musa I's visit to Mecca via Egypt

Questions 8–10 refer to the passage below.

(1) FIRST, THAT WE HAVE GRANTED TO GOD, and by this present charter have confirmed for us and our heirs in perpetuity, that the English Church shall be free, and shall have its rights undiminished, and its liberties unimpaired. That we wish this so to be observed, appears from the fact that of our own free will, before the outbreak of the present dispute between us and our barons, we granted and confirmed by charter the freedom of the Church's elections - a right reckoned to be of the greatest necessity and importance to it - and caused this to be confirmed by Pope Innocent III. This freedom we shall observe ourselves, and desire to be observed in good faith by our heirs in perpetuity.

(39) No free man shall be seized or imprisoned, or stripped of his rights or possessions, or outlawed or exiled, or deprived of his standing in any other way, nor will we proceed with force against him, or send others to do so, except by the lawful judgement of his equals or by the law of the land.

(40) To no one will we sell, to no one deny or delay right or justice.

The Magna Carta, 1215.

8. The demands for freedom both for the English church and from punishment reflect which of the following during this period?

(A) The extent of indentured servitude that existed at this time

(B) The tendency of the English king to exploit his power

(C) The abuses of the Roman Catholic church

(D) The ongoing conflict between religion and science

9. At the time of the signing of this document, which of the following was the dominant socioeconomic structure of European society?

(A) absolutism

(B) conservatism

(C) empiricism

(D) feudalism

10. This passage could be used as evidence for which of the following conclusions?

(A) England was among the first nations in Europe to use a written document to attempt to limit royal power

(B) The people of England had a better grasp on political struggles than did the people of other nations

(C) The barons of England were totally opposed to the existence of royalty

(D) The English church continued to decline as a result of the failure to enforce this charter

TIMELINE OF MAJOR DEVELOPMENTS, 1200 C.E.–1450

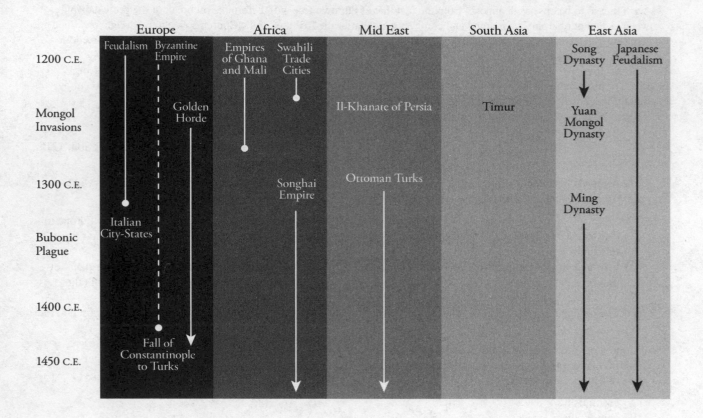

CHAPTER 6 DRILL EXPLANATIONS

1. **C** Knowing that the text was from a 13th-century Chinese source gives us some important clues. In the 13th century, China saw the beginning of the Yuan Dynasty—a time when China was ruled by the Mongols. The Mongols promoted cultural diffusion through well-maintained trade routes, which is consistent with (C). While (A) mentions the Mongols, it is incorrect, as the Mongols were largely tolerant of the cultures under their rule (and after all, Middle Eastern culture to this day contains elements from before the 13th century, so the Mongols surely did not destroy it). The references to the caliphate lead us to understand that the author is describing an Islamic culture, not a Christian one. Eliminate (B). While the author mentions the military, it does not address how it compares to any invading armies. Eliminate (D).

2. **D** The reference to chanting liturgy every seventh day points toward a Western Abrahamic religion since the king observes the Sabbath. This would point toward either Christianity or Islam. Eliminate (B) and (C). The reference to the caliphate and the knowledge that Antioch (in modern-day Syria) was under Muslim control should steer your thinking to Islam, (D), which is correct. Eliminate (A).

3. **A** Tributes were typically used to demonstrate loyalty to a ruling entity. Therefore, (A) is what you should be looking for. Tributes would not be of significant enough value to buoy the economy of an entire caliphate, so eliminate (B). Choice (C) is incorrect as tributes were collected following a conquest, as a way of maintaining peace. Finally, eliminate (D) since tributes confer dominance from one side of the relationship, not an equal exchange.

4. **C** This text was written in the 13th century, the start of Mongol dominance across Eurasia. Knowing this contextual information will lead you to (C), which is the correct answer. The Silk Road was strengthened and protected under Mongol watch, so (A) is incorrect. Christianity was largely relegated to Europe and the era of European imperialism was still a couple centuries away, so eliminate (D). Finally, recall that the Mongol empire was one of territory, infrastructure, and conquest, but not one that made many advances in the arts and sciences themselves (though they did allow for the spread of other cultures throughout their empire). Eliminate (B).

5. **C** For West Africans in the fourteenth century, there was only one empire available to join—the Mali Empire. Founded by Sundiata Keita, who led a revolt against the Soso in the thirteenth century, the Mali Empire was extraordinarily wealthy. It boasted extensive trading routes, two major trading centers (Timbuktu and Gao), and an administrative government that kept good order. The empire reached its peak at that time, then gradually decreased in relevance and power over the next two centuries.

6. **A** The Mali Empire was rich in two natural commodities prized by the rest of the world: gold and salt. Islamic traders from the Arabic lands made the long journey across northern Africa and the Sahara to trade for either or both—and the salt was often valued as much as the gold! There is little evidence of slavery at this point, so eliminate (B). The entire region was Islamic, the people were allowed freedom of worship, so it was mostly in name only; eliminate (C). Finally, punitive taxes were quite strongly enforced in the Mali Empire—after all, charging tax on every transaction is how the government of such a commerce-driven society becomes rich—so eliminate (D).

7. **D** The most famous king of the Mali Empire, Mansa Kankan Musa I, made a pilgrimage to Mecca (in modern-day Saudi Arabia) that set the Islamic world talking. On his way, his entourage stopped in Egypt, and evidently they spent so much gold in Cairo that the gold market was depressed for the next several years by the massive influx of the commodity. For centuries, his likeness was printed on maps bearing nuggets of gold. There is no evidence that (A), (B), or (C) were especially notable or even present in the Mali Empire.

8. **B** The English king at the time, King John, ruled through force, and his decisions weren't based on rule of law. The land-owning barons in England, particularly in the northeast, were wary of his excesses and began a rebellion. They marched on several major cities, capturing London, resulting in more defections to their cause. Only then did King John agree to sit down and negotiate, which is when they presented him with the Magna Carta. It's viewed as the first document that led to the establishment of a constitution, a parliament, and other such markers of a representative democracy. There is no evidence that the other answer choices are based in fact. Choice (D) in particular didn't occur for another four hundred years, when science finally rose to prominence.

9. **D** Feudalism dominated European life for nearly eight hundred years, from the Dark Ages through the Renaissance. Put broadly, it was a system of customs that were all centered around the rough division of society into three classes: the landowners (nobility), the clergy (priests), and the land-renters (serfs). Choice (A), absolutism, wouldn't exist for a few hundred more years, so eliminate it. Neither would (B), conservatism, or (C), empiricism, so eliminate those as well.

10. **A** The Magna Carta stands as the first European document in the medieval era to attempt to limit royal power. In fact, historians draw a line from this document to later ones, such as the English Bill of Rights, that also attempted to limit or at least redefine the power of the king. We don't know anything about the people of England versus the people of other European nations, so eliminate (B). The barons weren't necessarily opposed to the kingship in general, only to King John's unfair exploitation of power, so eliminate (C). The English church continued to grow in the centuries following, particularly in the sixteenth century, when Henry VIII separated the English church from Rome, forming the Anglican church. Eliminate (D).

Chapter 7
Period 2,
c. 1450 to c. 1750

Unit 3: Land-Based
Empires
Unit 4: Transoceanic
Interconnections

I. CHAPTER OVERVIEW

By 1450, global interaction really got cranking. The rise of Europe as a major player on the world scene was very important during this time period, and because the AP focuses so much on the interaction among cultures, most of the regions of the world in this chapter are discussed in terms of their relation to Europe.

As with the previous chapter, we suggest that you read through this chapter once, and then go back and focus on the things that you're not entirely clear about. To help you do that, here's the chapter outline:

I.   Chapter Overview

   You're reading it now.

II.   Stay Focused on the Big Picture

   Organize the many events that occurred during the 300 years covered in this chapter into some big-picture concepts.

III.   Unit 3: Land-Based Empires

   Here's how we've organized the information.

   A.   Major European Developments
   B.   Islamic Gunpowder Empires
   C.   Africa
   D.   Isolated Asia
   E.   Resistance

IV.   Unit 4: Transoceanic Interconnections

   Here's how we've organized it:

   A.   European Exploration and Expansion
   B.   The New World: Accidental Empire
   C.   Disease: The Ultimate Weapon of Mass Destruction
   D.   The Encomienda System
   E.   The African Slave Trade
   F.   The Columbian Exchange
   G.   The Commercial Revolution

V.   Technology and Innovations, 1450–1750

VI.   Changes and Continuities in the Role of Women

   Concubines, queens, and business women

VII.   Pulling It All Together

   Focus on the big-picture concepts now that you've reviewed the details.

II.   STAY FOCUSED ON THE BIG PICTURE

As you review the details of the civilizations in this chapter for each unit, stay focused on the following four big-picture concepts:

For **Unit 3**, ask yourself:

1.   Why did Europe become a dominant power during this time period? Was it because European nations vied for world dominance while other civilizations didn't, or because of technological superiority? Was it for some other reason? Why did some of the European nation-states develop vast empires while others did not? What motivated Europeans to explore, conquer, and colonize? There are lots of legitimate answers to these questions, and the content of this chapter will help you think about some of them.

2.   What were some of the differences among the ways in which non-European cultures interacted with Europe? What influences contributed to these differences? What were the consequences? You'll notice that European powers penetrated different parts of the globe to different degrees. Pay attention to why this was true—it will tell you a lot not only about Europe, but also about those individual non-European cultures as well.

For **Unit 4**, ask yourself:

3.   How did the global economy change during this time period? What was the impact on the world's civilizations? As you read, notice how economic considerations drove much of the world's interactions. Pay attention to how the larger global economy impacted the various regions of the globe.

4.   What were the impacts of global interaction on the environment? Conversely, what were the impacts of the environment on human societies? What ideas, diseases, plants, and animals traveled the globe along with human settlement? The need for new resources brought massive changes, but at the same time, the environment acted on human societies, sometimes with disastrous consequences. Pay attention to the effects of the 500-year period of global cooling that began around 1500 and resulted in shortages of crops, famines, and susceptibility to diseases.

III.   UNIT 3: LAND-BASED EMPIRES

A. Major European Developments

During the three centuries covered in this chapter, profound changes occurred on the European continent. These changes affected life on all levels: the way people viewed themselves (their past, their present, and their future potential), the way governments viewed their authority, the way religion intersected with politics and individuality, and the way Europeans thought about and interacted with the rest of the world.

By the end of these 300 years, the European countries had used their new technologies, new ideas of governing, and new forms of economic organization to become the dominant world powers. Much of their success was based on competition and rivalry as they raced to secure faster trade routes and new colonial possessions, and attempted to gain control of key resources. However, much of their success came at the expense of the land-based empires of Asia and the declining empires in the Americas.

While the previous chapter was all about interactions, this one covers the period of European maritime empire-building that resulted from those initial interactions across Asia and the Indian Ocean. As you review the enormous developments in Parts A and B below, think about how they were linked together and impacted each other.

Revolutions in European Thought and Expression

By the 1300s, much of Europe had been Christian for a thousand years. The feudal system had dominated the political and social structures for several hundred years, and the ancient classical civilizations of Greece and Rome had faded into the ancient past.

The history of the Middle Ages was dominated by local issues, a concern with salvation, territorial disputes, disease and famine, limited access to education, and small-scale trade. As you read in the last chapter, near the end of the Middle Ages, countries began to unify under centralized rule. The Crusades exposed Christians to the advanced Islamic civilizations, increased trade fueled contact with other parts of the world, and universities became great centers of learning. This increased contact with foreign powers, along with scholasticism, exposed Europeans not only to developments in the rest of the world but also to history. The Byzantine and Islamic Empires had preserved much of the heritage of ancient Greece and Rome, even as they built unique civilizations of their own and made huge contributions to ancient texts, especially in the areas of mathematics and science. As Europe expanded its worldview and interacted more frequently with these two empires, it placed a greater emphasis on its own classical past.

The combination of a rediscovered past and a productive present led to major changes in the way Europeans viewed the world and themselves. These new perspectives led to four massive cultural movements: the Renaissance, the Protestant Reformation, the Scientific Revolution, and the Enlightenment. These revolutions in expression and thought changed the world. In a span of just a few hundred years, Europe went from being a backward outpost on the perimeter of the major civilizations to the east to the home of some of the most dominant civilizations in the world.

We'll talk about the details of European global exploration and expansion later in this chapter. In the meantime, you should understand that this exploration and expansion were partly causing—and partly caused by—the major developments in thought and expression that are listed below.

1. The Renaissance: Classical Civilization Part II

After the Black Death abated and the population of Europe once again began to swell, the demand for goods and services began to increase rapidly. Individuals moved to the cities. A middle class made up of bankers, merchants, and traders emerged because of increased global trade. In short, Europe experienced an influx of money to go along with its newfound sense of history. It shouldn't be too surprising that a sizable chunk of this money was spent on recapturing and studying the past.

Humanism: A Bit More Focus on the Here and Now
In medieval Europe, thoughts of salvation and the afterlife so dominated personal priorities that life on Earth was, for many, something to be suffered through on the way to heaven rather than lived through as a pursuit of its own. As Europeans rediscovered ancient texts, they were struck with the degree that humanity—personal accomplishment and personal happiness—formed the central core of so much of the literature and philosophy of the ancient writers. The emphasis began to shift from fulfillment in the afterlife to participating in the here and now.

This is not to say that medieval Europeans had no concerns in the present or that early modern Europeans suddenly became hedonistic, focused on worldly pleasures. To the contrary, the Catholic Church and a focus on the afterlife remained dominant. However, Europeans were fascinated with the ancient Greek and Roman concepts of beauty and citizenship, and as a consequence they began to shift their focus to life on Earth and to celebrating human achievements in the scholarly, artistic, and political realms. This focus on human endeavors became known as **humanism**. Its impact was far-reaching because a focus on present-day life leads to a focus on individuals, and a focus on individuality inevitably leads to a reduction in the authority of institutions.

THE ITALIAN STATE SYSTEM
DURING THE RENAISSANCE

The Arts Stage a Comeback

The Renaissance literally means "rebirth," and this was nowhere more apparent than in the arts. In Italy, where powerful families in city-states such as Florence, Venice, and Milan became rich on trade, art was financed on a scale not seen since the classical civilizations of Greece and Rome. The **Medici** family in Florence, for example, not only ruled the great city and beyond (several family members not coincidentally became popes!), but turned it into a showcase of architecture and beauty by acting as patron for some of the greatest artists of the time, including **Michelangelo** and **Brunelleschi**.

Unlike medieval paintings, which often depicted humans as flat, stiff, and out of proportion with their surroundings, paintings of the Renaissance demonstrated the application of humanistic ideals learned from the ancients. Painters and sculptors such as **Leonardo da Vinci** and **Donatello** depicted the human figure as realistically as possible. Careful use of light and shadow made figures appear full and real. Many artists were so committed to this realism that they viewed and participated in autopsies to fully understand the structure of the human body.

Western Writers Finally Get Readers   Although printing was developed in China centuries earlier (remember which dynasty? The Song), movable type wasn't invented in Europe until the mid-1400s, when **Johannes Gutenberg** invented the printing press. Prior to Gutenberg's invention, the creation of books was such a long and laborious task that few were made. Those that were made were usually printed in Latin, the language of scholars and the Catholic Church. Because of this and the lack of public education, the typical person couldn't own books or even read.

With the invention of the **printing press**, all that changed. Books became easy to produce and thus were far more affordable. The growing middle class fueled demand for books on a variety of subjects that were written in their own **vernacular**, or native language, such as German or French. The book industry flourished, as did related industries such as papermaking, a craft that was learned from the Arabs, who learned it from the Chinese. More books led to more literate and educated people. The newly literate people desired more books, which continued to make them more educated, which again increased their desire for books, and so on. The most commonly circulated books and pamphlets were religious in nature. New translations of the Bible into vernacular languages encouraged public debate and personal interpretation of the Bible and helped usher in the Reformation.

2. The Protestant Reformation: Streamlining Salvation

You might recall from the previous chapter that during the Middle Ages, the Catholic Church was an extremely powerful force in Europe. While political power was diffused under the feudal system, and while the various European princes and political powers frequently clashed with the pope, emperors and princes knew that their power increased if the church blessed their reign. As a consequence, the pope wielded considerable political power.

The church was one of the most important institutions that unified ordinary people in Western Europe. It was a unifying force, an institution believed to be sanctioned by God. With such widely accepted credentials, the church held itself out as not only the undisputed authority on all things otherworldly, but also the ultimate endorsement on all things worldly. With one foot on Earth and the other in heaven, the pope—and with him the hierarchy of the Catholic Church—acted as the intermediary between man and God. Nearly everyone in Europe understood this clearly: to get to heaven, you had to proceed by way of the Catholic Church.

The church understood the power it had over the faithful. When it needed to finance its immense building projects plus pay for the huge number of Renaissance artists it kept in its employ, it began to sell **indulgences**. An indulgence was a piece of paper that the faithful could purchase to reduce time in purgatory (the place Catholics believed they would go after death). There, they would atone for their sins and then be allowed to enter heaven. Because purgatory was not thought of as a happy place to go, people greatly valued the concept of reducing their time there. Selling indulgences was not only a means of generating income, but also a way for the church to maintain power over its members.

During this time, landowning nobles grew increasingly resentful of the church, which had amassed an enormous amount of power and wealth and exploited a huge number of resources at the expense of the nobles. This resentment and mistrust fueled anti-church sentiments. The selling of indulgences propelled the frustration into the ranks of the peasant class and helped set the stage for confrontation. The selling of indulgences also confirmed to many the corrupt nature of the church.

Martin Luther: Monk on a Mission
In 1517, a German monk named **Martin Luther** nailed a list of 95 theses on a church door—a list that was distributed quickly and widely by aid of the newfangled printing press. His list outlined his frustrations with current church practices, including the church's practice of selling indulgences, which he said amounted to selling salvation for profit. Luther's frustrations had been building for some time. He had traveled to Rome, and was unnerved by the worldly nature of the city and the Vatican (the seat of the Catholic Church), which was in the midst of getting a Renaissance makeover—upgrades that were clearly paid for with money from churchgoers in far-away places.

Among Luther's many complaints was his insistence that church services should be conducted in the local languages of the people, not in Latin, a language that the German people didn't understand. To help in this effort, he translated the Bible into German so that it could be read and interpreted by everyone, as opposed to making people dependent on the church for biblical understanding. Luther's most significant claim was that salvation was given directly by God through grace, not through indulgences, and not through the authorization of the church. In other words, Luther suggested that the Bible teaches that people could appeal directly to God for forgiveness for sins and salvation. This revolutionary concept significantly reduced the role of the church as the exclusive middleman between God and man. In essence, the church was marginalized to an aid for salvation as opposed to the grantor of salvation.

Pope Leo X was outraged, and ordered Luther to recant, or formally retract, his theses. Meanwhile, Luther's ideas were spreading through much of northern Europe as the printing presses continued to roll. When Luther refused to recant, he was excommunicated. When he was allowed to address church leaders and princes at an assembly in Worms (1521), he refused to abandon his convictions. The pope called for his arrest, but a nobleman from Luther's hometown protected him, and Luther continued to write and spread his ideas.

Christianity Splits Again
The consequences of Luther's actions were enormous. Luther's followers began to refer to themselves as **Lutherans**, and began to separate themselves from the Catholic Church. What's more, other theologians began to assert their own biblical interpretations, some of which were consistent with Luther's; others were wildly different. Once the floodgates were opened, Luther had no control over the consequences.

John Calvin from France led a powerful Protestant group by preaching an ideology of predestination. Calvinist doctrine stated that God had predetermined an ultimate destiny for all people, most of whom God had already damned. Only a few, he preached, would be saved, and those people were known as the Elect. In the 1530s, the city of Geneva in Switzerland invited Calvin to construct a Protestant theocracy in their city, which was centrally located and near France. From there, Calvinist teachings spread and were as influential to successive Protestant Reformations as were the doctrines of Luther. **Calvinism**, for example, greatly influenced religious development in Scotland under John Knox, and in France with the growth of the Huguenots.

Henry VIII: An Epilogue
Henry VIII went on to marry five more wives and to father a son, who died young. His daughter Elizabeth, also a Protestant, rose to the throne, but more on that later when we discuss political developments in England.

In time, the Reformation spread to England, motivated by political as well as religious reasons. **King Henry VIII** did not have a son as heir to his throne and sought to end his marriage to Catherine of Aragon because of it. When the pope denied an annulment of the marriage, Henry VIII renounced Rome and declared himself the head of religious affairs in England. This sat well with those in England who already were becoming Protestants, but much of England remained Catholic. Nevertheless, Henry pushed forward and presided over what was called the **Church of England**, also known as the Anglican Church.

Focus On: Independent Thinking

The **Protestant Reformation** was a huge deal in world history. Its significance went well beyond the religious arena. While previous skirmishes between the pope and the nobles had been about papal political authority, Luther's challenges were theologically based and directed at the pope's religious role. Luther asserted that the people did not need the Catholic Church, or its priests, in order to interact with God; they needed only their Bibles. If the religious authority of the pope could be so openly and brazenly challenged, and commonly accepted understandings of God's relationship to man could be reevaluated and rearticulated, then people's understanding of other concepts might need to be reevaluated as well. Put simply, by challenging the pope, Luther made it acceptable to question the conventional wisdom of the church. With newly printed Bibles available in their own languages, laypeople could learn how to read and form their own relationships with God. As the common people became literate and better educated, more and more Europeans began to question both the world around them and the authority of the church. Europeans desired to search for their own answers to the questions of the universe. In short, the Protestant Reformation paved the way for revolutions in education, politics, and science.

The Counter-Reformation: The Pope Reasserts His Authority During the **Catholic Reformation** (also known as the **Counter-Reformation**) of the 16th century, the Catholic Church itself reformed, while also succeeding in winning back some of the souls it had lost to the fledgling Protestant denominations.

At first, the Catholic Church responded ineffectively to the new religious trends. However, when Luther refused to recant and German princes started to convert to Lutheranism, the Catholic Church began to institute reforms, which were led by Spain, a dedicated Catholic country. By banning the sale of indulgences, consulting more frequently with bishops and parishes, and training its priests to adhere to Catholic teaching more strictly, the Catholic Church regained some of its lost credibility. However, make no mistake, the Counter-Reformation was as much about reaffirming as it was about reforming, and the church made it clear that it was not bowing to Protestant demands but rather clarifying its position. Weekly mass became obligatory, and the supreme authority of the pope was reestablished. During this time, a former Spanish soldier and intellectual, **Ignatius Loyola**, founded the society of Jesuits, which was influential in restoring faith in the teachings of Jesus as interpreted by the Catholic Church. The **Jesuits** practiced self-control and moderation, believing that prayer and good works led to salvation. The pious example of the Jesuits led to a stricter training system and higher expectations of morality for the clergy. Because of their oratorical and political skills, many Jesuits were appointed by kings to high palace positions.

A group of church officials held a series of meetings known as the **Council of Trent** to direct the Counter-Reformation period from 1545 to 1563, dictating and defining the Catholic interpretation of religious doctrine and clarifying the Catholic Church's position on important religious questions such as the nature of salvation. During this period, "heretics" were once again tried and punished, and the Catholic Church reestablished Latin as the language to be used in worship.

The result? The Catholic Church staged an amazing comeback. The Counter-Reformation proved successful in containing the southward spread of Protestantism. By 1600, southern Europe (especially Italy, Spain, and Portugal), France, and southern Germany were heavily Catholic. Northern Germany and Scandinavia were mostly Lutheran. Scotland was Calvinist, as were pockets within central Europe and France. England, as mentioned previously, was Anglican.

The result of the result? Wars, of course. But more on that when we discuss developments in individual countries.

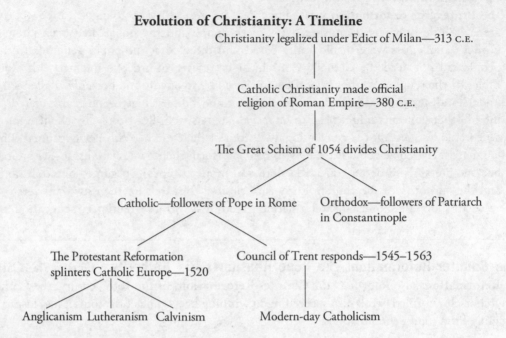

Evolution of Christianity: A Timeline

Christianity legalized under Edict of Milan—313 C.E.

Catholic Christianity made official religion of Roman Empire—380 C.E.

The Great Schism of 1054 divides Christianity

Catholic—followers of Pope in Rome

Orthodox—followers of Patriarch in Constantinople

The Protestant Reformation splinters Catholic Europe—1520

Council of Trent responds—1545–1563

Anglicanism Lutheranism Calvinism

Modern-day Catholicism

3. The Scientific Revolution: Prove It or Lose It

Prior to the Scientific Revolution, Europe and most of the world believed, as Aristotle asserted, that Earth was the center of the universe and that the sun, stars, and planets revolved around the earth. There certainly were numerous inconsistencies observed by scientists with regard to this theory, but most scientists continued to attempt to explain the inconsistency rather than investigate the theory itself. As Europe changed dramatically because of the Renaissance and the Protestant Reformation, and as the growth of universities gave structure to burgeoning questions about the world, educated Europeans began to examine the world around them with new vigor. The results were revolutionary.

The Copernican Revolution: A Revolution About Revolutions   Just as the Counter-Reformation was gaining momentum, **Nicolaus Copernicus** developed a mathematical theory that asserted that the earth and the other celestial bodies revolved around the sun and that the earth also rotated on its axis daily. This was pretty shocking stuff to many in the "establishment." Although most educated people had accepted the world was a sphere for centuries, even well before Columbus's voyage in 1492, the earth's position at the center of the universe was widely accepted. Copernicus's heliocentric theory of the solar system brought about much debate and much skepticism. In 1543, Copernicus published *On the Revolutions of the Heavenly Spheres* to prove his points, but it wasn't until Galileo—who discovered the moons of Jupiter with his telescope—that the Copernican model really took off.

In 1632, **Galileo** published his *Dialogue Concerning the Two Chief Systems of the World*. He wrote the work in Italian in order to reach a wide audience and defeat the defenders of Ptolemy (the scientist who promoted the earth as the center of the universe). He showed how the rotation of the earth on its axis produced the apparent rotation of the heavens, as well as how the stars' great distance from the earth prevented humans from being able to see their changed position as the earth moved around the sun. Galileo's proofs made it difficult for scholars to continue to accept the Ptolemaic model, which just so happened to be the model sanctioned by the Catholic Church. The church put Galileo on trial before the Inquisition in Rome for heresy and he was forced to recant. His book was placed on **The Index**, a list of banned heretical works. Nevertheless, while under house arrest, Galileo continued to research and document his findings.

> **Fun Fact**
> Astonishingly, Galileo's book remained on The Index until 1822!

The Scientific Method: In Search of Truth Recall that during the High Middle Ages and the early Renaissance, the scholastic method of reasoning was deemed the most reliable means of determining scientific meaning. Scholasticism was based on Aristotelianism and therefore used reason as the chief method of determining truth. Sometimes reason led to heresies, while other times reason was used to explain and complement faith, as was the case with Thomas Aquinas.

The scientific method was born out of the scholastic tradition, but it took that tradition to considerable new levels. Reason alone wasn't good enough. Under the scientific method, one had to prove what the mind concluded, document it, repeat it for others, and open it up to experimentation. At its highest stage, the scientific method required that any underlying principles be proven with mathematical precision.

Copernicus and Galileo, of course, were two fathers of the scientific method, but it took more than a century for the method to be widely used. There were many contributors. **Tycho Brahe** (1546–1601) built an observatory and recorded his observations, and **Francis Bacon** (1561–1626) published works on inductive logic. Both asserted that scientists should amass all the data possible through experimentation and observation and that the proper conclusions would come from this data. Then, **Johannes Kepler** (1571–1630) developed laws of planetary motion based on observation and mathematics. **Sir Isaac Newton** took it one step further. In *The Mathematical Principles of Natural Philosophy* (1697), he invented calculus to help prove the theories of Copernicus, Galileo, Bacon, and others. He also developed the law of gravity.

Together, these men and others developed a widely used system of observation, reason, experiment, and mathematical proof that could be applied to every conceivable scientific inquiry. With precise scientific instruments, such as the microscope and the telescope, a scientist could retest what another scientist had originally tested. Many scientific inquires were conducted with practical goals in mind, such as the creation of labor-saving machines or the development of power sources from water and wind. Francis Bacon, for example, argued that science was pursued not for science's sake but as a way to improve the human condition.

All of this eventually led to the Industrial Revolution, which will be discussed in the next chapter. In the meantime, however, you need to understand that the Scientific Revolution led to a major rift in society. While many highly educated Christians were able to hold on to their beliefs even as they studied science, many also began to reject the church's rigid pronouncements that conflicted with scientific findings. Many of these people either became **atheists** (who believe that no god exists) or **deists** (who believe that God exists but plays a passive role in life).

Deism: God as a Watchmaker The Scientific Revolution contributed to a belief system known as deism, which became popular in the 1700s. The deists believed in a powerful god who created and presided over an orderly realm but who did not interfere in its workings. The deists viewed God as a watchmaker, one who set up the world, gave it natural laws by which to operate, and then let it run by itself (under natural laws that could be proved mathematically). Such a theory had little place in organized religion.

The European Rivals

1. Spain and Portugal

As you read in the previous chapter, in 1469, **King Ferdinand**, from the Christian Kingdoms in northern Spain, and **Queen Isabella**, from the more Muslim regions of southern Spain, initiated the consolidation of Spanish authority under one house, and thereby created a nation-state that would become one of the world's most powerful forces over the next century. By aggressively supporting exploration (initially by underwriting Columbus's exploration and then later by establishing empires in the New World), Ferdinand and Isabella had a long-term impact on cultural world developments—they ensured the survival and expansion of the Spanish language and culture, including Catholicism, by extending them across the Atlantic. Ferdinand and Isabella also built a formidable naval fleet, allowing Spain to rule the seas for the next century.

Portugal: The Middleman of an Empire

As Spain focused on western exploration and its empire in the New World, the Portuguese continued their domination of coastal Africa, the Indian Ocean, and the Spice Islands. A small country with limited manpower, Portugal had to be content as the middleman of a "floating empire." It was an early player in the transatlantic slave trade, and it controlled sea routes and garrisoned trading posts; still, it was unable to exert control over large sections of the interior of Africa and India. Inevitably, Portugal could not maintain control of its far-flung colonies and lost control of them to the Dutch and British who had faster ships with heavier guns.

The international importance of Spain grew under **Charles V**, who inherited a large empire. Charles was from the Hapsburg family, which originated in Austria and, through a series of carefully arranged marriages (recall that divine right promoted intermarriage among royalty), created a huge empire stretching from Austria and Germany to Spain. While one set of Charles's grandparents were Hapsburgs, his other grandparents were Ferdinand and Isabella, who themselves had married to solidify the Spanish empire. Talk about family connections.

In 1519, Charles was elected Holy Roman Emperor by German princes, which meant that he then held lands in parts of France, the Netherlands, Austria, and Germany in addition to Spain. These possessions, plus the new colonies in the Americas, brought wars as well as riches. Spain fought France for control of Italy and the Ottoman Turks for control of Eastern Europe, which led to an expansion of Ottoman rule into much of Hungary (more on that later). In Germany, Charles defended Catholicism from the encroachment of Protestantism (recall that Spain was allied with the Catholic Church during the Counter-Reformation). Frustrated over trying to manage such an enormous empire at a time of expansion in the New World and revolution in Europe (the Protestant Reformation and Scientific Revolution, for example), he decided in 1556 to retire to a monastery and thereby abdicate the throne. He gave control over Austria and the Holy Roman throne of Germany to his brother, **Ferdinand I**. To his son, **Philip II**, he conferred the throne of Spain and jurisdiction over Burgundy (in France), Sicily, and the Netherlands as well as Spain's claim in the New World. Phillip II also gained control over Portugal.

Under Philip II, the Spanish Empire in the west saw some of its greatest expansion in the New World and a rebirth of culture under the Spanish Renaissance, but it also started showing signs of decay. A devoutly religious man, Philip oversaw the continuation of the **Spanish Inquisition** to oust heretics, led the Catholic Reformation against Protestants, and supported an increase in missionary work in the ever-expanding empire in the New World. Increasingly eager to develop their own empire, Dutch Protestants (of the Netherlands) revolted. By 1581, the mostly Protestant northern provinces of the Netherlands gained their independence from Spain and became known as the Dutch Netherlands. The mostly Catholic southern provinces remained loyal to Spain (this region would later become Belgium).

Exhibiting further signs of weakness, Spanish forces fighting for Catholicism in France fared poorly, and to the shock of many Spaniards, the English defeated and devastated the once mighty Spanish Armada as it tried to attack the British Isles. The defeat invigorated the English, who by the late 16th century were expanding their own empire, and signaled containment of Spanish forces.

Although Spain amassed enormous sums of gold from the New World, it spent its wealth quickly on wars, missionary activities, and maintenance of its huge fleets. By the mid-17th century, Spain still had substantial holdings, but its glory days had passed. England and France were well poised to replace it as the dominant European powers.

2. England

As you read earlier in the discussion of the Protestant Reformation, **King Henry VIII**, who ruled from 1509 to 1547, nullified the pope's authority in England, thereby establishing (under the 1534 **Act of Supremacy**) the Church of England and placed himself as head of that church. Henry took this action so that he could divorce his wife and marry Anne Boleyn in an effort to father a male heir. He didn't succeed in getting a male heir. Instead, he got another daughter, **Elizabeth I**, who oversaw a golden age in the arts known as the Elizabethan Age.

The **Elizabethan Age** (1558–1603) boasted commercial expansion and exploration and colonization in the New World, especially after the English fleet destroyed the Spanish Armada in 1588. During this time, the **Muscovy Company** was founded as the first joint-stock company, and the **British East India Company** quickly followed suit. Drake circumnavigated the globe. The first English colonists settled in the Roanoke colony in present-day Virginia. To top it all off, Shakespeare wrote his masterpieces. Simply put, England experienced a golden age under Elizabeth.

The religious battles that were unleashed by the Protestant Reformation still unsettled the region. Anglicans (Church of England) were battling Catholics, while other Protestant groups such as the Puritans were regularly persecuted. When **James I** came to power in 1607 after the death of Elizabeth, whose reign brought together the crowns of England and Scotland, he attempted to institute reforms to accommodate the Catholics and the Puritans, but widespread problems persisted. The Puritans (who were Calvinists) didn't want to recognize the power of the king over religious matters, and James reacted defensively, claiming divine right. It was at this point that many Puritans decided to cross the Atlantic. The Pilgrims' establishment of the Plymouth colony (1620) occurred during James's reign. Jamestown colony, as you might have guessed, was also founded during the reign of James I. The English aren't known for their innovative naming.

Charles I, son of James, rose to power in 1625. Three years later, desperate for money from Parliament, he agreed to sign the **Petition of Right**, which was a document limiting taxes and forbidding unlawful imprisonment. Charles ignored the petition after he secured the funds he needed and, claiming divine right, ruled without calling another meeting of Parliament for 11 years.

At home, Ferdinand and Isabella's work to expand Spanish culture and Catholicism led to the **Decree of Alhambra** in 1492, which called for the expulsion of all Spanish Jews who had not converted to Catholicism. In 1496, King Manuel I of Portugal created a similar policy—convert or leave. Suspicions that *conversos*, Jews who had converted to Catholicism, were not actually Catholic took an even more tragic turn in Lisbon on Easter day, 1506, as crowds publicly executed *conversos* and others suspected of being Jewish.

In 1640, when Scotland's resentment toward Charles resulted in a Scottish invasion of England, Charles was forced to call Parliament into session. Led by Puritans, this Parliament was known as the **Long Parliament** because it sat for 20 years from 1640 through 1660. The Long Parliament limited the absolute powers of the monarchy. In 1641, the parliament denied Charles's request for money to fight the Irish rebellion, and in response he led troops into the House of Commons to arrest some of the members. This sparked a civil war. Parliament raised an army, called the Roundheads, to fight the king. The Roundheads, under the leadership of **Oliver Cromwell**, defeated the armies of Charles I, who were called Cavaliers. The king was tried and executed. Oliver Cromwell rose to power, not as a monarch, but first as leader of what was called the **English Commonwealth**, and then after reorganizing the government, as **Lord Protector**.

When Cromwell ruled as Protector, he ruled with religious intolerance and violence against Catholics and the Irish. He encouraged Protestants to settle in Northern Ireland (this would cause many problems in future centuries). All of this caused much resentment, and after Cromwell died, Parliament invited Charles II, the exiled son of the now-beheaded Charles I, to take the throne and restore a limited monarchy. This is called the **Stuart Restoration** (1660–1688). A closet Catholic, Charles II acknowledged the rights of the people, especially with regard to religion. In 1679, he agreed to the **Habeas Corpus Act** (which protects people from arrests without due process). Following Charles II's death, his brother James II took over.

James II was openly Catholic, and he was unpopular. Like so many before him, he believed in the divine right of kings. In a bloodless change of leadership known as the **Glorious Revolution**, he was driven from power by Parliament, which feared he'd make England a Catholic country, and he fled to France. He was replaced in 1688 by his son-in-law and daughter, William and Mary, the Protestant rulers of the Netherlands, who promptly signed the **English Bill of Rights** in 1689. The Glorious Revolution ensured that England's future monarchs would be Anglican and that their powers would be limited.

Focus On: The Enlightenment Writers

Keep in mind that the Enlightenment writers were busy at work by this time. Hobbes published *Leviathan* in 1651 in response to the English Civil War, a time during which the monarch, Charles I, was beheaded. Hobbes's violent view of human nature and desire for an all-powerful ruler to maintain peace are completely understandable within the context of the English Civil War. While Hobbes missed the peaceful resolution of the war in the Glorious Revolution and the English Bill of Rights (1688–1689), John Locke did not. Locke's more optimistic view of human nature can be viewed in the context of the bloodless transition of power between James II and William and Mary. In addition, Locke's writings in *Two Treatises on Government* justified this change of leadership by suggesting that James II had violated the social contract. Political events in England during this time, and such events in general, cannot be separated from the development of social and political philosophy and vice versa.

3. France

After the Hundred Years' War (1337–1453) drove the English from France, the French began to unify and centralize authority in a strong monarchy. As elsewhere, however, religious differences stood in the way. France was largely Catholic, but during the Protestant Reformation, a group of French Protestants, known as **Huguenots**, developed into a sizable and influential minority. Throughout the mid- to late-16th century, Catholics and Huguenots bitterly fought each other, sometimes brutally, until, in 1598, **Henry IV** issued the **Edict of Nantes**, which created an environment of toleration. Henry IV was the first of the Bourbon kings, who ruled France for nearly two centuries until 1792.

Cardinal Richelieu, a Catholic, played an important role as the chief advisor to the Bourbons. His primary political role was to strengthen the French crown. While clashes erupted among Catholics and Huguenots (Protestants) in France, Richelieu did not seek to destroy the Protestants; he compromised with them and even helped them to attack the Catholic Hapsburgs of the Holy Roman Empire, an empire that he wanted to end in order to make France a stronger power in Europe. A new bureaucratic class, the *noblesse de la robe*, was established under Richelieu. The bureaucracy established by Richelieu and his successor, **Cardinal Mazarin**, prepared France to hold the strong position it would achieve in Europe under Louis XIV.

Louis XIV was four years old when he inherited the crown of France. His mother and Cardinal Mazarin ruled in his name until he reached adulthood, at which time he became one of the most legendary monarchs of European history. Louis XIV's long reign (1643–1715) exemplified the grandiose whims of an absolute monarchy. Calling himself the "Sun King" and "The Most Christian King," he patronized the arts as long as they contributed to the glorification of France and its culture, which became much admired and emulated. Ruling under divine right, he reportedly declared, "I am the State," and he built the lavish palace of Versailles to prove it. He never summoned the Estates-General, the lawmaking body, to meet. He revoked the Edict of Nantes, forcing many Huguenots to leave France. Perhaps most importantly, he appointed **Jean Baptiste Colbert** to manage the royal funds.

A strict mercantilist, Colbert wanted to increase the size of the French empire, thereby increasing the opportunity for business transactions and taxes. To accomplish this, France was almost constantly at war. For a while, warfare and mercantilist policies allowed France to increase its overseas holdings and gain the revenue needed for the extravagances of a king named for the Sun. However, the **War of Spanish Succession** (1701–1714) proved to be a disaster for the grand plans of France.

> ### Contrast Them: England and France in the 17th Century
> Unlike England, France was ruled by a series of strong and able monarchs under the Bourbon Dynasty. After the death of Elizabeth, England went from monarchy to Commonwealth to Restoration to Glorious Revolution. Hardly stable. On the other hand, France's Estates-General (a governing body representing clergy, nobles, merchants, and peasants) was not nearly as powerful as the English Parliament. It didn't even meet for the bulk of the 17th century because the French kings ruled successfully under the justification of divine right.

Recall that European royalty was intermarrying and reproducing. It turned out that the twisted branches of the royal family trees led to a situation in which, in 1701, one of Louis XIV's grandsons inherited the Spanish throne. This alarmed the rest of Europe, which feared that Spain, although substantially weaker than it had been in the previous century, and France, already quite powerful, would form an unstoppable combo-power, especially given their American holdings at the time (France owned a huge chunk of North America, Spain the bulk of Central and South America). It's a complicated story, but England, the Holy Roman Empire, and German princes all united under the perceived common threat, and 13 years later, the question of Spanish succession was settled. **Philip V**, the grandson, was able to rule Spain, but Spain couldn't combine with France, and France had to give up much of its territory to England, a country that then became even more powerful.

The bottom line is that Colbert and Louis XIV's many territorial invasions and wars proved costly and ineffective. France remained powerful, but by the 18th century, its position as a military power was weakening. Nevertheless, by 1750, its position as a center for arts was firmly established.

4. German Areas (The Holy Roman Empire, Sort of)

The situation in German and Slavic areas of central Europe during this time period was complicated. The Holy Roman Empire wasn't really in Rome but rather in present-day Austria and parts of Germany and surrounding regions because Italy was controlled by ruling families in the Italian city-states. The Holy Roman Empire geographically dominated the region, but was also still very feudal with lots of local lords running their own shows. Therefore, the Holy Roman Emperor was pretty weak. This is further complicated by the rise of the powerful Hapsburg family of Austria, which, as we already stated, kept intermarrying so that it dominated not only substantial territory within the Holy Roman Empire but also Spain and parts of Italy. It was complicated further by the fact that northern Germany was essentially a collection of city-states, such as Brandenburg, Saxony, and Prussia. Finally, remember that northern Germany went Lutheran during the Protestant Reformation, while southern areas of the Holy Roman Empire stayed Catholic, along with Spain and France. Got it? It's nutty, so we're going to hit only the highlights, or else your head will be spinning.

> **Contrast Them: Germany with Spain, England, and France**
>
> Germany unified under a central government much later than Spain, England, and France did. You'll read about German unification in the next chapter. You won't read about a huge German empire in the New World or a strong German monarchy, because for centuries Germany remained caught in a complicated web of rulers of the Holy Roman Empire, the Hapsburgs of Austria, and the princes of city-states. It was also a tangle of religious movements, because it was at the heart of the Protestant Reformation.

You need to grasp the following three things from this time period:

- The Holy Roman Empire lost parts of Hungary to the Ottoman Turks in the early 16th century (this is discussed in the section on the Ottoman Empire).

- The Thirty Years' War (1618–1648) devastated the region and significantly weakened the role of the Holy Roman emperors, leading to the rise of hundreds of nation-states in the region in the 19th century.

- By the 18th century, the northern German city-states, especially Prussia, were gaining momentum and power.

Now for a few of the details.

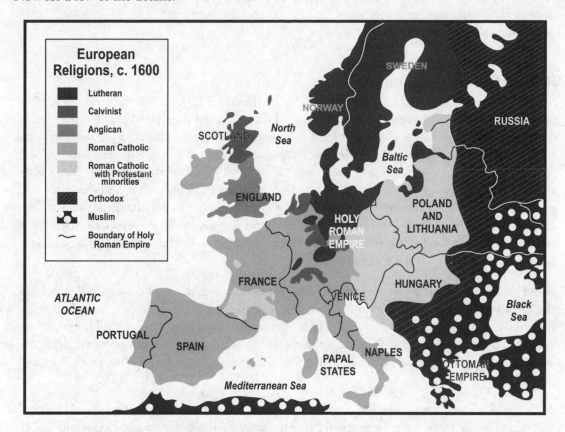

European Religions, c. 1600

- Lutheran
- Calvinist
- Anglican
- Roman Catholic
- Roman Catholic with Protestant minorities
- Orthodox
- Muslim
- Boundary of Holy Roman Empire

Religious Divisions Around 1600

In 1555, the **Peace of Augsburg** was intended to bring an end to the constant conflicts between Catholics and Protestants that engulfed the region during the Reformation and Counter-Reformation. The peace didn't last. The **Thirty Years' War** began in 1618 when the Protestant territories in Bohemia (which was under the rule of the Catholic Hapsburg clan) challenged the authority of the Holy Roman Catholic emperor, a situation that frequently arose prior to the Peace of Augsburg. This time, though, the conflict grew bigger than anything before it and developed into a huge religious and political war. Everyone seemed to want a piece of the action, including other countries such as France (under Richelieu), Denmark, and Sweden. Although this grew into a war between major European powers, the actual fighting stayed within the German empire, meaning that after 30 years of fighting, many parts of Germany were left depopulated and devastated. Some estimates suggest that the Holy Roman Empire lost one-third of its population during these 30 years, some 7 million people.

When the **Peace of Westphalia** was negotiated in 1648, the independence of small German states was affirmed, and Prussia became the strongest of them. The Holy Roman Empire was left barely limping along. Its territories had been reduced and its emperor, along with the Hapsburg family, was much less powerful. Somehow the Holy Roman Empire survived in name until 1806, but it hardly had any power after Westphalia.

The biggest beneficiary of the war was France. It became the most powerful country in Europe during the 17th century under Louis XIV, although, as you already read, it was weakened by the 18th century after the country overspent and overplayed its hand, particularly during the War of Spanish Succession. The other war beneficiary was Prussia, the German city-state centered in Berlin, which also controlled parts of Poland. Prussia eventually rose to dominate the German territories, unifying them into the powerful country of Germany, but you'll read about that in the next chapter.

Russia Out of Isolation

When the Turks conquered Constantinople and the Byzantine Empire fell, the center of Orthodox Christianity moved northward to Moscow, which was called the "Third Rome" (after Rome itself and then Constantinople). At around the same time, Russian leaders were overthrowing the Mongols. In 1480, **Ivan III** of Moscow refused to pay tribute to the Mongols and declared Russia free of Mongol rule. He, and later his grandson **Ivan IV**, established absolute rule in Russia, uniting it and expanding it ever eastward. They recruited peasants and offered them freedom from their feudal lords, known as **boyars**, if they agreed to settle in new lands to the east. The catch was that these peasants had to conquer the land themselves! Known as **Cossacks**, these peasant-soldiers expanded Russian territories in the 16th through the 18th centuries well into Siberia and southward to the Caspian Sea.

Ivan IV was such a strong leader and held such absolute power that he became known as **Ivan the Terrible** (not necessarily meaning bad, but instead formidable or impressive). Taking on the title of czar (Russian for "Caesar"), Ivan the Terrible expanded Russia's holding, but not without cost to the Russian people. By the 1560s, he ruled under a reign of terror, regularly executing anyone whom he perceived as a threat to his power, including his own son (executed in 1580).

After the death of Ivan IV in 1584, and with no strong heir to take the throne, Russia's feudal lords continually battled over who should rule the empire. The situation grew especially messy from 1604 to 1613, a period that historians refer to as the **Time of Troubles**, because one pretender to the throne would be killed by another pretender and yet another. In 1613, the madness subsided when **Michael Romanov** was elected czar by the feudal lords. The Romanov Dynasty added stability to the empire. It ruled until 1917.

Contrast Them: Russia and Western Europe

Despite the centralization of authority under the Ivans, Russia remained very much a feudal arrangement, with local lords exercising considerable power. While Western Europe basked in the glow of the Renaissance, explored and expanded its influence across oceans, and debated about religion, science, and government in a series of movements, Russia remained isolated from the west and pushed eastward instead. Its growth was territorial, but not intellectual or artistic. During the 15th, 16th, and most of the 17th centuries, it had nothing that could be labeled a Renaissance or Enlightenment. It wasn't part of the Renaissance because it was under the control of the Mongols at the time. It wasn't part of the Reformation because it wasn't part of the Catholic Church in the first place. So even though today we often see Russia as a European power, its history progressed along a very different path. It wasn't until the late 17th century that Russia turned its eyes westward.

Like the Ivans, the Romanovs consolidated power and often ruled ruthlessly. The peasants, now serfs, were practically enslaved people. By the late 1600s, the Romanovs had expanded the empire, with the help of the Cossacks, eastward through Siberia. By 1689, Russian territory spread from Ukraine (west of Moscow) to the Pacific Ocean, north of Manchuria.

Compare Them: Forced Labor Systems

Although slavery was not a new system, the demands of the newly global economy resulted in an expansion of systems of forced labor in the empires. At the same time, Russia's attempts to control their large land mass relied on the forced labor of the peasants or serfs. All three systems took advantage of the laborers and were frequently managed by harsh and brutal overseers. In the Spanish part of the New World, *haciendas* were established in which natives owed labor to their landlords—not unlike the feudalism of Europe. This system fell apart as the native populations diminished due to disease, and as natives converted to the Catholic faith. The Portuguese took advantage of the already thriving intra-African slave trade and transformed it into a transoceanic one. The majority of transported Africans wound up on plantations in Brazil and the Caribbean where life expectancy was just three to five years. Russian serfdom differed in that the Russian economy was domestic and both the laborers and the landowners were Russian.

At around this same time, **Peter the Great**, who ruled from 1682 through 1725, came to power. He was convinced he needed to Westernize Russia. He built Russia's first navy and founded St. Petersburg on the Baltic Sea as his new capital. The "window to the west," St. Petersburg became the home to hundreds of Western European engineers, scientists, architects, and artists who were recruited specifically to Westernize Russia. Women of the nobility were forced to dress in Western fashions. Men were forced to shave their beards. Most of the hard labor of building the great new city was accomplished, of course, by serfs turned enslaved people.

Under **Catherine the Great**, who ruled from 1762 until 1796, more enlightened policies of education and Western culture were implemented. Still, Russia suffered because Catherine fiercely enforced repressive serfdom and limited the growth of the merchant class. Catherine continued the aggressive westward territorial expansion, gaining ground in Poland and, most significantly, territory on the Black Sea. This advance ensured Russia's access to the Mediterranean to its south and west.

B. Islamic Gunpowder Empires

The history of the **Ottoman Empire** actually precedes 1450. You might recall from the previous chapter that the territories of the former Islamic Empire were overrun by the ubiquitous Mongols in the 13th century. Recall also that the Byzantine Empire, centered in Constantinople, controlled most of Turkey and influenced southeastern Europe and Russia. As the Mongol Empire fell, the Muslim Ottoman Empire, founded by **Osman Bey**, rose in Anatolia (eastern parts of Turkey) to unify the region and challenge the Byzantine Empire. As it grew in the 14th century, the Turks (as the Ottomans were called) came to dominate most of modern-day Turkey and eventually, in 1453, invaded Constantinople, thereby ending the Byzantine Empire. Perhaps 1450 isn't such an artificial boundary after all.

The Ottomans made Constantinople their capital city, renamed it Istanbul, and

Focus On: Westernization of Russia

Both Peter and Catherine are important because they positioned Russia for engagement with the rest of the world, particularly the Western world. By the late 18th century, Russia was in a significantly different position than it had been at the beginning of that century. It gained physical access to the West by both the Baltic and the Black Seas, and it gained cultural access to the West by actively seeking interaction. Unlike China and Japan, which repelled the West from their shores in the same time period, the Russians wanted to engage with and emulate the West.

converted the great cathedrals such as the Hagia Sophia into mosques. They installed solidified rule over conquered territory by handing over tracts of land called **timars** to aristocrats, thereby replacing local rulers with Ottoman officials. In the expanding empire, Christians and Jews were allowed to practice their religions, making the empire more tolerant than both the previous Islamic Empire and the other major regimes of the era. Within 100 years, the Ottomans conquered the expanse of the old Byzantine Empire, except for Italy westward. In other words, the Ottoman Empire extended from Greece eastward to Persia, and then all the way around the Mediterranean into Egypt and northern Africa.

As the empire grew, so too did religious persecution. To conquer large territories, the Ottomans employed a practice known as **devshirme**, in which they enslaved children of their Christian subjects and turned them into fighting warriors called Janissaries. In other cases, the Ottomans raised the enslaved children to become bureaucrats within the imperial government. Much of this expansion occurred during the reign of **Selim I**, who came to power in 1512. Significantly, Selim claimed that he was the rightful heir to Islamic tradition under the Arab caliphs. With that claim, and with such a huge empire, Istanbul became the center of Islamic civilization.

Just eight years later, **Suleiman I** (a.k.a. Suleiman the Magnificent) rose to power. He not only built up the Ottoman military, but also actively encouraged the development of the arts. For this reason, the Ottoman Empire experienced a golden age under his reign, which lasted from 1520 until 1566. During this time, the Ottomans tried to push into Europe through Hungary. You already read that the Holy Roman Empire was weakening during the Protestant Reformation. The Ottomans took advantage of this weakness; after taking parts of Hungary, the Turks tried to move into Austria. In 1529, the empire laid siege to Vienna, a significant European cultural center. Had the Turks successfully taken Vienna, who knows what the history of Western Europe would have been. From Vienna, the Turks could have easily poured into the unstable lands of the Holy Roman Empire, but it wasn't meant to be. Vienna was as far as the Turks ever got. Although Austrian princes and the Ottomans battled continually for the next century, the Ottomans were never able to expand much beyond the European territories of Byzantine influence.

The Safavids

It is worth mentioning the chief rivals of the Ottoman were their eastern neighbors, the Safavids. This centralized state was based on military conquest and dominated by Shia Islam. Its location between the Ottomans and the Mughals, in what is modern-day Iran, resulted in often contentious relationships between the Muslim states, alliances with European nations against the Ottomans, and a continuation of the long-standing rift between the Sunni and Shia sects.

Still, the Ottoman Empire lasted until 1922, making it one of the world's most significant empires. In that time, it greatly expanded the reach of Islam, while also keeping Eastern Europe in a constant state of flux. This allowed the powers of Western Europe to dominate, and once they started exploring the oceans, they were able to circumvent their eastern neighbors and trade directly with India, China, and their American colonies.

Remember the Mongols? After several false starts, in 1526, **Babur**, a leader who claimed to be descended from Genghis Khan but was very much Muslim, invaded northern India and swiftly defeated the Delhi Sultanate (also Muslim). Babur quickly established a new empire, known as the **Mughal Empire**, which dominated the Indian subcontinent for the next 300 years.

The Mughal Empire was distinctive for several reasons. First, within about 150 years, it had united almost the entire subcontinent, something that hadn't previously been done to the same extent. Recall that northern India experienced a series of invasions and empires, many of which you reviewed in the previous chapter. The same was not true of southern India. The Deccan Plateau in southern India had remained mostly isolated. It was there that Hinduism became very firmly established.

Babur's grandson, Akbar, who ruled from 1556 to 1605, was able to unify much of India by governing under a policy of religious toleration. Although Akbar gave the Muslim **zamindars** (landowners) the power to tax, as well as an army to enforce such taxation, he did allow Hinduism and Islam to be practiced openly. He eliminated the jizya, the head tax on Hindus that had been a source of great anger to the people, and tried to improve the position of women by attempting to eliminate sati, the practice in which high-caste Hindu women would throw themselves onto their husbands' funeral pyres. He even married a Hindu woman and welcomed Hindus into government positions.

For nearly 100 years, Hindus and Muslims increasingly lived side by side and, consequently, became more geographically mixed. The result was a golden age of art, architecture, and thought. Under **Shah Jahan**, Akbar's grandson, the **Taj Mahal** was built. However, after Akbar, two developments forever changed India.

The first was that religious toleration ended. When a new emperor, Aurangzeb, who was a very pious Muslim, came to the throne, he enacted pro-Muslim policies and waged wars of expansion to try to conquer the remaining portions of India still not under Mughal control. The Muslim government reinstated the jizya; Hindu temples were destroyed. The consequences of this development were significant for later centuries, but for the moment, understand that by 1700, Muslims began to persecute Hindus who were beginning to organize against their Muslim rulers and neighbors.

The second development was the arrival of the Europeans. In the early 17th century, the Portuguese and British were fighting each other for Indian Ocean trade routes. In the beginning, Portugal had established trade with the city of Goa, where it also sent Christian missionaries. By 1661, the British East India Company had substantial control of trade in Bombay. By 1691, the British dominated trade in the region and founded the city of Calcutta as a trading outpost. While the Mughal emperors were annoyed with the Europeans, they generally permitted the trade and regarded the Europeans as relatively harmless. Of course, the Industrial Revolution would turn Britain into an imperial superpower. But before 1750—the calm before the storm—India didn't feel particularly vulnerable to the Europeans, except in its port cities. It was a huge country with tons of resources united under strong Muslim rulers. It couldn't be conquered, right? At the time, Indians probably couldn't imagine that a century later, a British woman named Victoria would be crowned Empress of India.

Want More World History?
Check out our book *Fast Track: World History* for an essential and colorful review of all advance world history topics. Scan QR code to purchase or go to www.penguin-randomhouse.com/books/633975/fast-track-world-history-by-the-princeton-review/

C. Africa

Beginning in the 10th century, strong centralized states developed in southern and western Africa based on the wealth accumulated from trade. The trend of increased power continued with the transatlantic slave trade and the establishment of powerful kingdoms by the **Songhai**, and in the kingdoms of **Kongo and Angola**, among others. While you are not expected to know each of these kingdoms in detail, you should recognize the pattern of state-building and the relationship of Africa to both the Islamic world and the Europeans.

The sub-Saharan empire of Songhai was mentioned briefly in the previous chapter. Like its predecessors, Ghana and Mali, this was an Islamic state with economic ties to the broader Muslim world through the trans-Saharan trade of salt and gold. Like other empires, this was built on conquests and military force. Sunni Ali (ruled 1464–1493) consolidated his empire in the valley of the Niger River using an imperial navy, established a central administration, and financed the city of Timbuktu as a major Islamic center. Like all great empires, Songhai fell to a superior military force: Moroccans with muskets.

Adjacent to the Songhai Kingdom, the **Asanti** (Ashanti) Empire arose in 1670. Deriving its wealth from the gold trade, the Asanti Empire was more prepared to face invasions due to its highly organized military. Accordingly, the Asanti greatly expanded its territory.

On the west coast of Africa, the centralized kingdom of **Kongo** was bolstered by its trade with Portuguese merchants as early as the 1480s. The Europeans established close economic and political relationships with the king, a situation that initially worked to everyone's advantage. The kings of the Kongo converted to Catholicism, and **King Alfonso I** was particularly successful at converting his people. Over the long term, Portuguese tactics and the desire for enslaved people from the interior undermined the authority of the kings of Kongo and the state gradually declined. Eventually, there were outright hostilities and war between the two former allies and the kingdom was mostly destroyed.

South of Kongo, the Portuguese established a small trading post in Ndongo, or **Angola**, as early as 1575 for the sole purpose of expanding their trade in enslaved people from the interior. As a result, Angola grew into a powerful state and when the Portuguese attempted to further exert their authority and control, **Queen Nzinga** fiercely resisted. For 40 years, the warrior queen led her troops in battle, studied European military tactics, and made alliances with Portugal's Dutch rivals. Despite her efforts, in the end, she could not unify her rivals or overcome the superior weaponry of the Portuguese.

D. Isolated Asia

1. China

By 1368, the Ming Dynasty booted out the last of the Mongol rulers in China and restored power over the empire to the native Chinese. The Ming Dynasty ruled until 1644. During this time, the Ming built a strong centralized government based on traditional Confucian principles, reinstated the civil service examination, and removed the Mongol influence by reinvigorating Chinese culture.

In the early 15th century, the Chinese also did something quite extraordinary: they built huge fleets. **Zheng He**, a Chinese navigator, led fleets throughout southeast Asia and the Indian Ocean all the way to East Africa a century before the Europeans did the same. Had the Chinese continued to explore and trade, they may have become the dominant colonial power. Instead, within a few decades, the Chinese abruptly stopped their naval voyages. Increasingly, Chinese society turned inward.

The Ming government attempted to prop up its failing economy by changing easily counter-feited paper money to a "single-whip" system based on silver currency. Initially, Japan supplied the silver (much to the benefit of the shoguns in Japan), but with the discovery of American silver sources, China established trade relations with the Spanish through the Philippines. Although this exchange fueled a period of commercial expansion, inevitably the silver flooded the Chinese market, and the government was unable to control the resulting inflation.

By the 16th century, the Ming Dynasty was already in its decline, just as the Europeans were beginning to sail toward China. Pirates increasingly raided port cities, and the Portuguese set up shop in Macao. Still, the Chinese were able to keep the Europeans at a safe distance. However, internal problems persisted. By the 17th century, famines crippled the Chinese economy, and peasant revolts erupted against the increasingly powerless Ming rulers. In 1644, the Ming emperor invited a group of **Qing** warriors from nearby Manchuria to help him quell a peasant uprising, but instead, the Qing ousted the emperor. With that act, the Ming Dynasty ended and the Qing (or Manchu) Dynasty began. The **Manchus** ruled China until 1911.

Focus On: Environmental Change and Collapse

The new food crops that arrived in Europe, Africa, and Asia from the Americas (cassava, corn, peanuts, and pota-toes) were high in calories, easy to grow in previously uncultivated areas, and, as a result, allowed for massive population increases. These crops, along with new agricultural technologies and political stability, were initially a boon to China's economy and productivity. However, the new population levels could not be sustained over the long term, and a period of global cooling in the late 17th century put pressure on agricultural lands and hastened the collapse of the Ming Dynasty. In Europe, the arrival of potatoes finally stabilized a food supply and a population that had been devastated by centuries of cold weather, poor farming, and epidemic disease.

Because the Qing were from Manchuria, they were not ethnically Chinese. They attempted to remain an ethnic elite, forbidding the Chinese to learn the Manchu language or to marry Manchus. However, because the Manchus comprised a mere three percent of the population, they needed the help of ethnic Chinese to run the country. Therefore, the civil service examination gained new status. Even members of the lower classes were able to rise to positions of responsibility as the Manchus opened up the floodgates to find the best talent.

Since these emperors were not ethnically Chinese, they had to find ways to affirm their legitimacy in the eyes of the Chinese people. **Imperial portraits** of the emperors would be publicly displayed, often with items significant to Chinese history, such as books and other artifacts. Such images were reminiscent of the ancient Chinese tradition of ancestor veneration and helped solidify the authority of the ruling Manchus.

Manchu emperors were well steeped in Chinese traditions. Both **Kangxi**, who ruled from 1661 to 1722, and his chief successor, **Qianlong**, who ruled from 1735 to 1796, were Confucian scholars. Both emperors not only supported the arts, but also expanded the empire. Kangxi conquered Taiwan and extended the empire into Mongolia, central Asia, and Tibet. Qianlong added Vietnam, Burma, and Nepal to the vassal states of China.

In all of this expansion, the Chinese did not aspire to conquer the rest of the world, or even interact with it very much. They stayed focused on China and its surrounding neighbors. The

Manchus did trade with the Europeans and granted rights to the Portuguese, Dutch, and British, but they were vigilant about and successful at controlling trade relations through the mid-18th century. The Manchu were fierce protectors of their culture. When they felt threatened by European advances, they expelled the Europeans. In 1724, for example, Christianity was banned. In 1757, trade was restricted to just one city, Canton. Still, trade with Europeans was substantial. The Europeans bought large quantities of tea, silk, and porcelain. In exchange, the merchants received huge sums of silver, which created a new rising class of merchants in Chinese coastal cities.

2. Japan

In the 16th century, a series of shoguns continued to rule Japan while the emperor remained merely as a figurehead. As the century went on, Japanese feudalism began to wane and centralized power began to emerge. The shogun still ruled (as opposed to the emperor), but the power of the feudal lords was reduced. This centralization of power coincided with Japanese exposure to the West. In 1542, the Portuguese established trade with the empire (they also introduced guns to the Japanese). Within a decade, Christian missionaries streamed in. By the end of the century, not only had a few hundred thousand Japanese converted to Christianity, but the Jesuits took control of the port city of Nagasaki and trade flourished. Japan was well on its way to westernization.

In 1600, the trend changed dramatically. That year, **Tokugawa Ieyasu** established the Tokugawa Shogunate, a strict and rigid government that ruled Japan until 1868. The shogun further consolidated power away from the emperor and at the expense of the daimyo (feudal lords). Ieyasu claimed personal ownership to all lands within Japan and instituted a rigid social class model, inspired somewhat by Confucianism but in practice was more like the caste system. Four classes (warrior, farmer, artisan, and merchant) were established and movement among the classes was forbidden.

The Tokugawa period—also known as the **Edo period** because Tokugawa moved the capital to Edo (modern-day Tokyo)—was marked by a reversal in attitudes toward Western influences. Within two decades, Christians were persecuted. By 1635, a **National Seclusion Policy** prohibited Japanese from traveling abroad, and prohibited most foreigners from visiting Japan (limited relations were kept with China, Korea, and the Netherlands). In other words, Japan became increasingly secluded. The policy remained in place for nearly 200 years.

Tokugawa was very serious about this policy. He was worried that Japan would be overrun by foreign influences. Keep in mind that Spain had claimed the nearby Philippines and that the English and Portuguese kept trying to make their way into China. So, in 1640, when a group of Portuguese diplomats and traders sailed to Japan to try to negotiate with the emperor and convince him to open up a dialogue, the shogun had every member of the Portuguese delegation executed on the spot. The message was clear. Japan was off limits.

Contrast Them: India, China, and Japan on European Aggression

No doubt about it, under the Tokugawa Shogunate, the Japanese reacted most decisively against European colonialism. Both China and India allowed trade and European occupation of port cities, although in China it was increasingly limited under the Manchus. India was least suspecting of the Europeans and paid dearly for it. In the next chapter, you'll see the consequences of these three attitudes toward the Europeans: India was overrun, China was partially overrun, and Japan, after briefly falling prey to outside influence, turned the tables and became a colonizing empire itself.

The absence of foreign influences allowed Japanese culture to thrive. During this time period, Buddhism and Shintoism remained at the center of culture, and unique Japanese art forms also prospered. **Kabuki** theatre and a new form of poetry, **haiku**, became very popular. Artists dedicated themselves to the creation of richly detailed scrolls, wood-block prints, and paintings. In other words, under a strong central authority, Japanese culture underwent its own renaissance. Unlike the European Renaissance, however, it was strictly intended for domestic consumption.

E. Resistance

Large states expanded their power in the 17th century. At times, that expansion was met with considerable local resistance. The table below lists some key rebellions against some of the world's largest powers.

Rebellion	Location	Year	Challenged Power	Outcome
Ana Nzinga's Resistance	Ambundu Kingdoms of Ndongo and Matamba (modern-day Angola)	1641–1671	Portugal	Nzinga used strategic alliances and guerrilla tactics to resist the Portuguese colonizers; fighting continued a decade after her death before Nzinga's kingdoms were absorbed into Portuguese Angola.
Cossack Revolts	Modern-day Ukraine	17th and 18th centuries	Russian Empire	The Russian Empire encroached on the autonomous Cossack people; following a series of rebellions, the Cossacks eventually fell to Russia's expansionary ambitions.

Rebellion	Location	Year	Challenged Power	Outcome
Haitian Slave Rebellion	Haiti	1791–1804	France	A rebellion of enslaved people eventually led to the defeat of the French occupiers and independence for Haiti.
Maratha	India	1680–1707	Mughal Empire	Resisting the encroaching Islamic Mughal Empire, the Hindu Maratha Kingdom ultimately defeated its would-be occupiers and thus began the **Maratha Empire**, which spread across the subcontinent.
Maroon Societies	Caribbean and Brazil	17th and 18th centuries	Slave-owning societies in the Americas	Maroon communities formed by people who escaped slavery were often able to resist attempts at recapture and in several cases, signed treaties with frustrated authorities who accepted the Maroons' freedom.
Metacom's War	New England, United States	1675–1678	British colonists	Tensions over unfair trade practices by the colonists prompted this three-year war; the treaty to resolve the war aimed to restore a more equitable coexistence, though conflicts persisted.
Pueblo Revolts	Modern-day New Mexico, United States	1680	Spanish colonizers	The Native American Pueblo people pushed the Spanish colonizers out of New Mexico as a way to liberate themselves from the oppressive encomienda system. The victory was temporary, as the Spanish reentered the land a decade later.

IV.   UNIT 4: TRANSOCEANIC INTERCONNECTIONS

A. European Exploration and Expansion

Exploration before the late 15th century was largely limited to land travel. To be sure, ships were used on the Mediterranean and Indian Ocean trade routes for centuries, but they were linked up to land routes through Persia, Arabia, northern Africa, or central Asia on the Silk Road.

Eager to eliminate Muslim middlemen and discover more efficient trade routes to Asia, the Portuguese and their Iberian rivals, the Spanish, set out to sea. Advances in navigation, ship-building, and the development of gunpowder weapons allowed for increased sea travel. These "floating empires of the wind" soon controlled major shipping routes in the Indian Ocean, Indonesia, and the Atlantic Ocean.

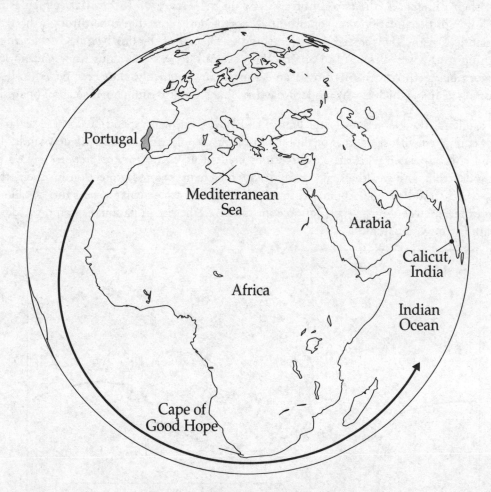

Portuguese Exploration in the 1500s

The increase in European trade encouraged by the formation of the Hanseatic League and the Crusades spawned a search for new, efficient trade routes on the seas. Portugal led the way because it was strategically situated near the coast of Africa, had long-standing trade relations with Muslim nations, and, most importantly, was led by a royal family that supported exploration (King John I of Portugal's most famous son was **Prince Henry the Navigator**). In

1488, Portugal financed a voyage by Bartholomew Dias, who rounded the tip of Africa (which became known as the Cape of Good Hope). In 1497, **Vasco da Gama** rounded the Cape of Good Hope, explored the east African kingdoms, and then went all the way to India, where he established trade relations.

Shortly thereafter, Spain, which had recently been unified under Isabella and Ferdinand, wanted in on the action. As you well know, in 1492 **Christopher Columbus** convinced them to finance a voyage to reach the east by going west. While those who were educated understood that the earth was a sphere, few people understood how large it was. Despite the fact that some scholars had accurately estimated the earth's size, most people, including Columbus, thought it was smaller. As a result, Columbus thought that China and India were located where the American continents are. He sailed, found Cuba and the islands that came to be known as the West Indies, and the exploration of the Americas was underway.

By 1494, Portugal and Spain were already fighting over land in the newly found Americas. To resolve their differences, the two countries drew up the **Treaty of Tordesillas**, which established a line of demarcation on a longitudinal (north-south) line that runs through the western Atlantic Ocean. They agreed that everything to the east of the line belonged to Portugal; everything to the west belonged to Spain. The western side was enormous (they had no idea how enormous at the time) so Spain became a mega-power quickly. Brazil happened to lie to the east of the line, which is why modern-day Brazilians speak Portuguese instead of Spanish.

Soon, England, the Netherlands, and France launched their own expeditions. These seafaring nations competed with each other by rapidly acquiring colonies and conquering new lands. The cost and risk associated with these explorations made it necessary for explorers to rely on the backing of strong and wealthy states. In addition, merchants wanted protection for their trade routes, which could also be acquired through allegiance to a particular sovereignty. Colonialism and the expansion of the trade routes contributed to the rise in nationalism and the development of strong monarchies.

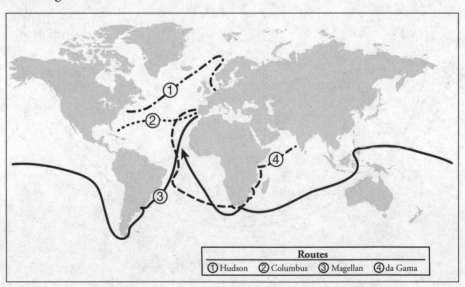

European Exploration in the Early 16th Century

Here's a quick list of other explorers.

- **Amerigo Vespucci**—He explored South America on several trips around 1500; he realized that the continent was huge and not part of Asia; America was named for him.

- **Ponce de Leon**—In 1513, he explored Florida for Spain in search of the fountain of youth.

- **Vasco de Balboa**—In 1513, he explored much of Central America for Spain; he laid sight on the Pacific Ocean.

- **Ferdinand Magellan**—In 1519, he sailed around the tip of South America to the Pacific Ocean for Portugal. He made it as far as the Philippines, where he died; his crew continued, however, and became the first to circumnavigate the globe.

- **Giovanni da Verrazzano**—In 1524, he explored the North American coast for France.

- **Sir Francis Drake**—In 1578, he became the first Englishman to circumnavigate the globe.

- **John Cabot**—In 1497, he explored the coast of North America for England.

- **Henry Hudson**—Beginning in 1609, he sailed for the Dutch, looking for a **Northwest Passage** to Asia. He explored the Hudson River and made claims to the area for the Dutch.

And Now a Word from Our Sponsors

Why, all of a sudden, were so many explorers sailing around the globe? Why didn't this happen sooner? In the late 15th century, innovation was combined with determination to apply new technologies to political and economic goals. In addition to advanced mapmaking techniques, the Age of Exploration was brought to you by the following fine products:

- **The Sternpost Rudder**—Invented in China during the Han Dynasty, the sternpost rudder allowed for better navigation and control of ships of increasing size. How did it end up in the hands of the Europeans? Trade, of course.

- **Lateen Sails**—These sails, invented during the early Roman Empire, allowed ships to sail in any direction, regardless of the wind. This was a huge improvement to ships that were dependent on the wind, especially in the Indian Ocean waters, where monsoons kept ships docked for long periods of time. Once these sails were used regularly on the Indian Ocean routes, they quickly became standard on transatlantic voyages.

- **The Astrolabe**—Sailors used this portable navigation device, developed in the Hellenic world around 150 B.C.E., to help them find their way. By measuring the distance of the sun and the stars above the horizon, the astrolabe helped determine latitude.

- **The Magnetic Compass**—Borrowed from the Chinese, who developed it during the Han Dynasty, the magnetic compass traveled west through trade with Arabs and allowed sailors to determine direction without staying in sight of land.

- **Three-Masted Caravels**—These large ships employed significantly larger lateen sails and could hold provisions for longer journeys in their large cargo rooms.

To be sure, many of these inventions existed prior to the 15th century, but so much of history is about timing. In the late 15th century, these inventions had converged on one continent, a continent that was fiercely competitive about trade routes, newly wealthy, increasingly organized under strong leaders, and racing with the innovation and imagination of the Renaissance. We've said it before and we'll say it again: the events of this time period are so interrelated that you can't separate them. The era needs to be understood as one giant glob of inseparable, indistinguishable forces.

B. The New World: Accidental Empire

Although Columbus failed to locate gold or spices in the Americas, the next generation of Spanish explorers found great wealth in the Aztec and Inca Empires. In 1519, **Hernando (Hernán) Cortés** landed on the coast of Mexico with a small force of 600 men. He found himself at the heart of the Aztec Empire, which you read about in the previous chapter. As you might recall, the Aztecs used the conquest of neighboring communities to secure humans for religious sacrifices. Many of these neighboring states loathed the Aztecs and were more than willing to cooperate with the Spaniards. Cortés alternatively subjugated or slaughtered those that were not.

Cortés, aided and guided by the resentful neighbors, first approached the magnificent Aztec capital of Tenochtitlan on horseback. Horses were as yet completely unknown in America (and in fact were introduced to the continent by Spanish conquistadores). Montezuma, the Aztec ruler, sent a gift of gold to appease this newcomer to his lands, but unfortunately for the Aztecs, this offering only fueled the appetite of the new conquerors. Because the Spaniards' sole motivation for exploring the New World was to acquire gold and spices, the Spanish didn't hesitate to seize Montezuma and begin a siege of Tenochtitlan.

C. Disease: The Ultimate Weapon of Mass Destruction

Although the Aztecs resisted the occupation and fought to rid their capital of the invaders, the Spanish had incredibly powerful weapons on their side, including diseases such as smallpox. These infections were completely new to the Americas, thanks to their geographic isolation prior to Europeans' arrival. The diseases quickly decimated the Aztecs, who had no natural resistance to them. The combination of disease, superior weapons, and assistance from Aztec enemies reduced the native population of the region from well over 20 million in 1520 to fewer than 2 million by 1580. Because so many of the deaths occurred in the first few years, the Spaniards were able to seize control of the empire by around 1525.

A similar fate met the Inca Empire. In 1531, **Francisco Pizarro** set out in search of the Incas with a tiny force of 200 men. Disease, superior weapons, and help from enemies quickly destroyed what little resistance the Incas could mount. In addition, Pizarro happened to land shortly after a very destructive civil war that had left the current emperor of the Incas in a shaky political position. By 1535, Pizarro was in control of the region.

Contrast Them: Expansion in the Americas Versus Empire-Building Elsewhere

We've talked about a lot of empires that expanded into far-reaching territories: the Romans, the Mongols, the Muslims, and the Macedonians, for example. In each of these cases, the empires either allowed existing cultural traditions to remain intact, or converted the existing population to their way of doing things, forcibly or not. By contrast, in the case of the Americas, the existing populations were largely wiped out. In addition, huge numbers of people moved in, far outnumbering the natives who had survived. Even the Mongols, who didn't hesitate to wipe out communities in their paths, didn't totally supplant the native populations the way the Europeans did in the Americas. Never before had an empire moved into such a vast territory that was so unpopulated (or, more accurately, depopulated). All of the other empires had to merge with, convert, or be converted by the existing populations. In the Americas, the Europeans created two new continents strictly in their own image.

D. The *Encomienda* System

Once Spain established a foothold in the New World, thousands of Spaniards arrived to build a new colonial empire. The colonial society was a hierarchical organization. At the top were the **peninsulares**, the select group of Spanish officials sent to govern the colonies. Below them, the *crillos,* or **creoles**, were people born in the colonies to Spanish parents. Because they weren't born in Spain, they were looked down upon by the Spanish monarchy and were consequently barred from high positions. Yet, because they were the children of Spaniards, the creoles were educated and wealthy, and after many generations, they were able to organize and demand recognition. They later became the leaders of the independence movements (more on that in the next chapter). Below the crillos were **mestizos**, those with European and Native American ancestry, followed by the **mulattos**, those with European and African ancestry. Finally, there were the native Americans, who had little or no freedom and worked on estates or in mines.

> In some regions of the New World, systems of forced labor already existed. For instance, the Inca used such a system known as *mit'a* for infrastructure projects. The Spaniards exploited this system and absorbed it into its *encomienda* structure.

To run the empire, the **viceroys**, who were appointed governors of each of the five regions of New Spain, established the *encomienda* system, which was a system of forced labor. The system provided the peninsulares with land and a specified number of native laborers. In return, the peninsulares were expected to protect the natives and convert them to Christianity. Shocked at the treatment of some of the natives, Christian missionaries appealed to the viceroys, emperor, and the Catholic Church to improve the natives' lot. Some in the empire agreed that reform was needed, but disastrously, the reform that was viewed as most important was the need for more workers. The reformers agreed to reduce the strain on the natives by bringing in new workers for the hardest jobs. Those new workers were enslaved Africans. Not only was this a cruel and ironic way to solve the problem (relieve the burden on one group of victims by creating a second group), but it also ended up not improving the lot of the natives. Within a few decades, both enslaved people and natives were at the bottom of the social structure, and neither had significant rights.

E. The African Slave Trade

Even before transatlantic voyages began, Europeans had begun exploiting a system of slavery that already existed in Africa. While many African tribes and nations practiced a form of slavery by requiring prisoners taken in battle to serve their captors for a period of time before being eventually released (when their captors judged that prisoners' honor, lost in battle, had been restored by their service), Europeans traded guns and other goods to African leaders in exchange for their surplus enslaved people but did not understand (or chose to ignore) the custom of eventual release. By the mid-15th century, the Portuguese were also capturing enslaved people while exploring the coasts of Africa. When the plantations (and mines) of the New World demanded more labor, the money-hungry empire builders knew where to go. So began a forced migration of people that would forever change the fate of millions of lives and the history of the New World.

Some African rulers cooperated with the slave trade, while others protested, but they were in a difficult position—as demand for the transatlantic slave trade increased, Europeans became increasingly ruthless in their methods, kidnapping Africans in their own raids or pitting groups against one another through control of the weapons trade. Kings and other leaders faced the choice of cooperating with the Europeans or seeing their people seized or slaughtered, so the slave trade expanded. Africans were rounded up, forced onto ships, chained together, taken below deck, and forced to endure the brutal **Middle Passage** to the Americas. By historians' best estimates, at least 13 million Africans were taken from the African continent and carried to the New World; approximately 60 percent went to South America, around 35 percent to the Caribbean, and about 5 percent to North America. Along the way, some suffocated from the hot, unventilated conditions below deck, others starved or died from outbreaks of disease, and yet others were killed attempting revolt or jumped overboard to their deaths, preferring suicide to the dishonor of slavery. Based on slave traders' existing records, historians believe average mortality rates were around 20 percent, though some voyages lost a much larger portion of their human cargo. Those who survived the journey were taken to the auction blocks, sold into slavery, and forced to work in plantation fields or in mines until their deaths, as were their children and their children's children.

Focus On: Demographic Shifts

The demographic changes of the 16th and 17th centuries were, in a word, huge. The Aztecs and Incas were wiped out. Large cities were depopulated. Europeans moved by the hundreds of thousands. Africans were forced to migrate by the millions. Cities in Europe swelled as the feudal system evaporated and urban, middle-class merchants lined their pockets with the fruits of trade and empire. By 1750, the continents of Europe, Africa, North America, and South America were unrecognizable from their 1450 portraits.

F. The Columbian Exchange

One consequence of the Spanish and Portuguese empires in the New World was what became known as the Columbian Exchange—the transatlantic transfer of animals, plants, diseases, people, technology, and ideas among Europe, the Americas, and Africa. As Europeans and Africans crisscrossed the Atlantic, they brought the Old World to the New and back again. From the European and African side of the Atlantic, horses, pigs, goats, chili peppers, and sugarcane (and more) flowed to the Americas. From the American side, squash, beans, corn, potatoes, and cacao (and more) made their way back east. Settlers from the Old World carried Bubonic Plague, smallpox, typhoid, influenza, and the common cold into the New and then carried Chagas and syphilis back to the Old. Guns, Catholicism, and enslaved Africans also crossed the Atlantic. With them, the enslaved people brought agriculture such as rice and okra, as well as elements of West African culture. Never before had so much been moved across the oceans, as ship after ship carried the contents of one continent to another.

The American food crops (cassava, corn, peanuts, and potatoes) that traveled east made population increases possible throughout Europe, Asia, and Africa. Urban populations and commercial interests grew throughout Europe and led to increased cultivation and enclosure of land. With increased cultivation came increased use of previously rural areas. Despite some threat of famine, shortages due to a long cooling period or "little ice age," and out-migration, overall the trend throughout much of northern Europe was that of a growing population.

Two key products of the Columbian Exchange were **sugar** and **silver**. Sugarcane roots had arrived in the Caribbean from India with Columbus, who saw an opportunity to monopolize a profitable crop in a new environment. Sugarcane production resulted in the development of plantations throughout the Spanish colonies and an increased need for enslaved or forced labor once the native populations of the islands declined. The results of the plantation system were brutal, dangerous labor and a transformation of the natural landscape.

The Spanish also monopolized the world's silver market from the mines they controlled in Mexico and in the Andes Mountain of Peru. This industry also resulted in a harsh system of forced labor: the previously mentioned *encomienda*. Like the sugar plantations, early silver mining depended on native labor until that grew too scarce to make a profit, when labor shifted to enslaved Africans provided by Portuguese traders.

More importantly, Spanish control of Latin American silver opened doors in Ming China. Spanish access to the Philippines, China, and the Pacific Ocean trade routes made the world a much smaller place.

G. The Commercial Revolution

The trading, empire building, and conquest of the **Age of Exploration** was made possible by new financing schemes that now form the basis of our modern economies. Though many elements had to come together at once for the new economy to work, timing was on the side of the Europeans, and everything fell into place.

First, the church gave in to state interests by revising its strict ban on what are now standard business practices, such as lending money and charging interest on loans. Once banking became respectable, a new business structure emerged: the **joint-stock company**, an organization created to pool the resources of many merchants, thereby distributing the costs and risks of colonization and reducing the danger for individual investors. Investors bought shares, or stock, in the company. If the company made money, each investor would receive a profit proportional to his or her initial investment. Because huge new ships were able to carry unprecedented cargoes, and because the goods were often outright stolen from their native countries, successful voyages reaped huge profits. A substantial middle class of merchants continued to develop, which in turn attracted more investors, and the modern-day concept of a stock market was well under way.

These corporations later secured royal charters for colonies, such as the Jamestown colony in Virginia, and funded them for business purposes. Even when they didn't establish colonies, monarchies granted monopolies to trade routes. The **Muscovy Company** of England monopolized trade routes to Russia, for example. The **Dutch East India Company** controlled routes to the Spice Islands (modern-day Indonesia).

Increased trade led to an early theory of macroeconomics for the nations of Europe. Under the theory of **mercantilism**, a country actively sought to trade, but tried not to import more than it exported; that is, it attempted to create a favorable balance of trade. Trade deficits forced dependencies on other countries, and therefore implied weakness. Of course, one country's surplus had to be met with another country's deficit. To resolve this dilemma, European countries were feverish to colonize. Colonies gave the mother country raw resources (not considered imports because the mother country "owned" them), while creating new markets for processed exports. To further aid the effort, monarchies promoted domestic industry and placed tariffs on imports from competing empires. As you'll see in the next chapter, once the Industrial Revolution was under way, mercantilism really took off.

It shouldn't be surprising that mercantilism fostered resentment in colonies. The colonial resources were shipped back to Europe while the colonists were forced to pay for products from Europe. Add taxes, and you've got major resentment. You already know that the American Revolution was in part due to colonial fury over this arrangement. One by one, beginning with America, European colonies revolted against the abuses by the unforgiving mercantilist economies of the European powers.

Oh Yeah…Remember Asia?

Recall that the original Portuguese explorers were trying to figure out a shortcut to India and China. Once they stumbled upon a couple of continents along the way and began wiping out native civilizations, building empires, and forcibly transporting millions of Africans to do hard labor, they forgot the original purpose of their exploration. In time, European explorers, armed with bottomless resources of energy and greed, remembered and pursued the East.

Asian colonization didn't really get rolling until the 19th century, so that will be covered in the next chapter. From the 16th through the 18th centuries, however, the Europeans managed to establish trade with the Asian empires, although it was more limited than they would have liked because of Asian protectionist policies and the difficulty of travel.

After making their way around the Cape of Good Hope, the Portuguese set up a trading post in Goa on the west coast of India. They also gained control over the Spice Islands by establishing naval superiority in the Straits of Malacca. In less than a century, however, other European powers coveted Asian riches. The Dutch, under the backing of the newly formed Dutch East India Company, conducted deliberate raids on Portuguese ships and trading posts. In the 17th century, the Dutch became the biggest power in the spice trades. Meanwhile, England and France set up trading posts in India.

As for China and Japan, both empires severely limited trade with the Europeans. Throughout this time period, the two Asian empires couldn't have been more unlike their European counterparts. They were highly isolationist. Not only did they not go out and try to find the rest of the world, they also pushed the rest of the world away when it came to find them. You'll read more about China and Japan in the next section.

Developments in Specific Countries and Empires, 1450–1750

It's dangerous to presume that because the Renaissance, the Protestant Reformation, the Scientific Revolution, the Enlightenment, and the Age of Exploration eventually had enormous consequences that they did so quickly, broadly, or in equal proportions. In reality, the major movements impacted different parts of Europe at different times and took a long time to penetrate all circles of society. Most people with power guarded it jealously, regardless of the intellectual or religious movements that brought their power into question. What's more, most of the peasant class didn't participate in the intellectual, scientific, or commercial developments because they weren't educated or in a position to be immediately impacted by the consequences.

Outside of Europe, the major developments of the time period also had widely varying consequences. In the previous section, we discussed the consequences on the Americas and on much of Africa. Lest you think the rest of the world remained passive in the face of European growth, it is important to note that powerful and centralized states were established (or reestablished) in the Middle East, India, China and Japan. The empires of Asia, too, had unique experiences, which are discussed in detail later in the chapter. As you review the developments in the European empires, keep in mind that most nations were led by monarchs, or sovereigns, who felt that the right to govern was ordained by God. Under this idea of divine right, it was essential for royal families to retain pure bloodlines to God, so intermarriage among royal families of different nations was common. Thus, the monarchies of one country also gained international influence as the ties of marriage and inheritance led to alliances.

Monarchies also contributed to the development of strong national loyalties, which led to many conflicts, internally and externally. The European wars of this time fall into three categories: religious fights between Protestants and Catholics, internal civil wars between a monarch and disgruntled nobles, and battles stemming from the trade disputes between rival nations. In the beginning of this era, Spain became the world's strongest nation with a powerful naval fleet and an extensive empire. As the balance of power in Europe shifted, the rival nations of England and France emerged as great powers.

V.   TECHNOLOGY AND INNOVATIONS, 1450–1750

Europe became a powerful force during this time period because of its willingness to adapt and use three key innovations that existed in other parts of the world: gunpowder weapons, navigation and ship-building technology, and finally the printing press (which developed independently in Germany). At a time when competition among the Europeans resulted in big risks and innovations, the Chinese and Japanese returned to more traditional lifestyles in order to maintain stability, and the Muslims, while retaining powerful land-based empires, allowed innovations in shipping and weaponry to pass them by.

The biggest impact of these new technologies was the expanded knowledge of the world that resulted from exploration by the European nations. Using their superior weapons and larger trading ships, the Europeans established new overseas trading empires, moved lots of plants and animals, enslaved and transported people across oceans, and generally transformed the interactions of the entire world. They fought wars with one another in Europe and—when they were unable to establish suitable trading relationships—went to war in the places they wished to conquer.

Increased contact meant the spread of new ideas and technology (such as the printing press), and the exposure to new cultures transformed both education and religion. The establishment of new Protestant churches in northern Europe increased the power of the kings and nation-states at the expense of the Catholic Church. Conversely, religious conflicts led to increased migrations from northern Europe and the resettlement of large numbers of colonists in the New World.

VI.   CHANGES AND CONTINUITIES IN THE ROLE OF WOMEN

A number of powerful women took charge of the most dominant empires of this time. These included Elizabeth I of England, Isabella of Spain, and Nur Jahan of Mughal, India. With the exception of Elizabeth, who chose never to marry, most of these women shared power with their husbands. In spite of the great power and visibility of these few elite women, for the most part the status and freedoms of women changed little from the previous period—legally they were often considered property of their husbands, inherited less than sons or brothers, and had few rights in legal or political spheres.

The biggest change in the lives of women came from the mixing of previously unknown cultures. The result of global exploration and colonization, these new relationships produced offspring considered mixed, or mestizo. Racial categories began to be more widely used in determining status or class hierarchy, and restrictions developed regarding marriages and legal relationships between classes. Changes in trade and production also placed a greater premium on male labor, and jobs that women had traditionally held, such as textile weaving, were increasingly dominated by men.

Some regions of the world served as exceptions to these general patterns but were still impacted by the global interactions. The forced migration of males in African societies resulted in a disproportionate number of females left behind in what were already matrilineal societies. These numbers reinforced polygyny, or multiple marriages. Although large numbers of men also migrated from Europe, the predominately Christian societies did not allow multiple marriages, and as the number of unmarried women increased, this created a problem in societies that regarded marriage as the goal of all women.

The non-European areas of the world tended to regard older or widowed women with both respect and superstition. In both Africa and many Native American societies, councils of older women were part of the political decision-making process. However, older women were also feared, as they couldn't necessarily be controlled. It was this need for control that led to a continuation of Neo-Confucianism values in eastern Asia. This social philosophy designated proper roles and virtues for women within the home with the understanding that if the home were stable so was the state.

In Europe, the revolutionary new ideas of the Renaissance and the Enlightenment included women, at least nominally. Education was more widely available to all classes, but opportunities for girls lagged far behind those for boys, and the highest levels of education were open only to males. Even the less hierarchical new Protestant religions limited the roles of women to wife and mother and did not have convents or monastic systems as alternatives to traditional roles. Eventually, the Protestant countries grew even more puritanical in their regulation of sex, marriage, and illegitimacy.

VII.   PULLING IT ALL TOGETHER

In the context of the Age of Exploration, "exploration" has lots of connotations. Of course, the most obvious is that it involved European exploration of the Americas and the beginnings of direct contact with Asia. But more than that, its exploration was also internal. In the Renaissance, Europe explored its own lost history. During the Protestant Reformation, it explored its relationship with God. During the Scientific Revolution, Europe explored the universe and the laws by which the universe functioned. During the Enlightenment, it explored the rights of man and the appropriate role of government, even as its empire depended on slavery. Finally, during the Commercial Revolution, Europe explored its potential.

Combined, these explorations were going in all directions—outward, upward, inward, backward to the past, forward to the future—and it was all going on simultaneously. If you're confused by the developments, you should be. It's hard to figure out which movements in which combination impacted which events. Historians haven't sorted it out either. It's open to debate.

What we can say is this: during the time period discussed in the chapter, Europe was where the energy was. There was so much change for so many reasons, that the boundaries of the continent couldn't contain it. Unlike China and Japan, which largely looked inward, and unlike the Islamic world, which didn't take to the seas or radically shake up religious and social orders, Europeans were dynamic at this particular time in history. They analyzed everything and were full of inconsistencies. At various points in history, other civilizations had at least as much energy and unrest, but because the Europeans had the technology, the political motivation, and the financial structure, they were able to quickly explode onto the world scene. Add in the evangelical nature of Christianity (an explicit desire to convert the world), and it's clear that the desire for expansion ran deep.

Some would say that European monarchs ruled absolutely during this time period and adopted a controlling, ethnocentric attitude with regard to the cultures they dominated. Perhaps this was precisely because Europe was in such cultural chaos itself. Who knows? We'll leave that to your further studies. In any case, it's hard to deny that even as Europeans explored their own history, culture, and structures to unprecedented degrees, they had little trouble marginalizing the complexities of others.

What About Non-European Cultures?
Why Was Their Interaction with the West So Varied?

There are lots of ways to answer these questions, but we'll get you started. China and Japan were both highly organized, confident civilizations. The contingencies of Europeans on their shores were modest. Because the Japanese and Chinese wanted desperately to preserve their own cultures, and because they had the power and sophistication to keep the Europeans, for the moment, at bay, that's precisely what they did. Why didn't the others?

In Africa, societies were fragmented. No centralized power existed, so the Europeans were harder to fend off. What's more, the Europeans weren't initially obsessed with penetrating the entire continent. Because they didn't have to overtake entire civilizations to achieve their goals, they were able to trade goods and abduct individuals one by one, with little concern for long-term impact on the continent.

In the Americas, of course, civilizations were quickly overwhelmed by European technology and disease. In the Ottoman Empire and Arabia, the interaction was somewhat limited because the Europeans weren't as dependent on the overland routes in their efforts to trade with India and China. This diminished the importance of the Middle East to the Europeans. What's more, because the Crusades ended unsuccessfully for the Europeans, trade with the Muslims was important, but conquest of the region was off the radar.

Finally, What About the Global Economy? How Did It Change?

Sailing, mercantilism, and private investment changed the global economy. Improvements in sailing diminished the need for the Asian land routes and connected the world like never before. Mercantilism and its dependence on the establishment of imperialism married economic and political developments. The establishment of joint-stock companies took major economic motivation out of the hands of governments and put it into the hands of the private sector. This meant that now thousands, tens of thousands, or even hundreds of thousands of people had a direct stake in trade routes and conquest. Because the benefits of economic prosperity were diffused among a larger group of individuals than ever before, governments began to lose their grip on controlling their own economies.

CHAPTER 7 KEY TERMS

Medici
Michelangelo
Brunelleschi
Leonardo da Vinci
Donatello
Johannes Gutenberg
printing press
vernacular
indulgences
Martin Luther
Pope Leo X
Lutherans
John Calvin
Calvinism
King Henry VIII
Church of England
Catholic Reformation
Counter-Reformation
Ignatius Loyola
Jesuits
Council of Trent
Tycho Brahe
Francis Bacon
Johannes Kepler
Sir Isaac Newton
atheists
King Ferdinand
Queen Isabella
Charles V
Ferdinand I.
Philip II
Spanish Inquisition
Decree of Alhambra
King Henry VIII
Act of Supremacy
Elizabeth I
Elizabethan Age
Muscovy Company
British East India Company
James I
Charles I
Petition of Right
Long Parliament
Oliver Cromwell
English Commonwealth

Lord Protector
Stuart Restoration
Habeas Corpus Act
Glorious Revolution
English Bill of Rights
Huguenots
Henry IV
Edict of Nantes
Cardinal Richelieu
Cardinal Mazarin
Louis XIV
Jean Baptiste Colbert
War of Spanish Succession
Philip V
Peace of Augsburg
Thirty Years' War
Peace of Westphalia
Ivan III
Ivan IV
boyars
Cossacks
Ivan the Terrible
Time of Troubles
Michael Romanov
Peter the Great
Catherine the Great
Ottoman Empire
Osman Bey
timars
devshirme
Selim I
Suleiman I
Babur
Mughal Empire
zamindars
Shah Jahan
Taj Mahal
Songhai
Kongo and Angola
Asanti
Kongo
King Alfonso I
Angola
Queen Nzinga
Zheng He

Qing
Manchus
Imperial portraits
Kangxi
Qianlong
Tokugawa Ieyasu
Edo period
National Seclusion Policy
Kabuki
haiku
Prince Henry the Navigator
Vasco da Gama
Christopher Columbus
Treaty of Tordesillas
Amerigo Vespucci
Ponce de Leon
Vasco de Balboa
Ferdinand Magellan
Giovanni da Verrazzano
Sir Francis Drake
John Cabot
Henry Hudson
Northwest Passage
The Sternpost Rudder
Lateen Sails
The Astrolabe
The Magnetic Compass
Three-Masted Caravels
Hernando (Hernán) Cortés
Francisco Pizarro
peninsulares
creoles
mestizos
mulattos
viceroys
encomienda
Middle Passage
sugar
silver
Age of Exploration
joint-stock company
Muscovy Company
Dutch East India Company
mercantilism

Chapter 7 Drill

See the end of the chapter for the answers and explanations.

Questions 1–5 refer to the image below.

1. This image most likely depicts which of the following?

   (A) A Portuguese caravel
   (B) A Viking longship
   (C) A Chinese junk
   (D) An Arabic dhow

2. Ships such as the one in the image were primarily salient to world history in that they

   (A) enabled Arabic control over the Indian Ocean
   (B) enabled diplomatic ties and cooperation across oceans
   (C) carried relatively large numbers of armed men, goods, and guns over long distances
   (D) facilitated Chinese colonialism

3. Which of the following were the most valuable goods by weight in international trade during the period in which the ship depicted would have been used?

   (A) Spices
   (B) Ivory and other animal products
   (C) Fraud and violence
   (D) Enslaved people

4. Ships such as the one in the image were most likely to be financed by

   (A) wealthy individual investors, such as aristocrats and factory owners
   (B) piracy and theft
   (C) letters of marque
   (D) royal beneficence or joint-stock companies

5. Which of the following most accurately characterizes the responses of the Chinese and Japanese Empires to the Age of Exploration?

   (A) Active participation in colonialism and trade
   (B) Passive participation in trade with European powers
   (C) Isolation and rejection of large-scale interaction with other states
   (D) Helpless victims of European colonial expansion

Questions 6–8 refer to the passage below.

God has created all these numberless people to be the simplest, without malice or duplicity, the most obedient, the most faithful to their natural Lords, and to the Christians, whom they serve, the most humble and patient, the most peaceful and calm, without strife or tumults, nor wrangling or querulous, as free from rancour, hate, and desire for revenge as any in the world.

They are likewise the most delicate people, weak and of feeble constitution, and they are less able than any other to bear fatigue, and they succumb readily to whatever disease attacks them… They are also very poor people, who have few worldly goods, nor wish to possess them.

Description of the indigenous people of the Americas.
From *A Short Account of the Destruction of the Indies*, by Bartolomé de las Casas. Written in 1542.

6. Indigenous people such as the ones described in the passage were NOT explicitly used by the Spanish Empire for which of the following purposes?

    (A) Reproduction
    (B) Agriculture
    (C) Mining
    (D) Domestic servitude

7. Which of the following represents the most successful indigenous uprising against Spanish colonizers in the seventeenth century?

    (A) The Mexican War of Independence
    (B) The Filipino Revolts
    (C) The Pueblo Revolts
    (D) The Cossack Revolts

8. For Europeans, which of the following represents a drawback of the Columbian Exchange?

    (A) a shortage of available workers to serve the *conquistadores* upon their return
    (B) a more limited range of food and beverage opportunities
    (C) increased death rates due to smallpox, typhoid, and influenza
    (D) the monetary inflation that occurred as a result of the arrival of so many new goods and precious metals

Questions 9–11 refer to the passage below.

It was about a year after the first breaking out of war that the tide of fortune began to turn, in some measure, in favor of the Russians. About that time the Czar gained possession of a considerable portion of the Baltic shore; and, as soon as she had done so, he conceived the design of laying the foundation of a new city there, with the view of making it the naval and commercial capital of his kingdom. This plan was carried most successfully into effect in the building of the great city of St. Petersburg.

From *History of Peter the Great, Emperor of Russia,* by Jacob Abbott, 1873.

9. The defeat of which of the following led to Russia's "possession of a considerable portion of the Baltic shore"?

   (A) The Ottoman Empire
   (B) The Safavid Dynasty
   (C) The Netherlands
   (D) Sweden

10. Which of the following conclusions about the period 1450–1750 C.E. is best supported by the passage?

   (A) Russia expanded its development as a civilization in order to expand the rights of its citizenry.
   (B) It was a period of growing absolute monarchy.
   (C) Europeans were threatened by the overwhelming growth of power to their East.
   (D) Empires began developing their own land instead of seeking new land.

11. The most important consequence of the events described in the passage was

   (A) The birth of the Russian Empire
   (B) The death of the tsarist Romanov regime
   (C) The beginning of European migration to Russia
   (D) The end of Russian militaristic expansion

TIMELINE OF MAJOR DEVELOPMENTS, 1450–1750

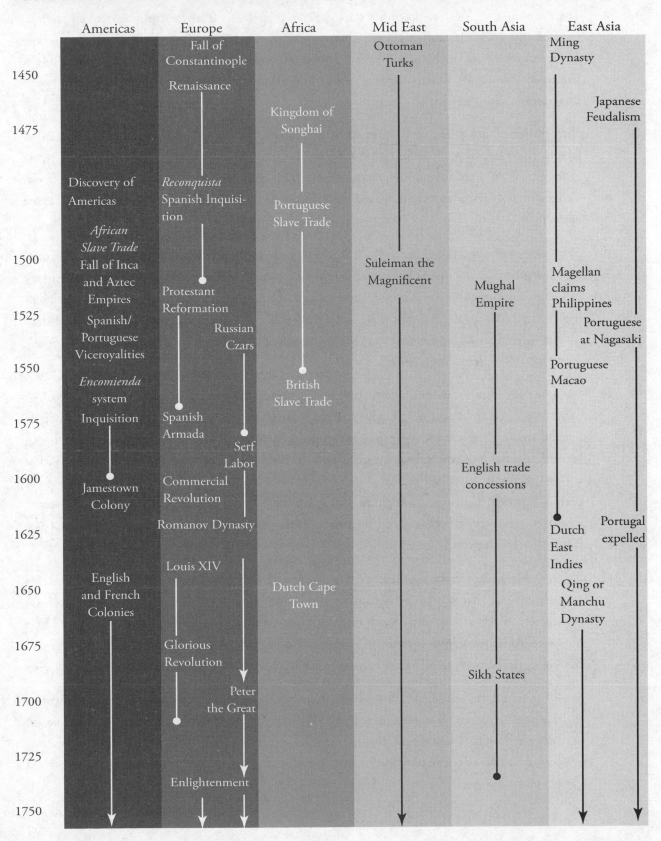

Americas	Europe	Africa	Mid East	South Asia	East Asia

1450 — Fall of Constantinople / Renaissance / Ottoman Turks / Ming Dynasty

1475 — Kingdom of Songhai / Japanese Feudalism

Discovery of Americas / *Reconquista* Spanish Inquisition / Portuguese Slave Trade

African Slave Trade Fall of Inca and Aztec Empires

1500 — Suleiman the Magnificent / Magellan claims Philippines

Spanish/Portuguese Viceroyalities / Protestant Reformation / Mughal Empire

1525 — Russian Czars / Portuguese at Nagasaki

Encomienda system

1550 — Portuguese Macao

British Slave Trade

1575 — Inquisition / Spanish Armada / Serf Labor

1600 — Jamestown Colony / Commercial Revolution / English trade concessions

1625 — Romanov Dynasty / Dutch East Indies / Portugal expelled

English and French Colonies / Louis XIV / Dutch Cape Town

1650 — Qing or Manchu Dynasty

1675 — Glorious Revolution

Sikh States

1700 — Peter the Great

1725

Enlightenment

1750

CHAPTER 7 DRILL EXPLANATIONS

1. **A** The prominent crosses on the ship's sails indicate that this is likely a European vessel, and the rows of gun ports for cannon cement that impression. In this era (the Age of Exploration), only European vessels routinely carried large numbers of gunpowder cannon, so eliminate (C) and (D). Viking longships, (B), were not sailing vessels, and in any case, were largely obsolete by the Age of Exploration. The answer is (A).

2. **C** Large sailing ships armed with broadside cannon made the Age of Exploration possible. Neither Islamic states nor China built or operated such vessels, so eliminate (A) and (D). The Age of Exploration was a period of fostered interaction between formerly separate peoples and states, but it was an age more of violent expansion than diplomatic cooperation, so (B) is incorrect. Choice (C) is the answer.

3. **A** This is more of a recall question, which might pop up on the AP World History: Modern Exam. This question is made more challenging by the fact that all of the listed "goods" were indeed very valuable. You can eliminate (C) first, since it's a practice rather than a trade good. Of the remaining choices, (A), spices, is the best answer. During this age, spices were worth many times their weight in gold in European markets. Ivory, (B), and enslaved people, (D), became substantially more valuable in trade after 1700.

4. **D** Large sailing ships armed with cannon were the single most expensive good during this period. (This would remain true until the advent of ships driven by steam.) Therefore, ships were generally beyond the reach of even very wealthy individuals. Eliminate (A). Piracy, though certainly popular and at times lucrative, generated wealth on the individual, not state, scale. Eliminate (B). For a long time, only states had the fiscal resources to build and equip such vessels. By the end of the period, however, joint-stock companies had come into their own and, by aggregating individual wealth in return for shares, allowed the private raising of sufficient capital for these ships. Choice (D) is therefore correct.

5. **C** Though they had their share of internal problems, the Ming and Qing dynasties ruled a powerful centralized state that was perfectly capable of resisting initial European advances. Therefore, (D) is incorrect. Neither power was much interested in expansion beyond their own borders, so (A) is incorrect. Although China engaged in some small-scale trade with European powers, Japan under the Tokugawa Shogunate sealed its borders to foreign powers. Therefore, (C) is correct.

6. **A** While some of the encomenderos—plantation owners—certainly used the indigenous servants to bear their children, it was never a formal objective of the Spanish Empire. Furthermore, in many portions of the New World, the indigenous population simply died out, mostly from disease, which is quite the opposite of reproduction. The other answer choices were roles that the enslaved indigenous tribes were expected to play, depending on region.

7. **C** The Pueblo Revolts occurred in New Mexico in the 1670s. The indigenous people of Pueblo San Juan united (using secret messages relayed through the number of knots in ropes!) and ejected their Spanish overlords. Their freedom only lasted 12 years, but it remains to this day the only successful native uprising against a colonizing power in North America. Choices (A) and (B) were even more successful, but they didn't occur until the nineteenth century, so eliminate both. Choice (D) took place in Russia, with no Spaniards involved whatsoever, so eliminate that too.

8. **D** When a society is flooded with wealth—either in currency or in hard goods—that society typically sees prices skyrocket. So happened with Europe during this era; as the exploitation of indigenous people in the New World increased, so did the harvesting of lumber, sugar, gemstones, and other goods. The arrival of these goods to the New World pushed up prices in Europe to unheard-of-levels in the span of a single generation, an event called the Price Revolution. Choices (B) and (C) are reversals, since Europeans experienced a greater range of food and beverage and a steady or even lowered rate of illnesses (unlike the indigenous counterparts, who suffered greatly). Eliminate (B) and (C). There is no evidence that there was a shortage of workers, so eliminate (A).

9. **D** The 21-year war with Sweden was the longest and most consequential event of Peter the Great's reign. The final defeat of Sweden granted Russia access to a long stretch of Baltic Sea, which granted it the ability to build both St. Petersburg and a navy. None of the other choices touch the Baltic Sea, so eliminate (A), (B), and (C).

10. **B** Peter the Great's reign over Russia was one of two great examples of absolute monarchy that arose in the seventeenth century, the other being Louis XIV of France. (Later, in the eighteenth century, Frederick the Great of Prussia would qualify.) Russia did expand its development as a civilization, but there were no rights extended to anybody, so eliminate (A). Europeans were not frightened of any power to the East, and certainly not Russia; in fact, European powers were busy trading with or conquering civilizations around the world. Eliminate both (C) and (D).

11. **A** The Russian Empire began as a direct result of Peter the Great's reign, both in his expansion of the land holdings and in his creation of a navy. In the centuries that followed, Russia used warfare against Sweden, Poland, Lithuania, and the Ottoman Empire (and others) to expand her holdings, so eliminate (D). Eliminate (B) because the tsarist Romanov regime would continue for another two centuries. Eliminate (C) because there was never any significant migration from Europe to Russia.

Chapter 8
Period 3,
c. 1750 to c. 1900

Unit 5: Revolutions

Unit 6: Consequences of
            Industrialization

I. CHAPTER OVERVIEW

Although this chapter covers only about 150 years, the world changed dramatically during that time. Europe's influence in the West waned even as it rose in the East. Napoleon tried to conquer Europe. Italy and Germany unified into modern nation-states. Japan became an imperial power. India was entirely overrun by the British. The United States rose to become a world power. The Industrial Revolution—the single biggest event of the time period—seemed to impact everything it touched, from political and economic developments, to the drive for colonial holdings in Africa and Asia, to daily life.

Here's the chapter outline:

I.   Chapter Overview

        You're in it.

II.   Stay Focused on the Big Picture

        Organize the major social, political, and economic changes that occurred during this time period into some big-picture concepts.

III.   Unit 5: Revolutions

        Here's how we've organized the information.

        A. The Enlightenment
        B. Enlightenment Revolutions in the Americas and Europe
        C. Industry and Imperialism
        D. Nationalist Movements and Other Developments
        E. The Growth of Nationalism

IV.   Unit 6: Consequences of Industrialization

        Here's how we've organized it:

        A. In Search of Natural Resources
        B. European Justification
        C. European Imperialism in India
        D. European Imperialism in China
        E. Japanese Imperialism
        F. European Imperialism in Africa
        G. The Berlin Conference
        H. U.S. Foreign Policy

V.   Technology and Innovations, 1750–1900

        Big machines, assembly lines, and new products.

VI.   Changes and Continuities in the Role of Women

        More education and more work!

VII.   Pulling It All Together

        Refocus on the big-picture concepts now that you've reviewed the historical details.

II. STAY FOCUSED ON THE BIG PICTURE

As you review the details of the developments in this chapter, stay focused on some big-picture concepts and ask yourself some questions.

For **Unit 5**, ask yourself:

1. Why did nationalism grow during this time period? How did the impact of nationalism vary among different countries? Whether in the Americas, Europe, or Asia, nationalism was a huge force. It sparked rebellions, independence movements, and unification movements. It also sparked domination and colonialism.

2. How and why does change occur? Stay focused on the complexity of social, political, and economic developments, as opposed to presuming that the dominant economic or political philosophies were shared universally among people in a certain country or region. Think about change as an evolving process in which certain ideas gain momentum, while other ideas lose steam but don't entirely die out.

For **Unit 6**, ask yourself:

3. How are the events of this time period interconnected? The Industrial Revolution and imperialism are not only interconnected but are connected to other developments in this time period as well. Stay focused on how developments in one region of the world had an impact on developments in another. Also, stay focused on how regional developments had a global impact through improvements in communication and transportation, as well as through colonialism.

4. How did the environment impact industrial and economic development? In Europe, the earliest phases of the Industrial Revolution were fueled by the resources available in England, so the resulting imperialism on a global scale was driven by the need for additional resources. Keep in mind the political and economic decisions that resulted in environmental change. At the same time, the environment impacted people. The general global cooling that began around 1500 C.E. put pressure on the populations of Europe and contributed to great poverty and peasant revolts, especially in the northern countries.

III.   UNIT 5: REVOLUTIONS

Focus On: The Church Defends Itself on Two Fronts

Both the Protestant Reformation and the Scientific Revolution challenged the absolute authority of the pope. The Reformation challenged the pope's authority on theological grounds; the Scientific Revolution challenged his authority on scientific and mathematical grounds. Don't presume that the Protestant Revolution was the main instigator of religious change during this time period. The religious implications of the Scientific Revolution were just as huge.

A. The Enlightenment

While the scientists put forth revolutionary ideas, the philosophers and social critics had a revolution of their own. **The Enlightenment** of the 17th and 18th centuries focused on the role of humankind in relation to government, ideas that greatly influenced the framers of the U.S. Constitution. Because the U.S. Constitution has since been a model for so many others across the globe, it's safe to say that the writers of the Enlightenment period changed the world.

Who were these Enlightenment writers? Here's an overview:

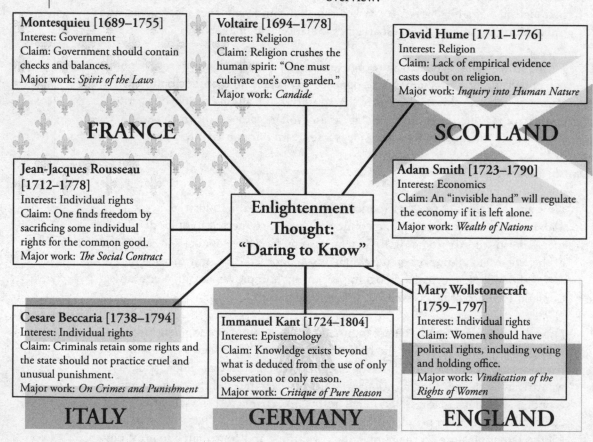

Montesquieu [1689–1755]
Interest: Government
Claim: Government should contain checks and balances.
Major work: *Spirit of the Laws*

Voltaire [1694–1778]
Interest: Religion
Claim: Religion crushes the human spirit: "One must cultivate one's own garden."
Major work: *Candide*

David Hume [1711–1776]
Interest: Religion
Claim: Lack of empirical evidence casts doubt on religion.
Major work: *Inquiry into Human Nature*

FRANCE

SCOTLAND

Jean-Jacques Rousseau [1712–1778]
Interest: Individual rights
Claim: One finds freedom by sacrificing some individual rights for the common good.
Major work: *The Social Contract*

Adam Smith [1723–1790]
Interest: Economics
Claim: An "invisible hand" will regulate the economy if it is left alone.
Major work: *Wealth of Nations*

Enlightenment Thought: "Daring to Know"

Cesare Beccaria [1738–1794]
Interest: Individual rights
Claim: Criminals retain some rights and the state should not practice cruel and unusual punishment.
Major work: *On Crimes and Punishment*

Immanuel Kant [1724–1804]
Interest: Epistemology
Claim: Knowledge exists beyond what is deduced from the use of only observation or only reason.
Major work: *Critique of Pure Reason*

Mary Wollstonecraft [1759–1797]
Interest: Individual rights
Claim: Women should have political rights, including voting and holding office.
Major work: *Vindication of the Rights of Women*

ITALY

GERMANY

ENGLAND

First a Little Background: Divine Right

During the High Middle Ages and through the Renaissance and Counter-Reformation, the church allied itself with strong monarchs. These monarchs came to power by centralizing authority, uniting people under a common banner of nationalism, forming empires by promoting exploration and colonization (much more on this later), and ruling with absolute authority. Because the vast majority of their populations were Christian, the best way to rule was to align oneself with God. Monarchs became convinced that God had ordained their right to govern, and that meant that people had a moral and religious obligation to obey them. This concept was known as the **divine right** of monarchs. James I of England, who ruled from 1603 to 1625, summed it up this way: "The king is from God and the law is from the King." His statement made it pretty clear that an illegal act was an ungodly act.

Because the pope also claimed to be ordained by God, the question of ultimate authority became very confusing indeed. During the Reformation, monarchs who resented the power of the church supported the reformists (Luther, Calvin, and others). Other monarchs, particularly in Spain and France, allied themselves with the church during the Counter-Reformation. In both cases, monarchs claimed to have divine right. Divine right could be used to support either position because the bottom line was that God supported whatever the monarchs chose.

Contrast Them: Divine Right and Mandate of Heaven

In the Zhou Dynasty (1046–256 B.C.E.) in China, the emperor ruled under what became known as a **Mandate of Heaven**, which sounds a whole lot like Divine Right, and it was except for an important difference. Under the Mandate of Heaven, the emperors believed they were divinely chosen, but would be given authority to rule only as long as they pleased heaven. If they didn't rule justly and live up to their responsibility, heaven would ensure their fall. Divine Right, on the other hand, was used to justify absolute rule without any corresponding responsibilities. Monarchs who ruled under a strict theory of Divine Right saw themselves as God's personal representatives, chosen specifically for the task of ruling. In other words, Divine Right was a privilege without any qualification, whereas the Mandate of Heaven was upheld only so long as rulers acted justly.

The Social Contract: Power to the People

During the 17th century, philosophers and intellectuals began to grapple with the nature of social and political structures, and the idea of the social contract emerged. The social contract held that governments were formed not by divine decree, but to meet the social and economic needs of the people being governed. Philosophers who supported the social contract theory reasoned that because individuals existed before governments did, governments arose to meet the needs of the people, not the other way around. Still, because different philosophers looked at human nature differently, they disagreed about the role of government in the social contract.

Thomas Hobbes (1588–1679), who wrote *Leviathan*, thought that people by nature were greedy and prone to violent warfare. Accordingly, he believed the role of the government under the social contract should be to preserve peace and stability at all costs. Hobbes therefore advocated an all-powerful ruler, or Leviathan, who would rule in such a heavy-handed way as to suppress the natural war-like tendencies of the people.

John Locke (1632–1704), who wrote *Two Treatises on Government*, had a more optimistic view of human nature, believing that mankind, for the most part, was good. Locke also believed that all men were born equal to one another and had natural and unalienable rights to life, liberty, and property. Since mankind was good and rational, and thus capable of self-rule, Locke believed the primary responsibility of the government under the social contract was to secure and guarantee these natural rights. If, however, the government ever violated this trust, thus breaking the social contract, the people were justified in revolting and replacing the government.

Rousseau's Legacy

Needless to say, Rousseau's beliefs not only had a tremendous effect on revolutionary movements in the colonies of the European empires, but also inspired the anti-slavery movement.

Jean-Jacques Rousseau (1712–1778) took the social contract theory to its furthest extreme, arguing that all men were equal and that society should be organized according to the general will, or majority rule, of the people, an idea he outlined in his famous work *The Social Contract* (1762). In a rational society, he argued, each individual should subject himself to this general will, which serves as the sovereign or ruling lawmaker. Under this philosophy, the individual is protected by the community, but is also free (or as free as one can be in organized society). He argues the essence of freedom is to obey laws that people prescribe for themselves.

Among the other Enlightenment thinkers and writers were Voltaire and Montesquieu. **Voltaire** espoused the idea of religious toleration. **Montesquieu** argued for separation of powers among branches of government. In all cases, Enlightenment writers didn't presume that government had divine authority, but instead worked backward from the individual and proposed governmental systems that would best serve the interest of the people by protecting individual rights and liberties.

While the real fruits of the Enlightenment were the revolutionary movements in the colonies and later in Europe, the new political ideas also affected the leadership of some 18th-century European monarchs. The ideals of tolerance, justice, and improving quality of life became guidelines for rulers known as **enlightened monarchs**, such as Joseph II of Austria and Frederick II of Prussia. To be sure, they still ruled absolutely, but they internalized the Enlightenment philosophy and made attempts to tolerate diversity, increase opportunities for serfs, and take on the responsibilities that their rule required.

Ironically, though the Enlightenment was a time of great intellectual and logical advancement, it was also a time of declining interest in new forms of art. The **Neoclassical Period**, which began in the middle of the 18th century, imitated the balanced, symmetrical style of ancient Greek and Roman architecture. This is the reason that many American federal buildings in Washington, D.C. are designed to look like Greek temples—that was the style when our country was founded.

B. Enlightenment Revolutions in the Americas and Europe

Two Revolutions: American and French

1. The American Revolution

For the most part, you won't need to know much about American history for the AP World History: Modern Exam. However, you will need to know about events in the United States that impacted developments in the rest of the world. The American Revolution is one of those events.

Britain began colonizing the east coast of North America during the 17th century. By the mid-18th century, British colonists in America felt threatened by France's colonial settlements on the continent. France and Britain were long-time rivals (archenemies in the Hundred Years' War and since), and they carried this rivalry with them into fights in America. The French enlisted the Algonquin and Iroquois tribes to fight alongside them against the encroaching colonists, but in 1763, England prevailed over the French in a war that was known in the colonies as the **French and Indian War** but known in Europe as the **Seven Years' War**. The British victory changed the boundaries of the two empires' American possessions, pushing French territory to the north while English territories expanded westward into the Ohio River Valley.

While the colonists were thrilled with the results of the war, the British felt the colonists had not adequately shared the burden. Of course, the colonists resented this, claiming that it was their efforts that made colonial expansion possible in the first place. At the same time, Britain's **George Grenville** and later **Charles Townshend** passed very unpopular laws on behalf of the British crown. These laws, including the **Revenue Act** (1764), the **Stamp Act** (1765), and the **Tea Act** (1773), were intended to raise additional funds for the British government. These laws created great unrest among the colonists, who not only felt the taxes were economically unfair, but also politically unjust: they had not been represented in Parliament when the laws had been passed. Thus arose the revolutionary cry, "No taxation without representation."

After the colonists dumped tea in Boston Harbor to protest the Tea Act, relations between crown and colonies deteriorated rapidly. On April 19, 1775, British troops battled with rebellious colonists in Lexington and Concord, and by the end of that bloody day, nearly 400 Britons and Americans were dead. The War of Independence had begun.

Independence Can't Happen Without a Little Paine The overwhelming majority of American colonists had either been born in England or were children of those born in England, and therefore many colonists felt ambivalent about—if not completely opposed to—the movement for independence. Even those who sought independence were worried that Britain was too powerful to defeat. One

Calling All History Buffs!
Taking the AP U.S. History Exam as well? You're in luck! Check out our *AP U.S. History Prep* for a comprehensive content review, strategy tips, and tons of practice.

Focus On: Causes and Consequences of the American Revolution

Don't worry too much about knowing the details of the American Revolution. You certainly don't need to know battles or even the personalities. Instead, understand that the Enlightenment had a huge impact because it not only helped to inspire the revolution itself, but also the type of government that was created after it succeeded. Also remember that mercantilist policies drove the American colonists nuts, as was the case in European colonies everywhere. These same forces—the Enlightenment and frustration over economic exploitation—are common themes in the world's revolutionary cries against colonialism throughout the 1800s.

student of the Enlightenment, **Thomas Paine**, urged colonists to support the movement. In his widely distributed pamphlet, *Common Sense*, he assailed the monarchy as an encroachment on Americans' natural rights and appealed to the colonists to form a better government. A mere six months later, Americans signed the **Declaration of Independence**. The printing press, the powerful tool of the Protestant Reformation, quickly became a powerful tool for the American Revolution as well.

France: More than Happy to Oblige

By 1776, as the war moved to the middle colonies and finally to the South, the Americans endured defeat after defeat. But in 1777, the French committed ships, soldiers, weapons, and money to the cause. France and England, of course, had been bickering for centuries, so the French leapt at the opportunity to punish England. In 1781, French and American troops and ships cornered the core of the British army, which was under the command of General George Cornwallis. Finding himself outnumbered, he surrendered, and the war was over. Within a decade, the Constitution and Bill of Rights were written, ratified, and put into effect. A fledgling democracy was on display.

2. The French Revolution

After the reign of Louis XIV, the Bourbon kings continued to reside in the lavish Versailles palace, a lifestyle that was quite expensive. More costly, however, were France's war debts. The War of Spanish Succession, the Seven Years' War, the American Revolution, you name it—France seemed to be involved in every major war both in Europe and abroad. With droughts damaging the French harvests and the nobility scoffing at spending restrictions, Louis XVI needed to raise taxes, but to do that he needed to get everyone on board. So, in 1789, he called a meeting of the **Estates-General**, a "governing body" that hadn't met in some 175 years. Bourbon monarchs, you'll recall, ruled under divine right, so no other input was generally seen as necessary. However, the king's poor financial situation made it necessary to call on this all-but-forgotten group.

The Estates-General: Generally a Mess

French society was divided into three estates (something like social classes). The First Estate comprised the clergy. Some were high ranking and wealthy; others were parish priests and quite poor. The Second Estate was made up of the noble families. Finally, the Third Estate comprised everyone else—peasant farmers and the small but influential middle class, or bourgeoisie, including merchants. The overwhelming majority (more than 95 percent) of the population were members of the Third Estate, but they had very little political power.

When Louis XVI summoned the Estates-General, he was in essence summoning representatives from each of these three estates. The representative nobles of the Second Estate came to the meeting of the Estates-General hoping to gain favors from the king in the form of political power and greater freedoms in the form of a new constitution. The representatives of the Third Estate (representing by far the greatest proportion of France's population), always suspicious of the nobility, wanted even greater freedoms similar to what they saw the former British colonies had in America. They went as far as suggesting to the king that the Estates-General meet as a unified body—all Estates under one roof. However, the top court in Paris, the *parlement*, ruled in favor of the nobility and ordered that the estates meet separately.

Frustrated at the strong possibility of being shut out of the new constitution by the other two estates, the Third Estate did something drastic on June 17, 1789—they declared themselves the **National Assembly**. The king got nervous, and forced the other two estates to join them in an effort to write a new constitution. But it was too little, too late. By then, peasants throughout the land were growing restless and were concerned that the king wasn't going to follow through on the major reforms they wanted. They stormed the Bastille, a huge prison in Paris, on July 14, 1789. From there, anarchy swept through the countryside and soon peasants attacked the nobility and feudal institutions.

By August, the National Assembly adopted the **Declaration of the Rights of Man**, a document recognizing natural rights and based on the ideas of the Enlightenment, the American Declaration of Independence, and particularly the writings of Jean-Jacques Rousseau. This declaration was widely copied and distributed across Europe, furthering the ideas of freedom, equality, and rule of law. The Assembly also abolished the feudal system and altered the monopoly of the Catholic Church by declaring freedom of worship. Meanwhile, the king and his family were taken to Paris, where the Third Estate revolutionaries could ensure that they wouldn't interfere with the work of the National Assembly. Perhaps most importantly, the French Revolution established the nation-state, not the king or the people (as in the United States), as the source of all sovereignty or political authority. In this sense, France became the first "modern" nation-state in 1789.

A New Constitution Causes Consternation

In 1791, the National Assembly ratified a new constitution, which was somewhat similar to the U.S. Constitution ratified just two years before, except that instead of a president, the king held on to the executive power. In other words, it was a constitutional monarchy, rather than a constitutional democracy. Those who wanted to abolish the monarchy felt cheated; those who wanted to retain the feudal structure felt betrayed.

Contrast Them: American and French Revolutions

The American Revolution involved a colonial uprising against an imperial power. In other words, it was an independence movement. The French Revolution involved citizens rising up against their own country's leadership and against their own political and economic system, and in that sense was more of a revolution. In other words, at the end of the American Revolution, the imperial power of England was still intact, and indeed the new United States was in many ways designed in the image of England itself. In contrast, at the end of the French Revolution, France itself was a very different place. It didn't simply lose some of its holdings. Instead, the king was beheaded and the socio-political structure changed.

That said, the word *revolution* aptly describes the American independence movement because the United States was the first major colony to break away from a European colonial power since the dawn of the Age of Exploration. What's more, the ideas adopted in the Declaration of Independence, the U.S. Constitution, and the French Revolution inspired colonists, citizens, and enslaved people across the globe. Quite revolutionary indeed!

Remember how most of the royalty in Europe intermarried? Well, it just so happened that Marie Antoinette, who was the wife of the increasingly nervous Louis XVI, was also the sister of the Emperor of Austria. The Austrians and the Prussians invaded France to restore the monarchy, but the French revolutionaries were able to hold them back. Continuing unrest led French leaders to call for a meeting to draw up a new constitution. Under the new constitution, the **Convention** became the new ruling body, and it quickly abolished the monarchy and proclaimed France a republic. Led by radicals known as the **Jacobins**, the Convention imprisoned the royal family and, in 1793, beheaded the king for treason.

The Reign of Terror: The Hard-Fought Constitution Gets Tossed Aside   While Prussia and Austria regrouped and enlisted the support of Great Britain and Spain, the Convention started to worry that foreign threats and internal chaos would quickly lead to its demise, so it threw out the constitution and created the **Committee of Public Safety**, an all-powerful enforcer of the revolution and murderer of anyone suspected of anti-revolutionary tendencies. Led by **Maximilien Robespierre** and the Jacobins, the Committee of Public Safety certainly wasn't a committee of personal safety, since it was responsible for the beheading of tens of thousands of French citizens. Even though the Committee was successful at controlling the anarchy and at building a strong national military to defend France against an increasing number of invading countries, after two years the French had enough of Robespierre's witch hunt and put his head on the guillotine. France quickly reorganized itself again, wrote a new constitution in 1795, and established a new five-man government called the **Directory**.

Napoleon: Big Things Come in Small Packages

The Height of Napoleon's Empire

While the Directory was not so great at implementing a strong domestic policy, the five-man combo was good at building up the military. One of its star military leaders was a teenager named **Napoleon Bonaparte**, who was a general by age 24. After military successes on behalf of the Directory, Napoleon returned to France and used his reputation and immense popularity to overthrow the Directory in 1799. He legitimized his actions by putting them before a popular vote, and once affirmed, he declared himself the First Consul under the new constitution (if you're counting, that makes four constitutions since the Revolution began).

Domestically, Napoleon initiated many reforms in agriculture, infrastructure, and public education. He also normalized relations with the church and restored a degree of tolerance and stability. Most importantly, his **Napoleonic Codes** (1804) recognized the equality of French citizens (meaning men) and institutionalized some of the Enlightenment ideas that had served as the original inspiration for many of the revolutionaries. At the same time, the code was also extremely paternalistic, based in part on ancient Roman law. The rights of women and children were severely limited under the code. Still, the code was a huge step forward in the recognition of some basic rights and in the establishment of rules of law. The code has since been significantly modified to reflect more modern sensibilities, but it is still in effect today, and has served as the model for many other national codes, especially in Europe.

Napoleon's biggest impact was external, not internal. In a stunning effort to spread France's glory throughout Europe and the Americas, Napoleon not only fended off foreign aggressors, but also made France an aggressor itself. Napoleon's troops conquered Austria, Prussia, Spain, Portugal, and the kingdoms within Italy. He dissolved the Holy Roman Empire, which was on its last legs anyway, and reorganized it into a confederacy of German states. In 1804, he crowned himself emperor of this huge new empire, fancying himself the new Charlemagne. By 1810, the empire was at its peak, but it didn't stay there for long. France lacked the resources to control a far-flung empire, and conflicts including an attempted blockade of powerful Britain cost it dearly. Nationalistic uprisings, such as unrest in Italy and fierce guerrilla warfare in Spain and Portugal, undermined Napoleon's power.

In 1812, Napoleon's greed got the better of him. He attacked the vast lands of Russia, but was baited into going all the way to Moscow, which the Russians then set aflame, preventing Napoleon from adequately housing his troops there. As winter set in and with no place to go, the troops had to trudge back to France and were attacked all along the way. Short on supplies, the retreat turned into a disaster. The army was decimated and the once-great emperor was forced into exile.

The leaders of the countries that had overthrown Napoleon met in Vienna to decide how to restore order (and their own power) in Europe. The principal members of the coalition against Napoleon were **Prince von Metternich** of Austria, **Alexander I of Russia**, and the **Duke of Wellington** of Britain. At first, disagreements among them prevented much progress. Hearing this, Napoleon returned from exile and attempted to regain power. His enemies, of course, rallied. At **Waterloo** in 1813, the allies united against their common threat. Defeating Napoleon decisively, they sent him to permanent exile on the island of St. Helena, where he later died. The allies eventually came to an agreement, in a meeting known as the **Congress of Vienna**, over what to do with France and its inflated territories.

The Congress of Vienna: Pencils and Erasers at Work   In 1815, the Congress decreed that a **balance of power** should be maintained among the existing powers of Europe in order to avoid the rise of another Napoleon. France was dealt with fairly: its borders were cut back to their pre-Napoleonic dimensions, but it was not punished militarily or economically. And although it rearranged some of the European boundaries and created new kingdoms in Poland and the Netherlands, the Congress also reaffirmed absolute rule, reseating the monarchs of France, Spain, Holland, and the many Italian states. While remarkably fair-minded, the Congress of Vienna ignored many of the ideals put forth by French revolutionaries and the rights established under France's short-lived republic. In other words, it essentially tried to erase the whole French Revolution and Napoleon from the European consciousness and restore the royal order.

Lots of Independence Movements: Latin America

The European colonies in Latin America were inspired by the success of the American Revolution and the ideas of the French Revolution. To be sure, there had been unsuccessful revolts and uprisings in the Latin American colonies for two or three centuries prior to those revolutions. In the early 19th century, however, the world order was different. Europe was in chaos because of the rise and fall of Napoleon, and this distracted the European powers from their American holdings, a development that gave rebellious leaders an opportunity to assert themselves more than they previously could have.

Haiti: Slave Revolt Sends France a Jolt

The first successful Latin American revolt took place in Haiti, a French island colony in the Caribbean. The French, true to their mercantilist policies, exported coffee, sugar, cocoa, and indigo from Haiti to Europe. French colonists owned large plantations and hundreds of thousands of enslaved people, who grew and harvested these crops under horrible conditions. By 1800, 90 percent of the population was enslaved and working on large plantations.

In 1801, as Napoleon was gaining momentum in Europe, **Pierre Toussaint L'Ouverture**, a former slave, led a violent, lengthy, but ultimately successful slave revolt. Enraged, Napoleon sent 20,000 troops to put down the revolt, but the Haitians were capable fighters. They also had another weapon on their side—yellow fever—that claimed many French lives. The French did succeed, however, in capturing L'Ouverture and imprisoning him in France, but by then they couldn't turn back the revolutionary tide. L'Ouverture's lieutenant **Jacques Dessalines**, also a former slave, proclaimed Haiti a free republic in 1804 and named himself governor-general for life. Thus, Haiti became the first independent nation in Latin America.

South America: Visions of Grandeur

In 1808, when Napoleon invaded Spain, he appointed his brother, Joseph Bonaparte, to the Spanish throne. This sent the Spanish authorities in the colonies into a tizzy. Who should they be loyal to? The colonists decided to remain loyal to their Spanish king and not recognize the French regime under Bonaparte. In Venezuela, they ejected Bonaparte's governor and, instead, appointed their own leader, **Simón Bolívar**. Tutored on the republican ideals of Rousseau during his travels to Europe and the United States, Bolívar found himself in the midst of a great opportunity to use what he learned. In 1811, Bolívar helped establish a national congress, which declared independence from Spain. Royalists, supporters of the Spanish crown, declared civil war. Bolívar proved to be a wily and effective military leader, and during the next decade, he won freedom for the area called Gran Colombia (which included modern-day Colombia, Ecuador, and Venezuela). Bolívar envisioned a huge South American country spanning across the continent, similar to the growing United States in North America, but it wasn't meant to be. In the following decades, the individual nation-states of northwestern South America formed their own governments.

Meanwhile, farther south in Argentina, the conflict between the French governor and those who still wanted to support the Spanish crown created another opportunity for liberation. **José de San Martin** was an American-born Spaniard (or Creole) who served as an officer in the Spanish army. In 1814, he began to put his extensive military experience to use—but for the rebels—taking command of the Argentinian armies. San Martin joined up with Bernardo O'Higgins of Chile and took the revolutionary movement not only through Argentina and Chile, but also to Peru, where he joined forces with Bolívar. The Spanish forces withered away. By the 1820s, a huge chunk of South America had successfully declared its independence from Spain.

Brazil: Power to the Pedros

Brazil, of course, was a Portuguese colony, and so when Portugal was invaded by Napoleon's armies in 1807, **John VI**, the Portuguese king, fled to Brazil and set up his royal court in exile. By 1821, Napoleon had been defeated and it was safe for John VI to return to Portugal, but he left behind his son, Pedro, who was 23 years old at the time, and charged him with running the huge colony. Pedro, who had spent most of his childhood and teenage years in Brazil and considered it home, declared Brazilian independence and crowned himself emperor the next year. Within a few more years, Brazil had a constitution.

In 1831, Pedro abdicated power to his son, **Pedro II**, who ruled the country through much of the 19th century. While he reformed Brazilian society in many ways and turned it into a major exporter of coffee, his greatest single accomplishment was the abolition of slavery in 1888 (which actually occurred under the direction of his daughter, Isabel, who was running the country while Pedro II was away). This action so incensed the landowning class that they revolted against the monarchy and established a republic in 1889.

Mexico: A Tale of Two Priests

As in other parts of Latin America, a revolutionary fervor rose in Mexico after the French Revolution, especially after Napoleon invaded Spain and Portugal. In 1810, **Miguel Hidalgo**, a Creole priest who sympathized with those who had been abused under Spanish colonialism, led a revolt against Spanish rule. Unlike in South America, however, the Spanish armies resisted effectively, and they put down the revolt at Calderon Bridge, where Hidalgo was executed.

Hidalgo's efforts were not in vain, however, because they put the revolution in motion. **José Morelos** picked up where Hidalgo left off and led the revolutionaries to further successes against the loyalists. Similar to what later happened in Brazil, the landowning class turned against him when he made clear his intentions to redistribute land to the poor. In 1815, he was executed.

It wasn't until 1821, after the landowning class bought into the idea of separation from Spain, that independence was finally achieved. In the **Treaty of Cordoba**, Spain was forced to recognize that its 300-year-old domination of Latin America was coming to an end. Mexico was granted its independence and Central America soon followed.

Inspiring Generations

Some colonized groups led acts of resistance that were ultimately put down by the oppressors, but went on to inspire countless other radicals who viewed the acts of their fallen leaders as inspiration to keep resisting.

Neocolonialism

Independent countries in Latin America that were still largely controlled by outside economic and political interests found themselves in a condition known as **neocolonialism**. Following independence movements in the 19th century, many Latin American nations saw significant increases in trade. However, the riches accumulated in these counties largely stayed within the confines of the wealthy, landowning class, inspiring working class movements to challenge these economic conditions.

One such movement occurred in Mexico. The **Mexican Revolution** began as a rejection of the 30-year dictatorship of **Porfirio Díaz**, who was seen as a pawn for landowners. He was defeated in an election by revolutionary aristocrat Francisco Madero. Madero was eventually overthrown in 1913 following a two-year presidency once he too was rejected by the revolutionary masses. The Mexican Revolution culminated in 1917 with the creation of Mexico's current constitution.

Inspiring Generations

RESISTANCE MOVEMENTS OF THE 19TH CENTURY			
Peru	**West Africa**	**United States**	**Sudan**
• **Túpac Amaru II** led a revolt in Peru against the Spanish occupiers. • Even though Amaru II was captured and executed, he continued to inspire Latin American resistance movements and served as a symbol of liberation for native peoples.	• **Samory Touré** established the Islamic Wassoulou Empire in 1878, going on to lead popular resistance to the French colonial presence. • Like Amaru II, Touré was captured, ending his imperial rule. However, following his death in 1900, his legacy continued to inspire local resistance to French colonialism.	• In the Dakota region, the Sioux performed a sacred ritual known as the **Ghost Dance** on their reservation as an act of resistance against the U.S. government. • The U.S. Army fired upon the Sioux upon mistaking the dance for a preparation for war. Despite fighting back, 300 Indians were killed.	• When Muhammad Ali of Egypt invaded the Sudan in 1819, he was opposed by the Sudanese who did not want to endure the heavy taxes, colonial rule, and less Islamist regime. • Led by Muhammad Ahmad, who anointed himself Mahdi, an Islamic messianic figure, the Sudanese **Mahadists** led a revolt that was ultimately stymied by the intervening British.

The Effects of the Independence Movements: More Independence than Freedom

While Europe was effectively booted out of many parts of the American continents during a 50-year time span beginning in about 1780, in some Latin American countries the independence from colonial power wasn't accompanied by widespread freedom among the vast majority of citizens. As in the United States, slavery still existed for decades. Peasants still worked on huge plantations owned by a few landowners. Unlike in the United States, however, a significant middle class of merchants and small farmers didn't emerge, and many of the Enlightenment ideas had influenced only the educated elite.

There were several reasons for this. The Catholic Church remained very powerful in Latin America, and while many of the priests advocated on behalf of the peasants and of the enslaved people (some martyred themselves for that cause), the church hierarchy as a whole protected the status quo. The church, after all, was one of the largest landowners in Latin America.

What's more, the economies of Latin America, while free from Europe politically, were still dependent on Europe economically. Latin American countries still participated in European mercantilism, often to their own detriment. They specialized in a few cash crops, exported almost exclusively to Europe, and then bought the finished products. In other words, most Latin American economies didn't diversify, nor did they broaden opportunities to a larger class of people, so innovation and creativity rarely took root.

There are notable exceptions. Chile diversified its economy fairly successfully, and Brazil and Argentina instituted social reform and broadened their economies to include a growing middle class. Ultimately, the hugely successful independence movements in Latin America didn't result in noticeable changes for a majority of the population for more than a century.

Comparison Chart of Independence Movements

	American Colonies 1764–1787	France 1789–1799	Haiti 1799–1804	Latin America 1810–1820s
Causes	Unfair taxation War debt Lack of representation	Unfair taxation War debt Social inequalities Lack of representation	French Enlightenment Social and racial inequalities Slave revolt	Social inequalities Removal of peninsulares Napoleon's invasion of Spain
Key Events	Boston Tea Party Continental Congress Declaration of Independence Constitution and Bill of Rights	Tennis Court Oath National Assembly Declaration of Rights of Man Storming Bastille Reign of Terror 5 Man Directory	Civil war Slave revolt Invasion of Napoleon	Peasant revolts Creole revolts Gran Colombia
Major Players	George III Thomas Paine Thomas Jefferson George Washington	Louis XVI Three Estates Jacobin Party Robespierre	Boukman Gens de Couleur Toussaint L'Overture Napoleon Bonaparte	Miguel Hidalgo Simón Bolívar José de San Martin Emperor Pedro I
Impacts	Independence Federal Democracy spreads—France, Haiti, Mexico	Rise of Napoleon Congress of Vienna Constitutional monarchy	Independence Destruction of economy Antislavery movements	Independence Continued inequalities Federal democracy (Mexico) Creole republics Constitutional monarchy (Brazil)

C. Industry and Imperialism

The Industrial Revolution, which began in the mid-18th century in Britain and spread rapidly through the 19th century, is inseparable from the Age of Imperialism, which reached its peak in the late 19th and early 20th centuries. Industrial technology had two enormous consequences. First, countries with industrial technology by definition had advanced military weapons and capacity, and were therefore easily able to conquer people who did not have this technology. Second, in order to succeed, factories needed access to raw materials to make finished products and markets to sell those finished products. Colonies fit both of these roles quite well.

Because the bulk of the western hemisphere freed itself from European control by the early 19th century (a lot more on this later), the industrial imperialists turned their eyes toward Africa and Asia, where exploitation was easy and markets were huge.

The Industrial Revolution

The Industrial Revolution began in Britain, helping to propel the country to its undisputed ranking as the most powerful in the 19th century. But Britain wasn't the only country that industrialized. The revolution spread through much of Europe, especially Belgium, France, and Germany, as well as to Japan and ultimately to the country that would eclipse Britain as the most industrialized—the United States. Still, since most of the developments occurred in Britain first, and since the social consequences that occurred in Britain are representative of those that occurred elsewhere, this section will focus heavily on the revolution in Britain. References to other countries will be made where warranted.

Agricultural Revolution Part II

Hopefully you remember that early civilizations came about, in part, because of an Agricultural Revolution that resulted in food surpluses. This freed some of the population from farming, and those people then went about the business of building the civilization. In the 18th century, agricultural output increased dramatically once again. This time, it allowed not just some people, but as much as half of the population to leave the farms and head toward the cities, where jobs in the new industrial economy were becoming available.

Keep in mind that agricultural techniques had been slowly improving throughout history. Since so many developments happened so quickly in the 18th century, this period was considered a revolution. Agricultural output increased for a whole host of reasons. Potatoes, corn, and other high-yield crops were introduced to Europe from the colonies in the New World. Farmers began using more advanced farming methods and technology, thereby increasing their crop yields. Through a process known simply as **enclosure**, public lands that were shared during the Middle Ages were enclosed by fences, which allowed for private farming and private gain.

What really cranked up the efficiency and productivity of the farms was the introduction of new technologies. New machines for plowing, seeding, and reaping, along with the development of chemical fertilizers, allowed farmers to greatly increase the amount of land they could farm, while decreasing the number of people needed to do it. **Urbanization** was a natural outgrowth of the increased efficiencies in farming and agriculture. In short, cities grew. In 1800, there were only about 20 cities in Europe with a population of more than 100,000. By 1900, 150 cities had similar populations, and the largest, London, had a population of more than 6 million.

Cities developed in areas where resources such as coal, iron, water, and railroads were available for manufacturing. The more factories that developed in favorable locations, the larger cities grew. In 1800, along with London, the Chinese cities of Beijing (Peking) and Canton ranked in the top three, but just 100 years later, 9 of the 10 largest cities in the world were in Europe or the United States.

Technological Innovations: The Little Engine That Could

Prior to the Industrial Revolution, most Europeans worked on farms, at home, or in small shops. Even after Britain started importing huge amounts of cotton from its American colonies, most of the cotton was woven into cloth in homes or small shops as part of an inefficient, highly labor-intensive arrangement known as the **domestic system**. Middlemen would drop off wool or cotton at homes where women would make cloth, which would then be picked up again by the middlemen, who would sell the cloth to buyers. All of this was done one person at a time.

However, a series of technological advancements in the 18th century changed all this. In 1733, John Kay invented the **flying shuttle**, which sped up the weaving process. In 1764, John Hargreaves invented the **spinning jenny**, which was capable of spinning vast amounts of thread. When waterpower was added to these processes, notably by Richard Arkwright and Edward Cartright in the late 18th century, fabric-weaving was taken out of the homes and was centralized at sites where waterpower was abundant. In 1793, when **Eli Whitney** invented the **cotton gin**, thereby allowing massive amounts of cotton to be quickly processed in the Americas and exported to Europe, the textile industry was taken out of the homes and into the mills entirely.

Although industrialization hit the textile industry first, it spread well beyond into other industries. One of the most significant developments was the invention of the **steam engine**, which actually took the work of several people to perfect. In the early 1700s, Thomas Newcomer developed an inefficient engine, but in 1769, **James Watt** dramatically improved it. The steam engine was revolutionary because steam could be used to generate power not only for industry but also for transportation. In 1807, **Robert Fulton** built the first **steamship**, and in the 1820s, **George Stephenson** built the first **steam-powered locomotive**. In the hands of a huge, imperial power like Britain, steamships and locomotives would go a long way toward empire building and global trade. Because Britain had vast amounts of coal, and because the steam engine was powered by coal, Britain industrialized very quickly.

But Wait, There's More!

During the next 100 years, enormous developments changed how people communicated, traveled, and went about their daily lives. These changes are far too numerous to list entirely, but we've picked a few major inventions and listed them below. It's unlikely you'll need to know all of these for the exam, but an understanding of the impact of the Industrial Revolution is perhaps best grasped by looking at the details. There isn't one item on the list below that you can deny has changed the world.

- **The Telegraph**—Invented in 1837 by Samuel Morse. Allowed people to communicate across great distances within seconds.
- **The Telephone**—Invented in 1876 by Alexander Graham Bell. Don't answer it while you're studying.
- **The Lightbulb**—Invented in 1879 by Thomas Edison. Kind of a big deal: now factories can run all night.
- **The Internal Combustion Engine**—Invented in 1885 by Gottlieb Daimler. If you've ever been in a car, you've personally benefited from the internal combustion engine.
- **The Radio**—Invented in the 1890s by Guglielmo Marconi, based on designs by Thomas Edison.

At the same time, there were huge advances in medicine and science. Pasteurization and vaccinations were developed. X-rays came onto the scene. **Charles Darwin** developed the concept of evolution by means of natural selection. The developments of this time period go on and on and on.

Compare Them: The Scientific Revolution and the Industrial Revolution

Both changed the world, of course. One was about the process of discovering, learning, evaluating, and understanding the natural world. The other was about applying that understanding to practical ends. In both cases, knowledge spread and improvements were made across cultures and across time. Even though patents protected individual inventions, one scientist or inventor could build on the ideas of colleagues who were tackling the same issues, thereby leading to constant improvement and reliability. This same collaborative effort is used today. Universities and research organizations share information among colleagues across the globe. The Internet, of course, allows data to be analyzed almost instantaneously by people all over the world.

The Factory System: Efficiency (Cough), New Products (Choke), Big Money (Gag)

The Industrial Revolution permitted the creation of thousands of new products from clothing to toys to weapons. These products were produced efficiently and inexpensively in factories. Under Eli Whitney's system of **interchangeable parts**, machines and their parts were produced uniformly so that they could be easily replaced when something broke down. Later, Henry Ford's use of the **assembly line** meant that each factory worker added only one part to a finished product, one after another after another. These were incredibly important developments in manufacturing. Although they made the factory system wildly profitable, they came with social costs. Man wasn't merely working with machines; he was becoming one. Individuality had no place in a system where consistency of function was held in such high esteem.

The factories were manned by thousands of workers, and the system was efficient and inexpensive primarily because those workers were way overworked, extremely underpaid, and regularly put in harm's way without any accompanying insurance or protection. In the early years of the Industrial Revolution, 16-hour workdays were not uncommon. Children as young as six worked next to machines. Women logged long hours at factories, while still having to fulfill their traditional roles as caretakers for their husbands, children, and homes.

This was a huge change from rural life. Whereas the farms exposed people to fresh air and sunshine, the factories exposed workers to air pollution and hazardous machinery. The farms provided seasonal adjustments to the work pattern, while the factories spit out the same products day after day, all year long. The despair and hopelessness of the daily lives of the factory workers were captured by many novelists and social commentators of the time (for example, Charles Dickens).

Focus On: The Family

The biggest social changes associated with industrialization were to the family. Both women and children became part of the workforce, albeit at lower wages, and in more dangerous conditions than their male counterparts. Workers were often dependent on companies for food, personal items, and housing—in factory-run boardinghouses. These new living arrangements removed workers from families and traditional structures. In many ways, this lessened the restrictions on young women and men. They were able to live away from home, manage their own incomes, and pursue independent leisure activities—going to theaters and dance halls, attending recitals, dining out in restaurants— all of which developed to support the new urban working class.

The emergence of a middle class also brought changes to the family. Home and work were no longer centered in the same space. Middle- and upper-class women were expected to master the domestic sphere, and thus remain private and separate from the realities of the working world. This was a time of great consumption as desirable products were mass produced and women were expected to arrange parlors and dining rooms with fancy tea cups and serving trays.

New Economic and Social Philosophies: No Shortage of Opinions

Industrialization created new social classes. The new aristocrats were those who became rich from industrial success. A middle class formed, made up of managers, accountants, ministers, lawyers, doctors, and other skilled professionals. Finally, at the bottom of the pyramid was the working class—and it was huge—made up of factory workers in the cities and peasant farmers in the countryside.

The rise of the industrial class had its origins in the concept of private ownership. **Adam Smith** wrote in *The Wealth of Nations* (1776) that economic prosperity and fairness is best achieved through private ownership. Individuals should own the means of production and sell their products and services in a free and open market, where the demand for their goods and services would determine their prices and availability. A **free-market system** (also known as **capitalism**), Smith argued, would best meet the needs and desires of individuals and nations as a whole. When governments remove themselves entirely from regulation, the process is called **laissez-faire capitalism**.

Contrast Them: Social Class Structures Before and After Industrialism

Keep in mind that throughout history, the wealthy class was small and the poorest class was huge, but industrialism gave it a new twist. Because of urbanization, people were living side by side. They could see the huge differences among the classes right before their eyes. What's more, the members of the working class saw factory owners gain wealth quickly—at their expense. The owners didn't inherit their position, but instead achieved success by exploiting their workers, and the workers knew it. In the past, under feudalism, people more readily accepted their position because, as far as they knew, the social structure was the way it had always been, and that's the way it was meant to be. If your dad was a farmer, you were a farmer. If your dad was the king, you were a prince. After industrialism, people saw for the first time the connection between their sacrifices and the aristocracy's luxuries.

Smith wrote his book in response to the Western European mercantilist practices that had dominated during the Age of Exploration. In the New World, monarchies—which were not only corrupt, but also highly inefficient—closely managed their economies. In the 19th century, European countries continued to develop their mercantilist philosophies (especially using colonies as a way of obtaining raw materials without having to import them from other countries and as a way of increasing exports). European countries also permitted and encouraged the development of private investment and capitalism through 1) allowing limited liability companies, which protect investors from suffering personal losses when their company loses money, and 2) the stock market, which allows individuals to invest capital into a company (and benefit when that company profits). These financial instruments gave way to the rise of major investment firms, such as the British East India Company.

While Adam Smith believed that free-market capitalism would lead to better opportunities for everyone, **Karl Marx**, a German economist and philosopher who spent a good part of his adult life living in poverty, pointed out that the factory workers had genuine opportunities but were being exploited as a consequence of capitalism. In other words, the abuses weren't merely the result of the way in which capitalism was practiced, but an inherent flaw in the system. In *The Communist Manifesto* (1848), Marx and Friedrich Engels wrote that the working class would eventually revolt and take control of the means of production. All the instruments of power—the government, the courts, the police, the church—were on the side of the rich against the workers. Once the class struggle was resolved by the massive uprising of the exploited, Marx predicted that the instruments of power wouldn't even be needed. The impact of Marxism was enormous, and served as the foundation of **socialism** and **communism**.

Marx and Engels were not just theorizing, they were also observing, and there was much discontent to support their view. In England in the early 1800s, groups of workers known as **Luddites** destroyed equipment in factories in the middle of the night to protest working conditions and pitiful wages. The government unequivocally sided with the business owners, executing some of the workers, while also enacting harsh laws against any further action.

At the same time, however, a greater number of people with influence (the middle class and the aristocracy) began to realize how inhumane the factory system had become and started to do something about it. These reformers believed that capitalism was a positive development, but that laws were needed to keep its abuses in check. In other words, they believed that the government needed to act on behalf of the workers as well as the factory owners. By the mid-19th century, there was a major split in thought among intellectuals and policymakers.

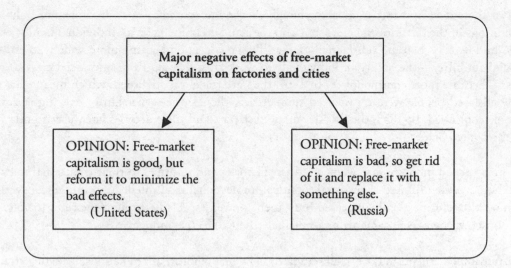

In Britain and the United States, where the impact of the Enlightenment was strong, democracy was developing, and the middle class was growing, reforms to the free-market system took root, lessening the negative impact of capitalism on workers. In other countries such as Russia, where absolute rule was strong and the peasant class extremely oppressed, reform was almost nonexistent. There, Marxist ideas grew popular among a small group of urban intellectuals—eventually including Vladimir Lenin—who believed they could lead a worker revolution and end the tyranny of the czars.

Elsewhere, Marxism impacted social thought and intermixed with capitalist thought to create economic systems that were partly socialist (in which the government owned some of the means of production) and partly capitalist (in which individuals owned some of the means of production). Most of Europe, including Britain after World War II, mixed socialist and capitalist ideas.

Capitalism and Enlightenment Combine: Reform Catches On

In the second half of the 19th century, after the abuses and social consequences of the Industrial Revolution became clear, a series of reforms occurred. The British Parliament passed laws, such as the **Factory Act of 1883**, which limited the hours of each workday, restricted children from working in factories, and required factory owners to make working conditions safer and cleaner. Meanwhile, **labor unions** were formed. The unions were vehicles through which thousands of employees bargained for better working conditions, or threatened to strike, thereby shutting down the factory. In addition, an increasing number of factory owners realized that a healthy, happy, and reasonably well-paid workforce meant a productive and loyal one.

All of these developments combined, though slowly and sporadically, to improve not only the conditions in the factories and cities, but also the standard of living on an individual family level. The middle class became substantially larger. Public education became more widely accessible. **Social mobility**—the ability of individuals to work their way up from one social class to the next—became more commonplace. In 1807, the slave trade was abolished, which meant that no new enslaved people were transported from Africa, though the ownership of existing enslaved people continued. In 1833, the British outlawed slavery, and three decades later, it was outlawed in the United States.

As men earned more money, women left the factories and returned to their traditional roles in the home, which limited their social, political, professional, and intellectual influence, even as democratic reforms greatly increased most men's power, especially through the right to vote. In response, women began organizing to increase their collective influence.

Despite improvements in the overall standards of living in industrialized nations, by 1900 extreme hardships persisted. In many cases, Europeans dreamed of starting over somewhere else, or escaping cruelties at home. From 1800 to 1900, nearly 50 million Europeans migrated to North and South America. Millions fled from famine in Ireland, or antisemitism in Russia, or poverty and joblessness in general.

D. Nationalist Movements and Other Developments

Two Unifications: Italy and Germany

One of the consequences of the Napoleonic era was that it intensified nationalism, or feelings of connection to one's own home, region, language, and culture. France, Spain, Portugal, Britain, and Russia, of course, had already unified and, in some cases, built enormous empires. But the Italian and German city-states were still very feudal, and were constantly at the center of warfare among the European powers. In the second half of the 19th century, however, all of that changed. With the wave of industrialization and all the changes that it inspired, as well as the nationalist sentiments that were still lingering decades after Napoleon's defeat, a drive to unify Italy and Germany resurfaced. Italy and Germany unified and eventually altered the balance of European power.

The Unification of Italy: Italians Give Foreign Occupiers the Boot

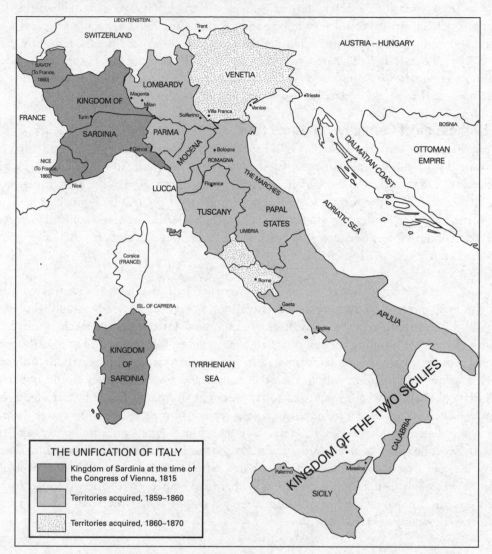

THE UNIFICATION OF ITALY

- Kingdom of Sardinia at the time of the Congress of Vienna, 1815
- Territories acquired, 1859–1860
- Territories acquired, 1860–1870

The Unification of Italy

In the mid-19th century, Italy was a tangle of foreign-controlled small kingdoms. Austria controlled Venetia, Lombardy, and Tuscany in the north. France controlled Rome and the Papal States in the mid-section. Only the divided kingdom of Sardinia (part of which was an island in the Mediterranean) was controlled by Italians.

In 1849, the king of Sardinia, **Victor Emmanuel II**, named **Count Camillo Cavour** his prime minister, and nationalism in Italy took off. Both Emmanuel and Cavour believed strongly in Italian unification. Through a series of wars in which Cavour sided with European powers that could help him boot out Austria from Italy, he managed to remove Austrian influence from all parts of Italy (except Venetia) by 1859. Meanwhile, **Giuseppe Garibaldi**, another Italian nationalist, raised a volunteer army and in 1860 his army overthrew the kingdom whose citizens pledged allegiance to Sardinia. So, by 1861, a large chunk of present-day Italy was unified, and it declared itself a unified kingdom under Victor Emmanuel.

In the following decade, the Italians managed to gain control of Venetia after siding with Prussia in its war against Austria (which previously controlled Venetia) and finally won control of Rome in 1870 when the French withdrew. Still, even though Italy was essentially unified, the boundaries of Europe were still very shaky. Some Italians thought that southern provinces of Austria and France were far more Italian than not and that those provinces were rightly part of Italy. What's more, Italy had a hard time unifying culturally because for centuries it had developed more regionally. Still, now unified, Italy was more able to assert itself on the world stage, a development that would impact Europe in the next century.

The Unification of Germany: All About Otto

The provinces that comprised Germany and the Austrian Empire (the Hapsburgs) hadn't been truly united since the decline of Charlemagne's Holy Roman Empire in the Middle Ages. Since the Peace of Westphalia (1648), which asserted the authority of regional governments, two areas in the region of the former Holy Roman Empire had politically dominated it: Prussia and Austria. Prussia, under the enlightened monarch Frederick the Great and his successors, achieved economic preeminence by embracing the Industrial Revolution. They also strongly supported education, which created a talented work force.

Many in Prussia wanted to consolidate the German territories into a powerful empire to rival the great powers of Europe, particularly Britain, France, and increasingly Russia. So, in 1861, the new king of Prussia, **William I**, appointed **Otto von Bismarck** prime minister with the aim of building the military and consolidating the region under its authority. In order to achieve this consolidation, Bismarck had to defeat Austria, which he did in only seven weeks, after he won assurances from the other European powers that they would not step in on Austria's behalf. Through more war and annexation, Bismarck secured most of the other German principalities, except for heavily Catholic regions in the south. So, the crafty Bismarck formed an alliance with the Catholic German states against aggression from France, and then, in 1870, provoked France to declare war on Prussia, starting the **Franco-Prussian War**—a war which, once won, consolidated the German Catholic regions under Prussian control. In 1871, the victorious Bismarck crowned King William I as emperor of the new German Empire, which was also known as the Second Reich ("second empire," after the Holy Roman Empire, which was known as the First Reich).

After unification, Germany quickly industrialized and became a strong economic and political power. Otto was not popular with everyone, especially socialists. In 1888, Germany crowned a new emperor, **William II**, who wanted to run the country himself. In 1890, he forced Bismarck to resign as prime minister and reestablished authority as the emperor. With the Industrial Revolution in Germany now running at full throttle, he built a huge navy, pursued colonial ambitions in Africa and Asia, and oversaw the rise of Germany into one of the most powerful nations in the world.

Nationalism was used as a force for unification, particularly in Europe. In fact, the Ottoman Empire attempted to ride the wave of nationalism to a reunified empire in the 19th century, though to less success than Italy and Germany. The weakening Ottoman Empire was buoyed by a movement called Ottomanism as individual regions strived to strengthen the once powerful state, rather than stand alone as weaker localities. However, in other places, locals harnessed the spirit of nationalism to inspire liberation from occupying forces.

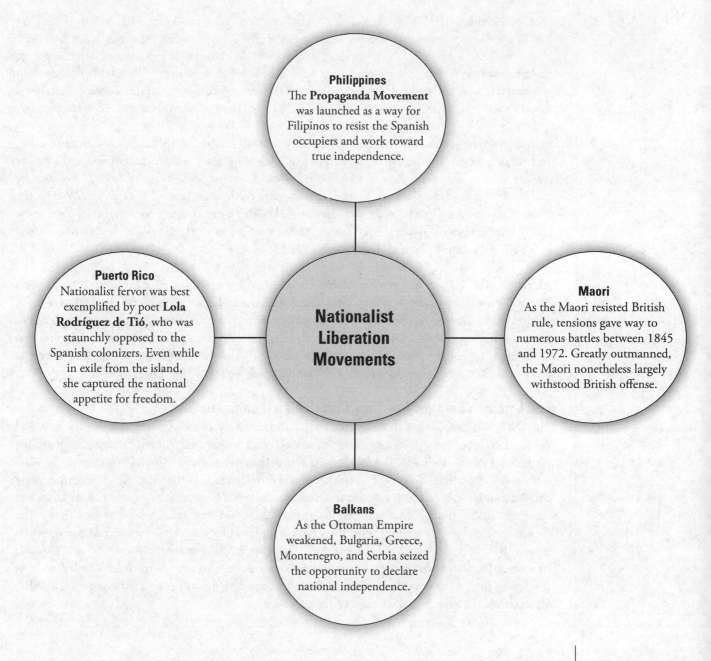

Philippines
The **Propaganda Movement** was launched as a way for Filipinos to resist the Spanish occupiers and work toward true independence.

Puerto Rico
Nationalist fervor was best exemplified by poet **Lola Rodríguez de Tió**, who was staunchly opposed to the Spanish colonizers. Even while in exile from the island, she captured the national appetite for freedom.

Nationalist Liberation Movements

Maori
As the Maori resisted British rule, tensions gave way to numerous battles between 1845 and 1972. Greatly outmanned, the Maori nonetheless largely withstood British offense.

Balkans
As the Ottoman Empire weakened, Bulgaria, Greece, Montenegro, and Serbia seized the opportunity to declare national independence.

Other Political Developments

Russia: Life with Czars

In the 19th century, Russia consolidated power over its vast territory by giving absolute power to its Romanov czars. The vast majority of the citizens were serfs with no rights, living an almost slavelike existence. Alexander I and Nicholas I frequently used the secret police to quash rebellions or hints of reform, despite the fact that an increasing number of Russians demanded change.

By the 1860s, long after the Enlightenment had had an effect on most developments in the West, **Alexander II** began some reforms. He issued the **Emancipation Edict**, which essentially abolished serfdom. It did little good. The serfs were given very small plots of land for which they had to give huge payments to the government to keep, so it was difficult for them to improve their lot. Some peasants headed to the cities to work in Russia's burgeoning industries, but there, too, the reforms that softened some of the harsher working conditions in the West hadn't made their way eastward. Whether in the fields or in the factories, the Russian peasants continued to live a meager existence, especially when compared to many of their Western European counterparts.

Still, during the second half of the 19th century, a small but visible middle class started to grow, and the arts began to flourish. In a span of just a few decades, Russian artists produced some of the greatest works of all time: Tolstoy wrote *Anna Karenina* and *War and Peace*, Dostoyevsky authored *The Brothers Karamazov*, and Tchaikovsky composed *Swan Lake* and *The Nutcracker*. Meanwhile, an intellectual class well-acquainted with political and economic thought in the rest of Europe began to assert itself against the monarchy. In 1881, Alexander II was assassinated by a political group known as **The People's Will**.

Alexander III reacted fiercely by attempting to suppress anything that he perceived as anti-Russian. Through a policy known as **Russification**, all Russians, including people in the far-flung reaches of the Empire that did not share a cultural history with most of Russia, were expected to learn the Russian language and convert to Russian Orthodoxy. Anyone who didn't comply was persecuted, especially Jews. Meanwhile, terrible conditions in the factories continued, even as production capacity was increased and greater demands were put upon the workers.

The Ottoman Empire: Are They Still Calling It an Empire?

The Ottoman Empire began its decline in the 16th century and was never able to gain a second wind. Throughout the 17th and 18th centuries, the Ottomans continually fought the Russians for control of the Balkans, the Black Sea, and surrounding areas. Most of the time, the Russians were victorious. So by the 19th century, not only was the Ottoman Empire considerably smaller and less powerful, but it was in danger of collapse. Greece, Egypt, and Arabia launched successful independence movements. This worried Britain and France, who feared that if the Ottoman Empire fell entirely, the Russian Empire would seize the chance to take over the eastern Mediterranean. So, for the next century, Britain and France tried to keep the Ottoman Empire going if only to prevent Russian expansion, as they did in the Crimean War in 1853. At the same time, of course, Britain and France increased their influence in the region. In 1882, for example, Britain gained control of Egypt.

E. The Growth of Nationalism

Nationalism was an enormous force on all continents during the time period covered in this chapter. Nationalism, broadly defined, is the desire of a people of a common cultural heritage to form an independent nation-state and/or empire that both represents and protects their shared cultural identity. It drove movements in Germany and Italy to unify. It drove movements in the Americas to declare independence. It drove resistance against European colonialism in India, China, and Africa, while it drove Europeans to compete with each other to promote national pride and wealth by establishing colonies in the first place. In China, it even drove peasant movements against the Manchu government, which was targeted for not representing the Han majority. It drove the French to unite behind Napoleon to attempt to take over Europe, and it drove the British to unite to try to take over the world. Nationalism drove the Japanese to quickly industrialize and the Egyptians to limit the power of the Ottomans.

In short, people all over the world began to identify strongly with their nation, or with the dream of the creation of their own nation. Even in the European colonies, and perhaps especially there, nationalism was growing. The oppressors used nationalist feelings to justify their superiority. The oppressed used nationalistic feelings to justify their rebellion.

IV. UNIT 6: CONSEQUENCES OF INDUSTRIALIZATION

A. In Search of Natural Resources

The factories of the Industrial Revolution created useful products, but to do so they required natural resources. Europe had its share of coal and iron ore used to provide power and make equipment for the factories, but raw materials such as cotton and rubber had to be imported because they didn't grow in the climates of Western Europe.

Industrial nations amassed incredible wealth by colonizing regions with natural resources, and then taking those resources without compensating the native peoples. The resources were sent back to Europe, where they were made into finished products. Then, the industrial nations sent the finished products back to the colonies, where the colonists had to purchase them because the colonial powers wouldn't let the colonies trade with anyone else. In short, the colonial powers became rich at the expense of the colonies. The more colonies a nation had, the richer it became.

Soon, Europe colonized nations on every other continent in the world. Europe became a clearinghouse for raw materials from around the globe while the rest of the world increasingly became exposed to Europe and European ideas. What's more, the need for raw materials transformed the landscape of the conquered regions. Limited raw materials depleted faster than at any time in human history. The Industrial Revolution, in addition to creating pollution, began to have an impact on the environment by gobbling natural resources.

With the newfound rush to mass produce their products, industrialists sought new sources for their raw materials. The more they looked abroad for their materials, the more countries with economic power increased their interest in an overseas presence.

> The British solidified its economic influence around the world by creating transnational companies. Similar to the way in which the Dutch East India Company gave the Dutch government a foothold in other parts of the world, the British-owned Hong Kong Shanghai Banking Corporation (HSBC) and later Unilever (a joint company based in Great Britain and the Netherlands) strengthened European economic power in Asia and Africa via **transnational businesses.**

B. European Justification

Even as progressives argued for an end to the slave trade and better working conditions in the factories, a huge number of Europeans—not just the industrialists—either supported or acquiesced in the colonization of foreign lands. Most Europeans were very ethnocentric and viewed other cultures as barbarian and uncivilized. Ironically, this ethnocentrism may have driven some of the social advancements within European society itself—after all, if you think of yourself as civilized, then you can't exactly brutalize your own people.

Two ideas contributed to this mindset. First, **social Darwinists** applied Charles Darwin's biological theory of natural selection to sociology. In other words, they claimed that dominant races or classes of people rose to the top through a process of "survival of the fittest." This meant that because Britain was the most powerful, it was the most fit, and therefore the British were superior to other races.

Second, many Europeans believed that they were not only superior, but that they had a moral obligation to (crassly said) dominate other people or (politely said) teach other people how to be more civilized—in other words, how to be more like Europeans. **Rudyard Kipling** summed it up in his poem "**White Man's Burden**." As European nations swallowed up the rest of the world in an effort to advance their economies, military strategic positioning, and egos, Kipling characterized these endeavors as a "burden" in which it was the duty of Europeans to conquer each "half-devil and half-child" so that they could be converted to Christianity and civilized in the European fashion. Never mind if the non-Europeans didn't want to be "civilized." The Europeans supposedly knew what was best for everyone.

"White Man's Burden"

This Kipling poem not only put forth the idea that European colonization and exploitation of other peoples was justified, it basically said that such actions were obligatory—a moral duty.

C. European Imperialism in India

As you know from the previous chapter, the Indian subcontinent had long been a destination for European traders eager to get their hands on India's many luxuries, such as tea, sugar, silk, salt, and jute (an extremely strong fiber used for ropes). By the early 18th century, the Mughal Empire was in decline after wars and religious conflict between Muslims and Hindus. Lacking a strong central government, India was vulnerable to influence from external powers.

In the 1750s, the rivalry between France and England reached a fever pitch. During the Seven Years' War (more on it later), the two countries battled each other in three theaters: North America, Europe, and India. England won across the board. The **British East India Company**, a joint-stock company that operated like a multinational corporation with exclusive rights over British trade with India, then led in India by **Robert Clive**, raised an effective army that rid

Contrast Them: Ethnocentrism in Europe and Elsewhere

To be sure, many cultures were ethnocentric. The Chinese, for example, believed their kingdom to be the Middle Kingdom, literally the "center of the world," and themselves ethnically superior to other races. Similar attitudes existed in Japan and in most major civilizations. The Europeans were hardly unique in their self-important attitudes. However, in their ability to act on those attitudes, they were dangerously unique. Armed with the most technologically advanced militaries and strong economic motives, the Europeans were quite capable of subjugating people whom they considered to be inferior, barbaric, or dispensable. Their success at doing so often reinforced the ethnocentric attitudes, leading to further colonialism and subjugation.

the subcontinent of the French. During the next two decades, Clive successfully conquered the Bengal region (present-day Bangladesh), quite a feat given that the East India Company was a corporation. It wasn't British troops who conquered the region, but corporate troops!

Over the next hundred years, the company took advantage of the weakening Mughals and set up administrative regions throughout the empire. In 1798, the large island of Ceylon (present-day Sri Lanka) fell to the British. In the early 1800s, the Punjab region in northern India came under British control, and from there the Brits launched excursions into Pakistan and Afghanistan.

The Sepoy Mutiny: Too Little, Too Late

To help administer the regions under its control, the East India Company relied on Sepoys, Indians who worked for the Brits, mainly as soldiers. By the mid-1800s, the Sepoys were becoming increasingly alarmed with the company's insatiable appetite for eating up larger and larger chunks of the subcontinent. What's more, the company wasn't very good about respecting the local customs of the Sepoys, and respected neither Muslim nor Hindu religious customs. When, in 1857, the Sepoys learned that their bullet cartridges (which had to be bitten off in order to load into the rifle) were greased with pork and beef fat, thus violating both Muslim and Hindu dietary laws, the Sepoys rebelled. The fighting continued for nearly two years, but the rebellion failed miserably.

The consequences were huge. In 1858, the British parliament stepped in, took control of India away from the East India Company, and made all of India a crown colony. The last of the Mughal rulers, **Bahadur Shah II**, was sent into exile, thereby ending the Mughal Empire for good. Nearly 300 million Indians were suddenly British subjects (that's as many people as are currently living in the United States). By 1877, Queen Victoria was recognized as Empress of India.

Full-Blown British Colonialism: England on the Indus

In the second half of the 19th century, India became the model of British imperialism. Raw materials flowed to Britain; finished products flowed back to India. The upper castes were taught English and were expected to adopt English attitudes. Christianity spread. Railroads and canals were built. Urbanization, as in Europe, increased dramatically. All of this came at the expense of Indian culture and institutions. Still, as the upper castes were Anglicized, they gained the education and worldly sophistication to begin to influence events. Increasingly, they dreamed of freeing India from British rule.

In 1885, a group of well-educated Indians formed the **Indian National Congress** to begin the path toward independence. It would take the impact of two world wars before they would get it. In the meantime, Indians, especially those who lived in the cities, continued to adapt to British customs while trying to hold on to their traditions.

D. European Imperialism in China

As you know, for much of its history, China was relatively isolationist. It traded frequently, but it didn't make exploration a high priority. It also expanded by conquering its neighbors, but never took this expansion beyond its own region of the globe. Up until the 1830s, China allowed the European powers to trade only in the port city of Canton, and it established strict limitations on what could be bought and sold. As the European powers, particularly the British, gained industrial muscle, they came barging in, this time with weapons and warships.

The Opium Wars: European Drug Pushers Force Their Right to Deal

In 1773, British traders introduced opium to the Chinese. By 1838, the drug habit among the Chinese had grown so widespread and destructive that the Manchu Emperor released an imperial edict forbidding the further sale or use of opium. Consistent with this edict, the Chinese seized British opium in Canton in 1839.

The British would have none of it. From 1839 to 1842, the two countries fought a war over the opium trade. This was known as the first **Opium War**. Overwhelmed by British military might, China was forced to sign the **Treaty of Nanjing**, the first of what came to be known as the "**unequal treaties**," by which Britain was given considerable rights to expand trade with China.

In 1843, Britain declared Hong Kong its own crown possession, a significant development that went beyond trading rights because it actually established a British colony in the region. In 1844, the Manchu Dynasty was forced to permit Christian missionaries back into the country.

When China resisted British attempts to expand the opium trade even further, the two countries fought a second Opium War for four years beginning in 1856. The Chinese defeat was humiliating. It resulted in the opening of all of China to European trade. Still, other than in Hong Kong, European imperialism in China was quite different from what it was in India and what it would be in Africa. In China, Britain fought more for trading concessions than for the establishment of colonies.

The Word Is Out: China Is Crumbling

The Opium Wars had a huge impact on the global perception of China. For centuries, the world knew that China was one of the more advanced civilizations. With the clear-cut British defeat of China with relatively few troops, the world realized that China was an easy target. What's more, the Chinese themselves knew that their government was weak, and so they, too, started to rebel against it. Internal rebellion started at the beginning of the 19th century with the **White Lotus Rebellions** led by Buddhists who were frustrated over taxes and government corruption. It continued through the middle of the century with the **Taiping Rebellion**. The Taipings, led by a religious zealot claiming to be the brother of Jesus, recruited an army nearly a million strong and almost succeeded in bringing down the Manchu government. The rebels failed, but the message was clear. China was crumbling from within and unable to stop foreign aggression from outside.

In the 1860s, the Manchu Dynasty tried to get its act together in what became known as the **Self-Strengthening Movement**, but it did no good. In 1876, Korea realized China was weak and declared its independence. Later, in the **Sino-French War** (1883), the Chinese lost control of Vietnam to the French, who established a colony there called French Indochina. If that wasn't enough, a decade later the Chinese were defeated in the **Sino-Japanese War**, when the rising imperial power of Japan wanted in on the action. In the **Treaty of Shimonoseki** (1895), China was forced to hand over control of Taiwan and grant the Japanese trading rights similar to those it had granted the Europeans. Japan also defeated the Koreans and took control of the entire peninsula.

Meanwhile, the European powers were rushing to establish a greater presence in China. By establishing **spheres of influence**, France, Germany, Russia, and of course Britain carved up huge slices of China for themselves. These spheres were not quite colonies. Instead, they were areas in which the European powers invested heavily, built military bases, and set up business, transportation, and communication operations. The Manchu Dynasty was still the governmental authority within the spheres.

By 1900, the United States, which had its own trading designs on Asia, was worried that China would become another India or Africa, and that the United States would be shut out of trade if the Manchu government fell and the Europeans took over the government. (Let's not forget the irony that the United States had barred the immigration of all Chinese laborers in the **Chinese Exclusion Act** of 1882.) Through its **Open Door Policy**, the United States pledged its support of the sovereignty of the Chinese government and announced equal trading privileges among all imperial powers (basically Europe and the United States).

The Boxer Rebellion: Knocked Out in the First Round

By the 20th century, nationalism among the Chinese peasants and local leadership was festering. Anti-Manchu, anti-European, and anti-Christian, the Society of Righteous and Harmonious Fists, or **Boxers**, as they came to be known, organized in response to the Manchu government's defeats and concessions to the Western powers and Japan. Infuriated, the Boxers' goal was to drive the Europeans and Japanese out of China. Adopting guerrilla warfare tactics, the Boxers slaughtered Christian missionaries and seized control of foreign embassies. Ultimately, however, they were not successful in achieving their aims. Instead, their uprising resulted in the dispatch of foreign reinforcements who quickly and decisively put down the rebellion. The Manchu government, already having made great concessions to the Europeans and Japanese, was then even further humiliated. As a result of the rebellion, China was forced to sign the **Boxer Protocol**, which demanded that China not only pay the Europeans and the Japanese the costs associated with the rebellion but also formally apologize for it as well.

Contrast Them: European Imperialism in China and India

Many European countries traded with India, but the British ultimately won out and established exclusive control. In China, the British dominated trade early on, and as they succeeded, more and more countries piled on.

In India, the British established a true colony, running the government and directing huge internal projects. In China, Europeans and the Japanese established spheres of influence, focusing on the economic benefits of trade with no overall governmental responsibilities. Therefore, when independence movements began in India, the efforts were directed against Britain, the foreign occupier. In contrast, when the people wanted to change the government in China, they targeted the Manchu Dynasty.

On its last legs, the Manchu Dynasty couldn't prevent the forces of reform from overtaking it from both within and without, and as a consequence, Chinese culture itself started to crumble. In 1901, foot binding was abolished. In 1905, the 2,000-year-old Chinese Examination System was eliminated. By 1911, the government was toppled and imperial rule came to an end. For the first time, under the leadership of Sun Yat-sen, a republic was established in China. More on this in the next chapter.

E. Japanese Imperialism

During the 17th and 18th centuries, Japan succeeded in keeping European influences away from its shores. It consequently built a highly ethnocentric, self-involved society that didn't even allow its own citizens to travel abroad. By the 19th century and the Industrial Revolution, the Europeans and the United States became so powerful and so crazed for markets that Japan found it hard to keep the westerners at bay. In 1853, **Commodore Matthew Perry** from the United States arrived in Japan on a steamboat, something the Japanese had never seen before, and essentially shocked the Japanese, who quickly realized that their isolation had resulted in their inability to compete economically and militarily with the industrialized world.

For a time, the West won concessions from Japan through various treaties such as the **Treaty of Kanagawa** (1854). These treaties grossly favored the United States and other countries. As in China, the nationalists grew resentful, but unlike the Chinese, the Japanese were organized. Through the leadership of the samurai, they revolted against the shogun who had ratified these treaties, and restored Emperor Meiji to power.

The Meiji Restoration: Shogun Out, Emperor In, Westerners Out

The **Meiji Restoration** ushered in an era of Japanese westernization, after which Japan emerged as a world power. By the 1870s, Japan was building railways and steamships. By 1876, the samurai warrior class as an institution had been abolished, and universal military service among all males was established.

The relative isolation of Japan during the Tokugawa Shogunate and the deliberate attempt to Westernize while strengthening Japanese imperial traditions during the Meiji led to a period of increased cultural creativity with rituals aimed at developing national identity. Much of this new identity was centered on military pageantry that celebrated Japanese victories over China and Russia in the early 20th century.

In the 1890s, Japanese industrial and military power really started to roll. It was now powerful enough to substantially reduce European and U.S. influence. It maintained trade, but on an equal footing with Western powers. Japan went through an incredibly quick Industrial Revolution. In 1895, Japan defeated China in a war for control of Korea and Taiwan. Japan was now an imperial power itself.

Compare Them: The Industrial Revolution in Europe and in Japan

The industrialization of Europe and Japan followed very similar paths, but Japan's was on fast forward. It managed to accomplish in a few decades what had taken Europe more than a century, in large part because it didn't have to invent everything itself—it just needed to implement the advances of Western industrialization. Still, the pattern was remarkably similar. Private corporations rose up, industrialists like the Mitsubishi family became wealthy, factories were built, urbanization increased dramatically, and reform was instituted. Japan learned from the Europeans quite well. If you can't beat an industrialized power, become one yourself.

F. European Imperialism in Africa

Unlike India and China, and to a certain degree Japan, Africa held little interest for most Europeans prior to the Industrial Revolution. To be sure, north of the Sahara, in Egypt and along the Mediterranean, Europeans had historical interest and impact. The vast interior of the continent remained unknown to the outside world. During the Age of Exploration, coastal regions of Africa became important to Europeans for limited trade, and also for strategic positioning, as stopping-off points for merchant ships en route to India or China. Most significantly, of course, Africa became the center of the slave trade.

The Slave Trade Finally Ends

As Enlightenment principles took root in Europe, larger and larger numbers of people grew outraged at the idea of slavery. Between 1807 and 1820, most European nations abolished the slave trade, although slavery itself was not abolished until a few decades later. In other words, no new enslaved people were legally imported from Africa, but those already in Europe or the New World continued to be enslaved until emancipation in the mid-19th century. In some cases, former enslaved people returned to Africa. Groups of former American enslaved people, for example, emigrated to Liberia, where they established an independent nation.

The Slave Trade Ends, Oppression Does Not

It's a terrible irony that as the slave trade ended in the 19th century, Europeans turned their attention to the continent of Africa itself. Within 50 years, Africans were subjugated again, but this time in their own homeland.

South Africa: Gold Rings, a Diamond Necklace, and a British Crown

Prior to the discovery of gold and diamonds in South Africa in the 1860s and 1880s, South Africa was valuable to the Europeans only for shipping and military reasons. The Dutch arrived first and settled Cape Town as a stopping point for ships on the way from Europe to India. In 1795, the British seized Cape Town, and the South African Dutch (now known as Boers or Afrikaners) trekked north-east into the interior of South Africa, settling in a region known as the Transvaal. When the Boers later discovered diamonds and gold in the Transvaal, the British quickly followed, fighting a series of wars for the rights to the resources. After years of bloody battles, known as the **Boer War** (1899–1902), the British reigned supreme, and all of South Africa was annexed as part of the ever-expanding British Empire. Of course, throughout this entire process, Africans were not allowed claims to the gold and diamonds, and were made to work in the mines as their natural resources were sent abroad.

Egypt: A New Waterway Makes a Splash

In theory, the Ottomans ruled Egypt from 1517 until 1882, although throughout the 19th century, Ottoman rule was extremely weak. Local rulers, called *beys*, had far more influence over developments in Egypt than the rulers in Istanbul. When Napoleon tried to conquer Egypt during his tireless attempt to expand France into a mega-empire at the turn of the 19th century, **Muhammad Ali** defeated the French and the Ottomans and gained control of Egypt in 1805. Egypt technically remained part of the Ottoman Empire, but as viceroy, Ali wielded almost exclusive control. During the next 30 years, he began the industrialization of Egypt and directed the expansion of agriculture toward cotton production, which was then exported to the textile factories of Britain for substantial profit.

Ali's Westernization attempts were temporarily halted by his grandson, **Abbas I**, but were rein-vigorated under subsequent rulers, who worked with the French to begin construction of the **Suez Canal**. The canal, when completed in 1869, connected the Mediterranean Sea to the Indian Ocean, eliminating the need to go around the Cape of Good Hope. Because Britain had a huge colony in India, the canal became more important to the British than to anyone else. As Egypt's finances went into a tailspin because of excessive government spending, Egypt started selling stock in its canal to raise money, stock that the British government eagerly gobbled up. By 1882, Britain not only controlled the Suez Canal, but had maneuvered its way into Egypt to such a degree that it declared it a British protectorate, which was essentially a colony except that Egyptians remained in political power.

Pushed out of Egypt, France focused on other parts of North Africa, particularly Algeria. The Italians, once they had unified as a country, also became interested in North Africa. The race for control of Africa was on.

G. The Berlin Conference

In 1884, Otto von Bismarck hosted the major European powers at a conference in Berlin intended to resolve some differences over various European claims to lands in the African Congo. By the end of the conference, the delegates had set up rules for how future colonization rights and boundaries would be determined on that continent. With rules in hand, the Europeans left the conference in haste. Each country wanted to be the first to establish possession in the various parts of Africa. Within three decades, almost the entire continent of Africa was colonized by Britain, France, Germany, Italy, Spain, Portugal, and Belgium. Only Ethiopia and Liberia remained independent of European rule by 1914.

While the Europeans added substantial infrastructure to the continent by building railroads, dams, and roads, they stripped Africa of its resources for profit and treated the natives harshly. Every colonial power except Britain exercised direct rule over its colonies, meaning Europeans were put in positions of authority and the colonies were remade according to European customs. The British, having their hands full with the huge colony in India and massive spheres of influence in China and elsewhere, permitted the native populations to rule themselves more directly and to more freely practice their traditional customs (similar to how the Roman Empire handled its far-flung territories).

Because the Berlin Conference of 1884 encouraged colonialism solely based on bargaining for political and economic advantage, the boundary lines that eventually separated colonial territories were based on European concerns, not on African history or culture. Therefore, in some situations, tribal lands were cut in half between two colonies controlled by two different European nations, while in other situations two rival tribes were unwillingly brought together under the same colonial rule. For a time, the disruption of traditional tribal boundary lines worked to the Europeans' advantage because it was difficult for the native Africans to organize an opposition within each colony. It did much more than thwart opposition; it disrupted the culture. Add in European schools, Christian missionaries, and Western business practices, and traditional African culture, as elsewhere in the global colonial swirl, started breaking apart.

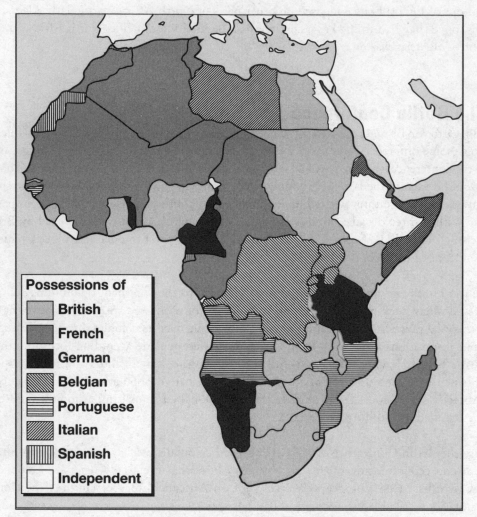

Possessions of

	British
	French
	German
	Belgian
	Portuguese
	Italian
	Spanish
	Independent

European Colonies in Africa, 1914

Compare Them: European Colonialism in Africa and Latin America

Colonialism in Africa was similar to that in the Americas in that boundary lines were determined by European agreements from abroad. In other words, there was total disregard for the societies that existed beforehand. Colonialism in Africa was similar to colonialism in America because multiple countries held claims to the land. Except for the colonies controlled by the British, the African colonies were governed by direct rule, similar to European rule of colonies in the Americas. This meant they sent European officials to occupy all positions of authority. Native traditions were overcome, not tolerated, and certainly not developed. This, of course, was in contrast to spheres of influence in China, for example, in which Europeans were generally more interested in making money rather than changing the entire culture.

H. U.S. Foreign Policy

After the wave of independence movements swept Latin America in the early 19th century, Europe found itself nearly shut out of developments in the entire western hemisphere—even as European countries were swiftly colonizing Africa and Asia.

To ensure that Europe wouldn't recolonize the Americas, U.S. President Monroe declared in his 1823 State of the Union Address that the Western Hemisphere was off-limits to European aggression. The United States, of course, wasn't the superpower then that it is today, so it was hardly in a position to enforce its declaration, which became known as the **Monroe Doctrine**. Britain, whose navy was enormous and positioned all over the globe, was fearful that Spain wanted to rekindle its American empire, so it agreed to back up the United States. As a result, the European powers continued to invest huge sums of money in Latin American business enterprises but didn't make territorial claims. In 1904, after European powers sent warships to Venezuela to demand repayment of loans, President Theodore Roosevelt added what came to be known as the **Roosevelt Corollary to the Monroe Doctrine**, which provided that the United States would intervene in financial disputes between European powers and countries in the Americas, if doing so would help to maintain the peace. While Latin American nations have at times benefited from the protection and oversight of their North American neighbor, the Monroe Doctrine also angered some Latin Americans, who saw the United States as exercising its own brand of imperialism in the region. This became clear when the United States incited Panamanians to declare their independence from Colombia, so that the United States could negotiate the right to build the **Panama Canal** in the Central American nation.

In 1898, a European power was dealt another blow in its efforts to maintain its footing in the Western Hemisphere. Spain, which still controlled both Cuba and Puerto Rico, was embroiled in conflict with Cuban revolutionaries when the United States, which sympathized with the Cubans, intervened and launched the **Spanish-American War** of 1898. In a matter of a few months, it was all over. The United States quickly and decisively destroyed the Spanish fleets in Cuba and in the Philippines, and thereby gained control of Guam, Puerto Rico, and the Philippines. Cuba was given its independence, in exchange for concessions to the United States, including allowing the creation of two U.S. naval bases on the island. The United States, henceforth, was considered to be among the world powers.

V. TECHNOLOGY AND INNOVATIONS, 1750–1900

Economic, political, and social changes occurred so rapidly in this 150-year period that it is difficult to keep track of them all. The flow chart in "Pulling It All Together" (see page 259) of this chapter provides a good outline of the causes and effects of these changes. Advances in power and transportation drove the Industrial Revolution. Steam provided consistent power for new factories. In transportation news, millions of miles of rail lines were laid throughout Europe, India, Africa, and eastern Asia. This facilitated the movement of resources and man-ufactured goods. The new industrial world required large numbers of laborers. In the latter half of the 19th century, this need, along with the abolition of slavery, resulted in large-scale migrations around the world. Europeans and east Asians immigrated to the Americas, and south Indians moved into other British-controlled territories.

This rapidly transforming world also resulted in the creation of new forms of entertainment for the urban working class, new literature and revolutionary new ideas, exhibitions, fairs and amusement parks, professional sports, as well as the first department stores with widely available consumer goods. Both English and Japanese women published novels, some of which were indictments of working class life. The rapid industrialization also created the need for new forms of job protection including unions and new ideas about the relationships between the social classes.

With industrialization came new imperialism and interactions. The arts and culture of Europe were influenced by contact with Asia and Africa, resulting in the development of new art forms. Meanwhile, the Japanese started to integrate Western styles into traditional art forms. The seemingly radical Impressionist period in 19th-century European painting was based on depictions of real life, while the modernist art movements included cubism, surrealism, and art nouveau.

New industrialization and imperialism also resulted in new reasons and new ways to make war. This period saw the development of automatic weapons, including the Maxim gun of the 1880s. The assembly line allowed for mass production of gasoline-powered automobiles and eventually the first tanks, which led to the massive destruction wrought on the battlefields of World War I.

VI.   CHANGES AND CONTINUITIES IN THE ROLE OF WOMEN

With all the dramatic transformations that took place in the 19th century, this was actually a low point in terms of women's rights. Education, real wages, and professional opportunities continued to be mostly inaccessible; however, the new intellectual and economic opportunities available to men did open doors for women, and movements began throughout the world to rally for women's political and legal rights.

Although women continued to be heavily restricted with few freedoms, political and legal barriers for men based on class or racial categories were mostly eliminated. However, women were not unaffected by the new Enlightenment ideals of freedom, equality, and liberty, and the earliest feminist writers emerged in Western Europe during this period. Both middle- and working-class women joined reform movements, labor unions, and socialist parties. Most important to these women was access to education, which was still denied to the majority of them due to ideas of mental inferiority based on Social Darwinism.

Although most Western countries opened university education to women, literacy rates in China and India—countries with long histories of secluding women—remained shockingly low well into the 20th century. However, male literacy in these regions was also low, and despite Christian missionary schools, it was not in the interest of the imperial powers to have a well-educated colonial populace.

Despite the challenges women faced during this period, the 19th century saw the beginnings of worldwide demands for women's liberation. Following the 1789 publication of the "Declaration of Rights of Man and Citizen" as a rallying cry for the French Revolution, playwright Olympia de Gouges penned her response—1791's "Declaration of the Rights of Woman and of the

Female Citizen." Her clarion call for inclusion of gender equality in the French Revolution landed her in the guillotine, but the document itself awakened generations of women's rights advocates in the coming century.

By the 1800s, many women in the United States were active in the abolitionist movement, and it was their exclusion from participation at a worldwide antislavery convention held in London in 1840 that convinced women like Elizabeth Cady Stanton and Lucretia Mott to hold the first women's rights convention in 1848 in Seneca Falls in upstate New York. Stanton and Mott, along with other reformers, published the Declaration of Rights and Sentiments of Women, which they modeled after the American Declaration of Independence. Their Declaration began, "We hold these truths to be self-evident, that all men and women are created equal...."

VII. PULLING IT ALL TOGETHER

From 1750 to 1900, so much happened in so many different places that it's easy to get lost unless you focus on major developments and trends. We suggest that you try to link up many of the events and movements in a flowchart. Once you start, you'll be amazed at how much is interconnected.

We've put together a sample flowchart for you. You may choose to connect developments quite differently from the way we have—there's certainly more than one way to link events together. That said, take a look at the chart and use it to help you begin to make your own.

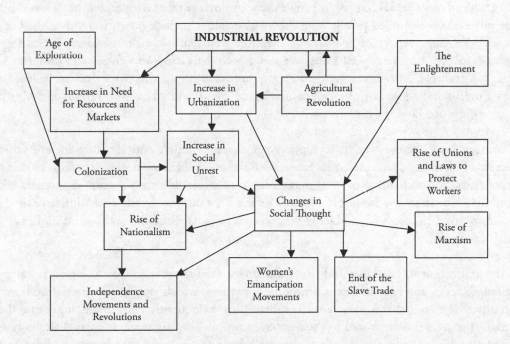

Of course, this chart doesn't begin to address many of the developments covered in this chapter. To include everything would require an enormous chart. In addition, developments were complicated and not entirely sequential. For example, there were two big rounds of independence movements and revolutions because there were two rounds of colonialism. The first round occurred after the Age of Exploration when the United States and Latin America declared their independence. The second round occurred after the Industrial Revolution and led to a race for new colonies in Asia and Africa. Those independence movements didn't occur until the 20th century.

Notice also that there are arrows going in both directions between the Agricultural Revolution and the Industrial Revolution—each led to more of the other. The greater the food surplus, the more a country could industrialize. The more it industrialized, the more it developed efficient machines and tools that could be used to increase agricultural production.

The Complex Dynamics of Change: Enough to Make Your Head Spin

During the time period covered in this chapter, there were many forces of change. Exploration. Industrialization. Education. The continuing impact of the Enlightenment. The end of slavery. Military superiority. Nationalism. Imperialism. Racism. Capitalism. Marxism. It's mind-boggling.

What's more, these changes were communicated faster than ever before. Trains and ships raced across continents and seas. Telegraph cables were laid and telephones were ringing. Think about how much faster Japan industrialized than England. Think about how much faster Africa was colonized than Latin America. Increases in transportation and communication had far-reaching consequences.

Urbanization, too, fueled change. As people came in closer contact with each other, ideas spread more quickly. Like-minded people were able to associate with each other. Individuals had contact with a greater variety of people, and therefore were exposed to more ideas. Increasingly, developments in the cities raced along at a faster pace than those in villages and on farms. In India, for example, British imperialism greatly impacted life in the cities. Indians learned to speak English and adopted European habits. In the countryside, however, Hindu and Muslim culture continued largely uninterrupted.

Of course, most change—even "revolutionary" change—didn't entirely supplant everything that came before it. For example, the Scientific Revolution challenged some assertions made by Catholicism, but both survived, and many sought to reconcile new scientific discoveries with traditional Christian teaching. Slavery was successfully outlawed, but that didn't mean that former enslaved people were suddenly welcomed as equals. Racism, both social and institutional, continued.

It's also important to keep in mind that individuals, even those who were the primary agents of change, acted and reacted based on multiple motives, which were sometimes at odds with each other. The United States declared its independence eloquently and convincingly, and then many of the signers went home to their enslaved people. Factory workers argued tirelessly for humane working conditions, but once achieved, happily processed raw materials stolen from distant lands where the interests of the natives were often entirely disregarded.

Change is indeed very complex, but it's also impossible to ignore. Life for virtually everyone on the globe was different in 1914 than in 1750. If you can describe how, you're well on your way to understanding the basics. If you can describe why, you're on your way to doing well on the exam.

CHAPTER 8 KEY TERMS

The Enlightenment
divine right
Mandate of Heaven
Thomas Hobbes
John Locke
Jean-Jacques Rousseau
Voltaire
Montesquieu
enlightened monarchs
Neoclassical Period
French and Indian War
Seven Years' War
George Grenville
Charles Townshend
Revenue Act
Stamp Act
Tea Act
Thomas Paine
Estates-General
Declaration of Independence
National Assembly
Declaration of the Rights of
    Man
Convention
Jacobins
Committee of Public Safety
Maximilien Robespierre
Directory
Napoleon Bonaparte
Napoleonic Codes
Prince von Metternich
Alexander I of Russia
Duke of
Wellington
Waterloo
Congress of Vienna
Pierre Toussaint L'Ouverture
Jacques Dessalines
Simón Bolívar
José de San
Martin
John VI
Pedro II
Miguel Hidalgo
José Morelos

Treaty of Cordoba
neocolonialism
Mexican Revolution
Porfirio Díaz
Túpac Amaru II
Samory Touré
Ghost Dance
Mahadists
enclosure
Urbanization
domestic system
flying shuttle
spinning jenny
cotton gin
Eli Whitney
steam engine
James Watt
Robert Fulton
steamship
George Stephenson
steam-powered locomotive
The Telegraph
The Telephone
The Lightbulb
The Internal Combustion
    Engine
The Radio
Charles Darwin
interchangeable parts
assembly line
Adam Smith
free-market system
capitalism
laissez-faire capitalism
Karl Marx
socialism
communism
Luddites
Factory Act of 1883
labor unions
Social mobility
Victor Emmanuel II
Count Camillo Cavour
Giuseppe Garibaldi
William I

Otto von Bismarck
Franco-Prussian War
William II
Propaganda Movement
Lola Rodríguez de Tió
Alexander II
Emancipation Edict
The People's Will
Russification
transnational businesses
social Darwinists
Rudyard Kipling
"White Man's Burden"
British East India Company
Robert Clive
Bahadur Shah II
Indian National Congress
Opium War
Treaty of Nanjing
    "unequal treaties"
White Lotus Rebellions
Taiping Rebellion
Self-Strengthening
    Movement
Sino-French War
Sino-Japanese War
Treaty of Shimonoseki
spheres of influence
Chinese Exclusion Act
Open Door Policy
Boxers
Boxer Protocol
Commodore Matthew Perry
Treaty of Kanagawa
Meiji Restoration
Boer War
Muhammad Ali
Abbas I
Suez Canal
Monroe Doctrine
Roosevelt Corollary to the
    Monroe Doctrine
Panama Canal
Spanish-American War

Chapter 8 Drill

See the end of the chapter for the answers and explanations.

Questions 1–5 refer to the maps below.

Select World Empires, c. 1800

Select World Empires, c. 1900

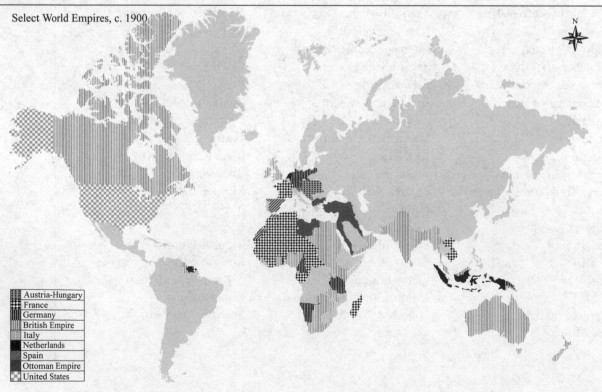

1. Which of the following best explains the increasing extent of European empires during the eighteenth and nineteenth centuries, as indicated in the maps?

   (A) Increasing economic vitality generated by technological innovation resulted in population growth and allowed for larger, better-equipped armies.
   (B) Centuries of warfare in Europe led to European generals and soldiers becoming the best in the world.
   (C) Other states were generally weaker and more internally divided than they had been in the past, and European states capitalized on that advantage.
   (D) It was a purely cultural phenomenon; the European will to power overcame all obstacles.

2. Which of the following best summarizes the intellectual underpinnings of European colonialism?

   (A) Europeans believed that the divinely ordained order of things was for Europeans to rule the earth.
   (B) There were none; colonialism was the result of pure greed.
   (C) Europeans believed that resources belonged to those who could make the best use of them; thus, the factories of Europe had a claim to the resources of the world.
   (D) The most powerful societies (and races) were believed to be the most fit and therefore had an obligation to rule over inferior societies.

3. Which of the following best summarizes the driving impulses behind most movements of national unification?

   (A) Similar political structures and solidarity among the noble classes led to the imposition of national unification from above.
   (B) Popular feelings of similarity, driven by a shared language and culture, led to pressure for national unification from below.
   (C) Economic arguments about larger common markets and the value of currency unions swayed bourgeois opinion and brought about unification.
   (D) Nations, like empires, were conquered; national unification in Europe was driven primarily by warfare.

4. Which of the following most accurately characterizes the changes in the map of Europe between 1800 and 1900?

   (A) Increasing nationalist pressures drove the unification of German polities as well as the unification of Italian polities, while Poland was divided between Russia, Germany, and the Hapsburg Monarchy.
   (B) The Hapsburg Monarchy successfully united the German states behind its rule, while Poland agreed to unify with Russia and Italy became an independent state.
   (C) There were no substantial changes in the map of Europe between 1800 and 1900.
   (D) Following defeat by the Russians, the Hapsburgs ceded much of the Balkan territories to the Ottoman Empire, while Germany and Italy became united, independent states.

5. Which of the following most accurately characterizes the changes in the map of North America between 1800 and 1900?

   (A) Canada's sale of Alaska to the United States complemented the results of the Louisiana Purchase and the Mexican-American War to lead to U.S. hegemony on the continent.
   (B) U.S. expansion to the west and south at the expense of France and Mexico led to the attainment of the present borders of the contiguous 48 states.
   (C) The collapse and disintegration of the Mexican Empire under Maximilian allowed Canadian and U.S. expansion into its former territories.
   (D) The Spanish-American War led to the United States occupying and annexing the bulk of Spanish imperial territories.

Questions 6–8 refer to the passage below.

The free-people of colour, though peaceful, were not inattentive to passing events: they sent a deputation to France, to claim their natural rights from the legislature.

It was about this time that M. Charles de Lameth, one of the deputies, made his well-known declaration:

"I am one of the greatest proprietors in St. Domingo, but I declare to you that, were I to lose all I possess, I should prefer it, rather than not recognize the principles that justice and humanity have consecrated; I declare myself in favor of the admission of the mixed races into administrative assemblies, and of the liberty of the blacks."

Such declarations appear to have inspired confidence in the colored population, who, thenceforward began to press their claims in the colony itself, though with little success; for one of their number, one Lacombe, was executed at the Cape for having signed a petition…

Notes on Haiti Made During a Residence in That Republic, by Charles MacKenzie, 1830. London, England.

6. The most significant global consequence of the Haitian Revolution was

   (A) the beginning of a French Empire in the Western Hemisphere
   (B) the acceptance of Black people into politics
   (C) the beginning of the end of the European slave trade
   (D) the weakening of the institution of slavery in the United States

7. Which of the following was NOT one of the causes of the Haitian Revolution?

   (A) Extreme violence committed against enslaved Haitians
   (B) The corruption of black Haitian leaders in the eighteenth century
   (C) The destabilization of France during the French Revolution
   (D) The announcement of the Declaration of the Rights of Man by the French National Assembly

8. Independence movements of the nineteenth century, like the one described above, often failed to bring meaningful change to the lives of formerly enslaved people. Which of the following does NOT explain this phenomenon?

   (A) The power of social reformers to push newly independent countries towards excessive liberalism
   (B) Failure to innovate or diversify economic activity
   (C) Economic dependence on former colonial powers
   (D) In Latin America, the power of the Catholic Church to influence policy and behavior

Questions 9–11 refer to the passage below.

Let us now suppose that the number of labourers still continues to increase…. [T]he very fact that a man is unable, by his own individual exertions, to comfortably provide sustenance for himself and his family, compels him to have recourse to the members of his own household in order to eke out a living, who thus become competitors with him for employment.

If, then, the number of labourers continued in this way to increase, and the demand for employment increased in proportion, as economists insist would be the case, employers would … take advantage of the necessities of the labourers and reduce their wages till they might be insufficient for bare subsistence…. [N]umbers of them would starve or become a charge on the community. Thus the effect would be in the highest way injurious.

I may be told that enlightened self-interest would always prevent the occurrence of such a disastrous result as I have here indicated. But I am not so sure of this.

From *Outlines of an Industrial Science,* by David Syme. 1877. London, England.

9. Which of the following is LEAST associated with the ideas stated in the passage above?

   (A) The hands-off approach of *laissez-faire* capitalism
   (B) The invisible hand of the market, as described by Adam Smith
   (C) The mid-nineteenth-century English labor union movement
   (D) The enclosure movement in rural areas

10. Syme describes an economic situation in which a surplus of laborers results in low pay by employers. Which of the following thinkers addressed this dilemma most directly in his writings?

    (A) Victor Emmanuel II
    (B) Karl Marx
    (C) Rudyard Kipling
    (D) John Locke

11. In addition to the topic discussed in the passage, another major consequence of the Industrial Revolution in Europe was

    (A) loss of colonial holdings
    (B) rapid urbanization
    (C) lack of social mobility
    (D) reduced emigration

TIMELINE OF MAJOR DEVELOPMENTS, 1750–1900

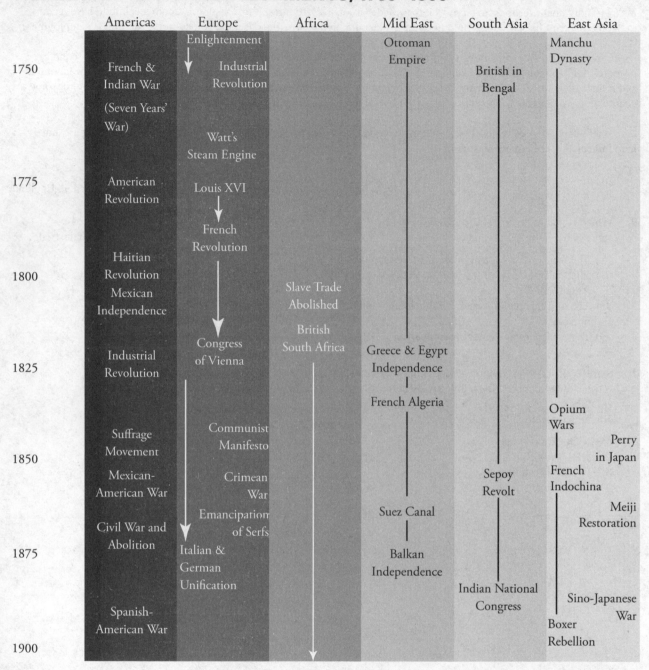

	Americas	Europe	Africa	Mid East	South Asia	East Asia
		Enlightenment		Ottoman Empire		Manchu Dynasty
1750	French & Indian War (Seven Years' War)	Industrial Revolution			British in Bengal	
		Watt's Steam Engine				
1775	American Revolution	Louis XVI				
		French Revolution				
1800	Haitian Revolution / Mexican Independence		Slave Trade Abolished / British South Africa			
1825	Industrial Revolution	Congress of Vienna		Greece & Egypt Independence / French Algeria		Opium Wars
1850	Suffrage Movement / Mexican-American War	Communist Manifesto / Crimean War			Sepoy Revolt	Perry in Japan / French Indochina / Meiji Restoration
1875	Civil War and Abolition	Emancipation of Serfs / Italian & German Unification		Suez Canal / Balkan Independence		
	Spanish-American War				Indian National Congress	Sino-Japanese War / Boxer Rebellion
1900						

CHAPTER 8 DRILL EXPLANATIONS

1. **A** Though this is a broad question, there are some straightforward ways to prune the answer choices. Choice (B) assumes that all other areas of the world had not experienced division and strife, which, while true for some areas over some times, does not describe this time period accurately. Similarly, (C) assumes that there was a novel and atypical degree of weakness and internal disunity across non-European states, which is an unwarranted assumption. Choice (D) makes an extreme claim—that it was only a cultural phenomenon. Extreme claims are typically incorrect, as, in this case, there are almost always multiple causes or influences on any historical phenomenon. Though cultural elements were likely relevant, the impact of the Industrial Revolution was far more relevant, so (A) is the best answer.

2. **D** While European colonialism was certainly motivated at least in part by greed, that was not a core element in the intellectual underpinnings of the phenomenon, which would be important in determining against whom and to what extent such greed ought be exercised (among other things). So (B) doesn't work. Similarly, while religion was not irrelevant to colonialism, it was no longer the guiding principle of state policy in this era, if indeed it ever was. Therefore, (A) is incorrect. When comparing the last two answer choices, remember that the defining characteristic of European colonialism was the creation of a racial hierarchy. Only (D) speaks to the core issue and is thus the best answer.

3. **B** Though commonalities of various kinds played a role in the rise of nationalism and ensuing national unification efforts, economics and political forms (whether a state was republican or monarchical in character, for example) were not substantial factors, and so (A) and (C) can be eliminated. Choice (D) may seem plausible, as many unification efforts did involve violence, but remember that the question is asking for what drove these movements, not how they were carried out. Thus, (B) is correct.

4. **A** The most straightforward approach here is to use your knowledge of European history to eliminate incorrect answers. The map of Europe changed substantially over the 19th century, so (C) does not make sense. Though Poland did lose much of its territory to Russia, this was an involuntary process; similarly, Prussia united the German states, not Austria-Hungary. Therefore, (B) is incorrect. Choice (D) is partially right; Germany and Italy did become united independent states during this time, but the first clause flips the script. The Ottoman Empire lost much of its European territory to Austria-Hungary following a series of military defeats rather than the other way around, so (D) is incorrect. Choice (A) successfully accounts for the disappearance of Poland and the unifications of Germany and Italy, and is thus the best answer.

5. **B** Be careful here; (A) is mostly correct, but remember that the United States bought Alaska from Russia, not from Canada. Choice (C) indicates that Mexico collapsed, which is incorrect. The Empire did end following Maximilian's execution, but the state itself neither collapsed nor disintegrated. While (D) is true in that the 1898 Spanish American War did lead to U.S. seizure of many of Spain's remaining colonial holdings, these were largely islands in Southeast Asia. There were no significant Spanish holdings on the North American continent by that time. Choice (B) correctly references the Louisiana Purchase and the Mexican-American War as leading to U.S. expansion in North America, and is therefore correct.

6. **C** While the establishment of a society owned and run by former slaves was an enormous accomplishment, it didn't inspire any successful slave rebellions elsewhere. (Even the German Coast Uprising in Louisiana, large though it may have been, was a failure.) However, it was a wakeup call to the world, particularly slaveowners, that Black people were not as complacent with slavery as had been assumed, and that the European slave trade wasn't going to continue without repercussions. Choice (A) is a reversal; the slave revolt ended dreams of a French empire in the Western Hemisphere, so eliminate it. Choice (B) simply never happened; eliminate that too. Choice (D) is another reversal; because of the Louisiana Purchase, the amount of land that was owned by the US doubled, which also doubled the need for enslaved people to work the land. Eliminate (D).

7. **B** Much of the Black political leadership in the eighteenth century consisted of free Black or mulatto people petitioning Paris for colonial reforms, or agitating enslaved people directly. There wasn't much room for obvious corruption in these instances, since corruption usually involves being close to political power. The other answers are all well-established contributing causes of the Haitian Revolution.

8. **A** The social reformers wished they had enough power to push their societies towards liberalism, but the fact was that many of the old institutions remained, even after independence. One of them was the Catholic Church, which in Latin America stood as an impediment to meaningful social change, since it represented the status quo, owned enormous tracts of land, and had never officially opposed slavery. Eliminate (D). Newly independent nations such as Colombia failed to diversify their economy outside of agriculture and mining, and thus never built a middle class, so eliminate (B). The goods they did produce, such as tobacco or coffee or rice, were often sold via exclusive trade agreements with the previous colonial powers, which prevented them from finding new partners, so eliminate (C).

9. **D** The Enclosure Movement was a push in the 18th and 19th centuries to transform public commons—meaning patches of public land that had been used for farming for centuries—into fenced-off, privately owned land, often used to grow items for sale and profit. It effectively killed off the last vestiges of the feudal system, ending the peasantry's association with the land. While this can be distantly connected to the problems of urban working class nearly a century later, this connection isn't nearly as strong as those of (A), (B), or (C). Those all exactly describe, in philosophical terms, the economic situation that gripped the second half of the nineteenth century. Eliminate (A), (B), and (C).

10. **B** In his writings, Karl Marx diagnosed the biggest problem contributing to the economic injustices of the nineteenth century: the fact that the working class lacked ownership of capital. His solution, however, was perhaps less feasible: the working class ought to rise up, seize control of the factories through revolution, and establish a workers' paradise. Choice (A) describes the first king of a united Italy; eliminate it. Also eliminate (C); Kipling was a poet, not an economist or political philosopher. Choice (D), famous Enlightenment philosopher John Locke, may or may not have agreed with the sentiment, but he died a century before the Industrial Revolution even began.

11.　**B**　Cities grew rapidly during the nineteenth century. After all, the growth of industrialization necessitated factories, and factories required access to large groups of workers. It's fair to say that the growth of cities, corporations, and industry all occurred together, at the same time. Choice (A) describes a loss of colonial holdings, but the British Empire actually added more many more colonial holdings during this time. Though France and Spain did give up their holdings in the Americas during this century, they did so for reasons unrelated to industry—mostly local revolutions. Eliminate (A). Social mobility skyrocketed, so eliminate (C). Ironically, however, Europeans began leaving Europe in massive numbers during this century—nearly 50 million—so eliminate (D).

Chapter 9
Period 4,
c. 1900 to Present

Unit 7: Global Conflict

Unit 8: Cold War and
    Decolonization

Unit 9: Globalization

You've (Almost) Made It!

Now that you've made it all the way to the last period covered on the exam (1900 to present), you're in the home stretch! Reward yourself by taking a break before diving into this chapter.

I. CHAPTER OVERVIEW

From 1900 onward, everything seemed to have global significance. Wars were called "world wars." Issues were thought of in terms of their worldwide impact, such as "global hunger" or "international terrorism." Organizations, such as the United Nations, formed to coordinate international efforts. Economies and cultures continued to merge to such a degree that eventually millions of people communicated instantaneously on the Internet, feeding a massive cultural shift known simply as "globalization."

It's a complex 120+ years. We'll help you sort through it. Here's how we organized this chapter:

I. Chapter Overview

    You're reading it now.

II. Stay Focused on the Big Picture

    This section will help you think about and organize the huge number of global events that have occurred over the past century.

III. Unit 7: Global Conflict

    This is the largest section of the chapter. In it, we plow through historical developments. If you're totally clueless on any part of this section, you might consider also reviewing the corresponding topic in your textbook. As you can see from the section titles, and as you hopefully remember from your history class, there were a bunch of very significant wars in the 20th century. As you study, worry more about the causes and consequences than about particular battles, although with regard to World War II, it's important to understand the general sequence of military and political events, so we've included quite a bit. Here's how we've organized the information:

    A. The World War I Era
    B. The World War II Era
    C. The Consequences

IV. Unit 8: Cold War and Decolonization

    Here's how we've organized it:

    A. Communism and the Cold War
    B. Power Grab: Soviets and Americans Want Everyone to Take Sides
    C. China: Communists Make Huge Gains
    D. The Cuban Revolution
    E. Cold War Tensions and Democratization in Latin America
    F. The Cold War Finally Ends
    G. Independence Movements and Developments in Asia and Africa

V.   Unit 9: Globalization

Here's how we've organized it:

A. International Terrorism and War
B. World Trade and Cultural Exchange
C. Environmental Change
D. Global Health Crises
E. The Age of the Computer

VI.   Changes and Continuities in the Role of Women

Finally, equal rights (in some places)

VII.   Pulling It All Together

Focus on the big-picture concepts now that you've reviewed the details.

II.   STAY FOCUSED ON THE BIG PICTURE

As always, connections, causation, and big-picture concepts are important. As you review the details of the 20th-century developments in this chapter, stay focused on the big picture, and ask yourself some questions.

For **Unit 7**, ask yourself:

1. How do nationalism and self-determination impact global events? As you review, notice how nationalism impacts almost every country that is discussed in this chapter. It serves as both a positive force in uniting people, and a negative force in pitting people against one another. Self-determination is closely linked with nationalism because it is the goal of most nationalists.

For **Unit 8**, ask yourself:

2. Are world cultures converging? If so, how? There's plenty of evidence that world cultures are, in fact, converging, especially with regard to technology, popular culture, and the Internet. On the other hand, there seems to be no shortage of nationalism or independence movements, which suggests that major differences exist. As you read the chapter, think about the forces that are making the cultures of the world converge and those that are keeping cultures separated.

For **Unit 9**, ask yourself:

3. How do increasing globalization, population growth, and resource use change the environment? Which resources are renewable and which are not? As the world grows ever more interconnected in trade and consumption of resources, think about what political, economic, and environmental decisions are made to maintain those trade relations.

III. UNIT 7: GLOBAL CONFLICT

A. The World War I Era

At the beginning of the 20th century, most of the world was either colonized by Europe, or was once colonized by Europe, so everyone around the world was connected to the instability on that small but powerful continent. This meant that when European powers were at war with each other, the colonies were dragged into the fight. To be sure, European rivalries had had a global impact for centuries, particularly during the colonial period. The Seven Years' War in the 18th century between the French and British, for example, impacted their colonial holdings everywhere. France, too, jumped in to help the United States in its revolution against the British. In 1914, a major fight among European powers had a far more substantial and destructive effect. The Industrial Revolution had given Europe some powerful new weapons plus the ships and airplanes that could be used to deliver them. Large industrial cities had millions of people, creating the possibility of massive casualties in a single bombing raid. A rise in nationalism fed a military build-up and the desire to use it. After the unifications of Germany and Italy, Europe simply had too many power-grabbing rivals. Not a good combination of factors if you like, well, peace.

Shifting Alliances: A Prewar Tally of European Countries

In the decades leading up to World War I, the European powers tried to keep the balance of power in check by forming alliances. The newly unified Germany quickly gained industrial might, but it was worried that France, its archenemy since the Franco-Prussian War in 1870, would seek revenge for its defeat. So, before he resigned from office, Otto von Bismarck created and negotiated the **Triple Alliance** among Germany, Austria-Hungary, and Italy in the 1880s. On the side, Bismarck also had a pact with Russia. Otto played to win.

Over the next few decades, the major players of Europe became so obsessed with a possible war that their generals were already putting plans into motion in the event of an outbreak. After William II ousted Bismarck from power in 1890, he ignored Russia and allowed previous agreements between the two countries to wither. With Russia now on the market for friends, France jumped at the chance to make an alliance. With France to the west and Russia to the east, a Franco-Russo alliance helped keep Germany in check. Meanwhile, Germany's 1905 **Schlieffen Plan** called for a swift attack on France through Belgium, an officially neutral country that had a growing relationship with Britain. By 1907, Britain had also signed friendly agreements with France and Russia, creating what became known as the Triple Entente. Clearly, everyone was anticipating the possibility of war, which was a pretty safe bet considering the contentious climate.

Trouble in the Balkans

Remember the Ottoman Empire? In the first two decades of the 20th century, it was still around, but it was in such bad shape that Europeans were calling it the "sick man of Europe." It kept losing territory to its neighbors. After Greece won its independence in 1829, the Slavic areas to the north of Greece, including Romania, Bulgaria, Serbia, and Montenegro began to win their independence as well. Bosnia and Herzegovina, however, were under the control of Austria-Hungary, as decided by the Berlin Conference of 1878, the same conference that led to the

European scramble to colonize Africa. Serbia wanted Bosnia and Herzegovina for itself. To complicate matters, Russia was allied with Serbia, a fellow Slavic country.

It was in this political climate that **Archduke Franz Ferdinand** of Austria-Hungary visited Sarajevo, the capital of Bosnia, in 1914. While there, **Gavrilo Princip**, a Serbian nationalist, shot and killed the Archduke and his wife. In an age when Europe was so tightly wound in alliances, suspicion, and rivalry that a sneeze could have set off a war, the dominos quickly started to fall. Austria-Hungary declared war on Serbia. Russia, allied with Serbia and then declared war on Austria-Hungary. Because Russia and Austria-Hungary were on opposite sides of the Triple Entente–Triple Alliance divide, the pressure mounted on France, Italy, Germany, and Britain to join in. Britain was reluctant to honor its commitments at first, but when Germany implemented the Schlieffen Plan and stormed through Belgium toward France, Britain joined the fray in order to protect France. Italy, on the other hand, managed to wiggle out of its obligations and declared itself neutral, but the Ottoman Empire took its place, forming with Germany and Austria-Hungary an alliance called the **Central Powers**.

> **The Shot That Started It All**
> The killing of Archduke Franz Ferdinand and his wife in Sarajevo was the catalyst for World War I.

World War I: The War to End All Wars?

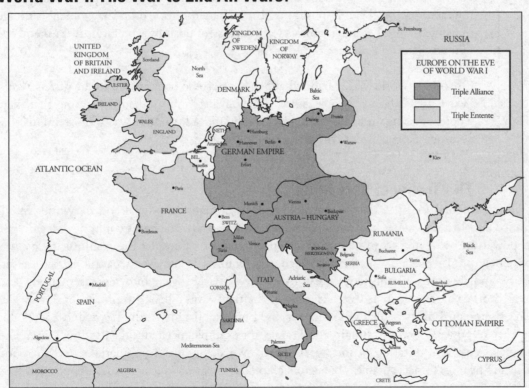

Europe on the Eve of World War I

Since the European powers had colonies or strong economic ties with most of the rest of the world, the original gunshot by a Serbian nationalist resulted in widespread casualties across the globe. More than 40 countries found themselves taking up arms, including Japan, which fought on the side of Britain, France, and Russia, now known as the Allies. In 1915, Italy managed to complete its about-face and joined the Allies as well.

The United States declared its neutrality at first, preferring to focus on its own internal affairs, a policy known as **isolationism**. When a German submarine (wow, technology came a long way quickly) sank the British passenger liner the *Lusitania* in 1915, killing more than 100 Americans who happened to be on board, public opinion in the United States shifted away from isolationism. The next year, as Germany tried to cut off all shipments to Britain, thereby starving the island country, it attacked U.S. merchant ships en route to Britain, further fueling American sentiment toward war. Then the **Zimmermann telegram** was intercepted. This telegram was a secret message sent between German diplomats suggesting that Mexico might want to join forces with Germany and thereby regain the territory it had lost to the United States in the Mexican-American War of 1846. U.S. President Woodrow Wilson learned of its contents soon after, and on April 2, 1917, America entered the war on the side of the Allies. On November 11, 1918, after brutal battles, trench warfare, and enormous loss of life, Germany and the Central Powers finally gave up.

The "War to End All Wars"

At the time, commentators referred to the Great War (World War I) as "the war to end all wars." They never imagined that another war would ravage the continent in less than two decades—a war that was even more devastating.

The consequences of the war were staggering. Eight-and-a-half million soldiers were killed. Around 20 million civilians perished. The social impact on the home front was substantial as well. Most governments took over industrial production during the war, while instituting price controls and rationing of products that were needed on the front lines. With huge numbers of men taking up arms, women moved into the factories to fill empty positions. This experience revved up the women's suffrage movement, and became the basis for a successful push by women in Britain and the United States to gain the vote after the war.

Of course, World War II hadn't happened yet, so no one referred to the war as World War I. Instead, most people called it the Great War, mistakenly thinking that there would never again be one as big or bloody. Indeed, the war was so horrendous that commentators called it "the war to end all wars."

The Treaty of Versailles

Signed in 1919, the **Treaty of Versailles** brought an official end to World War I. France and Britain wanted to cripple Germany economically, so that it could never again rise to power and threaten to invade other sovereign states of Europe. The resulting treaty was extremely punitive against Germany, which was required to pay war reparations, release territory, and downsize its military. It also divided Austria-Hungary into separate nations, and created other nations such as Czechoslovakia. The treaty was a departure from President Wilson's **Fourteen Points**, which were more focused on establishing future peace and a workable balance of power. However, Britain and France, for example, needed to justify the human and financial cost and duration of the war to their own demoralized populations and so found Wilson's proposal unacceptable. The victors blamed the war on Germany and then forced Germany to sign an extremely punitive treaty over the objections of the United States. The victors hoped that as a result, Germany would never threaten the security of Europe again. Instead, the treaty greatly weakened Germany's economy and bred resentment among the German population, laying the groundwork for the later rise of Adolf Hitler.

The League of Nations: Can't We All Just Get Along?

President Wilson was the voice of moderation at Versailles. He had hoped that the postwar treaties would be an opportunity to establish international laws and standards of fairness in international conduct. His Fourteen Points speech addressed these issues and called for the creation of a joint council of nations called the **League of Nations**. The leaders at Versailles agreed with the idea in principle, and they set out to create the organization to preserve peace and establish humanitarian goals, but when they got around to actually joining the league, many nations refused. England and France were tepid, while Germany and Russia initially scoffed at the idea (though later joined). Worse, the United States openly rejected it, a major embarrassment for President Wilson, who couldn't persuade the isolationist U.S. Congress that the league was a step toward lasting peace.

The Russian Revolution: Czar Out, Lenin In

By the time Nicholas II reigned (1894–1917), revolution was in the wind. The socialists began to organize. Nicholas tried to rally Russians around the flag by going to war with Japan over Manchuria in 1904, but the Russians suffered a humiliating defeat. On a Sunday in 1905, moderates marched on the czar's palace in a peaceful protest, an attempt to encourage him to enact Enlightened reforms, but Nicholas felt threatened and ordered his troops to fire on the protestors. The day has since been known as Bloody Sunday.

For the next decade, resentment among the working classes festered. In 1906, the czar attempted to enact legislative reforms by appointing a Prime Minister, Peter Stolypin, and by creating the Duma, a body intended to represent the Russian people, but every time the Duma was critical of the czar, he immediately disbanded it. In the end, the attempts at reform were too little, too late. The Romanov Dynasty would soon come to an end.

The **Russian Revolution** occurred even before World War I had ended. Russia entered the war with the world's largest army, though not the world's most powerful one, because the nation was not nearly as industrialized as its Western neighbors. Very quickly, the army began to suffer large-scale losses and found itself short on food, munitions, and good leadership. In February 1917, in the face of rising casualties and food shortages, **Czar Nicholas** was forced to abdicate his throne. The Romanov Dynasty came to an end. Under **Alexander Kerensky**, a provisional government was established. It was ineffectual, in part because it shared power with the local councils, called soviets, which represented the interests of workers, peasants, and soldiers. Although the provisional government affirmed natural rights (such as the equality of citizens and the principle of religious toleration—changes that were inconceivable under the czar), it wanted to continue war against Germany in the hope that Russia could then secure its borders and become a liberal democracy. The working classes, represented by the soviets, were desperate to end the suffering from the war. The idealism of the provisional officials caused them to badly miscalculate the depths of hostility the Russian people felt for the czar's war.

By 1918, the soviets rallied behind the socialist party, now called the **Bolsheviks**. Amid this turmoil, **Vladimir Lenin**, the Marxist leader of the party, mobilized the support of the workers and soldiers. He issued his **April Theses**, which demanded peace, land for peasants, and power to the soviets. Within six months, the Bolsheviks took command of the government. Under his vision of mass socialization, Lenin rigidly set about nationalizing the assets and industries of Russia. In March 1918, the soviets signed an armistice with Germany, the **Treaty of Brest-Litovsk**, which ceded a huge piece of western Russia to Germany, so Russia dropped out of World War I. It therefore wasn't part of the negotiations during the Treaty of Versailles.

In the Baltic republics of what would soon be called the **Soviet Union**, and in Ukraine, Siberia, and other parts of the former Russian Empire, counterrevolutionary revolts broke out. The Bolsheviks faced nonstop skirmishes between 1918 and 1921. To put down these struggles, the Bolsheviks created the **Red Army**, a military force under the command of **Leon Trotsky**. By 1918, the Red Army was a sizable force, and with the support of the peasants, it defeated the counterrevolutionaries. The counterrevolution had two lasting implications. First, the prolonged civil war deepened the distrust between the new Marxist state and its Western neighbors, who had supported the counterrevolutionaries. Second, the Bolsheviks now had a very powerful army, the Red Army, at its disposal.

Here Come the Turks

The Ottoman Empire, already on its last legs, made a fatal mistake by joining the losing Central Powers of World War I. During the war, Turkification, a process of reclaiming traditional Turkish culture, spawned a genocide of the Armenian minority and a shift away from Ottoman loyalty in favor of Turkish nationalism. In the peace negotiations, it lost most of its remaining land, and was therefore ripe for attack from the Greeks, who picked up arms in 1919. **Mustafa Kemal**, who later became known as **Ataturk**, "the Father of the Turks," led successful military campaigns against the Greeks, and then overthrew the Ottoman sultan. In 1923, Ataturk became the first president of modern Turkey. He successfully secularized the overwhelmingly Muslim nation, introduced Western-style dress and customs (abolishing the fez), changed the alphabet from Arabic to Latin, set up a parliamentary system (which he dominated), changed the legal code from Islamic to Western, and set Turkey on a path toward Europe as opposed to the Middle East. However, he instituted these reforms against opposition, and sometimes was ruthless in his determination to institute change.

B. The World War II Era

The Great War Part II

Even though World War II didn't get started until 1939, its causes were already well underway in the 1920s. In some ways, World War II isn't a separate war from World War I, but instead the Great War Part II.

Stalin: The Soviet Union Goes Totalitarian

Once the Soviets removed themselves from World War I, they concentrated on their own domestic problems. Lenin first instituted the **New Economic Policy (NEP)** in the early 1920s, which had some capitalistic aspects, such as allowing farmers to sell portions of their grain for their own profit. The plan was successful in agriculture, but Lenin didn't live long enough to chaperone its expansion into other parts of the Soviet economy. When Lenin died, the leadership of the Communist Party shifted to **Joseph Stalin**.

Stalin believed the NEP was ridiculously slow, so he discarded it. Instead, he imposed his **Five-Year Plans**, which called for expedient agricultural production by ruthlessly taking over private farms and combining them into state-owned enterprises, a process known as **collectivization**. The plans also advocated for the construction of large, nationalized factories. This process was achieved in the name of communism, but it was really totalitarianism. The people didn't share in the power or the profits, and had no choices regarding participation. Untold numbers died fighting to protect their farms. In Ukraine, millions died in famines that resulted when Stalin usurped crops to feed government workers at the expense of the farmers themselves.

Stalin's plans successfully industrialized the **USSR** (**Union of Soviet Socialist Republics**), the formal name for the Soviet Union, and improved economic conditions for the country as a whole, but Stalin relied on terror tactics, such as a secret police force, bogus trials, and assassinations. These murders peaked between 1936 and 1938. Collectively, they are sometimes referred to as the "Great Purge" because the government systematically killed so many of its enemies. Stalin also established labor camps to punish anyone who opposed him.

The Great Depression: Capitalism Crashes, Germany Burns

World War I was shockingly expensive. Countries spent more than $180 billion on armaments, boats, and trench warfare. Europe spent an additional $150 billion rebuilding. The massive scale of the war meant massive spending, at a level that nations had never experienced previously, and in the years following World War I, capitalism financed most of the recovery. As a consequence, the financial headquarters of the world shifted from London to New York, which had become a major center of credit to Europe during and after the war. In other words, Americans lent Europeans money, and lots of it.

It's hard to know for sure how many Soviet citizens were imprisoned or killed during the 1930s, especially because so many died as a result of famine during the collectivization process, but historians agree that millions of Soviets were slaughtered under Stalin's direction.

In particular, the economies of two countries relied on American credit: France and Germany. France had loaned huge sums of money to Russia, its prewar ally, but the Bolshevik government refused to honor the czar's debts, leaving France almost out of luck, except that Germany owed it a bunch of cash as well. Germany experienced extreme financial hardship because of the wartime reparations they were required to make under the Treaty of Versailles. Germany's answer was to use American credit to pay its reparations by issuing I.O.U.s to countries like France. France took these "payments," backed up by American credit and spent them on rebuilding its economy. From 1924 to 1929, this arrangement looked great on paper due to growth in both the United States and European economies. In many ways, the growth was artificial, based on loans that were never going to be repaid.

When the U.S. stock market crashed in October 1929, a spiral of monetary and fiscal problems called the **Great Depression** quickly escalated into an international catastrophe, and shattered the illusion of financial health in Europe. American banks immediately stopped extending credit. The effect was that Europe ran out of money, which it never really had in the first place. Germany couldn't pay its reparations without American credit, so France had no money either.

The depths of the depression were truly staggering. The United States and Germany were hit hardest. In both countries, almost one-third of the available workforce was unemployed. In the United States, out-of-work Americans rejected the dominant political party and in 1932 elected Franklin Roosevelt as president in a landslide election. Roosevelt and the United States Congress passed a series of laws known as the New Deal that consisted of heavy public spending with the purpose of creating jobs, reforms, and safety nets for struggling Americans. Other countries had much more fragile political structures. In places where democracy had shallow roots, such as Germany and Italy, whose shaky elective assemblies had been created only a decade earlier after World War I, the crisis resulted in the triumph of a political ideology that was anathema to the very spirit of democracy: fascism.

Fascism Gains Momentum

Between the First and Second World Wars, fascist parties emerged across Europe. They did not possess identical sets of beliefs, but they held a few important ideas in common. The main idea of **fascism** was to destroy the will of the individual in favor of "the people." In fact, the fascist corporatist economy organized private companies to be subservient to the state, ostensibly with the intention of curbing further economic downturn. Fascists wanted a unified society (as did the communists), but they weren't concerned with eliminating private property or class distinctions (the principal aim of communists). Instead, fascists pushed for another identity, one rooted in extreme **nationalism**, which often relied on racial identity.

Contrast Them: Fascism and Totalitarianism

Fascism is a subset of totalitarianism. A totalitarian dictator rules absolutely, attempting to control every aspect of life. Fascist rulers are a particular kind of totalitarian ruler, often regarded as extremely right-wing because they rely on traditional institutions and social distinctions to enforce their rule, and are extremely nationalistic. Their particular brand of nationalism is often based on racism. Communist totalitarian leaders like Stalin are often referred to as extreme left-wing because they seek to destroy traditional institutions and class distinctions, even as they retain absolute power themselves. Therefore, they're not referred to as fascist, but they're just as militaristic and controlling. Put another way, in their extreme forms, right-wing (fascist) and left-wing (communist) governments use the same tactics: totalitarianism. In both cases, all power rests in the hands of a single militaristic leader.

Fascism in Italy: Another Step Toward Another War

Italy was the first state to have a fascist government. The founder and leader was **Benito Mussolini**, who created the National Fascist Party in 1919. The party paid squads, known as **Blackshirts**, to fight socialist and communist organizations, an action that won over the loyalty of both factory owners and landowners. By 1921, the party seated its first members in the Italian parliament.

Although the fascists held only a few seats in the legislature, Mussolini demanded that King Victor Emmanuel III name him and several other fascists to cabinet posts. To rally support, Mussolini organized his paramilitary thugs to march to Rome and possibly attempt to seize power. If the king had declared martial law and brought in the army, most believe that the fascists would have scattered. However, the king was a timid man—facing economically troubling times—who was not unsympathetic to the fascist program. So, he named Mussolini prime minister, and the fascist march on Rome turned into a celebration.

As the postwar economy failed to improve, Italy was demoralized. Mussolini faced very little opposition to his consolidation of political power. He dabbled as a parliamentary leader for several months before completely taking over Parliament in 1922. He then implemented a number of constitutional changes to ensure that democracy no longer limited his actions, and, by 1926, Italy was transformed into a totalitarian fascist regime. To rally the people in a nationalistic cause, Italy started to focus on expansion, specifically in North Africa.

The Rise of Hitler

Immediately following the end of World War I, a revolt occurred in Germany when the emperor abdicated. Germany might well have become socialist at this point. Workers' and soldiers' councils (not unlike Russian soviets) formed in cities like Berlin. However, because the middle class in Germany was quite conservative and a large number of Germans had been relatively prosperous before the war, a socialist or communist system was rejected in favor of a fairly conservative democratic republic, called the **Weimar Republic**.

At the same time, Germany was in economic crisis, and Mussolini's success influenced Germany in many ways. The **National Socialist Party (Nazis)** rose to power in the 1920s, ushered in by the worldwide depression. As Germany's economy collapsed under the harsh reparations dictated by the Treaty of Versailles and the faltering world economy, German people increasingly rejected the solutions of the Weimar Republic's elected body, the **Reichstag**.

During this period **Adolf Hitler** rose to power as head of the Nazi Party. Like Mussolini's fascism, Hitler's Nazism inspired extreme nationalism and the dreams of renewed greatness for a depressed and divided country. Hitler's philosophies differed from Mussolini's in their emphasis on the superiority of one race over others. Well versed in Social Darwinism, Hitler was convinced that the Aryan race was the most highly evolved race, and that "inferior" races, such as Slavs and Jews, had "corrupted" the German race. He argued that Jews should be deported (later that changed to "eliminated") and that Germans should take over Europe.

The Nazi Party gained political power in the 1920s with Hitler as its guide, or *führer*. At first, the Nazis received votes democratically and participated in the Reichstag. In the early 1930s, as the Great Depression devastated the German economy, Hitler received increasing support. In the election of 1930, the Nazi Party increased its seats in Parliament tenfold. By 1932, the Nazis dominated German government and many who disagreed with Hitler still backed him, thinking he was the country's only hope. In 1933, Hitler became chancellor, or leader of the Reichstag. He then seized control of the government, known under his fascist rule as the **Third Reich**, and set his eyes on conquering Europe.

Contrast Them: Nationalism in Europe and in Its Colonies

Nationalism was a driving force throughout much of the 19th and 20th centuries, but it had a very different flavor in Europe and Japan than in most European and Japanese colonies. In Europe and Japan, nationalism fueled extreme racism, fascism, and domination. National pride became almost synonymous with national expansion and conquest of other peoples. In the colonies, nationalism meant self-determination, the ability to free the nation from rule by another and determine one's own destiny. National pride meant national sovereignty, not colonial or territorial expansion.

Appeasement: "Peace for Our Time," or Just Wishful Thinking?

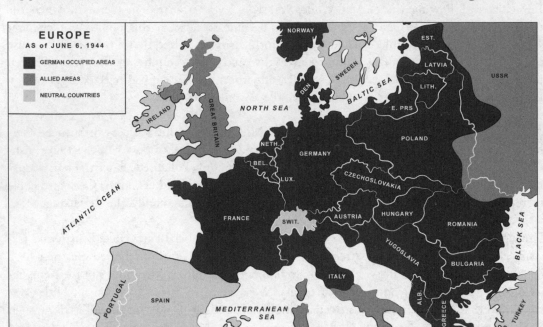

EUROPE
AS of JUNE 6, 1944

GERMAN OCCUPIED AREAS

ALLIED AREAS

NEUTRAL COUNTRIES

In 1933, Hitler began to rebuild the German military. This was a clear violation of the Treaty of Versailles—which was specifically intended to limit future German aggression—but the other nations of Europe, especially Britain and France, chose not to object, fearing another war. Later that year, Germany again snubbed world opinion by withdrawing from the League of Nations.

Meanwhile, Spain, which had established a parliamentary democracy in 1931, was in turmoil following the fall of the Spanish monarchy. In the summer of 1936, a group of army officers under the leadership of General **Francisco Franco** took control of large parts of Spain. Democratic loyalists organized to defend the state, and a brutal and divisive civil war ensued. Germany and Italy supported Franco's troops, called "nationalists." Although Franco was not a fascist, the Germans and Italians believed that the defeat of democracy in Spain was a step in the right direction.

France and Great Britain, still scarred from the loss of life and money in the Great War, adopted a nonintervention policy and refused to aid the supporters of the Spanish democracy. By 1939, Franco's troops captured Madrid and installed a dictatorship in Spain that managed to stay neutral throughout the war that soon erupted in Europe. The message was clear: Germany and Italy were more than willing to exercise their influence and support antidemocratic uprisings.

Meanwhile back in Germany in 1935, Hitler continued his policy of restoring Germany to its former world-power status by taking back the **Rhineland**, a region west of the Rhine River that had been taken away from Germany after World War I. Still, the rest of Europe stayed quiet. In 1937, he formed an alliance with the increasingly militant Japan. Then, in 1938, he annexed Austria and moved to reclaim the Sudetenland from Czechoslovakia. At the **Munich Conference of 1938**, which included Hitler, Mussolini, and Prime Minister **Neville Chamberlain** of England, Hitler was given the Sudetenland, without the consent of Czechoslovakia, in return for the promise to cease his expansionist activities. This incredibly optimistic (some would say stupid) policy is known as **appeasement**. Chamberlain agreed to give Hitler what he wanted as a means of avoiding war, believing German claims that it would be satisfied with Austria and the northern half of Czechoslovakia and would not expand further. Hitler, in fact, did stop his expansion—for one whole year. In 1939, Hitler invaded the remaining territories in Czechoslovakia.

The rest of Europe was shocked but didn't do anything to kick the Nazis out of Czechoslovakia. Instead, in March 1939, while Italy was invading Albania, Britain and France signed a non-aggression pact with Greece, Turkey, Romania, and Poland that provided that if any one of them were attacked, they'd all go to war.

Meanwhile, the Germans signed the **Nazi-Soviet Pact** in August of 1939. Stalin and Hitler agreed that Germany would not invade the Soviet Union if the Soviets stayed out of Germany's military affairs. Furthermore, the countries determined how Eastern Europe would be divided among them, giving Lithuania and eastern Poland to Germany and the remainder of Poland and Finland and the Baltic States to Russia. Stalin got a measure of security, and Hitler got a clear path by which to take Poland. With a secure agreement with the Soviet Union, German forces marched into Poland. Two days later, Britain realized that all diplomacy had failed and declared war on Germany, and France reluctantly followed suit. World War II had begun.

Meanwhile, in Japan...

Remember in the last chapter, when we discussed the Meiji Restoration and how Japan defeated China in a war for control of Korea and Taiwan, thus making Japan an imperial power? Well, later on after the Russo-Japanese War of 1904, the victorious Japanese kicked Russia out of Manchuria and established its own sphere of influence there. As if demonstrating that Japan was now an equal among European states, the British offered them an alliance in 1905, a treaty the Japanese gratefully accepted. Japan was now not just an imperial power but a world power.

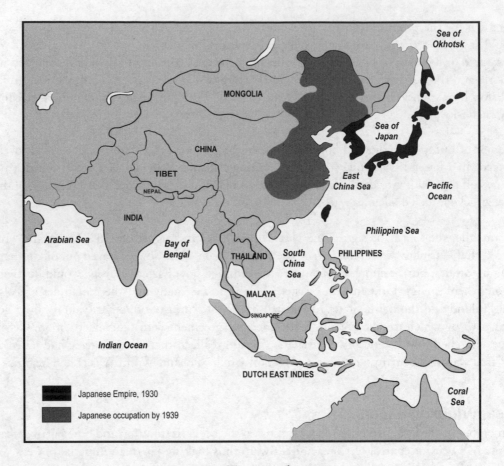

Japanese Territory by 1939

After World War I, in which Japan fought on the side of the Allies and was therefore one of the victors, Japan's economy and military really started to thrive. In 1915, during World War I, Japan sent a list of 21 demands to China, requiring China to give it trading rights and outright control over aspects of the government and economy, an act that was even more aggressive than some of the spheres of influence that had been established (and were still in effect) by the Europeans. In the 1920s, the country backtracked a little bit and focused on internal developments, softening its position toward China. By 1930, the Great Depression began to severely affect Japan and the Japanese militarists gained momentum, claiming that an empire would pull them out of the economic doldrums. In 1931, Japan invaded Manchuria, renaming it **Manchukuo** and establishing a colony there. After withdrawing from the League of Nations, Japan signed the **Anti-Comintern Pact** (against communism, specifically in Russia) with Germany in 1936, thereby forming the beginnings of an alliance that would eventually lead to a more formal one during World War II. In 1937, Japanese troops invaded China, pillaging towns and cities as they made their way down the eastern shore. One of the worst offenses was the aptly named "Rape of Nanjing," in which nearly 250,000 Chinese in the city of Nanjing were slaughtered in a matter of a few weeks by occupying Japanese forces. Japan's war with China eventually merged into the global conflagration of World War II that later started to burn in Europe.

A Quick Review of World War II

Hitler's forces were devastating. Their war tactic, known as **blitzkrieg** (literally "lightning war"), destroyed everything in its path with historically unprecedented speed. Poland's flat open plains were tragically well-suited for the German run. The swiftly moving German forces acquired so much territory in the west of Poland that Stalin was forced to mobilize quickly lest he lose the entire country to the German Reich. Within 10 days, Germany and Russia had divided Poland between them. Hitler then focused on the western front. In early 1940, Germany assaulted Holland and Belgium. Two days later, German forces entered France. Within a year, the Axis power controlled most of continental Europe.

Hitler assumed that Great Britain would crumble quickly after the fall of its ally, France. But a new leader, **Winston Churchill**, replaced Britain's more diplomatically minded Chamberlain. Churchill proved to be a resolute and fierce prime minister. He refused to cut a deal with Germany, so Hitler launched a massive air bombing campaign in 1940 known as the **Battle of Britain**, which pitted the superior numbers of the German air force against the smaller numbers of the Royal Air Force. The British succeeded in keeping the German army out, and with their newly devised handy tool known as radar, they managed a successful, though costly, defense of the island.

In the meantime, Italy attacked Greece but was unable to defeat the country until April 1941, when German armies rushed in to help out. The Nazi-Soviet Pact tacitly gave the Balkan state to Russia, so the takeover of Greece had serious consequences. Now that Germany had taken control of the Balkans, their previous agreement was moot, so they invaded the Soviet Union too for good measure, advancing quickly. The resulting movement of men and supplies into the Soviet Union relieved pressure on the desperate British, the only Allied nation still fighting (other than the Soviet Union, of course).

Meanwhile in the Pacific, Japan continued its expansion in China and invaded Indochina (Vietnam). For trade reasons, the United States viewed this action as hostile, but the United States still didn't want to get involved in the war, so it froze Japanese assets in the United States and imposed sanctions instead. At the same time, Japan entered into the **Tripartite Pact** with Rome and Berlin, ensuring worldwide implications for a war that had, up until that time, been two regional wars. Japan also planned to declare war against the United States if the United States refused to lift sanctions against Japan. The United States didn't, and on December 7, 1941, the Japanese bombed a U.S. naval station in Hawaii at **Pearl Harbor**. The United States was stunned, and promptly declared war against Japan, and in response, Germany declared war against the United States.

It took a while for the United States and Great Britain to coordinate a land attack against Germany because they needed a foothold in Europe from which to begin their assault. In the meantime, the Allies fought the Japanese in the Pacific and Germans and Italians in Africa while the United States also secretly worked on its **Manhattan Project**—the development of an atomic bomb. By 1943, the United States and Britain were ready for their European offensive, and they started it by taking control of Italy. The next year, English, American, and Canadian forces launched their biggest offensive, landing on the French beaches of Normandy on June 6, 1944, which is now known as **D-day**. With the help of French resistance forces, Allied Forces battled their way across northern France in the summer of 1944 and liberated France.

On the opposite side of Europe, the Red Army won a stunning victory against the Germans at Stalingrad in 1942 and advanced steadily west for three years. By May 1945, the Allied forces closed in on Hitler's troops from the eastern and the western fronts until they reached Berlin, ending the European theater of World War II. Hitler committed suicide.

The war in the Pacific continued to drag on for a few months. At great cost, the American forces defeated Japan from island to island in the South Pacific. But the Japanese refused to surrender, even though their fate was sealed. Believing that dropping an atomic bomb on Japan would end World War II quickly and result in fewer casualties than a prolonged war, **President Truman** of the United States ordered the dropping of an atomic bomb on the city of **Hiroshima** on August 6, 1945. The event marked the first time such a bomb had been used in warfare. The result was horrendous. More than 100,000 people were killed or injured and the city was completely leveled for miles. When the Japanese vowed to fight on, President Truman authorized the dropping of a second bomb on **Nagasaki** on August 9 with similar consequences. Japan finally surrendered and World War II was brought to a close.

C. The Consequences

The close of World War II brought with it enormous global changes. Since they are so numerous, it's best to think about them in broad categories.

The Holocaust Revealed

Outside of Germany, few knew just how horrible the Nazi regime was until after the war was over. In an ongoing slaughter known now as the **Holocaust**, but known in Nazi Germany as "The Final Solution," millions of Jews who lived in Germany and German-occupied lands were rounded up, blamed for every conceivable problem in society, and methodically killed in gas chambers and firing lines, their bodies disposed of in ovens and mass graves. As many as 6 million Jews were killed, making the Holocaust one of the largest acts of genocide in history (in addition, as many as 6 million Poles, Slavs, Gypsies, homosexuals, disabled people, and political dissidents were killed in the Holocaust). When the news of the atrocity spread after the war, public sympathy for the creation of Israel as a homeland for Jews rose sharply. More on that later.

The Peace Settlement

The United States and the Soviet Union became superpowers. Germany was occupied by the Allies—more on that later too. War crimes tribunals were established to prosecute and sentence Nazi officials. Japan was forced to demilitarize and establish a democracy. It did. It also embraced capitalism and became an economic powerhouse within a decade, but this time was friendly to the West.

Europe Torn to Shreds

In addition to a staggering loss of life (the Soviet Union alone lost more than 20 million soldiers and civilians), the infrastructure and communities of Europe were devastated. To help in the rebuilding effort, the United States instituted the **Marshall Plan** (named for George C. Marshall, the secretary of state who conceived of it) in 1947. The plan, in which billions of dollars of American money was made available for reconstruction, was offered to all European countries but only accepted by Western European nations. The plan worked: the economies of Western Europe recovered in less than a decade.

The Decline of Colonialism

European imperialism was already on the wane before World War II, but the war affected attitudes about empires, and inspired native populations to rise up against their oppressors. Much more on the decline of colonialism later in this chapter.

Big Changes for Women

Just as in World War I, in many countries, women worked outside the home during the war, raising money to support themselves or their families, while also helping the war effort. In Britain alone, more than three-fourths of adult women under age 40 were employed during the war. After the war, many women kept their jobs, or sought higher education, or otherwise began to broaden their horizons.

The Creation of International Organizations

After World War II, the Allies believed that a network of international organizations could reduce the probability that such a great war would break out again. The first of these international organizations was the **United Nations** (UN), established in 1945 to replace the failed League of Nations. Given more muscle than the League of Nations, the primary goal of the UN was simple: to mediate, and if necessary to intervene in, international disputes between nations. In 1948, as the world came to learn about the horrors of the Holocaust and other tragedies of the 20th century, the United Nations published a **Universal Declaration of Human Rights** that was notable for its attention to the dignity of children, women, and refugees. As time passed, the UN expanded beyond the realm of political conflicts and increasingly involved itself in the monitoring of human rights and other social problems. In addition to the UN, the World Bank, the International Monetary Fund, and the General Agreement on Trade and Tariffs (now known as the World Trade Organization) were formed to create and manage a more integrated global economy. The Allies believed that countries that were more connected economically would be less likely to invade one another.

The Start of the Cold War

Although they were allies during the war, the United States and the Soviet Union had very different worldviews. One was democratic and capitalist, the other totalitarian and communist. Neither wanted the other to spread its influence beyond its borders, so even before the war ended, they were strategizing on how to contain each other. This strategizing lasted for nearly 50 years, and the following section in this chapter explains the consequences.

IV. UNIT 8: COLD WAR AND DECOLONIZATION

A. Communism and the Cold War

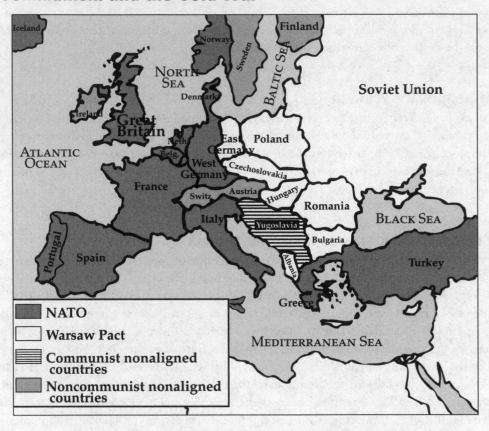

The Cold War in Europe

The **Cold War** lasted from 1945 through the early 1990s. Very few areas of the globe were unaffected. The two superpowers that emerged after World War II, the United States and the Soviet Union, not only vied for global domination, but also tried to pull the rest of the world into their standoff. Every time a government in any country across the globe changed hands, the Americans and Soviets evaluated it based on its leanings toward one side or the other, and in many cases actually tried to militarily influence the position it would take. All of this took place in the context of an arms race between the two superpowers in which nuclear arsenals became so massive that a global holocaust became possible at the touch of a button.

B. Power Grab: Soviets and Americans Want Everyone to Take Sides

After Germany was defeated, the U.S.-Soviet struggle immediately influenced the chain of events. The biggest conflict was over future security. Both superpowers wanted arrangements in Europe that made it more likely for their worldview to dominate. The United States promoted capitalism and variations on democracy. The Soviet Union promoted communism, which, as practiced by the Soviets at the time, also meant totalitarianism. A good chunk of Western Europe was solidly in the American camp, but the bigger question was Germany and parts of Eastern Europe.

According to plans drawn up by the Allies during conferences at **Yalta** and **Potsdam**, in February and July 1945 respectively, Germany and other parts of Eastern Europe were divided into temporary "spheres of influence," each to be occupied and rebuilt by respective members of the Allied forces. Germany was divided into four regions, each under the influence of one of four Allies: France, Britain, the United States, and the Soviet Union. Determined to protect its borders and ideology, the Soviet Union demanded that its neighboring states, places like Poland, Czechoslovakia, Hungary, Romania, and Bulgaria, be under its influence as well. The United States wanted those nations to have free elections. The Soviet Union refused and simply set up puppet states in those countries. This was the first hint of the beginning of the Cold War.

Meanwhile, in Germany in 1948, the French, British, and American regions merged into one, forming a democratic West Germany, while the Soviet Union's region became East Germany. The capital, Berlin, was on the eastern side, and within that city, an eastern and a western zone were created. The Soviets wanted all of Berlin to be within its control, so they cut off land access to Berlin from the west, an action known as the **Berlin Blockade**. The West retaliated by flying in food and fuel to the "trapped" western half of the city, an action known as the **Berlin Airlift**. Eventually, the Soviets relented and Berlin was divided in half. In 1961, the Soviets built a wall between the two halves, preventing East Berliners access to the West until the wall fell in 1989 (more on that later).

East Versus West

By the late 1940s, Europe was clearly divided into East and West, each under the influence of their respective superpowers.

East Germany, Poland, Czechoslovakia, Romania, and Hungary became part of the Eastern bloc, also called the **Soviet bloc** or Soviet satellites. Yugoslavia was communist as well, but established its own path, having testy relations with Moscow. Western Europe, including Britain, France, Italy, Belgium, the Netherlands, Norway, West Germany, and eventually Greece and Turkey, became part of the **Western bloc**.

Under the **Truman Doctrine** of 1947, the United States explicitly stated that it would aid countries threatened by communist takeovers. This policy is known as **containment**, as in "containing" your enemy. To this end, the Western bloc formed a military alliance of mutual defense called **NATO** (the North Atlantic Treaty Organization). In response, the Eastern bloc formed a military alliance known as the **Warsaw Pact**. For more than 40 years, the two alliances loaded their borders with weapons, first conventional, then nuclear, and dared the other to strike first. Churchill called the line between East and West the **Iron Curtain** because Western influence couldn't penetrate it and Easterners were rarely allowed to go to the Western bloc.

As for the rest of the world, the two superpowers quickly tried to influence developments to tip the balance of world power in their favor. Some countries allied with one side or the other (more on this later), but other countries, such as India, Ghana, and Indonesia, refused to take sides and sometimes accepted investment from both, a policy known as nonalignment. The nonalignment movement sought to build alliances among the world's former colonies that were beginning to experience their independence from foreign powers. In particular, African and Asian countries sought cooperative economic relations that would minimize their dependence on the world's superpowers. In 1955, the **Bandung Conference** invited leaders from Africa and Asia to meet in Indonesia in order to discuss such a partnership, a first step toward the **Non-Aligned Movement**.

Focus On: Nuclear Proliferation

Ever improving weapons technology was the force behind political strength in the 20th century. This was true from the devastated battlefields of World War I to the hot spots and standoffs of the Cold War. Beginning with the atomic bombs dropped on Japan in 1945, the Eastern and Western superpowers raced to develop superior weapons and defensive technologies. Despite attempts to limit nuclear technology to just five powers (China, Russia, the United States, Great Britain, and France) through the **Nuclear Nonproliferation Treaty** (1968) and the watchdog **International Atomic Energy Agency or IAEA** (1957), weapons development continued even after the collapse of the Soviet Union. Israel, India, and Pakistan chose not to participate in the treaty and now each has some nuclear weapons capacity. North Korea has continued to develop nuclear material in violation of treaty terms and both Iraq and Iran have attempted to build uranium enrichment programs. Only South Africa has voluntarily dismantled its nuclear weapons program.

The Cold War affected different countries in different ways. On the next several pages, you'll review how it impacted China, Korea, Vietnam, Cuba, and Europe.

C. China: Communists Make Huge Gains

China changed a lot after the fall of the Manchu Dynasty in 1911. Under the leadership of **Sun Yat-sen**, who led the **Chinese Revolution of 1911**, China became more Westernized in an effort to gain power and boot out the Europeans and Japanese, who had established spheres of influence in the country. Sun Yat-sen promoted his **Three Principles of the People**—nationalism, socialism, and democracy. It was hoped that nationalism would unite the people against foreign interests and give them a Chinese identity. State capitalism, or industrialization financed by the government, was useful in order to improve economic productivity and efficiency while not necessarily redistributing wealth, something Sun did not agree with. Although he advocated for a democratic system, Sun Yat-sen established a political party, the **Kuomintang (or KMT)**, which was dedicated to his own goals.

Sun Yat-sen didn't live long enough to see his plans implemented. His successor, however, **Chiang Kai-shek**, established the KMT as the ruling party of China, but only for a while. Throughout the 1920s and 1930s, two forces wreaked havoc on Chiang's plans. The Japanese Empire invaded Manchuria and made an effort to take over all of China in the late 1930s. Meanwhile, the communists, allied with the Soviet Union, were building strength in northern China. The communists joined the KMT in its fight against the Japanese, but at the same time were bitter rivals of the Kuomintang in the struggle to control the future of China.

During World War II, the United States pumped money into the KMT's efforts against Japan, while the Soviets weren't as active in their support for the communists' efforts against Japan, partly because they were focused on Germany. As you know, Japan was defeated. As in Europe, after the war, the powers of democracy and communism clashed, and the KMT and communists continued to fight the Chinese Civil War for the next four years.

By 1949, the communists under **Mao Zedong** had rallied millions of peasants in northern China and swept southward toward the Kuomintang strongholds, driving the Kuomintang farther and farther south until they finally fled to the island of Taiwan, where they established the **Republic of China**. The impact for mainland China was enormous. It became the **People's Republic of China**, the largest communist nation in the world under the leadership of Mao Zedong. The two Chinas have been separate ever since, and both claim to be the "real" China. Taiwan eventually developed into an economic powerhouse, but it lost its credibility as the true China when the United Nations and eventually the United States recognized the People's Republic of China as China in 1973. Taiwan has rejected China's efforts toward reunification, but nevertheless the two nations have grown close together, especially as the economies of both nations have grown stronger and stronger.

Mao Zedong: His Own Way

After the success of the Communist Revolution in China in 1949, its leader, Mao Zedong, collectivized agriculture and industry and instituted sweeping social reform using policies that were not unlike Stalin's Five-Year Plans. Most of these plans were relatively successful, and China greatly increased its productivity, especially in the steel industry. By the late 1950s, Mao implemented his **Great Leap Forward**, in which huge communes were created as a way of catapulting the revolution toward its goal of a true Marxist state. In reality, however, the local governments that ran the communes couldn't produce the ridiculously high agricultural quotas demanded by the central government. These local governments did what any fearful local government would—they lied about their production, leading to the starvation deaths of nearly 30 million Chinese people. By all accounts, it was more like a Great Stumble Backward. The successes of Mao's initiatives in the early 1950s were erased, and agriculture and industry failed to produce results. Part of the problem was that the Soviet Union—up until that time the only foreign supporter of China—pulled away and eventually withdrew its support. The Soviet Union not only wanted the world to become communist, but it wanted the world to be communist under its control. China wasn't following orders, so Soviet support for China cooled. The Sino-Soviet split left China on its own with its communal system in disarray.

Mao stepped back to focus on building the military—something that was essential if the country couldn't rely on Soviet support—while more moderate reformers tried to turn the country around. The progress was quick and substantial; elements of capitalism were introduced into the economy and, in 1964, China tested its first atomic bomb, adding to the global arms race that

War Against the West

Mao's Cultural Revolution was intended to rid China of all traces of Western influence and replace them with communist policies.

was quickly building around the world. Mao was unimpressed, however. A purist, Mao was upset that the country was straying from its communist path, and so, in 1966, he jumped back to the forefront of his government and promoted his most significant domestic policy, the **Cultural Revolution**. Mao's goal in the Cultural Revolution was to discourage anything approaching a privileged ruling class, as it existed in the West as well as among the Soviet communist elite. To accomplish this, Mao instituted reforms meant to erase all traces of a Western-influenced intelligentsia. Many universities were shut down for four years. The students and faculty, along with other "elites" including doctors, lawyers, and classically trained musicians, were sent to work on collective farms for "cultural retraining." In addition, many political dissidents were either imprisoned or killed. When the universities were reopened, the curriculum was reorganized to include only communist studies and vocational training. During this time, Mao's *Little Red Book*, a collection of his teachings on communism, became a popular symbol of the forced egalitarianism of the Cultural Revolution.

The whole plan failed miserably in advancing China economically or socially. By the early 1970s, China realized it needed to open itself up to Western ideas. In 1976, the new leadership under Deng Xiaoping quickly changed the education policy and began to focus on restructuring the economic policies.

Note the Change: Dynastic China to Communist China

For more than 2,000 years, Confucianism and a class structure dominated China. With the Communist Revolution, however, all traces of a class-based system were nearly erased. Traditional Chinese society valued large families, both because children were able to help on the farm and because Confucian philosophy gave identity to people based on their relationships—the parent/child relationship was one of the most important. When the communists took over, however, their program of collectivization made family farms obsolete. In addition, communists were not sympathetic to traditional values based on religious or philosophical beliefs that competed with the authority of the state. As the population of China continued to grow dramatically through the late 20th century, the communists took a practical approach to the overpopulation problem and began a propaganda campaign aimed at the use of contraception and abortion. By the late 1980s, faced with ever-increasing population figures, the Chinese government instituted a one-child-per-family policy. Reactions to the policy were severe. Many refused to abide by the policy in the first place. Others followed the law, but some of them killed their firstborn female infants in the hope of getting a male child the second time around. Opposition became more widespread and the government relaxed its policy.

The equality demanded in a classless society resulted in considerable advances for women. Husbands and wives were treated equally, at least as far as the law was concerned. Women gained the right to divorce their husbands. They obtained property rights. They received equal pay for equal work and were encouraged to pursue professional and vocational careers.

China Looks West: Likes the Money, Not So Sure About the Democracy

More recently, China's economy has been transformed from a strict communist command economy to one that includes elements of free-market capitalism. Deng Xiaoping's government entered into joint ventures with foreign companies in which the profits and business decisions were shared. In addition, Deng allowed for limited business and property ownership to stimulate hard work and innovation. The reforms have been wildly successful. China's economy is expanding faster than most of the economies of the world and reforms continue to be introduced slowly, giving the economy time to adjust to the changes. However, despite the economic reforms, the government continues to remain strictly communist in the political sense, and has frequently resisted government and social reforms. In 1989, one million demonstrators converged on Tiananmen Square, calling for democratic reform. In an event known as the **Tiananmen Square massacre**, the government sent troops and opened fire. Hundreds were killed. Today, while China continues to reform its economy and is rapidly becoming a major economic power-house, the possibility for democratic reforms is still unknown.

Division of Korea: The Cold War Turns Hot and Now Possibly Nuclear

Prior to World War II, Korea was invaded by Japan and annexed as part of the expanding Japanese Empire. After Japan was defeated in World War II, Korea was supposed to be reestablished as an independent nation, but until stability could be achieved and elections held, it was occupied by the Soviet Union and the United States in two separate pieces—the Soviet Union north of the 38th parallel and the United States south of it. This was very much like the way that Germany was split, and, similarly, the two superpowers couldn't agree on the terms of a united Korea.

In 1948, two separate governments were established—a Soviet-backed communist regime in North Korea and a U.S.-backed democracy in South Korea. Both superpowers withdrew their troops in 1949, but in 1950, North Korea attacked South Korea in an attempt to unite the two nations under a single communist government. The United Nations condemned the action and soon a multinational force, largely consisting of U.S. and British troops, went to the aid of the South Koreans. The UN forces made tremendous headway under **General MacArthur**, nearly reaching the Chinese border, but when it looked as if the North Koreans would be defeated, China entered the war on behalf of the communist North. The two sides battled it out along the 38th parallel, eventually leading to an armistice in 1953.

Today, the two nations remain separate and true to the political philosophies under which they were formed almost 70 years ago. The United States maintains a large military presence in South Korea, which has become an economic powerhouse. North Korea, meanwhile, has suffered through isolationist and just plain nutty rulers and massive food shortages, but has built up a huge military and acquired the technology to develop a nuclear bomb. It has already developed missiles capable of delivering those bombs to South Korea, Japan, China, or possibly even as far as the west coast of the United States. In October 2006, North Korea declared its first nuclear weapons test a success. Western scientists doubted its claims of success, but did confirm that some type of test had taken place. In response, the United Nations imposed additional, but largely symbolic, sanctions on North Korean imports (though China and Russia disagreed with the policy). Six-Party Talks (including the United States, North Korea, South Korea, China, Russia, and Japan) resumed, for the fifth time, and concluded with the agreement that North Korea was to shut down its reactor in July 2007 in return for extensive fuel aid. As of 2009, North Korea pulled out of the Six-Party Talks for good and has continued its nuclear enrichment program; as of February 2013, the country has detonated three nuclear devices. The failure of the international community to reach a resolution on the Korean peninsula in the early 1950s has created a modern-day crisis of nuclear proportions. The secretive nature of the North Korean regime has made it harder for international observers to gauge the communist nation's intentions, an especially frightening prospect for foreign observers who feared the instability the transfer of power could bring when Kim Jong-Il passed away in December of

> In May 2018, North Korea claimed that it would be dismantling its nuclear test site. Many experts remain skeptical about North Korea's commitment to denuclearize. At the time of publication, the future of diplomatic relations between the United States and North Korea remains uncertain, as does North Korea's alleged denuclearization.

2011. However, their fears were not realized as his son Kim Jong-un seems to be pursuing similar militaristic and aggressive policies toward the West as his father did.

Vietnam: The Cold War Turns Ugly

After World War II, the French tried to hold on to their colony of **Indochina**, but nationalists known as the **Vietminh** fought them back. By 1954, the Vietminh's guerrilla warfare techniques succeeded in frustrating the French, and an accord was signed in Geneva dividing the nation—you guessed it—into two pieces. The communists, under the leadership of **Ho Chi Minh**, gained control of the land north of the 17th parallel while **Ngo Dinh Diem** became the president of the democratic south. Under its new constitution, North Vietnam supported reunification of Vietnam as a communist state. Ho Chi Minh supported communist guerrillas in the south, and soon war broke out. France and the United States came to the aid of South Vietnam. Ho Chi Minh prevented them from taking over the north, but not before years of fighting led to hundreds of thousands of deaths. As United States forces finally withdrew in 1975, the North Vietnamese Army and communist **Viet Cong** fighters took control throughout South Vietnam. A peace agreement eventually led to the reunification of Vietnam as a communist state under the leadership of Ho Chi Minh. The long-range impact was significant for the region, the world, and the United States. The world witnessed the defeat of a superpower by a small but determined nation. Communism took a major step forward in the region. For the United States, the defeat affected foreign policy for decades, as the American public remained fearful of involving itself in "another Vietnam."

Genocide in Cambodia

Another Southeast Asian nation that welcomed communism was Cambodia. Fearing that its culture had been watered down by Western influences, particularly as the United States engaged in combat on Cambodian soil and involved itself in Cambodian elections during the war with Vietnam, communist faction **Khmer Rouge** rode popular support to take over the pro-Western government. Led by Pol Pot, the Khmer Rouge instituted a reeducation policy targeting the professional class and religious minorities. Nearly two million Cambodians were killed during the regime. Ironically, it was the Communist Vietnamese who put an end to Pol Pot's dictatorship in 1979.

Contrast Them: High-Tech Warfare and Guerrilla Warfare

High-tech warfare, such as fighter jets, missiles, and tanks, are not only sophisticated and effective, but also costly and logistically complicated. Generally, nations that have mastered high-tech warfare, like the United States, take months to position their weaponry and put together a war plan. Once implemented, high-tech warfare can be devastatingly efficient. **Guerrilla warfare**, on the other hand, is behind the scenes, stealthy, and much lower tech. Individuals or small groups fight site to site, disrupting their enemies' supply chains, or targeting seemingly random sites with small bombs and munitions. Each individual attack is generally less deadly, but since the attacks are flexible, random, and hard to predict, they can be very effective against a cumbersome, less flexible, high-tech opponent.

D. The Cuban Revolution

After Cuba won its independence from Spain during the Spanish-American War of 1898, the United States remained involved in Cuban affairs under the terms of the **Platt Amendment**, which also provided for the presence of U.S. military bases. During the following decades, the Americans invested heavily in Cuban businesses and plantations, but those investments generally only made the wealthy very rich with little or no benefit for the masses of peasants. From 1939 to 1959, the United States supported the **Batista Dictatorship** in Cuba, which continued the policies that benefited the wealthy landowners. In 1956, the peasants began a revolt under the leadership of **Fidel Castro**. Even the United States eventually withdrew its support of Fulgencio Batista. Using guerrilla warfare techniques, the revolutionaries made tremendous advances, and by 1959, Batista fled. The **Cuban Revolution** was hailed as a great success against a dictator.

Castro, the great promoter of democracy, took control of the government, suspended plans for an election, and established a communist dictatorship. By 1961, he had seized the industries, nationalized them, and executed his rivals. The United States became increasingly concerned about this communist dictatorship and imposed an economic embargo on Cuba—a move that strengthened Castro's ties with the Soviet Union and thus heightened U.S. fears. In an attempt to overthrow Castro, the United States trained and supported a group of anti-Castro Cuban exiles living in the United States. The United States was convinced that an invasion by these exiles would lead to a popular revolt against Castro, but it didn't work out that way. In 1961, **President Kennedy** authorized the **Bay of Pigs Invasion**, not with the full force of the mighty U.S. military, but with the small force of Cuban exiles, who were quickly captured after they landed, their revolt over before it began.

After the Bay of Pigs debacle, Cuba and the Soviet Union realized the United States might try something bigger next time around, so they mobilized. In 1962, U.S. spy planes detected the installation of Soviet missiles in Cuba, and Kennedy immediately established a naval blockade around the island, refusing to allow any more shipments from the Soviet Union. Kennedy made it clear to the world that if missiles were launched from Cuba, the United States would retaliate against the Soviet Union itself. The standoff became known as the **Cuban Missile Crisis**. For three months, the world waited to see who would back down, and on October 28, the Soviets said that they would remove the missiles in exchange for a promise from the Americans that they would not invade Cuba. The Americans agreed to the settlement. This was the closest brush the world has had with full-out nuclear war.

When the Soviet Union collapsed in the early 1990s, the Cubans lost their main financial backer. This was a huge loss because it amounted to billions of dollars of aid. Still, Castro managed to hang on to his power, but economic conditions in Cuba deteriorated sharply after the fall of communism in Europe. From 2006 to 2011, Fidel Castro gradually transferred his powers and responsibilities to his younger brother, Raúl, handing over first the presidency and then his position as First Secretary of the Communist Party of Cuba, which he had held since 1965. The elder Castro stepped down due to illness but periodically resurfaced in videos, demonstrating his continued presence as a political force in his brother's regime up until his death in November 2016.

E. Cold War Tensions and Democratization in Latin America

Despite independence movements, democratic elections, and developing economies, the United States maintained a heavy hand in Latin America whenever possible (remember the Roosevelt Corollary to the Monroe Doctrine?). Some of this was also the product of Cold War tensions. Marxism's anti-capitalist message had great appeal in less-developed countries and increased as U.S. investment in copper-mining and oil-drilling in the region intensified in the 1920s. Radical political parties developed in Mexico, Peru, Venezuela, Brazil, and much of Central America as complaints about imperial policies of the "**Good Neighbor**" to the north increased. As the United States confronted two world wars and the Great Depression, however, and Latin America became less of a priority, the region's nations took the opportunity to explore alternative paths to economic development. These took various forms: the stability of single-party rule (Mexico's PRI), the brutality of militaristic leaders (Argentina's Juan Perón and Chile's Augusto Pinochet) or the development of socialist democracies (Nicaragua and Guatemala). It was the latter that garnered the most attention from the United States—still in the midst of an ideological war with the Soviet Union—resulting in U.S.-backed coups, the use of Nicaragua as a staging ground for the Bay of Pigs invasion, and the targeting of the **Sandinista** guerrillas in Nicaragua and El Salvador during the 1980s.

Perhaps the biggest issues Latin America continues to face are their **export economies**. Reliance on products such as coffee, fruit, sugar, and oil has resulted in weak domestic economies and tremendous debt. While there is a long history of democracy throughout the region, the lag in economic development, increasing debt payments from loans dating back to the 1970s and 1980s, and out-migration continue to challenge the region. However, at the beginning of the 21st century, there has been tremendous growth throughout Latin America. Some is based on rising oil prices, but much can also be attributed to the development of new industries and trade agreements, both within Latin America and with the United States and Canada. Both Chile and Brazil are among the fastest-growing economies in the world.

Democracy has also taken interesting turns in Mexico and Venezuela in the last decade. The year 2000 was the first time a true multi-party election was held in Mexico since the formation of the state under the 1917 Constitution. The opposition, **PAN** or **National Action Party,** candidate won the presidency. Mexico had a second national election with an opposition slate in 2006 and again, the PAN candidate won, though the PRI won the most recent election in 2012. Venezuela, on the other hand, has amended its constitution to allow its socialist president Hugo Chavez a third term as the country has nationalized a number of industries including telephone and steel. In 2013, Chavez died and was succeeded by Nicolás Maduro, who has continued many of Chavez's policies.

F. The Cold War Finally Ends

THE FALL OF COMMUNISM
IN EASTERN EUROPE,
1989

Communist governments fall

Unrest in Soviet republics

The Fall of Communism in Eastern Europe

During the Cold War, the standard of living in Western Europe improved dramatically, despite economic swings. In Eastern Europe, behind the iron curtain, the massive state-run industries couldn't keep up with the innovations in the West. A growing divide between the "rich" West and the "poor" East was becoming obvious, and as it became obvious to the people who lived within the Eastern bloc, they began to revolt.

The revolt was as much about democracy and self-determination as it was about the economy. The Soviet Union was a huge patchwork of many different nationalities, many of which wanted to control their own destinies. What's more, an increasing number of people in the Eastern bloc countries that were controlled by the Soviet Union, such as Poland, were also itching for democratic and economic reform. By the 1980s, groups of reform-minded individuals began scratching that itch.

Poland: Solidarity Grows in Popularity

The decline of communism brought sweeping reform to Poland and its government, which had been trying for years to prevent the spread of anticommunist sentiment. In 1980, more than a decade before the fall of communism in the Soviet Union, a group of workers began the Solidarity movement under the leadership of **Lech Walesa**. Thousands of workers joined a strike for reform of the communist economic system. The government reacted by imposing martial law and arresting Lech Walesa, as well as other Solidarity leaders. Throughout the early- and mid-1980s, the government tried to suppress Solidarity. In 1988, the reform-minded Mieczyslaw Rakowski became the Premier of Poland. Solidarity was legalized and in 1989, a member of Solidarity, **Tadeusz Mazowiecki**, became prime minister in the first open elections since the end of World War II. In 1990, the Communist Party fell apart in Poland, just as it was falling apart throughout Eastern Europe, and Lech Walesa was elected president. During the 1990s, the economy improved swiftly as Poland introduced market-based reforms and a new democratic constitution. Poland formally completed its integration into the West by joining NATO in 1999 and the European Union in 2004. Quite a change.

German Reunification: All This, Just to Be Back Where It Started

The decline of communism in the Soviet bloc directly led to the reunification of Germany as a free-market democracy. East Germany cut ties with the Soviet Union and began negotiations with West Germany. Many Western nations feared that a united Germany would lead once again to a nationalistic regime, but the prospect for peace, economic and political reform, and an improved standard of living for the people of East Germany outweighed the concerns. When the Berlin Wall was torn down in 1989, signaling the fall of East Germany, a mass exodus of East Germans fled to the West. Businesses in East Germany continued to struggle because their outdated corporate structures, equipment, and machinery could not compete with the more efficient businesses in the western half of the nation. Unemployment was high in both halves of the newly united nation. Nevertheless, the government did not abandon its ambitious reconstruction program aimed at the modernization of the former East Germany and the establishment of nationwide communication and transportation lines. Germany has therefore continued to press forward and has since emerged as a leading economy in Europe.

Germany's Journey

Just in case you haven't been keeping track, in the last 90 years Germany went from being crushed in World War I, to being built up under fascist Nazis, to being crushed in World War II, to being occupied by four former enemies, to being divided in two, to being at the epicenter of the Cold War, to being reunified as a modern, capitalist-leaning, democratic nation. That's some pretty extreme historical whiplash!

During the final decade of the Soviet Union, the capitalist West leaned further into free market ideology, rejecting the measures that carried the United States and Great Britain through the hardships of the Great Depression through the early post-war years. By the early 1980s, British Prime Minister, **Margaret Thatcher** and American President **Ronald Reagan** made it clear that austerity, or limited government spending, was the way to further enrich the West, even as the Soviet Union began to crumble.

The Soviet Union Collapses: Glasnost, Perestroika, Kaput

When **Mikhail Gorbachev** came to power in the Soviet Union in 1985, he instituted policies of *glasnost* (openness) and urged a *perestroika* (restructuring) of the Soviet economy. He may not have realized it at the time, but he set in motion a tidal wave of change that he wouldn't be able to reverse. Legislation was passed to add elements of private enterprise to the economy. Nuclear arms treaties were signed with the United States. Gorbachev publicly and officially denounced the Great Purge, a huge deal because it showed that the Soviet Union was reevaluating itself. The list of reforms and changes goes on and on, but the bottom line is that within six years, Poland and other former Soviet satellites declared their separation from the USSR. The Soviet Union itself disintegrated in 1991. Russia became its own country again, while the other parts of the old Soviet Empire, such as Ukraine, Belarus, and Georgia, became independent nations.

Some observers were shocked by the degree to which so many different nationalities within the former Soviet Union wanted to form their own countries, and further shocked that most of the shifts in power happened relatively peacefully.

But there were exceptions. In the same region that sparked World War I 80 years prior—the Balkans—nationalistic movements within the former Yugoslavia led to "**ethnic cleansing**" in which Bosnian and Albanian Muslims were raped and slaughtered by Christian Serbians in what was simply the latest horrific chapter in a centuries-long regional and ethnic conflict. The violence eventually led to the involvement of UN troops during much of the 1990s. Even in Russia itself, nationalists in different regions, especially in Muslim-dominated **Chechnya**, want to break away, and have used guerrilla warfare and terrorist methods to advance their cause.

During the 1990s, most of the new countries in the former Soviet bloc, especially those in Eastern Europe, created constitutional democracies with economic systems based on variations of capitalism. Reform movements have occurred faster in some countries than in others, and adherents to communism have made themselves heard as the transition from state-owned to privately owned industries has resulted in high unemployment and corruption. Still, democracy seems to be taking a foothold in the region. Though much is uncertain about the future of the former Soviet bloc, a few things can be said for sure: by the end of 1991, the Cold War was over, the Warsaw Pact had disbanded, and the United States found itself as the world's only superpower.

Democracy and Authoritarian Rule in Russia

The new (old) country of Russia was (re)formed under a 1993 constitution. Although it had lost its Soviet satellite countries, this new Russian Federation was formidable in size, plentiful in natural resources, and full of corrupt Soviet bureaucrats looking to get rich under the new rules. On paper, the new Russia looks very much like a perfect **federal** state with three branches, checks and balances, and an independent court. In reality, Russia's abrupt introduction to both democracy and capitalism resulted in a 10-year period of corruption, high unemployment, deep poverty, widespread crime, and a nostalgia for Soviet-style control and discipline. The challenge for Russia's first president, **Boris Yeltsin**, was to reform the structures of both state and society. This was an enormous task, requiring completely new systems of government and trade.

Yeltsin resigned in 1999, and for the next eight years, former **KGB** agent **Vladimir Putin** headed the Russian state. He was elected president twice, in 2000 and 2004, and was appointed prime minister in 2008 by the newly elected president Dmitry Medvedev. This new style of Russian democracy has been marked by corruption and an authoritarian strengthening of the executive branch, limits on opposition candidates, and a crackdown on a free press. In a move that alarmed international observers, Putin announced in 2011 that he would run for a third presidential term in 2012, stretching his leadership to 16 years (and perhaps beyond?). Despite some protests in Russia, Putin defeated several challengers in March 2012 to return to the presidency. Russia's 21st-century economic growth has been considerable, but old habits die hard, and conflicts with the United States continue over plans for expansion of NATO, the placement of missiles in Eastern Europe, and the sale of technology to Iran.

Annexation of Crimea

In March of 2014, shortly after the successful Winter Olympic Games in Sochi, the Russian Federation annexed the region of Crimea in eastern Ukraine. Russia's continuing support of separatists within Ukraine and its military incursions into Ukrainian territory have led to the deaths of thousands of people and drawn widespread condemnation from the international community.

Contrast Them: "West" and "East"

During the Cold War, the terms "West" and "East" were frequently used to describe much of the world, especially the northern hemisphere. The "West," led by the United States, was generally democratic, generally capitalist, and generally prosperous. The "East," led by the Soviet Union, was communist, generally totalitarian, and generally substantially less prosperous in terms of per capita standard of living. Japan, incidentally, was part of the "West," because after World War II it developed along pro-Western, capitalist, generally pro-democracy lines. After the fall of communism in most of the world in the early 1990s, the terms began to lose their relevance. The West grew dramatically, but should Russia be considered part of the "West"? Clearly, most of its former satellites wanted to be considered as such. What's more, China, still communist, is transforming its economy and possibly irrevocably opening up its doors to the world, a movement called "Westernizing" but so far not leading to democratic reforms. As for the "East," nobody's sure what that refers to any more. Today, a new, perhaps overly general division between the "Western World" and the "Islamic World" is being used to describe world relations.

G. Independence Movements and Developments in Asia and Africa

After World War II, a wave of independence movements marked the beginning of the end of European imperialism. In an era when the United States and Western Europe were fighting a Cold War in part to defend people's right to choose their own futures (self-determination) under democratic systems, it became difficult for Western colonial powers to reconcile their post–World War II principles with their imperialist policies. More importantly, it was increasingly difficult for the subjugated peoples to tolerate their treatment, so they rose up and demanded independence.

The Indian Subcontinent

After the **Indian National Congress**, a mostly Hindu political party, was established in 1885 to increase the rights of Indians under colonial rule, and then the **Muslim League** in 1906 to advance the causes of Islamic Indians, it took years for momentum to build into an organized resistance to colonial power. In 1919, the **Amritsar massacre** catapulted the movement.

In Amritsar, 319 Indians, some Hindu and some Muslim, were slaughtered by British General Dyer during a peaceful protest in a city park. They were protesting the arrest of two of their leaders who also were doing nothing other than protesting, were unarmed, and entirely surprised by the attack. Because the park was walled, there was no way to escape from the attackers. By all accounts, the slaughter was unprovoked and entirely unwarranted. When news of the massacre spread, Indians joined the self-rule cause by the millions. It was now a full-fledged movement.

> **Gandhi's Influence on U.S. History**
> Gandhi's teachings partly inspired the civil disobedience of the U.S. civil rights movements led by Dr. Martin Luther King Jr.

During the 1920s, **Mohandas Gandhi** became the movement's most important voice and organized huge protests against colonial rule. Gandhi's philosophy of **passive resistance**, or civil disobedience, gained popular support in the struggle against British colonial rule. Instead of fighting with weapons, Gandhi's followers staged demonstrations and refused to assist the colonial governments. This included massive boycotts of British imperial goods as well as strikes, such as when hundreds of thousands of workers refused to act as labor for the British colonial government's salt factories. Gandhi's nonviolent teachings, and his success, became enormously influential.

At the same time, there was an increase in violence between Hindus and Muslims. While both groups worked together peacefully against the British, radical members of each group found it hard to tolerate the other. This disturbed Gandhi, who was raised Hindu but yearned for mutual respect among people of both religions. In the late 1920s, Gandhi began to call for Indian unity above religious considerations. Instead, the Muslim League actively pushed for the creation of a Muslim nation, and even bounced around a name for their future country: Pakistan.

Independence Won: Nations Two

After World War II, Britain finally granted independence to the Indian subcontinent. The long and relatively nonviolent struggle for independence had finally paid off. The terrible irony was that once independence was granted, the real bloodshed began. Radical Hindus and Muslims started killing each other.

There were two schools of thought regarding the newly independent subcontinent. The first, promoted by Mohandas Gandhi and, at first, the British, called for the establishment of a united India where both Hindus and Muslims could practice their religions. The second was a movement by **Muhammad Ali Jinnah**, whose aim was to partition the subcontinent and form a separate Muslim nation in the northern region, where Islam had become the dominant religion. The British eventually were convinced that a partition would save lives by separating people who seemed intent on killing each other, so when the British turned over the reigns to new leaders of independent India in 1947, it separated the country into thirds: India in the south and Pakistan in two parts, one to the northwest of India (Pakistan) and the other to the east (East Pakistan, currently Bangladesh).

Both parts of Pakistan were Muslim, while India was predominately Hindu, although officially secular. The result was chaotic. Millions of people moved or were forced to flee due to religiously motivated violence. Essentially, India and Pakistan exchanged millions of citizens, with practitioners of each religion moving to the nation where their religion was dominant. Nearly a half million people were killed as they migrated to their respective "sides." The move of so many people along religious lines only served to create an international conflict between Pakistan and India. Within a year, Gandhi himself was assassinated by a Hindu who was upset with Gandhi's secular motivations. Today, the two nations are still fighting, especially in Kashmir along their borders, where religious self-determination still remains the big issue. What's more, both countries have since become nuclear powers, and 2008 saw a significant increase in terrorism between the two nations as Pakistan became less stable.

Africa

After World War II, African nations also began to assert their independence. They were partly inspired by events in India and the rest of the world, but they were also motivated by the war itself. Hundreds of thousands of Africans fought for their colonial powers during the war. Many of them felt that if they were willing to die for their governing countries, then they had earned the right to live free.

South Africa became a significant British colony, complete with extensive investment in infrastructure and institutions. In 1910, the colony established its own constitution, and it became the Union of South Africa, still part of the British Commonwealth, but exercising a considerable amount of self-rule. Under the constitution, only white men could vote, so the native Africans had few rights. In 1912, educated South Africans organized the African National

Congress in an effort to oppose European colonialism and specific South African policies. This organization, of course, was similar to the Indian National Congress, which was established for similar ends.

After South Africa, the nations north of the Sahara were the next colonies to win independence. These nations had strong Islamic ties, and the mostly Muslim Middle East had already won its freedom in the decades prior (more on that later). Egypt, too, had won its independence early, in 1922, although it kept extremely close ties to Britain. In the 1950s, as the independence movement gathered steam in Africa, **Gamal Nasser**, a general in the Egyptian army, overthrew the king and established a republic. He nationalized industries, including the Suez Canal, and then became embroiled in Middle Eastern conflicts. Nasser's actions emboldened other Islamic nationalists to seek independence, and soon the African nations along the Mediterranean were free.

South of the Sahara, independence was a trickier issue. The problem was that while nearly everyone wanted independence, most of the colonies had been raped of their resources. There had been little investment in human beings. The vast majority of Africans were uneducated, or only educated through grammar school. Unlike in India, where a substantial number of upper-caste Indians were highly educated and even attended universities in Britain, many African nations had few natives who were skilled professionals: doctors, scientists, lawyers, diplomats, businesspeople. This meant that once the colonial powers left, there would be few people left with the education and skills to immediately take charge and begin to build a productive, self-sufficient society.

National unity among the natives was also difficult to foster because the boundaries of so many African colonies had been drawn according to European needs, and took no account of African history or needs. Africans within the same colony spoke different native languages and had differing, sometimes opposing, customs, histories, and loyalties. For all of these reasons, even after attaining their hard-won independence, many African nations struggled to build strong, stable, independent countries.

Decolonization and nation-building occurred in a variety of ways across Africa. The **Algerians** fought a bitter war for independence from France (1954–1962) while in the early 1960s Nigeria and **Ghana** negotiated their freedom into a Parliamentary governing style borrowed from England. After a series of military coups, they adopted presidential systems. **Kenya**, under the leadership of Jomo Kenyatta, negotiated its constitution with Great Britain after a brutal crackdown engineered by coffee planters unwilling to lose such profitable property. Others, such as **Angola** and **Belgian Congo**, overthrew colonial governments, only to become embroiled in civil wars or in Cold War tensions. **Zimbabwe** was among the last to establish African majority rule in 1980 (see following section on South Africa).

Fifty-three of Africa's 54 nations belong to the **African Union**, a political and economic confederation formed in 2001 to replace the **Organization of African Unity** or **OAU**. But success and stability are not guaranteed for any of these nations. **Chad**, **Sudan**, **Uganda**, **Somalia**, and **Rwanda** as well as the newly renamed **Democratic Republic of Congo** (former Zaire) have been wracked by ongoing and devastating civil wars since the turn of the 21st century. Attempts to form stable democracies have been thwarted by a reversion to "big man" politics, corruption, military coups, and escalating debt payments (to IMF and World Bank—see Alphabet Soup later in this chapter). Even relatively stable governments such as Kenya's have seen political violence escalate in recent years.

Economically, most of Africa is still rich in natural resources, albeit different ones from those the colonial powers were interested in. Palm oil and rubber have given way to petroleum and metals including nickel, cadmium, and lithium—prized for batteries to power cell phones, laptop computers, and hybrid cars. So, the former colonial powers plus some new industrial players (China!) remain interested and invested in the nations of Africa.

Note the Change: Globalization and the Rise of NGOs

NGOs, or nongovernmental organizations, have become an ever-increasing presence in our modern world. NGOs are typically private, often nonprofit, agencies that provide relief services and/or advocacy for groups that are generally not serviced or represented by their governments. Some familiar examples of NGOs include the International Committee of the Red Cross (ICRC), Doctors Without Borders, Amnesty International, and even the American Civil Liberties Union. It is often NGOs that lead relief efforts following natural disasters and during wars, particularly to countries and people who cannot afford to pay for such efforts. Organizations such as the World Wildlife Fund provide advocacy for the world's animals, which of course do not have any representation in the world's governments. But why have most of these organizations formed only in the years since World War II? Well, the major international governmental organizations that formed after World War II, such as the UN and World Bank, were criticized for representing the interests of only the world's wealthier and more powerful nations (as they had been created by the victors of the war), and so many well-meaning individuals formed private companies to fill needs that were not being met by the world's governments. Globalization, which has increasingly made it easier to communicate and travel around the world, has not only made it easier for NGOs to provide their services on a global scale, but has also made it much easier for them to raise the money needed to fund their operations.

Rwanda: Ethnic Genocide

The difficulties of establishing stable nations in Africa are exemplified by the situation in Rwanda. Ethnic strife, genocide, and human rights violations in Rwanda stem from conflicts between two groups: the **Tutsi** (15 percent of the Rwandan population) who governed the **Hutu** (85 percent of the Rwandan population) during German and Belgian colonial occupation. Belgian rule in particular exacerbated interethnic tensions, setting the stage for bloodshed as soon as colonial authorities withdrew. Upon Rwanda's independence in 1962, the Hutu revolted against the Tutsi leadership, leaving thousands dead and the two groups locked in bitter, bloody conflict. In 1973, a military coup by Juvenal Habyarimana unseated the government and eventually established a one-party republic in 1981. The military government worked to keep peace but encountered only modest success. That, too, was destroyed when Habyarimana's personal airplane was shot down over his presidential palace in 1994, assassinating the Hutu general. Almost immediately, conflict escalated, with the Hutu needing little encouragement to exact revenge on the Tutsi population whose leadership they blamed for the assassination. One hundred days of genocide left as many as 800,000 Tutsi dead, and by the following year, more than 2 million mostly Hutu refugees were sent or fled to neighboring Zaire, where many died from disease. The genocide and displacement in Rwanda ranks among the most devastating in recent history.

Compare Them: Independence in Africa and India

Both India and Africa successfully gained independence in the years following World War II, and both areas were tragically torn apart by ethnic and religious strife shortly following independence. In India, the tensions between Hindus and Muslims, which existed before the British colonized the subcontinent, reemerged as they departed. In many African nations, independence served only as an opportunity for long-held tribal hatreds to resurface in power struggles. The colonial powers, of course, were no better. They had been killing each other for thousands of years.

Developments in South Africa: The Rise and Fall of Apartheid

The year after the **South Africa Act** of 1909, the **Union of South Africa** was formed by combining two British colonies with two Dutch Boer republics, and although the British and Dutch colonists were given considerable rights to self-government, Black people were entirely excluded from the political process. In 1923, residential segregation was established and enforced. In 1926, Black people were banned from work in certain skilled occupations that white people wanted for themselves. When South Africa won independence from Britain in 1931, the racial policies didn't improve. In fact, a system of **apartheid** ("separation of the races") was established in South Africa in 1948 as an all-encompassing way of dividing Black (80 percent of the population) and white. By the late 1950s, apartheid was extended to the creation of homelands, areas of the country that were "set aside" for Black people. The homelands were in the worst parts of the country, and comprised less than 15 percent of the nation's land. The white people were given the cities, the resource-rich mines, and the best farmland. While many Black people were compelled to move to the homelands, others stayed in the cities, where they were segregated into Black slums. If this starts to sound like *District 9* (2009), there's a reason a sci-fi movie about segregating aliens was set in South Africa.

In response, the Black community organized. In the 1950s, **Nelson Mandela** became leader of the **African National Congress**, an organization determined to abolish apartheid. At first, he advocated peaceful protest, following the example of Gandhi. But in 1960, after the **Sharpeville massacre** in which 67 protesters were killed, the African National Congress supported guerrilla warfare. At Sharpeville, Black people were protesting a policy that forced them to carry passes to be in the cities in order to go to their jobs. The passes were issued at places of employment. This meant that if you worked and your wife didn't, you couldn't go into the city with her because she wouldn't have a pass. The massacre rallied the anti-apartheid movement. Mandela was arrested in 1964 for his role in anti-apartheid violence and sentenced to life imprisonment.

After decades of increasing pressure from the Black majority and the international community, South Africa finally released Mandela in 1990 and agreed to negotiate on the policy of apartheid. The government more than negotiated, it crumbled. In 1994, after apartheid was abolished, Mandela was elected president in the first free and open election in the nation's history.

The Middle East

After the fall of the Ottoman Empire and the creation of the modern nation of Turkey at the close of World War I, the Middle East, which was largely comprised of old Ottoman lands, was temporarily put under the control of the League of Nations. As if the two European power-houses didn't already control enough of the world, France was put in charge of Syria and Lebanon, while Britain got Palestine, Jordan, and Iraq. Persia (Iran) was already carved up into spheres of influence between Britain and Russia during the 19th century. As for Arabia, it united as a Saudi kingdom immediately following the fall of the Ottoman Empire.

The Middle East during the 20th century is complicated stuff, but a good chunk of the essential information involves the creation of the modern nation of Israel, so that's where we'll start.

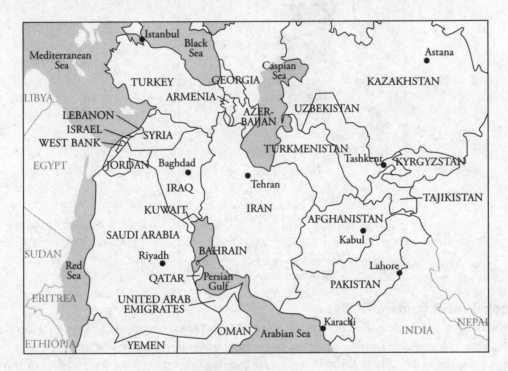

The Middle East

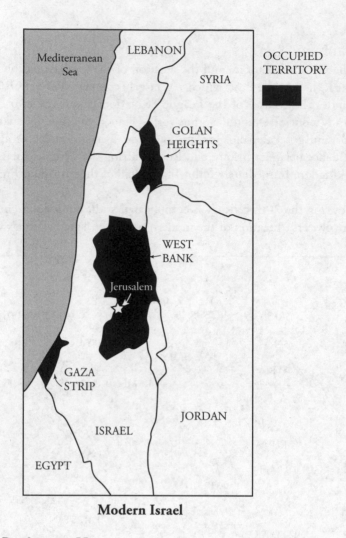

Modern Israel

Israel: Balfour Declares a Mess

At the time of the ancient Roman empire, the Hebrews (Jews) occupied lands in Palestine. As is the case everywhere else on the globe, between the Roman Empire and the events in this chapter, a series of conquests shifted power over the region a mind-numbing number of times. While a few Jews managed to stay in the region, most bolted for Europe or other areas as Palestine became increasingly entrenched in Islam. All the while, however, many Jews had wanted to return to what they believed was the "promised land." In the meantime, generation after generation of Muslim Palestinians had made that land home.

During World War I, **Zionists** (Jewish nationalists) living in Britain convinced **Arthur Balfour**, Britain's foreign secretary, that a Jewish homeland in Palestine was both desirable and just. He issued what became known as the **Balfour Declaration of 1917**, which explicitly stated the right for a home in Palestine for the Jewish people, but he also stated that it should in no way displace the Palestinians who currently lived there. As history would have it, Britain gained control of Palestine in 1920 as a mandate from the League of Nations—which meant that it was to govern on behalf of the League of Nations—and was therefore in a position to make good on its declaration.

The declaration was messy because it essentially provided that the Palestinians and Jews were to divide land that they both claimed. Not long after, many Jews, mainly Russian Jews fleeing violent, antisemitic mobs (**pogroms**), began streaming into Palestine. As their numbers grew, the Palestinians started to get uneasy. In the 1930s, huge numbers of Jews flooded the region to escape Germany as Hitler came to power. By the beginning of World War II, nearly 500,000 Jews had emigrated to Palestine. While Palestinians still outnumbered Jews, the Jewish population was now large enough to pull some serious weight, especially because money was pouring into the region from Jewish communities worldwide.

The Jewish Wait for a State Ends in 1948

In 1948, the United Nations (which had replaced the ineffectual League of Nations) officially created two Palestines, one for Jews and the other for Muslims (Palestinians). As soon as **David Ben-Gurion**, the first prime minister of Israel, announced the official creation of the Jewish homeland on May 14, 1948, Muslims from six Arab countries attacked Israel in what became known as the **1948 Arab-Israeli War**. However, the Israelis shocked and awed them with their quick organization and military capability. Within months, the Israelis controlled most of Palestine, including the Palestinian parts, while Jordan held the remaining portions (the **West Bank**). Suddenly, Palestinians were without a home. They had no land to call their own.

> **Sound Familiar?**
> The arrangement made between the Jews and Muslims in Palestine should sound familiar to you, as the same one was made between India and Pakistan. The Indians and Pakistanis have been fighting ever since.

As Jews flocked to Israel from all over the world, Israel and Arab countries continued to have skirmishes. In 1967, the amazingly short **Six-Day War** resulted in total victory for the Israelis, who took control of the West Bank from Jordan, the Sinai Peninsula and **Gaza Strip** from Egypt, and the **Golan Heights** from Syria. With the West Bank came control of the city of Jerusalem, Judaism's historical homeland. However, Muslims throughout the region resented Israeli control of the Dome of the Rock, a revered Islamic shrine dating back to the Abbasid caliphate which is also the site of the Temple Mount, an important Jewish historical site. The territorial gains resulted in new waves of Palestinian refugees to Jerusalem. In 1977, Israeli **Prime Minister Menachem Begin** and Egyptian **President Anwar Sadat** signed the **Camp David Accords**, an agreement that did not mention Golan Heights, Syria, or Lebanon, but which led to Israel pulling out of the Sinai and Egypt becoming the only Arab country yet to recognize Israel's right to exist. This was a huge blow to the Palestinians and other Arab nations. Sadat was assassinated and the lands gained in the Six-Day War remain some of the most contested in the region.

In the years since, the Israelis and the Palestinians have been fighting over the Israeli occupation of the West Bank, Golan Heights, and Gaza Strip. The **Palestine Liberation Organization (PLO)**, a group dedicated to reclaiming the land and establishing a Palestinian state, has so far been unsuccessful in negotiating a homeland. The efforts are complicated by the *intifada* (uprising), an on-again off-again movement that sometimes uses terrorism against Israeli citizens in an attempt to either destroy Israel or force it into withdrawal from the occupied territories.

In 2000, a new intifada reignited violence between Palestinians and the occupying Israeli forces. As suicide bombings became more frequent, newly elected Israeli prime minister **Ariel Sharon** approved the construction of a wall to be built between the Palestinian West Bank and Israel in order to protect Israelis against suicide attacks. Often compared to the Berlin Wall, Israel's protective wall has been criticized by some in the international community for employing such a draconian measure to fight terrorist attacks. Many in Israel, meanwhile, have pointed to the wall as a successful way to prevent needless violence and terrorism.

Not limiting itself to criticism, however, in 2003 the international community, led by the United States, the European Union, the UN, and Russia, proposed a "Roadmap to Peace," which outlined a set of goals to achieve peace in the region. Progress on the Roadmap remained stalled until the death of Palestinian president (and former PLO leader) **Yasser Arafat** in November 2004. Arafat had been consistently blamed by Israel and the United States for blocking such progress. Following his January 2005 election, Palestinian president **Mahmoud Abbas** quickly signed a cease-fire with Israel that effectively ended the *intifada* that began in 2000.

Under a "disengagement plan" adopted by the Israeli government, all Israeli settlers were supposed to have vacated the Gaza Strip by August 2005. Residents of the settlements who did not leave were forcibly removed by the Israeli army, a military action which greatly divided the Israeli public. Additional settlements were disbanded in the West Bank as part of the same plan. It is likely, however, that lasting peace will remain elusive until the Israelis and Palestinians can reach agreement on issues such as movement into and outside of the Palestinian Authority–controlled territories, the disarmament of militant groups, and the potential independence of a Palestinian state.

The situation is made even more complicated by limited financial stability and political divisions among Palestinians. The governing Palestinian Authority is divided into two factions: Fatah, a branch of the former Palestinian Liberation Organization, and Hamas. Translating to "Islamic Resistance Movement," Hamas was founded as an offshoot of the Muslim Brotherhood in 1987. Because of its open willingness to support terrorist tactics, Hamas is frequently the target of Israeli military attacks. Despite similar goals for a Palestinian state, Hamas and Fatah are deeply divided, and violent clashes occur with increasing frequency. After the creation of a unity government in 2006, Hamas led a coup in 2007 which concluded with a Hamas-imposed government in the Gaza Strip and a Fatah-run West Bank. Further complicating governance, in retaliation, President Mahmoud Abbas (Fatah) named Salam Fayyad prime minister. Hamas contended that Fayyad's appointment was illegitimate, as he was not voted into office. Israel's government—led by Prime Minister Benjamin Netanyahu—and the United States have shown willingness to work with Fatah. The United States and a number of European countries list Hamas as a terrorist organization and so do not negotiate with that party.

Israel's border with Lebanon and Syria remains another hotspot. Hezbollah, a militant Shia group backed by Syria and Iran, operates in the region. In 2006, Israel launched a major offensive against Hezbollah after two Israeli soldiers were captured in Israeli territory. These new hostilities threatened the stability of a country which had been the scene of intense fighting between Syrian, Israeli, and PLO forces throughout the 1980s and 1990s. Syria is widely seen to have a controlling hand in Lebanese politics. In 2005, when Prime Minister Rafiq Hariri was assassinated, fingers quickly pointed to Hezbollah and Syrian sources.

The Iranian Revolution: The Shah Gets Shooed

Reza Shah Pahlavi rose to power in 1925 by ousting the then-ruling shah, who had allowed Persia to fall under European spheres of influence. Taking a stance similar to the Japanese during the Meiji Restoration, Reza Shah decided that the best way to beat the Westernizers was to join them. Iran (formerly Persia) modernized slowly at first, but once the Europeans left after World War II, the Westernization efforts gained momentum, and in the 1960s, the shah instituted land and education reform known as the White Revolution (implying it would be bloodless), and increased the rights of women, including the right to vote. Women also pursued higher education and careers, and began to adopt Western dress. All of this infuriated many

Islamic fundamentalists who wanted to make the teachings of the Qu'ran the law of the land. Believing that the influence of the West was too strong, they sought to reverse the economic and social changes. Others believed that the shah was not reforming enough, especially with regard to the political system, which lacked significant democratic changes.

The shah reacted violently against dissent from both sides, pressing forward with his own mix of social and economic reform even in the face of strong public opposition. When **President Jimmy Carter** of the United States visited Iran to congratulate it on its programs of modernization and Westernization, the Islamic fundamentalists had had enough. In 1979, the shah was ousted from power during the **Iranian Revolution**, which sent Iran back to a theocracy led by *Ayatollah* ("Mirror of God") **Khomeini**. Iran is primarily Shia, and the ayatollah is the Shiite caliph (this was important during the Iran-Iraq War, as Iraq was ruled by Sunni Muslims). Immediately, modernization and Westernization programs were reversed, women were required to wear traditional Islamic clothing and to return to their traditional roles, and the Qu'ran became the basis of the legal system.

In 1980, soon after the revolution, Iraq invaded Iran following a series of border disputes between the two countries. Iran's position was further complicated by Iraqi leader Saddam Hussein's quiet support from the United States, which was still quite furious over Iran's taking of U.S. hostages during the revolution. Even with some U.S. support, the **Iran-Iraq War** turned into an eight-year war of attrition with neither side gaining much ground until a cease-fire was signed in 1988.

Since the Ayatollah Khomeini's death in 1989 (watch out—he was succeeded by the differently spelled **Ayatollah Khamenei**!), Iran has been characterized by a power struggle between powerful Islamic fundamentalist clerics and an increasingly vocal reform-minded and somewhat pro-Western minority. Most recently, however, Iran has caused international concern (particularly in the United States) by pushing ahead with efforts to develop what they deemed "peaceful" nuclear technologies, claiming they have a right as an independent nation to develop such technology as they see fit. Along with the International Atomic Energy Agency and the European Union, the United States is currently calling on Iran to sign an international agreement limiting or even eliminating its nuclear programs.

From 2005 until 2013, Tehran's ultra-conservative mayor **Mahmoud Ahmadinejad** was president of Iran. He was succeeded by the more politically moderate leader Hassan Rouhani. The American-led war in Iraq that began in 2003, the relationship of Iran and Iraq's Shia populations, and Iran's development of weapons programs and nuclear research have only complicated matters further.

Oil: Enormous Amounts of Goo

The Industrial Revolution was a huge bonanza for the Middle East. That's because they'd been sitting on more than two-thirds of the world's known oil reserves since the beginning of civilization. Prior to the Industrial Revolution, it was goo. After the Industrial Revolution, it was fuel. As multinational corporations rushed to the Middle East throughout the 20th century to obtain drilling and production rights, Middle Eastern governments such as those of Saudi Arabia, Kuwait, Iran, and Iraq started to earn billions of dollars annually. The oil also meant that the rest of the world had become very, very interested in the Middle East, because oil allowed the West to do one of its favorite things: drive. This world interest sometimes led to intervention and war.

Once the oil-producing nations of the Middle East realized how much power they wielded, they organized. In 1960, the region united with a few other oil-exporting nations, such as Venezuela, to form a petroleum cartel known as **OPEC** (Organization of Petroleum Exporting Countries). With three-quarters of the world's petroleum reserves, OPEC members collectively cut supply dramatically in the 1970s, sending the price of oil through the roof. Billions of extra dollars flowed into OPEC member nations' coffers. Nations such as Saudi Arabia used the extra money to modernize their infrastructures and spent billions on attempts to improve their agricultural sectors. Since the 1970s, OPEC hasn't been able to keep its members in line, and is therefore a much less powerful organization, but the individual members who make up the organization continue to wield huge power over the world economy.

> **Compare Them: Role of Women After the Chinese Revolution and Before the Iranian Revolution**
>
> In the West, women have benefited from substantial societal and legal changes, but the change has been gradual, over many generations. In China and Iran, the changes were quick. Within a single woman's lifetime, she went from an extremely traditional, oppressive society to one in which she could vote (in the case of Iran), dress less traditionally, divorce her husband, become educated, and pursue a career. Of course, after the Iranian Revolution, those reforms were reversed immediately. At that point, women in China and Iran were in completely different situations.

V. UNIT 9: GLOBALIZATION

A. International Terrorism and War

Since World War II and the formation of the United Nations, there has been increased interest in maintaining international security. Some of the organizations that are charged with this task are from the Cold War era: NATO, the United Nations, and the International Atomic Energy Agency. Others, such as the International Criminal Court in The Hague (formed in 2002) were formed to prosecute war crimes and crimes against humanity, no matter who committed them. Still others, including NGOs such as Amnesty International, Human Rights Watch, and Doctors Without Borders, serve to publicize issues that threaten human health and safety and provide aid to those in need.

War in the Gulf: Oil and Saddam Hussein

Iraq invaded Kuwait in August 1990 under the leadership of **Saddam Hussein** because Iraq wanted to gain control of a greater percentage of the world's oil reserves. Iraqi control of Kuwait would have nearly doubled Iraq's oil reserves to 20 percent of the world's total, and would have put it in good position to make advances on Saudi Arabia and the United Arab Emirates, actions that would have given Iraq control of more than half of the world's oil reserves. The world, especially the industrialized West, reacted immediately. In January 1991, the United Nations, and particularly the United States, sent forces to drive the Iraqis out of Kuwait in what we now call the **Persian Gulf War**. The immediate impact of their success was the liberation of Kuwait and the humiliation of Iraq, which was subjected to UN monitoring, severe limitations on its military activities, and economic sanctions. Nevertheless, Hussein remained in power, and the UN forces left the region without moving forward to oust him. Hussein held on to his brutal dictatorship for another 10 years while also, many argue, ignoring key elements of the peace treaty that allowed him to keep his power after his invasion of Kuwait.

In April 2003, a coalition of countries consisting primarily of the United States and Great Britain invaded Iraq to oust Saddam from power. Saddam's government quickly fell to coalition forces but Hussein himself was not captured until December of that year. Sovereignty was returned to a transitional government in June of 2004, and a new democratically elected government was formed in May 2005. However, since the initial invasion, Iraq has been increasingly plagued with sectional conflicts among Sunni, Shiites, and Kurds, the conflicts defined by suicide bombings against coalition forces and more and more against Iraqi forces and civilians of rival sects. Even amidst the violence, the Iraqi government ratified a new constitution in October 2005, followed by a general election in December 2005, with legislative seats distributed according to "proportional representation." This system allotted percentages of seats to women, Sunni Muslims, Kurdish Iraqis, as well as to the Shia majority. Despite delays in certifying the results of the December 2005 election, the newly elected government took office in May 2006, with **Jalal Talabani**, who is Kurdish, as president, and **Nouri al-Maliki**, who is Shia, as prime minister. The government has faced a number of challenges, and it remains to be seen whether it can successfully bring a violent insurgency to peaceful engagement in the political process. Even with the end of U.S. combat operations and the withdrawal of most coalition troops by the end of 2011, Iraq must also still contend with a number of opposing domestic and international interests as it tries to find stability in its new incarnation.

Taliban, Al Qaeda, Osama bin Laden

During the early 1980s, the Soviet Union sent thousands of troops to Afghanistan at the request of Marxist military leader **Nur Muhammad Taraki**, who had engineered a military coup against the previous government. Many Afghans opposed communism and Soviet intervention, however, and soon a massive civil war raged. Some of the resistors called themselves "holy warriors" and, with the aid of weapons from the Western powers who supplied the Cold War on every front, launched guerrilla attacks against the superior military might of the Soviet Union. As internal problems escalated in the Soviet Union, Gorbachev agreed to withdraw Soviet troops from the region and a peace accord was signed. While communism fell apart in the Soviet Union and Eastern Europe, the problems in Afghanistan continued. The decline of communism removed the Soviet threat, but warring factions vied to fill the power void.

The power that finally triumphed after 14 years of fighting and more than 2 million deaths was called the **Taliban**, an Islamic fundamentalist regime that captured the capital of Kabul in 1996. The new government imposed strict Islamic law and severe restrictions on women. It also provided safe haven for **Osama bin Laden**, the Saudi leader of an international terrorist network, known as **Al Qaeda**, which has a serious distaste for Saudi Arabia and the United States. It's believed that Al Qaeda's main issue with Saudi Arabia is that the ruling family is too cozy with the United States and that they have allowed U.S. troops to remain in the country since the Persian Gulf War, which amounts to the presence of infidels in a kingdom that is home to Islam's most holy sites. Al Qaeda despises the United States for what many believe are at least three reasons. First, the United States supports Israel, which the organization would like to see removed from the planet. Second, it has troops stationed in Saudi Arabia, and third, the United States is the primary agent of globalization, which Al Qaeda believes is infecting Islamic culture.

On **September 11, 2001**, Al Qaeda operatives managed to take control of four American passenger jets and fly two of them into the **World Trade Center** in New York City, one into the Pentagon in Washington, D.C., and one into a field in Pennsylvania. The towers of the World Trade Center fell to the ground, killing more than 2,500 civilians. The deaths of the people on all four planes and those killed at the Pentagon and the World Trade Center bring the total number of casualties to almost 3,000. The United States immediately launched a war on terrorism, targeting Al Qaeda and the Taliban. Within months, the Taliban was removed from power and U.S. and UN forces occupied the country of Afghanistan. Al Qaeda, on the other hand, still survives, though its leadership is being directly attacked and eliminated, most notably with the death of Osama bin Laden in May of 2011.

Although smaller in scale, suicide bombing and terrorist attacks (many linked to Al Qaeda and similar groups) continue regularly. They are a problem throughout the Israeli territories, between Sunni and Shia factions in Iraq, targeting tourists in the cities of Saudi Arabia, Egypt, and Turkey, and among Muslim separatists in Russia. Coordinated attacks occurred throughout Lebanon in 2004 and 2005, killing the former Prime Minister Rafiq Hariri (among others), while larger-scale attacks occurred in March 2004 on commuter trains in Madrid, Spain, in July 2005 on the London subway system, and the following July on trains in Mumbai (Bombay), India. Many of these attacks were linked to Islamic fundamentalists, who have also attacked Jewish and Christian minorities throughout Europe and the Middle East.

The Rise of ISIS

The recent rise of the so-called Islamic State (also known as IS, ISIL, or ISIS) in Iraq and Syria has led to constant instability in that region. ISIS has been especially effective at broadcasting its terrorist methods through online videos. The extremely graphic videos, which feature beheadings, shootings, and other executions, have led to nearly universal condemnation from the international community. The stated goal of ISIS is to revive a caliphate that unifies the entire Islamic world under ISIS's rule. Similarly, the terrorist group Boko Haram, whose name means "Western education is forbidden," has led to conflict and violence in West African countries such as Nigeria, Chad, Niger, and Cameroon. An alliance between ISIS and Boko Haram, which was formalized in 2015, will only worsen the terrorist problem in the Islamic world over the coming years.

B. World Trade and Cultural Exchange

The end of the Cold War removed the last obstacles to true global interaction and trade. Currencies were no longer tied to old alliances, and new business opportunities emerged. This deregulation, along with the development of systems of instantaneous communication such as the Internet, resulted in globally integrated financial networks. Commercial interdependence intensified in the 1980s as eastern Asia began to flex its industrial and commercial muscles.

Competition further drove global developments, and regional trading blocks such as the **North American Free Trade Agreement (NAFTA)** were created in the early 1990s. The European Economic Community (EEC), originally formed in 1957, transformed into the modern **European Union** (EU) tied to a single currency, the euro. The ease with which goods and ideas are transported across the world has resulted in cultures being more homogenous and integrated. This does not mean that local culture is lost, but it does mean that one can satisfy a craving for a Starbucks latte inside Beijing's Forbidden City. It also means almost instantaneous access to a wider range of music, art, literature, and information. Much of this is facilitated by the spread of English as the language of business and communication across the globe. This began in the 18th century with the far-flung colonies of the British Empire and continued with the emergence of the United States as a global power after World War II.

The **European Union,** or EU, was formed to give the United States some economic competition by banding Europe together in a single market. The real impetus to expand the powers of the EU came in the early 1990s when the collapse of the Soviet Union simultaneously opened Europe and left the United States unchallenged as the world's superpower. In 1989, the EU had 12 members; by 2011, it had 27, of which 10 were former Soviet satellite nations. The EU has three branches: executive, legislative, and judicial. Elections are held throughout Europe every five years. The formation of a monetary union, the **Eurozone**, in 1999, led all but three nations (UK, Sweden, and Denmark) to adopt a unified currency, the euro, in 2002.

While economic integration initially seemed relatively easy and produced a few boom years, in the crisis of the late 2000s (which began slightly earlier in Europe than in the United States), it became clear that stronger economies such as Germany's had borne the freight of weaker, over-extended economies such as Greece's, and by 2010, economic collapse in states such as Greece, Ireland, and Portugal threatened to destabilize the entire Eurozone. This has provoked sharp debates about economic integration that have now piled onto existing concerns about political and judicial integration, putting national interests and questions of sovereignty at stake.

Note the Change: The Threat of "McDonaldization"

Consider for a moment just how far and wide fast food culture has spread since the first McDonald's restaurant opened in California in the late 1930s. Take a quick jump over to McDonald's website and you can view the list of over 100 countries in which McDonald's has restaurants today, including Saudi Arabia, Pakistan, and Egypt. But why point out these Muslim countries? The so-called "McDonaldization" of the world can be used as both an example and a metaphor for the spread of what is predominantly a Western popular culture to the rest of the world. Many countries, such as India and even China, have embraced the fruits of Westernization, integrating and assimilating aspects of Western culture into their own. Other groups however, including fundamentalist movements in some Muslim countries, have rejected this "invasion" of modern Western culture, which they see as a threat to their traditional Islamic ways. Responses to the perceived threat of globalization have included many acts of international terrorism in an effort to fight encroachment as symbolized by the international spread of such Western cultural icons as Starbucks, Walmart, and Disney.

Global Culture

Globalization has also allowed for popular culture to be shared in communities throughout the world, creating a sense of cultural understanding as well as global togetherness. Some 20th-century examples of this include…

The Olympics	Countries from around the globe meet in one city every four years for this worldwide athletic showcase, which is derived from the ancient Greek athletic competitions.
World Cup Soccer	The world community meets in a single country every four years for a global soccer tournament, which resembles the Olympics.
Reggae	This is a form of Jamaican music created in the 1960s which gained worldwide popularity due as much to its focus on social issues as its infectious beats.
Bollywood	The global popularity of the American film industry based in Hollywood led to the creation of the Indian film industry based in Mumbai.
Social Media	This 20th-century development allows the world to connect through apps such as Facebook and Twitter. Social media has allowed information to travel instantly to people in every corner of the world, yet it has also been exploited by bad actors as a networking or recruiting tool.

To Be Rich Is Glorious: The Rise of China and India

"Socialism with Chinese Characteristics" or "To Be Rich Is Glorious" sums up Deng Xiaoping's plans for China after the death of Chairman Mao. Since normalized trade relations with the United States in the 1990s and acceptance into the World Trade Organization in 2001, China has become an industrial and economic juggernaut. What began with the creation of **special economic zones** exempt from the strict controls of communism in the late 1980s has become the world's warehouse and discount store! In the last 10 years, China's imports have increased from $82 billion (1999) to $338 billion (2008) built on a wide array of everyday consumer goods, toys, and apparel. This new and profitable industrial revolution has funded a building boom throughout China, brought the 2008 Olympic games to Beijing, and contributed to a rising and educated middle class who now shop and eat at 300 Starbucks and 800 McDonald's restaurants. Economic success has also led to a crackdown on Internet freedom. Politically, it is pretty much the same old China. The CCP allows some local elections and *The New York Times* is available online, but one party is clearly in charge and watching what you Google.

India, the world's largest democracy and one of its fastest-growing economies, has spent the past two decades making itself indispensable to the globally connected world. In 1991, India was broke, the leading contender for prime minister had been assassinated, and the country desperately needed a way to reinvent its economy and industries. Since loans from the IMF required economic reforms and austerity measures, major industries were privatized and others were publicly traded. India's greatest advantage is its highly educated and skilled population, yet the focus on traditional industry advocated by Gandhi had left India isolated and unable to compete globally. The desperation of 1991, at a time when technology and computer chip industries were developing in the United States, was a moment of opportunity for Indian investors and workers, many of whom had migrated to Silicon Valley. Indian entrepreneurs took these new ideas back to Indian companies such as Infosys and Tata, developed technology to route global calls, and built on the global demand for software, new technology, and support.

Both India and China are nuclear powers with two of the world's largest armies. Both are currently dealing with belligerent neighbors (Pakistan and North Korea), both have complicated relationships and history with Western powers, both have yet to deal with tremendous economic inequality and poverty within their borders, and as members of the G20 (see Global Alphabet Soup) both have figured out a way to keep growing while much of the industrialized world is in an economic slowdown.

Global Alphabet Soup

With globalization of trade come many agencies and organizations designed to protect and facilitate trade. The earliest of these were the International Monetary Fund, or IMF (1945), with 185 members and the World Bank (also founded in 1945), with 188 members. Both organizations were formed to stabilize world economic relationships and to loan financial assistance when needed. At the same time, the General Agreement on Tariffs and Trade, or **GATT**, was agreed upon to reduce barriers to international trade. GATT became the World Trade Organization, or WTO, in 1994. The WTO boasts 153 member states—most of the world's active trading nations—who adhere to the WTO's rules and regulations regarding trade relationships.

An organization of note is the **Group of Six**, or **G6**, created in 1975 as a forum for the world's major industrialized democracies. Its original members included the United States, Great Britain, West Germany, Italy, Japan, and France. They have since been joined by Canada in 1977, and by Russia in 1997, and were known as the **G8**. Recently, Russia was excluded from the forum by the other members in March 2014 as a result of its involvement in the 2014 Crimea crisis in Ukraine. The group has changed yet again and now meets as the **G7** group of nations. This informal summit of the world's most powerful leaders meets annually to discuss issues of mutual or global concern such as climate change, terrorism, and trade.

In addition to the G8, a group of 19 nations plus EU representatives make up the **G20,** or the Group of 20 Finance Ministers and Central Bank Governors. Beginning with the financial crises of the late 1990s, this group represents key industrialized as well as emerging economies.

C. Environmental Change

Until the 1980s, environmental issues focused on localized pollution or waste management, but along with global integration in every sector came global environmental concerns. Most recently, these concerns have focused on food; as suppliers become ever more distant from their consumers and trade agreements open up supply routes, safety regulations may not follow.

The "green revolution" of the 1950s and 1960s led to increased agricultural productivity through industrial means—chemical fertilizers and pesticides, biologically engineered foods, more efficient means of harvesting, and more marginal lands available for agriculture. While this resulted in inexpensive and plentiful food supplies, it destroyed traditional landscapes including rainforests in Indonesia and South America, reduced species diversity, and fostered social conflicts that might not have otherwise existed. As has been true throughout history, marginal lands cannot sustain the population increases they initially produce with new industrial technologies. This is especially notable in eastern and sub-Saharan Africa, where political and financial mismanagement contributed to widespread famines in the 1970s and 1980s.

Bottled water has become ubiquitous, but water is a crucial natural resource that is often carelessly managed by cities at the expense of their hinterlands. This is not a rapidly renewable resource and needs to be regulated for drinking and for agriculture. A similar pattern is seen with industrialized countries' consumption of oil—they want more and they want it cheap! Oil fuels industry, transportation, and heating of homes and businesses. The insatiable appetite for oil reserves on the part of industrialized democracies has led to strange political and economic alliances (see the previous section on the Middle East).

Finally, a quick note on global warming. It's getting warmer and human activities, including fuel consumption, heating, and cooling, are contributing to this. The outcome of these warming trends is uncertain. On the positive side, there will be longer growing seasons in temperate parts of the world, but the negative effects are more extreme conditions in marginal areas—longer periods of drought in some, flooding and disappearance of coastlines in others. The first Earth Summit on global climate change was held in 1992 in Rio de Janeiro. Five years later, the Kyoto Protocol was an attempt to make a global agreement on ways to reduce environmental damages, but because the United States has refused to ratify the Protocol (and Canada denounced it in 2011), it remains controversial and unable to function to its full potential. Industrialized nations continue to struggle with balancing potential damage to the environment with the growth potential of their business sector, and it is the business of production and consumption that has been of primary importance to policymakers.

D. Global Health Crises

Within globalization efforts, the relief of health crises is a primary focus. Nonprofit organizations such as the WHO (World Health Organization) work to lower infant mortality as well as to combat various diseases, such as malaria, tuberculosis, and influenza, which kill millions in third-world countries due to a lack of appropriate medical care and medicine. This problem has existed as far back as 1918, when a flu epidemic killed millions across the globe, but is still important today. Recent outbreaks of bird flu and swine flu, two strains of influenza passed from animals to humans, show that such epidemics, especially in countries without the United States' high level of sanitation, are still an issue.

AIDS is another notable global health crisis, especially in sub-Saharan Africa, where almost 25 percent of adults in some countries live with HIV (the virus that causes AIDS). While AIDS treatments can help those with the disease to live relatively normal lives, there is no cure as yet for this fatal illness, and only those in wealthier countries tend to have access to the most advanced treatments. Currently, global efforts to combat this health crisis are focused on prevention, and the WHO and other organizations are working on changing the social norms and behaviors of at-risk populations, particularly in Africa where the AIDS crisis is at its worst.

Other notable global health issues today include diseases that, in developed countries, are not a threat, such as cholera. New treatments for cholera, such as oral rehydration therapy, have drastically lowered mortality rates associated with the disease in Bangladesh, India, and neighboring countries. A severe outbreak of the Ebola virus in West Africa received global attention throughout 2014. As of this writing, the virus has claimed more than 10,000 lives, mostly in Liberia, Sierra Leone, and Guinea. When a few high-profile (but isolated) cases of Ebola appeared in Europe and the United States, strong national debates emerged about forced quarantines and open borders. Global health issues highlight the disparities that, despite the ongoing process of globalization, still exist today.

E. The Age of the Computer

The single most important technological advance since the 1980s is the rise of computers and, in turn, the Internet. Beginning in the 1970s, American companies such as Compaq and IBM developed new hardware, which allowed computers to shrink radically in size (by using a silicon chip to store data). The PC, or personal computer, became a reality, since this advance meant that computers no longer took up entire rooms. By the late 1980s, an early version of the Internet existed, though only those with advanced technical knowledge had access.

In the 1990s, more homes acquired computers; commercial software, such as web browsers and the services and programs offered by America Online, introduced the Internet to the American population at large, transforming both the home and the workplace. The Y2K scare, which involved a possible glitch in computers caused by the switch of dates to the new millennium, pointed out how dependent industry and society were on computers and the Internet. Y2K did not cause an actual crisis, and personal computers and similar technologies, including cell phones, are all the more crucial today to the personal and global business lives of many.

More recently, social media and the spread of the Internet have had huge ramifications worldwide. Social media platforms such as Twitter and Facebook have changed the way news is reported and have played a huge role in political developments in Middle Eastern countries, for example. During the "Arab Spring" of 2011, oppressive regimes in several nations were toppled due in part to the exposure—via social media—of the problems in those countries. Internet censorship exists in many nations, notably India and China, but overall this technology has served to bring people together both in business and in other aspects of life, changing the way we receive our news, take classes, and even shop. One current concern, however, is the growing gap in access between countries. The importance of the Internet and computer technology may serve as a barrier to globalization in countries without the infrastructure to join this "digital revolution."

The Internet has also raised the important issue of government surveillance and individual privacy. In 2013, Edward Snowden, an American computer specialist with access to classified documents, leaked information about the government's anti-terrorism measures to journalists. His revelations were astonishing. According to Snowden and the documents he released, the U.S. government had been collecting information from all of its citizens—not just terrorists or potential terrorists—and storing it in massive data centers. Such a surveillance system is considered by many privacy experts to be unconstitutional and unnecessary. Some in the government have denied the existence of such programs or claimed they are both legal and necessary to stop future terrorist attacks. For his part, Snowden fled the country and has been formally charged with crimes by the U.S. government for leaking the information. The problem was not limited to the United States, however. Similar revelations have sparked loud international debates in Europe, Asia, and Latin America and reveal the complicated nature of a world in which so much private information is accessible online.

VI.   CHANGES AND CONTINUITIES IN THE ROLE OF WOMEN

Finally, the upheavals and changes of the 20th century resulted in really dramatic changes in women's social, political, and economic roles. The integration and global connectedness of the world made access to education and political freedoms far more widespread, especially among the middle and upper classes. Change came more slowly to the lower and working classes, but still it came.

Politically, women gained the right to vote in many parts of the world by the first quarter of the 20th century. By 1930, that right had been gained by women in much of Latin America, India, China, Japan, and most of Europe. After World War II, most of the newly independent African countries included women's suffrage in their constitutions, and it is only in the most fundamentalist of the Middle Eastern countries that women still do not have the right to vote. However, having the right to vote differs significantly from having the education and opportunity to vote. In most Asian and African countries, female access to formal political power continues to be limited.

Contradictions also exist between theory and practice in communist and formerly communist countries. Under communism, everyone was equal, women played key roles in the Communist Revolutions in Russia, China, and Cuba, and educational opportunities were opened especially in professions such as medicine. Women were also generally given equal legal rights including those of inheritance, divorce, and child rearing. However, in reality, discrimination and gender issues continue. Almost all key positions within the Communist parties were and are held by men. In China, the one-child policy and mandatory sterilization disproportionately impact women and female children. State-sponsored sterilization was also common in Puerto Rico and India. Additionally, the end of communism and the loosening of economic restrictions seem to present more opportunities for men than for women.

Family structure changed dramatically in the 20th century, especially in the industrialized world. Birth rates dropped, birth control was widely available, and marriage rates declined as divorce and second marriages became more common. The 20th century also saw dramatic changes in the role of women at work. Beginning with wage labor in factories during the World Wars, women's presence in the workforce has become more widely accepted. A shift to profitable industries in chemicals, textiles, and electronics, has provided further economic opportunities for women. By the mid-1980s, education and access in Westernized and industrialized countries allowed women to participate fully in the work force. Women in agricultural economies, however, continued to have their labor under-enumerated. Throughout the world, women's pay has yet to fully equal that of male counterparts, nor are women compensated for the time they spend on a "second shift" as primary caregivers of young children.

VII.   PULLING IT ALL TOGETHER

You've read about a lot of stuff in this chapter. Two world wars. A cold war and all its consequences. The end of European imperialism. The rise of the United States as a superpower. Islamic fundamentalism in the Middle East. These are all huge issues. It's hard to discern immediately how you can connect them all together other than to say that there were a lot of wars and a lot of hatred. Nevertheless, beyond the morbidity and feelings of helplessness that a careful study of history can engender, there are also a lot of ways to think about history that can help you evaluate how people and the world function.

In the last chapter, we talked a lot about nationalism, and it certainly didn't stop in the 20th century. Nationalism not only led to fascism in Nazi Germany, but also to independence movements after World War II in India and Africa, and in Europe and Asia after the fall of the Soviet Union. Sometimes it was based on broad cultural characteristics—Gandhi, for example, unsuccessfully wanting everyone to look at themselves as Indians, not as Hindus or Muslims— and other times it was very narrowly defined—Serbs, for example, or Nazis.

Regardless of its forms, nationalism affected all of the major global events in the 20th century. In both World War I and World War II, the aggressors were highly nationalistic. The independence movements following World War II were nationalistic. And the Cold War, because it pitted two opposing worldviews that were so strongly identified with the nations of the Soviet Union and the United States, was arguably a nationalist struggle as well. National pride was on the line. In the end, superpower status was on the line, too.

By the late 20th century, whether because of nationalism or not, there was a huge number of independent nation-states. Each former colony in Africa was independent. Lots of new countries formed from the old Soviet Union. What's more, most of the countries were developing along democratic lines—though some along militaristic or Islamic theocratic lines—and capitalism seemed to be making huge gains after the fall of the Soviet Union, which leads us to the next question.

Is There Currently a Convergence of Cultures?

If you study history enough, you can argue for both sides. On the one hand, globalization is clearly occurring and has been for a long time. It's just that now it's happening a lot faster and penetrating more and more hidden parts of the globe. Centuries ago, trade, conquest, and exploration were forms of globalization because they brought people together, essentially "making the world smaller." Major movements like the Scientific Revolution, the Enlightenment, and the Industrial Revolution can certainly be categorized as shifts toward globalization because they weren't culturally specific, but rather could be applied nearly anywhere around the globe. They brought people closer together because they led to certain ways of thinking that were attractive and accepted by different kinds of people. If people start to agree on how the universe is organized or how governments should be organized, that is most certainly a convergence of cultures.

In the 20th century, globalization really took off. Aided by transportation, communication, and imperialism, anything produced in one country could be received in another. Popular examples of globalization are the appearance of the same multinational companies everywhere (seeing a McDonald's in Istanbul) and certainly the use of the Internet, but globalization is much broader than even these examples. Globalization has led to an interconnectedness of entire economies. The Great Depression in the 1930s proved that the economies of most industrialized nations were heavily intertwined. Today, the economies are so connected that a fall in stock prices in Tokyo will have an instantaneous impact on the stock market in the United States.

As more and more countries start to look the same (independent, democratic, constitutional), their economies function in similar ways (stock market, low barriers to trade, strong banking system), and their cultures look the same (educated people who know English, cell phones in their hands, Hollywood movies playing at theaters), it can be strongly argued that there is a convergence of cultures.

On the other hand, globalization doesn't necessarily mean convergence; it just means that everything is spread all around the globe all the time. It doesn't mean that people accept, like, or want what's being hurled at them. It just means that it's available. Some argue that globalization will lead to an increase in the number of people who lash out against it, sometimes aggressively or violently. Globalization isn't well received in Islamic fundamentalist countries, or in countries that are trying hard to maintain a historical cultural identity, like France.

More significantly, it can't be denied that the biggest movements of the 20th century were rooted in self-determination and nationalism. The whole point of self-determination is for nations to chart their own course. If self-determination and nationalism mean that a country is going to use its independence to do what every other country does, then why be independent in the first place? Clearly, people want to chart their own course. They fought wars for the right to do so. They must have done so for a reason. So it makes sense that globalization will have its limits. Moreover, isn't the world a whole lot less consolidated today than it was under European imperialism, when that small continent ruled the world? Doesn't that suggest the opposite of global convergence?

In the end, there's no right answer to this question. The challenge is not to accurately predict the future, but to have an understanding of history to make a reasonable, defendable argument about the direction that history seems to be taking. If you can discuss globalization, nationalism, and self-determination in the same essay or conversation without totally losing your mind, you have command enough of the issues and complexities to be confident in yourself. Keep reading, keep studying, and keep thinking.

CHAPTER 9 KEY TERMS

Triple Alliance
Schlieffen Plan
Archduke Franz Ferdinand
Gavrilo Princip
Central Powers
isolationism
Zimmermann telegram
Treaty of Versailles
Fourteen Points
League of Nations
Russian Revolution
Czar Nicholas
Alexander Kerensky
Bolsheviks
Vladimir Lenin
April Theses
Treaty of Brest-Litovsk
Soviet Union
Red Army
Leon Trotsky
Mustafa Kemal
Ataturk
New Economic Policy (NEP)
Joseph Stalin
Five-Year Plans
collectivization
USSR (Union of Soviet Socialist Republics)
Great Depression
fascism
nationalism
Benito Mussolini
Blackshirts
Weimar Republic
National Socialist Party (Nazis)
Reichstag
Adolf Hitler
Third Reich
Francisco Franco
Rhineland
Munich Conference of 1938
Neville Chamberlain
appeasement
Nazi-Soviet Pact
Manchukuo
Anti-Comintern Pact

blitzkrieg
Winston Churchill
Battle of Britain
Tripartite Pact
Pearl Harbor
Manhattan Project
D-day
President Truman
Hiroshima
Nagasaki
Holocaust
Marshall Plan
United Nations (UN)
Universal Declaration of Human Rights
Yalta
Potsdam
Berlin Blockade
Berlin Airlift
Soviet bloc
Western bloc
Truman Doctrine
containment
NATO (the North Atlantic Treaty Organization)
Warsaw Pact
Iron Curtain
Bandung Conference
Non-Aligned Movement
Nuclear Nonproliferation Treaty
International Atomic Energy Agency or IAEA
Sun Yat-sen
Chinese Revolution of 1911
Three Principles of the People
Kuomintang (or KMT)
Chiang Kai-shek
Mao Zedong
Republic of China
People's Republic of China
Great Leap Forward
Cultural Revolution
Tiananmen Square massacre
General MacArthur
Indochina
Vietminh

Ho Chi Minh
Ngo Dinh Diem
Viet Cong
Khmer Rouge
Guerrilla warfare
Platt Amendment
Batista Dictatorship
Fidel Castro
Cuban Revolution
President Kennedy
Bay of Pigs Invasion
Cuban Missile Crisis
"Good Neighbor"
Sandinista
export economies
PAN
National Action Party
Lech Walesa
Tadeusz Mazowiecki
Mikhail Gorbachev
Margaret Thatcher
Ronald Reagan
"ethnic cleansing"
Chechnya
Federal
Boris Yeltsin
KGB
Vladimir Putin
Indian National Congress
Muslim League
Amritsar massacre
Mohandas Gandhi
passive resistance
Muhammad Ali Jinnah
Gamal Nasser
Algerians
Ghana
Kenya
Angola
Belgian Congo
Zimbabwe
African Union
Organization of African Unity (OAU)
Rwanda
Chad
Sudan

Uganda

Somalia

Democratic Republic of
    Congo

Tutsi

Hutu

South Africa Act

Union of South Africa

apartheid

Nelson Mandela

African National Congress

Sharpeville massacre

Zionists

Arthur Balfour

Balfour Declaration of 1917

pogroms

David Ben-Gurion

1948 Arab-Israeli War

West Bank

Six-Day War

Gaza Strip

Golan Heights

Prime Minister Menachem
    Begin

President Anwar Sadat

Camp David Accords

Palestine Liberation
    Organization (PLO)

Ariel Sharon

Yasser Arafat

Mahmoud Abbas

President Jimmy Carter

Iranian Revolution

Ayatollah ("Mirror of God")
    Khomeini

Ayatollah Khamenei

Mahmoud Ahmadinejad

OPEC (Organization of
    Petroleum Exporting
    Countries)

Saddam Hussein

Persian Gulf War

Jalal Talabani

Nouri al-Maliki

Nur Muhammad Taraki

Taliban

Osama bin Laden

Al Qaeda

September 11, 2001

World Trade Center

North American Free Trade
    Agreement (NAFTA)

European Union (EU)

European Union

Eurozone

special economic zones

GATT

Group of Six (G6)

G7

G8

G20

Chapter 9 Drill

See the end of the chapter for the answers and explanations.

Questions 1–4 refer to the passage below.

"At present, we are concerned with a question which has immense importance for the party now and for the future—with how the cult of the person of Stalin has been gradually growing, the cult which became at a certain specific stage the source of a whole series of exceedingly serious and grave perversions of party principles, of party democracy, of revolutionary legality…Stalin originated the concept of 'enemy of the people.' This term automatically rendered it unnecessary that the ideological errors of a man or men engaged in a controversy be proven; this term made possible the usage of the most cruel repression, violating all norms of revolutionary legality, against anyone who in any way disagreed with Stalin, against those who were only suspected of hostile intent, against those who had bad reputations."

Nikita Khrushchev, Special Report to the 20th Congress of the Communist Party of the Soviet Union, 1956

1. Which of the following most clearly describes the "cruel repression" referenced in the passage?

   (A) Economic discrimination and severe social pressures

   (B) Mob violence initiated and directed by state officials

   (C) Persecution through the use of secret police, summary execution, and work camps

   (D) Exile or deportation out of the country for periods up to twenty years

2. Which of the following best characterizes the impact of the document from which this passage is drawn?

   (A) It marked an important thaw in social and political tensions.

   (B) It marked the beginning of a purge of the Communist Party under Stalin.

   (C) It marked the beginning of the end for McCarthyism.

   (D) It marked the de-Stalinization of the Chinese Communist Party.

3. Based on the passage and your knowledge of world history, which of the following offers the most accurate contrast between Stalin's mode of rule and that of Khrushchev?

   (A) Stalin governed through fear, while Khrushchev relied on revolutionary zeal among the workers to bring about true communism.

   (B) While Khrushchev established a democratic system of policy deliberation in the Soviet Union, Stalin ruled as a tyrant without input from the Party or the people.

   (C) Khrushchev restored the Party to the center of Soviet government under the so-called Nomenklatura system, while Stalin sidelined the Party through a tyrannical cult of personality.

   (D) Both Stalin and Khrushchev relied primarily on repression and terror to carry out their policies.

4. Which of the following best characterizes the Cold War in the 1950s?

   (A) U.S. economic and technological advances had led to a decisive U.S. advantage in the Cold War.

   (B) Infighting between China, Yugoslavia, and the Soviet Union over leadership of the communist bloc paralyzed the Warsaw Pact.

   (C) Advances in Soviet rocket technology gave the Soviet Union a clear advantage over the United States.

   (D) A combination of technological, industrial, and diplomatic factors interacted to generate a situation in which two evenly matched political blocs struggled for advantage over the other.

Questions 5~8 refer to the passage below.

A consideration of the above shows that there are certain features which are essential in a system of trenches. They must be strong, to resist heavy bombardment; they must be sited and designed to favor, by the utilization of oblique and enfilade fire of rifles and, above all, of machine guns, the development of the maximum volume of fire over any part of their front; they must be protected by a strong and well-hidden wire entanglement, in order to retain attacking infantry under this fire; they must provide protection for the garrison against weather and the effect of artillery fire.... Finally, the system of trenches must admit of immediate readjustment of the front, so that the effect of penetration at any point may be localized and need not weaken the hold of the defense on adjacent trenches.

Notes For Infantry Officers on Trench Warfare, compiled by the British General Staff. 1917.

5. It's often said World War I changed warfare forever. The "machine guns" mentioned in the passage were part of a group of new military technologies that included all of the following EXCEPT

(A) tanks
(B) cannons
(C) poison gas
(D) warplanes

6. Which of the following was most directly responsible for the rapid expansion of a local conflict in the Balkans to a massive continental war?

(A) The complex system of entangling national alliances
(B) The assassination of Archduke Francis Ferdinand
(C) The long history of religious factionalism
(D) The imperialistic drive to conquer foreign territory

7. To supply their troops on the front lines with necessary resources, European national governments undertook which of the following steps?

(A) They outlawed dangerous mining practices.
(B) They released controls on the price of goods.
(C) They refused women the right to vote.
(D) They seized the means of industrial production.

8. In the years following the war, as a result of the efforts put forward by troops like those mentioned in the passage, all of the following changes occurred EXCEPT

(A) the collapse of the Russian, Ottoman, and Austro-Hungarian Empires
(B) the rise of independence movements in European colonies
(C) the economic recovery experienced by participants in the war
(D) the arrival of communism and the formation of the Soviet Union

Questions 9–11 refer to the passage below.

The Indians won freedom in 1947 largely without using violence against the British. They did not succeed, however, in winning it without fighting one another. As the prospect of independence loomed, Hindus and Muslims jockeyed for power in the India that was to be....

After World War II, especially, the deadlock between Hindus and Muslims brought riots and mounting bloodshed. The British yielded to the Muslim demand for a new separate state for Muslims, Pakistan. Nehru and the Congress Party reluctantly agreed.... Old India was partitioned at independence.

The sequel to partition was an uprooting on a fantastic scale as Hindus and Sikhs fled from Pakistan to India and Muslims fled from India to Pakistan.

Introduction to India, by Beatrice Lamb, 1960.

9. The most significant consequence of the situation described in the passage has been

(A) the falling literacy rates in India that restrict its economic potential

(B) the destabilization of the region due to the two states' territorial and religious rivalries

(C) the establishment of Urdu as the official language of both countries

(D) the creation of the Indian National Congress

10. The increase in the region's population, particularly in India, has been made possible largely by

(A) the NGOs that have brought new medical facilities across the region

(B) the British Empire's generous policies towards members of the British commonwealth

(C) the Green Revolution that has dramatically increased the global food supply

(D) the new spirit of atheism that has gripped the Indian subcontinent

11. In context, the situation described in the passage can be best understood when viewed against the mid-twentieth-century backdrop of

(A) the global consequences of industrialization

(B) the growth of land-based empires in Asia

(C) the decolonization of many Asian and African countries

(D) the arrival of nuclear weapons to both nations

TIMELINE OF MAJOR DEVELOPMENTS SINCE 1900

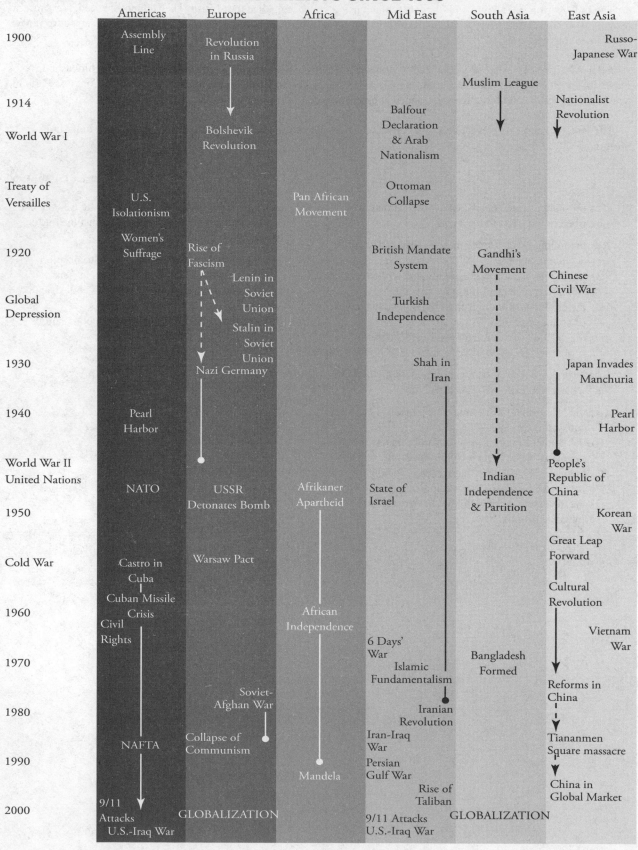

	Americas	Europe	Africa	Mid East	South Asia	East Asia
1900	Assembly Line	Revolution in Russia				Russo-Japanese War
1914				Balfour Declaration & Arab Nationalism	Muslim League	Nationalist Revolution
World War I		Bolshevik Revolution				
Treaty of Versailles	U.S. Isolationism		Pan African Movement	Ottoman Collapse		
1920	Women's Suffrage	Rise of Fascism		British Mandate System	Gandhi's Movement	Chinese Civil War
Global Depression		Lenin in Soviet Union		Turkish Independence		
		Stalin in Soviet Union				
1930		Nazi Germany		Shah in Iran		Japan Invades Manchuria
1940	Pearl Harbor					Pearl Harbor
World War II United Nations					Indian Independence & Partition	People's Republic of China
	NATO	USSR Detonates Bomb	Afrikaner Apartheid	State of Israel		
1950						Korean War
Cold War	Castro in Cuba	Warsaw Pact				Great Leap Forward
	Cuban Missile Crisis					Cultural Revolution
1960	Civil Rights		African Independence			Vietnam War
1970				6 Days' War	Bangladesh Formed	
				Islamic Fundamentalism		
1980		Soviet-Afghan War		Iranian Revolution		Reforms in China
	NAFTA			Iran-Iraq War		Tiananmen Square massacre
1990		Collapse of Communism		Persian Gulf War		
			Mandela	Rise of Taliban		China in Global Market
2000	9/11 Attacks U.S.-Iraq War	GLOBALIZATION		9/11 Attacks U.S.-Iraq War	GLOBALIZATION	

CHAPTER 9 DRILL EXPLANATIONS

1. **C** This question is essentially getting at a characterization of Stalinist repression. Use POE. Choice (A) is far too mild; this best describes the consequences suffered by those accused of Communist Party affiliations in the United States during the McCarthy era. Choice (B) does not match the legalism or the structure of Stalinism, being instead a good description of the repressive practices of Maoist China. Choice (D) does not accurately describe any repressive system used in any communist state in the first half of the 20th century, and thus is incorrect. Choice (C) does speak to the use of secret police as the main instrument of state repression, while also incorporating a description of the most common punishments: summary execution and sentencing to terms in the Gulag. Therefore, (C) is correct.

2. **A** Knowledge of important dates in Soviet history will help you here. This "Secret Speech," as it is known, took place in 1956, while Stalin died in 1953. Therefore, (B) cannot be correct, as Stalin had been dead three years before anyone in the Soviet Union summoned the courage to criticize him. Similarly, the Army-McCarthy hearings were in 1954, so McCarthyism was well on the decline before this speech was given; eliminate (C). Choice (D) is half-right: it did mark the beginnings of de-Stalinization, but only in the Soviet Union and its satellites. Stalin's legacy lasted much longer in Maoist China, and indeed Khrushchev's repudiation of Stalin was a driver of the Sino-Soviet split. Therefore, (A) is the best answer.

3. **C** For comparison questions, make sure both parts of the answer are correct. Look at (A), for example: while it is true that Stalin ruled by fear, Khrushchev did not return power to the workers and peasants of the Soviet Union. His government also relied on administrative repression and government action, though in a much different way; therefore, eliminate (A). Choice (B) is more difficult: although it is true that Khrushchev restored a measure of deliberative authority to Party bodies, governance did not become democratic; instead, it became oligarchic, so (B) is incorrect. Choice (D) mischaracterizes Khrushchev's government in the other direction: although the Soviet Union remained authoritarian, the atmosphere of terror that Stalin used to implement policy was dismantled under Khrushchev. Choice (C) accurately characterizes both the shift to an oligarchic system centered around the Party (the Nomenklatura system) and the tyrannical character of Stalin's cult of personality, so (C) is the correct answer.

4. **D** Choice (A) describes the Brezhnev era, which began much later in the Cold War. Choice (B) mischaracterizes the import of the lack of unity in the communist bloc: though Yugoslavia did break away, it was a minor state and, broadly speaking, this did not affect the Cold War. The Sino-Soviet split was more momentous but also came later (1961). Choice (C) may sound plausible due to Sputnik and related developments, but this was a public-relations measure rather than one that substantially shifted the balance of power in the Cold War one way or the other. Choice (D) best conveys the stalemate of the early Cold War, and is thus the correct answer.

5. **B** Cannons had been used for centuries in European warfare, dating back to the early Renaissance. They'd been used even earlier by the Ottomans, and were invented in the thirteenth century by the Song Dynasty in China. Choices (A), (C), and (D) all represent inventions of the late nineteenth or very early twentieth centuries, and all made their first appearance during World War I. Add other new arrivals such as machine guns, railways, submarines, and the telegraph, and you may start to understand why historians often view World War I as the single biggest turning point in the history of warfare.

6. **A** What should've been a small assassination of a local archduke escalated into a global conflict due a series of alliances that had been signed or agreed upon over the previous years. On one side: the German Empire and Austria-Hungary. On the other side: Russian Empire, France, and British Empire (only later did the United States join). The assassination of Archduke Ferdinand was the ignition, not the spread, so eliminate (B). Religious factionalism was irrelevant, so eliminate (C). While Europeans had just come out of the imperialistic era, it wasn't responsible for the system of alliances that provoked the long chain reaction.

7. **D** Across Europe, governments took control of the means of production, directing what the factories should produce, and thereby shifting their societies towards what was called "total war." No longer was warfare something distant from the population, performed by a small group of paid soldiers; the sheer size of WWI meant that the entire society had to reorient itself around the needs of the front lines. The other choices are all reversals. Dangerous mining practices were not outlawed— more resources than ever were needed for the war effort. Price controls were instituted, and women earned the right to vote shortly after the war concluded. Eliminated (A), (B), and (C).

8. **C** World War I damaged three major empires, irrevocably, so eliminate choice (A). Given the colonial powers' preoccupation with war on their own soil, independence movements in faraway European colonies such as India began to form; eliminate (B). Russia exited the war early in order to deal with its own internal eruptions, which transformed into the Bolshevik revolution and the creation of the Soviet Union, so eliminate (D). The correct answer, (C), ignores the economic struggles that Germany suffered in the decade following the war as it attempted to pay back reparations as demanded by the Treaty of Paris.

9. **B** Time has passed since the partition of the region, as described in the passage, but the rivalry between the two nations hasn't ended. India and Pakistan have been disputing the Kashmir region since 1947, and the conflict between Islam and Hindu beliefs continues to play a strong role in the unease. Literacy rates actually rose in each country after partition, so eliminate (A). Urdu is the official language of only Pakistan, so eliminate (C). The Indian National Congress was created in 1885, so eliminate (D).

10. **C** Through technological innovation, the Green Revolution brought hardier strains of rice and wheat to India. With a more reliable food supply, the population began to greatly increase. The NGOs (non-governmental organizations) have been active in India, but they certainly haven't been able to bring good medical care to the population (far from it!), so eliminate (A). The British Empire's policies towards members of its commonwealth may or may not be generous, but they certainly can't explain the explosion in population, so eliminate (B). Finally, there is no "spirit of atheism" in the region; India is the most religious country in the world, as measured in many ways, so eliminate (D).

11. **C** The era of the 1940s and 1950s saw a large number of colonies declare their independence from European powers: no less than 36, ranging from Singapore to Tanzania. In some areas the process was peaceful and orderly; in others, it was violent and chaotic. These movements represented the waning of Europe as the most powerful global power. In its place arose the Cold War between the two new superpowers: the U.S. and the Soviet Union. Choices (A) and (B) describe eras that occurred long before decolonization, so eliminate both. Choice (D) describes the arrival of nuclear weapons to Pakistan and India, but that didn't occur until the 1970s, so eliminate it.

Part VI
Additional
Practice Tests

Practice Test 2

Completely darken bubbles with a No. 2 pencil. If you make a mistake, be sure to erase mark completely. Erase all stray marks.

1.

YOUR NAME:
(Print)   Last   First   M.I.

SIGNATURE: _____   DATE: __ / __ / __

HOME ADDRESS: _____
(Print)   Number and Street

_____
City   State   Zip Code

PHONE NO.: _____

IMPORTANT: Please fill in these boxes exactly as shown on the back cover of your test book.

2. TEST FORM

_____

6. DATE OF BIRTH

Month		Day		Year	
○ JAN					
○ FEB	⓪	⓪	⓪	⓪	
○ MAR	①	①	①	①	
○ APR	②	②	②	②	
○ MAY	③	③	③	③	
○ JUN		④	④	④	
○ JUL		⑤	⑤	⑤	
○ AUG		⑥	⑥	⑥	
○ SEP		⑦	⑦	⑦	
○ OCT		⑧	⑧	⑧	
○ NOV		⑨	⑨	⑨	
○ DEC					

3. TEST CODE   **4. REGISTRATION NUMBER**

⓪	Ⓐ	Ⓙ	⓪	⓪	⓪	⓪	⓪	⓪	⓪	⓪
①	Ⓑ	Ⓚ	①	①	①	①	①	①	①	①
②	Ⓒ	Ⓛ	②	②	②	②	②	②	②	②
③	Ⓓ	Ⓜ	③	③	③	③	③	③	③	③
④	Ⓔ	Ⓝ	④	④	④	④	④	④	④	④
⑤	Ⓕ	Ⓞ	⑤	⑤	⑤	⑤	⑤	⑤	⑤	⑤
⑥	Ⓖ	Ⓟ	⑥	⑥	⑥	⑥	⑥	⑥	⑥	⑥
⑦	Ⓗ	Ⓠ	⑦	⑦	⑦	⑦	⑦	⑦	⑦	⑦
⑧	Ⓘ	Ⓡ	⑧	⑧	⑧	⑧	⑧	⑧	⑧	⑧
⑨			⑨	⑨	⑨	⑨	⑨	⑨	⑨	⑨

7. GENDER

○ MALE
○ FEMALE

The **Princeton** Review®

5. YOUR NAME

First 4 letters of last name				FIRST INIT	MID INIT
Ⓐ	Ⓐ	Ⓐ	Ⓐ	Ⓐ	Ⓐ
Ⓑ	Ⓑ	Ⓑ	Ⓑ	Ⓑ	Ⓑ
Ⓒ	Ⓒ	Ⓒ	Ⓒ	Ⓒ	Ⓒ
Ⓓ	Ⓓ	Ⓓ	Ⓓ	Ⓓ	Ⓓ
Ⓔ	Ⓔ	Ⓔ	Ⓔ	Ⓔ	Ⓔ
Ⓕ	Ⓕ	Ⓕ	Ⓕ	Ⓕ	Ⓕ
Ⓖ	Ⓖ	Ⓖ	Ⓖ	Ⓖ	Ⓖ
Ⓗ	Ⓗ	Ⓗ	Ⓗ	Ⓗ	Ⓗ
Ⓘ	Ⓘ	Ⓘ	Ⓘ	Ⓘ	Ⓘ
Ⓙ	Ⓙ	Ⓙ	Ⓙ	Ⓙ	Ⓙ
Ⓚ	Ⓚ	Ⓚ	Ⓚ	Ⓚ	Ⓚ
Ⓛ	Ⓛ	Ⓛ	Ⓛ	Ⓛ	Ⓛ
Ⓜ	Ⓜ	Ⓜ	Ⓜ	Ⓜ	Ⓜ
Ⓝ	Ⓝ	Ⓝ	Ⓝ	Ⓝ	Ⓝ
Ⓞ	Ⓞ	Ⓞ	Ⓞ	Ⓞ	Ⓞ
Ⓟ	Ⓟ	Ⓟ	Ⓟ	Ⓟ	Ⓟ
Ⓠ	Ⓠ	Ⓠ	Ⓠ	Ⓠ	Ⓠ
Ⓡ	Ⓡ	Ⓡ	Ⓡ	Ⓡ	Ⓡ
Ⓢ	Ⓢ	Ⓢ	Ⓢ	Ⓢ	Ⓢ
Ⓣ	Ⓣ	Ⓣ	Ⓣ	Ⓣ	Ⓣ
Ⓤ	Ⓤ	Ⓤ	Ⓤ	Ⓤ	Ⓤ
Ⓥ	Ⓥ	Ⓥ	Ⓥ	Ⓥ	Ⓥ
Ⓦ	Ⓦ	Ⓦ	Ⓦ	Ⓦ	Ⓦ
Ⓧ	Ⓧ	Ⓧ	Ⓧ	Ⓧ	Ⓧ
Ⓨ	Ⓨ	Ⓨ	Ⓨ	Ⓨ	Ⓨ
Ⓩ	Ⓩ	Ⓩ	Ⓩ	Ⓩ	Ⓩ

1. Ⓐ Ⓑ Ⓒ Ⓓ
2. Ⓐ Ⓑ Ⓒ Ⓓ
3. Ⓐ Ⓑ Ⓒ Ⓓ
4. Ⓐ Ⓑ Ⓒ Ⓓ
5. Ⓐ Ⓑ Ⓒ Ⓓ
6. Ⓐ Ⓑ Ⓒ Ⓓ
7. Ⓐ Ⓑ Ⓒ Ⓓ
8. Ⓐ Ⓑ Ⓒ Ⓓ
9. Ⓐ Ⓑ Ⓒ Ⓓ
10. Ⓐ Ⓑ Ⓒ Ⓓ
11. Ⓐ Ⓑ Ⓒ Ⓓ
12. Ⓐ Ⓑ Ⓒ Ⓓ
13. Ⓐ Ⓑ Ⓒ Ⓓ
14. Ⓐ Ⓑ Ⓒ Ⓓ
15. Ⓐ Ⓑ Ⓒ Ⓓ
16. Ⓐ Ⓑ Ⓒ Ⓓ
17. Ⓐ Ⓑ Ⓒ Ⓓ
18. Ⓐ Ⓑ Ⓒ Ⓓ

19. Ⓐ Ⓑ Ⓒ Ⓓ
20. Ⓐ Ⓑ Ⓒ Ⓓ
21. Ⓐ Ⓑ Ⓒ Ⓓ
22. Ⓐ Ⓑ Ⓒ Ⓓ
23. Ⓐ Ⓑ Ⓒ Ⓓ
24. Ⓐ Ⓑ Ⓒ Ⓓ
25. Ⓐ Ⓑ Ⓒ Ⓓ
26. Ⓐ Ⓑ Ⓒ Ⓓ
27. Ⓐ Ⓑ Ⓒ Ⓓ
28. Ⓐ Ⓑ Ⓒ Ⓓ
29. Ⓐ Ⓑ Ⓒ Ⓓ
30. Ⓐ Ⓑ Ⓒ Ⓓ
31. Ⓐ Ⓑ Ⓒ Ⓓ
32. Ⓐ Ⓑ Ⓒ Ⓓ
33. Ⓐ Ⓑ Ⓒ Ⓓ
34. Ⓐ Ⓑ Ⓒ Ⓓ
35. Ⓐ Ⓑ Ⓒ Ⓓ
36. Ⓐ Ⓑ Ⓒ Ⓓ

37. Ⓐ Ⓑ Ⓒ Ⓓ
38. Ⓐ Ⓑ Ⓒ Ⓓ
39. Ⓐ Ⓑ Ⓒ Ⓓ
40. Ⓐ Ⓑ Ⓒ Ⓓ
41. Ⓐ Ⓑ Ⓒ Ⓓ
42. Ⓐ Ⓑ Ⓒ Ⓓ
43. Ⓐ Ⓑ Ⓒ Ⓓ
44. Ⓐ Ⓑ Ⓒ Ⓓ
45. Ⓐ Ⓑ Ⓒ Ⓓ
46. Ⓐ Ⓑ Ⓒ Ⓓ
47. Ⓐ Ⓑ Ⓒ Ⓓ
48. Ⓐ Ⓑ Ⓒ Ⓓ
49. Ⓐ Ⓑ Ⓒ Ⓓ
50. Ⓐ Ⓑ Ⓒ Ⓓ
51. Ⓐ Ⓑ Ⓒ Ⓓ
52. Ⓐ Ⓑ Ⓒ Ⓓ
53. Ⓐ Ⓑ Ⓒ Ⓓ
54. Ⓐ Ⓑ Ⓒ Ⓓ

55. Ⓐ Ⓑ Ⓒ Ⓓ

AP® World History: Modern Exam

DO NOT OPEN THIS BOOKLET UNTIL YOU ARE TOLD TO DO SO.

At a Glance

Time
55 minutes
Number of Questions
55
Percent of Total Score
40%
Writing Instrument
Pencil required

Instructions

Section I, Part A of this exam contains 55 multiple-choice questions. Fill in only the ovals for numbers 1 through 55 on your answer sheet.

Indicate all of your answers to the multiple-choice questions on the answer sheet. No credit will be given for anything written in this exam booklet, but you may use the booklet for notes or scratch work. After you have decided which of the suggested answers is best, completely fill in the corresponding oval on the answer sheet. Give only one answer to each question. If you change an answer, be sure that the previous mark is erased completely. Here is a sample question and answer.

Sample Question

Chicago is a
(A) state
(B) city
(C) country
(D) continent

Sample Answer

Ⓐ ● Ⓒ Ⓓ

Use your time effectively, working as quickly as you can without losing accuracy. Do not spend too much time on any one question. Go on to other questions and come back to the ones you have not answered if you have time. It is not expected that everyone will know the answers to all the multiple-choice questions.

Your total score on the multiple-choice section is based only on the number of questions answered correctly. Points are not deducted for incorrect answers or unanswered questions.

At a Glance

Time
40 minutes
Number of Questions
3
Percent of Total Score
20%
Writing Instrument
Pen with black or dark blue ink

Instructions

Section I, Part B of this exam consists of 4 short-answer questions, of which you will answer 3. Answer all parts of Questions 1 and 2, and then choose to answer EITHER Question 3 or Question 4. Write your responses on a separate sheet of paper.

After the exam, you must apply the label that corresponds to the last short-essay question you answered—Question 3 or 4. For example, if you answered Question 3, apply the label ③ . Failure to do so may delay your score.

WORLD HISTORY: MODERN

Section I, Part A

Time—55 minutes

55 Questions

Directions: Each of the questions or incomplete statements below is followed by either four suggested answers or completions. Select the one that is best in each case and then fill in the appropriate letter in the corresponding space on the answer sheet.

Questions 1–3 refer to the passage below.

The study of literature and the practice of the military arts, including archery and horsemanship, must be cultivated diligently. "On the left hand literature, on the right hand use of arms," was the rule of the ancients. Both must be pursued concurrently. Archery and horsemanship are essential skills for military men. It is said that war is a curse. However, it is resorted to only when it is inevitable. In time of peace, do not forget the possibility of disturbances. Train yourself and be prepared.

The Edicts of the Tokugawa Shogunate: Excerpts from *Laws of Military Households* (Buke Shohatto), 1615

1. The excerpt above suggests that the military must adhere to which of the following characteristics?

   (A) Aggression
   (B) Piety
   (C) Brutality
   (D) Restraint

2. Instructions for military households can best be seen as evidence of which of the following characteristics of the Tokugawa period?

   (A) Strict social classes
   (B) Increased power to feudal lords
   (C) An openness to Western influence
   (D) Widespread allegiance to an emperor

3. The Tokugawa Shogunate focused primarily on which of the following?

   (A) Rapid industrialization
   (B) Eliminating foreign influence on Japan
   (C) Military conquest and expansion
   (D) Erasing the legacy of the shogun from Japanese culture

GO ON TO THE NEXT PAGE.

Questions 4–6 refer to the image below.

Thomas Jones Barker's *The Secret of England's Greatness*, 1863

This painting portrays Queen Victoria offering a bible to an African chief.

4. The painting suggests which of the following about England?

   (A) Victorian culture was intolerant of other religions.
   (B) The English crown justified imperialism on a moral basis.
   (C) England had little interest in the Berlin Conference.
   (D) The British economy relied upon the African slave trade.

5. Queen Victoria's reign can best be characterized by which of the following?

   (A) A drastic loss of imperial gains
   (B) Economic stagnation following the end of the Industrial Revolution
   (C) Liberal reform and decreasing power of the monarchy
   (D) Colonial expansion in Africa and a decreased presence in Asia

6. The painting most clearly reflects the concept of

   (A) Social Darwinism
   (B) Open Door Policy
   (C) "White Man's Burden"
   (D) mercantilism

GO ON TO THE NEXT PAGE.

Questions 7–10 refer to the passage below.

"As for the city of Karacorum I can tell you that, not counting the [Khan's] palace, it is not as large as the village of Saint Denis, and the monastery of Saint Denis is worth ten times more than that palace. There are two districts there: the Saracens' [Muslims] quarter where the markets are.... The other district is that of the Cathayans [Chinese] who are all craftsmen.

Apart from these districts there are the large temples of the court scribes. There are twelve pagan [Buddhist] temples belonging to the different nations, two mosques in which the law of Mihamet [Muhammad] is proclaimed, and one church surrounded by a mud wall and has four gates. At the east gate are sold millet and other grain, which is however seldom bought there; at the west sheep and goats are sold; at the south oxen and carts; at the north, horses."

Friar William of *Rubruck's The Journey of William of Rubrick* (1254)

7. Which of the following best characterizes the group governing the city of Karacorum?

(A) Mongols
(B) Muslims
(C) Chinese
(D) Christians

8. From the information given in the excerpt, which of the following best describes a policy of this city?

(A) Persecution of minority groups
(B) Command economy
(C) Heavy taxation
(D) Religious tolerance

9. The passage can best be described as which of the following?

(A) A historian documenting the structure of a government system
(B) A religious leader describing the diversity of his city
(C) An outsider reporting on his observation of a foreign city
(D) A government official criticizing an ongoing practice in a local district

10. The khans achieved most of their territory gains through which of the following methods?

(A) Economic influence
(B) Militarization
(C) Agricultural innovation
(D) Diplomacy

GO ON TO THE NEXT PAGE.

Questions 11–12 refer to the passage below.

"Upon their arrival they were honorably and graciously received by the grand Khan, in a full assembly of his principal officers. When they drew nigh to his person, they paid their respects by prostrating themselves on the floor. He immediately commanded them to rise, and to relate to him the circumstances of their travels, with all that had taken place in their negotiation with his holiness the pope. To their narrative, which they gave in the regular order of events, and delivered in perspicuous language, he listened with attentive silence. The letters and the presents from Pope Gregory were then laid before him, and, upon hearing the former read, he bestowed much commendation on the fidelity, the zeal, and the diligence of his ambassadors; and receiving with due reverence the oil from the holy sepulchre, he gave directions that it should be preserved with religious care. Upon his observing Marco Polo, and inquiring who he was, Nicolo made answer, This is your servant, and my son; upon which the grand Khan replied, "He is welcome, and it pleases me much," and he caused him to be enrolled amongst his attendants of honor. And on account of their return he made a great feast and rejoicing; and as long as the said brothers and Marco remained in the court of the grand Khan, they were honored even above his own courtiers. Marco was held in high estimation and respect by all belonging to the court. He learnt in a short time and adopted the manners of the Tartars, and acquired a proficiency in four different languages, which he became qualified to read and write."

Marco Polo's Travels, circa 1300 C.E.

11. The encounter described in the account above illustrates which of the following?

(A) The economic dominance of the Ottoman Empire

(B) The influence of Middle Eastern religious beliefs on the peoples of South Asia

(C) The lack of cooperation among major political groups in the High Middle Ages

(D) Amiable cultural exchange between Europe and Asia

12. Which of the following best characterizes one way in which the Mongol Empire was very different from the other major empires of the ancient and medieval worlds?

(A) The Mongols generally ignored or assimilated to the cultural identities of the people whom they conquered.

(B) The Mongols often took over territory without major destruction or bloodshed.

(C) The Mongols imposed their religious beliefs on the people whom they conquered.

(D) The Mongols had little interest in trading with their geographic neighbors.

GO ON TO THE NEXT PAGE.

Questions 13–15 refer to the image and passage below.

<u>Source 1</u>

Diagram of a Slave Ship from The Transatlantic Slave Trade, circa 1790

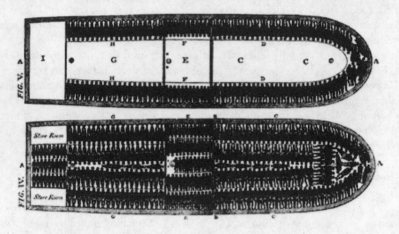

<u>Source 2</u>

"Are you *a man?* Then you should have an *human* heart. But have you indeed? What is your heart made of? Is there no such principle as compassion there? Do you never *feel* another's pain? Have you no sympathy? No sense of human woe? No pity for the miserable? When you saw the flowing eyes, the heaving breasts, the bleeding sides and tortured limbs of your fellow-creatures, was you a stone, or a brute? Did you look upon them with the eyes of a tiger? When you squeezed the agonizing creatures down in the ship, or when you threw their poor mangled remains into the sea, had you no relenting? Did not one tear drop from your eye, one sigh escape from your breast? Do you feel no relenting *now?* If you do not, you must go on, till the measure of your iniquities is full. Then will the great GOD deal with *you,* as you have dealt with *them,* and require all their blood at your hands."

Excerpt courtesy of the Rare Book Collection, Wilson Special Collections Library, UNC-Chapel Hill.

John Wesley, *Thoughts Upon Slavery,* 1774

13. The sentiment exhibited in <u>Source 2</u> reflects the concerns of which of the following groups?

    (A) The Puritans
    (B) The Freemasons
    (C) The Evangelicals
    (D) The Mormons

14. Which of the following most accurately depicts the historical context of the movements of goods and people during the centuries of transatlantic trade?

    (A) Enslaved people to the Americas; cotton, sugar, and tobacco to Europe; textiles, rum, and raw goods to Africa
    (B) Enslaved people to Africa; cotton, sugar, and tobacco to Europe; textiles, rum, and raw goods to the Americas
    (C) Cotton, sugar, and tobacco to the Americas; enslaved people to Europe; textiles, rum, and raw goods to Africa
    (D) Enslaved people to the Americas; cotton, sugar, and tobacco to Africa; textiles, rum, and raw goods to Europe

GO ON TO THE NEXT PAGE.

15. Which of the following correctly characterizes one consequence of the layout of transatlantic slave ships, as shown in <u>Source 1</u>?

(A) Many enslaved people died of disease in the crowded hulls of tightly packed ships.

(B) Slave ships often sank due to overcrowding and imbalanced weight allotment.

(C) Enslaved people were forced to assist in the rowing of the slave ships.

(D) Slave ships carried approximately equal numbers of enslaved people as crewmembers.

GO ON TO THE NEXT PAGE.

Questions 16–18 refer to the map and passage below.

<u>Source 1</u>

Map of European Colonies in Africa, early twentieth century

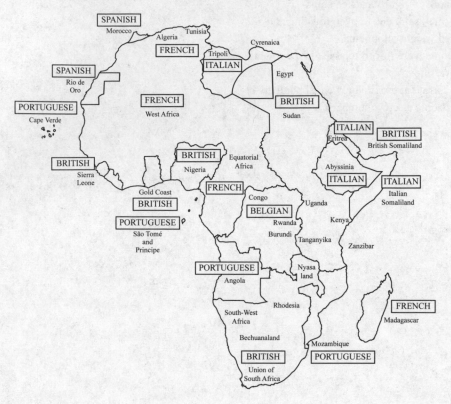

<u>Source 2</u>

"I repeat, that the superior races have a right because they have a duty. They have the duty to civilize the inferior races....In the history of earlier centuries these duties, gentlemen, have often been misunderstood; and certainly when the Spanish soldiers and explorers introduced slavery into Central America, they did not fulfill their duty as men of a higher race....But, in our time, I maintain that European nations acquit themselves with generosity, with grandeur, and with sincerity of this superior civilizing duty.

I say that French colonial policy, the policy of colonial expansion, the policy that has taken us under the Empire [the Second Empire, of Napoleon], to Saigon, to Indochina [Vietnam], that has led us to Tunisia, to Madagascar—I say that this policy of colonial expansion was inspired by...the fact that a navy such as ours cannot do without safe harbors, defenses, supply centers on the high seas....Are you unaware of this? Look at a map of the world."

Reprinted with permission of the Brooklyn College Department of History.

Jules Ferry, *On French Colonial Expansion*, 1884

GO ON TO THE NEXT PAGE.

16. The boundary lines on the map (Source 1) reflect which of the following?

    (A) Natural barriers such as rivers and mountain ranges
    (B) Traditional tribal divisions within African societies
    (C) Linguistic differences
    (D) European economic and political concerns

17. The references in <u>Source 2</u> to "superior races" and "inferior races" reflect which of the following attitudes?

    (A) The idea that the colonization of Africa would be profitable for European nations
    (B) The idea that European navies needed use of African ports
    (C) The idea that African peoples would benefit from European cultural influence
    (D) The idea that Africans and Europeans would have mutually beneficial cultural exchanges

18. Which of the following describes a negative short-term effect of the European colonization of Africa?

    (A) Famines occurred when African farmers were forced to grow crops for export.
    (B) Europeans built infrastructure such as roads and railways in the lands that they colonized.
    (C) Missionaries from Europe built schools for native populations.
    (D) Africa experienced a general improvement in medical care under European rule.

GO ON TO THE NEXT PAGE.

Questions 19–20 refer to the passage below.

"IN ORDER, most potent Sire, to convey to your Majesty a just conception of the great extent of this noble city of Temixtitlan, and of the many rare and wonderful objects it contains; of the government and dominions of Moctezuma, the sovereign: of the religious rights and customs that prevail, and the order that exists in this as well as the other cities appertaining to his realm: it would require the labor of many accomplished writers, and much time for the completion of the task. I shall not be able to relate an hundredth part of what could be told respecting these matters; but I will endeavor to describe, in the best manner in my power, what I have myself seen; and imperfectly as I may succeed in the attempt, I am fully aware that the account will appear so wonderful as to be deemed scarcely worthy of credit; since even we who have seen these things with our own eyes, are yet so amazed as to be unable to comprehend their reality."

[Thatcher, Oliver Joseph. The Ideas that have Influenced Civilization, in the Original Documents. Vol. 5. Milwaukee: The Roberts-Manchester Publishing Co., 1901. "Hernando Cortés: Letter Describing Mexico (1520)." *World History: The Modern Era,* ABC-CLIO, 2019, worldhistory.abc-clio.com/Search/Display/354563. Accessed 2 Apr. 2019.]

Hernando Cortés's letter to King Charles V of Spain (1520)

19. Which of the following best characterizes the activities that Cortés references in his letter?

(A) Peace building with neighboring tribes

(B) Communal ownership of all property

(C) Exclusion of women from economic life

(D) Expansionist policies

20. Cortés most likely followed up this excerpt with a description of which of the following findings?

(A) Aztec labor practices

(B) Religious diversity

(C) Majestic geography

(D) The presence of gold

GO ON TO THE NEXT PAGE.

Questions 21–24 refer to the image and passage below.

<u>Source 1</u>

Reconstruction of the Aztec Great Temple of Tenochtitlan, from 14th to early 16th century

<u>Source 2</u>

"This great city contains a large number of temples, or houses, for their idols, very handsome edifices, which are situated in the different districts and the suburbs; in the principal ones religious persons of each particular sect are constantly residing, for whose use, besides the houses containing the idols, there are other convenient habitations. All these persons dress in black, and never cut or comb their hair from the time they enter the priesthood until they leave it; and all the sons of the principal inhabitants, both nobles and respectable citizens, are placed in the temples and wear the same dress from the age of seven or eight years until they are taken out to be married; which occurs more frequently with the first-born who inherit estates than with the others. The priests are debarred from female society, nor is any woman permitted to enter the religious houses. They also abstain from eating certain kinds of food, more at some seasons of the year than others.

Among these temples there is one which far surpasses all the rest, whose grandeur of architectural details no human tongue is able to describe; for within its precincts, surrounded by a lofty wall, there is room enough for a town of five hundred families. Around the interior of the enclosure there are handsome edifices, containing large halls and corridors, in which the religious persons attached to the temple reside. There are fully forty towers, which are lofty and well built, the largest of which has fifty steps leading to its main body, and is higher than the tower of the principal tower of the church at Seville. The stone and wood of which they are constructed are so well wrought in every part, that nothing could be better done, for the interior of the chapels containing the idols consists of curious imagery, wrought in stone, with plaster ceilings, and wood-work carved in relief, and painted with figures of monsters and other objects. All these towers are the burial places of the nobles, and every chapel in them is dedicated to a particular idol, to which they pay their devotions."

Hernando Cortés, *Second Letter to Charles V*, circa 1520

GO ON TO THE NEXT PAGE.

21. Which of the following was an Aztec practice that took place at temples, such as that depicted in Source 1, and highly disturbed the Spanish conquistadors?

    (A) Human sacrifice
    (B) Grain storage
    (C) Burial rites
    (D) Trade and commerce

22. Which of the following describes the primary motivation of the Spanish conquest of the Aztec empire?

    (A) A desire to convert native populations to European cultural practices
    (B) A desire to establish trade networks in South America
    (C) A desire to establish permanent agricultural lands
    (D) A desire to acquire gold and spices

23. The description of Tenochtitlan's temples in Source 2 indicates that which of the following was true of Aztec society in the sixteenth century?

    (A) It was outward-focused and relied upon networks of ocean trade.
    (B) It was highly complex and contained large numbers of skilled artisans.
    (C) It was egalitarian in its treatment of women.
    (D) It had largely peaceful relations with neighboring civilizations.

24. Cortés's numerous references to "idols" in Source 2 illustrates which of the following conflicts between the Spanish conquistadors and the peoples of the New World?

    (A) Spanish monotheism versus Aztec polytheism
    (B) Spanish capitalism versus Aztec communalism
    (C) Spanish authoritarianism versus Aztec ethnocentrism
    (D) Spanish hedonism versus Aztec intellectualism

GO ON TO THE NEXT PAGE.

Questions 25–29 refer to the two charts below.

Coal Production in Japan from 1875–1905

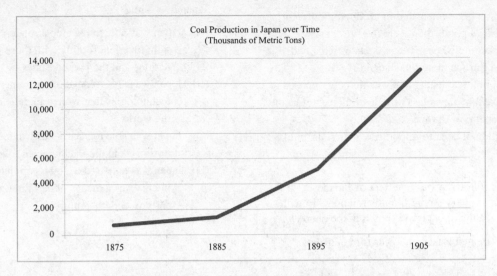

Coal Production in Japan over Time
(Thousands of Metric Tons)

Steamship Production in Japan from 1873–1905

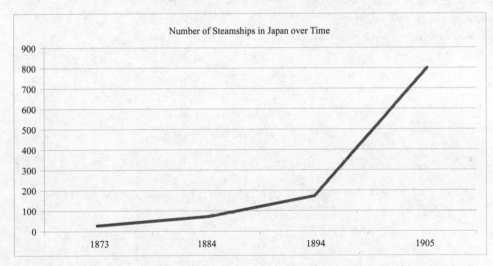

Number of Steamships in Japan over Time

25. Which of the following political eras in Japan best contextualizes the dramatic increases shown in the charts above?

(A) The Tokugawa Shogunate

(B) The Heian Era

(C) The Meiji Restoration

(D) The Showa Era

26. As an effect of the increased industrialization shown in the charts above, which of the following occurred in Japan in the late nineteenth century?

(A) The increased aggression of Japan toward the United States

(B) The weakening of Japanese imperial traditions

(C) The decrease in cultural creativity

(D) The abolition of the samurai warrior class

GO ON TO THE NEXT PAGE.

27. Based on the charts and your knowledge of world history, how was industrialization in Japan different from industrialization in Europe?

    (A) Japan was more interested in producing different industrial goods than were the Europeans.
    (B) Japan accomplished in a few decades what had taken Europe more than a century.
    (C) Japan's political leadership was fiercely opposed to the wealthy new class of industrialists, unlike the leadership in Europe.
    (D) Japan did not need to import raw materials, unlike Europe.

28. Which of the following was an effect of Japanese industrial and military strength on its relationship with its neighbors in the time period shown in the charts?

    (A) Japan defeated Russia in a war for control of Siberia.
    (B) Japan defeated China in a war for control of Korea.
    (C) Japan defeated France in a war for control of Indochina.
    (D) Japan defeated Britain in a war for control over Burma.

29. Which of the following was a long-term effect of the rapid growth of Japanese shipbuilding capability illustrated in the second chart ("Number of Steamships in Japan over Time")?

    (A) Japan was able to develop a modern navy that could fight on equal footing with those of European nations and the United States.
    (B) Japan was able to develop many new naval technologies that were unparalleled elsewhere in the world.
    (C) Japan was able to successfully defend German territories in the Pacific during World War I.
    (D) Japan was able to develop its civilian maritime interests as a means of demilitarization in the early twentieth century.

GO ON TO THE NEXT PAGE.

Questions 30–31 refer to the two passages below.

<u>Source 1</u>

"In the days of a great struggle against a foreign enemy who has been endeavoring for three years to enslave our country, it pleased God to send Russia a further painful trial. Internal troubles threatened to have a fatal effect on the further progress of this obstinate war. The destinies of Russia, the honor of her heroic Army, the happiness of the people, and the whole future of our beloved country demand that the war should be conducted at all costs to a victorious end.

The cruel enemy is making his last efforts and the moment is near when our valiant Army, in concert with our glorious Allies, will finally overthrow the enemy. In these decisive days in the life of Russia we have thought that we owed to our people the close union and organization of all its forces for the realization of a rapid victory; for which reason, in agreement with the Imperial Duma, we have recognized that it is for the good of the country that we should abdicate the Crown of the Russian State and lay down the Supreme Power."

Tsar Nicholas II, *Abdication*, March 15, 1917

<u>Source 2</u>

"History will not forgive revolutionaries for procrastinating when they could be victorious today (and they certainly will be victorious today), while they risk losing much tomorrow, in fact, they risk losing everything.

If we seize power today, we seize it not in opposition to the Soviets but on their behalf. The seizure of power is the business of the uprising; its political purpose will become clear after the seizure....

It would be an infinite crime on the part of the revolutionaries were they to let the chance slip, knowing that the salvation of the revolution, the offer of peace, the salvation of Petrograd, salvation from famine, the transfer of the land to the peasants depend upon them.

The government is tottering. It must be given the death-blow at all costs."

Vladimir Illyich Lenin, *Call to Power*, October 24, 1917

30. Czar Nicholas II's declaration of abdication in <u>Source 1</u> is best understood in light of which of the following?

   (A) Economic prosperity that fostered dislike of the aristocracy
   (B) Widespread dislike of Nicholas's tolerance of political dissidents
   (C) Large-scale military losses and resentment of the working classes
   (D) Persecution of religious minorities

31. What was the principal philosophical underpinning of Lenin's call to power in <u>Source 2</u>?

   (A) Capitalism
   (B) Mercantilism
   (C) Fascism
   (D) Marxism

GO ON TO THE NEXT PAGE.

Questions 32–33 refer to the image below.

Burning of the Plaine du Cap, 1791

This image depicts a rebellion in Haiti.

32. Which of the following events represents the historical context for the rebellion pictured above?

(A) The French Revolution

(B) The Congress of Vienna

(C) The Seven Years' War

(D) The Bourbon Restoration

33. Haiti's independence grew out of which of the following?

(A) A constitutional convention

(B) Internal conflicts among the various cultural groups

(C) A series of slave revolts

(D) An uprising against Jean-Jacques Dessalines

GO ON TO THE NEXT PAGE.

Questions 34–36 refer to the map below.

Trade Map of Africa, circa 15th century

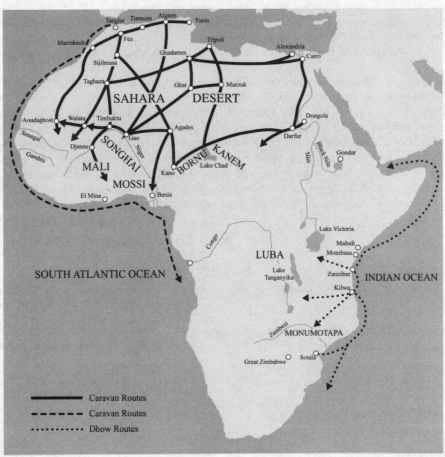

34. Who were the primary groups traversing the Sahara Desert to reach West Africa along the trade routes shown on the map?

    (A) Islamic traders
    (B) European traders
    (C) Chinese traders
    (D) Mongol traders

35. What was one significant effect of the Indian Ocean trade shown on the east side of the map?

    (A) The emigration of large numbers of Africans to southern Asia
    (B) The development of the Swahili language
    (C) The conversion of most of the coastal parts of eastern Africa to Christianity
    (D) The importation of gold from Arabia

36. What is the main reason that there were no significant trade routes in the central portion of the map?

    (A) The hostility of local tribes discouraged outsiders from entering.
    (B) The central part of Africa has no significant resources.
    (C) Linguistic barriers made trade difficult.
    (D) The harshness of the terrain made travel practically impossible.

GO ON TO THE NEXT PAGE.

Questions 37–38 refer to the passage below.

"The Romanists have, with great adroitness, drawn three walls round themselves, with which they have hitherto protected themselves, so that no one could reform them, whereby all Christendom has fallen terribly.

Firstly, if pressed by the temporal power, they have affirmed and maintained that the temporal power has no jurisdiction over them, but, on the contrary, that the spiritual power is above the temporal.

Secondly, if it were proposed to admonish them with the Scriptures, they objected that no one may interpret the Scriptures but the Pope.

Thirdly, if they are threatened with a council, they pretend that no one may call a council but the Pope…

…The second wall is even more tottering and weak: that they alone pretend to be considered masters of the Scriptures; although they learn nothing of them all their life. They assume authority, and juggle before us with impudent words, saying that the Pope cannot err in matters of faith, whether he be evil or good, albeit they cannot prove it by a single letter. That is why the canon law contains so many heretical and unchristian, nay unnatural, laws; but of these we need not speak now. For whereas they imagine the Holy Ghost never leaves them, however unlearned and wicked they may be, they grow bold enough to decree whatever they like. But were this true, where were the need and use of the Holy Scriptures? Let us burn them, and content ourselves with the unlearned gentlemen at Rome, in whom the Holy Ghost dwells, who, however, can dwell in pious souls only. If I had not read it, I could never have believed that the devil should have put forth such follies at Rome and find a following."

Martin Luther, *Address to the Nobility of the German Nation*, 1520

37. When the author of the passage above discusses the "second wall," to what is he referring?

   (A) The differing views of Catholics and Reformers on the appropriate definition of "Holy Ghost"

   (B) The differing views of Catholics and Reformers on the appropriate use and interpretation of biblical texts

   (C) The differing views of Catholics and Reformers on the appropriate theological belief about the divinity of Jesus

   (D) The differing views of Catholics and Reformers on the appropriate method of baptism

38. How is the "temporal power" mentioned in the passage best understood contextually?

   (A) A clerical or ecclesiastical authority

   (B) A legal or scholarly authority

   (C) A state or secular authority

   (D) A business or economic authority

GO ON TO THE NEXT PAGE.

Questions 39–41 refer to the passage below.

"We are not Europeans; we are not Indians; we are but a mixed species of aborigines and Spaniards. Americans by birth and Europeans by law, we find ourselves engaged in a dual conflict: we are disputing with the natives for titles of ownership, and at the same time we are struggling to maintain ourselves in the country that gave us birth against the opposition of the invaders. Thus our position is most extraordinary and complicated. But there is more. As our role has always been strictly passive and political existence nil, we find that our quest for liberty is now even more difficult of accomplishment; for we, having been placed in a state lower than slavery, had been robbed not only of our freedom but also of the right to exercise an active domestic tyranny… We have been ruled more by deceit than by force, and we have been degraded more by vice than by superstition. Slavery is the daughter of darkness: an ignorant people is a blind instrument of its own destruction. Ambition and intrigue abuses the credulity and experience of men lacking all political, economic, and civic knowledge; they adopt pure illusion as reality; they take license for liberty, treachery for patriotism, and vengeance for justice. If a people, perverted by their training, succeed in achieving their liberty, they will soon lose it, for it would be of no avail to endeavor to explain to them that happiness consists in the practice of virtue; that the rule of law is more powerful than the rule of tyrants, because, as the laws are more inflexible, every one should submit to their beneficent austerity; that proper morals, and not force, are the bases of law; and that to practice justice is to practice liberty."

Simón de Bolívar, *Message to the Congress of Angostura*, 1819

39. The passage is best understood in the context of which of the following political movements?

   (A) The fight for workers' rights in Central America
   (B) The fight for independence in South America
   (C) The fight for economic justice in the Caribbean
   (D) The fight for political autonomy in the Philippines

40. The author of this text expresses a belief in which of the following as requirements for a properly functioning legal system?

   (A) Truth and religion
   (B) Freedom and democracy
   (C) Intelligence and order
   (D) Morality and justice

41. Simón de Bolívar, the author of the passage, accomplished which of the following?

   (A) The first union of independent Latin American states
   (B) The first military victory of the War of 1812
   (C) The first military victory of the Spanish-American War
   (D) The first political coup by someone of mixed-race descent

GO ON TO THE NEXT PAGE.

Questions 42–45 refer to the two passages below.

Source 1

"We, men and women, who hereby constitute ourselves as the National Organization for Women, believe that the time has come for a new movement toward true equality for all women in America, and toward a fully equal partnership of the sexes, as part of the world-wide revolution of human rights now taking place within and beyond our national borders.

The purpose of NOW is to take action to bring women into full participation in the mainstream of American society now, exercising all the privileges and responsibilities thereof in truly equal partnership with men.

We believe the time has come to move beyond the abstract argument, discussion and symposia over the status and special nature of women which has raged in America in recent years; the time has come to confront, with concrete action, the conditions that now prevent women from enjoying the equality of opportunity and freedom of which is their right, as individual Americans, and as human beings."

National Organization for Women, *Statement of Purpose*, 1966

Source 2

"The long-term goal of Gay Liberation, which inevitably brings us into conflict with the institutionalized sexism of this society, is to rid society of the gender-role system which is at the root of our oppression. This can only be achieved by eliminating the social pressures on men and women to conform to narrowly defined gender roles. It is particularly important that children and young people be encouraged to develop their own talents and interests and to express their own individuality rather than act out stereotyped parts alien to their nature.

As we cannot carry out this revolutionary change alone, and as the abolition of gender roles is also a necessary condition of women's liberation, we will work to form a strategic alliance with the women's liberation movement, aiming to develop our ideas and our practice in close inter-relation. In order to build this alliance, the brothers in gay liberation will have to be prepared to sacrifice that degree of male chauvinism and male privilege that they still all possess."

Gay Liberation Front, *Manifesto*, 1971

42. Source 2 endorses which of the following as the most important way to achieve the goals discussed in the passage?

   (A) Lessening the pressures of gender conformity
   (B) Forming a strategic alliance with the women's liberation movement
   (C) Sacrificing chauvinism and privilege
   (D) Encouraging youth to expand their individuality

43. Source 1 suggests that which of the following was true about the women's movement in 1966?

   (A) It had succeeded in achieving all of its goals.
   (B) It was ready for more abstract discussions.
   (C) It was not a movement supported by men.
   (D) It had not achieved full equality for all segments of society.

44. According to the text, the authors of Source 2 see which of the following as an obstacle to achieving gay liberation?

   (A) Rigid societal gender roles
   (B) Conflicts with the women's rights movement
   (C) Societal privileging of some races over others
   (D) Inequity in pay scales

45. Which of the following do both Source 1 AND Source 2 identify as obstacles to their aims?

   (A) The lack of concrete action
   (B) Inequality between the sexes
   (C) Male chauvinism and privilege
   (D) New movements and alliances for equality

GO ON TO THE NEXT PAGE.

Questions 46–48 refer to the passage below.

"Instead of encouraging education for Arab girls in Algeria, the French administration has closed the schools that existed prior to the [1830] conquest, allowed conservative Muslim men to shut down those schools for girls that were established after the conquest, and thus the capital of Algeria has not had a single [academic] school for native girls for thirty-five years. When the rector of the Academy of Algiers, Monsieur Jeanmarie, opened a class where young Arab girls could receive education, these girls proved so prodigiously intelligent that the French became alarmed. The French said that these young girls when they graduate from school would no longer want to stay at home in seclusion."

"Women and Algeria" by Parisian feminist Hubertine Auclert, published November 22, 1896 in *Le Radical*.

46. Which of the following historical backdrops gives context to Auclert's commentary on women in Algeria?

    (A) Utopianism
    (B) Communism
    (C) Industrialism
    (D) Colonialism

47. The conquest referenced in the passage above involved a conflict between France and which of the following entities?

    (A) The Mughal Empire
    (B) The Safavid Empire
    (C) The Ottoman Empire
    (D) The Songhai Empire

48. Auclert suggests that which of the following was a fear held by French officials?

    (A) Education can lead a person to challenge an unjust system.
    (B) Religious diversity would lead to instability.
    (C) The French would interact with native girls.
    (D) The Algerian education system was doomed for failure.

GO ON TO THE NEXT PAGE.

Questions 49–50 refer to the passage below.

"Workers, peasants, soldiers, youth, pupils!
Oppressed and exploited compatriots!
The Communist Party of Indochina is founded. It is the party of the working class. It will help the proletarian class lead the revolution in order to struggle for all the oppressed and exploited people. From now on we must pin the Party, help it and follow it in order to implement the following slogans:
1. To overthrow French imperialism, feudalism, and the reactionary Vietnamese capitalist class.
2. To make Indochina completely independent.
3. To establish a worker-peasant and soldier government.
4. To confiscate the banks and other enterprises belonging to the imperialists and put them under the control of the worker-peasant and soldier government.
5. To confiscate all of the plantations and property belonging to the imperialists and the Vietnamese reactionary capitalist class and distribute them to poor peasants."

[Ho Chi Minh. Selected Writings: 1920–1969. Hanoi: Foreign Languages Publishing House, 1977, 39–41. "Ho Chi Minh: Program for the Communists of Indochina (1930)." World History: The Modern Era, ABC-CLIO, 2019, worldhistory.abc-clio.com/Search/Display/354599. Accessed 2 Apr. 2019.]

Ho Chi Minh's "Program for the Communists of Indochina" (1930)

49. Ideas similar to those expressed in the passage have directly contributed to the development of which of the following aspects of late twentieth-century decolonization movements?

(A) A rise in pan-nationalism
(B) An appeal to communism
(C) The development of national congresses
(D) The implementation of free market principles

50. Ho Chi Minh's vision of Vietnam in the passage differs most strongly from the social structure of which of the following?

(A) Cuba
(B) South Korea
(C) Laos
(D) Romania

GO ON TO THE NEXT PAGE.

Questions 51–53 refer to the passage below.

"Upon this a question arises: whether it be better to be loved than feared or feared than loved? It may be answered that one should wish to be both, but, because it is difficult to unite them in one person, it is much safer to be feared than loved, when, of the two, either must be dispensed with. Because this is to be asserted in general of men, that they are ungrateful, fickle, false, cowardly, covetous, and as long as you succeed they are yours entirely; they will offer you their blood, property, life, and children, as is said above, when the need is far distant; but when it approaches they turn against you. And that prince who, relying entirely on their promises, has neglected other precautions, is ruined; because friendships that are obtained by payments, and not by greatness or nobility of mind, may indeed be earned, but they are not secured, and in time of need cannot be relied upon; and men have less scruple in offending one who is beloved than one who is feared, for love is preserved by the link of obligation which, owing to the baseness of men, is broken at every opportunity for their advantage; but fear preserves you by a dread of punishment which never fails."

Nicolo Machiavelli, *The Prince*, circa 1513 C.E.

51. Which of the following best characterizes the author's attitude in the passage?

   (A) Cynicism about the loyalty of a ruler's subjects
   (B) Optimism about the fair-mindedness of political leaders
   (C) Criticism of the religious establishment
   (D) Ambivalence about the future of his economic prospects

52. Machiavelli's treatise is best understood in the context of which of the following?

   (A) A time of burgeoning economic prosperity among the lower classes of Italian society
   (B) A time of increasing religious devotion among the elite Italian scholars
   (C) A time of intense political conflict among warring Italian city-states and other factions
   (D) A time of collegial cooperation between scholars and ecclesiastical authorities in Italy

53. The political philosophy espoused in the text above is different from those of the medieval period in which of the following ways?

   (A) It accepted the notion that monarchs were justified in asserting their authority.
   (B) It was a pragmatic rather than an ethical or religious ideology.
   (C) It stressed the importance of looking back to the classical past.
   (D) It did not rely upon strong concepts of equality across class boundaries.

GO ON TO THE NEXT PAGE.

Questions 54–55 refer to the two passages below.

Source 1

"It is impossible to demand that an impossible position should be cleared up by peaceful revision and at the same time constantly reject peaceful revision. It is also impossible to say that he who undertakes to carry out these revisions for himself transgresses a law, since the Versailles "Diktat" is not law to us. A signature was forced out of us with pistols at our head and with the threat of hunger for millions of people. And then this document, with our signature, obtained by force, was proclaimed as a solemn law."

Adolf Hitler, speech to the Reichstag, September 1, 1939

Source 2

"We shall not flag or fail. We shall go on to the end. We shall fight in France, we shall fight on the seas and the oceans, we shall fight with growing confidence and growing strength in the air, we shall defend our island, whatever the cost may be. We shall fight on the beaches, we shall fight on the landing grounds, we shall fight in the fields and in the streets, we shall fight in the hills; we shall never surrender."

Winston Churchill, speech before Parliament, June 4, 1940

54. What is the historical background for Adolf Hitler's condemnation of the Treaty of Versailles mentioned in Source 1?

(A) Hitler's belief that Poland's territorial borders should not be violated

(B) A rising intolerance of ethnic and political minority groups

(C) A widespread belief in Germany that it had been unfairly treated at the end of World War I

(D) Hitler's attempted collaboration with Italian leader Benito Mussolini

55. Winston Churchill's speech in Source 2 is best understood in the context of which of the following?

(A) British support for growing resistance movements in Eastern Europe

(B) British trade deals with American manufacturers of military hardware

(C) British appeasement of the Axis powers

(D) British fears about a possible invasion attempt by Nazi Germany

GO ON TO THE NEXT PAGE.

WORLD HISTORY: MODERN

SECTION I, Part B

Time—40 minutes

Directions: Answer Question 1 **and** Question 2. Answer **either** Question 3 **or** Question 4.

Use complete sentences; an outline or bulleted list alone is not acceptable. On test day, you will be able to plan your answers in the exam booklet, but only your responses in the corresponding boxes on the free-response answer sheet will be scored.

Use the illustration below to answer all parts of the question that follows.

Illustration of James Watt's Mechanical Steam Engine, 1764

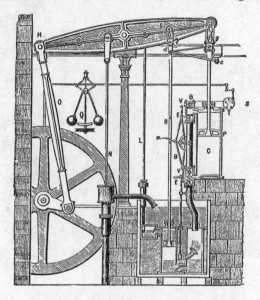

1. a) Identify TWO specific technological advances that benefited from the development of the Watt engine.

   b) Explain ONE specific long-term effect of the introduction of the Watt engine on each of the technological advances you identified in part (a).

   c) Identify ONE reason for the decline of Watt's specific steam engine.

GO ON TO THE NEXT PAGE.

Use the image below to answer all parts of the question that follows.

Poster of the *Sputnik* launch in 1957

The above poster celebrates the tenth anniversary of the Sputnik launch in 1957, in which the Soviet Union successfully launched a satellite into space.

2. a) Identify how the "space race" between the United States and the Soviet Union had its origins in the Cold War nuclear arms race.

   b) Using TWO specific examples, explain how the end of communism changed the relationship between the United States and the former Soviet Union.

   c) Explain ONE effect that the space race had upon the daily lives of people in the United States and/or the Soviet Union.

GO ON TO THE NEXT PAGE.

Question 3 or 4

Directions: Answer **either** Question 3 **or** Question 4.

Answer all parts of the question that follows.

3. a) Explain TWO factors that led to the emergence of a Mongol Empire.

b) Identify and explain TWO specific ways in which the Mongols assimilated into foreign cultures during the thirteenth and fourteenth centuries.

c) Identify ONE specific custom initiated by the Mongols that outlasted their own empire.

GO ON TO THE NEXT PAGE.

Use the passage below to answer all parts of the question that follows.

"The greatest improvement in the productive powers of labor, and the greater part of the skill, dexterity, and judgment with which it is anywhere directed, or applied, seem to have been the effects of the division of labor....To take an example, therefore, the trade of the pin-maker; a workman not educated to this business, nor acquainted with the use of the machinery employed in it, could scarce, perhaps, with his utmost industry, make one pin in a day, and certainly could not make twenty. But in the way in which this business is now carried on, not only the whole work is a peculiar trade, but it is divided into a number of branches, of which the greater part are likewise peculiar trades. One man draws out the wire, another straights it, a third cuts it, a fourth points it, a fifth grinds it at the top for receiving, the head; to make the head requires two or three distinct operations; to put it on is a peculiar business, to whiten the pins is another; it is even a trade by itself to put them into the paper; and the important business of making a pin is, in this manner, divided into about eighteen distinct operations, which, in some factories, are all performed by distinct hands, though in others the same man will sometimes perform two or three of them."

Adam Smith, *The Wealth of Nations*, 1776

4. a) Identify and describe TWO specific historical examples from 1750 to the present day that illustrate the benefits of the division of labor as described in the text.

    b) Identify and describe ONE critique of Adam Smith's view of labor.

    c) Identify ONE general benefit that Europe enjoyed as a result of the division of labor in the nineteenth century.

END OF SECTION I

The Exam

AP® World History: Modern Exam

SECTION II: Free Response

DO NOT OPEN THIS BOOKLET UNTIL YOU ARE TOLD TO DO SO.

Instructions

The questions for Section II are printed in the Questions and Documents booklet. You may use that booklet to organize your answers and for scratch work, but you must write your answers in this Section II: Free Response booklet. No credit will be given for any work written in the Questions and Documents booklet.

The proctor will announce the beginning and end of the reading period. You are advised to spend the 15-minute period reading the question and planning your answer to Question 1, the document-based question. If you have time, you may also read Questions 2, 3, and 4.

Section II of this exam requires answers in essay form. Write clearly and legibly. Circle the number of the question you are answering at the top of each page in this booklet. Begin each answer on a new page. Do not skip lines. Cross out any errors you make; crossed-out work will not be scored.

Manage your time carefully. The proctor will announce the suggested time for each part, but you may proceed freely from one part to the next. Go on to the long essay question if you finish Question 1 early. You may review your responses if you finish before the end of the exam is announced.

After the exam, you must apply the label that corresponds to the long-essay question you answered—Question 2, 3, or 4. For example, if you answered Question 2, apply the label ② . Failure to do so may delay your score.

At a Glance

Total Time
1 hour, 40 minutes
Number of Questions
2
Writing Instrument
Pen with black or dark blue ink

Question 1 (DBQ): Mandatory
Suggested Reading and Writing Time
60 minutes
Percent of Total Score
25%

Question 2, 3, or 4 (Long Essay): Choose ONE Question
Answer either Question 2, 3, or 4
Suggested Time
40 minutes
Percent of Total Score
15%

WORLD HISTORY: MODERN

SECTION II

Total Time—1 hour, 40 minutes

Question 1 (Document-Based Question)

Suggested reading and writing time: 1 hour

It is suggested that you spend 15 minutes reading the documents and 45 minutes writing your response. Note: You may begin writing your response before the reading period is over.

Directions: Question 1 is based on the accompanying documents. The documents have been edited for the purpose of this exercise.

In your response you should do the following.

• Respond to the prompt with a historically defensible thesis or claim that establishes a line of reasoning.

• Describe a broader historical context relevant to the prompt.

• Support an argument in response to the prompt using at least six documents.

• Use at least one additional piece of specific historical evidence (beyond that found in the documents) relevant to an argument about the prompt.

• For at least three documents, explain how or why the document's point of view, purpose, historical situation, and/or audience is relevant to an argument.

• Use evidence to corroborate, qualify, or modify an argument that addresses the prompt.

Begin your response to this question at the top of a new page in the separate Free Response booklet and fill in the appropriate circle at the top of each page to indicate the question number.

GO ON TO THE NEXT PAGE.

1. Using the documents and your knowledge of world history, evaluate how governments and international organizations responded to the consequences of World War II after it ended in 1945.

Document 1

Source: Preamble to the Charter of the United Nations, 1945.

WE THE PEOPLES OF THE UNITED NATIONS DETERMINED

- to save succeeding generations from the scourge of war, which twice in our lifetime has brought untold sorrow to mankind, and

- to reaffirm faith in fundamental human rights, in the dignity and worth of the human person, in the equal rights of men and women and of nations large and small, and

- to establish conditions under which justice and respect for the obligations arising from treaties and other sources of international law can be maintained, and

- to promote social progress and better standards of life in larger freedom,

AND FOR THESE ENDS

- to practice tolerance and live together in peace with one another as good neighbours, and

- to unite our strength to maintain international peace and security, and

- to ensure, by the acceptance of principles and the institution of methods, that armed force shall not be used, save in the common interest, and

- to employ international machinery for the promotion of economic and social advancement of all peoples,

HAVE RESOLVED TO COMBINE OUR EFFORTS TO ACCOMPLISH THESE AIMS

Accordingly, our respective Governments, through representatives assembled in the city of San Francisco, who have exhibited their full powers found to be in good and due form, have agreed to the present Charter of the United Nations and do hereby establish an international organization to be known as the United Nations.

GO ON TO THE NEXT PAGE.

Document 2

Source: Preamble to the Constitution of Japan, 1946.

We, the Japanese people, acting through our duly elected representatives in the National Diet, determined that we shall secure for ourselves and our posterity the fruits of peaceful cooperation with all nations and the blessings of liberty throughout this land, and resolved that never again shall we be visited with the horrors of war through the action of government, do proclaim that sovereign power resides with the people and do firmly establish this Constitution. Government is a sacred trust of the people, the authority for which is derived from the people, the powers of which are exercised by representatives of the people, and the benefits of which are enjoyed by the people. This is a universal principle of mankind upon which this Constitution is founded. We reject and revoke all constitutions, laws, ordinances, and rescripts in conflict herewith. We, the Japanese people, desire peace for all time and are deeply conscious of the high ideals controlling human relationship and we have determined to preserve our security and existence, trusting in the justice and faith of the peace-loving peoples of the world. We desire to occupy an honored place in an international society striving for the preservation of peace, and the banishment of tyranny and slavery, oppression and intolerance for all time from the earth. We recognize that all peoples of the world have the right to live in peace, free from fear and want. We believe that no nation is responsible to itself alone, but that laws of political morality are universal; and that obedience to such laws is incumbent upon all nations who would sustain their own sovereignty and justify their sovereign relationship with other nations. We, the Japanese people, pledge our national honor to accomplish these high ideals and purposes with all our resources.

Document 3

Source: Preamble to the Constitution of India, 1949.

We, the people of India, having solemnly resolved to constitute India into a sovereign socialist secular democratic republic and to secure to all its citizens:

JUSTICE, social, economic and political;

LIBERTY of thought, expression, belief, faith and worship;

EQUALITY of status and of opportunity; and to promote among them all FRATERNITY assuring the dignity of the individual and the unity and integrity of the Nation;

In our constituent assembly this twenty-sixth day of November, 1949, do hereby adopt, enact, and give to ourselves this constitution.

GO ON TO THE NEXT PAGE.

Document 4

Source: Preamble to the Constitution of France, 1958.

The French people hereby solemnly proclaim their dedication to the Rights of Man and the principle of national sovereignty as defined by the Declaration of 1789, reaffirmed and complemented by the Preamble to the 1946 Constitution.

By virtue of these principles and that of the free determination of peoples, the Republic offers to the Overseas Territories that express the will to adhere to them new institutions based on the common ideal of liberty, equality, and fraternity and conceived with a view to their democratic evolution.

Document 5

Source: Vietnamese Declaration of Independence, 1945.

… for more than eighty years, the French imperialists, abusing the standard of Liberty, Equality, and Fraternity, have violated our Fatherland and oppressed our fellow citizens. They have acted contrary to the ideals of humanity and justice. In the field of politics, they have deprived our people of every democratic liberty…

For these reasons, we, members of the Provisional Government, representing the whole Vietnamese people, declare that from now on we break off all relations of a colonial character with France; we repeal all the international obligations that France has so far subscribed to on behalf of Vietnam and we abolish all the special rights the French have unlawfully acquired in our Fatherland. The whole Vietnamese people, animated by a common purpose, are determined to fight to the bitter end against any attempt by the French colonialists to reconquer their country. We are convinced that the Allied nations, which at Tehran and San Francisco have acknowledged the principles of self-determination and equality of nations, will not refuse to acknowledge the independence of Vietnam. A people who have courageously opposed French domination for more than eight years, a people who have fought side by side with the Allies against the Fascists during these last years, such a people must be free and independent. For these reasons, we, members of the Provisional Government of the Democratic Republic of Vietnam, solemnly declare to the world that Vietnam has the right to be a free and independent country—and in fact is so already. The entire Vietnamese people are determined to mobilize all their physical and mental strength, to sacrifice their lives and property in order to safeguard their independence and liberty.

GO ON TO THE NEXT PAGE.

Document 6

Source: Universal Declaration of Human Rights, 1948.

Article 1.
All human beings are born free and equal in dignity and rights. They are endowed with reason and conscience and should act towards one another in a spirit of brotherhood.

Article 2.
Everyone is entitled to all the rights and freedoms set forth in this Declaration, without distinction of any kind, such as race, colour, sex, language, religion, political or other opinion, national or social origin, property, birth or other status. Furthermore, no distinction shall be made on the basis of the political, jurisdictional or international status of the country or territory to which a person belongs, whether it be independent, trust, non-self-governing or under any other limitation of sovereignty.

Article 3.
Everyone has the right to life, liberty and security of person.

Article 4.
No one shall be held in slavery or servitude; slavery and the slave trade shall be prohibited in all their forms.

Article 5.
No one shall be subjected to torture or to cruel, inhuman or degrading treatment or punishment.

Article 6.
Everyone has the right to recognition everywhere as a person before the law.

Document 7

Source: Final Report to the Secretary of the Army on the Nuremberg War Crimes Trials United States, 1949.

The documents and testimony of the Nuremberg record can be of the greatest value in showing the Germans the truth about the recent past, quite apart from the judgments and sentences pronounced on individual defendants. The judgments, and the principles of law on which they were based, must obviously be considered in a world setting, and not in a purely German context. There is little chance that the judgments and principles of Nuremberg will be of much benefit in Germany if they fail to win more than lip-service in the world at large.

END OF DOCUMENTS FOR QUESTION 1

GO ON TO THE NEXT PAGE.

Question 2, 3, or 4 (Long Essay)

Suggested writing time: 40 minutes

Directions: Answer Question 2 **or** Question 3 **or** Question 4.

In your response you should do the following.

- Respond to the prompt with a historically defensible thesis or claim that establishes a line of reasoning.

- Describe a broader historical context relevant to the prompt.

- Support an argument in response to the prompt using specific and relevant examples of evidence.

- Use historical reasoning (e.g., comparison, causation, continuity or change over time) to frame or structure an argument that addresses the prompt.

- Use evidence to corroborate, qualify, or modify an argument that addresses the prompt.

2. Evaluate the extent to which the arrival of Islam can be considered a pivotal point in the history of the Indian subcontinent. In the development of your argument, consider what changed and what stayed the same after Islam's arrival in India.

3. Evaluate the extent to which the split between the Roman Catholic and Protestant churches in the sixteenth century can be considered a pivotal point in the history of Christianity. In the development of your argument, consider what changed and what stayed the same after this split within Christianity.

4. Compare and contrast the effectiveness of two anti-colonial movements in the late nineteenth and twentieth centuries. In the development of your argument, explain what was similar about the effectiveness of the two movements and what was different.

WHEN YOU FINISH WRITING,
CHECK YOUR WORK ON SECTION II IF TIME PERMITS.

STOP
END OF EXAM

Practice Test 2:
Answers and
Explanations

PRACTICE TEST 2 ANSWER KEY

1.	D		29.	A
2.	A		30.	C
3.	B		31.	D
4.	B		32.	A
5.	C		33.	C
6.	C		34.	A
7.	A		35.	B
8.	D		36.	D
9.	C		37.	B
10.	B		38.	C
11.	D		39.	B
12.	A		40.	D
13.	C		41.	A
14.	A		42.	A
15.	A		43.	D
16.	D		44.	A
17.	C		45.	B
18.	A		46.	D
19.	D		47.	C
20.	C		48.	A
21.	A		49.	B
22.	D		50.	B
23.	B		51.	A
24.	A		52.	C
25.	C		53.	B
26.	D		54.	C
27.	B		55.	D
28.	B			

PRACTICE TEST 2 EXPLANATIONS

Section I, Part A: Multiple-Choice Questions

1. **D** The reference to resorting to war only when it is inevitable should lead us to the correct answer, restraint, (D). This, of course, is the opposite of aggression and brutality, so eliminate (A) and (C). The text doesn't reference adherence to religious precepts, so piety is incorrect. Eliminate (B).

2. **A** Tokugawa Ieyasu instituted a rigid social class model which included four classes (warrior, farmer, artisan, and merchant). This text is a testament to rigidity of the social classes, as strict behavioral rules were offered to households within the warrior class, along with the other classes. Choice (A) is correct. Other changes instituted by Tokugawa Ieyasu included the diminishment of feudal power (he confiscated all land), largely closing off Japan to the Western world (and persecuting westerners, particularly Christians, within Japan), and turning ruling power to the shogun (not the emperor). Therefore, (B), (C), and (D) are all incorrect.

3. **B** The Tokugawa Shogunate became increasingly secluded. In fact, in 1635, a National Seclusion Policy prohibited Japanese from traveling abroad, and prohibited most foreigners from visiting Japan. Choice (B) correctly points to this priority of Edo-period Japan. The rejection of western influence also kept industrialization from reaching Japan until the end of the shogunate. Eliminate (A). This rejection also gave Japan little need for military expansion. Eliminate (C). Finally, the Tokugawa Shogunate lifted the shogun to a position above that of the emperor. It could hardly be said that this period erased the legacy of the shogun. Choice (D) is incorrect.

4. **B** The image shows Queen Victoria offering a Bible to an African chief. Symbolically, this refers to the queen "offering" Christianity (and by extension, Western culture) in order to "civilize" the native population of Africa. This shifted the view of imperialism to a moral imperative. Choice (B) is correct. While the painting depicts the queen favoring Christianity, there is no evidence in the image that the British were actively intolerant of other religions. Eliminate (A). This painting was created decades before the Berlin Conference (in which the powers of Europe met to divide up African regions for colonial purposes), and it shows Great Britain's interest in imperialism, so (C) is incorrect on a number of levels. The slave trade had already been banned at the time this painting was created, so eliminate (D).

5. **C** British Parliament gained much power during the second half of the 19th century stemming from the Chartism movement. This would best align with (C), which is the correct answer. The British Empire was expanding only during the 19th century, so eliminate (A). Further, the Industrial Revolution was still going strong through the 19th century, putting Great Britain's economy at the top of all of the world's economies. Choice (B) is incorrect. While Great Britain did experience colonial expansion in Africa, (D) is only half correct. Recall colonial India and the Opium Wars in China. Eliminate it.

6.   **C**   The concept of "saving" native people with Western Civilization is at the heart of the concept of "White Man's Burden." Choice (C) is correct. Social Darwinism is the belief that certain people are inferior to others (similar to how Darwinism works in the natural world). However, the painting was created only a couple years after Darwin's *Origin of Species* was published and the concept of Social Darwinism was still several years away. Eliminate (A). The Open Door Policy refers to an early 1900s policy that allowed Western nations to do business in China, despite China's protests. Eliminate (B). Finally, (D) is incorrect since mercantilism is an economic concept, and the painting does not feature any references to economic concepts.

7.   **A**   The reference to the Khan's palace in the first sentence should immediately bring your thoughts to the Mongols (recall leaders such as Kublai Khan and Genghis Khan). Choice (A) is correct. While Muslims and Chinese are mentioned in the text, these are references to groups living within "districts" under the rule of the Khan. Eliminate (B) and (C). The city of Karacorum was actually the capital of the Mongol Empire, located in modern-day Mongolia, far from any place of Christian dominance in the 13th century (note the reference to the simple mud-walled church). Eliminate (D).

8.   **D**   The description of Buddhist temples, two mosques, and a church show that there was diversity in religious practice in Karacorum. You may also recall from studying the Mongol Empire that it was tolerant of local customs. Choice (D) is correct. Accordingly, (A) must be incorrect, as it appears the religious groups are freely practicing their traditions in Karacorum. The only mention of the economy occurs in the final sentence when the author describes what is sold in the city. However, there is no evidence of this being a command (government directed) economy. Eliminate (B). Finally, nothing in the text refers to taxation, so (C) is also incorrect.

9.   **C**   Be careful here. While (B) seems tempting (there is a religious leader describing the diversity of the city), the religious leader is not a citizen of the city, making that answer incorrect. Rather, Friar William is an outsider (hence the title of the text, *The Journey of Friar William of Rubruck*). Choice (C) is correct because it refers to an outsider reporting on a city. As far as we know, Friar William is not a historian and he doesn't delve into the governmental structure, so (A) is incorrect. Finally, eliminate (D) because Friar William is a visitor, certainly not a government official, in Karakorum.

10.   **B**   While Karakorum was the home base of the Mongol Empire, the Mongols had expanded all over Asia. This was accomplished with well-trained armies ruthlessly invading new territories. Choice (B) is correct. The Mongols weren't known for their economic or agricultural innovations, though their maintenance of trade routes allowed economic and agricultural ideas to spread. Eliminate (A) and (C). Finally, eliminate (D) as the sheer brutality of the Mongol's military strategies would undermine any claim to the use of diplomacy.

11.   **D**   The account of Marco Polo's travels from Venice to China, which may or may not be completely factual, illustrates the European perspective of a man encountering a Mongol ruler and being well received at that ruler's court. The exchange of ideas and languages mentioned in the text makes (D) the best answer.

12. **A** One of the unique characteristics of the Mongols was that unlike other major civilizations of the ancient and medieval worlds, the Mongols conquered vast territories of diverse peoples without imposing their own cultural imprint upon the people whom they conquered. Generally, after the initial conquest had taken place, the Mongols left people alone to pursue their own cultural and religious practices as before. Choice (A) is therefore the best answer.

13. **C** There had always been antislavery sentiment among certain religious groups, particularly in England and the United States, but the date of the passage in question (1774) indicates that the author was probably associated with the growing evangelical movement in the late 18th century. In addition to their religious fervor, evangelical groups historically supported many social justice movements such as the fight against slavery. Therefore, (C) is the best answer. Choice (A) is too early chronologically. Choice (B) is a decent option, but the Freemasons were not generally known for their abolitionist views. Mormonism was not founded until the 1820s, so (D) is chronologically too late.

14. **A** The networks and movements of goods and people around three continents are often referred to as the "Triangular Trade." The classical understanding of this theory holds that enslaved people were brought from Africa to the Americas, where the use of enslaved Africans was essential to growing cash crops, which were then shipped to Europe, where those goods or products made from those goods were used to purchase more enslaved people in Africa. Therefore, (A) is the best answer.

15. **A** The owners of slave ships involved in the transatlantic passage wanted to make their voyages as profitable as possible, which meant cramming as many enslaved people as possible into the ships. For the slaves, this meant a minimum of space in which to move and unbearable conditions that bred disease and death. Choice (A) is the best answer.

16. **D** The European colonization of Africa was decided by powerful individuals in Europe with very little concern for Africans' best interests. Even today, many of the national boundaries in Africa are reflective of decisions made in Europe during the late 19th century and do not necessarily reflect cultural, religious, tribal, or linguistic differences among African peoples. Choice (D) is the best answer.

17. **C** The attitude of the speaker in Source 2 clearly indicates that he views Europeans and European culture as inherently better than Africans and African culture. Unfortunately, this attitude was widespread in the 19th century. Choice (C) is the best answer.

18. **A** European colonists often forced African farmers to produce certain types of goods that were intended for export rather than local use. This policy led to numerous famines across Africa during the late 19th and early 20th centuries. Choice (A) is correct.

19. **D** The Aztecs used the conquest of neighboring communities as a policy for both political and religious purposes. Therefore, (D) is correct. Choice (A) describes the opposite of what the Aztecs did. Eliminate it. Be care with (B). This describes the Inca, who eschewed the concept of private property. Eliminate it. Aztec women could inherit property and even held a limited role in commerce. Eliminate (C).

20. **C** While describing his experience in the city of Tenochtitlan (Temixititlan), Cortés closed the excerpt with the statement "even we who have seen these things with our own eyes, are yet so amazed as to be unable to comprehend their reality." It would naturally follow that he would try his best to describe the city. Choice (C) is correct. The passage does not have any interest in describing labor, so (A) is incorrect. There is also no mention of religion, so eliminate (B). While gold may be part of the majesty of the city, this is not explicitly referenced. Eliminate (D).

21. **A** While scholars do not know how common human sacrifice was, there is solid archaeological evidence to support the reports from Spanish conquistadors that the Aztecs performed ritual sacrifices of human beings at temples such as the one at Tenochtitlan. Therefore, (A) is the best answer. (The Spanish viewed the Aztec practice as barbaric and "un-Christian.")

22. **D** It is true that the Spanish tried to convert the Aztecs to Christianity, (A), and established farms in the New World, (C). However, the primary motivation for the Spanish conquest was to obtain gold, spices, and other valuable goods, making (D) the best answer. The Aztecs lived in Central, not South America, so (B) is also incorrect.

23. **B** Cortés's description of the grandeur and architectural mastery of the temple at Tenochtitlan supports other accounts from the 16th century, as well as archaeological evidence that points to the Aztecs being highly advanced, with well-developed institutions and vast building programs. Therefore, (B) is the best answer.

24. **A** When Cortés refers to the "idols" in Tenochtitlan's temples, he is referring to the statues and other symbols representing the many Aztec deities worshiped in those temples. This polytheism on the part of the Aztecs was one of the principal sources of conflict between those in the New World and the Spanish conquistadors, who were predominantly Catholic (and thus monotheistic). Choice (A) is correct.

25. **C** The Meiji Restoration, which began in the late 1800s, was a period of reform in which the previously isolationist Japan began to welcome Western influence and initiate a rapid industrialization process. The charts show a concurrent rise in coal production and the number of steamships, illustrating the period of technological and industrial growth that occurred under the Meiji Restoration. Thus, (C) is the best answer.

26. **D** By 1876, the Japanese warrior class had been abolished in favor of a policy of required military service for all adult males, making (D) the best answer. Choice (A) is not correct because many Japanese emigrated to the United States during the late 19th century. (Aggression toward Japanese in the United States occurred later, during World War II.) Choices (B) and (C) are both backward and thus incorrect.

27. **B** Because the process of industrialization started so much later in Japan than it did in Europe, Japan was able to use technologies that had been developed in Europe without reinventing the wheel. Japan was thus able to industrialize much more quickly than Europe, making (B) the best answer.

28.   **B**   By the 1890s, Japan's military had become quite strong. In a move of imperial-style expansion, Japanese forces defeated the Chinese and gained control over Korea. Choice (B) is correct.

29.   **A**   Japan's increased shipbuilding capability coincided with a rise of nationalism, and the country began a rapid process of militarization in the early 20th century. Although it played a relatively small role in World War I, even by the 1910s Japan had proven to the world that it was an equal in terms of military power. (Of course, Japan's navy played a huge role in the Pacific Theater of World War II a few decades later.) Choice (A) is the best answer.

30.   **C**   The Russian Revolution and the abdication of Czar Nicholas II were precipitated by a number of factors. Chief among these were Russia's military losses to the Japanese, as well as the food shortages and other economic woes that followed, leading to the working classes' resentment of the aristocracy. Choice (C) is the best answer.

31.   **D**   Lenin was the leader of the Bolshevik party, which adhered to Marxist/Communist philosophical ideologies. Both before and after the czar was forced from power, Lenin advocated an uprising among the working classes ("proletariat") and a radical change in Russia's system of government and economics. Choice (D) is the best answer.

32.   **A**   The ideology that spawned the French Revolution both inspired and justified a revolution of French rule by Haitian slaves. Choice (A) is correct. Both the Congress of Vienna and the Bourbon Restoration occurred in the decades following the Haitian Revolution, so they would not represent the context of the slave revolt in Haiti. Eliminate (B) and (D).

33.   **C**   The Haitian Revolution was not accomplished through a constitutional convention—eliminate (A)—but rather through a former slave, Toussaint L'Ouverture, who led slave rebellions against the French occupiers of Haiti. Choice (C) is correct. Various cultural groups (indigenous, Black, Europeans, and groups of mixed ethnicity) largely cooperated in fighting against France. Eliminate (B). Choice (D) is incorrect because Jacques Dessalines was not a French occupier. He was L'Ouverture's lieutenant.

34.   **A**   It was the Islamic traders who had the motivation and the desert skills to cross the treacherous Sahara Desert to reach the kingdoms of Songhai and Mali in the Middle Ages, making (A) the best answer. Europeans, (B), did travel to West Africa, but not through the desert.

35.   **B**   As Muslim traders came from the Middle East and southern Asia to the east coast of Africa, they brought with them the Arabic language. Swahili is, in fact, a hybrid of traditional African Bantu languages and Arabic, making (B) the best answer.

36.   **D**   Most of central Africa consists of jungle and mountains, so travel there was (and still is) quite difficult. It was not until the modern era that outsiders explored central Africa using the great river systems as a means of transportation. Choice (D) is the answer.

37. **B** When he refers to the "second wall," Luther is protesting the fact that in the 16th century, the Catholic Church held very conservative views about who had the authority to interpret the Bible. One of the impetuses for the Protestant Reformation was the development of the printing press, which led to the ability of more people to read the Bible for themselves in their own languages. Choice (B) is the best answer.

38. **C** When speaking of a "temporal power," Luther means a secular or state authority rather than a religious or spiritual one. One of the complaints of Luther and other Reformers was that the Catholic Church was not subject to any authority beyond the Pope. Choice (C) is correct.

39. **B** The author of this speech, Simón de Bolívar, was a famous military man and politician who led the fight for independence in large parts of South America. Therefore, the best answer is (B).

40. **D** In the last sentence of the passage, the author states that "proper morals, and not force, are the bases of law; and that to practice justice is to practice liberty." Choice (D) is correct.

41. **A** Simón de Bolívar successfully led a movement that resulted in the creation of several independent nations, including Venezuela and Colombia. His grand vision was to unify these separate nations politically, and he was president of this union, known as Gran Colombia, for more than a decade. Choice (A) is correct.

42. **A** This question is challenging, as all of the tactics named are drawn directly from the text. The task is to determine which one is the *most important*. Choice (C) is likely the easiest to eliminate, as this is characterized in the text as a precursor to an alliance with the women's liberation movement rather than an end in itself. Choices (B) and (D) can also be eliminated, as they refer to ways to eliminate gender roles rather than the main goals of the movement that are discussed in the passage. According to the text, the only way to achieve the goals of the Gay Liberation movement is to eliminate social pressure to conform to gender roles, so (A) is the best answer.

43. **D** Source 1 states that there are "conditions that now prevent women from enjoying the equality of opportunity and freedom of which is their right," making (D) the best answer. Choice (A) is incorrect for the same reason, and (B) and (C) are both contradicted by the text.

44. **A** Source 2 states that the goal of Gay Liberation is "to rid society of the gender-role system which is at the root of our oppression," making (A) the best answer. Choice (B) is incorrect because the gay rights and women's rights movements were aligned. Choices (C) and (D) are not mentioned in the passage.

45. **B** In order to successfully answer this question, you need to choose the obstacle that is explicitly identified by BOTH sources. A lack of concrete action, (A), is mentioned as a problem only in Source 1, so eliminate it. The idea of forming new movements and alliances for equality appears in both sources, but as a positive measure to achieve their goals, not as an obstacle; eliminate (D). Choice (C) identifies an issue that, while plausible as an obstacle to the aims of both movements, is not mentioned in Source 1 and thus is incorrect. Choice (B) is therefore the best answer.

46. **D** The control that France had over Algerian citizens was due to colonialism. Choice (D) is correct. Utopianism and communism were terms that came from Marxist thought in the mid 19th century, but they did not influence the conditions of the Algiers. In fact, Marx was a critic of colonialism. Eliminate (A) and (B). At the time this passage was written, Algeria was still over a half century from its (post-colonial) industrialization. Choice (C) is incorrect.

47. **C** Algeria had been, before the French arrived, part of the Ottoman Empire. In 1830, France invaded Algeria and took it as a colony. Choice (C) is correct. The Safavid and Songhai empires had long ceased to exist by 1830, so eliminate (B) and (D). Finally, (A) is incorrect as the Mughal Empire was based in India, which would not have put Algeria (in Northern Africa) under its control.

48. **A** Auclert writes, "The French said that these young girls when they graduate from school would no longer want to stay at home in seclusion." This suggests that their education helps them to realize the injustice of the French occupation. Choice (A) is therefore correct. The passage also suggests that for this reason, the education system might be quite effective, which would contradict (D). The passage does not reference religion, so (B) is incorrect. There is also no mention of how French and Algerian girls interacted with one another. Eliminate (C).

49. **B** In the late 20th century, several anticolonial movements looked toward Marxist ideology as a blueprint out of their colonial condition. What Ho Chi Minh provides in this passage is one such example (confiscating properties belonging to the imperialists and distributing them to poor peasants). Choice (B) best aligns with this ideology. Further, Ho Chi Minh's text directly opposes free market capitalism, so (D) can be eliminated. Pan-nationalism was indeed a decolonization movement but did not by definition involve the redistribution of property as advocated by the passage. Eliminate (A). India was an example of a place that developed a national congress as part of a decolonization movement, but again, this is not referenced in the passage provided. Choice (C) is therefore incorrect.

50. **B** Ho Chi Minh is advocating a communist economy in this passage (putting banks under worker-peasant control, redistributing property among the poor). Therefore, we can eliminate any answer choices that had communist systems. Cuba, Laos, and Romania all became communist in the post–World War II era. Eliminate (A), (C), and (D). All that remains is (B), which is correct. South Korea remained an ally to the capitalist West during the Cold War.

51. **A** In the passage, Machiavelli states that "this is to be asserted in general of men, that they are ungrateful, fickle, false, cowardly, covetous." Because people are disloyal to their rulers, according to this line of thinking, it is better for rulers to be feared than to be loved (so as to ensure obedience). Thus, (A) is the best answer.

52. **C** At the time that this passage was written, Italy was governed by independent city-states that were often at war with each other, with the church, and with other nations such as France and Spain. Machiavelli's treatise is thus in some ways a reaction to the political uncertainty of his day, making (C) the best answer.

53. **B** In contrast to the scholars of the medieval period, who were much more religious-minded and concerned with morality, Machiavelli's worldview was more practical. Instead of relying upon abstract religious or philosophical arguments about what was right and wrong, Machiavelli focused on real-world situations (and some thought he was cruel and manipulative as a result). Choice (B) is the best answer.

54. **C** It was widely felt in Germany that the Treaty of Versailles had treated Germany poorly at the conclusion of World War I. While there are many causes behind the start of World War II, one of the principal ones was the Nazi Party's aggressive foreign policy, which, in part, was a reaction to a perception of national humiliation following World War I. Choice (C) is correct.

55. **D** In 1940, Britain was experiencing a grave threat from Nazi Germany. Hitler had already annexed large portions of Europe, and Britain was in a fight for its life. In particular, the Nazis conducted intense bombing campaigns of Britain's major cities. Churchill's speech is an example of the British leader's attempt not only to prepare his people for the possible trouble faced by the nation, but also to inspire them toward victory over the Axis Powers. Choice (D) is the best answer.

Section I, Part B: Short-Answer Questions

Question 1

a)   The Watt engine contributed in many ways to the Industrial Revolution, but two obvious and direct technological advances are:

- Robert Fulton's steamship

- George Stephenson's locomotive

b)   The long-term effects can include the following:

- Bolstered by steamships and locomotives, global trade accelerated dramatically.

- Employment spiked due to the creation of steam-powered factories and mills.

- The rise of factories and mills, as well as the efficiency of travel, transformed Europe's population from rural to largely urban.

- Due to the ample amount of coal in Great Britain, the empire industrialized quickly and went on to lead an imperial age.

- Asian nations' share of global manufacturing declined (Indian and Egyptian textiles, for example).

c)   There are a few different reasons:

- The primary reason for the decline of the steam engine was the invention of the internal combustion engine, which was more powerful.

- The manpower and equipment needed to run a steam engine became expensive when compared with later innovations.

- Watt's engine in particular featured low-pressure design, but it was superseded by a high-pressure design later in the nineteenth century.

Question 2

The photograph shows the culmination of the space race, a competition of technology between the United States and the Soviet Union during the Cold War.

a) The Cold War brought about a game of one-upmanship between the two superpowers. In the arms race, each side wished to show the other its dominance in technology and military power, as well as its economic superiority. These same goals drove the space race. The Americans became especially alarmed when the Soviet satellite *Sputnik* was launched in 1957, demonstrating the possibility of delivering a long-range nuclear warhead.

b) The end of the Cold War in 1989 brought about opportunities for U.S.-Russian partnerships including:

- the reduction of nuclear weapons (START I in 1991)

- military alliances, such as standing against Iraq in the 1991 Gulf War

- collaboration in space exploration

c) The competition in the skies had an impact on the following things back on earth:

- Both countries began to train their respective citizens for engineering and science.

- Both countries expanded the number of jobs available in technology and manufacturing.

- A greater awareness of outer space resulted in a flurry of creative works about space, including films (such as *2001: A Space Odyssey*) and science fiction novels.

Question 3

a) The Mongols' emergence as a Eurasian power can be attributed to any of the following:

- Genghis Khan managed to unify several warring tribes of Mongolia and led the Mongol invasion of China in 1234, which was the beginning of the enormous Mongolian conquests. The Mongol Empire eventually spanned from the Pacific Ocean to Eastern Europe.

- The Mongols' elite military capabilities were unique for the time. Soldiers were trained to fight on horseback and used violent, aggressive tactics until their enemies surrendered.

- When the Mongols ruled in China, the underlying bureaucracy remained. The Mongols brought in foreign government administrators, but the lower-level support and service jobs were kept by locals, which helped maintain a certain stability in government.

b)   The Mongols, who were illiterate, nomadic people prior to their conquests and education reforms brought about by Genghis Khan, eventually became assimilated into the cultures of the people they defeated. Focus on ways their military dominance allowed for this assimilation:

- The empire that stretched all the way across Asia allowed for the exchange of goods, ideas, and culture from one distant region to another.

- Mongol control of the central Asian Silk Routes increased the interaction between Europe and Asia.

- Genghis Khan also established the first pony express and postal system and gave tax breaks to teachers and clerics within his empire.

- Because the Mongol Empire was so enormous and conquered so many different kinds of civilizations, it did not attempt to force a unified religion or way of life on its people.

- In many cases, Mongols assimilated into the cultures they conquered. For example, in Persia, most Mongols became Muslim.

c)   Aside from the destruction and the killing, the Mongol Empire carried a lasting effect on its conquered regions in many ways:

- It engendered religious tolerance. The Mongols effortlessly absorbed Buddhism, Daoism, and other religions into their empire.

- The Mongol Empire established trade routes between Europe and Asia that later built an era of increased prosperity for both regions. Europeans could obtain a huge variety of new, imported consumer goods.

- These same trade routes later carried the bubonic plague from Asia to Europe, devastating the European continent. Whoops, sorry!

- It helped unify Russia. This was because the center of the Russian Orthodox Church was moved from Kiev, Ukraine to Moscow, Russia after the Mongols sacked Kiev. This boosted Moscow's importance.

Question 4

a)   Adam Smith discusses division of labor, which is commonly understood as assembly line production (although Henry Ford's moving assembly line as we know it did not arise until 1913). The division of labor benefited unskilled laborers who could now find jobs in factories by performing a simple task. You can cite any of the following examples (among others):

- The Portsmith Block Mills aided the British Navy during the Napoleonic Wars by creating parts for the ships.

- Nasmyth, Gaskell, and Company mass-produced locomotives in England in the 19th century.

- Muhammad Ali's textile mills in Egypt

- Development of railroads in Tsarist Russia

- Richard Garrett and Sons' Long Shop, which mass produced steam engines (1852)

- Henry Ford's automotive assembly line (1913)

b) Possible critiques of Smith's laissez-faire economics could be found in the following:

- Karl Marx, a German economist and philosopher who spent a good part of his adult life living in poverty, pointed out that the factory workers had genuine opportunities but were being exploited as a consequence of capitalism.

- Other Utopian socialists, such as Charles Fourier, are fair game on this question.

- A group of 19th-century British workers known as Luddites destroyed equipment in factories in the middle of the night to protest working conditions and pitiful wages.

c) Not counting any specific historical examples as asked by part a), the division of labor carried many general benefits:

- It increased production. European civilization began to produce more goods, at a faster rate, than any previous civilization, ever.

- It increased profits. Granted, these profits weren't evenly shared, but they at least existed. This did eventually result in an increased standard of living and a growing middle class—both good things!

- It decreased costs of production. Making a pair of socks, for example, had never been done as cheaply, which made it easier to sell socks at lower prices, which meant more people could afford to buy those socks.

Section II: Document-Based Question (DBQ)

A strong essay for this prompt would acknowledge the common goal of human rights present in all seven documents, while distinguishing between the motivations behind each document. For instance, Documents 1 and 2 explicitly reference the horrors of the Second World War and express the necessity of human rights in avoiding such conflicts in the future. Another perspective is offered by Documents 6 and 7, which contend that human rights are bigger than individual nation-states, and that the world community has a responsibility in ensuring human rights. Documents 3 and 5, on the other hand, express many of the same goals as the earlier documents, yet do so through the lens of post-colonialism. Accordingly, the documents from both India and Vietnam place an emphasis on the concepts of liberty and equality. A strong essay would show the commonalities between these documents, and highlight the key differences that informed their creation. The trickiest document might be Document 4. The creation of France's Fifth Republic is both a reaction to the Second World War and colonialism. The Fifth Republic established a strong presidency, which was not present when Hitler invaded France. But the Fifth Republic was more immediately a reaction to France's defeat in Indochina as well as the Algerian revolt—both of which showed the tenuousness of maintaining colonies in the post–World War II era. A strong essay would recognize that this document would fit into both aforementioned categories.

Long Essay

Question 2

For this essay, you should develop a thesis statement that claims Islam had either a significant or minor impact on the Indian subcontinent. To be considered a "pivotal point," the emergence of Islam will have to have changed the region (i.e., governmental rule or religious influence) in ways that would not have occurred had the religion not emerged. To decide this, weigh your evidence:

What changed:

- The governmental structure of northern India changed quite drastically. The Delhi Sultanate instilled a ruling style more consistent with the caliphates of the Middle East.

- Islam spread throughout much of northern India, as some of the sultans were offended by the polytheism of Hindus. Hindu temples were sometimes destroyed, and occasionally violence erupted in communities.

- Despite the differences between the Islamic and Hindu cultures, significant progress in infrastructure and educational systems swept India into the future. Colleges were founded and irrigation systems were vastly improved.

- A couple centuries after the Delhi Sultanate, the Mughal Empire had united almost the entire subcontinent, something that hadn't previously been done to the same extent. Hindus and Muslims increasingly lived side by side and, consequently, became more geographically mixed. The result was a golden age of art, architecture, and thought.

What stayed the same:

- Hinduism remained, as many Hindus were allowed, under law, to continue practicing their religion. This did, however, come at a cost—non-Muslims were charged a tax known as jizya.

- While a considerable number of Hindus in northern India converted to Islam, the vast majority of Hindus in southern India held on to their traditions, mostly due to the existence of the Deccan Plateau that largely kept southern India isolated from the goings-on in the North.

- The Mughal emperor Akbar instilled religious toleration, allowing Hindus to practice openly across the empire. However, it must be mentioned that under the new emperor, Aurangzeb, the practice of Hinduism was once again regulated and conflicts between the groups reignited.

Question 3

In this essay, you should determine whether the changes of the Protestant Reformation outweigh the status quo. Using the evidence enumerated in your outline, create a thesis that argues the Reformation can be considered a pivotal point or that the Reformation did not actually change the history of Christianity in a significant way. Either way, discuss both sides of the issue and let your analysis explain why the evidence shows your thesis to be correct. Here are some of the pieces of evidence you should consider.

What changed:

- While Christianity existed across Europe, the synchronicity of faith in Western Christianity faded away as the church went into different directions (in terms of practice and belief) in Germany, England, and Switzerland.

- Luther asserted that the people did not need the Catholic Church, or its priests, in order to interact with God; they needed only their Bibles. If the religious authority of the pope could be so openly and brazenly challenged, and commonly accepted understandings of God's relationship to man could be reevaluated, then people's understanding of other concepts might need to be reevaluated as well. By challenging the pope, Luther made it acceptable to question the conventional wisdom of the church.

- The Counter-Reformation. The Church was forced to clarify its positions on certain religious questions during the Council of Trent, and the emergence of the Jesuits refocused a corrupted clergy toward values such as morality and piety.

What stayed the same:

- Papal power remained intact. The pope's influence throughout most of Western Europe was still significant.

- The simultaneous existence of Catholicism and Protestantism illustrated the strength of Christendom within Europe. Despite the wars that arose from this split, the dominance of Christianity in the Western World did not change from this event.

Question 4

In this essay, you must juxtapose the similarities and differences between two movements. You can tackle this essay in a number of ways. You may introduce the two movements in your introductory paragraph, and then use one body paragraph to show similarities and one to show differences. Another approach would be to use one body paragraph to discuss one movement, your second body paragraph to discuss the other movement (while highlighting some similarities and differences), and a third body paragraph to demonstrate a general argument about whether these movements are mostly similar or different. Choose two movements that you feel most confident writing about. Here are some anti-colonial movements that fall within the time period and will fit this question well:

- Boxer Rebellion in China

- Mohandas Gandhi's independence movement in India

- South Africa's independence (won in 1931)

- Algerian independence from France

- Jomo Kenyatta's leadership in helping Kenya separate from Great Britain

- Vietnamese opposition to France

HOW TO SCORE PRACTICE TEST 2

Section IA: Multiple Choice

_____ × 1.090 = _____
Number Correct   Weighted
(out of 55)   Section I Score
                                  (Do not round)

Section IB: Short Answer

Question 1:
_____ × 3.3333 = _____
(out of 3)   (Do not round)

Question 2:
_____ × 3.3333 = _____
(out of 3)   (Do not round)

Question 3 or 4:
_____ × 3.3333 = _____
(out of 3)   (Do not round)

AP Score Conversion Chart World History	
Composite Score Range	AP Score
107–150	5
90–106	4
73–89	3
56–72	2
0–55	1

Section II: Document-Based Question

Question 1:
_____ × 5.3571 = _____
(out of 7)   (Do not round)

Section II: Long Essay

Question 2, 3, or 4:
_____ × 3.750 = _____
(out of 6)   (Do not round)

Composite Score

_____ + _____ + _____ + _____ = _____
Weighted   Weighted   Weighted   Weighted   Composite Score
Section IA   Section IB   DBQ   Long   (Round to the
Score   Score   Score   Essay   nearest whole
                                                      Score   number

Practice Test 3

The Princeton Review®

Completely darken bubbles with a No. 2 pencil. If you make a mistake, be sure to erase mark completely. Erase all stray marks.

1.

YOUR NAME: _____
(Print)
　　　　　　　Last　　　　　　　First　　　　　　M.I.

SIGNATURE: _____　DATE: ___/___/___

HOME ADDRESS: _____
(Print)
　　　　　　　　　　Number and Street

_____
　City　　　　　　State　　　　　　Zip Code

PHONE NO.: _____

IMPORTANT: Please fill in these boxes exactly as shown on the back cover of your test book.

5. YOUR NAME

First 4 letters of last name				FIRST INIT	MID INIT
Ⓐ	Ⓐ	Ⓐ	Ⓐ	Ⓐ	Ⓐ
Ⓑ	Ⓑ	Ⓑ	Ⓑ	Ⓑ	Ⓑ
Ⓒ	Ⓒ	Ⓒ	Ⓒ	Ⓒ	Ⓒ
Ⓓ	Ⓓ	Ⓓ	Ⓓ	Ⓓ	Ⓓ
Ⓔ	Ⓔ	Ⓔ	Ⓔ	Ⓔ	Ⓔ
Ⓕ	Ⓕ	Ⓕ	Ⓕ	Ⓕ	Ⓕ
Ⓖ	Ⓖ	Ⓖ	Ⓖ	Ⓖ	Ⓖ
Ⓗ	Ⓗ	Ⓗ	Ⓗ	Ⓗ	Ⓗ
Ⓘ	Ⓘ	Ⓘ	Ⓘ	Ⓘ	Ⓘ
Ⓙ	Ⓙ	Ⓙ	Ⓙ	Ⓙ	Ⓙ
Ⓚ	Ⓚ	Ⓚ	Ⓚ	Ⓚ	Ⓚ
Ⓛ	Ⓛ	Ⓛ	Ⓛ	Ⓛ	Ⓛ
Ⓜ	Ⓜ	Ⓜ	Ⓜ	Ⓜ	Ⓜ
Ⓝ	Ⓝ	Ⓝ	Ⓝ	Ⓝ	Ⓝ
Ⓞ	Ⓞ	Ⓞ	Ⓞ	Ⓞ	Ⓞ
Ⓟ	Ⓟ	Ⓟ	Ⓟ	Ⓟ	Ⓟ
Ⓠ	Ⓠ	Ⓠ	Ⓠ	Ⓠ	Ⓠ
Ⓡ	Ⓡ	Ⓡ	Ⓡ	Ⓡ	Ⓡ
Ⓢ	Ⓢ	Ⓢ	Ⓢ	Ⓢ	Ⓢ
Ⓣ	Ⓣ	Ⓣ	Ⓣ	Ⓣ	Ⓣ
Ⓤ	Ⓤ	Ⓤ	Ⓤ	Ⓤ	Ⓤ
Ⓥ	Ⓥ	Ⓥ	Ⓥ	Ⓥ	Ⓥ
Ⓦ	Ⓦ	Ⓦ	Ⓦ	Ⓦ	Ⓦ
Ⓧ	Ⓧ	Ⓧ	Ⓧ	Ⓧ	Ⓧ
Ⓨ	Ⓨ	Ⓨ	Ⓨ	Ⓨ	Ⓨ
Ⓩ	Ⓩ	Ⓩ	Ⓩ	Ⓩ	Ⓩ

2. TEST FORM

_____

6. DATE OF BIRTH

Month		Day		Year	
◯ JAN					
◯ FEB	⓪	⓪	⓪	⓪	
◯ MAR	①	①	①	①	
◯ APR	②	②	②	②	
◯ MAY	③	③	③	③	
◯ JUN		④	④	④	
◯ JUL		⑤	⑤	⑤	
◯ AUG		⑥	⑥	⑥	
◯ SEP		⑦	⑦	⑦	
◯ OCT		⑧	⑧	⑧	
◯ NOV		⑨	⑨	⑨	
◯ DEC					

3. TEST CODE　　4. REGISTRATION NUMBER

⓪	Ⓐ	Ⓙ	⓪	⓪	⓪	⓪	⓪	⓪	⓪	⓪
①	Ⓑ	Ⓚ	①	①	①	①	①	①	①	①
②	Ⓒ	Ⓛ	②	②	②	②	②	②	②	②
③	Ⓓ	Ⓜ	③	③	③	③	③	③	③	③
④	Ⓔ	Ⓝ	④	④	④	④	④	④	④	④
⑤	Ⓕ	Ⓞ	⑤	⑤	⑤	⑤	⑤	⑤	⑤	⑤
⑥	Ⓖ	Ⓟ	⑥	⑥	⑥	⑥	⑥	⑥	⑥	⑥
⑦	Ⓗ	Ⓠ	⑦	⑦	⑦	⑦	⑦	⑦	⑦	⑦
⑧	Ⓘ	Ⓡ	⑧	⑧	⑧	⑧	⑧	⑧	⑧	⑧
⑨			⑨	⑨	⑨	⑨	⑨	⑨	⑨	⑨

7. GENDER

◯ MALE
◯ FEMALE

The Princeton Review®

---

1. Ⓐ Ⓑ Ⓒ Ⓓ
2. Ⓐ Ⓑ Ⓒ Ⓓ
3. Ⓐ Ⓑ Ⓒ Ⓓ
4. Ⓐ Ⓑ Ⓒ Ⓓ
5. Ⓐ Ⓑ Ⓒ Ⓓ
6. Ⓐ Ⓑ Ⓒ Ⓓ
7. Ⓐ Ⓑ Ⓒ Ⓓ
8. Ⓐ Ⓑ Ⓒ Ⓓ
9. Ⓐ Ⓑ Ⓒ Ⓓ
10. Ⓐ Ⓑ Ⓒ Ⓓ
11. Ⓐ Ⓑ Ⓒ Ⓓ
12. Ⓐ Ⓑ Ⓒ Ⓓ
13. Ⓐ Ⓑ Ⓒ Ⓓ
14. Ⓐ Ⓑ Ⓒ Ⓓ
15. Ⓐ Ⓑ Ⓒ Ⓓ
16. Ⓐ Ⓑ Ⓒ Ⓓ
17. Ⓐ Ⓑ Ⓒ Ⓓ
18. Ⓐ Ⓑ Ⓒ Ⓓ

19. Ⓐ Ⓑ Ⓒ Ⓓ
20. Ⓐ Ⓑ Ⓒ Ⓓ
21. Ⓐ Ⓑ Ⓒ Ⓓ
22. Ⓐ Ⓑ Ⓒ Ⓓ
23. Ⓐ Ⓑ Ⓒ Ⓓ
24. Ⓐ Ⓑ Ⓒ Ⓓ
25. Ⓐ Ⓑ Ⓒ Ⓓ
26. Ⓐ Ⓑ Ⓒ Ⓓ
27. Ⓐ Ⓑ Ⓒ Ⓓ
28. Ⓐ Ⓑ Ⓒ Ⓓ
29. Ⓐ Ⓑ Ⓒ Ⓓ
30. Ⓐ Ⓑ Ⓒ Ⓓ
31. Ⓐ Ⓑ Ⓒ Ⓓ
32. Ⓐ Ⓑ Ⓒ Ⓓ
33. Ⓐ Ⓑ Ⓒ Ⓓ
34. Ⓐ Ⓑ Ⓒ Ⓓ
35. Ⓐ Ⓑ Ⓒ Ⓓ
36. Ⓐ Ⓑ Ⓒ Ⓓ

37. Ⓐ Ⓑ Ⓒ Ⓓ
38. Ⓐ Ⓑ Ⓒ Ⓓ
39. Ⓐ Ⓑ Ⓒ Ⓓ
40. Ⓐ Ⓑ Ⓒ Ⓓ
41. Ⓐ Ⓑ Ⓒ Ⓓ
42. Ⓐ Ⓑ Ⓒ Ⓓ
43. Ⓐ Ⓑ Ⓒ Ⓓ
44. Ⓐ Ⓑ Ⓒ Ⓓ
45. Ⓐ Ⓑ Ⓒ Ⓓ
46. Ⓐ Ⓑ Ⓒ Ⓓ
47. Ⓐ Ⓑ Ⓒ Ⓓ
48. Ⓐ Ⓑ Ⓒ Ⓓ
49. Ⓐ Ⓑ Ⓒ Ⓓ
50. Ⓐ Ⓑ Ⓒ Ⓓ
51. Ⓐ Ⓑ Ⓒ Ⓓ
52. Ⓐ Ⓑ Ⓒ Ⓓ
53. Ⓐ Ⓑ Ⓒ Ⓓ
54. Ⓐ Ⓑ Ⓒ Ⓓ

55. Ⓐ Ⓑ Ⓒ Ⓓ

The Exam

AP® World History: Modern Exam

DO NOT OPEN THIS BOOKLET UNTIL YOU ARE TOLD TO DO SO.

At a Glance

Time
55 minutes
Number of Questions
55
Percent of Total Score
40%
Writing Instrument
Pencil required

Instructions

Section I, Part A of this exam contains 55 multiple-choice questions. Fill in only the ovals for numbers 1 through 55 on your answer sheet.

Indicate all of your answers to the multiple-choice questions on the answer sheet. No credit will be given for anything written in this exam booklet, but you may use the booklet for notes or scratch work. After you have decided which of the suggested answers is best, completely fill in the corresponding oval on the answer sheet. Give only one answer to each question. If you change an answer, be sure that the previous mark is erased completely. Here is a sample question and answer.

<u>Sample Question</u>   <u>Sample Answer</u>

Chicago is a
(A) state
(B) city
(C) country
(D) continent

Use your time effectively, working as quickly as you can without losing accuracy. Do not spend too much time on any one question. Go on to other questions and come back to the ones you have not answered if you have time. It is not expected that everyone will know the answers to all the multiple-choice questions.

Your total score on the multiple-choice section is based only on the number of questions answered correctly. Points are not deducted for incorrect answers or unanswered questions.

At a Glance

Time
40 minutes
Number of Questions
3
Percent of Total Score
20%
Writing Instrument
Pen with black or dark blue ink

Instructions

Section I, Part B of this exam consists of 4 short-answer questions, of which you will answer 3. Answer all parts of Questions 1 and 2, and then choose to answer EITHER Question 3 or Question 4. Write your responses on a separate sheet of paper.

After the exam, you must apply the label that corresponds to the last short-essay question you answered—Question 3 or 4. For example, if you answered Question 3, apply the label ③ . Failure to do so may delay your score.

WORLD HISTORY: MODERN

Section I, Part A

Time—55 minutes

55 Questions

Directions: Each of the questions or incomplete statements below is followed by either four suggested answers or completions. Select the one that is best in each case and then fill in the appropriate letter in the corresponding space on the answer sheet.

Questions 1–3 refer to the passage below.

"For these were a people who emerged from the confines of China, and attacked the cities of Turkistan, like Kashghar and Balisaghun, and thence advanced on the cities of Transoxiana, such as Samarqand, Bukhara and the like, taking possession of them, and treating their inhabitants in such wise as we shall mention; and of them one division then passed on into Khurasan, until they had made an end of taking possession, and destroying, and slaying, and plundering, and thence passing on . . . even to the limits of Iraq, whence they marched on the towns of Adharbayjan and Arraniyya, destroying them and slaying most of their inhabitants, of whom none escaped save a small remnant; and all this in less than a year; this is a thing whereof the like hath not been heard."

Muslim historian ibn al-Athir's description of invasions of Islamic territories (c. 1230)

1. The invaders described by the historian went on to create which of the following Chinese dynasties?

   (A) Song
   (B) Yuan
   (C) Ming
   (D) Qing

2. The passage can best be used as evidence for which of the following trends that took place during the thirteenth century?

   (A) Widespread cultural diffusion through military expansion
   (B) A use of violence to suppress religious expression
   (C) The disruption of trade networks
   (D) The rise of the Gunpowder Empires

3. Which of the following additional pieces of information would be most directly useful in assessing the extent to which the developments reflected in the passage represented a long-term threat to Islamic culture?

   (A) Information on the administrative policies of Islamic empires
   (B) Information on military strategies used by Islamic empires to fend off attacks
   (C) Information on the specific practices of Islamic culture
   (D) Information on changes in the number of practitioners of Islam from the thirteenth through twentieth centuries

GO ON TO THE NEXT PAGE.

Questions 4–7 refer to the image below.

Sixteenth-century Byzantine fresco that portrays the invasion of Constantinople by the Turks

[Ilona Budzbon/iStockphoto.com *Siege of Constantinople, 1453*. World at War: Understanding Conflict and Society, ABC-CLIO, 2019]

4. The image best illustrates which of the following trends in the period circa 1450–1750?

   (A) The disruption of communication between the Islamic world and Europe

   (B) The dominance of Islamic empires due to the use of gunpowder

   (C) The inability for Islam to spread into the continent of Europe

   (D) The decline of Christendom

5. Which of the following was a consequence of the event portrayed in the image?

   (A) Orthodox Christianity ceased to exist in Europe.

   (B) The artistic and architectural legacy of the Byzantines was largely lost.

   (C) Moscow became Orthodox Christianity's most prominent city.

   (D) Muslims and Orthodox Christians shared control of the city of Constantinople.

6. Which of the following best describes why Constantinople was a desirable city to control?

   (A) The city stood at the crossroads of Europe and Asia, which offered both economic and military benefits.

   (B) As the center of Christianity, the city held enormous influence throughout all of Europe.

   (C) Its Mediterranean location gave it trade access to Northern Africa and the Middle East.

   (D) Constantinople had long been viewed as the primary center of the Indian Ocean trade network.

7. Which of the following best describes the policy the Turks had towards non-Islamic religious groups within the Ottoman Empire?

   (A) Non-Muslims were immediately subjected to formal conversions.

   (B) Religious tolerance was practiced as a way to keep regional groups under Ottoman control unlikely to rebel.

   (C) Religious groups were each given small positions in the civil service as a way to seek diverse sources of wisdom.

   (D) Minority groups, such as Christians and Jews, were initially permitted to practice their religions, but were later persecuted.

GO ON TO THE NEXT PAGE.

Questions 8–11 refer to the passage below

"At the beginning of the new year the rulers of each village came to Cuzco, bringing their quipus, which told how many births there had been during the year, and how many deaths. In this way the Inca and the governors knew which of the Indians were poor, the women who had been widowed, whether they were able to pay their taxes, and how many men they could count on in the event of war, and many other things they considered highly important. The Incas took care to see that justice was meted out, so much so that nobody ventured to commit a felony or theft. This was to deal with thieves, rapists, or conspirators against the Inca."

Pedro de Cieza de Leon's *Chronicles of the Incas* (1540)

8. A historian researching the governmental structure of the Inca would most likely find this passage useful as a source of information about which of the following?

   (A) Population changes among the Inca civilization
   (B) The most common crimes experienced by the Incan people
   (C) The intricate bureaucracy of the Inca
   (D) How the government punishes serious crime

9. The author's mention of the *quipus* refers to which of the following technologies?

   (A) A threaded device used for counting
   (B) A medical device used during childbirth
   (C) A religious item that was used for honoring rulers
   (D) A mathematical innovation that was used primarily for calculating taxes

10. Inca women were not excluded from the labor force as they were in other parts of the world because agricultural labor in South America was made more difficult by which of the following environmental constraints?

    (A) A lack of beasts of burden
    (B) No reliable water access
    (C) Mountainous terrain
    (D) Limited precipitation

11. The author's reference to military preparedness best reflects which of the following characteristics of the Inca Empire?

    (A) Its development of military technologies, such as gunpowder
    (B) Its vulnerability to invasions
    (C) Its priority of land expansion
    (D) Its lack of a systematic theology

GO ON TO THE NEXT PAGE.

Questions 12–15 refer to the passage below

"To the Merchants, Clothiers and all such as wish well to the Staple Manufactory of this Nation.

The Humble ADDRESS and PETITION of Thousands, who labour in the Cloth Manufactory.

SHEWETH, That the Scribbling-Machines have thrown thousands of your petitioners out of employ, whereby they are brought into great distress, and are not able to procure a maintenance for their families, and deprived them of the opportunity of bringing up their children to labour: We have therefore to request, that prejudice and self-interest may be laid aside, and that you may pay that attention to the following facts, which the nature of the case requires.

The number of Scribbling-Machines extending about seventeen miles south-west of LEEDS, exceed all belief, being no less than one hundred and seventy! and as each machine will do as much work in twelve hours, as ten men can in that time do by hand, (speaking within bounds) and they working night-and-day, one machine will do as much work in one day as would otherwise employ twenty men."

1786 petition by the Leeds (England) Woolen Workers

12. This petition is best understood in the context of which of the following?

   (A) England's change from an agricultural economy to a manufacturing economy
   (B) England's transfer of political power from the crown to the parliament
   (C) The European era of revolutions
   (D) England's rapid automation of labor

13. Which of the following was a consequence of the technology targeted in this petition?

   (A) The election of Marxist politicians to parliament
   (B) The loss of Great Britain's strong economic standing in the world
   (C) An expansion of job opportunities for the British working class
   (D) The eradication of the domestic system

14. According to the author of the petition, why might the Scribbling-Machines have "deprived them of the opportunity of bringing up their children to labour"?

   (A) The loss of job opportunities meant that English workers would choose to have fewer children.
   (B) Unhappy with the ineffective trade unions, workers decided to shift their careers away from manual labor.
   (C) Children cannot do the same work as their parents if that work is obsolete.
   (D) The machine's technology necessitated laws that prohibited child labor.

15. A historian would most likely use this passage to illustrate which of the following?

   (A) The effects that the early part of the Industrial Revolution had on the textile industry
   (B) The benefits that automation had on English society
   (C) Reasons that the British Parliament began to investigate child labor
   (D) The unwavering support workers showed toward the merchants and clothiers

GO ON TO THE NEXT PAGE.

Questions 16–19 refer to the passage below.

"The Chinese are all infidels: they worship images, and burn their dead just like the [Hindus]. The King of China is a Tartar, and one of the descendants of [Ghenghis] Khan...In all the Chinese provinces, there is a town for the [Muslims], and in this they reside. They also have cells, colleges, and mosques, and are made much of by the Kings of China...

When we approached this city [of Hangzhou] we were met by its judge, the [elders] of Islamism, and the great merchants. The [Muslims] are exceedingly numerous here. This whole city is surrounded by a wall: each of the six [districts of Hangzhou] is also surrounded by a wall. In the first reside the guards, with their commander. I was told that, in the muster-rolls, these amount to twelve thousand...In the second division are the Jews, Christians, and the Turks who worship the sun: these are numerous, their number is not known: and theirs is the most beautiful city. Their streets are well disposed, and their great men are exceedingly wealthy. There are in the city a great number of [Muslims], with some of whom I resided for fifteen days; and was treated most [honorably]..."

Ibn Battuta, *Voyages,* 1332–1346 C.E.

16. The observations expressed in the passage are best seen as evidence for which of the following in Yuan China?

    (A) Policies of religious toleration
    (B) Instatement of foreigners as provincial administrators
    (C) Mongol assimilation into Chinese culture
    (D) Military pressures from internal unrest

17. Which of the following conclusions about the period 600 C.E.–1450 C.E. is most directly supported by the passage?

    (A) Long-distance contact between civilizations stagnated.
    (B) New religious traditions overturned prior lasting religious beliefs.
    (C) The empires of steppe nomads united trade links across Eurasia.
    (D) Technological developments spread across trade routes.

18. Which of the following changes to Chinese policies regarding trade occurred under the Ming Dynasty of China?

    (A) The Chinese government restricted foreign merchants to specific sites in the coastal cities.
    (B) The Chinese government monopolized the production and sale of key resources, such as salt and iron.
    (C) The Chinese government endorsed Chinese merchants to conduct trade missions abroad.
    (D) The Chinese government abandoned Confucian principles to allow merchants a greater participation in local government.

19. Compared to the observations expressed in the passage, Mongol administration of its Russian domains in the period 600 C.E. to 1450 C.E. differed in that it

    (A) was only tolerant of Orthodox Christianity, while the Mongol administration in China favored many religious traditions
    (B) relied heavily on tribute from the Russian principalities, while the Mongol administration in China emulated a centralized Chinese bureaucratic state
    (C) was viewed favorably by its subjects, while the Mongol administration in China encountered immense domestic unrest
    (D) stimulated Russian export of trade goods to China, while the Mongol administration in China intentionally curtailed Chinese economic activity

GO ON TO THE NEXT PAGE.

Questions 20–23 refer to the passages below.

"…Whereas a certain controversy exists between the said lords, their constituents, as to what lands, of all those discovered in the ocean sea up to the present day, the date of this treaty, pertain to each one of the said parts respectively; therefore, for the sake of peace and concord, and for the preservation of the relationship and love of the said King of Portugal for the said King and Queen of [Spain]…their said representatives, acting in their name…covenanted and agreed that a boundary or straight line be determined and drawn north and south, from pole to pole, on the said ocean sea, from the Arctic to the Antarctic pole.

And all lands, both islands and mainlands…discovered…on the eastern side of the said bound… shall belong to, and remain in the possession of, and pertain forever to, the said King of Portugal and his successors. And all other lands, both islands and mainlands…discovered…on the western side of the said bound…shall belong to, and remain in the possession of, and pertain forever to, the said King and Queen of [Spain] and to their successors."

Treaty of Tordesillas between Spain and Portugal, 1494

20. This treaty is best understood in the context of which of the following?

   (A) The Dark Ages
   (B) The Age of Exploration
   (C) The Enlightenment
   (D) The Industrial Revolution

21. The "western side of the said bound" refers to which geographic region?

   (A) The Americas
   (B) Africa
   (C) East Asia
   (D) The Indian subcontinent

22. The purpose of this treaty is to do which of the following?

   (A) Establish mutually beneficial trade practices
   (B) Bring about an end to a centuries-long state of war
   (C) Create a military alliance
   (D) Avoid potential conflict between two nation-states

23. Based on the passage and your knowledge of world history, the treaty most strongly influenced which of the following developments?

   (A) Nationalism
   (B) Humanism
   (C) Colonialism
   (D) Social Darwinism

GO ON TO THE NEXT PAGE.

Questions 24–27 refer to the passage below.

"The question as to who, and what, is responsible for African underdevelopment can be answered at two levels. Firstly, the answer is that the operation of the imperialist system bears major responsibility for African economic retardation by draining African wealth and by making it impossible to develop more rapidly the resources of the continent. Secondly, one has to deal with those who manipulate the system and those who are either agents or unwitting accomplices of the said system. The capitalists of Western Europe were the ones who actively extended their exploitation from inside Europe to cover the whole of Africa."

Walter Rodney, historian, *How Europe Underdeveloped Africa*, 1974

24. Rodney's argument in the passage is most likely a response to which of the following developments of the period 1450 to 1750 C.E.?

   (A) The colonization of the interior of Africa by European powers
   (B) The expansion of the African diaspora to the New World
   (C) The spread of Christianity into Sub-Saharan Africa
   (D) The importation of New World products into Africa

25. Which of the following would best support the author's assertion that Western European capitalists were responsible for African underdevelopment?

   (A) The aggressive expansion of the slave trade to provide labor for Caribbean sugar plantations
   (B) The continuous sale of enslaved Africans by Arabian merchants into the Mediterranean market
   (C) The establishment of Cape Colony by the Dutch East India Company
   (D) The growth of trade links between Europe and Ethiopia

26. Based on your knowledge of world history, which of the following contributed LEAST to Europe's ability to penetrate Africa in the period 1750 to 1900 C.E.?

   (A) The invention of the machine gun
   (B) The invention of vaccines for tropical diseases
   (C) The development of the joint-stock company
   (D) The invention of steam-powered ships

27. Which of the following best explains the importance of trading contacts with Europeans for Sub-Saharan Africans in the period 1450 to 1750 C.E.?

   (A) Sub-Saharan Africans relied on European merchants to sustain population growth through the constant importation of New World foodstuffs.
   (B) Sub-Saharan Africans consolidated new states and kingdoms by trading with the Europeans for firearms.
   (C) Sub-Saharan Africans depended on European merchants as the sole purchasers of slaves.
   (D) Sub-Saharan Africans allied with European powers to evict Muslim and Arab merchant princes from encroaching on their sovereignty.

GO ON TO THE NEXT PAGE.

Questions 28–30 refer to the map below.

Plan of the City of Batavia, Capital of the Dutch East India Company on the Island of Java, 1667 C.E.

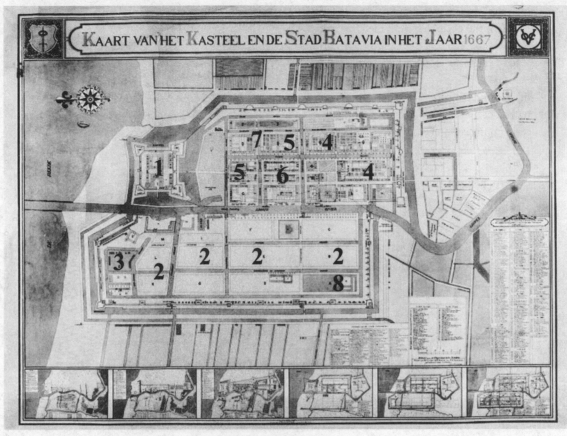

Image courtesy of Tropenmuseum, part of the National Museum of World Cultures

Legend	
1. Fort	4. Marketplace
2. Residence Blocks	5. Muslim Mosque
3. Dutch East India Company Administration Building	6. Calvinist Chapel
	7. Buddhist Stupa
	8. Garrison Barracks

28. Based on the map and your knowledge of world history, which of the following likely encouraged the development of the city of Batavia?

    (A) The presence of Muslims and Buddhists on the island of Java brought Dutch missionaries to convert them to Calvinism.

    (B) The natural harbor provided ample room for shipyards and docks.

    (C) The Dutch East India Company evaluated the site of the city to be an easily defended outpost in Indonesia.

    (D) The city produced an ample supply of spices.

29. The layout of the city as shown in the map most clearly demonstrates which of the following developments of the time period?

    (A) European trade companies developed urban centers in areas in which they traded frequently.

    (B) Populations rose on account of the spread of New World crops.

    (C) New sanitation techniques were implemented in urban centers to protect against disease.

    (D) Cities served as sites of manufacture and production of trade goods.

GO ON TO THE NEXT PAGE.

30. The variety of places of worship shown on the map of Batavia was most likely the result of which of the following broader processes from 600 to 1450 C.E.?

(A) The split in the Muslim world following the usurpation of the Caliphate from the Umayyads by the Abassids

(B) The spread of religions along heavily frequented trade routes

(C) The Crusades and the spread of Christian influence into traditionally Muslim lands

(D) The successful invasion of Java by the Mongolians

GO ON TO THE NEXT PAGE.

Questions 31–35 refer to the passage below.

"The quicksilver mines of Huancavelica are where the poor Indians are so harshly punished, where they are tortured and so many Indians die; it is there that the noble caciques [headmen] of this kingdom are finished off and tortured. The same is true in all the other mines: the silver mines of Potosi [and others]. . . . The owners and stewards of the mines, whether Spaniards, mestizos, or Indians, are such tyrants, with no fear of God or Justice, because they are not audited and are not inspected twice a year. . . .

And they are not paid for the labor of traveling to and from the mines or for the time they spend at the mines. The Indians, under the pretext of mining chores, are made to spend their workdays herding cattle and conveying goods; they are sent off to the plains, and the Indians die. These Indians are not paid for their labor, and their work is kept hidden.

And [the mine owners] keep Indian cooking women in their residences; they use cooking as a pretext for taking concubines. . . . And they oblige the Indians to accept corn or meat or chicha [corn beer]. . . at their own expense, and they deduct the price from their labor and their workdays. In this way, the Indians end up very poor and deep in debt, and they have no way to pay their tribute.

There is no remedy for all this, because any [colonial official] who enters comes to an agreement with the mine owners, and all the owners join forces in bribing him. . . .Even the protector of the Indians is useless;. . . he [does not] warn Your Majesty or your royal Audiencia [court] about the harms done to the poor Indians."

Excerpt from *The First New Chronicle and Good Government* [abridged], by Felipe Guaman Poma de Alaya. Selected, translated, and annotated by David Frye. Copyright 2006 Hackett Publishing Company. Reprinted with permission from the publisher.

Felipe Guaman Poma de Ayala, *The First New Chronicle and Good Government*, circa 1610

31. The views expressed in the passage are best seen as evidence for which of the following in the society of Spanish South America?

    (A) The formal adoption of debt slavery as a means to clear debts

    (B) The absence of corruption among elites

    (C) The king's lack of interest in the welfare of Native American subjects

    (D) The imposition of social stratification based on origin of birth

32. Which of the following conclusions about the period 1450–1750 C.E. is most directly supported by the passage?

    (A) The population of the Americas declined.

    (B) Silver flows from the Americas went principally to Europe and Asia.

    (C) The religious traditions and social customs of the New World were dramatically altered by the arrival of Europeans.

    (D) Intermarriage between Spanish colonists and natives led to equality between the races.

33. Compared to the practices in the excerpt, English treatment of the natives in the New World <u>differed</u> in that they

    (A) viewed the natives as true equals as they settled the Americas

    (B) were confused by the natives' lack of a notion of land ownership

    (C) widely did not condone intermingling with the natives

    (D) used the natives exclusively for harvesting cash crops, like tobacco and cotton

34. Which of the following changes to the Spanish policies towards Native Americans occurred on account of the practices described in the passage?

    (A) The replacement of native laborers in the mines with an almost exclusively African slave workforce

    (B) The foundation of viceroyalties to allow for more effective royal administration of native relations

    (C) The promulgation of royal decrees insisting on more humane treatment of the natives

    (D) The enfranchisement of all natives by local Spanish elites in the colonies

35. The production of the mines mentioned in the passage most directly contributed to which of the following in the period 1450–1750 C.E.?

    (A) The prosecution of a variety of wars by the Spanish Hapsburgs across the world

    (B) The development of a vibrant merchant class in Spain

    (C) A decrease in patronage of religious activities by the monarchs of Spain

    (D) A decrease in the frequency of voyages of exploration undertaken by the Spanish

GO ON TO THE NEXT PAGE.

Questions 36–39 refer to the two passages below.

Source 1

"The Sovereign Congress of Venezuela, to which authority the people of the Republic of the New Granada have voluntarily stood by.
Considering:

1.   That united in a single Republic, the provinces of Venezuela and the New Granada have all proportions and ways to elevate themselves to a higher grade of power and prosperity.
2.   That constituted in separate republics, for any more stronger the ties that these have united them, so far from taking advantages of so many advantages, they would hardly consolidate and make respect their sovereignty.
3.   That these truths, highly penetrated by superior talented men and of an enlightened patriotism, had moved the governments of both republics to convene in a reunion that the vicissitudes of wars decreed and decree the following fundamental Law of the Republic of Colombia:

ARTICLE 1. The Republics of Venezuela and New Granada are from this day on united in a single one under the glorious title of Republic of Colombia....
ARTICLE 4. The Executive Power of the Republic will be vested on the President and in case of his defect a Vice President and his replacement will be appointed interimly by the acting Congress."

Fundamental Law Establishing Gran Colombia, passed by the Congress of Angostura convened by Simón Bolívar, 1819

Source 2

"IN THE NAME OF THE HOLY TRINITY.
TITLE 1 - Of the Empire of Brazil, its Territories, Government, dynasty, and Religion.

Art. 1. The EMPIRE of Brazil is the political association for all Brazilian citizens. These will form a free and independent nation, and will not form any other union or federation, which may cause it to lose its own Independence.

Art. 2. Its territory is divided into provinces in the form in which it currently finds itself; these may be subdivided, as is required for the good of the state.

Art. 3. Its government is a Hereditary Monarchy, constitutional, and Representative.

Art. 4. The prevailing dynasty is that of the Lord Dom Pedro I, the sitting Emperor and Perpetual Defender of Brazil.

Art. 5. The Catholic Apostolic Roman Religion will continue to be the religion of the Empire. Followers of all other religions are allowed to worship within their households, or particular houses for that intent, so long as there is nothing indicating this on the exterior of the Temple."

Constitution of the Empire of Brazil, March 25, 1824

36.   Taken together, the two sources best illustrate which of the following aspects of political philosophy in the period circa 1750–1900 C.E.?

(A)   Constitutions around the world decreed representative governments for their citizens.
(B)   Monarchs exerted a great deal of influence in their nations' governments.
(C)   Military dictatorships often supplanted democratic governments.
(D)   Industrialization propelled societies to demand more social obligations from their governments.

37.   Which of the following is most directly responsible for the creation of these constitutions?

(A)   Nationalist movements advocating pan-Americanism
(B)   Revolts organized by provincial elites in Latin American nations
(C)   Aboriginal natives gathering the support of provincials to create constitutions
(D)   Colonial powers preparing their colonies for independence

GO ON TO THE NEXT PAGE.

38. Which of the following would most undermine the expectations expressed in Article 1 of Source 1?

(A) Intervention by the United States and European powers in the independence of Latin American countries

(B) Nationalism in Latin America pressing for stronger unity between the former Spanish colonies of South America

(C) Slave rebellions fragmenting newly independent Latin American states

(D) Sectionalism of elites in the various territories of newly independent Latin American states

39. Which of the following inferences about religion in the period 1750–1900 c.e. is supported by Source 2?

(A) Religious uniformity was expected of the citizens of most states in the period.

(B) Religious toleration gained acceptance with the laws of most states in the period.

(C) Religious authority was the basis of the divine right of monarchs to rule their states in the period.

(D) Religious influence on the populations of states declined due to scientific advancements.

GO ON TO THE NEXT PAGE.

Questions 40–43 refer to the passage below.

"MAHATMA GANDHI'S MESSAGE"

REMAIN NON-VIOLENT

The following message was sent by Mahatma Gandhi from Waltair:—

Maulana Mohamed AH was arrested at Waltair under sections 107 and 108 to be called upon to give security, to be of good behaviour for one year. The place and date of trial is unknown.

The Begum Saheba and Mr. Hayat were permitted to see him after arrest.

He and I were going to address a meeting outside the station. He was arrested. I continued going to the meeting and addressed them. There is no cause for sorrow, but every cause for congratulation. There should be no hartal. Perfect peace and calmness should be observed. I regard the arrest as a prelude to Swaraj and the redress of the Khilafat and the Punjab wrongs, if we can remain non-violent. Retain Hindu-Muslim Unity despite the madness of some Moplahs, and fulfil the Swadeshi programme.

I hope every Indian, man or woman, will completely boycott foreign cloth and take up spinning or weaving during every spare minute.

By striving like the Maulana, be insistent on religious and national rights.

Let us earn imprisonment. I am conscious of the Maulana's innocence and I am sure the imprisonment of the innocent will enable the nation to reach the cherished goal."

Mohandas Gandhi, *The Pilgrims' March,* 1921

40. The boycott mentioned in the <u>fifth paragraph</u> is best understood in the context of which of the following historical developments?

   (A) Indian protectionism from the importation of large quantities of foreign manufactured goods
   (B) Indian efforts towards self-rule and independence
   (C) Indian labor's collectivization and agitation for better working conditions
   (D) Indian efforts to maintain a non-aligned status during the Cold War

41. The instructions indicated in the <u>fourth paragraph</u> to remain nonviolent most likely inspired which of the following historical developments?

   (A) The Zionist movement that created the modern state of Israel
   (B) The independence movements that freed the states of southeast Asia from colonial rule
   (C) The civil rights movements that changed the legal status of minorities in the United States
   (D) The communist movement that changed the government of Cuba

42. Which of the following historical developments from the period 1450–1750 C.E. most inspired the instructions indicated in the <u>fifth paragraph</u> to boycott foreign cloth?

   (A) The conquest of India by rival Muslim empires
   (B) The development of joint-stock companies
   (C) The importation of food crops from the New World
   (D) The African slave trade

43. Which of the following historical developments most assisted the ultimate success of the boycott mentioned in the <u>fifth paragraph</u>?

   (A) Pressure on colonial powers by the Soviet Union to retreat from their colonies
   (B) The Great Depression that started in 1929
   (C) The decolonization process already underway in Africa
   (D) World War II

GO ON TO THE NEXT PAGE.

Questions 44–47 refer to the passage below.

"To slacken the tempo would mean falling behind. And those who fall behind get beaten. But we do not want to be beaten. No, we refuse to be beaten! One feature of the history of old Russia was the continual beatings she suffered because of her backwardness. She was beaten by the Mongol khans. She was beaten by the Turkish beys. She was beaten by the Swedish feudal lords. She was beaten by the Polish and Lithuanian gentry. She was beaten by the British and French capitalists. She was beaten by the Japanese barons. All beat her—because of her backwardness, because of her military backwardness, cultural backwardness, political backwardness, industrial backwardness, agricultural backwardness. They beat her because it was profitable and could be done with impunity. You remember the words of the pre-revolutionary poet: 'You are poor and abundant, mighty and impotent, Mother Russia.' Those gentlemen were quite familiar with the verses of the old poet. They beat her, saying: 'You are abundant,' so one can enrich oneself at your expense. They beat her, saying: 'You are poor and impotent,' so you can be beaten and plundered with impunity. Such is the law of the exploiters—to beat the backward and the weak. It is the jungle law of capitalism. You are backward, you are weak—therefore you are wrong; hence you can be beaten and enslaved. You are mighty—therefore you are right; hence we must be wary of you.

That is why we must no longer lag behind."

Joseph Stalin, speech delivered at the first All-Union Conference of Leading Personnel of Socialist Industry, February 4, 1931

44. The speech as a whole is best understood in the context of which of the following historical developments?

   (A) Stalin's drive to motivate Soviet industry for the Winter War with Finland
   (B) Stalin's push to make the Soviet Union a nuclear nation
   (C) Stalin's implementation of Five-Year Plans for the Soviet economy
   (D) Stalin's purges of dissidents and other political prisoners

45. The reference to the "continual beatings" most directly supports which of the following decisions in later Soviet foreign policy?

   (A) The invasion of Afghanistan
   (B) The creation of the Warsaw Pact
   (C) The imposition of the Brezhnev Doctrine against anti-Soviet protesters in Europe
   (D) The declaration of war against Japan at the end of World War II

46. Stalin's efforts to advance Russia as justified by his mention of the "continual beatings" were vindicated by which of the following historical events?

   (A) The Space Race with the United States
   (B) The Polish-Soviet War in the early 1920s
   (C) The Western intervention in the Russian Civil War
   (D) The German invasion of Russia in 1941

47. Based on the passage and your knowledge of world history, Stalin's speech is most strongly influenced by which of the following?

   (A) Appeasement
   (B) Fascism
   (C) Communism
   (D) Secret treaties

GO ON TO THE NEXT PAGE.

Questions 48–51 refer to the table below.

**Gross Domestic Product (Total Economic Output)
of Japan from Selected Years**

Year	GDP (million yen)	GDP per capita
1934	17,422	255
1937	19,949	282
1940	22,848	312
1942	23,445	322
1944	22,538	303
1946	13,083	173
1955	25,399	282

48. Which of the following best explains the changes illustrated in the table from 1937 to 1942?

   (A) Government spending on wars waged against China and the Western Allies
   (B) Military takeover of the civilian government
   (C) The conquest of Manchuria
   (D) Embargos and other sanctions imposed by the United States

49. Which of the following best explains the changes illustrated in the table from 1942 to 1946?

   (A) The destruction of Japanese industrial assets during wartime
   (B) Trade with other Japanese-affiliated states in the Pacific
   (C) Nationwide strikes and protests
   (D) Greater use of forced labor

50. Which of the following best explains the changes illustrated in the table after 1946?

   (A) The reintroduction of constitutional democracy
   (B) The presence of American troops in Japan and the Korean War
   (C) Greater interference in Japanese politics by communist agents
   (D) Economic investment in newly independent Asian nations

51. What conclusion would be best supported by the data presented in the table?

   (A) The Japanese economy expanded only between 1934 and 1955.
   (B) The average economic output of the Japanese population returned to 1937 levels by 1955.
   (C) Wartime only stimulated the Japanese economy.
   (D) The Japanese government's war goals were to secure resources in Asia to sustain economic expansion.

GO ON TO THE NEXT PAGE.

Questions 52–55 refer to the passage below.

"**Article 1**

The Parties undertake, as set forth in the Charter of the United Nations, to settle any international dispute in which they may be involved by peaceful means in such a manner that international peace and security and justice are not endangered, and to refrain in their international relations from the threat or use of force in any manner inconsistent with the purposes of the United Nations.

Article 2

The Parties will contribute toward the further development of peaceful and friendly international relations by strengthening their free institutions, by bringing about a better understanding of the principles upon which these institutions are founded, and by promoting conditions of stability and well-being. They will seek to eliminate conflict in their international economic policies and will encourage economic collaboration between any or all of them.

Article 3

In order more effectively to achieve the objectives of this Treaty, the Parties, separately and jointly, by means of continuous and effective self-help and mutual aid, will maintain and develop their individual and collective capacity to resist armed attack…

Article 5

The Parties agree that an armed attack against one or more of them in Europe or North America shall be considered an attack against them all and consequently they agree that, if such an armed attack occurs, each of them, in exercise of the right of individual or collective self-defence recognised by Article 51 of the Charter of the United Nations, will assist the Party or Parties so attacked by taking forthwith, individually and in concert with the other Parties, such action as it deems necessary, including the use of armed force, to restore and maintain the security of the North Atlantic area."

North Atlantic Treaty, April 4, 1949

52. The treaty is most clearly an example of which of the following?

(A) A reduction of barriers to trade across international borders

(B) A secret treaty to maintain the balance of power in Europe

(C) Reconstruction efforts to rebuild Europe after World War II

(D) A response to aggression from outside of Western Europe

53. Based on the treaty, the United Nations mentioned in the first paragraph is an example of which of the following?

(A) An organization dedicated to asserting an ideological tenet over the world

(B) An organization opposed to the use of force between nations in any situation

(C) An organization dedicated to providing avenues of arbitration of disputes for the nations of the world

(D) An organization dedicated to expanding free trade across international borders

54. Which of the following best explains why the North Atlantic Treaty was signed by its participating countries?

(A) Because of new enfranchisement laws, citizens demanded their countries join in alliance with other nations.

(B) The threat from opposing states was sufficient enough to join in alliance for the sake of protection.

(C) The opportunity to retake colonies lost after World War II could be acted on only through military alliance with other countries.

(D) A monopoly on nuclear warfare capabilities compelled nations to join the alliance out of fear.

55. The North Atlantic Treaty in the passage above most clearly supports which of the following concepts?

(A) Capitalism

(B) Collective defense

(C) Mutually assured destruction

(D) Communism

GO ON TO THE NEXT PAGE.

WORLD HISTORY: MODERN

SECTION I, Part B

Time—40 minutes

Directions: Answer Question 1 **and** Question 2. Answer **either** Question 3 **or** Question 4.

Use complete sentences; an outline or bulleted list alone is not acceptable. On test day, you will be able to plan your answers in the exam booklet, but only your responses in the corresponding boxes on the free-response answer sheet will be scored.

Use the map below to answer all parts of the question that follows.

Colonization Map of Africa in 1914

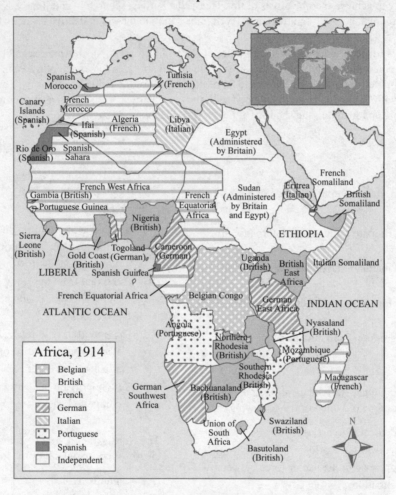

1. a) Identify and explain TWO factors in the period 1750–1900 C.E. that enabled European powers to carve up almost the entirety of Africa by 1914.

   b) Identify and explain ONE reason European powers colonized only the coast of Africa during the period 1450–1750 C.E.

   c) Identify and explain ONE effect of imperialism upon African life by the end of the nineteenth century.

GO ON TO THE NEXT PAGE.

Answer all parts of the question that follows.

2. a) Identify and explain TWO ways in which governments consolidated their power during the period 1750–1900 c.e. Use specific examples from one or more states or empires.

   b) Identify and explain TWO ways in which the consolidation of power during the period 1750-1900 c.e. was challenged.

   c) Identify and explain ONE major effect upon East Asia of the consolidation of European power during the period 1750 to 1900.

GO ON TO THE NEXT PAGE.

Question 3 or 4

Directions: Answer **either** Question 3 **or** Question 4.

Use the image below to answer all parts of the question that follows.

Shen Du, Tribute Giraffe with Attendant, 1414 c.e.

This piece of art was commissioned by the Yongle Emperor of the Ming Dynasty to commemorate a giraffe given as tribute to him in the same year by the king of Bengal, an East Indian kingdom centered on modern Bangladesh.

3. a) Identify and explain ONE factor that caused the king of Bengal to pay tribute to the Yongle Emperor.

   b) Identify and explain ONE way in which the king of Bengal most likely acquired a giraffe to pay as tribute to the Yongle Emperor.

   c) Identify and explain ONE benefit that paying tribute to the Yongle Emperor would carry for the Bengali people.

GO ON TO THE NEXT PAGE.

Use the two passages below to answer all parts of the question that follows.

<u>Source 1</u>

"The Westernization of Russia under Peter the Great was a fundamental shift of Russian society, transferring its focus away from the east and towards the west. In so doing, he achieved a complete transformation of Russian society, transforming it from a largely agricultural land of powerful aristocrats into an industrial society with a powerful king at the helm of state and loyal, Western oriented nobles to support his rule."

<u>Source 2</u>

"Peter the Great's Russia, at his passing in 1725, was fundamentally no different a society than it was when Peter took the throne. Peter rightly saw that Russia's existential threats were in the west and south, and no longer in the east, and they required a more advanced army and a more powerful Tsar than Russia had ever had before. Once his reforms were complete, Russia enjoyed an army the rival of its neighbors, but the success of his reforms can be called into question as the Romanov dynasty was pushed to extinction almost two centuries later."

4. a) Identify and explain ONE piece of historical evidence that would support Source 1's evaluation of the success of Peter the Great's reforms.

b) Identify and explain ONE piece of historical evidence that would support Source 2's evaluation of the success of Peter the Great's reforms.

c) From the two evaluations above, select the one that, in your opinion, is more accurate to the true success of Peter the Great's reforms of Russia. Briefly explain your choice using additional evidence beyond that used to answer (a) or (b).

END OF SECTION I

AP® World History: Modern Exam

SECTION II: Free Response

DO NOT OPEN THIS BOOKLET UNTIL YOU ARE TOLD TO DO SO.

At a Glance

Total Time
1 hour, 40 minutes
Number of Questions
2
Writing Instrument
Pen with black or dark blue ink

Question 1 (DBQ): Mandatory
Suggested Reading and Writing Time
60 minutes
Percent of Total Score
25%

Question 2, 3, or 4 (Long Essay): Choose ONE Question
Answer either Question 2, 3, or 4
Suggested Time
40 minutes
Percent of Total Score
15%

Instructions

The questions for Section II are printed in the Questions and Documents booklet. You may use that booklet to organize your answers and for scratch work, but you must write your answers in this Section II: Free Response booklet. No credit will be given for any work written in the Questions and Documents booklet.

The proctor will announce the beginning and end of the reading period. You are advised to spend the 15-minute period reading the question and planning your answer to Question 1, the document-based question. If you have time, you may also read Questions 2, 3, and 4.

Section II of this exam requires answers in essay form. Write clearly and legibly. Circle the number of the question you are answering at the top of each page in this booklet. Begin each answer on a new page. Do not skip lines. Cross out any errors you make; crossed-out work will not be scored.

Manage your time carefully. The proctor will announce the suggested time for each part, but you may proceed freely from one part to the next. Go on to the long essay question if you finish Question 1 early. You may review your responses if you finish before the end of the exam is announced.

After the exam, you must apply the label that corresponds to the long-essay question you answered—Question 2, 3, or 4. For example, if you answered Question 2, apply the label 2. Failure to do so may delay your score.

This page intentionally left blank.

GO ON TO THE NEXT PAGE.

WORLD HISTORY: MODERN

SECTION II

Total Time—1 hour, 40 minutes

Question 1 (Document-Based Question)

Suggested reading and writing time: 1 hour

It is suggested that you spend 15 minutes reading the documents and 45 minutes writing your response. Note: You may begin writing your response before the reading period is over.

Directions: Question 1 is based on the accompanying documents. The documents have been edited for the purpose of this exercise.

In your response you should do the following.

- Respond to the prompt with a historically defensible thesis or claim that establishes a line of reasoning.

- Describe a broader historical context relevant to the prompt.

- Support an argument in response to the prompt using at least six documents.

- Use at least one additional piece of specific historical evidence (beyond that found in the documents) relevant to an argument about the prompt.

- For at least three documents, explain how or why the document's point of view, purpose, historical situation, and/or audience is relevant to an argument.

- Use evidence to corroborate, qualify, or modify an argument that addresses the prompt.

Begin your response to this question at the top of a new page in the separate Free Response booklet and fill in the appropriate circle at the top of each page to indicate the question number.

GO ON TO THE NEXT PAGE.

1. Using the following documents and your knowledge of world history, analyze the roles and perceptions of women in the Chinese and Vietnamese revolutions of the twentieth century.

Document 1

Source: He Zhen, wife of the anti-Manchu leader Liu Shipei, 1908.[1]

…those of us who are women suffer untold bitterness and untold wrongs in order to get hold of this rice bowl. My fellow women: do not hate men! Hate that you do not have food to eat. Why don't you have any food? It is because you don't have any money to buy food. Why don't you have any money? It is because the rich have stolen our property…

There is now a kind of person who says that if women only had a profession, they would not fear starvation. Middle-class families, for example, are sending their daughters to school….Then if they get married they can become teachers. They won't need to rely on men in order to survive. Likewise, families that are very poor are sending their daughters and daughters-in-law to work in factories….However, as I see it schools too are owned and operated by certain people, and if you teach in a school, then you are depending on those people in order to eat. Factories too are built by investors, and if you work in a factory, you are depending on its owners in order to eat….

I have a good idea that will exempt you from relying on others while still finding food naturally. How? By practicing communism. Think of all the things in the world. They were either produced by nature or by individual labor. Why can rich people buy them but poor people cannot? It is because the world trades with money….If every single woman understands that nothing is more evil than money, and they all unite together to cooperate with men to utterly overthrow the rich and powerful and then abolish money, then absolutely nothing will be allowed for individuals to own privately.

---

[1] Excerpt from *Sources of Chinese Tradition: From 1600 Through the Twentieth Century,* compiled by Wm. Theodore de Bary and Richard Lufrano, 2nd ed., vol. 2 (New York: Columbia University Press, 2000), 389–392. © 2000 Columbia University Press.

GO ON TO THE NEXT PAGE.

Document 2

Source: Sharon L. Sievers, "Women in China, Japan, and North Korea," 1988.[1]

The following quotations are taken from Vietnamese and Chinese revolutionary writings and interviews with women involved in revolutionary movements in each country. They express the women's goals, their struggle to be taken seriously in the uncharacteristic political roles they had assumed, and some of the many ways women found self-respect and redress for their grievances as a result of the changes wrought by the spread of the new social order.

"Women must first of all be masters of themselves. They must strive to become skilled workers…and, at the same time, they must strictly observe family planning. Another major question is the responsibility of husbands to help their wives look after children and other housework."

"We intellectuals had had little contact with the peasants and when we first walked through the village in our Chinese gowns or skirts the people would just stare at us and talk behind our backs. When the village head beat gongs to call out the women to the meeting we were holding for them, only men and old women came, but no young ones. Later we found out that the land-lords and rich peasants had spread slanders among the masses saying 'They are a pack of wild women. Their words are not for young brides to hear.'"

"Brave wives and daughters-in-law, untrammelled by the presence of their menfolk, could voice their own bitterness, encourage their poor sisters to do likewise, and thus eventually bring to the village-wide gatherings the strength of 'half of China' as the more enlightened women, very much in earnest, like to call themselves. By 'speaking pains to recall pains,' the women found that they had as many if not more grievances than the men, and that given a chance to speak in public, they were as good at it as their fathers and husbands."

"In Chingstun the work team found a woman whose husband thought her ugly and wanted to divorce her. She was very depressed until she learned that under the Draft Law [of the Communist party] she could have her own share of land. Then she cheered up immediately. 'If he divorces me, never mind,' she said. 'I'll get my share and the children will get theirs. We can live a good life without him.'"

[1] Excerpt from Sievers, Sharon L. "Women in China, Japan, and Korea," in *Restoring Women to History: Teaching Packets for Integrating Women's History into Courses on Africa, Asia, Latin America, the Caribbean, and the Middle East*, edited by Cheryl Johnson-Odim and Margaret Strobel (Bloomington, IN: Organization of American Historians, 1988).

GO ON TO THE NEXT PAGE.

Document 3

Source: Florence Ayscough, *Chinese Women: Yesterday and Today,* 1938.

TRADITIONAL WOMEN

"To be unassuming, to yield; to be respectful, to revere, to think first of other people afterwards herself, if she performs a kind action, to make no mention thereof, if she commits a find, to make no denial; to endure reproach, treasure reproof, to behave with veneration and right fear; such demeanor is described as exemplify humility and adaptability....

To lie down to sleep when it is late, to be at work, early, from dawn till dark not to shirk puffing forth strength, to bend the mind to domestic affairs, nor to evade such, be they troublesome or easy, to accomplish that which must be done, to be orderly, to systematize the way of conduct; such behavior is said to be absorption in diligent too....

To be sedate in manner, of upright purpose, to serve her lord her husband; to keep herself pure, composed, not being given to misplaced jest or laughter; free from pollution, reverently to arrange the wine and food to be placed before tablets of progenitors, ancestors, the oblations of dead forefathers....

Nothing equals in importance the imperative duty of obedience! If the mother-in-law say, 'It is not so' and it be so, assuredly, it is right to obey her order. If the mother-in-law say, 'It is so' even if it not be so, nevertheless, act in accordance with the command. Do not think of opposing, or of discussing what is, what is not; do not struggle to divide the crooked from the straight. This is what is called the imperative duty of obedience. The ancient book Nu Hsien-Patterns for Woman states: 'A wife is like the shadow from high sunlight, the echo following sound.'

MODERN WOMEN

"'...You'd better think it over and choose some other job. Driving tractors is no work for a slip of a girl like you.'

The man in charge of registration for the tractor-drivers' training class had clearly made up his mind that I was unsuitable. I felt angry because it seemed unjust that he should try and turn me down without even a trial.

'Let me take the entrance examination anyway,' I said. 'If I fail, I shall have nothing more to say.'

I passed the examination. In the six years that followed I achieved my ambition of becoming a tractor-driver, worked for a while as instructor to a women's tractor-drivers team, and became the vice-director of the Shuangchiao State Farm near Peking. That is still my work today."

GO ON TO THE NEXT PAGE.

Document 4

Source: Huy Oánh, "Produce and Prepare to Fight the War" (*SẤN XUẤT VÀ SẤN SÀNG CHIẾN ĐẤU*), Vietnam, 1966.

Image reprinted courtesy of The British Library

Document 5

Source: Phan Boi Chau, Vietnamese nationalist leader, "The New Vietnam," 1907.

With regard to education, that of the military and women is the most important…

Women will become good mothers, loving wives, knowledgeable in literature and poetry, well trained in commerce; they are also expert educators of our children and efficient assistants to our soldiers. A good mother will have nice children; she will be a virtuous wife to a perfect husband. Moreover in politics women will possess many rights. Only with education will one know how to neglect one's private interests in order to take care of the public good, so as to make one's country accumulate its riches and increase its strength. A country that has no patriotic women is bound to be subjugated by another country…In all matters related to finance, in industrial schools…in trading outlets, in banks…it is best to employ well-educated women. They will strive to serve the country as much as men. Their pride and dignity will be equal to men's…Every woman in the country should of course endeavor to become a good mother, a virtuous wife, but also a talented woman…Women shall not be inferior to men. That's the aim of women's education.

GO ON TO THE NEXT PAGE.

Document 6

Source: Communist political pamphlet, 1930.

Oh, unhappy patriots, let us struggle alongside our men. Let us destroy the French capitalists, the mandarins, in order to establish a social government that will give us freedom, equality, and happiness…Let us work and act energetically in order to achieve the Revolution, to obtain equality, between men and women.

Document 7

Source: Statement by Le Duan, Vietnamese communist party politician, speech at the Vietnamese Women's Fourth Congress, 1974.

The Viet Nam Fatherland owes its heroic sons and daughters to the contributions of heroic, undaunted, faithful and responsible mothers. For many centuries, the Vietnamese mothers have handed down to us the mettle of the Trung Sisters and Lady Trieu, the tradition of industrious labour and love of country and of home. We can rightly be proud of our Vietnamese mothers.

END OF DOCUMENTS FOR QUESTION 1

GO ON TO THE NEXT PAGE.

Question 2, 3, <u>or</u> 4 (Long Essay)

Suggested writing time: 40 minutes

Directions: Answer Question 2 <u>or</u> Question 3 <u>or</u> Question 4.

In your response you should do the following.

- Respond to the prompt with a historically defensible thesis or claim that establishes a line of reasoning.

- Describe a broader historical context relevant to the prompt.

- Support an argument in response to the prompt using specific and relevant examples of evidence.

- Use historical reasoning (e.g., comparison, causation, continuity or change over time) to frame or structure an argument that addresses the prompt.

- Use evidence to corroborate, qualify, or modify an argument that addresses the prompt.

2. Evaluate the extent to which the Opium Wars of the nineteenth century can be considered a turning point in world history. In the development of your argument, explain what changed and what stayed the same from the period before the Opium Wars to the period after the Opium Wars.

3. Evaluate the extent to which the development of joint-stock companies in the sixteenth century c.e. can be considered a turning point in world history. In the development of your argument, explain what changed and what stayed the same from the period before the development of joint-stock companies in the sixteenth century c.e. to the period after the development of joint-stock companies in the sixteenth century c.e.

4. Evaluate the extent to which the emergence of the Industrial Revolution in the nineteenth century c.e. can be considered a turning point in world history. In the development of your argument, explain what changed and what stayed the same from the period before the emergence of the Industrial Revolution in the nineteenth century c.e. to the period after the emergence of Industrial Revolution in the nineteenth century c.e.

WHEN YOU FINISH WRITING,
CHECK YOUR WORK ON SECTION II IF TIME PERMITS.

STOP
END OF EXAM

Practice Test 3:
Answers and
Explanations

PRACTICE TEST 3 ANSWER KEY

1.	B		29.	A
2.	A		30.	B
3.	D		31.	D
4.	B		32.	A
5.	C		33.	C
6.	A		34.	C
7.	D		35.	A
8.	C		36.	A
9.	A		37.	B
10.	C		38.	D
11.	C		39.	B
12.	D		40.	B
13.	D		41.	C
14.	C		42.	B
15.	A		43.	D
16.	A		44.	C
17.	C		45.	B
18.	A		46.	D
19.	B		47.	C
20.	B		48.	A
21.	A		49.	A
22.	D		50.	B
23.	C		51.	B
24.	B		52.	D
25.	A		53.	C
26.	C		54.	B
27.	B		55.	B
28.	C			

PRACTICE TEST 3 EXPLANATIONS

Section I, Part A: Multiple-Choice Questions

1. **B** If there is one group who should come to mind when thinking of invasions across 13th-century Asia, it should be the Mongols. The Mongols ruled China as the Yuan Dynasty. Choice (B) is correct. The Song Dynasty was overthrown by the Mongols so (A) is incorrect. Also eliminate (C), as the Ming took over China following the fall of the Mongols. The Qing Dynasty is also incorrect as it proceeded the Ming. Eliminate (D).

2. **A** The Mongol Invaders, while not being known for many advancements in science or art themselves, allowed for the spread of various cultures throughout Eurasia due to its control and maintenance of trade routes. That cultural diffusion can be chalked up to the incredible militaristic expansion of the Mongols. Choice (A) is correct. Eliminate (C) as the Mongols protected and expanded, rather than disrupted, trade routes. Choice (B) is incorrect since the Mongols were quite tolerant of the religious practices of its conquered people. Choice (D) is incorrect since the Gunpowder Empires came after Mongol rule. In fact, the first of the Gunpowder Empires, the Ottoman, arose from the ashes of the former Mongol Empire in Eastern Europe and Western Asia.

3. **D** The Mongols were known for being tolerant of religions under their rule; however, to learn more about whether the Mongols were ever a long-term threat to Islam, one simply needs to look at whether the population of Muslims in the world had increased or decreased in the long run following the Mongol conquests. Choice (D) says exactly this. The administrative policies, other than maybe tolerance of local religions, would not tell us much. Further policies are not as useful as actual data of population changes. Eliminate (A). Similarly, military strategies would not be relevant to the long-term effects the Mongols had on Islam. Eliminate (B). Finally, the practices of Islamic culture, on their own, would not help a historian assess the impact that Mongols had on Islamic culture. Some more information about how practice may have changed during this period would be necessary. Eliminate (C).

4. **B** The Turks' invasion of Constantinople was the beginning of the Ottoman Empire, the first of the "Gunpowder Empires." Choice (B) is correct. As the invasion of Constantinople placed the capital city of an Islamic empire in Europe, it could hardly be said that there was a disruption of communication between Europe and the Islamic world. Choices (A) and (C) are incorrect. While Islam had moved into Eastern Europe, Christianity still had a strong hold over the rest of Europe during this period (and was expanding overseas). Eliminate (D).

5. **C** Following the invasion of Constantinople, the city became an Islamic stronghold, forcing the Eastern Orthodox leadership out. Eliminate (D). The most populous city of Eastern Orthodox Christians was now Moscow. Therefore, (C) is correct. Choice (A) is incorrect because it is too extreme. There were other places in Europe, such as Greece, where Orthodox Christianity was still thriving. Much of the Byzantine artistic and architectural legacy was simply adopted by the Ottomans

(transforming the Hagia Sophia into a mosque is probably the most well-known example of this). Eliminate (B).

6. **A** Constantinople (now Istanbul) sits on the Bosporus Strait, which runs through the northern part of modern-day Turkey and separates the European and Asian continents. This is most consistent with (A), which is the correct answer. Choice (B) is not totally correct because, while Constantinople was the center of Eastern Orthodox Christianity, it was not the center of Christendom—the Catholic Church was centered in Rome. Constantinople is not on the Mediterranean Sea (it's on the Aegean Sea) and *definitely* not on the Indian Ocean. Eliminate (C) and (D).

7. **D** In the expanding Ottoman Empire, Christians and Jews were allowed to practice their religions, but as the empire grew, so too did religious persecution. For instance, the Ottomans enslaved children of their Christian subjects and turned them into fighting warriors, known as Janissaries. Choice (D) is correct. Choices (A), (B), and (C) are incorrect because none of them accurately capture the nature of the changing attitudes toward religious minorities in the Ottoman Empire.

8. **C** References to counting the population, paying taxes, and dealing with crime are evidence that the Inca had a complex governmental structure. This shows the presence of an Incan bureaucracy, so (C) is correct. The text does not give the reader specific information about the population changes, so (A) is incorrect. The passage also does not go into specific detail on how common certain crimes were or how those crimes were dealt with. Eliminate (B) and (D).

9. **A** Since the quipus were described as telling "how many births there had been during the year," it would make sense that they were a counting device. Choice (A) is correct. The text only mentions the device used for keeping track of the number of childbirths, not that it was used for the process of childbirth. Choice (B) is incorrect. There is no reference to religion. Eliminate (C). Taxes are mentioned later in the text, so (D) is incorrect.

10. **C** Located in the Andes mountains, the Inca could use all the human labor they had available—women included—to work the land. Choice (C) is correct. While there were not many domesticated animals available in the mountainous Incan Empire, (A) is incorrect because it is too extreme. There is, after all, the notable exception of the llama! Choice (B) is incorrect as the Inca had access to the Pacific Ocean as well as an intricate river system (such as the Amazon). Finally, many parts of the Incan empire are in a rainforest, which experiences an equatorial climate with lots of rain. Eliminate (D).

11. **C** The Inca were expansionist, as the rulers sought their place in the afterlife based on new land they conquered. Choice (C) is correct. The Inca did not develop gunpowder, which made it vulnerable to the Spanish. Eliminate (A). The mountainous terrain and dense rainforest made the Incan Empire relatively secure from land invasions, so (B) is incorrect. The Inca had an intricate religion, which would make (D) incorrect.

12. **D** The workers who penned this petition are protesting losing their jobs due to the new machines. Therefore, this passage is to be understood in the context of the automation of labor. Choice (D) is correct. Choice (A) is incorrect but may seem tempting because it is easy to associate automation with manufacturing. However, the move toward manufacturing had already occurred, bolstered by

human labor. Choice (B) is incorrect because the rapid empowerment of parliament happened in the following century, and more importantly, is not terribly relevant to this issue. The same can be said for the European era of revolutions. Eliminate (C).

13. **D** The highly labor-intensive arrangement known as the domestic system ultimately came to its end with the automation of labor. Choice (D) is therefore correct. Marx was not even alive at this time, so (A) is incorrect. The British had the strongest economy of the 19th century as it expanded its empire around the world, so eliminate (B). Finally, (C) is incorrect because the machines referenced in this passage led to the loss of jobs due to the automation of labor.

14. **C** The automation of labor led to a loss of jobs, ultimately making several occupations obsolete. Therefore, the authors of the petition are in part expressing their dismay that they will not be able to bring up their children to do the same work. Choice (C) is correct. There is no evidence that the working class did not have any more children. Eliminate (A). Unions were still in their infancy at the time this petition was written and were still illegal. The circumstances that the authors of this petition are responding to likely led to the strengthening of the union movement. Therefore, (B) is incorrect. The text does not address the issue of child labor. Eliminate (D).

15. **A** This text gives an important insight into how textile laborers reacted to the accelerating automation of labor in the early part of the Industrial Revolution. Choice (A) is therefore correct. Eliminate (B) and (D) since the perspective offered in this text decries the new machinery. There is no reference to child labor, so eliminate (C).

16. **A** Ibn Battuta's description of Hangzhou mentions that a variety of religions were practiced in the city. Choice (A) supports this idea and is the correct answer. Eliminate (B) because the passage does not explicitly state that these non-Mongolians are administrators. Eliminate (C) because there is no evidence of Mongolian assimilation in this passage. Finally, eliminate (D) because there is no mention of the population revolting, just lots of city guards.

17. **C** Ibn Battuta managed to travel throughout the Muslim world and even beyond. Eliminate (A) because it contradicts the ideas in the passage. Eliminate (B) and (D) because the passage neither indicates that new religions displaced old beliefs nor mentions new technologies. Choice (C) is the best answer.

18. **A** The Ming Dynasty arose out of the ashes of Mongol mismanagement and followed a policy of restricting outside influences in China, lest foreigners retake the country. The choice that best aligns with this idea is (A). Eliminate (B), as this first occurred in the Han Dynasty and is not a Ming innovation. Eliminate (C) because after the voyages of Zheng He, the Ming government ceased to finance seaborne voyages of significance. Eliminate (D), as the Ming actually followed Neo-Confucian policies.

19. **B** The Mongols ruled Russia as if it were a protection racket, exacting tribute from the Russian principalities but leaving direct administration to the princes themselves. This matches (B). Eliminate (A) because the Russian Mongols eventually converted to Islam. Eliminate (C) because the Russians chafed under Mongol rule and revolted themselves. Finally, eliminate (D) because the Mongols stimulated Chinese production and economic activity as much as possible for their own taxation purposes.

20. **B** The Treaty of Tordesillas was created to clearly establish which lands would be settled by Spain and which would be settled by Portugal. This race to settle lands was characteristic of the Age of Exploration. Choice (B) is correct. This period occurred following the Dark Ages. In fact, exploration was one of the trends that moved Europe out of the Dark Ages. Eliminate (A). The Enlightenment and the Industrial Revolution were still a few centuries away, so (C) and (D) are incorrect.

21. **A** The boundary in question cuts right through the Atlantic Ocean. To the west is what we refer to as the Western Hemisphere—the Americas. Choice (A) is correct. Africa, East Asia, and the Indian subcontinent are all to the east of the Atlantic Ocean. Eliminate (B), (C), and (D).

22. **D** The treaty references that it is created "for the sake of peace and concord." This most closely aligns with (D). There is no reference to trade, so (A) is incorrect. Spain and Portugal were not engaged in a centuries-long war, so eliminate (B). There is no mention in the text of a military alliance, so eliminate (C).

23. **C** As Spain and Portugal spread their influence around the world, they established colonies. Choice (C) is correct. While there was no doubt national pride underpinned some of the exploration, Nationalism, as a political and social movement did not really arise until the 18th century. Eliminate (A). Humanism was an artistic and philosophical focus on human endeavors, so it would be unrelated to this treaty. Eliminate (B). Social Darwinism (and its namesake Charles Darwin) was still several centuries away, so (D) is also incorrect.

24. **B** Rodney's argument is that Europe's colonization efforts, compounded with the capitalist system, impoverished Africa. Eliminate answer choices that do not reflect this argument, such as (C) and (D). Historically, the Europeans only settled the coastlines between 1450 and 1750, so (A) is also incorrect. The answer is (B).

25. **A** Here, you should be looking for an answer choice that has to do with the slave trade, a root cause of Africa's underdevelopment. Eliminate (B), as it does not deal with Western European exploitation of the slave trade. Eliminate (C) because it is not necessarily a byproduct of the slave trade. Choice (D) is too limited, so eliminate it. The best answer here is (A).

26. **C** The question is asking for the choice that contributed LEAST to Europe's ability to penetrate Africa between 1750 and 1900. Choice (C), the development of the joint-stock company, did not occur during this time period, so it cannot have contributed to Europe's penetration of Africa. Therefore, (C) is the answer.

27. **B** Sub-Saharan African states relied largely on trade with Europe to purchase guns necessary to capture other enslaved people and expand their own state structures. Eliminate (C), as Europeans were not the only buyers of enslaved people. Eliminate (D) because it refers to Muslim and Arab merchants specifically and not the whole of sub-Saharan Africa. Eliminate (A) because it implies that New World foods were constantly shuttled into Africa to feed the population of the continent; while New World foods were brought into Africa, after the initial contact, Africans grew New World foods in Africa itself. Therefore, (B) is correct.

28. **C** The map depicts the Dutch East India Company's capital at Batavia. Note that the city is focused on a fort and a garrison barracks along the exterior at prominent positions; this should help you identify (C) as the correct answer. Eliminate (A) because the Dutch did not focus much on converting people. Eliminate (B) because the map's legend does not include shipyards or docks. Eliminate (D) because the legend lacks any mention of spices.

29. **A** The map's legend and title mention that the Dutch East India Company had a capital and administration at Batavia. Eliminate (B) because the map does not indicate any population growth; it shows only that there are many residence blocks. Eliminate (C) because the legend does not mention sanitation structures. Eliminate (D) because the legend does not include factories or production centers.

30. **B** As indicated by the legend, there is a Buddhist stupa and a Muslim mosque in the city. Recall that Buddhism and Islam made their way to Indonesia during the period 600–1450 C.E. via trade routes. Eliminate (A) because the caliphates did not control Indonesia. Eliminate (C) because the crusaders did not reach Indonesia. Eliminate (D) because the Mongolians did not succeed in their invasion of Java. Choice (B) is the best answer.

31. **D** The passage discusses the treatment of aboriginal natives in South America by the Spanish in their silver mines. Recall that in the Spanish colonies, a caste system existed according to race and birthplace, which is closest to (D). Eliminate (B), as it is a reversal of what is stated in the passage. Eliminate (C) because the letter is written to the king, who is ostensibly worried about his subjects in the last sentence. Eliminate (A) because it is less directly supported in the passage than (D).

32. **A** The passage indicates that many of the natives sent to the mines did not return. Eliminate (B) because the passage does not say where the silver was spent. Eliminate (C) because the passage does not discuss social transformations. Eliminate (D) because the passage does not indicate that there were any feelings of equality between Spaniards and natives. The best answer is (A).

33. **C** The English did not intermarry with the natives like the Spaniards did, and their colonies were largely distinct from native settlements. Therefore, (C) is correct. Eliminate (A), which is demonstrably false. Eliminate (B) because wars between English colonists and natives over land were common. Eliminate (D) because the English also employed enslaved Africans for cash-crop harvesting in the southern colonies.

34. **C** The passage discusses the mistreatment of natives in the Spanish mines, and the fact that the mit'a system and other such forms of exploitation killed a great many natives. The Spanish monarchy actually banned such exploitative measures and tried to impose laws demanding humane treatment. Therefore, (C) is correct.

35. **A** The mines in the passage produced silver, as stated in the first paragraph. The Spanish government relied on the silver shipments from the New World to finance its far-flung military efforts. Eliminate (B) because the Spanish never created the kind of merchant class that existed in England or the Netherlands. Eliminate (C) as well, since the Spanish monarchs were staunch supporters and patrons of Catholicism. Finally, eliminate (D) because the Spanish sent their galleons on voyages of exploration far and wide. The correct answer is (A).

36. **A** Both sources mention legislatures, so eliminate (B). Choice (C) is true, but not reflected in either of the passages. Choice (D) is also not mentioned in either passage, so eliminate it. Choice (A), the idea that constitutions around the world established representative governments, is correct.

37. **B** Latin American independence movements were typically organized by the native-born elites and not the European-born aristocrats, so eliminate (C) and (D). Choice (A) is the opposite of what actually transpired, so eliminate it. Choice (B) is the answer.

38. **D** The former Spanish colonies, once free, were united for a brief time but later split ways due to irreconcilable differences stemming from their vast distances from each other; eliminate (B). While the United States and Europe did intervene in Latin American affairs, those interventions were not typically designed to fragment Latin American states, so eliminate (A). Slavery existed in some of the Spanish colonies, but the revolutions were inspired by Enlightenment ideals that usually involved freeing the enslaved people, so eliminate (C). Choice (D) is correct.

39. **B** Source 2, the Constitution of the Empire of Brazil, claims that Catholicism is the state religion of Brazil but allows for religious toleration for other creeds as well, so eliminate (A). Choice (C) is not explicitly mentioned in Source 2, so eliminate (C). Choice (D) is true of the period but not reflected in the source, so eliminate it. Choice (B) is correct.

40. **B** The passage discusses Gandhi's nonviolent protests as a tool to gain independence from Great Britain. Eliminate (A), (C), and (D), as these lack any connection to the independence movement. Choice (B) is the answer.

41. **C** Eliminate (B) and (D), as they involve violent revolutions, which is not what the question is asking for. Eliminate (A), as Zionism was a force before the Indian nonviolent protest movement was underway. Choice (C) is the best answer.

42. **B** The boycott of foreign cloth referred to in the passage was intended to help free India from foreign rule. Therefore, eliminate any answer choice that would not result in foreigners coming to rule India. Choices (C) and (D) fall into this category, so eliminate them. While the Mughals did make gains in India during this period, the ultimate rulers of India were the British via the British East India Company, so eliminate (A). Choice (B), the development of joint-stock companies, is correct.

43. **D** As mentioned above, the goal of the boycott of foreign cloth was to free India from British rule, so eliminate any answer choice that does not involve weakening British resolve to abandon India. Choice (C), decolonization, occurred after the Indian independence movement, so it can be eliminated. Choice (B) strengthened Britain's resolve to hold onto its colonies, so it too can be eliminated. Choice (A) is plausible but not as strong as (D), especially since more direct Soviet pressure to decolonize came after World War II, during the Cold War. Choice (D) is correct.

44. **C** Stalin's speech is an exhortation to the managers of industry to quicken the pace of production and technological advancement. Eliminate (A) because the speech mentions nothing of offensive war. Eliminate (B) because the development of a Soviet nuclear bomb occurred much later than the speech. Eliminate (D) because the speech makes no mention of political prisoners or dissenters. Choice (C) is the answer.

45. **B** According to this speech, Stalin firmly believed that foreign nations attacked Russia because it was weak. Therefore, any foreign policy that would provide a buffer and strength to Russia proper was in Russian interests. You can eliminate (A) because the Soviets invaded Afghanistan to prop up a socialist government. Eliminate (C) because the protesters that the Soviets crushed were trying to gain independence for their countries. Eliminate (D) because the Soviets attacked Japan to gain territory and have a say in the postwar Far East.

46. **D** Stalin's drive for Russia's advancement may have come at a grave cost, but it definitely put the Soviets in a much better position to withstand full-scale war in World War II. Eliminate (A) because the Soviet Union ultimately gave up the Space Race after the United States landed men on the moon. Eliminate (B) and (C) because they took place earlier than Stalin's speech. Choice (D) is therefore the best answer.

47. **C** Stalin was the leader of the Soviet Union at the time of his speech, and his lambasting of capitalist and monarchist foreign aggressors clearly shows communist sympathies. Therefore, (C) is correct. Eliminate (A) because appeasement is more often applied to the Western democracies' relationship to Adolf Hitler's territorial demands. Eliminate (B) because fascism is the form of government followed by Mussolini and Hitler, not Stalin. Eliminate (D) because secret treaties are a hallmark of World War I, not II.

48. **A** The table shows that the Japanese economy grew from 1937 to 1942. Eliminate answer choices that would cause the economy to decline or are outside the time period. Choices (B) and (D) would cause the economy to decrease its output, so they can be eliminated. Choice (C) occurred outside the time period and can be eliminated as well. Choice (A) is therefore the answer.

49. **A** The table shows that the Japanese economy collapsed between 1942 and 1946. Eliminate any answer choices that would cause the economy to grow or are outside the time period. Choice (B) would cause the economy to grow and can be eliminated. Choices (C) and (D) are possible, but neither is as strong as the literal destruction of Japanese industry by Allied forces, (A). Therefore, eliminate (C) and (D) and choose (A).

50. **B** The table shows that the Japanese economy grew after 1946, so eliminate answer choices that are outside the time period or would cause the economy to decline. Choice (C) might be true, but it is not historically accurate. Choice (D) is outside the time period of the table. Choice (A) is a good answer, but democracy alone cannot guarantee economic growth. The Japanese economic miracle after World War II is most credited to the Korean War, so (B) is the best answer.

51. **B** The table shows the Japanese economy grew and fell depending on its success in wartime. Eliminate (A) and (C), as these are demonstrably false based on the table. Choice (D) is true, but not mentioned in the table. Therefore, choose (B).

52. **D** The North Atlantic Treaty is the document responsible for the creation of NATO, the U.S.-centered alliance bloc in the Cold War. Eliminate (A) because NATO is focused on defense, not trade. Eliminate (B) because secret treaties occurred during World War I, not the Cold War. Eliminate (C), as it invokes the Marshall Plan, which was economic aid to Europe, not military defense as stated in the document.

53. **C** The United Nations is mentioned in the first paragraph as a forum for peaceful settlements of conflict. Eliminate (A) because it invokes NATO or the Warsaw Pact, not the United Nations. Eliminate (B) because the fourth paragraph states that the UN allows for self-defense of nations. Eliminate (D) because the passage mentions nothing about trade. Choice (C) is correct.

54. **B** NATO was founded to provide defense against the Soviet Union for Western nations, which best aligns with (B). Eliminate (A) because many of the participating nations in NATO had largely enfranchised populations to begin with. According to the document, NATO is a defensive alliance, so eliminate (C). Eliminate (D) because the Soviet Union acquired atomic weapons in 1949, breaking the U.S. monopoly.

55. **B** NATO is a treaty that reflects (B), collective defense—the idea that an attack on one member is an attack on all. Eliminate (A) because NATO countries are typically capitalist, but a capitalist economy is not necessary for membership. Eliminate (C) because mutually assured destruction is what happens when two nuclear parties have large enough arsenals to eradicate each other—the document doesn't support this reading at all. Eliminate (D) because the "communist" alliance in the Cold War was the Warsaw Pact, not NATO.

Section I, Part B: Short-Answer Questions

Question 1

A successful response for this question will discuss the impact of the Industrial Revolution on European expansionism and how the "New Imperialism" of the later 19th century differed from the colonial efforts of the previous centuries.

a)   A successful response must include TWO of the following:

- The development of various technologies, such as steamships, machine guns, and rifles, as well as health developments like quinine and sanitary innovations, that helped advance European efforts to colonize the interior of Africa

- The growing sense of nationalism and international competition among European nations, making the establishment of colonies essential to becoming a great power

- The necessity for markets and more raw resources for the ever-growing demand of industries back home

- The developments of new philosophies, such as Social Darwinism, that advocated European dominance over the entire world

b)   A successful response must include ONE of the following:

- The commercial interests of Europeans, which were satisfied by coastal enclaves, such as the Portuguese fort systems along the coasts of Angola and Mozambique

- The usefulness of Africa as a resupply station for boats en route to India, such those of the Dutch in South Africa

- The prevalence of disease and other maladies that kept Europeans out of the jungles of Africa

- The relative strength of native African empires, such as the Ashanti in West Africa, the Xhosa or Zulu in South Africa, and Kongo in Southwest Africa

c) African life was changed immeasurably by the colonization of the continent by European powers:

- African laborers were hired to build roads, railroads, and communication networks. Though these workers were no longer pursuing subsistence farming, their wages were still very low.

- For those workers who did remain in agriculture, European powers demanded the farmers move towards cash crops. In practice, this usually meant that Africans begin to work in European-controlled colonial plantations at very low wages.

- With no concern for traditional cultures, Europeans carved the continent into arbitrary nations (often named after themselves, such as Rhodesia). The borders of these countries didn't consider pre-existing tribal relations. This often pushed rival tribes into the same colonial administration, which had serious effects in the twentieth century.

- Africans were often forced to convert to Christianity.

- The most talented or wealthy Africans often sought education in Europe, and dressed according to European customs.

Question 2

a) A good response to this question must contextualize the period 1750–1900 C.E. and major developments within this period with specific historical examples. A successful answer must include TWO of the following:

- **The Industrial Revolution and other advanced technologies:** States that harnessed industrialism and the rapid advances it brought benefited the most, as they were able to organize their societies through railroads, steamships, communications technologies, and so on. Great Britain is the perfect example of this.

- **Nationalism**: States like Germany, Italy, France, Japan, and the various Balkan nations that revolted from the Ottoman Empire all used nationalism to legitimize themselves as nation-states. The belief that one's country should be the home of one's own nationality drove governments to harness their citizens' patriotism, which in turn made the governments stronger.

- **Liberalism and Enlightenment ideals**: Many nations in this period saw enfranchisement of their populations and even the establishment of republics, as in the cases of France and Great Britain. Former New World colonies saw their independence achieved through Enlightenment ideals, and countries like the United States, Mexico, and even Haiti relied on these ideals as the basis for their existence.

- **Militarization**: Not all governments relied on liberal ideas of democracy and representation. Nations like Russia, Austria, and Qing China used brute military force to control their populations and suppress dissent. Military power was augmented by industrial technology, and as the weapons of war became more potent, this power was effective but not long-lasting.

b) There were several ways that people challenged the power of governments in the period between 1750 and 1900, but you need to write about only TWO of them. You may want to include the following:

- The French Revolution saw the Third Estate demand a larger voice in government, challenging the absolute power of the French throne.

- Independence movements occurred throughout Latin America.

- The wave of revolutions moved across Europe in 1848.

- Socialists challenged the primacy of industrialization.

c) There are a number of different possible responses to this question:

- Manufacturing power passed from East Asia to Europe. In the early 1700s, China was one of the biggest producers of goods in the world. By 1900, after the Industrial Revolution (spearheaded by England), Europe had firmly snatched that crown.

- Political control also passed from East Asia to Europe. China, for example, began the period relatively sovereign. By 1900, as a result of the Opium Wars, China ended the period on its knees, handing over control of Hong Kong to the British.

- In Asia, government-led efforts to reform and modernize economies and militaries were faced with resistance from conservative segments of society.

Question 3

A successful response will discuss Ming voyages of naval exploration, such as those headed by the admiral Zheng He, and relate those to China's ability to exact tribute from the states it dominated in the Indian Ocean.

a) A good response will discuss Zheng He's voyages, the advanced technology that Ming China had at this point in history, the buoyancy of the Ming economy, or the strength of the Ming military, especially fresh from its victory against the Mongolian overlords of the Yuan Dynasty.

b) A good response will discuss how Bengal was part of the same trade network frequented by Arab, Chinese, and Indian merchants between East Africa and India.

c) A good response will discuss the tribute as the attempt to guarantee a reduced tax rate, a favored trade status, or protection against further military actions.

Question 4

a) To successfully answer part (a), you should discuss Peter the Great's reforms—either those of the nobility and how he imposed Westernization in order to use the nobles' power to his benefit, or economic reforms involving the importation of Western technologies to allow Russia to internally produce guns and other advanced technology.

b) A good answer to (b) will discuss how Peter the Great's reforms preserved the nature of Russian society by leaving the autocratic Tsar and the greater magnates as the sole powerholders in the Russian empire. None of Peter's reforms bettered the status of the serfs—even though serfdom in Western Europe was on the decline—or helped to generate a strong capitalist tradition.

c) A successful answer to part (c) will involve justifying your answer to either (a) or (b), while also adding another example and explaining how these examples justify your judgment of Peter's Westernizing reforms.

Section II: Document-Based Question (DBQ)

A strong essay for this prompt will touch on the key differences between Vietnamese and Chinese documents. Many of the Vietnamese documents involve nationalism and a desire for independence from France, while the Chinese documents stress a desire for social equality and a drive for a better standard of living, as well as the abolishment of the imperial system. The essay should also establish the idea that communist ideals fit well with women's desire for gender equality and equal opportunity, especially with respect to educational opportunities. Women were employed in jobs outside of the home, but they were not always welcomed in these roles at first, as demonstrated in Document 3. A particularly difficult document to interpret might be Document 4. Note that the figure is an armed woman. The artist is calling for women to not only be involved in the war as belligerents, but, according to the title, to produce. Since the figure is accompanied by livestock, the term *produce* appears to refer to agricultural output. This image therefore seems to be evidence of the gender equality present in Vietnamese communism.

Long Essay

Question 2

A successful essay will discuss the importance of the Opium Wars and their impact on history. An essay that argues the importance of the Opium Wars would discuss the isolationism of China. China was pretty self-sufficient and did not need many outside trading partners. The British crowbarred their way in by introducing opium to China. The drug became so widespread in China that the Manchu Emperor released an imperial edict forbidding the further sale or use of opium. The British would have none of it. From 1839 to 1842, the two countries fought a war over the opium trade. This was known as the first Opium War. Overwhelmed by British military might, China was forced to sign the Treaty of Nanjing, the first of what came to be known as the "unequal treaties," by which Britain was given considerable rights to expand trade with China. An essay arguing for the importance of the Opium Wars would be sure to analyze the huge impact on the global perception of China. For centuries, the world knew that China was one of the more advanced civilizations. With the clear-cut British defeat of China with relatively few troops, the world realized that China was an easy target, and many nations forced China to open up for trade. China was ultimately defeated by Japan, which was starting its own imperial conquests.

If the essay seeks to downplay the importance of the Opium Wars, it would be necessary to analyze the inevitability of the downfall of the Manchus, whether the Opium Wars took place or not. For instance, you could argue that Korea declaring its independence, or Vietnam doing the same, was inevitable due to an ongoing perceived weakness in China. Further, internal unhappiness with the Manchu government was swelling in the mid-19th century. The Manchu Dynasty couldn't prevent the forces of reform from overtaking it from both within and without, and as a consequence, Chinese culture itself started to crumble. In 1901, foot binding was abolished. In 1905, the 2,000-year-old Chinese Examination System was eliminated. By 1911, the government was toppled and imperial rule came to an end. For the first time, under the leadership of Sun Yat-sen, a republic was established in China.

Question 3

A strong essay will discuss the importance of joint-stock companies with respect to their function in history. Countries like France, England, and the Netherlands founded various companies, the East India companies the most notable of them, to help finance the costs of colonization. Other European states like Portugal and Spain, however, did not rely on private financing but rather used public monies to sponsor colonization efforts. An essay that argues that joint-stock companies had a strong effect on world history should use evidence to show that the English, French, and Dutch were ultimately more successful in their empire-building efforts than the Spanish and Portuguese.

An essay that argues that joint-stock companies were of *less* importance should use evidence to show that the colonization efforts of the Spanish and Portuguese were of no less importance or less successful than company-sponsored efforts and had great significance in history, as well. An essay that takes this position might contend that the governments would ultimately absorb these companies and, therefore, that governments, not private industry, ultimately sponsored colonization efforts.

Question 4

A successful essay will discuss the Industrial Revolution and its various effects on world history. An essay in favor of the Industrial Revolution as an important moment in history will emphasize the dramatic transformation of human society that industrialization brought; almost every aspect of society was affected by the massive technological strides that resulted from industrialization. Furthermore, the Industrial Revolution confirmed the primacy of Europe over the world; by the end of the 19th century, it was clear that European nations dominated almost the entire world or had a massive influence on the cultures of those nations that remained independent.

An essay seeking to downplay the importance of the Industrial Revolution will argue that the industrial transformation of the 19th century was merely accelerated by the Industrial Revolution, and that the foundation of this transformation was laid during the Age of Discovery, which resulted in global interactions and a fully linked world. An essay that subscribes to this view might argue that gender roles were, in many cases, not affected, or that the transformative processes of the 19th century were not evenly distributed around the world, but rather were mostly localized in Europe and places influenced by European culture.

HOW TO SCORE PRACTICE TEST 3

Section IA: Multiple Choice

$$\underline{\hspace{4cm}} \times 1.090 = \underline{\hspace{4cm}}$$

| Number Correct (out of 55) | Weighted Section I Score (Do not round) |

Section IB: Short Answer

Question 1:

$$\underline{\hspace{4cm}} \times 3.3333 = \underline{\hspace{4cm}}$$
(out of 3)   (Do not round)

Question 2:

$$\underline{\hspace{4cm}} \times 3.3333 = \underline{\hspace{4cm}}$$
(out of 3)   (Do not round)

Question 3 or 4:

$$\underline{\hspace{4cm}} \times 3.3333 = \underline{\hspace{4cm}}$$
(out of 3)   (Do not round)

AP Score Conversion Chart World History	
Composite Score Range	AP Score
107–150	5
90–106	4
73–89	3
56–72	2
0–55	1

Section II: Document-Based Question

Question 1:

$$\underline{\hspace{4cm}} \times 5.3571 = \underline{\hspace{4cm}}$$
(out of 7)   (Do not round)

Section II: Long Essay

Question 2, 3, or 4:

$$\underline{\hspace{4cm}} \times 3.750 = \underline{\hspace{4cm}}$$
(out of 6)   (Do not round)

Composite Score

$$\underline{\hspace{3cm}} + \underline{\hspace{3cm}} + \underline{\hspace{3cm}} + \underline{\hspace{3cm}} = \underline{\hspace{3cm}}$$

| Weighted Section IA Score | Weighted Section IB Score | Weighted DBQ Score | Weighted Long Essay Score | Composite Score (Round to the nearest whole number |

Practice Test 4

The **Princeton Review®**

Completely darken bubbles with a No. 2 pencil. If you make a mistake, be sure to erase mark completely. Erase all stray marks.

1.

YOUR NAME: _____
(Print)   Last   First   M.I.

SIGNATURE: _____   DATE: __ / __ / __

HOME ADDRESS: _____
(Print)   Number and Street

_____
City   State   Zip Code

PHONE NO.: _____

IMPORTANT: Please fill in these boxes exactly as shown on the back cover of your test book.

2. TEST FORM

3. TEST CODE   **4. REGISTRATION NUMBER**

Test Code columns: 0-9 on left and right, with middle columns A/B/C/D/E/F/G/H/I, J/K/L/M/N/O/P/Q/R

Registration Number: 0-9

5. YOUR NAME

First 4 letters of last name				FIRST INIT	MID INIT
A	A	A	A	A	A
B	B	B	B	B	B
C	C	C	C	C	C
D	D	D	D	D	D
E	E	E	E	E	E
F	F	F	F	F	F
G	G	G	G	G	G
H	H	H	H	H	H
I	I	I	I	I	I
J	J	J	J	J	J
K	K	K	K	K	K
L	L	L	L	L	L
M	M	M	M	M	M
N	N	N	N	N	N
O	O	O	O	O	O
P	P	P	P	P	P
Q	Q	Q	Q	Q	Q
R	R	R	R	R	R
S	S	S	S	S	S
T	T	T	T	T	T
U	U	U	U	U	U
V	V	V	V	V	V
W	W	W	W	W	W
X	X	X	X	X	X
Y	Y	Y	Y	Y	Y
Z	Z	Z	Z	Z	Z

6. DATE OF BIRTH

Month	Day	Year
JAN		
FEB	0 0	0 0
MAR	1 1	1 1
APR	2 2	2 2
MAY	3 3	3 3
JUN	4	4 4
JUL	5	5 5
AUG	6	6 6
SEP	7	7 7
OCT	8	8 8
NOV	9	9 9
DEC		

7. GENDER
- MALE
- FEMALE

The **Princeton Review®**

1. A B C D
2. A B C D
3. A B C D
4. A B C D
5. A B C D
6. A B C D
7. A B C D
8. A B C D
9. A B C D
10. A B C D
11. A B C D
12. A B C D
13. A B C D
14. A B C D
15. A B C D
16. A B C D
17. A B C D
18. A B C D

19. A B C D
20. A B C D
21. A B C D
22. A B C D
23. A B C D
24. A B C D
25. A B C D
26. A B C D
27. A B C D
28. A B C D
29. A B C D
30. A B C D
31. A B C D
32. A B C D
33. A B C D
34. A B C D
35. A B C D
36. A B C D

37. A B C D
38. A B C D
39. A B C D
40. A B C D
41. A B C D
42. A B C D
43. A B C D
44. A B C D
45. A B C D
46. A B C D
47. A B C D
48. A B C D
49. A B C D
50. A B C D
51. A B C D
52. A B C D
53. A B C D
54. A B C D

55. A B C D

AP® World History: Modern Exam

SECTION I, PART A: Multiple Choice

DO NOT OPEN THIS BOOKLET UNTIL YOU ARE TOLD TO DO SO.

At a Glance

Time
55 minutes
Number of Questions
55
Percent of Total Score
40%
Writing Instrument
Pencil required

Instructions

Section I, Part A of this exam contains 55 multiple-choice questions. Fill in only the ovals for numbers 1 through 55 on your answer sheet.

Indicate all of your answers to the multiple-choice questions on the answer sheet. No credit will be given for anything written in this exam booklet, but you may use the booklet for notes or scratch work. After you have decided which of the suggested answers is best, completely fill in the corresponding oval on the answer sheet. Give only one answer to each question. If you change an answer, be sure that the previous mark is erased completely. Here is a sample question and answer.

Sample Question   Sample Answer

Chicago is a   Ⓐ ● Ⓒ Ⓓ
(A) state
(B) city
(C) country
(D) continent

Use your time effectively, working as quickly as you can without losing accuracy. Do not spend too much time on any one question. Go on to other questions and come back to the ones you have not answered if you have time. It is not expected that everyone will know the answers to all the multiple-choice questions.

Your total score on the multiple-choice section is based only on the number of questions answered correctly. Points are not deducted for incorrect answers or unanswered questions.

SECTION I, PART B: Short Answer

At a Glance

Time
40 minutes
Number of Questions
3
Percent of Total Score
20%
Writing Instrument
Pen with black or dark blue ink

Instructions

Section I, Part B of this exam consists of 4 short-answer questions, of which you will answer 3. Answer all parts of Questions 1 and 2, and then choose to answer EITHER Question 3 or Question 4. Write your responses on a separate sheet of paper.

After the exam, you must apply the label that corresponds to the last short-essay question you answered—Question 3 or 4. For example, if you answered Question 3, apply the label ③ . Failure to do so may delay your score.

WORLD HISTORY: MODERN

Section I, Part A

Time—55 minutes

55 Questions

Directions: Each of the questions or incomplete statements below is followed by either four suggested answers or completions. Select the one that is best in each case and then fill in the appropriate letter in the corresponding space on the answer sheet.

Questions 1–2 refer to the passage below.

At Buda I made my first acquaintance with the Janissaries; this is the name by which the Turks call the infantry of the royal guard. The Turkish state has 12,000 of these troops when the corps is at its full strength. They are scattered through every part of the empire, either to garrison the forts against the enemy, or to protect the Christians and Jews from the violence of the mob. There is no district with any considerable amount of population, no borough or city, which has not a detachment of Janissaries to protect the Christians, Jews, and other helpless people from outrage and wrong.

[Forster, C. T., and F. H. B. Daniel, eds. *The Life and Letters of Ogier Ghiselin de Busbecq, vol. I.* London: Kegan Paul, 1881.

"Ogier Ghiselin De Busbecq: on Ottoman Soldiers (Ca. 1554)." *World History: Ancient and Medieval Eras*, ABC-CLIO, 2019.]

Flemish ambassador Ogier Ghiselin de Busbecq's description of Ottoman soldiers (c. 1554)

1. The Janissaries mentioned in the passage are best understood as which of the following?

    (A) An informal group of citizen soldiers who volunteered to serve on an as-needed basis
    (B) Mercenaries for hire that created instability within the Ottoman Empire
    (C) A standing military that overthrew the sultan
    (D) An elite army that had historical origins as enslaved Christians

2. A historian would most likely use this passage in the treaty to illustrate which of the following?

    (A) How the Turkish military compared to foreign militaries
    (B) The violence deployed toward Christians and Jews by the Ottoman government
    (C) The aftereffects of the Ottoman conquest of Hungary
    (D) The methods used for training Janissaries

GO ON TO THE NEXT PAGE.

Questions 3–6 refer to the passage below.

"Many of those slaves we transport from Guinea to America are prepossessed with the opinion, that they are carried like sheep to the slaughter, and that the Europeans are fond of their flesh; which notion so far prevails with some, as to make them fall into a deep melancholy and despair, and to refuse all sustenance, tho' never so much compelled and even beaten to oblige them to take some nourishment: notwithstanding all which, they will starve to death; whereof I have had several instances in my own slaves both aboard and at Guadalupe."

[John Barbot, "Some Memoirs of the Life of Job, the Son of Solomon ," in Thomas Astley and John Churchill, eds., Collection of Voyages and Travels (London, 1732).

Firsthand account of John Barbot, an agent for the French Royal African Company (1732)

3. Barbot's account is best understood in the context of which of the following?

   (A) The colonization of South America
   (B) The development of North African trade networks
   (C) The dominance of French colonial holdings in the Americas
   (D) The transatlantic exchange of people, crops, animals, goods, and technology

4. The need for human labor during the Age of Exploration was most directly a consequence of which of the following?

   (A) The difficulty of growing crops in the Americas
   (B) The lack of automated industrial technology
   (C) The introduction of sugar crops to the New World
   (D) The discovery of gold deposits in the Americas

5. Which of the following was an important continuity underlying the interaction described in the passage?

   (A) The use of violence to create and maintain European colonies
   (B) Widespread opposition to the slave trade
   (C) The mutually beneficial relationship between laborers and manufacturers
   (D) The cooperation between European colonizers and Native American populations

6. Which of the following additional pieces of information would be most directly useful in assessing the extent to which Barbot's account was representative of most examples of human trafficking during the eighteenth century?

   (A) A list of the most common ports used for the slave trade
   (B) Statistics regarding survival rates of enslaved people during the Age of Exploration
   (C) Laws regarding human trafficking in the eighteenth century
   (D) Maps that portray the routes of different slave ships

GO ON TO THE NEXT PAGE.

Questions 7–9 refer to the passage below.

"Nature hath made men so equal in the faculties of the body and mind, as that, though there be found one man sometimes manifestly stronger in body or of quicker mind than another, yet when all is reckoned together the difference between man and man is not so considerable as that one man can thereupon claim to himself any benefit to which another may not pretend as well as he. For, as to the strength of body, the weakest has strength enough to kill the strongest, either by secret machination or by confederacy with others that are in the same danger with himself."

Thomas Hobbes, *Leviathan* (1651)

7. Hobbes's *Leviathan* was written in the context of which of the following European events?

   (A) The Counter Reformation
   (B) The War of Spanish Succession
   (C) The Glorious Revolution
   (D) The English Civil War

8. The excerpt above offers a central argument for which Enlightenment-era development?

   (A) The Invisible Hand
   (B) Social contract theory
   (C) Divine Right of Kings
   (D) Communism

9. Which of the following emerged in large part due to the ideas outlined in *Leviathan*?

   (A) The Industrial Revolution
   (B) The English Civil War
   (C) A wave of rebellions against European monarchies
   (D) Marxist reforms across Europe

GO ON TO THE NEXT PAGE.

Questions 10–14 refer to the passage below.

"My little homestead in the city, which I recently insured for £2,000 would no doubt have shared the common fate, as the insurance companies will not make good that which is destroyed by the Queen's enemies. And although I have a farm of 50 acres close to the town, no doubt the crops and premises would have been destroyed. In fact, this has already partly been the case, and I am now suing the Government for damages done by a contingent of 1,500 natives that have recently encamped not many hundred yards from the place, who have done much damage all around."

Letter from a British citizen to his sister during the Anglo-Zulu War, South Africa, 1879

10. Incidents such as those described by the author of the letter were used by the British government to do which of the following?

    (A) Issue a *casus belli* to go to war with the Kingdom of Zulu

    (B) Tax the Zulu kingdom to cover damages attributed to them

    (C) Sever its responsibility to protect citizens who chose to live in South Africa

    (D) Liberate the Zulus from British colonialism

11. Which of the following reasons explains why European citizens moved in large numbers to Zulu lands in 1867?

    (A) The British crown offered incentives to those who would establish homesteads in the unsettled lands of South Africa.

    (B) The Zulu created attractive trade ports along the Indian Ocean.

    (C) The Berlin Conference clarified boundaries, thus making it logistically sound for Europeans to move to the African colonies.

    (D) A diamond rush ensued following the discovery of diamonds on Zulu lands.

12. Which of the following was a direct effect of the expanding British presence in South Africa in the late nineteenth century?

    (A) South Africa became the most economically successful of all the British colonies.

    (B) Great Britain was penalized at the Berlin Conference with a loss of land.

    (C) The British engaged in a war with South African decedents of the Dutch.

    (D) British settlers created an independent nation.

13. A historian researching nineteenth-century conflicts in South Africa would most likely find this letter a useful source for information about which of the following?

    (A) The diffusion of cultural practices throughout South Africa

    (B) Economic boons present in British colonies

    (C) Daily challenges of Afrikaners during the colonial period

    (D) Unforeseen consequences of British imperialism

14. The inclusion of the author's pending litigation with the British government serves to do which of the following?

    (A) Highlight the extent of the author's property losses

    (B) Express his opposition to the ongoing war

    (C) Belittle British officials

    (D) Place blame on both his home country as well as the Zulus

GO ON TO THE NEXT PAGE.

Questions 15–18 refer to the image below.

Chinese Poster, 1958

"Brave the wind and the waves; everything has remarkable abilities."

Image courtesy of ChinesePosters.net.

15. Which economic philosopher most influenced the message of this poster?

(A) John Stuart Mill
(B) Adam Smith
(C) Karl Marx
(D) David Ricardo

16. Which of the following is NOT a result of the Great Leap Forward's outcomes?

(A) China strengthened its alliance with the Soviet Union.
(B) The Cultural Revolution was initiated.
(C) The Chinese adopted elements of capitalism.
(D) The Chinese changed their focus to military matters.

17. In what way was the Great Leap Forward different from the Soviet Union's Five-Year Plan?

(A) The Great Leap Forward focused only on industrial production, while the Five-Year Plan also took on agricultural production.
(B) Unlike the Soviet Union, China was unable to successfully industrialize during this period.
(C) Mao utilized a process of collectivization in his plan, a technique eschewed by Stalin.
(D) Historians attribute mass starvation to the Great Leap Forward, but do not see similar consequences to the Five-Year Plan.

18. The images on the poster best reflect which of the following ambitions of the People's Republic of China?

(A) To cut off ties with the non-communist world
(B) To have all citizens contribute to China's industrialization
(C) To launch the Cultural Revolution
(D) To form a friendlier alliance with Taiwan

GO ON TO THE NEXT PAGE.

Questions 19–20 refer to the image below.

Illustration of Power Loom Weaving, 1835

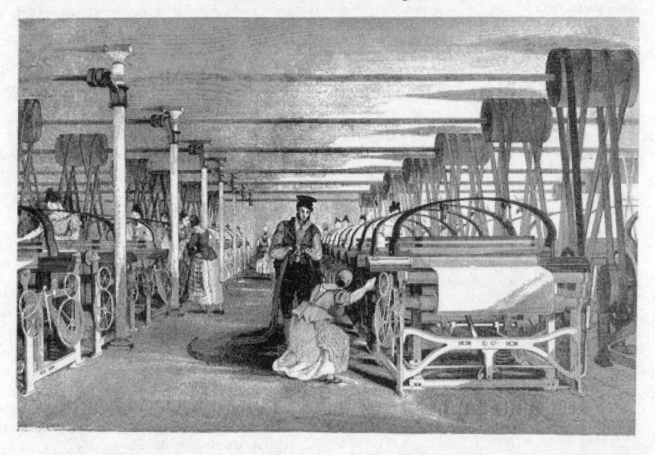

19. The device in the image had an impact most similar to which of the following technologies?

(A) The cotton gin

(B) The quipu

(C) Movable type

(D) Three-field system

20. Which of the following additional pieces of information would be most useful in addressing the extent to which the developments reflected in the image represented a long-term change to the English economy?

(A) Information on which companies profited most from power loom weaving

(B) Information on how the power loom functions

(C) Information on population shifts from rural to urban locations

(D) Information on women's roles within the textile factories

GO ON TO THE NEXT PAGE.

Questions 21–24 refer to the passage below.

"In Northern India the existence of separate States at this period is usually little more than a question of words. A zamindar who paid revenue to the Mogul was clearly in a position of dependence, and if he wished to establish a claim to sovereignty, the first step was to refuse, or omit to pay revenue. Such an omission might, however, arise from various other causes, and it is probable that in Rajputana, Central India, and Chota Nagpur there were numerous chiefs and tribes occupying what constitutional lawyers would regard as an anomalous position, sometimes paying the stipulated revenue, sometimes in open rebellion, and sometimes enjoying practical independence because the Mogul authorities found it inconvenient to undertake active measures of coercion."

W.H. Moreland, historian, on the policies of the Mughal (Mogul) Empire in *India at the Death of Akbar*, 1920

21. Which of the following characteristics most accurately defines the "zamindar[s]" mentioned in the passage?

(A) Muslim landowners

(B) Buddhist peasants

(C) Sikh nobility

(D) Hindu aristocrats

22. Zamindars had an ability "to establish a claim to sovereignty" largely due to the Mughal Empire's policy of

(A) religious toleration

(B) universal taxation

(C) martial law

(D) suffrage

23. The author's description of revenue collection in the Mughal Empire is best seen as evidence for which of the following generalizations?

(A) Only people of certain religions were required to pay revenue to the empire.

(B) Geographical differences may have influenced which groups pay taxes.

(C) Revenue collection was the only source of funds by which the Mughal Empire operated.

(D) The case of Rajputana was a typical one in the Mughal Empire.

24. The changes experienced by the zamindars under the Mughal throne are most similar to those faced by

(A) feudal lords under the Holy Roman Empire

(B) Russian peasants under the Romanovs

(C) Qing warriors under the Manchu Dynasty

(D) the daimyo under Emperor Tokugawa

GO ON TO THE NEXT PAGE.

Questions 25–28 refer to the passage below.

"I travelled thence to 'Aden, the port of Yemen, on the coast of the ocean. It is surrounded by mountains and can be approached from one side only; it has no crops, trees, or water, but has reservoirs in which rainwater is collected. The Arabs often cut off the inhabitants from their supply of drinking-water until they buy them off with money and pieces of cloth. It is an exceedingly hot place. It is the port of the Indians, and to it come large vessels from Kinbayat [Cambay], Kawlam [Quilon], Calicut and many other Malabar ports [on the south-west coast of India]. There are Indian merchants living there, as well as Egyptian merchants. Its inhabitants are all either merchants, porters, or fishermen. Some of the merchants are immensely rich, so rich that sometimes a single merchant is sole owner of a large ship with all it contains, and this is a subject of ostentation and rivalry amongst them. In spite of that they are pious, humble, upright, and generous in character, treat strangers well, give liberally to devotees, and pay in full the tithes due to God."

From *Travels in Asia and Africa*, 1325–1354 by Ibn Battuta; translated and edited by H. A. R. Gibb. Copyright © 1929 by Broadway House. Reproduced by permission of Taylor & Francis Books UK.

Ibn Battuta describing his travels, circa 1325–1354 C.E.

25. Which of the following led directly to the development of the economic system described in the passage?

    (A) Military campaigns
    (B) Meteorological phenomena
    (C) Competition with European trade networks
    (D) The presence of highly developed port cities

26. The views expressed in this journal passage are best seen as evidence of which of the following concerning medieval Islamic societies?

    (A) The absence of religious orthodoxy
    (B) Hostility toward outsiders
    (C) Limited economic opportunities
    (D) The supremacy of piety

27. The tone of the passage best reflects which of the following developments in the Indian Ocean trade network?

    (A) The ability of commerce to foster cultural diffusion
    (B) The superiority of Arabian port cities
    (C) The increasing difficulty caused by language barriers
    (D) The overproduction of cash crops

28. Ibn Battuta's experiences were LEAST similar to the experiences of which of the following?

    (A) Zheng He
    (B) Marco Polo
    (C) Lorenzo de Medici
    (D) Xuanzang

GO ON TO THE NEXT PAGE.

Questions 29–32 refer to the cartoon below.

Frank Leslie's Illustrated Newspaper, 1882

THE ONLY ONE BARRED OUT. Enlightened American Statesman.
—"We must draw the line *somewhere*, you know."

29. The conflict addressed in the cartoon is best understood in the context of which of the following?

(A) The imperial interests of the United States

(B) A dramatic increase in migration

(C) A stagnation in global trade

(D) The burgeoning human rights movement

30. Which late-nineteenth/early-twentieth century policy is most similar to the one depicted in the cartoon?

(A) Open Door Policy

(B) White Australia Policy

(C) Meiji Restoration

(D) Russification

31. For which reason does the cartoonist imply that the United States discriminated against Chinese immigrants?

(A) Fear of overpopulation

(B) Concerns about communism

(C) To avoid competition in the labor market

(D) Revenge for the Boxer uprising

32. Which of the following would the cartoonist argue is an undesirable characteristic in a migrant coming to the United States?

(A) Temperance

(B) Racial designation

(C) Industriousness

(D) Political radicalism

GO ON TO THE NEXT PAGE.

Questions 33–35 refer to the passage below.

"Indeed, as both the fatwas of distinguished [scholars] who base their opinion on reason and tradition alike and the consensus of the Sunni community agree that the ancient obligation of extirpation, extermination, and expulsion of evil innovation must be the aim of our exalted aspiration, for "Religious zeal is a victory for the Faith of God the Beneficent"; then, in accordance with the words of the Prophet (Peace upon him!) "Whosoever introduces evil innovation into our order must be expelled" and "Whosoever does aught against our order must be expelled," action has become necessary and exigent..."

Letter from Ottoman Sultan Selim I to Safavid Shah Ismail I, 1514

33. The letter from Selim I is most clearly an example of which of the following?

   (A) The maintenance of military supremacy at all costs
   (B) Expanding tensions between religious sects
   (C) Factors that brought about the collapse of the Ottoman Empire
   (D) Peacemaking efforts among the Islamic empires

34. The Safavids drew the ire of Islamic empires such as the Ottoman and the Mughal Empires primarily because the Safavids

   (A) were an expansionist empire geographically located between two other expansionists
   (B) rejected the central tenets of Islam
   (C) enslaved Christians, and turned them into Safavid fighters
   (D) were ruled by Ismail, who proclaimed himself to be a Caliph

35. The empire founded by Ismail I can be best characterized by which religious tradition?

   (A) Sufi
   (B) Sikh
   (C) Sunni
   (D) Shi'a

GO ON TO THE NEXT PAGE.

Questions 36–38 refer to the image below.

World War II Era Poster from the Soviet Union, 1917

This poster reads "Young Men and Women, Defend the Freedom, Motherland, and Honor that was Won by your Fathers."

36. This poster draws directly on its audience's experiences of which of the following events?

   (A) The Great Purge
   (B) The Yalta Conference
   (C) World War I
   (D) The Russian Revolution

37. The image is best seen as evidence for which of the following?

   (A) Anti-American sentiment at the dawn of the Cold War
   (B) The use of propaganda to drive support for World War II
   (C) Russian regret over exiting World War I
   (D) The results of Soviet collectivization

38. The Soviet Union's view of nationalist fervor depicted in the painting is evidence of which of the following contrasts to Marx's view of communism?

   (A) The Soviet Union saw communism as developing most effectively within a single country, while Marx envisioned it as an international movement.
   (B) The Soviet Union saw communism as primarily a militaristic philosophy, while Marx argued for a peaceful approach.
   (C) The Soviet Union saw communism as being fully realized by 1917, while Marx predicted the proletariat revolt to occur much later.
   (D) The Soviet Union saw communism as a theoretical concept, while Marx attempted to implement a communist society.

GO ON TO THE NEXT PAGE.

Questions 39–43 refer to the passage below.

"Above all, we want equal political rights, because without them our disabilities will be permanent. I know this sounds revolutionary to the whites in this country, because the majority of voters will be Africans. This makes the white man fear democracy.

But this fear cannot be allowed to stand in the way of the only solution which will guarantee racial harmony and freedom for all. It is not true that the enfranchisement of all will result in racial domination. Political division, based on colour, is entirely artificial and, when it disappears, so will the domination of one colour group by another. The [African National Congress] has spent half a century fighting against racialism. When it triumphs it will not change that policy.

This then is what the [African National Congress] is fighting. Their struggle is a truly national one. It is a struggle of the African people, inspired by their own suffering and their own experience. It is a struggle for the right to live.

During my lifetime I have dedicated myself to this struggle of the African people. I have fought against white domination, and I have fought against black domination. I have cherished the ideal of a democratic and free society in which all persons live together in harmony and with equal opportunities. It is an ideal which I hope to live for and to achieve. But if needs be, it is an ideal for which I am prepared to die."

Nelson Mandela, 1964

39. Which of the following explains why Mandela feels that his idea "sounds revolutionary to the whites in this country"?

    (A) White South Africans had not yet known independence from Britain.
    (B) Many white South Africans had already supported increasing Black rights before the Sharpeville Massacre.
    (C) White South Africans were unfamiliar with a democratic form of government.
    (D) The political power of white citizens would be tempered by the larger number of Black voters.

40. Which of the following policies is characteristic of South Africa at the time of Mandela's speech?

    (A) Political allegiance to Juvenal Habyarimana
    (B) Dual sovereign governments separating British and Dutch regions of the country
    (C) Universal adult franchise with open elections
    (D) Black citizens being forced to carry identification within city limits

41. This passage is most clearly an example of which of the following?

    (A) A response to failed unification attempts
    (B) A plea to change a government policy
    (C) A proposal to increase the standing of Africa in the modern world
    (D) Ardent opposition to the influence of capitalism in Africa

42. The inclusion of the African National Congress in Mandela's argument is intended to do which of the following?

    (A) Show an opposing viewpoint
    (B) Advocate for the status quo
    (C) Give historic context to a struggle
    (D) Show solidarity with other African nations

43. Mandela's argument in the passage most clearly opposes which of the following ideologies?

    (A) Apartheid
    (B) Communism
    (C) Neocolonialism
    (D) Pan-Africanism

GO ON TO THE NEXT PAGE.

Questions 44–47 refer to the passage below.

"The real grievance of the worker is the insecurity of his existence; he is not sure that he will always have work, he is not sure that he will always be healthy, and he foresees that he will one day be old and unfit to work. If he falls into poverty, even if only through a prolonged illness, he is then completely helpless, left to his own devices, and society does not currently recognize any real obligation towards him beyond the usual help for the poor, even if he has been working all the time ever so faithfully and diligently. The usual help for the poor, however, leaves a lot to be desired, especially in large cities, where it is very much worse than in the country."

Otto von Bismarck, 1884

44. According to the passage and your knowledge of world history, this speech led to the creation of laws that did which of the following?

   (A) Limited work hours in factories
   (B) Established public health care and pensions
   (C) Displaced citizens in the overpopulated city to the countryside
   (D) Forced early retirement for aging workers

45. Otto von Bismarck likely made this speech in reaction to which of the following issues?

   (A) Social acceptance of child labor
   (B) Declining life expectancy in Germany
   (C) Criticisms of German trade tariffs
   (D) Negative effects attributed to industrial capitalism

46. How would twentieth-century economist John Maynard Keynes suggest that society address Otto von Bismarck's evaluation of workers in Germany?

   (A) Keynes would recommend government intervention in order to maintain aggregate demand.
   (B) Keynes would suggest helping elderly workers, but claim that the government should not intervene in most circumstances.
   (C) Keynes would caution against government intervention in personal economic matters.
   (D) Keynes would advocate doing nothing because he felt poverty in rural areas was actually more severe than it was in cities.

47. The long-term effects of Otto von Bismarck's speech include which of the following?

   (A) Development of socialized programs throughout much of Europe
   (B) Disunity of the German states
   (C) Communist overhaul of the eastern parts of Germany
   (D) A decrease in German economic output

GO ON TO THE NEXT PAGE.

Questions 48–50 refer to the passage below.

"His Majesty the Emperor of China and His Majesty the Emperor of Japan, desiring to restore the blessings of peace to their countries and subjects and to remove all cause for future complications… have agreed to the following articles:—

ARTICLE I.
Independence of Korea.—China recognizes definitely the full and complete independence and autonomy of Korea, and in consequence the payment or tribute and the performance of ceremonies and formalities by Korea to China, in derogation of such independence and autonomy, shall wholly cease for the future.

ARTICLE II.
Cession of part of Fengtien Province.—China cedes to Japan in perpetuity and full sovereignty the following territories together with all fortifications, arsenals, and public property thereon:
(a) The southern portion of the province of Fengtien
(b) The island of Formosa, together with all islands appertaining or belonging to said island of Formosa."

["Treaty of Shimonoseki (1895)." *World at War: Understanding Conflict and Society,* ABC-CLIO, 2019, worldatwar.abc-clio.com/Search/Display/768350. Accessed 2 Apr. 2019.]

Treaty of Shimonoseki (1895)

48. Based on the concessions in the treaty, what was most likely the outcome of the conflict it resolved?

(A) Japan had defeated China in a military operation.
(B) A war between China and Japan ended in a stalemate.
(C) Japan assisted China in putting down a rebellion.
(D) China handily defeated the Japanese army.

49. Which of the following was an important long-term effect of the Treaty of Shimonoseki?

(A) Korea became two nations, separated at the 38th parallel.
(B) Taiwan remained under Chinese jurisdiction.
(C) China was secluded from foreign trade.
(D) Japan began its systematic development of a Pacific empire.

50. This treaty occurred within the context of which of the following continuities of nineteenth-century Chinese history?

(A) Chinese military and economic expansion
(B) China's concession of land and spheres of influence to outside entities
(C) China's transition to a communist government
(D) Increased autonomy given to the Chinese emperor

GO ON TO THE NEXT PAGE.

Questions 51-55 refer to the passage below.

"The colonial world is a world cut in two…In the capitalist countries a multitude of moral teachers, counselors and 'bewilderers' separate the exploited from those in power. In the colonial countries, on the contrary, the policeman and the soldier, by their immediate presence and their frequent and direct action maintain contact with the native and advise him by means of rifle butts and napalm not to budge. It is obvious here that the agents of government speak the language of pure force. The intermediary does not lighten the oppression, nor seek to hide the domination; he shows them up and puts them into practice with the clear conscience of an upholder of the peace; yet he is the bringer of violence into the home and into the mind of the native."

The Wretched of the Earth by Frantz Fanon (1961)

51. The mention that "the agents of government speak the language of pure force" is best understood in the context of which of the following twentieth-century continuities?

   (A) The ongoing practice of colonial expansion
   (B) The inability of the agents of government to communicate with local populations
   (C) The dehumanization of people in developing nations
   (D) Cold War tensions

52. Fanon's interpretation of the colonial world as presented in the passage was most strongly influenced by which of the following?

   (A) Marxism
   (B) Anticolonialism
   (C) Social Darwinism
   (D) Nationalism

53. The colonized nations described by Fanon experienced difficulty building stable, independent countries for which of the following reasons?

   (A) They were unable to secure independence from their European colonizers.
   (B) Most colonized nations had been resistant to democratic constitutions.
   (C) Colonized nations had few natural resources of their own with which to build a strong economy.
   (D) National boundaries had been drawn by Europeans with no regard for shared languages or cultures.

54. The process of African decolonization was most accelerated by which of the following factors?

   (A) A series of treaties made with European colonizers
   (B) Pan-nationalism
   (C) Increased wealth in colonized countries
   (D) Political stability

55. All of the following statements are factually accurate. Which most likely informs Fanon's view of the two worlds discussed in the passage?

   (A) Fanon dedicated part of his life to helping Algerians fight for their independence against France.
   (B) Fanon encountered racism while fighting in the French Free Forces during World War II.
   (C) Fanon had experience living in colonized nations as well as in France.
   (D) The Algerian fight for independence was a stressor that contributed to the fall of the French Fourth Republic.

GO ON TO THE NEXT PAGE.

WORLD HISTORY: MODERN

SECTION I, Part B

Time—40 minutes

Directions: Answer Question 1 **and** Question 2. Answer **either** Question 3 **or** Question 4.

Use complete sentences; an outline or bulleted list alone is not acceptable. On test day, you will be able to plan your answers in the exam booklet, but only your responses in the corresponding boxes on the free-response answer sheet will be scored.

Use the map below to answer all parts of the question that follows.

Extent of the British Empire in 1900

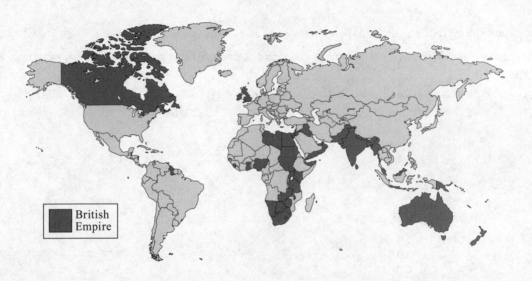

British Empire

1. a) Identify and explain TWO ways that the expansion of the British Empire changed a particular region or regions.

   b) Identify and explain ONE reason that the British Empire experienced a decline.

   c) Identify and explain ONE method that the British Empire used to maintain control of its colonies.

GO ON TO THE NEXT PAGE.

Use the passage below to answer all parts of the question that follows.

"The fact that we can release atomic energy ushers in a new era in man's understanding of nature's forces. Atomic energy may in the future supplement the power that now comes from coal, oil, and falling water, but at present it cannot be produced on a basis to compete with them commercially. Before that comes there must be a long period of intensive research. It has never been the habit of the scientists of this country or the policy of this government to withhold from the world scientific knowledge. Normally, therefore, everything about the work with atomic energy would be made public.

But under the present circumstances it is not intended to divulge the technical processes of production or all the military applications. Pending further examination of possible methods of protecting us and the rest of the world from the danger of sudden destruction."

President Harry Truman, speech informing American citizens that an atomic
weapon had been used against Japan, August 6, 1945

2. a) Identify and explain ONE way that the speech reflects the complexity of atomic technology.

b) Identify and explain TWO ways in which the development of this weapon impacted international relations following the Second World War.

c) Identify and explain ONE factor that led to the development of atomic weapons.

GO ON TO THE NEXT PAGE.

Question 3 or 4

Directions: Answer **either** Question 3 **or** Question 4.

Answer all parts of the question that follows.

3. a) Identify and explain TWO ways in which improved transportation technology led to cultural diffusion during the period 1200 to 1450 C.E. Use specific examples from one or more civilizations.

   b) Identify and explain TWO motivations for increased cultural interactions during the period 1200 to 1450 C.E. Use specific examples from one or more civilizations.

   c) Identify and explain ONE reason for the rise of nation-states in Europe during the period 1200 to 1450 C.E. Use a specific example from one or more civilizations.

GO ON TO THE NEXT PAGE.

Use the image below to answer all parts of the question that follows.

Phillip Veit, Germania, 1848

4. a) Identify and explain ONE symbol in the painting that represents German nationalism.

b) Identify and explain ONE factor that brought about nationalist fervor in Germany.

c) Select a nationalist movement (besides that of Germany), state its primary goal, and explain whether, in your opinion, it succeeded in its goal. Briefly explain your choice using evidence.

END OF SECTION I

AP® World History: Modern Exam

SECTION II: Free Response

DO NOT OPEN THIS BOOKLET UNTIL YOU ARE TOLD TO DO SO.

At a Glance

Total Time
1 hour, 40 minutes
Number of Questions
2
Writing Instrument
Pen with black or dark blue ink

Question 1 (DBQ): Mandatory
Suggested Reading and Writing Time
60 minutes
Percent of Total Score
25%

Question 2, 3, or 4 (Long Essay): Choose ONE Question
Answer either Question 2, 3, or 4
Suggested Time
40 minutes
Percent of Total Score
15%

Instructions

The questions for Section II are printed in the Questions and Documents booklet. You may use that booklet to organize your answers and for scratch work, but you must write your answers in this Section II: Free Response booklet. No credit will be given for any work written in the Questions and Documents booklet.

The proctor will announce the beginning and end of the reading period. You are advised to spend the 15-minute period reading the question and planning your answer to Question 1, the document-based question. If you have time, you may also read Questions 2, 3, and 4.

Section II of this exam requires answers in essay form. Write clearly and legibly. Circle the number of the question you are answering at the top of each page in this booklet. Begin each answer on a new page. Do not skip lines. Cross out any errors you make; crossed-out work will not be scored.

Manage your time carefully. The proctor will announce the suggested time for each part, but you may proceed freely from one part to the next. Go on to the long essay question if you finish Question 1 early. You may review your responses if you finish before the end of the exam is announced.

After the exam, you must apply the label that corresponds to the long-essay question you answered—Question 2, 3, or 4. For example, if you answered Question 2, apply the label ②. Failure to do so may delay your score.

GO ON TO THE NEXT PAGE.

WORLD HISTORY: MODERN

SECTION II

Total Time—1 hour, 40 minutes

Question 1 (Document-Based Question)

Suggested reading and writing time: 1 hour

It is suggested that you spend 15 minutes reading the documents and 45 minutes writing your response. Note: You may begin writing your response before the reading period is over.

Directions: Question 1 is based on the accompanying documents. The documents have been edited for the purpose of this exercise.

In your response you should do the following.

• Respond to the prompt with a historically defensible thesis or claim that establishes a line of reasoning.

• Describe a broader historical context relevant to the prompt.

• Support an argument in response to the prompt using at least six documents.

• Use at least one additional piece of specific historical evidence (beyond that found in the documents) relevant to an argument about the prompt.

• For at least three documents, explain how or why the document's point of view, purpose, historical situation, and/or audience is relevant to an argument.

• Use evidence to corroborate, qualify, or modify an argument that addresses the prompt.

Begin your response to this question at the top of a new page in the separate Free Response booklet and fill in the appropriate circle at the top of each page to indicate the question number.

GO ON TO THE NEXT PAGE.

1. Using the following documents and your knowledge of world history, discuss the barriers women have faced for more equal treatment in modern society. Consider the goals and methods of such campaigns.

Document 1

Source: Anna Manning Comfort, *The Public 2*, 1899.

Home Burdens of Uncle Sam

"Take up the white man's burden" –

The Negro, once our slave!

Boast lightly of his freedom,

This problem still is grave.

We scoff and shoot and lynch him,

And yet, because he's black,

We shove him out of office

And crowd him off the track.

"Take up the white man's burden" –

Yes, one of them is sex.

Enslaved are your brave women,

No ballot, while you tax!

Your labors and your conflicts,

Columbia's daughters share,

Yet still denied the franchise,

Quick give! be just! deal fair!

GO ON TO THE NEXT PAGE.

Document 2

Source: From the *Women's Charter*, adopted at the Founding Conference of the Federation of South African Women,
  Johannesburg, 1954.

This organisation is formed for the purpose of uniting women in common action for the removal of all political, legal, economic, and social disabilities. We shall strive for women to obtain:

1. The right to vote and to be elected to all State bodies, without restriction or discrimination.

2. The right to full opportunities for employment with equal pay and possibilities of promotion in all spheres of work.

3. Equal rights with men in relation to property, marriage and children, and for the removal of all laws and customs that deny women such equal rights.

4. For the development of every child through free compulsory education for all; for the protection of mother and child through maternity homes, welfare clinics, crèches and nursery schools, in countryside and towns; through proper homes for all, and through the provision of water, light, transport, sanitation, and other amenities of modern civilisation.

5. For the removal of all laws that restrict free movement, that prevent or hinder the right of free association and activity in democratic organizations, and the right to participate in the work of these organisations.

6. To build and strengthen women's sections in the National Liberatory movements, the organisation of women in trade unions, and through the peoples' varied organisation.

7. To cooperate with all other organisations that have similar aims in South Africa as well as throughout the world.

8. To strive for permanent peace throughout the world.

Document 3

Source: *The Plight of Women's Work in the Early Industrial Revolution in England and Wales*, evidence taken by
  Children's Employment Commission, 1841.

Miss — has been for several years in the dress-making business. The common hours of business are from 8 A.M. 'til 11. P.M. in the winters; in the summer from 6 or half past 6 A.M. 'til 12 at night. During the fashionable season, that is from April 'til the later end of July, it frequently happens that the ordinary hours are greatly exceeded; if there is a drawing room or grand fete, or mourning to be made, it often happens that the work goes on for 20 hours out of the 24, occasionally all night. . . . The general result of the long hours and sedentary occupation is to impair seriously and very frequently to destroy the health of the young women. The digestion especially suffers, and also the lungs: pain to the side is very common, and the hands and feet die away from want of circulation and exercise.

Miss — is sure that there are some thousands of young women employed in the business in London and in the country. If one vacancy were to occur now there would be 20 applicants for it. Thinks that no men could endure the work enforced from the dress-makers.

GO ON TO THE NEXT PAGE.

Document 4

Source: Aung San Suu Kyi, Nobel Prize Laureate, excerpts from keynote address at APC Conference, 1995.

For millennia women have dedicated themselves almost exclusively to the task of nurturing, protecting, and caring for the young and old, striving for the conditions of peace that favour life as a whole. To this can be added the fact that, to the best of my knowledge, no war was ever started by women. But it is women and children who have always suffered most in situations of conflict. Now that we are gaining control of the primary historical role imposed on us of sustaining life in the context of the home and family, it is time to apply in the arena of the world the wisdom and experience thus gained in activities of peace over so many thousands of years. The education and empowerment of women throughout the world cannot fail to result in a more caring, tolerant, just, and peaceful life for all.

Document 5

Source: Raja Rammohan Roy, *A Second Conference Between an Advocate for, and an Opponent of the Practice of Burning Widows Alive*, 1820.

Advocate:

I alluded. . . to the real reason for our anxiety to persuade widows to follow their husbands, and for our endeavors to burn them pressed down with ropes: viz., that women are by nature of inferior understanding, without resolution, unworthy of trust, subject to passions, And void of virtuous knowledge; they, according to the precepts of the Sastra, are not allowed to marry again after the demise of their husbands, and consequently despair at once of all worldly pleasure; hence it is evident, that death to these unfortunate widows is preferable to existence; for the great difficulty which a widow may experience by living a purely ascetic life, as prescribed by the Sastras, is obvious; may bring disgrace upon her paternal and maternal relations, and those that may be connected with her husband. Under these circumstances, we instruct them from their early life in the idea of the beatitude of their relations, both by birth and marriage, and their reputation in this world. From this many of them, on the death of their husbands, become desirous of accompanying them; but to remove every chance of their trying to escape from the blazing fire, in the burning them we first tie them down to the pile.

GO ON TO THE NEXT PAGE.

Document 6

Source: *Pravda* (Soviet Newspaper), "On the Path to a Great Emancipation," March 8, 1929.

Capitalist "democracy" has not and cannot give freedom to working and laboring women. Working women in all bourgeois countries are economically and politically enslaved. Middle class conventionality has a tenacious vice-grip on daily life. Advanced women workers and revolutionary women proletarians are persecuted. The most brutal blows of capitalist "rationalization," unemployment, and hunger in the midst of plenty descend upon the female half of the proletariat. Fascism, Catholicism, and reformism with increasingly thoroughness exploit the historical backwardness of women workers in order to split apart the proletarian ranks and strengthen the position of imperialism. The temples of "national government"—what a thing to talk about!—are protected by stone walls which prevent the participation of working women.

Document 7

Source: Argentine feminist Maria Eugenia Echenique, "The Emancipation of Women," 1876.

When emancipation was given to men, it was also given to women in recognition of the equality of rights, consistent with the principles of nature on which they are founded, that proclaim the identity of soul between men and women. Thus, Argentine women have been emancipated by law for a long time. The code of law that governs us authorizes a widow to defend her rights in court, just as an educated woman can in North America, and like her, we can manage the interests of our children, these rights being the basis for emancipation. What we lack is sufficient education and instruction to make use of them, instruction that North American women have; it is not just recently that we have proclaimed our freedom. To try to question or to oppose women's emancipation is to oppose something that is almost a fact, it is to attack our laws and destroy the Republic.

So let the debate be there, on the true point where it should be: whether or not it is proper for women to make use of those granted rights, asking as a consequence the authorization to go to the university so as to practice those rights or make them effective. And this constitutes another right and duty in woman: a duty to accept the role that our own laws bestow on her when extending the circle of her jurisdiction and which makes her responsible before the members of her family.

END OF DOCUMENTS FOR QUESTION 1

GO ON TO THE NEXT PAGE.

Question 2, 3, or 4 (Long Essay)

Suggested writing time: 40 minutes

Directions: Answer Question 2 **or** Question 3 **or** Question 4.

In your response you should do the following.

- Respond to the prompt with a historically defensible thesis or claim that establishes a line of reasoning.

- Describe a broader historical context relevant to the prompt.

- Support an argument in response to the prompt using specific and relevant examples of evidence.

- Use historical reasoning (e.g., comparison, causation, continuity or change over time) to frame or structure an argument that addresses the prompt.

- Use evidence to corroborate, qualify, or modify an argument that addresses the prompt.

2. Evaluate the extent to which resistance to colonialism in the nineteenth and twentieth centuries transformed national identities. In the development of your argument, explain what changed and what stayed the same from the period before the resistance to colonialism in the nineteenth and twentieth to the period after the resistance to colonialism in the nineteenth and twentieth centuries.

3. Evaluate the extent to which the emergence of Enlightenment philosophies in the seventeenth century c.e. transformed European culture. In the development of your argument, explain what changed and what stayed the same from the period before the emergence of Enlightenment philosophy in the seventeenth century c.e. to the period after the emergence of Enlightenment philosophy in the seventeenth century c.e.

4. Evaluate the extent to which the Cold War transformed Latin American culture. In the development of your argument, explain what changed and what stayed the same from the period before the Cold War to the period after the Cold War began.

WHEN YOU FINISH WRITING,
CHECK YOUR WORK ON SECTION II IF TIME PERMITS.

STOP
END OF EXAM

Practice Test 4:
Answers and
Explanations

PRACTICE TEST 4 ANSWER KEY

1.	D	29.	B
2.	C	30.	B
3.	D	31.	C
4.	C	32.	D
5.	A	33.	B
6.	B	34.	A
7.	D	35.	D
8.	B	36.	D
9.	C	37.	B
10.	A	38.	A
11.	D	39.	D
12.	C	40.	D
13.	D	41.	B
14.	D	42.	C
15.	C	43.	A
16.	A	44.	B
17.	B	45.	D
18.	B	46.	A
19.	A	47.	A
20.	C	48.	A
21.	D	49.	D
22.	A	50.	B
23.	B	51.	C
24.	D	52.	A
25.	B	53.	D
26.	D	54.	B
27.	A	55.	C
28.	C		

PRACTICE TEST 4 EXPLANATIONS

Section I, Part A: Multiple-Choice Questions

1. **D** To conquer large territories, the Ottomans enslaved children of their Christian subjects and turned them into fighting warriors, known as Janissaries. Therefore, (D) is correct. Eliminate (A) since the Janissaries were not informal, and for at least the earliest members, were not voluntary. Choices (B) and (C) are incorrect, as the Janissaries worked for the sultan.

2. **C** Following the Ottoman conquest, the city of Buda, which was located in Hungary (think of modern-day Budapest) was occupied by Ottoman militants (the Janissaries). This gives some insight into life in Buda following the Ottoman invasion. Choice (C) is correct. There is no comparison to other militaries, so eliminate (A). This passage describes how the government protected Christians and Jews from the violence of the mob, not perpetrated the violence. Eliminate (B). There are no training methods covered in this text, so (D) is incorrect.

3. **D** The author is referring to the Atlantic slave trade, which would fall under the categories listed in (D), the correct answer. Colonies in South America had already been established at the time this passage was written, so eliminate (A). The focus of this passage is on the transatlantic slave trade, not trade routes within North America, which would make (B) incorrect. While the French had significant colonial holdings in the Americas, it could hardly be considered "dominant" especially as compared to the Spanish. Eliminate (C).

4. **C** Sugarcane roots had arrived in the Caribbean from India with Columbus, who saw an opportunity to monopolize a profitable crop in a new environment. Sugarcane production resulted in the development of plantations throughout the Spanish colonies and an increased need for enslaved labor once the native populations of the islands declined. This precipitated the slave trade from Africa. Choice (C) is correct. The colonists had little trouble growing a variety of crops in the New World, hence the need for labor. Eliminate (A). The Columbian Exchange began centuries before the Industrial Revolution, so automated industrial technology was not an option anyhow. Eliminate (B) since it is ahistorical. Gold deposits in the Americas were not as plentiful as the explorers had hoped—certainly not enough to necessitate extra labor. Eliminate (D).

5. **A** The author describes the fear of enslaved people due to the brutality they experience en route to the New World from Africa (Guinea to America) and while enslaved by using the simile "like sheep to the slaughter." This is consistent with the mention of violence in (A), which is the correct answer. While opposition to the slave trade existed, the passage does not explicitly reference it to justify (B) as a correct answer. Eliminate it. The "laborers" (enslaved people) did not benefit at all from this exchange. Eliminate (C). Most Native American populations actively resisted the efforts of European colonizers. Eliminate (D).

6. **B**   Barbot describes the brutality and fear experienced by enslaved people in the Atlantic slave trade. Data about the brutality would include findings on how many enslaved people survived the trans-Atlantic trip, which is consistent with (B). Ports for the slave trade and the various routes the ships undertook would be irrelevant to Barbot's claims about the human experiences of the enslaved people on the ships. Eliminate (A) and (D). Whether or not laws existed regulating the slave trade, the brutality was still real, and therefore those laws would not give insight into the accuracy of Barbot's account. Eliminate (C).

7. **D**   Thomas Hobbes published *Leviathan* in 1651 in response to the English Civil War, a time during which the monarch, Charles I, was beheaded. Hobbes's violent view of human nature and desire for an all-powerful ruler to maintain peace are completely understandable within the context of the English Civil War. Choice (D) is correct. The Counter Reformation was a Catholic response to the Protestant Reformation and took place a century before Hobbes wrote *Leviathan*, so (A) is incorrect. The Glorious Revolution followed several decades after Hobbes penned this text, so (C) is incorrect. Finally, the War of Spanish Succession was even later than the Glorious Revolution, so (B) is also incorrect.

8. **B**   Thomas Hobbes thought that people by nature were greedy and prone to violent warfare. Accordingly, he believed the role of the government under the social contract should be to preserve peace and stability at all costs. Choice (B) is correct. The Invisible Hand is associated with another Enlightenment-era thinker, Adam Smith, and is an economic, rather than political, theory. Eliminate (A). The Enlightenment was a time that began to move past and reject the idea of the Divine Right of Kings. So while Hobbes advocated for a powerful king, he did so under the guise of social contract theory, not because kings were divinely ordained. Eliminate (C). The idea of communism, as theorized by Karl Marx, came two centuries after *Leviathan*, and is therefore not from the Enlightenment era. Choice (D) is incorrect.

9. **C**   The ideas from the Enlightenment (not just from Hobbes, but also John Locke and Jean-Jacques Rousseau) influenced a wave of revolutions, such as in the United States, France, Haiti, and across Europe at the turn of the 19th century. Each of those revolutions had one thing in common: they were rebellions against a European monarch. Choice (C) is correct. The Industrial Revolution was beginning at this period, as well, but did not emerge from social contract theory, but rather from technological innovations. Choice (A) is incorrect. Hobbes wrote *Leviathan* in reaction to the English Civil War, so that was not an event that emerged from this text. Eliminate (B). While Marxist reforms may have eventually grown out of the ashes of the European rebellions, they are not traced back to *Leviathan* as directly as the revolutions against European monarchs. Choice (D) is incorrect.

10. **A**   *Casus belli*, (A), is just a Latin term that means "reason for war." The British cited conflicts between the colonial settlers and the native Zulu population to demonstrate that the native population was the aggressor. This was important to the British, as a successful war campaign would increase British influence in South Africa.

11. **D** As the saying goes, imperial conquest is motivated by the three G's: God, glory, and gold. While none of these is mentioned in the answer choices, (D), diamonds, supports the idea that conquests were often motivated by a desire for riches. Be aware of your timelines, as (C) includes the Berlin Conference, which did not occur until 1884.

12. **C** More famous than the Anglo-Zulu War is the Boer War (1899–1902). The British came into conflict with some of the earlier European settlers of South Africa, the Boers (or Afrikaners), who are Dutch descendants. Choice (C) is correct.

13. **D** The letter describes the difficulties that one settler encountered upon arriving in South Africa. The British settled South Africa, among other colonies, with little regard for the population that already lived there. There is no evidence for the diffusion of the two cultures, so eliminate (A). The author discusses the economic difficulties he experiences, so there is no discussion of a boon; eliminate (B). You can also eliminate (C), as the author is British, not Afrikaner, and does not mention Afrikaners. Thus, the best answer is (D).

14. **D** The author not only tells his sister of his conflict with the Zulu, but he also expresses frustration with the fact that the insurance company will not cover his losses. He is therefore going to sue the British government. The author seems caught in the middle and has conflicts with both parties. The amount of exact loss is not mentioned, so eliminate (A). He does not give an opinion on the war, so (B) is incorrect. While the author is critical of the British government, he does not specify any officials and merely says that he is suing the British government in general, so eliminate (C). Choice (D) is the best answer.

15. **C** The poster, which is propaganda for the Great Leap Forward, represents Mao Zedong's vision for China. Since China became a communist nation under Mao, the obvious influence should be Karl Marx, (C).

16. **A** The Great Leap Forward ultimately failed to industrialize China, due in no small part to diminished support from the Soviet Union, which was not pleased with the direction in which China was taking communism. The failure of the Great Leap Forward led to some radical changes for China, including the Cultural Revolution, (B); the adoption of some capitalist practices, (C); and the beefing up of its military, (D). Therefore, eliminate (B), (C), and (D), and choose (A).

17. **B** Both the Great Leap Forward and the Five-Year Plan sought to propel industrial and agricultural output, but China was unable to industrialize in the way that the Soviet Union was able to. Eliminate (A). Choice (C) is also incorrect because collectivization, the government takeover of businesses, was the method that drove both plans. The Five-Year Plan led to starvation, particularly for the farmers, as Stalin prioritized feeding government workers, so eliminate (D). Choice (B) is correct.

18. **B** The poster shows citizens from all walks of life in China contributing to industry and agriculture, which is consistent with (B).

19. **A** The power loom automated the process of weaving fabric. Therefore, the correct answer will be a technology that automates labor. Choice (A) is therefore correct because the cotton gin allowed massive amounts of cotton to be quickly processed in the Americas and exported to Europe. The quipu is a threaded counting device used by the Inca. It did not automate labor. Eliminate (B).

Movable type led to the printing press but was not an automation of labor in the same way that the machines of the Industrial Revolution were. Choice (C) is incorrect. Finally, the three-field system made agriculture more efficient during the European Middle Ages but did not automate labor. Eliminate (D).

20. **C** With the automation of fabric development, the textile industry was taken out of the homes and into the mills entirely. This led to a movement of people to cities as they looked for jobs in mills (the rural jobs were disappearing in favor of automation). Choice (C) is therefore correct. Knowing which companies did best during this period would not be useful in assessing a long-term change in England (outside of those studying the history of a particular company perhaps). Eliminate (A). The specific functionality of the power loom, outside of the fact that it automates labor that was previously done by humans, is irrelevant to looking at long-term economic trends in England. Choice (B) is incorrect. Finally, the factory roles associated with the different sexes is not relevant to long-term changes in the English economy unless accompanied by information, for instance, about whether women were a smaller or larger part of the changing economy. Still the movement of population is the far more relevant issue here. Eliminate (D).

21. **D** The *zamindars* were nobles in India at the time the Islamic Mughal Empire was established. Since they were native to India, it can be reasonably concluded that they were Hindu, which is (D).

22. **A** The Mughal Empire was notable for its religious toleration, (A), a key to success on the subcontinent that was already populated by Hindus. The passage makes it clear that not all zamindars paid taxes, so eliminate (B). Choices (C) and (D) were not characteristic of the Mughal Empire, so eliminate them.

23. **B** The passage mentions zamindars who lived in areas that the Mughal authorities found "inconvenient" to travel to in order to collect revenue. Therefore, (B) is the correct answer. As the passage notes, these places, such as Rajputana, were anomalous (uncommon), so eliminate (D). The passage does not indicate that tax collection was the only source of revenue, so get rid of (C). Nor is there any mention of whether other religions had to pay taxes or not. Eliminate (A).

24. **D** For this question, you are looking for a group that had a similar experience to the zamindars. That is, you are looking for a group that had its traditional aristocratic power challenged by a new regime. This would describe the daimyo, (D), in Japan when the Tokugawa Era began. Lords kept their land and relatively important place in society under the Holy Roman Empire, so (A) is not similar to the zamindars. Peasants never had significant power in Russia, so eliminate (B). Choice (C) is not similar because the Qing warriors represented the Manchu Dynasty; eliminate (C).

25. **B** The Indian Ocean trade network depended primarily on one thing: monsoons. These seasonal winds pushed boats from west to east in one part of the year, and from east to west six months later. The network was driven by the need for trade, not military conquest, so eliminate (A). Choice (C) is incorrect, as there was no competition with Europe. In fact, at the time, the Indian Ocean was far busier a trade route than any route in Europe. The development of the port cities was actually a function of there being a thriving trade network, not a cause of it, so (D) is incorrect. Choice (B) is the answer.

26. **D** The final sentence states that despite the pursuit of wealth, the traders were "pious, humble, [and] upright," which matches (D). The attention to tithes would indicate at least some degree of religious orthodoxy, so eliminate (A). The network welcomed cultures from all over the Indian Ocean, including Zoroastrians and Hindus; eliminate (B). There were vast economic opportunities, so (C) is also incorrect. Choice (D) is the answer.

27. **A** Ibn Batutta focuses on the presence of Indian and Egyptian merchants living in a port city on the Arabian Peninsula. This indicates the presence of cultural diffusion, (A). While this journal passage takes place in Aden, there is no discussion of whether such cities were superior to others along the Indian Ocean, so eliminate (B). The trade network is successful despite the many languages present, so (C) does not make sense. There is no evidence of crop overproduction, so get rid of (D).

28. **C** Ibn Batutta was an explorer. Each answer choice is an explorer with the exception of Lorenzo de Medici, who was a statesman from the Italian Renaissance. Therefore, (C) is the answer.

29. **B** The Chinese Exclusion Act was created when the United States wanted to limit access to Chinese immigrants who were coming to the United States in search of work. The spike in Chinese immigrants was consistent with much of the world. This increase in migration, (B), was the result of an increased ability to travel, as well as search for more labor opportunities.

30. **B** You are looking for a policy that excluded a particular people from migrating to a particular country. This would be the White Australia Policy, (B), which allowed only English-speaking immigrants (typically from United Kingdom nations) to enter Australia. Eliminate (A), as the Open Door Policy was a trade policy with China. The Meiji Restoration was the process of Japanese modernization by adopting Western influence, so get rid of (C). Russification is not correct, as it refers to the process of non-ethnic Russians forced to take on characteristics of Russian culture; eliminate (D).

31. **C** The migrant depicted in the cartoon who is not allowed to enter the United States has a bag called "Industry." This indicates that he is being discriminated against due to his industriousness, which some Americans feared would keep Americans out of jobs. The choice that reflects this idea is (C). The cartoon states that communists are welcome, so eliminate (B). There is no evidence in the cartoon for either overpopulation or the Boxer Rebellion, so (A) and (D) are incorrect.

32. **D** The migrant who carries with him both temperance and industriousness is not allowed in the door. The cartoonist criticizes the American policy for not rewarding these characteristics, which might suggest that the cartoonist favors them. Eliminate (A) and (C). There is no evidence of racial designation, so (B) is incorrect. The cartoonist includes a list of problematic characteristics that Americans seem to have no problem allowing in the country. Many of these characteristics are politically radical, such as Communist, Fenian (Irish radical), and Hoodlum. Therefore, (D) is the answer.

33. **B** At its core, the tensions between Selim and Ismail go back centuries to the initial Sunni-Shi'a rift. This is apparent in the text when Selim references the fatwa (Islamic religious ruling), as well as the opinions of the Sunni community, against those who "introduce evil" (presumably the Shi'a). Choice (B) is correct.

34. **A** The Safavids were located in Persia, smack dab between the Mughal Empire (India) and the Ottoman Empire (Eastern Europe, Northern Africa, and the Levant). This idea matches (A). The Safavids were devout Muslims, so eliminate (B). Choice (C) is incorrect, as it describes a practice utilized by the Ottoman Empire. Choice (D) does not make sense, as Shi'a Muslims would never proclaim there to be a caliph who was not appointed by God from Muhammad's direct family lineage. Selim, by contrast, was named caliph under the Sunni tradition.

35. **D** Persia, since the earliest Muslims lived there, has been largely Shi'a, (D). Accordingly, the Safavid Empire was Shi'a. Selim, the author of the letter, is writing as a Sunni, a group that has long rivaled the Shi'a.

36. **D** Use Process of Elimination (POE). The reference to 1917 should draw your attention to either World War I or the Russian Revolution. Eliminate (A) and (B). Knowing that the Russians experienced terrible losses during World War I and left the war to tend to the revolution happening back home, and the fact that the text refers to freedom, motherland, and honor that was "won," (C) must be incorrect. Choice (D) is correct. The Russian Revolution is the event the poster is referring to.

37. **B** The caption, which labels the poster as World War II era is the biggest clue here. The intention of the poster is to refer to the gains made by the Bolsheviks in 1917 as a way to convince Russians of the importance of the current war. Choice (B) is correct. The tenor of the poster is pride, not regret, so eliminate (C). Since the poster is from World War II, the Cold War has not yet begun. Choice (A) is incorrect. Finally, eliminate (D) since there is no reference to collectivization, the Russian government takeover of private farms during the 1930s.

38. **A** Upon publishing their ideas about communism, Marx and Engels developed the First and Second Internationals, loose federations of the world's socialist parties heavily influenced by Marxism, in order to facilitate the spread of Marxist ideas worldwide. They envisioned a worldwide proletariat revolution. By contrast, the Bolsheviks, fearful of the instability present in the rest of Europe, saw success by focusing inward, at least until the Cold War. Choice (A) is correct because it best articulates this contrast. Both the Soviet Union and Marx saw communism as an economic system, not a militaristic one. Further, Marx did not advocate only peaceful methods for the proletariat to seize power. Eliminate (B). Marx saw the proletarian revolution as imminent at the time of his writing. Choice (C) is incorrect. Finally, eliminate (D), as the Soviet Union obviously by attempting to create a communist state saw the philosophy as more than just theoretical.

39. **D** In the opening paragraph, Mandela explains that the "majority of voters would be Africans." This would take away significant voting power from white citizens. Therefore, (D) is correct. South Africa had been independent since 1910, so (A) is incorrect. There was not significant support among white citizens in favor of increasing rights for Black people, so eliminate (B). Choice (C) is not correct because South Africa had a democratic form of government, but it discriminated against its Black citizens.

40. **D** One of the forms of discrimination during apartheid in South Africa was that Black people could live only in certain, undesirable regions. Those regions were not in the city and so Black citizens had to carry identification to justify their presence in a city. Choice (D) is correct. Juvenal Habyarimana was a Rwandan statesman, and therefore unrelated to this speech. Eliminate (A). There had not been separate Dutch and British regions in quite some time, so (B) is incorrect. In the first paragraph, Mandela makes it clear that Black people could not vote in South Africa at the time. Therefore, there was no universal adult franchise, and you can eliminate (C).

41. **B** Mandela considers the fight against apartheid "a struggle for the right to live." His speech is, indeed, a plea to change a government policy. Choice (B) is correct. There had been no unification attempts in South Africa since 1910, so eliminate (A). Mandela does not mention Africa in relation to the modern world nor does he bring up capitalism. Eliminate (C) and (D).

42. **C** Nelson Mandela notes that the African National Congress "has spent half a century fighting against racialism." Mandela was pointing to the length of time the fight for justice had gone on. This aligns with (C). Eliminate (A) because the viewpoint of the African National Congress is also his own. Mandela advocates a change in South Africa's policies; therefore, he does not advocate for the status quo. Eliminate (B). There is no mention of other African nations, so (D) is incorrect.

43. **A** Choice (A) makes sense because apartheid was the government-sanctioned policy of racial discrimination used in South Africa. Use POE to get rid of the incorrect answer choices. Mandela stands against all forms of colonialism, but the focus of this passage is the elimination of racist policies in South Africa. Eliminate (C). There is no mention of socialism or communism, so eliminate (B). Pan-Africanism is the belief that Africans should unite for optimal social, political, and economic outcomes. This is an ideology that Mandela would support, so eliminate (D). Choice (A) is the answer.

44. **B** Otto von Bismarck focuses on the difficulties that both age and poor health present. These concerns gave way to better health care and pensions (payment for retired workers). Therefore, (B) is correct.

45. **D** Industrial capitalism has given way to many hardships, some of which are outlined by Otto von Bismarck in this passage. Therefore, (D) is correct. There is no mention of child labor, which had already been addressed decades earlier, so eliminate (A). There is no evidence of a declining life expectancy in Germany. Further, the scientific breakthroughs of the 19th century would increase life spans. Eliminate (B). Choice (C) is incorrect because Bismarck never mentions tariffs.

46. **A** Keynesian economics is critical of the free market's ability to solve all economic problems. Instead, it advocates for governments to create demand (people's ability and willingness to spend money). Choice (A) reflects this idea. If the government can aid in both health-care costs and in post-retirement income, people would have more disposable income to keep the economy healthy. Choices (B), (C), and D) are incorrect because they contradict Keynesian economics.

47. **A** Throughout the 20th century, European nations adopted systems to ensure essential needs for its citizens—a type of socialism. Therefore, (A) is correct. Germany stayed unified (and free from a communist government) until the end of World War II, so eliminate (B) and (C). Germany remained the strongest industrial nation in mainland Europe until World War I, so (D) is incorrect.

48. **A** A key clue here is that China is giving up territory ("China cedes to Japan"), making it clear that China lost in this conflict. Choice (A) is correct. A Process of Elimination (POE) approach would also work: the fact that China ceded territory would lead to the elimination of (B) and (D). Choice (C) is also incorrect because the treaty implies that China and Japan opposed each other, not cooperated.

49. **D** As China ceded East Asian territory to Japan, Japan began expanding around the Pacific Rim, beginning to create its empire. Choice (D) is correct. Korea did not divide into two nations until the Cold War, nearly 60 years later. Eliminate (A). Formosa, now known as Taiwan, is ceded to Japan in the final part of the excerpt. Therefore, (B) is incorrect. Finally, (C) is incorrect, as an important continuity faced by China at this point in history was the contrast between its desire to stay isolated and the actions of Japan, Russia, the United States, and the nations of Europe to force China into trade relationships.

50. **B** Even though the Chinese Qing Dynasty wished to stay autonomous and largely isolated from trading with the rest of the world, European powers were rushing to establish a greater presence in China. By establishing spheres of influence, France, Germany, Russia, and of course Britain carved up huge slices of China for themselves. Choice (B) is correct. The fact that China wished to stay economically isolated undermines the economic half of (A). Eliminate it. China did not become a communist nation until after World War II. Choice (C) is incorrect. Finally, eliminate (D) as the Qing Dynasty saw the Chinese emperor's power diminish. In fact, the Qing Dynasty saw the final emperor of China.

51. **C** Fanon argues that the colonizers exercise "pure force" over the colonized. This rule through violence is most consistent with (C), which states that people in developing nations (largely those that were colonized or only recently liberated) were dehumanized. Eliminate (A), as by 1961, much of the formerly colonized world was in a process of decolonization. Local populations in colonized nations learned the language of the colonizers, so (B) would not make much sense. Eliminate it. While the Cold War was ongoing, and the world powers were trying to create allies from the developed world, those tensions were not directly the context for Fanon's remarks. Rather, he is referring to the ongoing use of violence in the developing world. Therefore, eliminate (D).

52. **A** A Process of Elimination (POE) approach would be the best tool on this question. You may not be 100% certain about whether Fanon was influenced by Marxism, so hold on to (A) for the time being. However, it is clear that Fanon opposed colonialism in all forms, so (B) is definitely incorrect. Further, Social Darwinism was used to justify unequal treatment of people based on such determinants as skin color and ethnicity. This is hardly an appropriate position for an anticolonialist. Eliminate (C). Pan-nationalism was an approach used by many African anticolonial movements, so (D) may seem tempting. Hold on to it. Now compare (A) and (D). Look for evidence in the text to support either. Fanon's critique of what he refers to as "capitalist countries" is a strong indicator of Marxism. There is no such indicator of nationalism in this text. Eliminate (D). Choice (A) is correct.

53. **D** The Berlin Conference created boundary lines that separated colonial territories based on European concerns, not on African history or culture. Therefore, in some situations, tribal lands were cut in half between two colonies controlled by two different European nations, while in other situations two rival tribes were unwillingly brought together under the same colonial rule. Choice (D) is correct. The nations that Fanon is describing were already liberated at this point (an era of decolonization) or were about to be. Eliminate (A). Many decolonized nations attempted democratic reform following their independence. Choice (B) is incorrect. As you may recall from your study of world history, African nations were full of natural resources, which was one of the primary reasons European nations sought to create colonies there in the first place. Choice (C) is incorrect.

54. **B** Pan-Africanism, the belief that Africans should unite for optimal social, political, and economic outcomes, was a form of pan-nationalism championed by many leaders of the African independence movements. Choice (B) is correct. While some former colonies created treaties following wars of independence, this did not characterize most of African decolonization. Eliminate (A). There was no dramatic increase in wealth in the colonized countries since they were being run by outside nations which would have benefited from any new wealth. Choice (C) is incorrect. Due to the ill-thought-out boundaries from the Berlin Conference, there was not widespread political stability throughout Africa during the time of decolonization. Choice (D) is incorrect.

55. **C** Fanon describes both the colonized world and the capitalist world in this text. His references to both types of nations come from his time in France as well as his time in colonies, such as Algeria. Choice (C) is correct. Choices (A) and (B) are incorrect because they do not speak to Fanon's experience in the developed world. Choice (D) is not relevant to the lives experienced in two types of societies. Eliminate it.

Section I, Part B: Short-Answer Questions

Question 1

a) There are plenty of changes that the British Empire brought to the world, but you need to write about only TWO of them. You can include any of the following:

- Colonizing regions around the world (South Africa, sub-Saharan Africa, India, North America, China, Australia) and exploiting natural resources in those regions

- Spreading of the technologies of the Industrial Revolution (automated labor) around the world. Feel free to choose any of the technologies to mention here.

- Spreading language (English) and religion (Christianity) to its colonies

b)   You need to identify and explain ONE reason for the decline of the British Empire. You may choose to focus on the following:

- The devastation of both World Wars took its toll on Great Britain, which emerged from the First World War sharing its position as the world power with a number of other countries. The Second World War led to further decline in the power of the British vis-à-vis the United States, a former colony.

- The decolonization movements, particularly following the Second World War, saw colonized people rise against Great Britain and demand their independence.

c)   There are a number of different responses to this question:

- Crown-appointed governors lived in the colony and ran day-to-day affairs on behalf of the government.

- In certain cases, the British Empire linked its colonies together via trade, which benefited some of the colonized people (mostly merchants), who then worked to maintain the status quo.

- Sometimes, force was used to suppress colonial uprisings, as in the Sepoy Rebellion in India from 1857 to 1859.

- In places that never fully accepted British imperialism, such as China, the British Empire was satisfied with wielding large cultural and political influence, though not direct colonial control.

Question 2

a)   The complexities of atomic technology are actually outlined in the text. Contrast the benefits of atomic technology (energy) with the destructive qualities of atomic technology.

b)   Discuss any of the following:

- arms race

- leverage for power (North Korea, Iran)

- threat of terrorist groups using the technology

- the idea that local conflicts deserve international attention (Kashmir, Koreas)

c)   Many things led to the unfortunate development of atomic weaponry:

- Discovery of new materials such as uranium and plutonium

- Government support of research, particularly in Western laboratories such as the University of Chicago

- The rise of Hitler to power in Germany, which caused many of its scientists to defect to the U.S. to work on its nuclear technology

Question 3

a) The ability to travel greater distances had a significant impact on cultural diffusion. Have your pick of any of the following. (Remember, you need to identify and explain TWO ways in which traveling longer distances affects cultural diffusion.)

- Christianity: The power of the papacy ensured the strength of Christianity in all reaches of Europe.

- Islam: Journey to Mecca connected Dar al-Islam via the introduction of crops (cotton, sugar, citrus) to new cultures; scholarship (Greek science and philosophy) was reintroduced to Europe via Muslim Spain; Ibn Battuta traveled the Islamic world and shared his experiences through his journal.

- Judaism: The Diaspora stretched from Europe to the Mediterranean to Central Asia along the Silk Road.

- Africa: Islam spread from Northern Africa through Sub-Saharan regions; Bantu languages spread (most famously Swahili, which is a combination of Bantu language and Arabic); Arabs and Berbers trained camels to haul travelers long distances across the Sahara; cities were established to facilitate trade (Timbuktu).

- Europe: Islamic scholars read and translated the works of the ancient Greeks; Marco Polo brought products and ideas from China and Central Asia back to Europeans; cities were established to facilitate trade (Venice, Novgorod).

- India: Supremacy of Hinduism is challenged by the introduction of Islam; Hindus known as Rajputs launched a resistance, which led to military and technology innovations from both Hindus and Muslims; cities were established to facilitate trade (Calicut).

- Arabia/Persia: Merchants traveled the Silk Road; horses were trained to travel across the steppes; cities, such as Baghdad, facilitated trade.

- Americas: Mesoamerican groups (such as Maya) and Andean groups (such as Inca) both traded and exchanged traditions outside their borders; cities were established to facilitate trade (Cahokia, Tenochtitlan).

- East Asia: East Asian technologies such as gunpowder, printing, and paper were brought to Islamic regions as well as Western Europe; Zheng He explored regions along the Indian Ocean, collecting goods, ideas, and tributes to bring back to China; trade cities were frequented by Arab traders (Hangzhou, Melaka).

b) You need to identify TWO primary reasons for cultural interactions, though the specific examples you can cite are pretty numerous.

- War: Remember that many cultural interactions occurred through military conquests. The Mongols are the most likely group to first pop into your mind. But don't forget some other conflicts from this period, such as the Muslims and Rajputs, and the entrance of the Ottoman armies into Europe via Hungary.

- Economic interests were also at play: The South Asian trade networks, especially the Indian Ocean routes that connected the Swahili Coast with Arabia, India, and Southeast Asia, led to increased wealth along the routes. Similarly, the Silk Road, connecting China to the Mediterranean Coast contained many profitable outposts.

c) Several civilizations unified themselves into a single political entity during this era:

- England began to unify itself with the signing of the Magna Carta, which laid the foundation for Parliament

- France unified in response to creeping English presence on French soil. Nothing brings people together like a common enemy!

- Slightly outside the era, Spain was unified in the last part of the fifteenth century by Queen Isabella marrying King Ferdinand (of Aragon), ejecting the Moors, and waging a campaign of torture against non-Christian Spaniards called the Inquisition.

- Russia unified itself after a long period of occupation by a branch of the Mongols, managing to maintain its own Eastern Orthodox Church in the meantime. Later, Ivan III expanded Russian territory and declared himself czar.

Question 4

This painting should be a familiar image of nationalist romanticism.

a) The symbols you may notice on *Germania* are as follows:

- sword: strength

- broken chains: unshackled; freedom

- sunrays: rebirth; optimism

- oak leaf crown: symbol of heroism since the ancient Romans and Greeks

- the striped flag (black/red/gold tricolor, had this been a color image): symbol of German nationalists

b) There are many causes of German nationalism that go back many centuries, but focus on the 19th century:

- The Volkisch movement forged a sense of community among the German-speaking peoples by appealing to their sense of culture by publishing stories from the German countryside (Brothers Grimm) and composing operas and symphonies based on German folk tunes (Richard Wagner).

- The development of methods of transportation made it easier to interact with other German-speaking people.

- The spread of *Anschluss* (reunification with Austria, a German speaking nation-state)

- Early 19th-century nationalism arose from anger over the Napoleonic invasion of the German states.

c) You can choose other 19th-century movements (Italy, France, Greece, Ireland, Philippines, Argentina, and others); anticolonial movements (19th-century India, Boxer Rebellion, Ghost Dance); and post-colonial movements (Ho Chi Minh in Vietnam, Kwame Nkrumah in Ghana, or the Indian National Congress). And remember, you are not limited to just these.

Section II: Document-Based Question (DBQ)

To present a strong understanding of these documents, it is important to highlight the universal nature of the oppression of women. The authors of these documents discuss a variety of struggles that women have faced in the previous two centuries. A couple of the documents stem from existential threats, such as war-torn Myanmar (Document 4) and the expectation for widows to self-immolate at their husbands' funerals (Document 5). Document 6 inserts the struggle of women into the Cold War by providing the Soviet view of how capitalism stands in the way of emancipation. Document 7 gives us a unique view by using Argentina as a case study in which equal rights are written into the law, but many women, having internalized a traditional view of womanhood, are reluctant to take advantage of those rights.

Others represent the struggle for enfranchisement and fair practices in the workplace. While each speaker advocates for women's rights, an effective essay will pay attention to the cultural and historical differences among each document in order to best highlight the universality of the theme. Ultimately, you should investigate how the speakers view the ways in which equality between women and men would ultimately change the world.

Long Essay

Question 2

Each of the decolonization movements from this time period arose for a very specific reason. While some were rooted in nationalism, others were rooted in liberal reform and economic freedom. Some were a mix of all these things. Be sure that, no matter which examples you use, you ultimately tie your content back to a thesis that asserts the impact the movement had on the colonized peoples' national identities. Your essay should mention at least some of the following:

- Franz Fanon's organizing and resistance efforts in Algeria

- The Boxer Rebellion in China

- Gandhi's Indian resistance to the British Empire

- Vietnamese opposition to France

- Jomo Kenyatta's role in the liberation of Kenya from Great Britain

- South African Independence

- Kwame Nkrumah's work in Ghana

- Efforts of the Indian National Congress

- The Native American Ghost Dance movement

Question 3

For this essay, your thesis needs to connect the ideas of the Enlightenment to real outcomes. You may want to focus on how the ideas that influenced revolutions (American, French, Haitian, etc.), inspired monarchs to implement significant changes (enlightened absolutists), or laid the foundation for modern democracy. Depending on which Enlightenment topics you wish to focus on, your essay should mention at least some of the following:

- It's difficult to overstate the extent to which Enlightenment philosophers shaped the establishment of Western governments. Thomas Hobbes, who had a less than optimistic view of humankind, saw states and, by extension, governments as necessary to keep people from harming one another. John Locke built on this idea, claiming that citizens are connected through a *social contract,* which allows people to maintain life, liberty, and property. Montesquieu went further with the concept of the social contract, applying it to human reason; reason gives way to law. The application of reason to law also led him to outline the idea of separation of powers. You can tie this pretty neatly to Russia's Catherine the Great, who codified Russian law after reading the works of Montesquieu.

- Enlightenment philosophy also lends itself to a discussion of individual rights. Jean-Jacques Rousseau wrote that people could find freedom only by consenting to the general will through a social contract. Mary Wollstonecraft extended the idea of individual rights to the plight of women, arguing for suffrage. In Italy, Cesare Beccaria wrote about the rights of the accused, revolutionizing how we view crime, trials, and punishments. Frederick II of Prussia put some of these ideas into practice, including the cessation of capital punishment.

- Religion, specifically Christianity, had governed European thought processes for centuries. The Scientific Revolution called some of these assumptions into question. Accordingly, Enlightenment philosophers also questioned the centrality of religion. Voltaire, a deist, felt that religion limited human freedom. David Hume, an atheist, found Christian doctrine untenable due to a lack of empirical evidence. In response, enlightened absolutist Joseph II of Austria sought to limit the influence of the Catholic Church.

- Adam Smith revolutionized economics with his idea of the Invisible Hand. The legacy of this idea can be found in the Industrial Revolution and the development of free-market capitalism.

Question 4

In this essay, you should frame your argument in a way that shows how the pressure for developing nations to choose sides during the Cold War affected the countries of Latin America. While some countries allied with the United States (as capitalist democracies), others sided with the Soviet Union's communism. This became an especially tenuous situation, as the Latin American countries were close geographic neighbors to the United States. As the United States and the Soviet Union pressured countries for their allegiance, revolutionary movements bred from ideologies ranging from nationalism to Marxism drove significant change in Latin America. You may want to focus on some of the following cases:

- As the United States supported Cuba's Batista dictatorship, resentment among the working class in Cuba grew. A communist revolution ousted Batista and installed Fidel Castro as its dictator. Cuba became the Soviet Union's ally with the closest geographical presence to the United States.

- Radical political parties, rejecting the neocolonialism that benefited their aristocracy, had developed in Mexico, Peru, Venezuela, among other nations. The anti-capitalist message of the communist parties found great appeal among the lower classes.

- Radical opposition to the United States fomented in Nicaragua and El Salvador, countries in which the United States intervened as it targeted the Sandinistas.

- Guatemala democratically elected Jacabo Árbenz, who had fought to end unfair labor practice by the U.S.-backed United Fruit Company and was seen as a communist leader by the American government. The United States staged a coup d'état to oust the president, which launched a civil war between the Guatemalan government and left-wing revolutionaries that lasted more than 30 years.

- Some countries, such as Argentina, sought a "Third Way" to avoid choosing between two sides. Juan Perón ruled Argentina with a brutal militaristic dictatorship in his goal to be self-sufficient and maintain friendly relations with both the United States and the Soviet Union.

HOW TO SCORE PRACTICE TEST 4

Section IA: Multiple Choice

_____ × 1.090 = _____
Number Correct   Weighted
(out of 55)   Section I Score
                                (Do not round)

Section IB: Short Answer

Question 1:

_____ × 3.3333 = _____
(out of 3)   (Do not round)

Question 2:

_____ × 3.3333 = _____
(out of 3)   (Do not round)

Question 3 or 4:

_____ × 3.3333 = _____
(out of 3)   (Do not round)

AP Score Conversion Chart World History	
Composite Score Range	AP Score
107–150	5
90–106	4
73–89	3
56–72	2
0–55	1

Section II: Document-Based Question

Question 1:

_____ × 5.3571 = _____
(out of 7)   (Do not round)

Section II: Long Essay

Question 2, 3, or 4:

_____ × 3.750 = _____
(out of 6)   (Do not round)

Composite Score

_____ + _____ + _____ + _____ = _____
Weighted   Weighted   Weighted   Weighted   Composite Score
Section IA   Section IB   DBQ   Long   (Round to the
Score   Score   Score   Essay   nearest whole
                                                    Score   number

NOTES

NOTES

NOTES

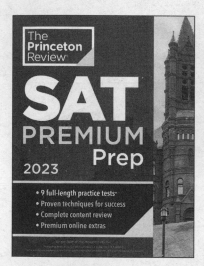

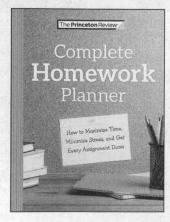